the
visual
food
lover's
guide

QA INTERNATIONAL

WILEY

JOHN WILEY & SONS, INC.

"The Food Lover's Guide" created and produced by

QA International
329, rue de la Commune Ouest, 3ᵉ étage
Montréal (Québec) H2Y 2E1 Canada
T: 514.499.3000
F: 514.499.3010

www.qa-international.com

This book is adapted from "Dictionnaire encyclopédique des aliments," Solange Monette, Les Éditions Québec Amérique inc.

John Wiley & Sons, Inc.
CREDITS

Publisher
Natalie Chapman

Senior Editor
Linda Ingroia

Senior Editorial Assistant
Charleen Barila

Production Manager
Michael Olivo

Graphic Design
Holly Wittenberg

Library of Congress Cataloging-in-Publication Data

The visual food lover's guide/QA International.
    p. cm.
  Based on The Visual food encyclopedia.
  Includes index.
  ISBN 978-0-470-50559-5 (pbk.)
  1. Food--Encyclopedias--Pictorial works. 2.
Cookery--Encyclopedias--Pictorial works. I. Québec Amérique
International.
  TX349.V534 2009
  641.503—dc22

                      2009009690

Photo Credits
Cooking how-to photos © Studio Focus-Pocus
All food (except the images obtained through iStockPhoto.com, listed below):
© Ilva Beretta, 2008. All rights reserved. www.luculliandelights.com
p. 27 turnips © John Peacock; p. 44 olives © Gerri Hernández; p. 73 radicchio
© Matteo De Stefano; p. 104 yams © YinYang; p. 142 tofu © Daniel Bendjy;
p. 191 lemons © Sergei Didyk; p. 230 watermelons © Klaudia Steiner; p. 265 nori
© Agata Malchrowicz; p. 273 bolete mushrooms © Szelmek; p. 312 breads
© Camilo Jimenez; p. 360 salmon © Liza McCorkle; p. 390 lobsters © Darren Baker;
p. 421 basil © Kjell Brynildsen; p. 480 lamb chops © Joe Biafore; p. 519 chicken
© Don Bayley; p. 586 olive oil © Maria Toutoudaki

Printed in China
10 9 8 7 6 5 4 3 2 1   14 13 12 11 10 09
PO 395, Version 1.0.2

CREDITS

Publisher
Caroline Fortin

Editorial Directors
François Fortin
Martine Podesto

Executive Editors
Serge d'Amico
Claire de Guillebon

Editorial Assistants
Ophélie Delaunay
Julie Lepage
Myriam Morneau

Nutrition Consultants
Marie Breton Dt. P.
Isabelle Emond Dt. P.

Graphic Design
Louis Beaudoin
Josée Noiseux
Anne Tremblay

Computer Graphics Artists
Jean-Yves Ahern
Pascal Bilodeau
Jocelyn Gardner
Marc Lalumière
Rielle Lévesque
Michel Rouleau
Mamadou Togola

Page Setup
Émilie Corriveau
Mélanie Giguère-Gilbert
Danielle Quinty

Computer Programming
Pascal Laniel
Martin Lemieux

Prepress
Julien Brisebois
François Hénault
Karine Lévesque

Production
Nathalie Fréchette

Research
Nathalie Daneau
Gilles Vézina

Coordination/Photo Retouching
Josée Gagnon

Cook
Laurent Saget

Translation
ECHOES TRANSLATIONS/Marta Serrano Estruch

Proofreading
Veronica Schami Editorial Services

the visual food lover's guide

Includes essential information on
how to buy, prepare, and store
over **1,000** types of food

QA INTERNATIONAL

WILEY

JOHN WILEY & SONS, INC.

Table of contents

For your reference

WEIGHT*

Ounces (oz)	Pounds (lb)	Grams (g)
1	1/16	30
1.8	1/9	50
2	1/8	60
3	1/5	90
3.5	2/9	100
4	1/4	120
5	1/3	140
6	2/5	170
7	5/12	200
8	1/2	230
9	3/5	260
10	2/3	290
12	3/4	340
16	1	450
35	2 1/4	1000 (1 kg)

VOLUME*

	Ounces (oz)	Millilitres (ml)
1 teaspoon	1/5	5
1 tablespoon	1/2	15
1/8 cup	1	30
1/4 cup	2	60
1/3 cup	2 1/2	80
2/5 cup	3	100
1/2 cup	4	120
2/3 cup	5 1/2	160
3/4 cup	6	180
1 cup	8	250
4 cups (1 quart)	32	1000 (1 l)

TEMPERATURE*

Degrees Fahrenheit	Degrees Celsius	Degrees Fahrenheit	Degrees Celsius
-0.5	-18	225	105
10	-12	250	120
20	-6	275	135
30	0	300	150
40	4	325	160
50	10	350	175
60	15	375	190
70	20	400	205
80	25	425	220
90	30	450	230
100	40	475	245
125	52	500	260
150	65	525	270
175	80	550	290
200	90	575	300

*These measures are rounded.

LENGTH*

Imperial	Metric
2/5 in.	1 cm
1 in.	2.5 cm
1 ft.	30.5 cm
3 3/10 ft. or 40 in.	1 m

HEALTH PROPERTIES

Antiarthritic: a substance that prevents arthritis
Antiseptic: a substance that prevents or alleviates infections
Cholagogue: a substance that promotes the elimination of bile
Depurative: a substance that purifies the body by promoting the elimination of toxins and wastes
Digestive: a substance that promotes digestion
Diuretic: a substance that promotes the flow of urine
Emmenagogue: a substance that promotes or regulates menstrual flow
Expectorant: a substance that promotes the oral elimination of respiratory secretions
Laxative: a substance that promotes the excretion of feces
Remineralizing: foods that replenish the body's supply of minerals
Tonic: a food that fortifies or stimulates the body
Vermifuge: a food or substance that promotes the elimination of intestinal worms

Vegetables

Vegetables are classified according to the part of the plant that is eaten:

- **bulb vegetables:** garlic, leek, onion, scallion, shallot, etc.
- **root vegetables:** beet, burdock, carrot, celeriac, malanga, parsnip, radish, rutabaga, salsify, turnip, etc.
- **fruit vegetables:** avocado, bell pepper, chayote, cucumber, eggplant, okra, olive, squash, tomato, etc.
- **leaf vegetables:** cabbage, chicory, cress, dandelion, lettuce, nettle, radicchio, sorrel, spinach, etc.
- **stem vegetables:** asparagus, bamboo shoot, cardoon, celery, chard, fennel, fiddlehead, kohlrabi, etc.
- **tuber vegetables:** cassava, Chinese artichoke, Jerusalem artichoke, jícama, potato, sweet potato, taro, yam, etc.
- **flower vegetables:** artichoke, broccoli, broccoli rabe, cauliflower, etc.

TIPS FOR COOKING VEGETABLES

Vegetables should be cooked as briefly as possible, as they become bland and mushy if overcooked, and lose vitamins and minerals. Cut vegetables into similar-sized pieces so that they cook evenly. Reduce cooking time if vegetables are to be reheated or served cold, since the cooking process will continue while they are hot. The cooking process can be stopped by running vegetables under cold water, but this also leads to the loss of vitamins and minerals.

Keep peeled or sliced vegetables covered while cooking to prevent them from drying out. Only add salt or other seasonings at the end of cooking, as salt can leave dark spots on vegetables, while herbs and spices lose their flavor or can become overly intense. Only use a small amount of water to cook fibrous vegetables. Fresh vegetables often do not need any water, as too much water increases cooking time and leads to nutrient loss. It is not necessary to add water to frozen vegetables. Eggplant, cassava, potato, squash and tomato should be pricked before being baked in the oven. This allows steam to escape and prevents the vegetables from bursting.

Cooking vegetables in the microwave oven preserves the color and flavor of vegetables better than any other cooking method.

:: Boiling

Boiling consists of cooking vegetables in boiling water. Place vegetables in a cooking pot large enough for them to cook evenly. Add vegetables once the water has come to a full boil and keep the heat on high so that the water returns to a boil quickly. Then lower the heat so that the vegetables are cooked at a simmer. Cover vegetables while cooking to reduce cooking time and the evaporation of volatile substances. Green vegetables, however, should be cooked uncovered; otherwise, the acids they contain become concentrated and destroy their chlorophyll, which makes them lose their color.

Adding an alkaline ingredient (such as baking soda) to the cooking water of green vegetables preserves their color, but this is not recommended, as it makes the vegetables turn soft, affects their taste, destroys their thiamine content and accelerates the loss of vitamin C. To prevent the loss of color in green vegetables, reduce cooking time or choose another cooking method.

Adding an acidic ingredient (vinegar, citrus juice, dry wine, cider) preserves the color and firmness of red and white vegetables. Vegetables that discolor easily (artichoke, salsify), once cut or peeled, should be cooked in a mixture of flour (1 tablespoon/15 ml), water (3 tablespoons/45 ml) and the juice of half a lemon added to 4 cups (1 l) of boiling salted water.

Salt draws out water from vegetables, which is also why it tenderizes them. Added at the beginning of cooking, it makes the vegetable juices run, leading to a loss of nutrients. Salt also becomes more concentrated over the course of the cooking time. It should not be used with vegetables that have a high water content (mushrooms, cucumbers, tomatoes, etc.) and is not recommended for several others (red cabbage, bell peppers, etc.), where it leads to a loss of flavor and firmness.

Boiling significantly reduces the flavor and nutritional value of vegetables. Use only a small amount of water and reserve the cooking liquid for soups and sauces.

:: Steaming
Steaming consists of using the heat released from a small amount of boiling water. Place vegetables in a single layer in a steamer or steam basket about 1 in. (2.5 cm) above just-simmering water. Only add the vegetables to the steamer when the water starts to boil. Cover. When the lid vibrates or releases steam, lower the heat to keep the water just at simmering point. Steaming vegetables takes slightly longer than boiling, but results in less loss of nutrients and flavor.

:: Pressure-cooking
Pressure-cooking consists of cooking within an airtight container. In a pressure cooker, the temperature rises above boiling point, so vegetables cook very rapidly. Observe cooking times scrupulously, down to the minute.

:: Quick-braising
Quick-braising consists of cooking vegetables in their own juice after sautéeing in a small amount of fat or oil. A small amount of liquid (water, wine, tomato sauce, cooking juices, etc.) can be added if desired at the beginning to get the process started. Cover and cook over a low heat to blend flavors well and obtain vegetables that are tender. This method is especially recommended for squash, mushrooms, tomatoes, onions and shallots.

:: Braising
Braising consists of cooking foods slowly, covered, over a low heat, after sautéeing in fat or oil. Cook vegetables whole or in pieces. Braise vegetables by themselves or with a piece of meat to create tasty combinations. Braising especially suits harder vegetables (fennel, cardoon, artichoke, cabbage, celery, etc.).

:: Dry-heat cooking
Dry-heat cooking uses the heat of an oven or barbecue. Cook vegetables whole in their skin or cut into pieces. Prick eggplant and potato or slash their skin in a few places so that they don't burst from internal pressure. Cooking with dry heat makes vegetables tender, juicy and tasty, and limits the loss of nutrients, especially if the skin is left on. Adding an acid or alkaline ingredient is not useful.

:: Stir-frying
Stir-frying makes use of a light, quick frying or steaming process, or a combination of the two. Group vegetables according to their cooking time and fry them quickly in oil over a very high heat, beginning with those requiring the longest cooking time. Cook very briefly to seal in nutrients and preserve color, texture, flavor and nutritional value. Add aromatics such as ginger or garlic, if desired. To combine the frying process with steaming, reduce the heat slightly and add a small amount of liquid (water, tamari sauce, stock, etc.). Blend with cornstarch to make a sauce. Cook covered. Stir-frying suits firmer vegetables such as cauliflower, broccoli and carrots.

:: Deep-frying
Deep-frying consists of cooking at high temperature by immersing food in liquid fat, usually oil. Use peanut, safflower or soybean oil. Keep the temperature of the oil between 300°F and 350°F (150°C-175°C); it must not rise above 425°F (215°C), as the oil may catch fire. Dry vegetables well or encase them in a coating (floured, breaded—dipping in flour, beaten egg and bread crumbs—or battered). Plunge the vegetables into the oil, beginning with those requiring the longest cooking time. Cooked vegetables rise to the surface. Drain, then blot on paper towel. Frying adds a large amount of fat to vegetables without improving their nutritional value.

:: Microwaving

Microwaving utilizes ultrashort waves in a specially designed oven. Use microwave-safe containers for cooking. Place vegetables that require longer cooking time at the edge of the cooking dish, and those that cook more quickly at the center (large pieces of vegetable can be placed on paper towel). Cooking time varies depending on the wattage, size and settings of the oven (check the manufacturer's manual). Microwaving is generally quicker than cooking in a traditional oven. Check whether food is done to avoid overcooking, and return for further cooking if necessary.

Keep in mind

- The more food there is, the longer the cooking time will be.

- The more water, fat or carbohydrate a vegetable contains, the more quickly—or sometimes unevenly—it will cook.

- The more water there is in the pot, the longer the cooking time will be.

- Food at room temperature takes less time to cook than chilled or frozen food.

- Food cooks better if placed in the center of the oven (most microwave ovens have a rotating plate that allows food to be cooked more evenly).

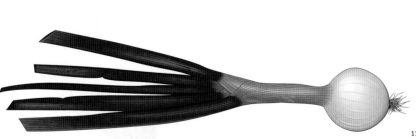

TIPS FOR FREEZING VEGETABLES

Most vegetables freeze well. They first need to be blanched. Only a few vegetables with high levels of acidity do not need to be blanched. Blanching consists of boiling raw vegetables for variable lengths of time (the length of time varies according to the type and size of vegetable), then cooling and draining them. To blanch vegetables:

1. Bring a large quantity of water to a boil—16 cups (4 l) of water for about 1 lb (500 g) of vegetables or 32 cups (8 l) of water for 1 lb (500 g) of leaf vegetables.
2. Place the vegetables in a metal basket or cheesecloth so they can be removed from the water easily and quickly.
3. When the water is at full boil, immerse the vegetables, cover and start timing the blanching process. The water should quickly return to a boil.
4. When the blanching time is up, cool the vegetables by plunging them immediately in very cold water (50°F/10°C) and leave them just long enough to cool (do not oversoak them).
5. Drain vegetables and seal in freezer bags, squeezing out all of the air. On the bag, write the name of the vegetable, the quantity and the date of freezing. Freeze quickly at a temperature of -0.5°F (-18°C) or less. Vegetables can generally be stored in a freezer for up to one year. The nutritional value of a properly blanched and frozen vegetable is comparable to a freshly cooked vegetable.

Most vegetables do not need to be defrosted before cooking, although some do need to be partly or completely defrosted. It is even preferable to avoid defrosting completely to limit the loss of flavor and nutritional value. To defrost vegetables, leave them in their sealed bag either at room temperature or in the fridge. Allow more time for defrosting in the fridge.

To cook, add vegetables once water has come to a full boil, cover, wait for the water to return to a boil, then reduce heat. The cooking time is shorter than for fresh vegetables, as the vegetables have already been partly cooked during the blanching process.

TIPS FOR PRESERVING VEGETABLES

Homemade vegetables must be pressure-cooked. Like all foods low in acid (meat, seafood, etc.), vegetables can become very toxic if they are only sterilized in boiling water. The botulism toxin is attracted to low-acid environments, and is only destroyed at around 250°F (120°C), a temperature achieved only through pressure-cooking. Only tomatoes are acidic enough to be adequately sterilized in boiling water.

Chive

Allium schoenoprasum and *Allium tuberosum*, Liliaceae

An aromatic plant originally from the East. **Chive** (*Allium schoenoprasum*) is the smallest member of the onion family. It has long green needlelike leaves and a very mild flavor. The **garlic chive** (*Allium tuberosum*) is a common ingredient in Asian cooking. It has a stronger flavor than the variety of chives cultivated in the West.

chive

garlic chive

BUYING

:: **Choose:** chives with fresh, green, firm leaves.

SERVING IDEAS

 Chives and garlic chives are used to flavor hot and cold dishes. They add flavor and serve as a garnish for vinaigrettes, mayonnaise, salads, dips, vegetables, soups, sauces, cheeses, omelettes, pasta dishes, tofu, fish, seafood, meat and poultry. They are preferably added at time of serving.

PREPARING

Chop chives finely using scissors.

NUTRITIONAL INFORMATION

water	92%
protein	0.1 g
carbohydrates	0.1 g
fiber	0.1 g
calories	1
	per 0.1 oz/3 g

PROPERTIES: Chive juice is used as an anthelmintic remedy.

STORING

:: **In the fridge:** a few days.
:: **In the freezer:** as is.

Scallion

Allium fistulosum, Liliaceae

An aromatic plant originally from southwestern Siberia. The scallion, also called "green onion," has a slight bulge at its base; the white part is fleshy and the long, green leaves are narrow and hollow. It has a slightly pungent flavor.

scallion

Scallion

BUYING

 :: Choose: scallions with fresh, green leaves and a pleasant smell.

SERVING IDEAS

 The green part of the scallion is used at the end of cooking to flavor hot and cold dishes. It adds flavor and serves as a garnish for vinaigrettes, mayonnaise, salads, dips, vegetables, soups, sauces, cheeses, omelettes, pasta dishes, tofu, fish, seafood, meat and poultry. It can be used in place of chives (reduce quantity). The white part is used in the same way as onion.

PREPARING

Finely chop scallion stems using scissors or with a knife.

NUTRITIONAL INFORMATION

water	90.5%
protein	1.9 g
fat	0.4 g
carbohydrates	6.5 g
fiber	1.7 g
calories	34
	per 3.5 oz/100 g

GOOD SOURCE (RAW): vitamin C and potassium.
CONTAINS (RAW): vitamin A, iron, folic acid, zinc and phosphorus.
PROPERTIES: Scallion juice is used as an anthelmintic remedy.

STORING

:: In the fridge: a few days.
:: In the freezer: as is.

Leek

Allium porrum, Liliaceae

Originally from central Asia, the leek is a vegetable with a delicate and subtle flavor, milder and sweeter than the onion. The section that grows underground is the "white" and tender part of the leek. The green leaves that are cut off near where they start to separate form the "green" of the leek.

BUYING

:: Choose: straight, firm, intact leeks, without any brown spots, and with leaves that are a deep green.
:: Avoid: leeks with a cracked or swollen base, or with dehydrated or discolored leaves.

leek

PREPARING

 Clean the leek carefully.

1 Remove outer leaves if they are no longer fresh.

2 Remove the part of the root with threads attached as well as the top part of the leaves.

3 Make a lengthwise incision into the leek down to ¾-1¼ in. (2-3 cm) from the base.

4 Spread the leaves apart and wash them carefully in cold water. Drain.

COOKING

Leeks only need a short amount of cooking time. Choose leeks of the same thickness for even cooking.
:: Boiled: whole or split, 15-20 min; sliced, 20-25 min.
:: Baked or **braised:** 25-35 min.
:: Sautéed: 3-5 min.
:: Stewed: 10-15 min.

NUTRITIONAL INFORMATION

	raw
water	83%
protein	1.5 g
fat	0.3 g
carbohydrates	14 g
fiber	1.8 g
calories	61
	per 3.5 oz/100 g

EXCELLENT SOURCE: folic acid.
GOOD SOURCE: potassium and iron.
CONTAINS: vitamin C, vitamin B$_6$, magnesium, copper and calcium.
PROPERTIES: laxative, antiarthritic, antiseptic, diuretic and tonic. It is used to cleanse the digestive system.

STORING

:: At room temperature: 1-3 months, unwashed, in a cool place with a humidity level of 90%-95%.
:: In the fridge: raw, about 2 weeks.
:: In the freezer: 3 months, whole (blanch 2 min before) or sliced. Cook without defrosting for better flavor.

SERVING IDEAS

 Leek is eaten raw or cooked. It is often used raw in salads, finely chopped. Cooked leek is prepared in the same way as asparagus. It is excellent with vinaigrette, cream and potatoes. Leek works very well cooked with veal, ham and cheese; it combines well with lemon, basil, sage, thyme and mustard. Its leaves are used to flavor stocks and stews, and can be used in place of chive or shallot. The white of the leek is used to flavor court bouillons and cooking juices.

Shallot

Allium ascalonicum, Liliaceae

A bulb probably originally from the Near East. It has a more fragrant and subtle flavor than onion and is not as harsh as garlic. The same size as a garlic bulb, it contains two or three cloves. There are several varieties of shallots. The **French gray shallot**—or "common shallot"—is small and elongated, with gray skin, a purplish head, and firm and pungent flesh. The **Jersey shallot**—or "red shallot"—is a short, rounded bulb, with reddish skin and veined flesh that is not as pungent. The **banana shallot** is an elongated bulb with a coppery color.

French gray shallot

BUYING

:: **Choose:** firm shallots with dry skin.
:: **Avoid:** shallots that have sprouted, soft shallots or with spots on the skin.

SERVING IDEAS

Shallot is eaten raw or cooked. It is an ingredient in béarnaise, Bercy and red-wine sauces. It is used in salads, with fish and with broiled or sautéed meat. It is used to flavor *beurre blanc* (a white wine or vinegar and butter sauce), soups, vinaigrettes and vegetables. The green stems can be used in the same way as chives. The bulbs can be used to flavor vinegars or oils.

COOKING

:: **Sautéed:** soften shallot over a very gentle heat (do not allow it to brown or burn).

NUTRITIONAL INFORMATION

	raw
water	80%
protein	0.3 g
carbohydrates	1.7 g
calories	7
	per 0.35 oz/10 g

PROPERTIES: mineralizing, aperitive and stimulant. It is used to relieve burns and insect bites.

STORING

:: **At room temperature:** 1 month, in a dark, cool, dry and well-ventilated place.
:: **In the fridge:** 15 days. When cut, wrap in plastic film or place in a container and cover with olive oil (oil can be used for cooking).

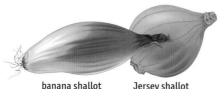

banana shallot   Jersey shallot

Garlic

Allium sativum, Liliaceae

A plant originally from central Asia. Garlic has a particularly persistent flavor that stays on the breath and produces sweat. The bulb or "head" of garlic is formed of smaller sections, commonly called cloves. Each head may contain 12-16 cloves. The most common varieties are the **white garlic** or "softneck garlic"; the **pink garlic** and the **purple garlic**, only the skin of which is colored; and the **rocambole (hardneck) garlic**, which has a milder flavor.

white garlic

BUYING

:: **Choose:** plump and firm heads of garlic with intact skin and no sprouts or spots. Garlic is available in a variety of forms (flakes, powder, paste, etc.), but it is best to use fresh garlic for the most flavor.

PREPARING

To peel garlic more easily, lightly crush cloves under the flat side of a knife. Cut them in half and remove the green shoot sometimes found in the middle; the shoot makes garlic difficult to digest and is responsible for the odor it leaves on the breath. The flavor of garlic doesn't appear until it is cut, crushed or chopped. The more finely it is cut, the stronger its taste will be.

NUTRITIONAL INFORMATION

water	59%
protein	0.6 g
fat	0.1 g
fiber	0.1 g
carbohydrates	3 g
calories	13
	per 0.3 oz/9 g (3 cloves)

EXCELLENT SOURCE: selenium.

PROPERTIES: diuretic, carminative, stomachic, tonic, antispasmodic, antiarthritic, antiseptic, anthelmintic and antibiotic. Garlic is said to relieve various illnesses such as bronchitis, gout, hypertension and digestive problems.

Garlic

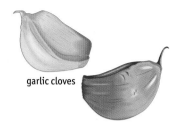

garlic cloves

SERVING IDEAS

Garlic is used mainly as a condiment. It flavors vinaigrettes, soups, vegetables, tofu, meat, stews, charcuterie (sausages and deli meats), marinades, etc. Raw, chopped or crushed, garlic is used to make aioli (garlic mayonnaise), rouille (a red pepper sauce), tapenade (olive paste), pistou (a green herb sauce like pesto), pesto sauce and garlic butter. Meats such as lamb roasts can be stuffed with cloves of garlic.

For a delicate hint of garlic, rub a raw garlic clove, peeled and cut in half, on the inside of a salad bowl or a fondue pot. To flavor oil, add a few cloves of lightly crushed garlic. The green stems of fresh garlic can also be used in place of shallots or chives.

Chew parsley, mint or coffee beans to freshen the breath after eating garlic.

STORING

:: At room temperature: 6 months, in a dry, well-ventilated, cool or temperate place, around 30°F (0°C) and a humidity level no higher than 60%. Garlic stems can be braided and hung several months in an airy spot.

:: In the freezer: 2 months, as is, with its outer skin removed.

COOKING

For maximum flavor, only add garlic at the end of cooking. For a more discreet, nutty flavor that won't have such an effect on breath, leave garlic whole and cook without peeling or cutting. Avoid browning garlic when frying, as this destroys almost all of its flavor and makes it bitter. This bitterness will transfer to other foods.

pink garlic

Onion

Allium cepa, Liliaceae

Spanish onion

A plant originally from central Asia and Palestine. The strength of the onion depends on the variety and the climate. The **Spanish onion** is one of the mildest. The **white onion** is mild and sweet. The **red onion** is the sweetest and the **yellow onion** is the strongest. The **Vidalia** onion is a large pale yellow onion native to Vidalia, Georgia. They are sweet and juicy.

The **green onion** or "new onion" is sold fresh in bundles. These are also known as scallions (see p. 13).

Some people find onion difficult to digest (especially raw). Onion affects the breath, which can be freshened by chewing parsley, mint or coffee beans. The aroma of the onion comes from its volatile essential oil, which is rich in allyl sulfides.

BUYING

:: **Choose:** firm onion, with no sign of sprouting or mold, a good dry, smooth and crackly outer skin, and a neck that is as small as possible. Onions are often treated with radiation to prevent germination, which is rarely indicated on the packaging. Onion is available in dried form, as flakes or powder, sold as is or seasoned (for example, onion salt). Some of these products contain more salt than onion.

NUTRITIONAL INFORMATION

	raw
water	89.7%
protein	1.2 g
fat	0.2 g
carbohydrates	8.6 g
fiber	1.6 g
calories	38
	per 3.5 oz/100 g

CONTAINS: potassium, vitamin C, folic acid and vitamin B_6. Onions contain substantially the same amount of vitamins and minerals when cooked.

PROPERTIES: diuretic, antibiotic, antiscorbutic, stimulant and expectorant. It is used to treat flu, intestinal parasites, gallstones, diarrhea and rheumatism.

Onion

PREPARING

Completely remove the section at the base of the onion with roots attached to make separating the layers of the onion easier. A cut onion loses its juice; avoid preparing it too far in advance or leaving on a counter or wooden surface that it might impregnate with its juice. To remove the smell of onion from hands, rub with lemon juice or vinegar. Avoid chopping onion in a processor, as it turns into a purée. The more finely an onion is chopped the more quickly it cooks, but the more flavor it loses.

Preparing onions is often accompanied by watery eyes, caused by the breakdown of onion cells when cut; these cells release sulfurous substances that, in contact with the surrounding air, create a new molecule, allyl sulfate, that irritates the eye. The stronger the onion, the more it stings the eyes. There are several suggested tricks for preventing tears:

- Use a very sharp knife and stand as far away from the onion as possible.
- Chill the onion for 1 hr in the fridge or 15 min in the freezer to slow down the action of the enzyme.
- Protect the eyes so they are not in direct contact with the irritant.
- Cut the onion under a stream of cold water to dissolve the irritating molecules, which are water-soluble.

white onion

STORING

The length of time onions keep depends on the variety. The "stronger" the onion is and the less water it contains, the better it will keep.

:: At room temperature: keep onions in a cool, dry place (yellow onions: 2-3 months; red onions: 2-6 weeks). Keep onions away from potatoes, as they absorb their moisture, which makes them rot and develop. Avoid keeping cut onions; they lose their vitamins and can spoil, as they oxidize rapidly.

:: In the fridge: green onions, 1 week.

:: In the freezer: peeled and chopped. Onions soften when defrosted and lose flavor.

Onions can be dried: cut into thin slices, place on a cookie sheet and put in the sun for 2-3 days, then dry in a 200°F (90°C) oven for about 10 min, or dry in a food dehydrator for a few hours 150°F-160°F (65°C-70°C).

SERVING IDEAS

Onion is used cooked or raw, especially when mild. The flavor of raw sliced onion can be softened by boiling for a few minutes (cool under cold water) or by soaking in cold water or vinegar. Yellow onion is an essential ingredient in onion tart, French onion soup and dishes prepared à la soubise and Nicoise-style. Onion can be served as a gratin, deep-fried, stir-fried, with cream or stuffed. It is used as a condiment in hot or cold dishes, cooked or raw, chopped, minced or cut into rings. Studded with a clove, onion adds flavor to stews or stocks.

Small onions can be glazed or preserved in vinegar. They are added whole to stews or slow-cooked dishes (for example, beef burgundy).

COOKING

Cooking brings out the sweetness in onion and makes it lose its sulfurous enzymes, making it milder.

:: Sautéed: sauté onions briefly without browning them to retain their crisp texture.

red onion

green onion

Water chestnut

Eleocharis dulcis, Cyperaceae

The aquatic bulb of a plant originally from southern China. The bulb is encased in a coarse dark brown skin; the crunchy, juicy, sweet and perfumed white flesh is covered in a thin brown skin. Water chesnut is most familiar in North America as a canned food imported from China and sold in specialty food stores.

water chestnut

BUYING

:: **Choose:** water chestnuts that are fresh and very hard.

:: **Avoid:** bruised water chestnuts or ones that have soft spots.

SERVING IDEAS

Water chestnuts are eaten raw (*Eleocharis dulcis* species only) or cooked. Raw water chestnuts are served as an hors d'oeuvre or as part of a light meal. Cooked water chestnuts are delicious by themselves, coated in butter. They add an unusual crunchy note to many dishes, in particular soups, mixed salads, fruit salads, sautéed tofu or vegetable-based dishes, pasta dishes and quiches, meat, poultry and seafood. They are delicious cooked with rice and spinach, then gratinéed.

Water chestnut purée can be added to chicken stock with onions, apples and a light cream, or to potato, sweet potato or winter squash.

NUTRITIONAL INFORMATION

	raw	canned
water	74%	86%
protein	1.5 g	1.1 g
fat	0.2 g	0.1 g
carbohydrates	24 g	12 g
calories	107	50
		per 3.5 oz/100 g

EXCELLENT SOURCE: potassium.
CONTAINS: riboflavin, magnesium and phosphorus (raw), potassium and iron (canned).
PROPERTY: tonic.

PREPARING

Wash fresh water chestnuts carefully to remove all traces of mud, remove any soft or brown sections and discard damaged or fermented chestnuts.

Water chestnuts may be peeled before or after cooking. There is less waste if they are peeled after cooking, but this will affect the color of the flesh. To peel before cooking: place the water chestnuts in a saucepan, cover with boiling water and boil 4-5 min. Drain, then peel using a sharp knife to remove their thin brown skin. Drop into water to which some lemon juice has been added to avoid discoloring. To peel after cooking, first make a cross-shaped incision into the flat base.

COOKING

Cooking makes water chestnuts slightly sweeter and preserves their crunchy texture.

:: **Boiled:** add a little lemon juice to the cooking water to prevent browning. They can also be cooked in stock or a half-and-half mixture of water and milk.

:: **Stir-fried:** first boil (5 min) or steam (7-8 min) the water chestnuts.

Water chestnuts can be used whole, halved, sliced, diced, julienned or puréed.

STORING

Water chestnuts are fairly fragile, so it is best to store them unpeeled.

:: **In the fridge:** 2 weeks, in a container and covered with water. Fresh, unwashed water chestnuts can also be placed 2 weeks in a paper bag and stored in the coldest part of the fridge. They need to be checked regularly, as they can start to dry out or ferment. Peeled water chestnuts keep for 2-3 days. Refrigerate any uneaten canned water chestnuts in water, replacing with fresh water every day.

:: **In the freezer:** 6 months, raw and unpeeled or 1 year, cooked and puréed (1 tablespoon/ 15 ml of butter or honey can be added to the purée before freezing to prevent it from separating). Stir the purée once defrosted to restore its even consistency.

Beet

Beta vulgaris, Chenopodiaceae

A plant with a fleshy root probably originally from North Africa. There are three principal varieties of beets. The **garden beet** is a more or less fleshy beet with a thin, smooth skin and usually a bright red flesh with large colorful wavy or crinkly edible leaves. The **fodder beet** is used as cattle feed. The **sugar beet** ("red beet") is turned into sugar or alcohol.

red beet

BUYING

:: **Choose:** firm, smooth beets with no spots or bruises and a good deep red color.
:: **Avoid:** very large beets or ones with long roots, as they can be woody.

COOKING

Wash the beets under running water without damaging the skin; brush gently if necessary. Cook the beets whole without peeling or breaking the skin, leaving the roots on and ¾-1¼ in. (2-3 cm) of the tops.
:: **Boiled or steamed:** depending on the size of the beets, allow 30-60 min cooking time.
:: **Baked:** this method keeps the flavor and highlights the color.
To check for doneness, run the beets under a stream of cold water, the skin will come off easily if they are well cooked. Avoid pricking beets with a fork or knife as they will then lose color during cooking. Only add salt at the end of cooking, as salt will discolor them.

STORING

:: **At room temperature:** 2-4 weeks. Store leaves or roots with 2-3 in. (5-8 cm) of stem in a cool (30°F/0°C) and humid (90%-95%) environment.
Beets keep longer in the ground or in a winter cellar, but they tend to harden.
:: **In the fridge:** fresh beets, 2-4 weeks. Unwashed leaves, 3-5 days, in a loosely closed or perforated plastic bag.
:: **In the freezer:** cook prior.

NUTRITIONAL INFORMATION

	cooked	cooked leaves
water	89%	90.9%
protein	2.6 g	1.1 g
fat	0.2 g	0.1 g
carbohydrates	5.5 g	6.7 g
fiber	2.9 g	2.2 g
calories	27	31
		per 3.5 oz/100 g

BEET BULB

EXCELLENT SOURCE: potassium and vitamin A.
GOOD SOURCE: vitamin C, riboflavin and magnesium.
CONTAINS: iron, copper, calcium, thiamine, vitamin B$_6$, folic acid, zinc and niacin.
PROPERTIES: aperitive and easily digested. Beets relieve headaches and are useful against flu and anemia.

BEET LEAVES

EXCELLENT SOURCE: potassium.
GOOD SOURCE: folic acid and magnesium.
CONTAIN: iron.

SERVING IDEAS

 Beets can be eaten raw, cooked, canned or pickled in vinegar.

Raw beets are peeled, sliced or grated and, if desired, seasoned. Cooked beets can be eaten hot or cold; they are often dressed with a vinaigrette or used in salads. Their leaves are delicious cooked and are prepared in the same way as spinach or chard.

Beets can also be used as a coffee substitute; finely sliced beets are dried, roasted, then powdered.

The beet is the basis of borscht, an eastern European soup traditionally served with sour cream.

Beet juice stains fingers easily; a little lemon juice will remove marks (or use gloves to avoid this problem). It can also color urine and stools.

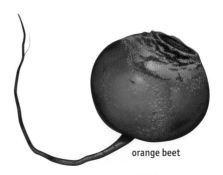
orange beet

Turnip

Brassica rapa, Cruciferae

A root vegetable of European origin, the turnip belongs to a family that also includes cabbage, mustard and radish. The fleshy part of the turnip is covered with a thin skin, the upper part of which forms a reddish or purple ring. The tops of the turnip plant are edible. Turnip is often confused with rutabaga. It can be told apart by its leaves, which are rough and hairy.

turnip

BUYING

:: **Choose:** a firm, heavy, unwrinkled turnips without spots or bruises. The tops (if still attached) should be firm and green.
:: **Avoid:** large turnips, which can be bitter and woody.

SERVING IDEAS

Turnip is delicious in soups and stews, puréed or stuffed and braised. When tender, turnip is cooked with cream, with Mornay sauce or in a gratin. It can be eaten raw or cooked in a salad. Its tops are prepared in the same way as spinach.

STORING

:: **In the fridge:** 1-3 weeks, unwashed, tops removed, in a loosely closed or perforated plastic bag. Place tops 4-5 days in a loosely closed or perforated plastic bag.
:: **In the freezer:** blanch 2 min or cook and turn into a purée.

COOKING

:: **Boiled:** 10-15 min.
:: **Steamed:** a little longer than boiling time, depending on the size of the vegetable. Turnip becomes high in calories when fried.

NUTRITIONAL INFORMATION

	raw
water	92%
protein	0.9 g
fat	0.1 g
carbohydrates	6.2 g
fiber	1.8 g
calories	27
	per 3.5 oz/100 g

TURNIP BULB
GOOD SOURCE: vitamin C and potassium.
CONTAINS: folic acid.
PROPERTIES: revitalizing, diuretic, antiscorbutic, refreshing, emollient and pectoral. The sulfurous substances in turnip may cause flatulence.

TURNIP LEAVES
GOOD SOURCE: vitamin A, vitamin B, vitamin C, potassium and magnesium.

PREPARING

Brush, peel and wash the turnips just prior to cooking to avoid browning. If the turnips are very fresh, not too large and unwaxed, peeling is not necessary. It is preferable to blanch turnips 10 min before preparing them, as they become more digestible, retain more nutritional value and will emit less odor.

Parsnip

Pastinaca sativa, Apiaceae

A root vegetable originally from the Mediterranean region. Its texture resembles that of a turnip and the top part of the plant is similar to celery. Its yellow-white, fruity flesh has a nutty taste.

parsnip

BUYING

:: **Choose:** firm and smooth parsnips with no bruises and fairly small in size.

SERVING IDEAS

Parsnips are prepared in the same way as carrots, salsify or turnips, which they can replace in most recipes. They are delicious puréed, fried, served cold with vinaigrette, glazed in the same way as carrots or as a vegetable side dish. They can be eaten raw or in soups or stews. Parsnips have more flavor if cooked whole and not for too long (approximately the same cooking time as carrots).

PREPARING

Brush and peel the parsnips (only if waxed). Their thin skin can be easily removed after cooking, especially if the parsnips are cooked whole or they are older. The flesh darkens on contact with air; it must be cooked as soon as it is cut or placed in water with a little lemon juice or vinegar. It may be necessary to remove the core of older or large parsnips, as these are often hard, woody and tasteless.

NUTRITIONAL INFORMATION

	cooked
water	77.7%
protein	1.3 g
fat	0.3 g
carbohydrates	19.5 g
fiber	4 g
calories	55
	per 3.5 oz/100 g

Parsnips have a high level of carbohydrate, much higher than carrots, which makes them sweet and relatively high in calories.

EXCELLENT SOURCE: potassium and folic acid.
CONTAINS: vitamin C, magnesium, pantothenic acid, copper, phosphorus and vitamin B_6.
PROPERTIES: disintoxicant, emmenagogic, antirheumatic and diuretic.

STORING

:: **In the fridge:** 4 weeks, wrapped and placed in a loosely closed or perforated plastic bag with a sheet of paper towel.
:: **In the freezer:** blanch whole parsnips 5 min or cut parsnips 3 min.

Carrot

Daucus carota, Apiaceae

A root vegetable originally from the Middle East and central Asia. Carrots may be either long or rounded depending on the variety. They can be orange, white, yellow, red, purple or black.

carrot

BUYING

:: **Choose:** firm, colorful carrots with stiff, well-colored tops (stalks and leaves).
:: **Avoid:** limp carrots with damp or sprouting parts.

STORAGE

:: **At room temperature:** place carrots in a dark, cool (35°F/1°C), humid (93%-98% humidity), and well-ventilated environment. Do not store carrots near vegetables that emit a lot of ethylene gas, such as pears, apples or potatoes (which speeds up ripening).
:: **In the fridge:** 1-3 weeks, in a loosely closed or perforated plastic bag.
:: **In the freezer:** 1 year at -0.5°F/-18°C. Blanch whole carrots 5 min or cut carrots 3 min.

PREPARING

Wash or brush the carrots; peel if older. Remove the bitter green part near the stems. Cut into sticks, rounds, chunks, or julienne strips or dice, slice or grate.

NUTRITIONAL INFORMATION

	raw	cooked
water	87.8%	87.4%
protein	0.9 g	1.2 g
fat	0.1 g	0.1 g
carbohydrates	3.2 g	10.5 g
fiber	3.2 g	1.9 g
calories	43	45
		per 3.5 oz/100 g

EXCELLENT SOURCE: vitamin A (raw and cooked) and potassium (raw).
GOOD SOURCE (COOKED): potassium.
CONTAINS: vitamin C and thiamine (raw), copper (cooked), vitamin B_6, folic acid and magnesium (raw and cooked).
PROPERTIES: diuretic, mineralizing, anthelmintic, antidiarrheal, tonic and antianemic. Carrots play a role in maintaining good eyesight. Raw grated carrots can be applied as a remedy to relieve burns. Their juice seems to be beneficial for the liver. Excessive consumption of carrots may cause skin to develop a yellow hue.

SERVING IDEAS

Raw carrots are eaten plain, in salads, and as an hors d'oeuvre, or used in cake and cookie batters. Cooked carrots are prepared à la jardiniere (cut into chunks and cooked with other garden vegetables), glazed or puréed with butter or cream. They are used in soups, stews, quiches, soufflés and omelettes.

Celeriac

Apium graveolens var. *rapaceum,* Apiaceae

A root vegetable originally from the Mediterranean, celeriac is a variety of celery. It has an irregular shape, covered with small root clumps. Its brownish skin is rough and thick. The white crunchy flesh has a slightly pungent flavor.

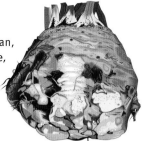

celeriac

BUYING

:: **Choose:** a heavy, firm, intact celeriac, without bruises.

:: **Avoid:** hollow-sounding celeriac with a diameter of more than 4½ in. (12 cm) or weighing more than 1 lb (500 g).

SERVING IDEAS

Celeriac is eaten raw, cut into slices, diced or grated (often dressed with a mustard-flavored mayonnaise or *remoulade* sauce). It can be cooked and made into a purée, by itself or with other vegetables. It adds flavor to soups and stews. It is well suited to braising and is delicious covered in a Mornay or béchamel sauce and gratinéed.

PREPARING

Wash then peel celeriac, or peel after cooking. To prevent the flesh from turning brown, sprinkle with vinaigrette or lemon juice as soon as it is cut, or cook immediately.

STORING

:: **In the fridge:** a few weeks, without its leaves, in a loosely closed or perforated plastic bag.

Celeriac can also be kept at near-freezing temperature.

NUTRITIONAL INFORMATION

	raw	cooked
water	88%	92.3%
protein	1.5 g	1 g
fats	0.3 g	0.2 g
carbohydrates	9.2 g	5.9 g
calories	39	25
		per 3.5 oz/100 g

EXCELLENT SOURCE (RAW): potassium.
GOOD SOURCE: vitamin C, phosphorus, vitamin B$_6$ and magnesium (raw), iron and potassium (cooked).
CONTAINS (COOKED): vitamin C, phosphorus, vitamin B$_6$ and magnesium.
PROPERTIES: aperitive, diuretic, depurative, stomachic, mineralizing and tonic.

COOKING

Avoid overcooking.
:: **Boiled:** 10-15 min.
:: **Steamed:** 12-18 min.
Adding an acidic substance to the cooking liquid (1 teaspoon/5 ml of lemon juice or vinegar) prevents it from oxidizing.

Black radish

Raphanus sativus var. *niger,* Cruciferae

A root vegetable probably originally from the eastern Mediterranean region. The black radish can be almost as pungent as horseradish, which is a close relative. Its flesh is very white, firm, and not as juicy as the red radish.

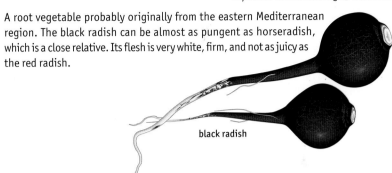

black radish

BUYING

 :: Choose: very firm black radishes, without any spots or cracks. The tops, if still attached, should be a bright green.

SERVING IDEAS

 Black radishes are rarely eaten as is. To salt, grate or slice black radishes thinly or into sticks, sprinkle with salt, mix well then cover the bowl and let rest for 1 hr, then rinse, drain, and prepare according to the recipe. They can then be flavored with shallots and sour cream, used in salads, or served with a *remoulade* sauce (mustard-flavored mayonnaise). Black radishes are very decorative when their skins are left on. When cooked, their flavor is similar to rutabaga. They are used in soups, stews, and omelettes and with tofu.

PREPARING

Scrape, brush and peel black radishes.

NUTRITIONAL INFORMATION

PROPERTIES: the extracted juice of black radishes is said to be antiscorbutic and antiallergic. It is used as a sedative for the nerves and a tonic for the respiratory system. It is used to treat the liver, dyspepsia, cholelithiasis, urinary lithiasis, lung conditions (coughs, chronic bronchitis, asthma), whooping cough, rheumatism, arthritis, gout and eczema.

COOKING

 :: Stir-fried: 10-25 min cooking time, depending on freshness.

STORING

:: In the fridge: several weeks, unwashed, without their tops, in a loosely closed or perforated plastic bag.

Radish

Raphanus sativus, Cruciferae

A root vegetable probably originally from western Asia. There are several species of radish. The **red radish** has a white, cream-colored or reddish flesh that is juicy and crunchy, and has edible leaves. The **black radish** (p. 31) has a flavor that is more pungent than the red radish. The **white radish** (p. 33) is also known as "daikon."

radish

BUYING

:: **Choose:** firm radishes with smooth skin and no spots or bruises. The radish tops, if still attached, should be bright green.
:: **Avoid:** large radishes.

SERVING IDEAS

Radishes are eaten raw (as an hors d'oeuvre, with dips, in salads, and sandwiches), marinated or cooked. They are used in soups, pot roasts, omelettes or stir-fries. Fresh and tender radish leaves are prepared in the same way as spinach. They can be used in a soup or potato mash, or dried and infused. Radish sprouts have a pungent flavor similar to watercress. They can be used in soups, sandwiches and omelettes, and to flavor tofu and fish (add at the last minute).

PREPARING

Peel radishes if a less pungent flavor is desired. Remove roots and leaves, then rinse them in a large quantity of water and drain. Radishes are eaten whole, sliced, in sticks, diced, chopped or grated.

NUTRITIONAL INFORMATION

	raw
water	95%
protein	0.6 g
fat	0.5 g
carbohydrates	3.6 g
fiber	2.2 g
calories	17
	per 3.5 oz/100 g

GOOD SOURCE (RAW): vitamin C and potassium.

CONTAINS (RAW): folic acid.

PROPERTIES (RAW): antiseptic, antiarthritic, antiscorbutic, antirachitic, antirheumatic and aperitive. Radishes seems to aid digestion, and treat bronchitis, asthma, scurvy, demineralization, as well as the liver and gallbladder. Some people find radishes difficult to digest.

COOKING

Adding an acidic substance to the cooking liquid intensifies the color of radishes. Alkaline substances reduce their color.

STORING

:: **In the fridge:** 1 week, unwashed, with tops removed, in a loosely closed or perforated plastic bag.

Daikon

Raphanus sativus var. *longipinnatus*, Cruciferae

A root vegetable probably originally from the eastern Mediterranean region. Daikon is a white-fleshed winter radish, crunchy and juicy with a relatively mild taste. It is also known as "Japanese" or "Chinese" radish, or "winter radish." There are several sweet-fleshed varieties.

daikon

BUYING

:: Choose: firm and shiny daikons, with no spots or bruises. The tops, if attached, should be a bright green.

:: Avoid: very large daikons and those with opaque skin.

SERVING IDEAS

Daikons are eaten raw as an hors d'oeuvre, with dips, in salads and sandwiches. Grated and dressed with vinaigrette, vinegar or lemon juice, they can be used as an accompaniment to vegetables, poultry, seafood or fish. Cooked daikon is used in the same way as turnip, especially in soups. It can also be added to stir-fries. Daikon tops, prepared in the same way as spinach, can be added to salads or soups.

Daikon seeds can be sprouted. They have a pungent flavor, similar to watercress. They can be added, at the last minute, to soups, sandwiches and omelettes, and to flavor tofu and fish.

In Asia, daikons are cooked or preserved in salt. They are used in soups or fried with other foods. Their flavor becomes milder during cooking.

NUTRITIONAL INFORMATION

water	94.5%
protein	0.3 g
carbohydrates	1.8 g
calories	8
	per 1.75 oz/50 g

CONTAINS (RAW): vitamin C and potassium.
PROPERTIES: antiseptic, diuretic, aperitive and tonic.

STORING

Daikon is fragile.

:: In the fridge: without their tops, placed in a loosely closed or perforated plastic bag (3-4 days maximum if to be eaten raw or 1 week if intended to be cooked).

PREPARING

Brush daikon or thinly peel the part that is going to be used. It can be grated, cut into sticks, diced, julienned or sliced finely, or puréed after cooking.

red winter radish

green winter radish

Rutabaga

Brassica napus var. *napobrassica,* Cruciferae

A root vegetable that is the result of a cross between the savoy cabbage and the turnip. It is usually yellowish in color, but white-fleshed varieties also exist. Rutabaga has a stronger taste than turnip; it can be distinguishable by a protruding section at the top of the root to which the leaves are attached.

rutabaga

BUYING

:: **Choose:** a firm and heavy rutabaga, with no spots and not too large.

SERVING IDEAS

 Rutabaga is eaten raw or cooked. It is eaten in soups, stews and soufflés. It can be used in place of turnip in most recipes. Rutabaga benefits from the addition of a sauce or cream. Puréed rutabaga is mixed with mashed potato and carrot.

PREPARING

Peel then cut the rutabaga. Remove the heart if it is brown in color. The stronger the rutabaga smells, the sharper its flavor will be. To soften the flavor, blanch it 5 min before cooking.

STORING

:: **In the fridge:** 3 weeks, unwashed, in a loosely closed or perforated plastic bag.
:: **In the freezer:** blanch 2 min, or cook then turn into a purée.

NUTRITIONAL INFORMATION

	cooked
water	90%
protein	1.1 g
fat	0.2 g
carbohydrates	7.7 g
fiber	2.1 g
calories	34
	per 3.5 oz/100 g

EXCELLENT SOURCE: potassium.
GOOD SOURCE: vitamin C.
CONTAINS: magnesium, folic acid and phosphorus.
PROPERTIES: mineralizing and diuretic.

COOKING

:: **Boiled:** 15 min.
:: **Steamed:** slightly longer cooking time than if boiled.

Malanga

Xanthosoma sagittifolium, Araceae

The tuber of a plant originally from the northern part of South America and the Caribbean. Malanga belongs to a family of decorative plants related to the philodendron. The impressive leaves of the malanga plant are edible. The tuber, irregular in shape, is covered with a thin smooth skin that may be covered in hair or small roots, depending on the variety. Its firm, crunchy and slightly viscous flesh can be white, yellow, orange, pink or reddish in color. It has a strong, slightly earthy and vaguely nutty flavor. Malanga is high in starch.

malanga

BUYING

:: **Choose:** a very firm malanga with no mold or soft spots. Make a small slice with the fingernail to check whether the flesh is juicy.

SERVING IDEAS

Malanga is only eaten cooked. It is grated and cooked in crepes or made into fritters (*acras*), Caribbean-style. Use in moderation, as its strong taste can overpower other foods. It is delicious fried or with a sauce. Its starch is used in the manufacturing of alcohol.
Malanga leaves are cooked in the same way as spinach or used to wrap foods that are then cooked in the oven.

STORING

Malanga is fragile.
:: **In the fridge or at room temperature:** keep leaves several days in the fridge in a loosely closed or perforated plastic bag. Wipe it with a damp cloth before storing.

NUTRITIONAL INFORMATION

water	66%
protein	1.7g
fat	0.3 g
carbohydrates	31 g
calories	132
	per 3.5 oz/100 g

CONTAINS: thiamine, vitamin C, iron and phosphorus. Several malanga varieties contain acrid, irritating substances that are neutralized when cooked.

PREPARING

Peel the malanga, then cover with cold water if not using immediately.

COOKING

:: **Boiled:** 20 min. It can be used as is, as a side dish or puréed.
Malanga can first be boiled or steamed, then added to a stew or soup at the end of cooking.

Salsify

Tragopogon porrifolius and *Scorzonera hispanica,* Compositae

Root vegetables that are originally from the Mediterranean region, **salsify** (*Tragopogon porrifolius*) and **black** (or "Spanish") **salsify** (*Scorzonera hispanica*) are closely related. Their mild and sweet flavor is often compared to that of oysters. Some say they have a slight asparagus or artichoke taste, with an aftertaste of coconut. The leaves of the salsify plant are edible; the young shoots have a slight Belgian endive taste. Black salsify is less woody and tastier than salsify.

salsify

black salsify

BUYING

:: **Choose:** firm, medium-sized salsify, with no damp parts.

SERVING IDEAS

Salsify and black salsify are delicious in soups and stews or in a gratin, with béchamel or cheese sauce. They can be eaten cold, dressed with a vinaigrette. Salsify goes well with potato, leek, celery, onion and spinach. They are delicious braised with veal, poultry or fish; they can be glazed in the same way as carrots.

PREPARING

Both varieties of salsify oxidize when peeled or cut. Immerse them in water mixed with a little lemon juice or vinegar or boil them whole for 15 min before peeling or preparing. Their skin can temporarily stain hands when peeling.

STORING

Both varieties of salsify are best used fresh.
:: **In the fridge:** several days, unwashed in a loosely closed or perforated plastic bag.

NUTRITIONAL INFORMATION

	cooked
water	81%
protein	2.7 g
fat	0.2 g
carbohydrates	15.4 g
fiber	3.1 g
calories	80
	per 3.5 oz/100 g

SALSIFY

GOOD SOURCE: potassium.
CONTAINS: vitamin B_6, vitamin C, magnesium, folic acid and phosphorus.
PROPERTIES: salsify contains inulin (a carbohydrate close to starch), which is suitable for diabetics to eat, as it does not affect blood sugar levels. Salsify is blood thinning and has a decongestant effect on the liver and kidneys. It can cause flatulence. Delicate persons or those eating salsify for the first time should only eat a small amount.

COOKING

 Cook briefly so that the flesh does not become mushy.
:: **Steamed:** 10-15 min (recommended cooking method).
:: **Boiled:** 8-12 min.

Burdock

Arctium lappa, Compositae

Tall plant probably originally from Sibera or the Caucasus. The fruit of the burdock plant are bracts ending in small hooks. Burdock is also known under its Japanese name, *"gobo."* The edible parts of the plant are its young shoots, its large, pale green oval leaves and its roots, whose flavor is similar to salsify.

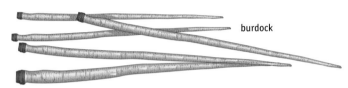

burdock

BUYING

:: **Choose:** firm burdock, measuring about ¾ in. (2 cm) wide and 15¾ in. (40 cm) long.

PREPARING

To remove burdock's bitter aftertaste, soak for 5-10 min in salted water before cooking. Clean well to remove any soil residue and cook unpeeled. To prevent the flesh from discoloring, cook as soon as it is cut, or soak for a few minutes in cold water to which a little lemon juice or vinegar has been added. It can be grated, cut into thin slices or diced.

SERVING IDEAS

Burdock is used as a vegetable or to flavor stews and marinades. It can also be stir-fried or used as a soup ingredient. The young shoots and leaves can be braised; the leaves can also be cooked as a leaf vegetable.

NUTRITIONAL INFORMATION

	boiled
water	76%
protein	2.1 g
fat	0.2 g
carbohydrates	21 g
calories	88
	per 3.5 oz/100 g

EXCELLENT SOURCE: potassium.
GOOD SOURCE: magnesium.
CONTAINS: phosphorus, iron and calcium.
PROPERTIES: sudorific, diuretic, depurative, choleretic and used against cancer. Burdock purifies the blood and is effective as an ointment on skin problems.

STORING

:: **In the fridge:** several days, wrapped in damp paper towel, then placed in a loosely closed or perforated plastic bag.

Eggplant

Solanum melongena, Solanaceae

The fruit of a plant originally from India, eggplant is a berry that is eaten as a vegetable. There are several varieties of eggplants. The **purple-skinned eggplant**, which has an elongated form like a large pear, is the most well-known variety. The **Asian** or "Chinese" **eggplant** refers to several varieties that can be as small as an egg, long and thin, or resemble a cluster of grapes. The thin, shiny, smooth skin can be dark or light purple, cream, white, green or orange. The yellowy-white flesh is spongy and contains small brownish edible seeds.

common eggplant

BUYING

:: Choose: a firm, heavy eggplant, with smooth, evenly colored skin. To test for ripeness, press sides gently: if the imprint remains visible, the eggplant is ready to eat.
:: Avoid: an eggplant with wrinkled, dull skin or with brown spots.

NUTRITIONAL INFORMATION

	raw
water	92%
protein	1.2 g
carbohydrates	6.3 g
fiber	1.5 g
calories	27
	per 3.5 oz/100 g

GOOD SOURCE: potassium.
CONTAINS: folic acid, copper, vitamin B_6 and magnesium.
PROPERTIES: diuretic, laxative and calming.

SERVING IDEAS

Eggplant is delicious hot or cold. It can be stuffed, broiled, gratinéed, stewed, skewered or puréed. It is cooked with tomatoes, garlic and olive oil, as in ratatouille, *baba ghanoush* (eggplant dip) or moussaka. Some Asian varieties can be eaten raw in a salad.

western eggplant

PREPARING

Prepare eggplant quickly or sprinkle it with lemon juice if it is left standing, as its flesh discolors quickly when cut. It is a good idea to cut large eggplants, sprinkle them liberally with salt and let sit for 1 to 2 hrs to remove some of their water content and bitterness. Eggplant can also be soaked in water for about 15 min, peeled, or simply cooked as is when using a less bitter variety.

STORING

Eggplant should be handled with care, as it is easily damaged. It is very sensitive to changes in temperature.

:: **In the fridge:** 1 week. Remove any wrapping as quickly as possible and place the eggplant in a loosely closed or perforated plastic bag.

:: **In the freezer:** 6-8 months, blanch or steam prior to freezing.

COOKING

Blanch the eggplant for a few minutes before cooking. Avoid adding salt, especially at the beginning of cooking time.

:: **Fried:** coat slices of eggplant in flour, beaten egg and bread crumbs for deep or pan-frying. Coating eggplants reduces fat absorption.

:: **Baked:** prick the eggplant so that it doesn't burst. Cook whole and unpeeled at 350°F (175°C) for 15-25 min depending on size. It can also be halved (make incisions in the flesh) so that it cooks evenly. Stuffed, it will take 35-60 min at 350°F (175°C) to cook. Cut into slices or chunks, eggplant cooks in 15-20 min. It can be brushed with a little olive oil and seasoned.

:: **Steamed** or **microwaved**.

:: **Grilled** or **broiled**: cook 4 to 6 inches from the heat source until browned on both sides. Brush with oil if it looks dry.

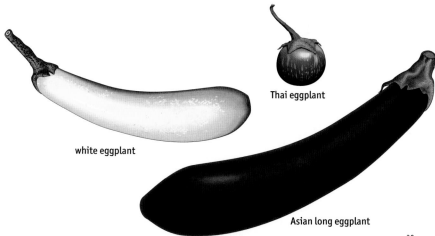

Thai eggplant

white eggplant

Asian long eggplant

Avocado

Persea americana, Lauraceae

The fruit of the avocado tree, originally from Central or South America. The flesh of the avocado is creamy, with a butterlike consistency and a slightly nutty flavor. The skin is not edible. Avocado varies in shape, color and size depending on the variety. The **Hass avocado** is oval in shape, with a rough black or purple-brown skin that is shiny when ripe. The **Fuerte**, **Zutano** and **Bacon avocados** are also oval in shape, with shiny green skin. The "**cocktail**" **avocado** is miniature-sized and has no pit.

Hass avocado

BUYING

:: **Choose:** an avocado that is rather heavy for its size, not too hard, and without dark spots or bruises. It is ready to eat when it yields to slight finger pressure.

:: **Avoid:** very soft avocado.

PREPARING

Cut the avocado in two, lengthwise, using a stainless steel knife. If the flesh clings to the pit, separate the two halves by gently twisting them in opposite directions, then remove the pit by embedding a knife in its center or using a spoon. Sprinkle the flesh with lemon juice to avoid the flesh discoloring.

NUTRITIONAL INFORMATION

	raw
water	74.3%
protein	2 g
fat	15.3 g
carbohydrates	7.4 g
fiber	2.1 g
calories	161
	per 3.5 oz/100 g

EXCELLENT SOURCE: potassium and folic acid.
GOOD SOURCE: vitamin B$_6$.
CONTAINS: magnesium, pantothenic acid (B$_5$), vitamin C, copper, niacin, iron, vitamin A and zinc.
PROPERTIES: very nutritious and high in energy. Avocado is said to be beneficial for the stomach and intestines.

SERVING IDEAS

 Avocado is usually eaten raw, since it does not cook well. Only add at the end of cooking time and avoid boiling, as it quickly loses its flavor.

Avocado is often served as is, simply cut in half with the cavity filled with vinaigrette, mayonnaise or lemon juice seasoned with salt and pepper. Avocado is used in sandwiches and salads. It is cooked in hot or cold soups and in desserts (ice cream, mousse, fruit salad, etc.). It is often stuffed with seafood or chicken. Guacamole, an avocado mash seasoned with hot pepper, pimiento, onions, spices and lime juice, and served with tortillas, is an essential dish in Mexican cooking.

STORING

:: At room temperature: place in a paper bag if you wish to speed up the ripening process.

:: In the fridge: ripe avocado, 2-3 days. If the avocado is cut, sprinkle the exposed part of the avocado with lemon juice to avoid the flesh discoloring and keep 1-2 days.

:: In the freezer: puréed with lemon juice, about 1 year.

Bacon avocado

Bell pepper

Capsicum annuum, Solanaceae

The fruit of a plant originally from Latin America, bell pepper (or "sweet pepper") is a more or less fleshy pod enclosing a quantity of whitish seeds in its internal cavity. There are several varieties, with different shapes, colors and tastes. The **green pepper** is picked before reaching full maturity, as green peppers left on the vine turn yellow, then red as they ripen. The **purple**, **brown** and **black peppers** turn green again if they are left on the plant. The **red** and **orange peppers** are the sweetest. Bell peppers ripened on the plant are sweeter and more aromatic.

green pepper

BUYING

:: **Choose:** a firm, shiny, brightly colored bell pepper, smooth and fleshy, with no spots or soft parts. The flesh should yield to slight pressure.

SERVING IDEAS

Bell pepper is eaten raw or cooked. Raw bell pepper is eaten plain, with dips or as an hors d'oeuvre, or in salads. Cooked bell pepper is used in soups, omelettes, with tofu, stews, on skewers, in rice and pasta dishes, pizzas and Portuguese and Mexican recipes. It works well with chicken, rabbit, ham, tuna and eggs. It is used to make pickles, gazpacho, *piperade* (an egg dish with stewed peppers) and ratatouille. It is often served stuffed.

NUTRITIONAL INFORMATION

water	92.2%
protein	0.9 g
fat	0.2 g
carbohydrates	6.4 g
fiber	2 g
calories	27
	per 3.5 oz/100 g

RED AND GREEN PEPPERS
EXCELLENT SOURCE: vitamin A and C (especially red peppers).
GOOD SOURCE: potassium.
CONTAIN: vitamin B_6 and folic acid.
PROPERTIES: stomachic, diuretic, stimulant, digestive and antiseptic.

STORING

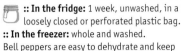 **:: In the fridge:** 1 week, unwashed, in a loosely closed or perforated plastic bag.
:: In the freezer: whole and washed.
Bell peppers are easy to dehydrate and keep for at least a year when dried. They can also be marinated.

COOKING

Cooking brings out the sweetness of bell peppers. Avoid overcooking, as they lose their color and nutrients. Cooking makes brown, black or purple bell peppers turn green.
:: Roasted or **grilled:** cook 6-10 min over open flame, rotating frequently, until skin blackened. Remove skin with knife, cut out stem and core and remove excess seeds.

PREPARING

Remove the stem, core and seeds, then cut the bell pepper into rings, strips, chunks or dice. When stuffing a bell pepper, cut around the stem and remove; take out the seeds and core, cut out any hard whitish ribs, stuff, then replace the stem. To reduce cooking time, blanch the bell pepper before emptying and filling it.
To remove the skin of a bell pepper, place it under the broiler and broil evenly for 10-12 min, turning frequently, until the skin bubbles and blackens. Cover the bell pepper with a damp cloth or place it in a paper bag until cool, then peel using a knife and rinse under running water.

yellow pepper

red pepper

Olive

Olea europaea, Oleaceae

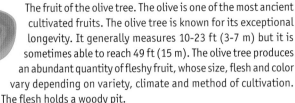

The fruit of the olive tree. The olive is one of the most ancient cultivated fruits. The olive tree is known for its exceptional longevity. It generally measures 10-23 ft (3-7 m) but it is sometimes able to reach 49 ft (15 m). The olive tree produces an abundant quantity of fleshy fruit, whose size, flesh and color vary depending on variety, climate and method of cultivation. The flesh holds a woody pit.

green olives

Green olives are picked when they have reached their normal size, just before they change color. **Black olives** are picked when ripe. They are dark purple in color, almost black.

Olives are inedible in their natural state. They contain a very bitter chemical compound that irritates the digestive system. To become edible, olives have to be marinated and undergo various treatments, which vary according to the region and the variety. The table olive must be medium to large in size, or 0.10-0.18 oz (3-5 g); the pit must be able to be removed easily, and the skin must be thin, flexible and resistant to shocks and brine solutions. Green olives are prepared according to two types of procedures: the Spanish method, which involves fermentation, and the American method, without fermentation. The Greek "salting" method only applies to black olives.

Olives can also be preserved in salt. This method results in wrinkled olives but the skin remains intact; their taste is fruity and slightly bitter.

Once they are ready to be consumed, olives are left in the barrel or packed into containers. Some are pitted and stuffed, especially with bell pepper, onion, almond or anchovy and even seasoned with spices. They can also be cut into halves, quarters or slices, chopped or turned into a paste.

< olives (raw)

Olive

BUYING

 Olives are sold loose, in jars or in cans. Check that olives sold loose are handled and stored with care.

STORING

:: **At room temperature:** 1 year, in a sealed container.

:: **In the fridge:** opened containers. Place olives bought loose in a closed container. Green olives and black salt-dried olives do not keep as long.

SERVING IDEAS

Olives are popular as hors d'oeuvres. They are also used in salads and with meat and poultry. They are an ingredient in a multitude of cooked dishes, in particular tapenade (black olive paste seasoned with capers and anchovy), pizza and stews. Olives play a role in many Mediterranean dishes such as Spanish tapas, and Nicoise- and Provencale-style dishes.

To soften the harshness or saltiness of olives, boil them for about 15 min (they will, however, lose some of their aroma). Some or all of the liquid in which olives are kept may also be replaced with water or a mixture of water and vinegar seasoned with garlic, thyme, oregano, etc.

NUTRITIONAL INFORMATION

	marinated green	black
protein	28 g	16 g
fat	2.5 g	2.5 g
carbohydrates	0.3 g	1.5 g
fiber	0.9 g	0.5 g
calories	23	25
		per 3.5 oz/100 g

GREEN AND BLACK OLIVES

CONTAIN: fats (12%-30%), iron (black olives).

TRACES: vitamins and minerals.

PROPERTIES: laxative, aperitive and cholagogic.

OLIVE OIL

PROPERTIES: used externally, it is said to be effective against hair loss and boils.

OLIVE LEAVES

PROPERTIES: astringent, hypotensive and hypoglycemic.

black olives

Cucumber

Cucumis sativus, Cucurbitaceae

The fruit of a plant originally from southern Asia. There are several varieties of cucumber. The so-called English or European varieties are longer; the American varieties are rounder.

The color of cucumber skin ranges between green and white. It can be smooth, ribbed or rough but is always shiny. Some varieties have bumps that can be prickly. The pale, cool and crunchy flesh is slightly bitter and contains a number of edible seeds whose size and quantity vary depending on the variety.

Gherkin, dill or pickling cucumber refers to cucumber varieties that are picked when still immature and firm in order to make into pickles.

American cucumber

BUYING

 :: Choose: a firm cucumber with a bright green color and of medium size.

:: Avoid: a bruised cucumber, one with yellow spots or that is too big (as it may be bitter or bland and contain many hard seeds).

STORING

Cucumber is sensitive to changes in temperature.

:: In the fridge: 3-5 days, as is or cut and well wrapped (as its taste is absorbed by surrounding food items).

NUTRITIONAL INFORMATION

water	96%
protein	0.5 g
fat	0.1 g
carbohydrates	2.9 g
fiber	0.7 g
calories	13
	per 3.5 oz/100 g

EXCELLENT SOURCE: potassium, vitamin C and folic acid.

PROPERTIES: diuretic, depurative and calming. Puréed and mixed with other ingredients, cucumber flesh is used to make masks for skin treatments.

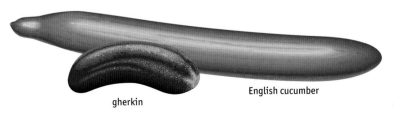

gherkin

English cucumber

Cucumber

SERVING IDEAS

Grated or cut lengthwise, sliced or diced, raw cucumber can be used with vinaigrette, yogurt or sour cream, or stuffed with seafood. It is also served as a salad. Cucumber can also be preserved, marinated or cooked. When cooked, it is prepared in the same way as zucchini, which it can replace in most recipes. It is excellent as a soup; it can accompany meat and fish and be added to stews, gratinéed or served with béchamel sauce. It can be sautéed or braised.

PREPARING

Remove cucumber seeds if hard. The skin may be left on, especially if the cucumber is very fresh, not too large and has not been waxed. It can be salted to reduce its water content and bitterness. It should be well drained so that the dish it is added to does not become watery.

Winter melon

Benincasa hispida, Cucurbitaceae

The fruit of a plant originally from Malaysia, the winter melon is related to the squash, the melon and the cucumber. The sweet, firm and tasty flesh encloses seeds inside a cavity. It is also called "white gourd," "ash gourd" or "wax gourd."

winter melon

BUYING

:: **Choose:** a firm, unbruised winter melon. Some large varieties of winter melon are sold in pieces, but some of the smaller ones are sold whole.

PREPARING

Remove the skin and the fibrous part of the winter melon containing the seeds. Cut the melon into pieces of the same size for even cooking.

NUTRITIONAL INFORMATION

	cooked
water	96%
protein	0.5 g
fat	0.2 g
carbohydrates	2.9 g
fiber	0.8 g
calories	40
	per 3.5 oz/100 g

CONTAINS: vitamin C.

SERVING IDEAS

Winter melon is used in soups and stir-fries or is preserved. It can often replace squash or pumpkin and is used as an accompaniment to spicy foods. The young leaves and floral buds, as well as the fried seeds, are edible.

STORING

:: **At room temperature:** several weeks, whole, in a cool, dry, dark place. It can also be stored 6 months at a temperature of 55°F-60°F (13°C-15°C) with a humidity level of 70%-75%.

Bitter melon

Momordica charantia, Cucurbitaceae

The fruit of a plant originally from India, the bitter melon is related to the squash, the melon and the cucumber. It is sometimes also called "bitter gourd" or "balsam pear." The rather dry flesh holds seeds. Its high level of quinine gives it a bitter taste that increases with its level of maturity. A mature bitter melon is yellow or orange.

bitter melon

BUYING

:: **Choose:** a firm, dark green bitter melon with no mold.

STORING

:: **In the fridge:** well wrapped, 1 week.

PREPARING

Peel the bitter melon (unless salting), cut in two lengthwise and remove the seeds and white part. Cut the flesh into pieces of the same size for even cooking. To reduce the bitterness of the melon, blanch it for a few minutes or salt it (leave for 30 min then rinse under water).

NUTRITIONAL INFORMATION

water	94%
protein	1 g
fat	0.2 g
carbohydrates	3.7 g
fiber	14 g
calories	17
	per 3.5 oz/100 g

SERVING IDEAS

Bitter melon can't be eaten raw. In China, it is steamed or used as an ingredient in a dish containing pork, onion, ginger and black bean sauce. It is also added to Chinese soups. In India, it is used alone or combined with lentils or potatoes, and seasoned with turmeric and cumin. It is often marinated.

Okra

Abelmoschus esculentus, Malvaceae

The fruit of a plant probably originally from Africa, okra is related to the hibiscus, mallow and cotton plants. Okra has edible skin that is smooth or slightly velvety, depending on the variety. The inside of the vegetable is divided into sections enclosing green or brownish edible seeds. Okra contains a moist substance that is released when the pod is broken. It has a subtle flavor and an unusual texture.

okra

BUYING

 :: Choose: well-colored okra that are tender but firm, without spots or bruises, up to 4 in. (10 cm) in length.

SERVING IDEAS

Okra is eaten raw or cooked. It can be prepared like asparagus or eggplant, which it can replace in most recipes (reduce cooking time). It goes well with tomatoes, onions, bell peppers and eggplant, as well as with the following herbs and spices: curry, coriander, oregano, lemon and vinegar. Cold, blanched okra is eaten as a salad or with vinaigrette dressing. Okra is an ingredient in several Creole dishes or as a side dish to chicken. Okra is used to thicken soups and stews. For this purpose, it should be added 10 min before the end of the cooking time.

COOKING

Okra can be cooked by itself or with other vegetables.

:: Braised or **boiled**.

:: Steamed: 8-15 min.

:: Breaded, then **fried**, **sautéed** or **marinated**.

Okra discolors in iron or copper saucepans.

NUTRITIONAL INFORMATION

	cooked
water	90%
protein	22 g
fat	0.2 g
carbohydrates	7.2 g
fiber	3.2 g
calories	32
	per 3.5 oz/100 g

EXCELLENT SOURCE (COOKED): potassium.

GOOD SOURCE (COOKED): magnesium and folic acid.

CONTAINS (COOKED): vitamin C, thiamine, vitamin B_6, zinc, vitamin A, calcium, phosphorus and niacin.

PROPERTIES: digestive, slightly laxative and emollient.

PREPARING

Gently rub any okra that has a velvety covering. Clean, then drain; remove the stem and tip if cooking whole. Cooked okra can be cut into rounds to thicken dishes.

STORING

:: In the fridge: 2-3 days, in a paper bag, or in paper towel, then inside a loosely closed or perforated plastic bag.

:: In the freezer: whole, blanch for 2 min before.

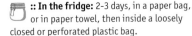

Tomato

Lycopersicon esculentum, Solanaceae

The fruit of a bushy and sometimes climbing plant, originally from Mexico and Central America. Tomato varies in color, taste, shape and size according to the variety. The **cherry tomato** has a diameter of 1-1³/₁₆ in. (2.5-3 cm). The yellow (or pear) tomato resembles a small pear. Yellow tomatoes are slightly less acidic than red. The **plum tomato** (or Italian or Roma tomato) resembles a small egg. The **grape tomato** is a baby plum tomato. The **common tomato** has a rounded shape, measures 2³/₈-4³/₄ in. (6-12 cm) in diameter and weighs about 2.5-3.5 oz (75 g-1 kg). The **green tomato** is medium-sized and highly flavored. The **genetically modified tomato** is

common tomato

a tomato whose genes have been altered for longer keeping. The **hydroponic tomato** was created by American agriculturists in 1984 in response to the industry's need for an easily harvested and packaged tomato.

BUYING

:: **Choose:** intact tomatoes without cracks or wrinkles, firm but yielding to slight pressure, with a bright color and pleasant smell.
:: **Avoid:** soft, spotted or damaged tomatoes. Tomatoes bought at the end of summer are best, as they are picked when ripe.

NUTRITIONAL INFORMATION

	raw red tomato	cooked red tomato
water	93.8%	92.2%
protein	0.8 g	1.1 g
fat	0.3 g	0.4 g
carbohydrates	4.6 g	5.8 g
fiber	1.2 g	1.5 g
calories	21	27
		per 3.5 oz/100 g

GOOD SOURCE: vitamin C and potassium.
CONTAINS: folic acid and vitamin A.
PROPERTIES: aperitive, diuretic, energizing, antiscorbutic, disintoxicating and mineralizing.

grape tomatoes

Tomato

SERVING IDEAS

The tomato is eaten raw or cooked. Raw tomato is eaten as is, dressed with vinaigrette or in salads, hors d'oeuvres and sandwiches. Cherry tomato is used raw, often for decorative effect.

The tomato can be stuffed, made into jam or used in soups, sauces, omelettes, risottos, pot roasts and marinades. It is an essential ingredient in ratatouille, gazpacho, pizza and *caponata* (a Mediterranean vegetable stew). It works very well with garlic, shallot, basil, tarragon, thyme, bay leaf, oregano and cumin. It is delicious with olives, bell peppers and eggplant.

Tomatoes are a perfect accompaniment to tuna and sardines as well as beef, chicken, veal or eggs, and are also featured in many Italian sauces and dishes.

Green tomatoes, edible when cooked, are often sautéed, fried or marinated. Tomatoes can be made into juice, sauce or coulis, or be puréed or crushed.

Tomatoes can also be dried and preserved in a container covered with oil, preferably olive.

STORING

:: At room temperature: 1 week, away from sunlight. Do not wash them until using. Wrapping green tomatoes individually in paper or covering them with a cloth speeds up the ripening process. Then, they can be kept a few weeks.

:: In the fridge: to slow the ripening process (2-3 days). Have tomatoes at room temperature for about 30 min before eating, for better flavor.

:: In the freezer: blanch whole tomatoes 30-60 sec and run under cold water before removing the skin, without letting them soak. Tomatoes can be cooked gently for 5-6 min or until tender with salt and sugar (1 teaspoon/5 ml each) before freezing.

To can tomatoes, use a sterilizing process and put the preparation in the appropriate sterilized jars. Add 1 tablespoon (15 ml) of bottled lemon juiced for every 2 cups (500 ml) of tomatoes, or $\frac{1}{5}$ teaspoon (1 ml) of citric acid. Add ¼ teaspoon (2 ml) of salt. Add these ingredients after the tomatoes are in the jar.

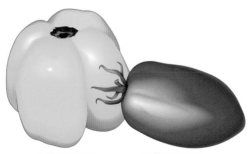

yellow tomato   Italian tomato

PREPARING

Wash tomato. Peel, seed and trim, if desired, according to how they will be used.

:: To peel: plunge tomato for 15-30 sec in boiling water (don't let it cook or soak), cool it or run under cold water. A colander or metal basket will make this process easier. A very ripe tomato can be peeled immediately. Cut into the skin, grab the skin between the thumb and the blade of a knife, and pull away.

:: To seed: cut tomato in half and squeeze out the juice and seeds, then remove any remaining seeds.

:: To trim: remove the hard part of the tomato that holds the stalk by cutting a circle around it.

COOKING

Avoid cooking tomatoes in aluminum receptacles, as this may lead to corrosion. Add a little sugar or honey during cooking to neutralize the acidity of tomatoes. Cook tomatoes over a very gentle heat so that they do not become difficult to digest.

:: Broiled or **baked:** 8-15 min. Slice in half and place cut-side up in pan.

:: Sautéed or **fried.**

cherry tomatoes   pear tomato

Tomatillo

Physalis ixocarpa, Solanaceae

The fruit of a plant probably originally from Mexico. The tomatillo is related to the tomato, eggplant, bell pepper and potato. This fruit is a berry that is firmer and glossier than the tomato, but is covered with a paper-thin husk. Usually picked green, it can become purple or yellowish when mature. Tomatillo is slightly gelatinous and acidic and its taste is a little stronger than other varieties of *Physalis,* in particular the winter cherry (p. 166).

tomatillo

BUYING

:: Choose: firm tomatillos with a uniform color. If the husk is still attached, it should be crisp (a sign of maturity), and without any mold.

SERVING IDEAS

The tomatillo is usually cooked, but it can also be eaten raw as is, in salads or added to gazpacho or guacamole. In Mexico, the *mole verde* sauce is based on tomatillo, and used with meat, tacos, burritos, enchiladas, etc.

With its unusual appearance, tomatillo can be used for decorative purposes; open its skin slightly or turn it upside down on its stem.

PREPARING

Remove the husk then wash the tomatillo just before using, carefully cleaning the base of the stem, where a sticky substance is found. Remove the core.

NUTRITIONAL INFORMATION

	raw
water	91.7%
protein	0.9 g
fat	1.2 g
carbohydrates	6 g
calories	32
	per 3.5 oz/100 g

GOOD SOURCE: potassium.
CONTAINS: vitamin C, magnesium, niacin and thiamine.
PROPERTIES: antipyretic, diuretic, antirheumatic and depurative.

STORING

:: At room temperature: 2 days.
:: In the fridge: 1 week.
:: In the freezer: cook prior to freezing.

Squash

Cucurbita spp., Cucurbitaceae

The fruit of a plant related to the melon and the cucumber. There are two main categories of squash: summer squash and winter squash.

SUMMER SQUASH

Summer squash are fragile. They have tender skin that is edible, as are their seeds. There are several varieties of summer squash. The **zucchini** is also called courgette. Its white, watery flesh does not have a lot of flavor and contains a smaller or greater amount of seeds. It is tasty when small: 6-8 in. (15-20 cm) long.

straightneck squash   zucchini

The **marrow squash** looks like a large zucchini. The **crookneck squash** and the **straightneck squash** have yellow flesh. In Europe, the crookneck squash is called "Italian squash." These squash are tastiest when they are 8-10 in. (20-25 cm) long. The straightneck squash is the result of a human genetic improvement on the crookneck squash. The skin of the **pattypan squash** is not as tender as the zucchini. When very ripe, the skin whitens and hardens and must be removed. The pale, firm and slightly sweet flesh is not as watery as the zucchini, and its flavor is reminiscent of artichoke. Pattypan squash is tastiest when it measures 3-4 in. (8-10 cm) in diameter. Very small pattypan squash can be preserved in vinegar.

crookneck squash

marrow squash

WINTER SQUASH

The orange flesh of winter squash is drier, more fibrous and much sweeter than summer squash and becomes soft when cooked. The skin of winter squash is not edible. There are several varieties of winter squash. The **butternut squash** is best when it measures 8-12 in. (20-30 cm) in length with a base of about 4¾ in. (12 cm) in diameter. Its soft flesh is more or less sweet and very orange. Any greenish tinge of the skin indicates that the squash is not ripe. The **Hubbard squash** has dense, dry flesh that is not as sweet and less orange than the flesh of most other winter squash. It keeps for 6 months.

pattypan squash

Squash

The **turban squash** has dry orange-yellow or gold-yellow flesh, dense but soft, very sweet, with a slight nutty flavor. The **buttercup squash** has soft and sweet orange flesh. It keeps for about 1 month. The **acorn squash** or "pepper squash" has quite pale orange-yellow flesh that is fine and not stringy, with a nutty and peppery taste. This squash is best when it measures about 4¾ in. (12 cm) in length and 8 in. (15-20 cm) in diameter. It keeps for 30-50 days.

Some squash varieties are not as common, such as the **banana squash**. Its orange flesh is firm and not stringy. It is often sold in cut pieces, as are the **mammoth squash** and **sweet dumpling squash**.

The **pumpkin** and the **European winter squash** are often confused. The stalk of the North American pumpkin is hard and woody, with five angular sides, without any bulging at its connection point. The stalk of the European winter squash is tender, spongy, cylindrical in shape and flared where it connects. These squash are distinguished by their flesh, which is a little denser, with a stronger taste than other winter squash. Rarely used just as a vegetable, they are often cooked into soups, desserts or jams. Their quite dark orange-yellow flesh is dry and sweet. Their seeds are highly prized; those of the Tripletreat variety have no husks. Pumpkin can be substituted for or combined with other squash.

pumpkin

European winter squash   turban squash   buttercup squash

BUYING

SUMMER SQUASH
:: **Choose:** firm, intact squash with glossy skin, without marks or cracks.
:: **Avoid:** squash that is too large or small, dull, or with spots.

WINTER SQUASH
:: **Choose:** a firm, intact squash, heavy for its size, with dull skin. Whole squash should still have part of its connecting stem attached.
:: **Avoid:** a squash that is split, or whose skin has brown or soft spots.

NUTRITIONAL INFORMATION

	cooked summer squash	cooked winter squash
water	93.7%	89%
protein	0.9 g	0.9 g
fat	0.3 g	0.6 g
carbohydrates	4.3 g	8.8 g
fiber	1.6 g	2.8 g
calories	20	39
		per 3.5 oz/100 g

Winter squash contains more carbohydrates and is thus higher in calories than summer squash.
EXCELLENT SOURCE: potassium and vitamin A.
CONTAIN: vitamin C, folic acid, pantothenic acid and copper.

mammoth squash

banana squash

sweet dumpling squash

Hubbard squash

Squash

SERVING IDEAS

SUMMER SQUASH

Summer squash is eaten raw or cooked. Raw summer squash is eaten plain or with dips. It is used in appetizers, salads and sandwiches, or marinated. Grated and mixed with eggs, flour and seasoning, it can be made into great crepes. Summer squash can be cooked in its own juice with garlic, onions and tomatoes. It can also be stuffed and cooked in the oven, gratinéed, braised, fried coated in batter or bread crumbs or broiled. It is used in soups, stews, quiches and omelettes. It can replace cucumber in most recipes.

The flowers of the squash and zucchini plant are edible. They have a delicate taste and add flavor and a decorative effect to soups, fritters, crepes, omelettes, rice, seafood and poultry. They are lightly fried over high heat or stuffed and then cooked in the oven.

WINTER SQUASH

Winter squash is used in soups, stews, couscous and curries. Cooked and puréed, it can be combined with potato mash or made into soups. Winter squash is used to make pies, cakes, muffins, cookies, desserts, soufflés and creams. It can replace sweet potato in most recipes.

COOKING

:: Boiled: cut squash into ¾-1½ in. (2-4 cm) cubes, use only a little water and cook 10-15 min until tender. Prick a whole, unpeeled squash in several places, cover with water and boil for 1 hr. This method does not yield the best results.

:: Steamed: cut the squash in half, into slices or chunks, season with salt and place on a rack in a large saucepan (15-40 min, depending on the size of the pieces). This method of cooking is recommended.

:: Baked: use unpeeled squash, cut in half (or into quarters if large). Put a little oil or butter in the cavity, season with salt and pepper, sprinkle with nutmeg and cinnamon or any other spices. Pour a little water, orange or lemon juice into the cavity and place the squash in a dish containing ¾-2 in. (2-5 cm) water (30-60 min, until tender). Brown sugar, honey or maple syrup can be put in the cavity of the squash, or they can be stuffed. Add cheese for a gratin.

:: Microwaved: cut winter squash in two, remove seeds from inside the cavity, cover with plastic wrap or place in a suitable plastic bag, and cook on the highest setting for 10-15 min, depending on size, or until tender.

squash flower

butternut squash

PREPARING

SUMMER SQUASH

Wash, then cut off ends. Leave squash whole, grate or cut into halves, dice, julienne strips or slices. Squash can be halved lengthwise, hollowed out and stuffed. It is often salted, especially if its water content could upset the balance of a dish.

:: To salt: slice the squash more or less thickly, arrange on a shallow plate, sprinkle liberally with coarse salt and let stand (20-30 min). Rinse the slices in a colander under cold running water. Dry and prepare according to the recipe.

WINTER SQUASH

Wash the squash. Peel and remove the seeds of very ripe squash. This squash does not need to be salted. It needs more cooking time. As its flavor is not as subtle, it is used in soups or stews, or as a mash.

STORING

SUMMER SQUASH

:: In the fridge: 1 week, in a loosely closed or perforated plastic bag. Do not wash until just before using.

:: In the freezer: 3-4 months, cut into ½ in. (1 cm) slices and blanched for 2 min. Its flesh becomes softer after defrosting.

WINTER SQUASH

:: At room temperature: 1 week-6 months, depending on the variety, in an environment sheltered from cold, heat and light, with a temperature of 50°F-60°F (10°C-15°C) and a humidity level of 60%. Leave part of the stem that connected the squash to the plant and remove any soil residue.

:: In the fridge: 1-2 days, cut or cooked. Wrap pieces of raw squash in plastic wrap.

:: In the freezer: cooked and puréed.

1 Cut squash in two. Remove seeds and fibers using a spoon. Reserve and dry seeds.

2 Cut the squash into two or four sections before peeling. If the recipe allows, leave the skin on during cooking (essential if stuffing the squash or if the skin is very hard).

acorn squash

Dried squash seeds

SERVING IDEAS

 Dried squash seeds are used plain or roasted, whole, chopped or ground. They are eaten as is or mixed with walnuts, almonds, peanuts and dried fruit. They can be added to salads, pasta dishes, sauces and vegetables.

PREPARING

:: Roasting squash seeds:
1. Remove seeds from the cavity of the squash; dry using a paper towel.
2. Spread seeds on a cookie sheet and let dry at room temperature a few hours or for a few days.
3. Place seeds in the oven (350°F/175°C) until golden. Shake them a few times. Coat with oil and salt.
4. Remove seeds from the oven and the cookie sheet to stop the cooking process.
5. Cool and dry the seeds before storing in an airtight container, or they will become moldy.

NUTRITIONAL INFORMATION

	winter squash seeds
water	7%
protein	33 g
fat	42 g
carbohydrates	13.4 g
fiber	13.8 g
calories	522
	per 3.5 oz/100 g

Dried squash seeds are very nutritious and high in energy. Roasted with oil, they usually contain saturated acids and are even higher in energy than when plain.

EXCELLENT SOURCE: magnesium, iron, phosphorus, zinc, copper, potassium, niacin and folic acid.

GOOD SOURCE: riboflavin and thiamine.

CONTAIN: pantothenic acid.

PROPERTIES: diuretic. Dried squash seeds contribute to the relief of urinary infections and prostate problems. They are also said to be an aphrodisiac.

STORING

:: At room temperature: in a cool, dry place, protected from insects or rodents.
:: In the fridge: chopped or ground seeds.
:: In the freezer.

hulled pumpkin seeds

whole pumpkin seeds

Spaghetti squash

Cucurbita pepo, Cucurbitaceae

The fruit of a plant originally from North or Central America. The spaghetti squash's flesh, which ranges in color from pale yellow to green, resembles spaghetti when separated with a fork after cooking. Its flavor is similar to summer squash.

spaghetti squash

BUYING

:: **Choose:** a hard, intact spaghetti squash, without any bruises or green color.

COOKING

:: **Baked** or **boiled:** prick the whole squash in several places and cook for 1 hr in the oven at 350°F (175°C), or 30-45 min in boiling water. It is ready when it is soft. Overcooking makes the flesh bland and mushy. Spaghetti squash can also be cut in half lengthwise (remove the seeds found in the center cavity). Cook in the oven, cut side up, for 30-45 min. In boiling water, cook 20 min. It is ready when the flesh breaks off in threads.
:: **Microwaved:** cut the squash in two and remove the seeds. Place one half in the oven, cut side up, and cover with plastic wrap with one corner lifted up. Cook each half separately on the highest setting (6-8 min) or until the flesh separates easily.

NUTRITIONAL INFORMATION

	cooked
water	92.3%
protein	0.7 g
fat	0.3 g
carbohydrate	6.5 g
fiber	1.4 g
calories	27
	per 3.5 oz/100 g

CONTAINS: potassium, vitamin C and pantothenic acid.

SERVING IDEAS

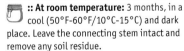

Spaghetti squash can replace spaghetti in most recipes. It can also be used as an ingredient in soups and stews. Cooked and cooled, it is served as a salad, dressed with vinaigrette or mayonnaise. Raw, it is eaten grated (squeeze to remove excess water).

STORING

:: **At room temperature:** 3 months, in a cool (50°F-60°F/10°C-15°C) and dark place. Leave the connecting stem intact and remove any soil residue.
:: **In the fridge:** cut or cooked.
:: **In the freezer:** raw and grated, or cooked. Spaghetti squash decreases in volume when defrosted.

Chayote

Sechium edule, Cucurbitaceae

The fruit of a plant originally from Mexico and Central America that is used as a vegetable. Chayote, also known as "mirliton," has a thin, rough, edible skin that can be light green, dark green or yellowish-white. Its pale, firm and crunchy flesh does not have a strong flavor and has a high water content. It encloses a pit that can sprout inside the fruit and is edible when cooked.

chayote

BUYING

 :: Choose: a firm chayote without any marks.

:: Avoid: chayote whose skin is too thick.

SERVING IDEAS

Chayote is eaten raw in salads or served as is, with a vinaigrette dressing. When cooked, it can be covered in a sauce and gratinéed.

Once it is ripe (when the seed starts to sprout), the chayote is peeled and cooked, ready to be used in Creole-style dishes (*acras* and gratins). It is an ingredient in soups and stews, it can be stir-fried, stuffed, used in marinades and chutneys, etc. Chayote can be used in place of summer squash in most recipes.

Sugar, lime juice, cinnamon and nutmeg can be added to a chayote compote as a dessert.

COOKING

The mild flavor of the chayote is better if it is still slightly crisp after cooking.

:: Boiled or steamed: 10-15 min.

NUTRITIONAL INFORMATION

water	93%
protein	0.6 g
fat	0.5 g
carbohydrates	5.1 g
fiber	0.7 g
calories	24
	per 3.5 oz/100 g

GOOD SOURCE (RAW): potassium.
CONTAINS (RAW): vitamin C, folic acid, vitamin B$_6$, copper and magnesium.

STORING

:: In the fridge: a few weeks, wrapped in plastic wrap.

PREPARING

 Peel the chayote before or after cooking. A sticky substance appears when the chayote is peeled, so it is preferable to wear gloves or peel under running water.

Spinach

Spinacia oleracea, Chenopodiaceae

spinach

A plant probably of Persian origin. Spinach is harvested when the leaves are still young and tender, before the floral stem appears.

BUYING

:: **Choose:** fresh, dark green spinach with tender, supple leaves.

:: **Avoid:** dull, yellowed, limp or waterlogged spinach.

PREPARING

Wash spinach carefully just before using. Do not let spinach soak. Place in a container, cover with water and gently shake; change the water if necessary. Remove any large stems, as they cook more slowly than the leaves if left whole.

COOKING

Cook using the water remaining on leaves after they have been washed and shaken gently, 1-3 min on a high heat in a covered saucepan. Add spinach to simmered dishes at the end of cooking time. Pressure-cooking or steaming spinach is not recommended. To avoid oxidizing spinach, use glass or stainless steel containers and utensils. Overcooked spinach acquires a brownish color.

STORING

:: **In the fridge:** 4-5 days, raw and unwashed. Cooked spinach does not keep well.

:: **In the freezer:** blanch for 2 min before. Avoid defrosting completely before using.

NUTRITIONAL INFORMATION

	raw
water	91.6%
protein	2.9 g
fat	0.3 g
carbohydrates	3.5 g
fiber	2.6 g
calories	23
	per 3.5 oz/100 g

EXCELLENT SOURCE (RAW): folic acid, vitamin A, potassium and magnesium.

GOOD SOURCE (RAW): vitamin C and iron.

CONTAINS (RAW): riboflavin, vitamin B_6, calcium, copper, zinc, niacin and phosphorus.

PROPERTIES (RAW): mineralizing, antiscorbutic and antianemic.

SERVING IDEAS

Spinach is eaten raw (in salads and sandwiches) or cooked (plain, with butter and lemon juice, with Mornay or béchamel sauce or cream, or in a gratin). It can be made into a purée, by itself or with potato. It goes well with milk and eggs (in omelettes and quiches). It is a classic accompaniment to veal, poultry and fish, and it is also used as an ingredient in stuffings, soufflés and gratins. Spinach is the vegetable used in dishes prepared Florentine-style.

Sorrel

Rumex acetosa and *Rumex patientia,* Polygonaceae

Plants originally from northern Asia and Europe, sorrel and patience dock are two varieties of the same species. They have a sharp, acidic flavor. There are two principal varieties of sorrel. **Common sorrel** or "garden sorrel" (*Rumex acetosa*) has large, tender leaves that are bright green in color. **Patience dock** (*Rumex patientia*) is larger than common sorrel and its rounded leaves are rough and less flavorful; it is often considered to be a weed.

common sorrel

BUYING

:: **Choose:** sorrel with firm, shiny green leaves and thin stems.

SERVING IDEAS

Sorrel can be eaten raw or cooked. Its acidic, lemony flavor is refreshing in a salad (use young leaves). It is cooked and prepared in the same way as spinach and is delicious in soups and sauces.

Sorrel soup is a classic dish in many countries. Sorrel sauce works well with poultry, eggs and quiches. It is a traditional accompaniment to fish (shad, pike) and veal. Puréed, it can be used in a potato or legume mash.

Its acidity can be softened by mixing with lettuce leaves or adding cream.

NUTRITIONAL INFORMATION

	raw sorrel
water	92.9%
protein	1.9 g
fat	0.8 g
carbohydrates	3.1 g
	per 3.5 oz/100 g

EXCELLENT SOURCE: vitamin C, magnesium, vitamin A and potassium.

GOOD SOURCE: iron.

CONTAINS: phosphorus.

Sorrel contains substantially the same amount of vitamins and minerals whether raw or cooked.

PROPERTIES: diuretic, revitalizing, refreshing, aperitive, digestive, antiscorbutic and slightly laxative. Sorrel and patience dock contain relatively high levels of oxalic acid, a toxic substance; consume in moderation.

PREPARING

Wash sorrel just before using; do not leave to soak. In a container, cover sorrel with water and shake gently; change the water if necessary. Sorrel is often cooked without its stems. To remove, fold the leaf lengthwise and pull on the stem.

LEAF VEGETABLES

COOKING

Steaming sorrel increases its bitterness. Avoid cooking in aluminum or cast-iron pans (discoloring). Use a stainless steel knife.

STORING

Sorrel is fragile.
:: In the fridge: 1-2 days, in a loosely closed or perforated plastic bag (1-2 days).
:: In the freezer: cook before freezing.

Nettle

Urtica dioïca and *Urtica urens*, Urticaceae

An edible plant with stinging hairs, originally from Eurasia. Its flavor is more or less pungent depending on the variety. The most common are the **stinging nettle** (*Urtica dioïca*), sometimes called "common nettle" or "bull nettle," whose leaves are used by themselves or mixed with sorrel; and the **dwarf nettle** (*Urtica urens*), sometimes called "small nettle" or "annual nettle," which is especially used in salads.

dwarf nettle

BUYING

Nettle is picked before the stems harden. Gloves can be used, or avoid touching the tips of the leaves.

SERVING IDEAS

 Nettle leaves lose their sting when cooked or dried. Nettle is used in the same way as spinach. It is delicious as a soup, with potato, leek, watercress, cabbage or legumes. It is braised with onion, garlic and nutmeg.
More tender nettle leaves and less pungent varieties can be used raw, finely chopped.

NUTRITIONAL INFORMATION

protein	5.5 g
fat	0.7 g
carbohydrates	7 g
calories	57
	per 3.5 oz/100 g

GOOD SOURCE: iron, calcium, potassium, magnesium, vitamin A and vitamin C.
PROPERTIES: astringent, tonic, digestive, galactogenic, depurative, diuretic and antirheumatic. It is used as a mouthwash (for mouth infections) or a decoction (for hair loss or dandruff).

STORING

Nettle is fragile.
:: In the fridge: place unwashed nettle in a loosely closed or perforated plastic bag.

Dandelion

Taraxacum officinale, Compositeae

A plant originally from Europe, North Africa, central and northern Asia and North America. Dandelion, from the French term *dent-de-lion* (lion's tooth), has jagged leaves with pale stems containing a milky sap like a flower stem. Wild dandelion leaves are smaller and more bitter than cultivated varieties.

dandelion

BUYING

:: **Choose:** dandelion with fresh leaves and roots attached (for better keeping).
:: **Avoid:** dandelion with dry, dull or limp leaves.

SERVING IDEAS

Young dandelion leaves are added raw to salads. The bitter flavor of dandelion works well with hazelnut or olive oil, raspberry or wine vinegar. It is delicious dressed with a hot vinaigrette (which tenderizes the fibrous texture of the leaves and softens their bitterness). In France, dandelion salad traditionally contains small pieces of bacon, vinegar and garlic croutons. Braised dandelion is an accompaniment to pork (ham, bacon or smoked pork).
Dandelion buds are marinated, the flowers are made into wine and the roots are used as a coffee substitute.

STORING

It is best to use dandelion as quickly as possible.
:: **In the fridge:** maximum 5 days in a loosely closed or perforated plastic bag.
:: **In the freezer:** blanch 2 min before. Avoid defrosting completely before using.

NUTRITIONAL INFORMATION

	raw leaves
water	85.6%
protein	1.6 g
fat	0.4 g
carbohydrates	5.3 g
fiber	2 g
calories	26
	per 1 cup (250 ml)

EXCELLENT SOURCE: vitamin A.
GOOD SOURCE: vitamin C and potassium.
CONTAINS: iron, calcium, riboflavin, thiamine, magnesium, vitamin B_6, folic acid and copper.
PROPERTIES: depurative, diuretic, tonic, aperitive, antiscorbutic and decongestant. Dandelion is used to relieve ulcers, hepatitis and itching. The bitter substances found in the root are responsible for its stimulating effect on the liver and gallbladder. The root is said to have slightly laxative properties. Dandelion can cause benign skin eruptions in sensitive people.

PREPARING

 Wash dandelion just before using. Blanch 1-2 min before using to reduce bitterness.

Purslane

Portulaca oleracea, Portulaceae

A very common plant in the relatively warm areas of central Europe, North and South America, with a slightly acidic and pungent taste. Purslane stems have a rubbery consistency.

purslane

BUYING

:: **Choose:** purslane with firm leaves and stems.

SERVING IDEAS

Purslane is eaten raw or cooked. Tender stems can be prepared in the same way as spinach or cardoon. Its leaves, which are more tender the closer they are to the top of the stem, are prepared in the same way as watercress. Purslane flavors and garnishes soups, sauces, mayonnaise, omelettes and stews. It is excellent with grated carrot or mashed potatoes, and is served with lettuce and tomatoes. Purslane stems and leaves can be marinated in vinegar. In Middle Eastern countries, purslane is an ingredient of *fattoush* salads.

NUTRITIONAL INFORMATION

water	93%
protein	1.6 g
fat	0.1 g
carbohydrates	3.6 g
calories	17
	per 3.5 oz/100 g

EXCELLENT SOURCE: potassium and magnesium.
GOOD SOURCE: vitamin A.
CONTAINS: vitamin C, calcium and iron.
PROPERTIES: diuretic, anthelmintic, depurative and emollient. The high water content of purslane makes it thirst-quenching.

STORING

Purslane is very fragile; use as soon as possible.

Lamb's lettuce

Valerianella olitoria, Valerianaceae

A plant probably originally from the Mediterranean region. There are several varieties of lamb's lettuce, some of which have a nutty flavor. Lamb's lettuce is very tender and delicate-tasting. Also called mâche.

lamb's lettuce

Lamb's lettuce

BUYING

:: **Choose:** lamb's lettuce with fresh, green, glistening leaves.

:: **Avoid:** lamb's lettuce with limp leaves that have lost some of their green.

Lamb's lettuce is usually sold in small bunches, with its roots still attached.

SERVING IDEAS

Lamb's lettuce is delicious by itself, in salads with nuts, apples or beets, or combined with tender lettuces (like Boston and Bibb). Do not use vegetables or a vinaigrette with an overly strong flavor, so that its mild flavor is not masked. Nut oil with lemon juice and salt will bring out its delicate taste. Lamb's lettuce can be used as a garnish for soup. For this purpose, chop finely and add at the end of cooking. It adds color to omelettes, potato salads and rice salads (add when serving). It can be incorporated into poultry stuffings.

STORING

Lamb's lettuce is highly perishable.

:: **In the fridge:** 2 days, wrapped in paper towel, then place in a loosely closed or perforated plastic bag. It is best eaten as soon as possible after purchase.

NUTRITIONAL INFORMATION

	raw
water	93%
protein	2 g
fat	0.4 g
carbohydrates	3.6 g
calories	21
	per 3.5 oz/100 g

EXCELLENT SOURCE (RAW): vitamin A, vitamin C and potassium.

GOOD SOURCE (RAW): iron and vitamin B_6.

CONTAINS (RAW): copper, zinc, folic acid, magnesium and phosphorus.

PROPERTIES (RAW): diuretic, revitalizing and laxative.

PREPARING

Remove lamb's lettuce roots. At time of serving only, wash lamb's lettuce gently, changing the water if necessary (do not let the leaves soak). Dry leaves carefully. Season at time of serving.

Arugula

Eruca sativa, Crucifereae

A very aromatic plant originally from Europe and western Asia belonging to the same family as cress, radish and mustard. Arugula's strong flavor is reminiscent of cress.

arugula

BUYING

:: **Choose:** arugula with fresh, tender leaves that are a solid green color and well defined.

:: **Avoid:** arugula with limp, yellowed or spotted leaves.

SERVING IDEAS

 Raw or cooked arugula flavors and garnishes salads, soups, mayonnaise, sandwiches, potato salads and pasta dishes. As a purée, it can be used in soups or sauces.

PREPARING

Remove the roots and fibrous stems of the arugula. Wash carefully (only just before using), without letting it soak.

NUTRITIONAL INFORMATION

	raw
water	92%
protein	0.3 g
carbohydrates	0.4 g
fat	0.1 g
calories	3
	per 0.35 oz/10 g (125 ml)

PROPERTIES: stimulant, diuretic and stomachic.

STORING

Use arugula as soon as possible after purchase.

:: **In the fridge:** 2-3 days, wrapped in damp paper towel and placed in a loosely closed or perforated plastic bag. It can also stand with its stems in a container with cold water, changed daily.

Cress

Nasturtium officinale and *Lepidium sativum,* Crucifereae

A plant probably originally from the Middle East. Cress has a strong tangy and peppery flavor. The most well-known species are **watercress** (*Nasturtium officinale*) and **garden cress** (*Lepidium sativum*).

watercress

BUYING

:: **Choose:** cress with fresh, tender, green leaves.

:: **Avoid:** cress with limp, yellowed or spotted leaves.

Cress is sold in bunches.

SERVING IDEAS

 Watercress leaves (mustardy taste) are enjoyed in salads. Garden cress (more pungent) flavors salads, sauces and sandwiches. As cress has a strong flavor, it should be used in moderation. It flavors and garnishes mayonnaise, dips, pasta dishes and tofu. Cress is cooked and prepared in the same way as spinach. It is also used in soups.

Cress

NUTRITIONAL INFORMATION

	raw
water	95%
protein	2.3 g
fat	0.1 g
carbohydrates	1.3 g
fiber	1.8 g
calories	11
	per 3.5 oz/100 g

EXCELLENT SOURCE: vitamin C, vitamin A and potassium.
CONTAINS: calcium, magnesium, riboflavin, vitamin B_6 and phosphorus.
PROPERTIES: tonic, diuretic, aperitive, depurative, antiscorbutic, mineralizing, antianemic and anthelmintic.

PREPARING

Remove cress roots. When about to use, pick over and wash carefully. To wash, cover with water in a container and shake gently; change the water if necessary and do not let the cress soak.

garden cress

STORING

Cress is very fragile.
:: In the fridge: 1-2 days, wrapped in damp paper towel and placed in a loosely closed or perforated plastic bag. To extend its keeping time, place in a container with the stems in cold water, changed daily.

Radicchio

Cichorium intybus var. *foliosum,* Compositeae

A plant originally from northern Italy, radicchio is a variety of red chicory. It can be the size of a Boston lettuce or a Belgian endive. It has a slightly bitter and acidic taste.

radicchio

LEAF VEGETABLES

BUYING

 :: Choose: radicchio with a firm and intact base, compact and well-colored leaves, and without brown discoloration.

PREPARING

Remove the radicchio's core, separate the leaves, remove any brown parts, wash, then dry.

SERVING IDEAS

 Radicchio is eaten raw or cooked. Raw radicchio can hold raw dipping vegetables, olives, cheese, etc. It can also be combined with other lettuces. Cooked radicchio flavors soups, rice, legumes, pasta dishes, omelettes and tofu. It can be roasted whole on a skewer. It can replace or be combined with Belgian endive and escarole.

NUTRITIONAL INFORMATION

	raw
water	93%
protein	0.6 g
fat	0.2 g
carbohydrates	1.8 g
calories	16
	1 cup (250 ml)

CONTAINS: folic acid, potassium, copper and vitamin C.
PROPERTIES: aperitive, depurative, diuretic, stomachic, mineralizing and tonic.

STORING

:: In the fridge: 1 week, unwashed, in a loosely closed or perforated plastic bag. Eat as soon as possible after purchase.

Chicory

Cichorium spp., Compositeae

A plant probably originally from the Mediterranean region. There are several varieties of chicories. The **wild chicory** is very bitter and has short stems that are formed of green jagged leaves similar to dandelion. It is eaten as a salad vegetable when young and tender. The **curly endive** is mainly eaten as a salad vegetable. Its green, narrow, very lacy and pointed leaves grow in rosette form. It has whitish or reddish ribs and is relatively bitter. The **escarole** has large leaves with slightly jagged edges. It is often affected by an infection that browns the ends of its leaves, especially in the middle; these brown parts must be discarded.

curly endive

Chicory

BUYING

:: Choose: chicory with a pale center, surrounded by firm, shiny, crisp leaves that are very curly and vivid green.

SERVING IDEAS

Chicory and escarole are used in the same way as lettuce or spinach, which they can replace or be combined with. Raw, they are especially served as a salad, dressed with a vinaigrette or mayonnaise. They form an interesting mix with other greens.

Chicory can be braised or added to soups at the end of cooking time for flavor. It can also be braised then gratinéed, used in flans, quiches or béchamels.

PREPARING

Wash chicory and escarole quickly in a large quantity of water without letting it soak, only just before using. Remove any withered leaves and hard sections. Cut and season only just before using.

STORING

:: In the fridge: 1 week. Place chicory or escarole in a loosely closed or perforated plastic bag or wrap loosely in a damp cloth. Avoid placing in sealed containers, as it may become rotten. Dry as much as possible before storing.

If the chicory and escarole are a little wilted, they can be refreshed by being plunged in ice water.

NUTRITIONAL INFORMATION

	wild chicory	curly endive and escarole
water	92%	94%
protein	1.7 g	1.2 g
fat	0.3 g	0.2 g
carbohydrates	4.7 g	3.4 g
calories	23	17
	per 3.5 oz/100 g	

WILD CHICORY
EXCELLENT SOURCE: folic acid, potassium and vitamin A.
GOOD SOURCE: vitamin C, pantothenic acid and copper.
CONTAINS: magnesium, calcium, iron, riboflavin, vitamin B_6 and zinc.

CURLY ENDIVE AND ESCAROLE
EXCELLENT SOURCE: folic acid and potassium.
GOOD SOURCE: vitamin A.
CONTAIN: pantothenic acid, vitamin C, zinc, iron, copper and calcium.
PROPERTIES: aperitive, depurative, diuretic, stomachic, anthelmintic, cholagogic, mineralizing and tonic. Chicory "coffee" is said to be slightly laxative and to have a tonic effect on the intestines.

escarole

radicchio

Endive

Cichorium intybus, Compositeae

A plant created in the 19th century by a Belgian botanist. There are two principal varieties of endives. **White endive** has crunchy leaves that are a creamy white color with a slightly bitter taste. **Red endive** is a cross between the white endive and red radicchio. Its flavor is milder than the white endive. It cannot be cooked, as it loses its color and particular flavor.

endive

BUYING

:: **Choose:** firm endive with compact, creamy white leaves, five times longer than wide, with only two outer leaves visible.
:: **Avoid:** soft endive with green leaves or whose ends have browned.

STORING

Endive is best when very fresh.
:: **In the fridge:** 5-7 days, in a loosely closed or perforated plastic bag or wrapped loosely in a damp cloth.

COOKING

:: **Braised:** 30-45 min.
:: **Steamed:** 25-35 min.

NUTRITIONAL INFORMATION

	raw
water	95%
protein	1 g
fat	0.1 g
carbohydrates	3.2 g
calories	15
	per 3.5 oz/100 g

EXCELLENT SOURCE: folic acid.
GOOD SOURCE: potassium.
CONTAINS: vitamin C, pantothenic acid, riboflavin and zinc.
PROPERTIES: aperitive, depurative, diuretic, digestive, cholagogic, remineralizing and tonic.

SERVING IDEAS

Endive is eaten raw or cooked. Raw, it is often served as a salad, dressed with a vinaigrette or mayonnaise. The hollow leaves can be stuffed with cheese, and it is also mixed with other greens. Endive can be braised, quick-braised and covered with béchamel sauce or simply dressed with butter and seasoned with fresh herbs (for example, parsley, chives, tarragon, chervil). It can also be quick-braised and wrapped in ham, then gratinéed.

PREPARING

Endive does not need to be washed; the outer leaves can be wiped with a damp cloth. Do not let it soak in water, as this makes it bitter. It should be cut and seasoned just before using to avoid browning through contact with the air. Leave endive leaves whole or slice them. To separate the leaves, cut a small cone about 1 in. (2.5 cm) in size out of the base of the endive, where the bitterness is concentrated.

Lettuce

Lactuca spp., Compositeae

A plant originally from the eastern Mediterranean region and western Asia. There are many varieties of lettuce. **Crisphead lettuce** has outer leaves that are green and crunchy, with leaves that are more yellow or white at the center. The most well-known crisphead lettuce is iceberg lettuce. **Butterhead lettuce** has very tender leaves. The most well-known butterhead lettuces in North America are Bibb lettuce and Boston lettuce. **Green leaf lettuce** is a non-head lettuce with curly, wavy leaves. It covers several varieties, all with long, large leaves that are tender and tasty. Some have a slightly nutty taste. **Romaine** or **cos lettuce** has long, firm, very crisp leaves with an even green color. The leaves have a central rib

Boston lettuce

that is rigid, fibrous and especially crunchy. **Celtuce** (also called "asparagus" or "stem lettuce") is a cross between celery and lettuce. Its flavor is reminiscent of both of these vegetables.

Lettuce

NUTRITIONAL INFORMATION

	Boston	iceberg	green leaf	cos	celtuce
water	95.6%	95.9%	94%	94.9%	94.5%
protein	0.7 g	0.6 g	0.8 g	1 g	0.5 g
fat	0.1 g	0.1 g	0.2 g	0.1 g	0.2 g
carbohydrates	1.3 g	1.2 g	2.1 g	1.4 g	2.2 g
calories	8	8	11	9	13

per 1 cup (250 ml)

GOOD SOURCE: folic acid.
CONTAINS: vitamins and mineral salts (the greener the lettuce, the more it contains).
PROPERTIES: aperitive, analgesic, emollient and calmative. It is recommended for insomnia, coughs and nervous or sexual excitement.

PREPARING

Remove the lettuce core to separate the leaves more easily. Remove any wilted outer leaves and hard parts. Wash lettuce carefully to remove dirt and insects. Some varieties, including green leaf lettuce, require meticulous cleaning. Wash the leaves, changing the water if necessary, by shaking them gently and without letting them soak. Drain carefully. Tear lettuce into pieces by hand rather than using a knife, as this will discolor the edges. Do not remove lettuce from the fridge or add dressing until serving to avoid it going limp. If the lettuce is too bitter, it can be blanched by being plunged in boiling water for a few minutes.

BUYING

 :: **Choose:** lettuce with a tight head and shiny, firm, crunchy leaves.
:: **Avoid:** limp, dull, waterlogged lettuce with discolored or yellowed parts, or whose ends are dried out or browned.

romaine or cos lettuce

SERVING IDEAS

Lettuce is most often eaten raw, but it can also be cooked. Raw lettuce is mainly served as a salad, dressed with vinaigrette or mayonnaise, or used in sandwiches. Combining several varieties of lettuce in a salad improves its look, flavor and nutritional value. Romaine lettuce is used in the classic Caesar salad. Lettuce is often braised or used in soups. Finely shredded lettuce leaves added to a soup at the end of the cooking time add a delicate flavor to the broth. Puréed lettuce leaves also make an excellent soup.

STORING

:: In the fridge: wash green leaf lettuce and romaine lettuce before refrigerating. Other lettuces should only be washed just before using. Wrap lettuce loosely in a damp cloth or in an airtight container (3-5 days for romaine lettuce, 1-2 weeks for iceberg lettuce and 2-3 days for Boston and green leaf lettuce). Keep lettuce away from fruits or vegetables that emit a lot of ethylene (apples, pears, bananas, cantaloupes and tomatoes), as this gas browns the leaves. Lettuce can be crisped by plunging in cold water.

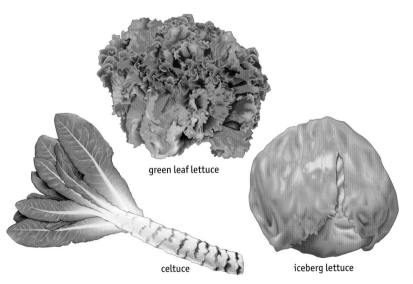

green leaf lettuce

celtuce

iceberg lettuce

Violet

Viola odorata, Violaceae

A plant belonging to the pansy family. The leaves and flowers of the violet plant are used for both culinary and medicinal purposes.

violet

BUYING

 Violets are available in specialty grocery stores.

STORING

 Use violet flowers and leaves as soon as possible after purchase.
:: **In the fridge:** a few days.

NUTRITIONAL INFORMATION

PROPERTIES: expectorant. Violet is said to relieve migraines and fever. Made into a tea, it is said to be a mild sedative.

SERVING IDEAS

Fresh, dried or preserved violets garnish salads (add vinaigrette first), pastries and beverages. They can flavor desserts or be added to poultry or fish stuffings. Violet essence is used to perfume cakes, ice cream, confectionery and liqueurs.

Nasturtium

Tropaeolum majus, Tropaeolaceae

A plant originally from South America with edible leaves, flowers and buds. The common species of nasturtium is low and compact. Its flowers are bright yellow, orange or red.

nasturtium

BUYING

 Nasturtiums are available in specialist grocery stores.

STORING

 Use nasturtium leaves and flowers as soon as possible after purchase.

NUTRITIONAL INFORMATION

PROPERTIES: stimulant, expectorant, antiscorbutic, diuretic and used topically. The seeds are said to have a purgative effect.

SERVING IDEAS

 Young nasturtium leaves and flowers are added to salads (add vinaigrette first). The flowers can also garnish soups, vegetables, poultry, fish, meat, pastries and beverages. The buds and green fruit are preserved in tarragon vinegar and can be used in place of capers.

Cabbage

Brassica oleracea, Crucifereae

A plant of thick overlapping leaves that may or may not form a head, may be smooth or curly, and colored green, white or red. There are almost 400 varieties of cabbage, differing widely in shape, type and color. There are cabbages with inflorescences (broccoli, p. 113; cauliflower, p. 111), with stems (kohlrabi, p. 95; kale, p. 83; collards, p. 82; Chinese cabbage, p. 85) and with smooth or curly leaves (savoy cabbage, green, white and red cabbages).

green head cabbage

BUYING

:: **Choose:** heavy, compact cabbage with brilliant, well-colored and crunchy leaves.
:: **Avoid:** cabbage with spotted, cracked or damaged leaves.

COOKING

Use only a small amount of water (³⁄₈-³⁄₄ in./1-2 cm in the cooking pot) and, if cooking white cabbage, add an acid ingredient (vinegar, lemon juice). Add the cabbage once the water has come to a boil; cook grated cabbage 5-8 min and quartered cabbage 10-15 min. Cut red cabbage with a stainless steel knife to prevent discoloration. To make into a salad, dress with a little vinegar after slicing thinly. Adding an acidic ingredient to the cooking liquid brings out the color of cabbage, whereas too much water drains its color.

NUTRITIONAL INFORMATION

	raw	cooked
water	93%	93.6%
protein	1.2 g	1.0 g
fat	0.2 g	0.2 g
carbohydrates	5.4 g	4.8 g
fiber	1.8 g	1.7 g
calories	24	21
	per 3.5 oz/100 g	

EXCELLENT SOURCE (RAW): vitamin C and folic acid.
GOOD SOURCE: potassium (raw and cooked) and vitamin C (cooked).
CONTAINS: vitamin B_6 (raw) and folic acid (cooked).
PROPERTIES: anticancerous, antidiarrheal, antiscorbutic, antibiotic, mineralizing and aperitive. Its juice is very effective in treating stomach ulcers. In herbal medicine, it is used to treat over 100 illnesses.

Cabbage

PREPARING

Wash cabbage after removing its fibrous or damaged outer leaves. If it contains worms, soak for 15 min in salted or vinegared water.

SERVING IDEAS

Cabbage can be eaten raw, cooked or preserved. Raw cabbage can be grated or sliced; it is delicious as a salad. Cabbage can be quick-braised, steamed, braised, sautéed, stuffed, etc. It is used in soups, stews and stir-fries. It works well cooked with carrots, onions and potatoes as well as bacon and sausages. Sauerkraut is made from preserved cabbage.

savoy cabbage

red head cabbage

white head cabbage

STORING

 :: At room temperature: keep cabbage in a cold room with 90%-95% humidity levels and a temperature close to 30°F (0°C) and no higher than 35°F (2°C).

:: In the fridge: about 2 weeks, in the vegetable compartment or in a loosely closed or perforated plastic bag. Cover and avoid putting it near foods that could absorb its smell .

:: In the freezer: blanch grated cabbage 1 min and cabbage cut into wedges 2 min. The texture softens when defrosted.
Cabbage can be dehydrated.

Sea kale

Crambe maritima, Crucifereae

A plant originally from western Europe whose leaves and stalks are edible.

sea kale

NUTRITIONAL INFORMATION

	cooked
water	95%
protein	1.4 g
carbohydrates	0.8 g
	per 3.5 oz/100 g

PROPERTIES: diuretic and antiscorbutic.

COOKING

 :: Steamed: 10 min.

STORING

 :: In the fridge: 2-3 days.
:: In the freezer: 1 year. Blanch before freezing.

SERVING IDEAS

Boiled sea kale is delicious with a flavored sauce or sautéed with garlic. Its blanched stems are edible and are prepared in the same way as asparagus, coated in butter or a light sauce; they are best when about 8 in. (20 cm) long. Sea kale can be eaten raw with vinaigrette.

A plant originally from the eastern Mediterranean region or Asia.

Collards

Brassica oleracea var. *viridis*, Crucifereae

A plant originally from the eastern Mediterranean region or Asia. Collards belong to the cabbage family. Their smooth, thick, ribbed leaves are flat or curly on the edge, depending on the variety. The ribs down the middle of the leaves are tough and unpleasant to eat. Collards have a strong flavor, though they are milder than kale.

collards

BUYING

:: **Choose:** collards with firm, well-colored and relatively small leaves, without any spots or mold.

SERVING IDEAS

Fresh collards are added sparingly to salads. To soften their taste, blanch before cooking. Collards can be prepared in the same way as spinach. They work well with barley, brown rice, kasha, potatoes and legumes. They are used in soups, stews, omelettes and quiches. They are delicious with sauce and made into a gratin or puréed (by themselves or with potato, sweet potato or legumes). They can be quick braised with smoked pork. The leaves can be served with butter and lemon juice.

PREPARING

Wash collards well under running water. Separate each leaf from the central rib and discard the rib unless the collards are young and tender.

NUTRITIONAL INFORMATION

	raw	cooked
water	90.5%	92%
protein	1.6 g	1.4 g
fat	0.2 g	0.2 g
carbohydrates	7.1 g	6.1 g
calories	31	27
		per 3.5 oz/100 g

EXCELLENT SOURCE: vitamin A (raw and cooked).
GOOD SOURCE: vitamin C (raw).
CONTAIN: potassium and folic acid (raw), vitamin C and potassium (cooked).

COOKING

:: **Steamed, quick-braised** or **stir-fried**.

STORING

Collards are best eaten as soon as possible after purchase.

:: **In the fridge:** several days, unwashed, wrapped in damp paper towel and placed in a loosely closed or perforated plastic bag.
:: **In the freezer:** blanch 2-3 min before.

Kale

Brassica oleracea var. *acephala f. sabellica,* Crucifereae

A plant probably originally from the Mediterranean region. Kale has large, fibrous, very curly leaves, ranging in color from pale green to dark green and sometimes even blue-green, with a strong flavor.

kale

BUYING

:: **Choose:** kale with firm, well-colored and relatively small leaves, without spots or mold.

SERVING IDEAS

Kale is rarely eaten raw. It can be added sparingly to salads. It lends its strong taste to soups and stews. Blanch before cooking to soften the taste. Kale is delicious with a sauce and gratinéed or puréed (by itself or with potatoes).

PREPARING

Remove the outer leaves and core of the kale and separate the leaves. Wash well under running water to remove any soil and insects it may contain.

COOKING

:: **Boiled** or **steamed:** 20-30 min.
:: **Braised**, **stuffed** or **stir-fried**.

NUTRITIONAL INFORMATION

	raw	cooked
water	84.5%	91%
protein	3.3 g	1.9 g
fat	0.7 g	0.4 g
carbohydrates	10 g	5.6 g
fiber	1.5 g	2.0 g
calories	50	32
		per 3.5 oz/100 g

EXCELLENT SOURCE: vitamins A and C (raw and cooked), potassium (raw).

GOOD SOURCE: vitamin B_6 and copper (raw), potassium (cooked).

CONTAINS: folic acid, calcium and iron (raw and cooked), thiamine, riboflavin, niacin and zinc (raw), copper and vitamin B_6 (cooked).

STORING

Kale is best eaten as soon as possible as possible after purchase.

:: **In the fridge:** 5-10 days, unwashed with well-packed leaves in a loosely closed or perforated plastic bag.

:: **In the freezer:** blanch 2-3 min before.

Salad savoy

Brassica oleracea var. *acephala,* Crucifereae

Salad savoy is a close relative of kale and
ornamental kale. The color of its leaves varies
from purplish-pink to cream, green or white. It is
more tender than cabbage and firmer than lettuce. Its
flavor is reminiscent of broccoli or cauliflower.

salad savoy

BUYING

:: Choose: salad savoy with firm, well-
colored leaves, without spots or mold.

SERVING IDEAS

 Salad savoy is eaten raw (in salads) or
cooked (soups, rice, legumes, pasta
dishes, omelettes and tofu). As salad savoy is
very decorative, it is used to line serving plates
or for containing dips, appetizers, cheese,
potato salad, rice salad and fruit salad.

STORING

It is best to eat salad savoy as soon
as possible after purchase.

:: Refrigerated: 1 week, unwashed, wrapped
in damp paper towel and placed in a loosely
closed or perforated plastic bag.

NUTRITIONAL INFORMATION

water	92%
protein	2.1 g
fat	0.4 g
carbohydrates	3 g
calories	12
	per 3.5 oz/100 g

EXCELLENT SOURCE: vitamin A, vitamin C,
potassium, phosphorus, calcium and iron.

PREPARING

Separate each leaf from the base. Cut
out and discard the tough stems. Wash
under running water.

COOKING

Keep cooking time short to retain color,
flavor and nutritional value.

:: Steamed, **quick-braised** or **stir-fried**.

Brussels sprouts

Brassica oleracea var. *gemmifera,* Crucifereae

A plant whose origins are obscure. It is said to have developed near
Brussels, hence its name. Brussels sprouts grow in tight formation at
the base of a series of leaves arranged along a stem.

Brussels sprouts

BUYING

:: **Choose:** green, firm and compact Brussels sprouts, with no yellow leaves and of similar size.

SERVING IDEAS

Brussels sprouts are only eaten cooked. They can be served with butter, with béchamel sauce, as a gratin, in soups and stews, stir-fried and puréed with potato. They can also be served cold as a salad.

PREPARING

Remove base and any wilted leaves, then wash the Brussels sprouts in water. Soak for 15 min in water to which a little lemon juice or vinegar has been added, in case there are any worms.

STORING

:: **In the fridge:** 3-4 days, unwashed in a loosely closed or perforated plastic bag.
:: **In the freezer:** 1 year. Blanch small sprouts 3 min and larger sprouts 5 min.

NUTRITIONAL INFORMATION

	cooked
water	87%
protein	2.5 g
fat	0.5 g
carbohydrates	8.7 g
fiber	4.3 g
calories	39
	per 3.5 oz/100 g

EXCELLENT SOURCE: vitamin C, folic acid and potassium.
CONTAINS: vitamin B$_6$, iron, thiamine, magnesium, vitamin A, phosphorus and niacin.
PROPERTIES: antineoplastic.

COOKING

Brussels sprouts are cooked whole with a small cross-shaped incision made at the base (for more even and faster cooking).
:: **Boiled:** 8-12 min in 3/8-3/4 in. (1-2 cm) water.
:: **Steamed** or **braised:** about 15 min (according to desired tenderness).

Chinese cabbage

Brassica rapa, Crucifereae

Plants probably originally from China and eastern Asia. There are three principal varieties in the West. The **Chinese white cabbage**, also named "petsay" or "napa," has a high water content. It is less fibrous with a milder flavor than ordinary cabbage. The **bok choy**, or "pak choi," has juicy, crunchy, mild-tasting stems and leaves whose flavor is not as strong as head cabbage. The **kai-lan** is also called "Chinese broccoli" or "Chinese kale." Its leaves and flowering stems are edible. It is the most delicate cabbage.

Chinese white cabbage

Chinese cabbage

BUYING

:: **Choose:** Chinese cabbage with compact, firm and fresh stems, with no brown spots. The leaves can be slightly soft.

SERVING IDEAS

Chinese white cabbage is eaten raw in salads. Its stems can be used in place of celery. Cooked, it flavors soups, simmered dishes, pasta dishes and stir-fries. Marinated Chinese cabbage can be served as a side salad. To salt Chinese cabbage, sprinkle liberally with salt and stir occasionally. Wait a few hours, drain and eat with a vinaigrette (garlic, ginger, green onion, rice vinegar, soy sauce, sugar, salt and cayenne pepper).

Bok choy is eaten raw, cooked or marinated. Cut the base and leafy part and remove the stems. Trim into large chunks. Bok choy is delicious stir-fried (cook the stems for a few minutes and add the leaves right at the end). Bok choy is added to soups, gratinéed, combined with rice or served as a side dish. The stems can be used in place of celery and the leaves in place of spinach or chard.

Kai-lan is eaten raw or cooked. It is prepared and used like broccoli; it only requires short cooking time. It can be stir-fried.

NUTRITIONAL INFORMATION

	cooked Chinese white cabbage	cooked bok choy
water	95%	95.5%
fat	0.2 g	0.2 g
protein	1.5 g	1.6 g
carbohydrates	2.4 g	1.8 g
fiber		1.6 g
calories	13	12
		per 3.5 oz/100 g

COOKED CHINESE WHITE CABBAGE
GOOD SOURCE: vitamin C, folic acid and potassium.
CONTAINS: vitamin A.
COOKED BOK CHOY
EXCELLENT SOURCE: potassium and vitamin A.
GOOD SOURCE: vitamin C and folic acid.
CONTAINS: vitamin B_6, calcium and iron.
KAI-LAN
EXCELLENT SOURCE: vitamin A, vitamin C, calcium and iron.

STORING

:: **In the fridge:** keep in a loosely closed or perforated plastic bag. Even if it can be kept 2 weeks, use Chinese white cabbage as soon as possible. Bok choy and kai-lan keep for a few days. Wash bok choy and Chinese white cabbage only when using.

bok choy

kai-lan

Asparagus

Asparagus officinalis, Liliaceae

A plant originally from the eastern Mediterranean region, asparagus is in fact the young shoot (less commonly called the "turion" or "spear") that emerges from the underground stem called the "crown." Asparagus is divided into three groups. The **green asparagus** is the most common. The **white asparagus** is more tender but has less taste. The **purple asparagus** has a very fruity flavor.

green asparagus

BUYING

:: **Choose:** firm, stiff asparagus with compact heads and a vivid color, with no rust-colored parts, that are a similar size (for more even cooking).

:: **Avoid:** yellowed asparagus with limp stems and flowering heads.

SERVING IDEAS

Asparagus can be served warm or hot (with butter or hollandaise sauce) or cold (with a vinaigrette, mayonnaise or mustard sauce). It can be puréed and turned into soup, cream or soufflé. Cut into pieces or whole, it is used to garnish omelettes, quiches, salads or pasta dishes and can be stir-fried.

COOKING

Avoid lengthy cooking of asparagus, as it can become mushy and lose flavor, color and nutritional value.

:: **Boiled:** cook asparagus tied together in a bundle.

:: **Steamed:** a recommended cooking method. Preferably use an asparagus pot (a tall pot in which the asparagus can be placed upright) to protect the more fragile tips.

:: **Microwaved.**

Asparagus are cooked when they are tender but still firm. To stop the cooking process, immediately plunge the asparagus in cold water, but do not let the asparagus soak. Avoid cooking asparagus in iron pots, as the high level of tannin in asparagus reacts with the iron and alters its color.

Asparagus

NUTRITIONAL INFORMATION

	raw
water	92%
protein	2.6 g
fat	0.3 g
carbohydrates	4.2 g
calories	24
	per 3.5 oz/100 g

EXCELLENT SOURCE: folic acid.
CONTAINS: vitamin C, potassium, thiamine, riboflavin, vitamin B$_6$, copper, vitamin A, iron, phosphorus and zinc.
PROPERTIES: diuretic. Asparagus is said to be laxative, mineralizing and tonic.

STORING

Asparagus is very fragile.
:: In the fridge: 3 days, wrapped in a damp cloth and placed in a loosely closed or perforated plastic bag.
:: In the freezer: 9 months, blanched and placed in a plastic bag.

PREPARING

Before cooking asparagus, remove the bottom part of the stem (this part can be puréed or used for soups, for example). Wash well in cold water to remove any sand or soil.

1 Cut off the bottom part of the asparagus with a sharp knife.

2 Peel the asparagus from the tip to the base.

3 Tie the asparagus into a bunch with string.

4 Tied up with string, the asparagus can be easily removed from the pot when cooked.

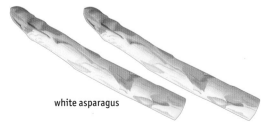

white asparagus

STEM VEGETABLES

< green asparagus

Bamboo shoot

Phyllostachys spp., Gramineae

A plant originally from Asia. The leaves, heart and sugary fluid that flows from the stems are also edible. All bamboo species should only be eaten cooked, as they contain toxic substances that are destroyed during cooking.

BUYING

In Western countries, bamboo shoots are mostly available dried or canned (in water or vinegar) from specialty food stores. They can sometimes be bought fresh in Asian markets.

SERVING IDEAS

Canned bamboo shoots are edible without further cooking. They can be chopped and boiled, sautéed or braised as an accompaniment to meat and fish or any Asian dish. Sold in slices or sticks, they are used in hors d'oeuvres, soups and simmered dishes. In Japan, bamboo shoots are used in sukiyaki.

STORING

:: **In the fridge:** several days. Place any uneaten canned bamboo shoots in an airtight container and cover them with cold water. Change water every 1-2 days.

NUTRITIONAL INFORMATION

	canned
water	94%
protein	1.8 g
fat	0.4 g
carbohydrates	3.2 g
calories	19
	per 3.5 oz/100 g

CONTAINS: potassium.

COOKING

:: **Boiled:** cut into sticks, cubes or slices and simmer in lightly salted water until tender (about 30 min). Prepare according to the recipe.

peeled bamboo shoot   bamboo shoot

Cardoon

Cynara cardunculus, Compositeae

Plant originally from the Mediterranean region with long flexible branches and woody outer stems that are hard and covered with soft spines. The flavor of cardoon is reminiscent of artichoke, celery or salsify.

cardoon

BUYING

:: **Choose:** cardoon with firm, crisp, creamy-white stems that are quite large and fleshy.

STORING

:: **In the fridge:** 1-2 weeks, the base of the cardoon rolled in paper towel and placed in a loosely closed or perforated plastic bag or paper bag.

COOKING

Blanching cardoon before cooking tenderizes the vegetable and reduces its bitterness. Using a peeler, remove the strings from each external stem. Cut the stems into pieces 4-4¾ in. (10-12 cm) long and add 1-2 teaspoons (5-10 ml) of vinegar to boiling water to avoid blackening. Pieces of cardoon can discolor during preparation, but it becomes even more discolored during cooking.
:: **Boiled:** blanch 10-15 min or cook completely 30 min. Drain, then prepare according to the recipe.

NUTRITIONAL INFORMATION

	cooked
water	93.5%
protein	0.8 g
fat	0.1 g
carbohydrates	5.3 g
calories	22
	per 3.5 oz/100 g

EXCELLENT SOURCE: potassium.
GOOD SOURCE: magnesium.
CONTAINS: calcium and iron.
PROPERTIES: calmative.

SERVING IDEAS

Cardoon cannot be eaten raw. It is cooked with cream, gratinéed, fried or puréed with potato. It is used as a side vegetable or in soups and stews. It is eaten cold with vinaigrette or mayonnaise.

Chard

Beta vulgaris var. *cicla,* Chenopodiaceae

A plant related to the beet, but only its stems (ribs) and leaves are eaten. Often compared to spinach, chard leaves have a less pronounced taste. They are a plain or rippled green color on top of tender and crunchy white or red stems.

Swiss chard

BUYING

:: **Choose:** chard with firm stems that have no brown marks and crisp, well-colored leaves.

SERVING IDEAS

Chard is eaten raw (the young leaves in salads) or cooked (hot or cold). It can be cooked whole, or the stems and leaves can be cooked separately. Chard stems can be sauced (Mornay, hollandaise) or dressed with a vinaigrette, and can replace Chinese cabbage in sautéed dishes or used in a soup or stew. The leaves are prepared like spinach and can act as a substitute.

PREPARING

Wash chard carefully. Cut off the bottom part of the stems and remove any stringy fibers that stand out.

STORING

:: **In the fridge:** 4 days, unwashed, in a loosely closed or perforated plastic bag.
:: **In the freezer:** blanch leaves 2 min before freezing. Chard stems do not freeze.

NUTRITIONAL INFORMATION

	raw	cooked
water	92.7%	92.7%
protein	1.8 g	1.9 g
fat	0.2 g	0.1 g
carbohydrates	3.7 g	4.1 g
fiber	1.6 g	2.1 g
calories	19	20
		per 3.5 oz/100 g

EXCELLENT SOURCE: vitamin C (raw), vitamin A, magnesium and potassium (raw and cooked).
GOOD SOURCE (COOKED): vitamin C and iron.
CONTAINS: iron and folic acid (raw), copper, riboflavin, vitamin B$_6$ and calcium (raw and cooked).
PROPERTIES: the leaves are said to be laxative and diuretic.

COOKING

Blanch chard stems (1-2 min) or sprinkle them with lemon juice or vinegar to stop them from blackening. Avoid iron or aluminum pots.
:: **Baked** or **braised:** chard stems 20-30 min.
:: **Steamed** or **boiled:** 5-8 min for stems and leaves. Cook separately if the stems are over ½ in. (1.5 cm) wide.

rhubarb chard

Fennel

Foeniculum vulgare, Apiaceae

A plant originally from the Mediterranean region, also called "sweet fennel" or "Florence fennel." Fennel has a mild and slightly sweet flavor reminiscent of aniseed or licorice. It is composed of a pale green or white bulb formed from interwoven leaves, and topped with stems decorated with a multitude of feathery leaves.

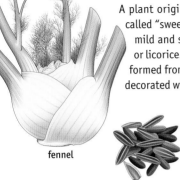

fennel

fennel seeds

BUYING

:: **Choose:** a firm, round, perfumed fennel that is white with no marks and with good stalks. The stalks and leaves, sometimes sold by themselves, should be fresh and green.

SERVING IDEAS

Remove any hard fennel leaves before using. Fennel is delicious with cream or yogurt. Raw fennel is cut into slices, thin slivers or sticks and used in salads. Blanched fennel can be braised or sautéed with other vegetables or by itself. It can be prepared with cream, as a gratin, or broiled and served with lemon. It accompanies other vegetables, legumes, rabbit, pork, lamb, beef, seafood and fish.

Fennel seeds flavor cheese, bread, soups, sauces, pastries and wine.

The leaves are traditionally associated with fish, but they can be used as an herb in several other dishes.

NUTRITIONAL INFORMATION

	raw	seeds
water	90.2%	8.8%
protein	1.3 g	0.3 g
fat	0.2 g	0.2 g
carbohydrates	7.2 g	1.1 g
calories	31	7
		per 3.5 oz/100 g

EXCELLENT SOURCE (RAW): potassium.
CONTAINS (RAW): vitamin C, folic acid, magnesium, calcium and phosphorus.
PROPERTIES (RAW): aperitive, diuretic, antispasmodic, stimulant and anthelmintic. Fennel is said to help reduce flatulence, relieve gastric pain and break down fatty and indigestible foods.

STORING

:: **In the fridge:** about 1 week.
:: **In the freezer:** blanch before freezing (flavor will be reduced).
The leaves can be dried in a microwave oven (30 sec-2 min).

93

Fiddlehead

Matteuccia struthiopteris and *Osmunda cinnamomea*, Polypodiaceae

The curled head of a young fern shoot, also called a "crozier." Only the fiddleheads of some species are edible, including that of the ostrich fern (*Matteuccia struthiopteris*) and the cinnamon fern (*Osmunda cinnamomea*). In Japan, bracken fern fiddleheads are broiled before being used to neutralize the carcinogenic substances they can contain. Bracken fiddleheads have a more bitter flavor than ostrich fern fiddleheads.

fiddleheads

BUYING

:: **Choose:** fresh, tightly rolled fiddleheads that are firm, green, with their brown scales attached and about ¾-1½ in. (2-4 cm) in diameter on a short stem. Fiddleheads are bought fresh, frozen or preserved.

SERVING IDEAS

The head and a small part of the stem are eaten. Fiddleheads are eaten cooked (hot or cold) and sometimes raw. They are delicious with butter, vinaigrette or covered in hollandaise, cheese or béchamel sauce, whether gratinéed or not. They are served as a side dish, salad or soup, in pasta dishes, omelettes and stews.
Never eat fiddleheads that are no longer curled up.

PREPARING

Rub fiddleheads with hands to remove the scales. They can also be placed in a bag and shaken. Wash carefully, dry, then prepare. Wash just before using.

NUTRITIONAL INFORMATION

water	62%
protein	2.5 g
fat	0.3 g
carbohydrates	3.3 g
calories	20
	per 3.5 oz/100 g

GOOD SOURCE: potassium.
CONTAINS: vitamin C, niacin and iron.

COOKING

:: **Boiled:** in salted boiling water (5-7 min).
:: **Steamed** or **quick-braised:** 5-10 min, according to desired tenderness.

STORING

Fiddleheads are fragile.
:: **In the fridge:** wrap fiddleheads in paper towel, then place in a loosely closed or perforated plastic bag (1-2 days).
:: **In the freezer:** blanch 1-2 min, immerse in cold water, dry well and spread on a cookie sheet to freeze, then place in a sealed container. Cook without defrosting.

Kohlrabi

Brassica oleracea var. *gongylodes,* Crucifereae

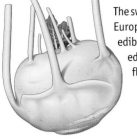

The swollen stem of a plant apparently originally from northern Europe. Kohlrabi has a bulbous base with stems that end in edible leaves. It can be pale green, white or purple, with an edible skin. Its sweet and crunchy flesh has a subtle radish flavor, while the stems and leaves taste like cabbage.

kohlrabi

BUYING

 :: Choose: a smooth kohlrabi with no spots and a diameter of no more than 2¾ in. (7 cm). The leaves, if still attached, should be firm and well colored.

SERVING IDEAS

Kohlrabi is eaten raw as is, with dips, as a salad or dressed with vinaigrette. Cooked kohlrabi is served as a side dish, used in soups and stews, puréed or stuffed. It is steamed, peeled or unpeeled, and served with lemon juice and butter. It is delicious with a sauce or sour cream, as a gratin or cooked with ginger and garlic.

PREPARING

Kohlrabi can be peeled before cooking or, more easily, after cooking. To eat raw, remove stems, then peel, removing all of the fibrous layer underneath the skin. Kohlrabi can be grated or julienned, diced, sliced or cut into chunks.

NUTRITIONAL INFORMATION

	raw
water	91%
protein	1.7 g
fat	0.1 g
carbohydrates	6.2 g
fiber	1 g
calories	27
	per 3.5 oz/100 g

EXCELLENT SOURCE: vitamin C and potassium.
CONTAINS: vitamin B$_6$, folic acid, magnesium and copper.
Kohlrabi leaves are rich in vitamin A.

COOKING

 :: Boiled or **steamed:** peel after cooking (20-30 min or until tender).
:: Braised, sautéed, roasted, or **baked:** peel before cooking.
Cook leaves only briefly and dress with lemon juice and butter.

STORING

:: In the fridge: about 1 week, without its leaves, in a loosely closed or perforated plastic bag. The leaves keep 1-2 days.

Celery

Apium graveolens var. *dulce,* Apiaceae

A plant originally from the Mediterranean region whose stalks (or ribs), leaves, roots and seeds are used. The fleshy, ridged stalks join at the base to form a "head" of celery. The inside of the celery, called the "heart," is the most tender part. There are several varieties of celery, with stalks that are more or less green or white. **White celery** is favored by Europeans and **green celery** has been adopted by North Americans.

green celery

BUYING

:: **Choose:** celery with glossy, firm, crisp stems. The leaves, if still attached, should be a good green color.

:: **Avoid:** celery with limp or damaged stems that have brown scars or yellowed leaves.

PREPARING

Cut off the base of the celery, wash stalks under running water, then cut into the desired length. If needed or desired, the fibrous strings on the outside of the celery stalk can be removed; this can be done by cutting into the celery just under the surface at the top or bottom of the stalk and pulling on the stringy thread.

NUTRITIONAL INFORMATION

	raw	cooked
water	95%	94%
protein	0.8 g	0.8 g
fat	3.8 g	4 g
carbohydrates	9.2 g	5.9 g
calories	15	17
	per 3.5 oz/100 g	

EXCELLENT SOURCE: potassium.
CONTAINS: vitamin C, folic acid and vitamin B_6.
PROPERTIES: aperitive, diuretic, depurative, stomachic, mineralizing, antiscorbutic, antiseptic, antirheumatic and tonic. Celery is said to lower blood pressure by lowering the level of stress hormones. Celery juice applied as a compress encourages the healing of ulcers and wounds. Celery seeds are used to treat flu, colds, insomnia, indigestion and arthritis.

SERVING IDEAS

Celery is eaten raw or cooked. Raw celery is often served as an hors d'oeuvre stuffed with cheese, seafood preparations, poultry or eggs. It is also used in salads and sandwiches. Cooked celery flavors soups, sauces, stews, pasta dishes, tofu, quiches, omelettes and rice dishes. It is also served as a side dish when braised, gratinéed, dressed with béchamel sauce or with butter. Celery leaves add flavor to dishes. They can be used chopped or whole, fresh or dried, in salads, soups, sauces or court bouillon. Whole or ground celery seeds are used in stuffings, poached vegetables, savory cookies, marinades and sauces.

STORING

:: **At room temperature:** wrap unwashed celery with its roots (if still attached) in a loosely closed or perforated plastic bag and place in a cool (30°F/0°C) and very humid spot.

:: **In the fridge:** 1 week, in a loosely closed or perforated plastic bag, in a damp cloth or in a closed container.

The base of the celery head can be stood in cold salted water. Avoid keeping peeled and cut celery in water, as soaking leads to a loss in nutritional value. To crisp celery, moisten it slightly and refrigerate for a few hours.

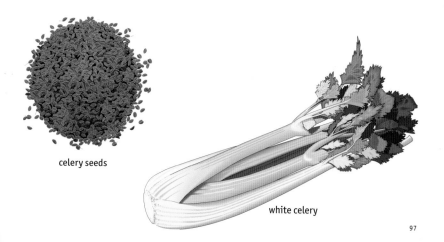

celery seeds

white celery

Cassava

Manihot esculenta and *Manihot dulcis,* Euphorbiaceae

The tuber of a shrub with large palmlike leaves, originally from northeastern Brazil and southwestern Mexico. Cassava has white, yellow or reddish flesh beneath a brown skin. Coned or cylindrical in shape, it looks like a sweet potato when small. There are several varieties of cassava. The **bitter cassava** (*Manihot esculenta*) owes its taste to the large amount of hydrocyanic acid it contains. It is only edible after being treated in various ways. It is from this high-starch variety of cassava that tapioca is obtained. The **sweet cassava** (*Manihot dulcis*) contains less hydrocyanic acid than bitter cassava.

sweet cassava

BUYING

 :: Choose: cassava without any mold or sticky parts and little damage.

:: Avoid: strong-smelling cassava or with parts with a gray-blue color.

STORING

 Cassava is fragile.

:: In the fridge: fresh, a few days.

:: In the freezer: peeled and cut before freezing.

SERVING IDEAS

 Sweet cassava is eaten plain, in the same way as potato or sweet potato, which it can replace in most recipes.

Broiled cassava flour, spiced and garnished with onions, raisins and cashews, is served as a side dish.

A flour is extracted from sweet cassava that is used to make sauces, breads, stews, flatbreads and cakes.

Tapioca's lack of flavor makes it very useful for thickening soups, sauces, stews, pies, fruit and puddings, as it takes on the flavor of the dish it is added to. Tapioca cooked in milk forms the base of delicious desserts.

NUTRITIONAL INFORMATION

	dry minute tapioca	*dry pearl tapioca*	*raw cassava*
water			68.5%
protein	0.2 g	0.1 g	3.1 g
carbohydrates	15.6 g	26.6 g	26.9 g
fat			0.4 g
fiber		0.4 g	0.1 g
calories	64	102	120
	per 1 oz/30 g	*per 1 oz/30 g*	*per 3.5 oz/100 g*

EXCELLENT SOURCE: vitamin C, potassium, iron and magnesium.
GOOD SOURCE: thiamine and vitamin B$_6$.
CONTAINS: folic acid, niacin, copper, calcium, phosphorus, riboflavin and pantothenic acid.
PROPERTIES: cassava contains more calories than potato, as it has a higher level of carbohydrates.

PREPARING

To reduce the toxicity of cassava, soak after it has been peeled and grated or cut into pieces. Cut the tuber into 2 or 3 large chunks, slice lengthwise, then remove the skin using a knife. After peeling, wash cassava well under running water.

COOKING

Cook cassava in a pot filled with fresh water; cover to prevent evaporation. Boiling or roasting whole cassava or cassava pieces neutralizes the enzyme responsible for producing the hydrocyanic acid. Stir tapioca during cooking to prevent lumps forming.

minute tapioca

Potato

Solanum tuberosum, Solanaceae

A plant tuber. Potato varieties differ in shape, color, size, flavor and starch content. Their pale or yellowish flesh is covered with a skin that may be red, brown, yellow, green or purple-blue. Mostly round, long or smooth, potato tubers are scattered with small "eyes," from which the buds emerge. Potatoes are fragile and easily damaged.

new potatoes

BUYING

:: **Choose:** firm, intact potatoes, with no sprouts or green parts.
Paper bags are preferable to plastic bags, which must be perforated to allow moisture to escape and prevent the potatoes from rotting. Potatoes are sometimes sold prewashed; these are more expensive and more difficult to store.

PREPARING

Discard any potato that is more than 50% green, as it will be bitter and inedible. Brush potato well if it is to be cooked in its skin, remove eyes and any trace of green. New potatoes do not need to be peeled; cook them as is or brush them. To avoid the flesh blackening, cook potato as soon as it is cut or place in cold water until using. This brief soaking time prevents the disintegration of the potato if the water is changed for cooking.

STORING

:: **At room temperature:** 9 months, at a temperature no higher than 40°F (4°C). Potatoes can also be kept about 2 months in a dark, dry, cool and ventilated place at a temperature of 45°F-50°F (7°C-10°C). Avoid keeping potatoes in a pantry at room temperature, as this encourages sprouting and dehydration.

:: **In the fridge:** new potatoes, cooked potatoes or very old potatoes, 1 week. Keep them away from strongly flavored foods such as onions.

Potato can also be dried or preserved.

TUBER VEGETABLES

NUTRITIONAL INFORMATION

	raw	baked (skin on)	boiled (skin on)	boiled (peeled)	fried (deep-fried)	potato chips
protein	2.1 g	2.3 g	1.9 g	1.7 g	4.0 g	6.6 g
carbohydrates	18 g	25.2 g	20.1 g	20 g	39.6 g	48.5 g
fat	0.1 g	0.1 g	0.1 g	0.1 g	10.6 g	35.4 g
fiber	1.5 g	2.3 g	1.5 g	1.4 g	0.8 g	1.4 g
vitamin C	19 mg	13 mg	13 mg	7 mg	11 mg	58 mg
calories	79	109	87	86	315	539

per 3.5 oz/100 g

Raw potato contains 79.4% water.

EXCELLENT SOURCE: potassium.

GOOD SOURCE: vitamin C (decreases by 40% over the first 2 months of storage).

CONTAINS: vitamin B$_6$, copper, niacin, magnesium, folic acid, iron and pantothenic acid.

PROPERTIES: raw potato juice is said to be antispasmodic, diuretic, antiscorbutic and cicatrizing. It can be used as a calmative and to relieve gastric ulcers. Potato is used to treat inflammations, sunburn and other burns, and cracked skin.

Exposure to light or sun can lead potatoes to form green spots that may contain solanin, a toxic alkaloid substance. In small doses, it may cause stomach cramps, headaches or diarrhea; in larger doses, it can affect the nervous system.

SERVING IDEAS

Potatoes are eaten cooked, most popularly as French fries, mashed potatoes, roasted or baked. It accompanies meat, poultry and fish. Its flavor can be enhanced with cheese, onion and fresh or dried herbs and spices. Potato works well in soups, stews and omelettes. It is a basic ingredient of croquettes, *quenelles* (a type of dumpling) and gnocchi. Potato can be used in elaborate and refined dishes such as mashed potato enriched with egg yolk and piped into shapes for baking, soufflés, soups and stews. For a good potato purée, add peeled potatoes to cold water and bring to a boil, then add salt. Drain when cooked, then mix in butter and hot milk with a wooden spatula. The more milk or cream is added and the more the potatoes are beaten, the lighter the mash will be.

Potato is made into a starch used in pastries, charcuterie (deli meats) and puddings, and is used to bind and thicken. Potato is the basic ingredient of vodka.

Potato

COOKING

:: **Boiled** or **steamed:** whole with their skin in a very small amount of salted boiling water (adding lemon juice helps keep their whiteness); cover the pot and make sure the potatoes don't stick together. Whole potatoes take 20-30 min to cook in boiling water and 30-45 min to steam. Potatoes cut into pieces will cook in 10-15 min in water or over steam.

The cooking liquid can be used in soups and sauces.

For fluffy mashed potatoes, boil, then dry the potatoes first. Use a potato masher or mill for best results.

:: **Baked:** prick potatoes with a fork to allow the steam to escape; wrap in aluminum foil to cook more slowly. Unwrapped potatoes will be drier. A medium-sized potato will cook in 40-50 min at 425°F (215°C) or about 70 min at 350°F (175°C).

:: **Microwaved:**
1. Prick the whole, unpeeled potato in several places to avoid bursting and place on a piece of paper towel.
2. Cook on a high setting for 3-4 min (if more than one potato is being cooked at the same time, the cooking time should be increased).
3. Turn once during cooking, if the microwave oven does not have a revolving plate.
4. Let rest 2 min wrapped in paper towel before serving.

Marfona potato (white)

All blue potato

Desiree potato (red)

:: **Fried:** the best results are achieved using potatoes with a low water content. Peel potatoes or leave unpeeled, and cut into more or less thin strips of equal size, no more than ⅜ in. (1 cm) thick or the fries will be very greasy.

Peeled potatoes should be rinsed in water but must not soak; dry carefully to avoid spitting when they are immersed in the hot oil.

The frying liquid should be a fat or oil that can tolerate temperatures of 350°F (175°C) without breaking down (see *Oil*, p. 590). The oil level when cold should reach one-third of the way up the frying container.

Preheat the frying oil to 325°F-350°F (160°C-175°C); oil that is hot enough will sputter. Immerse potatoes in the oil in small batches so that the temperature of the frying liquid does not drop too much, as this makes the fries softer and greasier. The heat can be increased to compensate for the drop in temperature, but the cooking must be monitored so that it is lowered again once the heat has returned to its maximum temperature. There are two possible cooking methods: in one stage or in two stages for crunchier fries. To cook in two stages, cook the potatoes in the first stage for 5-6 min in frying liquid at 300°F-325°F (150°C-160°C) and remove them before they take on a golden color; drain and cool. Return them to fry 2-3 min at 350°F (175°C), until golden. Blot on paper towel; only add salt when serving.

The frying liquid must be in good condition otherwise it becomes noxious. Filter the oil and store it in the fridge or in a cool place. Discard oil that is very dark, thick and rancid, or that smokes before reaching 300°F (150°C). Do not add fresh oil when the oil level is too low, as the quality of the new oil will be altered very quickly by the stale oil.

Fries cooked in the oven are lower in fat. For oven fries, coat potatoes in hot oil (1 tablespoon/15 ml per 1 cup/250 ml of potato) and cook at 450°F (230°C) for about 8 min. Lower the heat to 375°F (190°C) and cook until tender, or broil 15-20 min 3 in. (8 cm) from the heat source, moving them about from time to time.

Frozen fries can be deep-fried or baked in the oven (often soft and greasy, undercooked and rather insipid). Frozen fries rarely taste as good as fresh fries and often contain additives (check the list of ingredients).

Taro

Colocasia esculenta, Araceae

The tuber of a plant probably originally from Southeast Asia, taro belongs to a family of ornamental plants related to the philodendron and dieffenbachia. Some varieties have an elongated shape and resemble sweet potato, others are rounded and resemble celeriac. The large leaves and young shoots of taro are edible blanched. Its sweet floury flesh, colored cream, white or gray-mauve, is sometimes veined with pink or brown.

taro

BUYING

:: Choose: very firm taro without any mold or soft parts. Make a small incision in the flesh to check for juiciness.

SERVING IDEAS

Taro is only eaten cooked and is best served very hot, as its texture changes as it cools. It is used in the same way as potato. Taro thickens soups and stews and absorbs their flavors. It is delicious fried or with a sauce. Grated taro can be cooked as pancakes. Taro pieces cooked in syrup are served as *entremets* or a dessert.
Taro is ground into a starch. The leaves are cooked in the same way as spinach or are used to wrap food cooked in the oven.

STORING

Taro should be eaten as soon as possible after purchase, as it quickly goes soft.
:: At room temperature: place taro in a cool, dark, dry and well-ventilated spot.
:: In the fridge: wipe leaves with a damp cloth and keep several days in a loosely closed or perforated plastic bag.

NUTRITIONAL INFORMATION

	cooked
water	64%
protein	0.4 g
fat	0.2 g
carbohydrates	34.5 g
calories	142
	per 3.5 oz/100 g

EXCELLENT SOURCE: potassium.
CONTAINS: magnesium, phosphorus and iron.

COOKING

:: Boiled: 20 min.
:: Baked: 25 min, basting frequently with butter or sauce to prevent the flesh drying out.
:: Steamed or **microwaved**.
Add steamed or boiled taro to a soup or stew at the end of cooking time.

PREPARING

Peel taro, then cover with cold water if it is not to be used immediately. Taro contains a sticky fluid that can irritate the skin; peel wearing gloves or under running water.

< yams

Yam

Dioscorea spp., Dioscoreaceae

The tuber of a climbing plant whose place of origin is unknown. Yam is one of the most widely eaten foods in the world and is a staple food in several countries, in particular South American and Caribbean countries.

Yam can be elongated or round in shape. Its flesh can be white, yellow, ivory, pink or pink-brown. Its thick skin ranges from white to pink to blackish-brown and can be hairy or rough. Its flavor is more earthy and not as sweet as some sweet potato varieties.

Chinese yam

BUYING

 :: **Choose:** firm, intact yams, without mold or soft parts.

SERVING IDEAS

Yam is prepared in the same way as potato and can be substituted for potato or sweet potato in many recipes. It is fried, used in soups and stews, grated and made into cakes or bread. Boiled or puréed yam has little flavor. Spices are added to it; it is cooked with other foods or covered in sauce. Yam softens the highly seasoned and spicy flavors of Caribbean dishes. Cooked in the oven, yams dry out and benefit from being served with a sauce. Small yams can be cooked in their skin.

COOKING

Yam is mainly eaten cooked.
:: **Boiled:** peeled and cut into cubes, in salted water (10-20 min).

NUTRITIONAL INFORMATION

	raw
water	70%
protein	1.5 g
fat	0.1 g
carbohydrates	28 g
fiber	3.9 g
calories	116
	per 3.5 oz/100 g

EXCELLENT SOURCE: potassium.
CONTAINS: vitamin C, vitamin B$_6$, thiamine, copper, folic acid, magnesium and phosphorus.
PROPERTIES: some wild varieties of yam contain a steroid used in the pharmaceutical industry to manufacture contraceptives. Yam has a higher level of starch than potato, which makes it more floury.

STORING

:: **At room temperature:** store yams in a dark, cool, dry and well-ventilated spot. Avoid keeping yams in plastic bags.

Jícama

Pachyrhizus tuberosus and *Pachyrhizus erosus,* Fabaceae

The tuber of a plant originally from Mexico, Central and South America. There are two varieties of jícamas. The **Pachyrhizus tuberosus** jícama is the largest. It is originally from the Amazon region. Very juicy, it is almost always eaten raw. The **Pachyrhizus erosus** jícama, originally from Mexico and Central America, is smaller. It is eaten raw or cooked.

Depending on the variety, jícama can resemble a turnip with slightly flattened ends. Its skin is not edible; inside is a juicy, crunchy and sweet flesh with a mild flavor reminiscent of water chestnut.

jícama

BUYING

:: **Choose:** a firm, medium- or small-sized jícama, with thin, undamaged skin. Make a small incision in the skin with the fingernail to check its thickness as well as the juiciness of the flesh.

SERVING IDEAS

Jícama is eaten raw (as a salad, with dips and as an hors d'oeuvre) or cooked. It is sliced thinly, dressed with lemon or lime juice and sprinkled with chili seasonings and salt for a typically Mexican appetizer. It adds a crunchy note to soups, vegetables, rice, tofu, quiches, meat, poultry, seafood and fruit salads. It is delicious in stews or sweet-and-sour dishes, as it absorbs other flavors. It can be used in place of bamboo shoots or water chestnuts in most recipes.

NUTRITIONAL INFORMATION

water	85%
protein	1.4 g
carbohydrates	12.8 g
calories	55
	per 3.5 oz/100 g

COOKING

Jícama is cooked like potatoes, or by frying lightly and quickly.

STORING

:: **At room temperature:** several weeks, in a cool, dry spot.

:: **In the fridge:** 3 weeks, whole and not wrapped. 1 week, cut, in a loosely closed or perforated plastic bag.

PREPARING

It is easier to peel jícama with a knife. Once peeled, it can be grated, diced, julienned or sliced.

Sweet potato

Ipomoea batatas, Convolvulaceae

The tuber of a plant originally from Central America, sweet potato is not related to the potato, despite what one may think. There are over 400 varieties of sweet potato. Its thin edible skin, smooth or rough, can be white, yellow, orange, red or purple; its flesh is white, yellowish or orange. The different varieties of sweet potato are divided into two groups, those with dry flesh and those with moist flesh.

sweet potato

BUYING

:: **Choose:** firm sweet potatoes with no soft spots, cracks or bruises.

:: **Avoid:** refrigerated sweet potatoes.

SERVING IDEAS

Sweet potato is always eaten cooked. It can replace winter squash in most recipes, and is used to make cakes, pies, bread, puddings, marmalades, cookies and muffins. Sweet potato is cooked in croquettes, gratins, soufflés and with cream. It works well with cinnamon, honey, coconut, nutmeg and lime. Sweet potato works very well as a side dish for pork, ham and poultry. It is particularly delicious baked in the oven or mashed. Sweet potato can be dried and made into flakes or chips. Alcohol, starch and flour are also extracted from sweet potatoes.

NUTRITIONAL INFORMATION

	cooked, boiled (peeled)
water	73%
protein	1.6 g
fat	0.3 g
carbohydrates	24.3 g
fiber	2.5 g
calories	105
	per 3.5 oz/100 g

EXCELLENT SOURCE: vitamin A (the more colored the sweet potato, the more vitamin A it contains).

GOOD SOURCE: potassium.

CONTAINS: vitamin C, vitamin B_6, riboflavin, copper, pantothenic acid and folic acid. Higher in starch than potato, it contains more or less the same amount of carbohydrate.

PREPARING

Peel the sweet potato if it is waxed or dyed. To prevent the flesh blackening in contact with the air, place cut sweet potato in cold water until using or cook as quickly as possible (cover completely with water).

STORING

Handle sweet potatoes with care.
:: At room temperature: 7-10 days, in a cook, dark, well-ventilated spot, at less than 65°F (20°C).
:: In the fridge: cooked, 1 week.
:: In the freezer: cook before freezing.

COOKING

:: Microwaved: whole and unpeeled. Prick in several places, wrap in paper towel and cook on a high setting for 5-7 min; turn when half cooked and let rest for 2 min before serving.
:: Baked: whole and in its skin, prick in several places to prevent it bursting and cook for 45-60 min, until tender.
:: Boiled: boil for 20-30 min, then peel.

Jerusalem artichoke

Helianthus tuberosus, Compositeae

The tuber of a plant originally from North America. The yellow-white flesh of the Jerusalem artichoke is crunchy, juicy and sweet with a delicate flavor and covered in a thin edible skin. This is also called "sunchoke."

Jerusalem artichoke

BUYING

:: Choose: small, firm Jerusalem artichokes with intact skin.
:: Avoid: Jerusalem artichokes with any hint of green or that have started sprouting.

PREPARING

To avoid Jerusalem artichokes blackening when cut, soak in water to which some lemon juice or vinegar has been added. They are often cooked unpeeled after being carefully cleaned (they can be peeled after cooking).

SERVING IDEAS

Jerusalem artichoke is eaten raw (as a salad and hors d'oeuvre), cooked or marinated. It can be made into a purée, a gratin or served with cream. Cooked Jerusalem artichoke can be used in place of water chestnuts and potatoes. It is used in soups, stews, pancakes and fritters. It works well with leeks and poultry.
Jerusalem artichoke can be made into alcohol or dried and made into a very nutritious flour.

STORING

 Jerusalem artichokes are fragile; handle with care.

:: **In the fridge:** 2 weeks, unwashed, in a loosely closed or perforated plastic bag with some paper towels to eliminate excess moisture.

Jerusalem artichokes can also be marinated.

COOKING

Cook Jerusalem artichoke only briefly, as its flesh can become mushy. Avoid cooking Jerusalem artichoke in an aluminum or iron pot, as it discolors in contact with these metals.

:: **Baked:** whole (30-45 min, depending on size).

:: **Steamed:** 10-15 min.

:: **Boiled:** 8-12 min.

:: **Sautéed:** 5-7 min. Add at the last minute if cooking in a wok.

NUTRITIONAL INFORMATION

	raw
water	78%
protein	2 g
fat	2 g
carbohydrates	17.4 g
fiber	1.6 g
calories	76
	per 3.5 oz/100 g

EXCELLENT SOURCE: potassium.

GOOD SOURCE: iron and thiamine.

CONTAINS: niacin, phosphorus, copper, magnesium, folic acid and pantothenic acid.

PROPERTIES: disinfectant, energizing and galactogenic. Jerusalem artichoke contains inulin, a carbohydrate close to starch, that can cause gas in some people. Delicate individuals or those eating Jerusalem artichoke for the first time should only eat a small portion.

Chinese artichoke

Stachys spp., Labiaceae

A swelling of the tuberous rhizomes of a plant originally from Japan. Chinese artichoke tubers have thin, edible skin. Their very delicate and slightly sweet flavor is reminiscent of salsify or artichoke, which is reflected in its name.

Chinese artichoke

BUYING

:: **Choose:** firm, unwrinkled Chinese artichokes whose ends are evenly colored.

PREPARING

 Do not peel Chinese artichoke. To clean, place in a bag with coarse salt, shake vigorously, then wash.

SERVING IDEAS

Chinese artichoke is used and prepared in the same way as potato, Jerusalem artichoke or salsify. It can be boiled, quick-braised, fried, preserved in vinegar or puréed. It is eaten in salads or cooked with other vegetables. It is often blanched prior to cooking (2 min), and is delicious sautéed in butter or served with cream.

NUTRITIONAL INFORMATION

protein	2.7 g
carbohydrates	17.3 g
calories	80
	per 3.5 oz/100 g

STORING

Chinese artichokes are fragile; they dry out quickly.

:: In the fridge.

Cauliflower

Brassica oleracea var. *botrytis,* Cruciferae

A plant composed of a compact head (also called the "curd"), formed of several undeveloped inflorescences that are attached to a short central stem. Cauliflower is covered with several layers of green leaves attached to the stem. The small, tender, inner leaves, which are yellow-green in color, are edible. Cauliflower is usually white, but some varieties are purplish in color (they turn green during cooking). Purple cauliflower is very close to broccoli; it cooks more quickly than white cauliflower and has a milder flavor.

cauliflower

BUYING

:: Choose: a cauliflower with a firm, compact head that is creamy white in color, with well-colored green leaves still attached.
:: Avoid: discolored cauliflower with brown spots or that has started to flower.

PREPARING

Remove the outer leaves and the core, and leave the small green leaves. Separate the cauliflower florets from the main stem, keeping part of the stem; keep florets whole or cut them into sections if they are very large. Wash under running water or soak in slightly salted or vinegared water in case any worms are present.

Cauliflower

NUTRITIONAL INFORMATION

	raw	cooked
water	92%	92.5%
protein	2 g	1.9 g
fat	0.2 g	0.2 g
carbohydrates	5 g	4.6 g
fiber	1.8 g	1.8 g
calories	24	24
		per 3.5 oz/100 g

EXCELLENT SOURCE: vitamin C, folic acid and potassium (raw), vitamin C and potassium (cooked).
GOOD SOURCE (COOKED): folic acid.
CONTAINS: niacin (raw), copper (cooked), vitamin B$_6$ (raw and cooked).
PROPERTIES: anticancerous. Cauliflower is the most digestible member of the cabbage family.

COOKING

Cauliflower cooks very quickly. Monitor its cooking closely, as it can disintegrate and become pasty, which leads to a loss of flavor and nutritional value.
:: Boiled: add a bread crust to the cooking liquid to absorb some of its odor.
:: Steamed.
:: Stir-fried.
:: Microwaved.

SERVING IDEAS

 Cauliflower is eaten raw or cooked. Raw, it is eaten as is, with dips, in hors d'oeuvres or salads. Cooked, still firm, cauliflower is eaten hot or cold. It is used as a side vegetable or in soups, stews, pasta dishes, omelettes and quiches. It is delicious covered in Mornay, hollandaise or béchamel sauce and gratinéed. Cooked and puréed, it can be incorporated into soufflés or soups. Cauliflower is also an ingredient in marinades, relishes and chutneys. It can replace broccoli in most recipes.

STORING

:: In the fridge: about 10 days, unwashed, in a loosely closed or perforated plastic bag. Cooked, 2-3 days (cauliflower is more fragile).
The older the cauliflower is, the stronger its taste and odor become.
:: In the freezer: blanch (3 min) prior to freezing. It will be more watery when defrosted.

purple cauliflower

Broccoli

Brassica oleracea var. *italica,* Crucifereae

A plant originally from southern Italy, broccoli can be green, white or purple. There are several other varieties, in particular the broccoflower, which is close to cauliflower, and the Romanesco broccoli, which is the result of a cross between broccoli and cauliflower.

broccoli

BUYING

:: **Choose:** a firm, well-colored broccoli with compact florets. The outer leaves should be green with firm stems.

:: **Avoid:** broccoli that has flowered, yellowed, or wilted, that has spots or is losing its buds.

SERVING IDEAS

Broccoli is eaten raw as is, with dips, in hors d'oeuvres or as a salad. Cooked broccoli, still firm, may be served hot or cold. It is delicious dressed with a vinaigrette, covered with béchamel, Mornay or hollandaise sauce and gratinéed, with butter or puréed. It is served as a side dish or used in soups, stews, stir-fries, omelettes, soufflés, quiches and pasta dishes. It works well in recipes for cauliflower.

PREPARING

Remove broccoli leaves that are wilted or tough, but keep the small, more tender leaves. The tougher leaves can be added to soups and stews. Leave heads whole or cut them into florets if they are very large (for more rapid and even cooking). Wash the broccoli in water or soak 15 min in lightly salted or vinegared water.

NUTRITIONAL INFORMATION

	cooked
water	90.6%
protein	2.9 g
carbohydrates	5.1 g
fat	0.4 g
fiber	2.6 g
calories	28
	per 3.5 oz/100 g

EXCELLENT SOURCE (COOKED): vitamin C and potassium.

GOOD SOURCE (COOKED): folic acid.

CONTAINS (COOKED): vitamin A, magnesium, pantothenic acid, iron and phosphorus.

PROPERTY: anticancerous.

COOKING

Broccoli stems cook more slowly than the heads. They can be cooked by themselves for a few minutes. Peel, make cuts lengthwise or cut into chunks if very thick.

:: **Boiled** or **steamed:** whole (10-15 min). Add a very small amount of sugar to keep the green color.

:: **Stir-fried.**

:: **Microwaved.**

STORING

:: **In the fridge:** 2-5 days.

:: **In the freezer:** 1 year at -0.5°F/-18°C. Blanch before freezing.

Broccoli rabe

Brassica rapa var. *ruvo* or *italica,* Crucifereae

A plant originally from the Mediterranean region, with a slightly bitter taste. The stems, leaves, floral buds and flowers are all edible. The stems have a milder flavor than the leaves.

broccoli rabe

BUYING

:: **Choose:** small, firm broccoli rabe, with few buds or open flowers.
:: **Avoid:** broccoli rabe with limp stems, or leaves that are wilted or yellowed.

SERVING IDEAS

Raw broccoli rabe is prepared in the same way as broccoli, which it can replace in most recipes (the strong flavor of raw broccoli rabe is not always liked). Cooked broccoli rabe is eaten hot (covered in béchamel sauce or cheese, then gratinéed, or dressed with lemon juice and butter) or cold (dressed with a vinaigrette). Broccoli rabe adds a pungent note to blander foods, such as tofu, pasta dishes and potatoes. Quick-braising can make broccoli rabe bitter.

STORING

:: **In the fridge:** 1 week, unwashed, in a loosely closed or perforated plastic bag.

NUTRITIONAL INFORMATION

	raw
water	89%
protein	3.6 g
carbohydrates	5.9 g
fiber	1.5 g
calories	32
	per 3.5 oz/100 g

PREPARING

Wash broccoli rabe well. Remove the base of the stems, leave the rest whole or cut into pieces. The leaves can be separated from the stems, which take longer to cook.

COOKING

:: **Boiled:** cook stems in a very small amount of water (1 min), then add the leaves and buds (2-4 min).
Broccoli rabe can be blanched 1 min, but that reduces its flavor.

Artichoke

Cynara scolymus, Compositeae

The bud of a plant derived from the thistle, originally from the Mediterranean region. The edible parts of the artichoke are its heart (the base) and the bottom part of the leaves (its bracts). The fuzzy "choke" inside the heart is not eaten. Artichoke species differ in shape and color. The purple Provence, or *poivrade,* artichoke is fairly small and has a less developed choke; it can be eaten raw.

artichoke

BUYING

:: **Choose:** a compact, heavy artichoke with hard, tight leaves and a good green color.
:: **Avoid:** an artichoke with discolored leaves or black spots at the tip, or that are open.
It is also possible to buy preserved artichoke hearts ready to eat, packed in brine, fresh water or with vinegar.

COOKING

Avoid cooking artichoke in an aluminum or iron pot, as it turns gray. Whole artichoke is ready when its center leaves detach easily. Before serving, drain the artichoke by turning it upside down.
:: **Baked**.
:: **Boiled:** cook artichokes in salted water for 35-45 min, depending on size. Cover totally to avoid blackening. A plate can be placed on top of the artichokes to keep them at the bottom of the pot, or cover with a cloth.
:: **Steamed**.
Artichoke hearts can be cooked in water to which a little lemon juice or vinegar has been added (prevents blackening). Cook over very gentle heat (15-20 min), until they are easily pierced with a knife blade.

NUTRITIONAL INFORMATION

	cooked
water	84%
protein	3.5 g
fat	0.2 g
carbohydrates	11.2 g
calories	50
	per 3.5 oz/100 g

EXCELLENT SOURCE: potassium and magnesium.
GOOD SOURCE: folic acid.
CONTAINS: vitamin C, copper, iron, phosphorus, niacin, vitamin B_6, zinc, pantothenic acid and calcium.
PROPERTIES: aperitive, blood purifier, antitoxic and diuretic. Artichoke is said to stimulate the production of bile and to be excellent for the liver. Its therapeutic effects are best obtained from infusing the large jagged leaves (and not the bract leaves, which are eaten).

Artichoke

FLOWER VEGETABLES

PREPARING

purple Provence artichoke

Wash the artichoke under running water and soak in water to which a little vinegar has been added. The pointed ends of the leaves can be removed by cutting off about ⅜ in. (1 cm) with scissors.

1 Break off the artichoke stem, which allows the hard fibers to be removed from the base.

2 Remove the outer leaves from around the base, leaving the tender ones.

3 Cut across the artichoke leaves two-thirds along the length.

4 Remove the remains of the leaves from the base of the artichoke and cut into a regular shape.

5 Rub the base with a cut lemon to avoid oxidation and keep artichokes in lemon water.

STORING

:: In the fridge: 4-5 days, unwashed, in a loosely closed or perforated plastic bag . If it has its stem, place upright in water. A cooked artichoke keeps 24 hr.
:: In the freezer: cooked artichoke hearts, 6-8 months.

SERVING IDEAS

Cooked artichoke is eaten hot, warm or cold. Remove leaves one by one and scrape the fleshy base through the teeth. When all the leaves have been removed, a central pink- or mauve-colored cone and the choke can be removed to reveal the heart, which can then be eaten. The leaves and the heart can be dipped in mayonnaise. Artichoke hearts are used in salads and hors d'oeuvres or as a garnish.

Whole artichoke can be stuffed and cooked in the oven. It is delicious covered with béchamel, butter or hollandaise sauce, or cooked Nicoise-style (with tomato and other flavorings such as garlic, olives and basil).

Legumes

The term "legume" refers both to the plants whose fruit is enclosed in a pod and to the family these plants belong to (*Leguminosae*). The legumes represent a vast family of plants including more than 600 genera and more than 13,000 species.

TIPS FOR PREPARING LEGUMES

Most dried legumes must be soaked before cooking. Soaking rehydrates dried legumes (called "pulses"), reduces their cooking time and preserves their vitamins and minerals. It also reduces gas-related problems. Some legumes do not need soaking. Legumes are generally soaked for 6-8 hr, but this soaking time can be shortened or omitted if using a pressure cooker. Dried legumes can be soaked in large quantities and a portion of them frozen.

:: Long soaking

Discard damaged beans and any foreign matter. Wash dried legumes several times in cold water and leave to soak. Discard any impurities or beans that float to the surface. Place the dried legumes in a large bowl, cover with three parts water to one part legumes and let soak overnight in a cool place or in the fridge.

:: Quick soaking

Place in 3-4 cups (750-1,000 ml) water for 1 cup (250 ml) of dried legumes (about 6.5 oz/185 g), then bring gently to a boil. Let simmer for 2 min, cover and remove from heat. Let rest for 1-2 hr, until the beans have swollen in size. Drain and cook according to the recipe. If using a microwave oven, place dried legumes in a dish large enough to contain them when they swell; cover with cold water and cook on the highest setting for 8-10 min or until they boil. Continue to boil for 2 min, then let rest for 1 hr.

There are some precautions that can be taken to reduce gas problems provoked by legumes:

• Remove the outer skin of dried legumes before eating.
• Do not use the soaking water for cooking; the soaking water can also be changed a few times, or cook the legumes for 30 min, then change the cooking water and cook until very tender. Changing the cooking or soaking water does, however, lead to a loss of nutrients; this can be reduced by adding a little food yeast at time of serving.
• Cook slowly and thoroughly.
• Chew well and avoid finishing the meal with a sweet dessert, or adding sweet ingredients during the cooking of the legumes.

TIPS FOR COOKING LEGUMES

After soaking, legumes can be cooked on the stovetop, in the oven or in a pressure cooker.

:: Cooking on the stovetop and in the oven

This slow-cooking method is best if the legumes are cooked with other ingredients, as they will then absorb all of the flavors. Cover dried legumes with cold water, bring to a boil, reduce heat and let simmer until the legumes are tender (usually about 2 hr).

:: Cooking in a pressure cooker

This method of cooking is quicker, but is best when there are not many cooking ingredients and seasonings added at the beginning of cooking. Pressure-cooking involves certain risks, especially for dried legumes that produce higher amounts of scum, such as soybeans, lima beans and the various peas. It is not recommended for lentils and split peas. For good results:

- Add a little oil to the cooking liquid to prevent scum from forming (the valve and pressure regulator could become blocked). Beans cooked in the pressure cooker should be brought to a boil uncovered, then remove any scum that forms. Lower the heat, let simmer and cover with the lid to pressure-cook; time cooking carefully once the desired pressure is reached.
- Do not cook too large a quantity of dried legumes (do not fill the pressure cooker more than one-third of its volume), as most double or triple their size during cooking.
- Do not cook over a high heat. Run the pot under cold water as soon as the cooking time is over. Always clean the valve and pressure regulator well after use to prevent them from becoming blocked (if they become blocked, put the pressure cooker under cold water immediately and clean them).

To reduce cooking time and make legumes tender, some baking soda can be added to the cooking or soaking liquid. However, this destroys part of the legumes' thiamine content, reduces the absorbability of their amino acids and often alters their flavor. Adding a little seaweed slightly reduces the cooking time, tenderizes dried legumes and adds to their nutritional value.

Salt and acid ingredients (tomato, vinegar, lemon juice) are added at the end of cooking time, as they harden dried legumes and extend cooking time. If more water needs to be added during cooking, use boiling water.

Do not cook two varieties of legume at the same time, even if in principle they require the same cooking time; they will rarely cook evenly. Cook separately. Most legumes contain substances that diminish their nutritional value, but cooking the legumes well eliminates these substances.

Bean

Phaseolus spp., Leguminosae

The fruit of a plant originally from Central and South America. The word "bean" refers to the fruit, the seed and the plant that produces them. The pods of most bean varieties can be eaten fresh (before reaching full maturity). Once they are mature, they are no longer edible; the beans are podded and the seeds, called legumes,

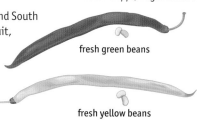

fresh green beans

fresh yellow beans

can be used fresh or dried, and cooked. The pods can be green (sometimes with purple or red stripes), yellow or purple (becoming green when cooked). They can be long and narrow, straight or slightly curved. Some varieties are stringless, such as snap beans.

White beans include numerous varieties. The **white kidney bean** is kidney-shaped and quite large with blunt ends. The small white bean is not as large. The **Great Northern bean**, medium in size, is not as kidney-shaped as the white kidney bean, and is rounder, with rounded ends. The **cannellini bean** (very prized in Italy) is slightly kidney-shaped with blunt ends. The **white pea bean**, or "navy bean," is the size of a pea and oval in shape. And the **cranberry bean**, or "borlotti bean," is large, round and not too mealy, a creamy white color with pink or brown streaks. Very popular in Europe and also known as the "coco bean," it is used in stews and for the French bean dish *cassoulet*. White bean varieties are interchangeable in most recipes. They are not as strongly flavored as red beans, and they take on the flavor of the dishes they are cooked in.

The **pinto bean** loses its markings during cooking and takes on a pink color and creamy texture. It can be used in place of red kidney beans and adds color to dishes. It is delicious made into a purée. The **Roman bean** is highly regarded in Italy, where it is called *"fagiolo romano."* Becoming evenly colored when cooked, it has a mild texture and it absorbs the flavors of the foods it is cooked with. It can be used in place of pinto or red kidney beans. The **red kidney bean** has a mild texture and flavor and is used in simmered dishes, where it absorbs the flavors. It is used in chili con carne and is often canned; it can be used in place of Roman or pinto beans. The **flageolet bean** is less floury than most other legumes. Often called a *"fayot"* bean

pinto beans

flageolet beans

in Europe, in France it is served with roast lamb. It is mostly available dried or canned. The **black bean** (or "turtle bean") represents a staple of American cuisine as well as that of Central America and Mexico. In Mexican cuisine, it is used in *frijoles refritos* (refried beans), in *burritos* and *enchiladas*, or in soups and salads.

black beans

BUYING

:: **Choose:** firm, crisp fresh beans, with a good green or golden yellow color, without bruises or brown spots and regular in shape. A little moisture when snapped indicates freshness.

:: **Avoid:** beans that are overripe or too old, as they will be hard and mealy.

COOKING

Fresh green and purple beans need to be cooked with care, as they can lose their color. Cooking time varies depending on the method used, the size of the beans and whether they are whole or cut into pieces. Keep cooking time brief; they will be tastier, more nutritious and more colorful.

:: **Boiled** or **steamed:** 5-15 min.

Dried beans are cooked after soaking. Cooking times vary from 1½ to 2 hr, according to the variety.

STORING

:: **In the fridge:** place fresh unwashed beans 2-3 days in a loosely closed or perforated plastic bag.

:: **In the freezer:** 12 months. Blanch cut fresh beans 3 min and whole fresh beans 4 min.

PREPARING

Wash fresh beans just before using; break off each end and remove the string (if necessary).

Roman beans

fresh green beans

Bean

NUTRITIONAL INFORMATION

	raw fresh bean	cooked fresh bean	boiled dried white bean	boiled dried pinto bean	boiled dried red bean
water	90.3%	89.2%	63.0%	64.0%	66.9%
protein	1.8 g	1.9 g	9.7 g	8.2 g	8.7 g
fat	0.1 g	0.3 g	0.3 g	0.5 g	0.5 g
carbohydrates	7.1 g	7.9 g	25.0 g	25.6 g	22.8 g
fiber	1.8 g	2.4 g	6.3 g	8.6 g	7.4 g

per 3.5 oz/100 g

RAW FRESH BEAN

GOOD SOURCE: potassium and folic acid.
CONTAINS: vitamin C, magnesium, thiamine, iron, vitamin A and niacin.
TRACES: copper, phosphorus and calcium.

COOKED FRESH BEAN

EXCELLENT SOURCE: potassium.
GOOD SOURCE: folic acid.
CONTAINS: vitamin C, magnesium, iron, vitamin A and copper.
PROPERTIES: diuretic, depurative, tonic and antiinfective.

DRIED BEAN

EXCELLENT SOURCE: potassium and folic acid.
GOOD SOURCE: magnesium and iron.
CONTAINS: copper, phosphorus, zinc, thiamine, niacin and vitamin B_6.

SERVING IDEAS

Fresh beans are more often eaten cooked (hot or cold) than raw. They are served as a side dish or used in salads, soups, stews, marinades and stir-fries. They are delicious as a gratin or dressed with a sauce or vinaigrette. They work well with tomato, thyme, oregano, rosemary, mint, marjoram, mustard, anise, nutmeg and cardamom.
Dried beans are eaten hot or cold, whole or puréed, used in soups, salads, sandwich spreads and main dishes. They are also cooked as a dessert.
Dried bean purée can be served as a side dish or used as a base for croquettes or patties, for example.

red kidney beans

Lima bean

Phaseolus lunatus, Leguminosae

The fruit of a plant originally from South America. The pods contain 2-4 beans whose size varies from tiny to very large, depending on the variety. The beans can be white, red, purple or black, even-colored or streaked; the most common lima beans are cream or green-colored. Lima beans are tasty with a mealy texture.

lima beans

BUYING

 :: Choose: fresh, clean, shiny lima beans. Shelled lima beans should be plump with tender green or green-white skin.

:: Avoid: wrinkled, spotted or yellowed lima beans.

STORING

:: At room temperature: the lima bean loses its flavor and becomes slimy. The podded beans are highly perishable.

COOKING

Avoid lengthy cooking, as lima beans become mushy.

:: Pressure-cooked: 15 min for the large-bean variety and 10 min for small beans. They produce a lot of scum during cooking, which is dangerous in the pressure cooker, as the valves and safety regulator can become blocked (see *Introduction*, p. 118).

:: Boiled: 15-25 min (fresh beans) and about 1½ hr (dried bean, depending on size).

NUTRITIONAL INFORMATION

	boiled
water	69.8%
protein	7.8 g
fat	0.4 g
carbohydrates	20.9 g
fiber	7.2 g
calories	115
	per 3.5 oz/100 g

EXCELLENT SOURCE: folic acid and potassium.
GOOD SOURCE: magnesium and iron.
CONTAINS: thiamine, phosphorus, zinc, copper, niacin and pantothenic acid.
The lima bean is a very good source of fiber. As they lack certain amino acids, lima bean proteins are incomplete (see *Food Complementarity Theory,* p. 277).

SERVING IDEAS

Immature lima beans are eaten fresh, with or without their pod; they are also served as a vegetable. Fresh lima beans are used in salads, soups and stews like succotash (made with corn and cream). They are suited to all sorts of dishes. The mild taste of lima beans means that they do not mask delicate flavors in a dish. Puréed, they can replace potatoes. They can also be sprouted.

Mung bean

Phaseolus aureus or *Vigna radiata,* Leguminosae

mung beans

The fruit of a plant originally from India. Mung bean pods contain dwarf seeds that can be green (most common variety), golden yellow, brown, olive green or purple-brown, evenly colored or streaky. Mung bean sprouts are used in Western countries.

BUYING

 Fresh mung bean sprouts are sold in plastic bags. They can also be bought cooked, in cans.

SERVING IDEAS

 Mung beans are used in the same way as other legumes, which they can replace or be used in combination with.

The mung bean sprout is a basic ingredient of chop suey and is used in salads and Asian-style dishes.

The immature pods can be prepared and cooked in the same way as green beans.

COOKING

Whole or split, soaking is not necessary.

:: **Boiled:** 45-60 min.

:: **Pressure-cooked:** with soaking (5-7 min), without soaking (10 min).

NUTRITIONAL INFORMATION

	raw sprouts	boiled
water	90.4%	72.7%
protein	3.1 g	7.0 g
fat	0.2 g	0.4 g
carbohydrates	5.9 g	19.2 g
fiber	1.5 g	2.5 g
calories	30.8	105.4
		per 3.5 oz/100 g

EXCELLENT SOURCE: folic acid.

GOOD SOURCE: potassium and magnesium.

CONTAINS: thiamine, iron, zinc, phosphorus, copper and pantothenic acid.

Mung beans are a source of fiber.

As they lack certain amino acids, mung bean proteins are incomplete (see *Food Complementarity Theory,* p. 277).

Urad

Phaseolus mungo or *Vigna mungo,* Leguminosae

The fruit of a plant originally from Asia, also known as "black gram" or "Chinese black bean." The urad pods enclose seeds that are black, grayish, brown or dark green. Inside they are a white, creamy color.

urad

SERVING IDEAS

 Immature urad pods are often used as vegetables. With a soft texture and strong taste, urad is prepared in the same way as other legumes. In Asia, they form the basis of the highly regarded black bean sauce. In India, they are hulled, split and used with rice to make a sort of flatbread (*dhosa*) or the spiced lentil purée (*dal*). Ground into a flour, urad is used to make confectionery, flatbreads and bread.

COOKING

:: **Boiled:** 1½ hr.
:: **Pressure-cooked:** with soaking (15 min), without soaking (20-25 min).

NUTRITIONAL INFORMATION

	boiled
water	72.5%
protein	7.6 g
fat	0.6 g
carbohydrates	18 g
fiber	1 g
calories	105
	per 3.5 oz/100 g

EXCELLENT SOURCE: folic acid and magnesium.
GOOD SOURCE: potassium.
CONTAINS: phosphorus, iron, thiamine, zinc, copper, niacin, pantothenic acid, riboflavin and calcium.
As they lack certain amino acids, urad proteins are incomplete (see *Food Complementarity Theory*, p. 277).

Adzuki bean

Phaseolus angularis or *Vigna angularis,* Leguminosae

The fruit of a plant originally from Asia. Adzuki bean pods hold tiny seeds that are usually a brownish red, but can also be black, light yellow, green or gray. They can be plain or streaky-colored and have a white *hilum* (the ridge where the bean was connected to the pod).

COOKING

Soak in cold water (2-3 hr).
:: **Boiled:** simmer (1½-2 hr).
:: **Pressure-cooked:** with soaking (20 min), without soaking (20-25 min).

adzuki beans

Adzuki bean

SERVING IDEAS

Immature adzuki bean pods are used in the same way as green beans. Adzuki beans are also dried and used in the same way as other legumes. They have a delicate flavor and are often served with rice. Adzuki beans are made into a paste in Asian countries (red bean paste), which is an ingredient in both savory and sweet dishes. This paste can be used in place of tomato paste.

The adzuki bean is used as a coffee substitute, and it can be puffed or sprouted. Milled adzuki beans are used as a flour in cakes, soups and milk substitutes.

NUTRITIONAL INFORMATION

	boiled
water	66%
protein	7.5 g
fat	0.1 g
carbohydrates	25 g
fiber	8 g
calories	127
	per 3.5 oz/100 g

EXCELLENT SOURCE: potassium.
GOOD SOURCE: magnesium, zinc, phosphorus and copper.
CONTAINS: iron and thiamine.
Adzuki beans are very high in fiber.
As they lack certain amino acids, adzuki bean proteins are incomplete (see *Food Complementarity Theory*, p. 277).

Runner bean

Phaseolus coccineus or *Phaseolus multiflorus,* Leguminosae

The fruit of a plant probably originally from Mexico or Central America. Runner bean pods contain white beans streaked with red or red beans streaked with black.

runner beans

SERVING IDEAS

Mature runner beans are eaten fresh or dried. They are cooked and prepared in the same way as red kidney beans. Runner beans work well with onions, tomatoes and tuna. The unripe pods are edible.

COOKING

Soak for several hours.
:: Boiled: 1-1½ hr.
:: Pressure-cooked: with soaking (10-15 min), without soaking (15-20 min).

NUTRITIONAL INFORMATION

	cooked
water	12%
protein	23 g
fat	2 g
carbohydrates	70 g
fiber	5 g
calories	385
	per 3.5 oz/100 g

As they lack certain amino acids, runner bean proteins are incomplete (see *Food Complementarity Theory*, p. 277).

Lupine bean

Lupinus albus, Leguminosae

The fruit of a plant, some varieties of which are originally from the Mediterranean region and others from North or South America. The white lupine bean is probably the most widely eaten. The pods enclose 3-6 seeds that are a dull pale yellow and are generally packed tightly together.

white lupine beans

PREPARING

Most lupine beans should be treated, in order to neutralize the alkaloid substances that make them bitter:

1. Cover 2 cups (500 ml) of lupine beans with 6 cups (1.5 l) of cold water, then leave them to soak 12 hr.
2. Drain the lupine beans, rinse and cover them again with fresh water.
3. Cook the lupine beans gently until tender (about 2 hr). Check for doneness by inserting the point of a knife.
4. Drain the lupine beans, cover them again with cold water and let them cool completely.
5. Drain again, cover them once again with cold water, mix in 2 tablespoons (30 ml) of salt and place in a cool spot (not in the fridge). Leave to soak 6-7 days, changing the salted water twice a day.
6. Once the bitterness is gone, keep the lupine beans in the fridge in salted water in an airtight container.
7. To serve the lupine beans, drain the amount needed and serve as is or dressed with lemon juice, with or without their skin.

NUTRITIONAL INFORMATION

water	71%
protein	15.5 g
fat	2.9 g
carbohydrates	9.9 g
fiber	0.7 g
calories	119
	per 3.5 oz/100 g

The white lupine bean is very nutritious.

GOOD SOURCE (BOILED): magnesium, potassium and zinc.

CONTAINS (BOILED): phosphorus, copper, thiamine, iron and calcium.

As they lack certain amino acids, white lupine bean proteins are incomplete (see *Theory of Food Complementarity,* p. 277).

SERVING IDEAS

Lupines are served plain as an appetizer in the same way as olives, especially in Italy and the Middle East. They are made into a flour used in soups, sauces, cookies, pasta dishes and bread. Lupine beans can be roasted and ground to make a coffee substitute.

Lentil

Lens esculenta or *Lens culinaris,* Leguminosae

The fruit of a plant probably originally from central Asia. The short, flat and oblong pods contain 1 or 2 seeds. Lentils are divided into two groups, according to their size: the large lentil (*macrospermae)* and the small lentil (*microspermae)*. One of the most well-known varieties in the West is the round **European lentil** that has a biconvex disk shape and is green or

green lentils

brown in color, still with its skin. The **Egyptian** or **red lentil** has no skin and is smaller and more round. Lentils can vary in shape, color, texture and flavor, depending on the species.

SERVING IDEAS

Dried lentils are used to prepare nutritious soups; they are also used in salads and main dishes. They are made into a purée, often used to make croquettes. In India, lentils and rice are often paired together. Lentils can be sprouted or made into flour, to make flatbreads and protein supplements (combined with grain flour).

PREPARING

Lentils do not need to be soaked. Wash carefully, as they often contain small stones. Lentils are digested more easily if added to boiling water.

NUTRITIONAL INFORMATION

	dry, boiled
water	69.6%
protein	9.0 g
fat	0.4 g
carbohydrates	20 g
fiber	3.9 g
calories	116
	per 3.5 oz/100 g

EXCELLENT SOURCE: folic acid and potassium.
GOOD SOURCE: iron and phosphorus.
CONTAINS: magnesium, zinc, thiamine, copper, niacin, vitamin B_6 and pantothenic acid.

COOKING

Avoid cooking lentils for too long, as this turns them into a purée.
:: Boiled: 60 min for brown lentils and 15-20 min for orange lentils.
:: Pressure-cooked: 15-20 min for brown lentils and about 5 min for orange lentils. When cooking lentils, add a little oil; this prevents the formation of scum, which can block the safety and pressure valves (see *Introduction,* p. 118).

red lentils

Dolichos bean

Vigna spp. or *Dolichos lablab,* Leguminosae

There are several varieties of dolichos beans. The **black-eyed pea** is originally from North Africa. The different varieties range in color from white to red, brown, black, yellow-green or cream. They can be plain-colored, streaky or marbled. The **yardlong bean**, or "asparagus bean," is originally from central Africa. It has a flavor that is similar to the green bean and asparagus. The **lablab bean**, or "hyacinth bean," is probably originally from India, where it has been eaten for a very long time. It is also enjoyed in Africa, Central America, South America and Asia.

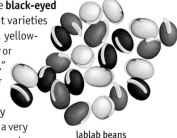

lablab beans

COOKING

BLACK-EYED PEA
:: **Boiled:** about 1 hr. Avoid overcooking, which easily turns them into a purée.
:: **Pressure-cooked:** 10 min with soaking; 10-20 min without soaking.

black-eyed peas

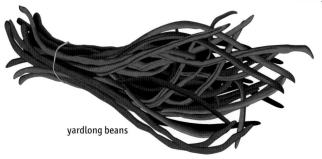

yardlong beans

Dolichos bean

NUTRITIONAL INFORMATION

	cooked black-eyed pea	boiled yardlong bean	fresh and boiled lablab bean
water	70%	68.8%	86.9%
protein	7.7 g	8.3 g	2.9 g
fat	0.5 g	0.5 g	0.2 g
carbohydrates	20.8 g	21.1 g	9.2 g
fiber	9.6 g	2 g	1.8 g
calories	116	118	49
			per 3.5 oz/100 g

BLACK-EYED PEA

EXCELLENT SOURCE: folic acid.

GOOD SOURCE: potassium, magnesium, iron and thiamine.

CONTAINS: phosphorus, zinc, copper, niacin, pantothenic acid and vitamin B_6.

YARDLONG BEAN

EXCELLENT SOURCE: folic acid, magnesium and potassium.

GOOD SOURCE: iron, phosphorus and thiamine.

CONTAINS: zinc, copper, pantothenic acid and vitamin B_6.

LABLAB BEAN

EXCELLENT SOURCE: copper.

GOOD SOURCE: potassium and magnesium.

CONTAINS: riboflavin, iron and phosphorus.

Dolichos beans are a source of fiber.

As they lack certain amino acids, their proteins are incomplete (see *Food Complementarity Theory*, p. 277).

SERVING IDEAS

 Dolichos beans resemble common beans and can be used in the same way, fresh or dried.

The pods of the black-eyed pea are edible before they are fully mature and are often served as a green vegetable. The leaves and roots are also edible. Black-eyed peas can be used in soups and salads, cooked in patties or slow-cooked. They are made into a purée or sprouted.

The yardlong bean is most often eaten fresh, like the green bean. Less juicy and less sweet, its stronger flavor is more like dried beans. Stir-frying especially suits yardlong beans. The dried seeds are prepared in the same way as the seeds of other legumes.

The lablab bean, once dried, is used in the same way as other legumes, which it can replace in most recipes. Dried and then ground into a flour, it is used in bread, or to make cooked balls as well as porridge. It can also be sprouted. Fresh lablab beans are used in the same way as green beans.

Broad bean

Vicia faba, Leguminosae

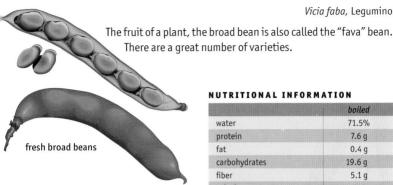

The fruit of a plant, the broad bean is also called the "fava" bean. There are a great number of varieties.

fresh broad beans

NUTRITIONAL INFORMATION

	boiled
water	71.5%
protein	7.6 g
fat	0.4 g
carbohydrates	19.6 g
fiber	5.1 g
calories	110
	per 3.5 oz/100 g

EXCELLENT SOURCE: folic acid.
GOOD SOURCE: potassium and magnesium.
CONTAINS: copper, phosphorus, zinc, iron, thiamine and riboflavin.
The broad bean is high in fiber.
As they lack certain amino acids, their proteins are incomplete (see *Food Complementarity Theory,* p. 277).

COOKING

Cook fresh or dried broad beans with or without their skin. To remove the skin, plunge the broad beans in boiling water for a few minutes, drain, then cool under running water. The skin can also be removed after the beans have been soaked for 12-24 hr (refresh water several times).
Dried broad beans require about 2½ hr cooking time. If skinned, they only need 8-12 hr soaking and about 1½ hr cooking. Fresh broad beans need to be cooked about 20 min.
:: Pressure-cooked: about 20 min with soaking; about 25 min without soaking.

SERVING IDEAS

The broad bean is mealy with a strong flavor. Young and fresh broad beans are sometimes eaten raw, without the thick skin, which contains tannins that leave a bitter taste. Fresh or dried, they are delicious in soups and simmered dishes, whole or puréed. Broad beans can be popped and eaten as an appetizer, like popcorn. Cooked broad beans can be eaten cold, whole or puréed. They are especially used in hors d'oeuvres, salads and sandwich spreads. The immature pods are edible, and are used in the same way as green beans.

dried broad beans

Pea

Pisum sativum, Leguminosae

The fruit of a plant originally from central Asia and Europe. The green, smooth pods are straight or slightly bent, rounded or flat, and hold seeds of variable size, round in shape or slightly square. Usually green, these seeds can be grayish, whitish or brownish. Fresh peas are called "green peas," and when dried, "dried peas." The latter are sold whole or in halves, when they are called "split peas." Split peas come in green and yellow varieties.

Round peas, used by the frozen-food industry, are more mealy and less sweet than **wrinkled peas**, which are mostly used for canning.

Snow peas have sweet and crunchy edible pods. Only the flat ones are good to eat.

Sugar-snap peas have tasty pods even when the green peas are well formed.

wrinkled pea pods

BUYING

GREEN PEAS

:: Choose: fresh green peas with smooth pods containing a good number of peas that are not too large, and are shiny and bright green in color.

Fresh green peas are rare and rather expensive.

SNOW PEAS

:: Choose: snow peas that are not too large with firm pods, crunchy and intact, and a good bright green color.

:: Avoid: snow peas with limp, wrinkled, yellowed or spotted pods.

Snow peas are mainly sold fresh.

snow peas

PREPARING

Before shelling fresh green peas, run them briefly under cold water, then break off the upper part of the pod and pull on the string found where the two pod-halves join (some varieties don't have a string). Repeat at the other end, separate the pods and remove the peas. Green peas do not need to be washed.

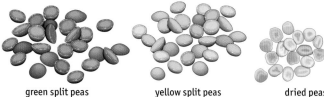

green split peas   yellow split peas   dried peas

NUTRITIONAL INFORMATION

	cooked green peas	cooked dried peas	cooked snow peas
water	77.9%	69.5%	88.9%
protein	5.4 g	8.4 g	3.3 g
fat	0.2 g	0.4 g	0.2 g
carbohydrates	15.6 g	21.1 g	7.0 g
fiber	6.7 g	4.0 g	2.8 g
			per 3.5 oz/100 g

COOKED GREEN PEAS

GOOD SOURCE: folic acid, potassium, thiamine and magnesium.

CONTAIN: vitamin C, zinc, vitamin B$_6$, niacin, iron and phosphorus.

DRIED PEAS

EXCELLENT SOURCE: potassium and folic acid.

GOOD SOURCE: thiamine.

CONTAIN: magnesium, zinc, iron, copper, phosphorus and pantothenic acid.

As they lack certain amino acids, peas proteins are incomplete (see *Food Complementarity Theory*, p. 277).

COOKED SNOW PEAS

EXCELLENT SOURCE: vitamin C.

GOOD SOURCE: potassium.

CONTAIN: iron, folic acid, magnesium, thiamine, pantothenic acid, vitamin B$_6$ and phosphorus.

SERVING IDEAS

Snow peas and very young and very fresh green peas can be eaten raw; cooking makes them sweeter.

Cooked fresh green peas can be combined with carrots or asparagus tips. They accompany meat and poultry. They can be made into soups. Cold peas can be used in a mixed salad. Frozen green peas are used in the same way as fresh green peas.

Snow peas are used in the same way as green beans, which they can replace in most recipes. Raw snow peas are used in salads and hors d'oeuvres. Cooked snow peas are prepared in the same way as fresh peas. They are excellent in stir-fries.

Whole dried peas are cooked in soups, traditionally with a ham bone and cubed ham. Puréed split peas are used in soups and can accompany main dishes.

COOKING

FRESH GREEN PEAS
Cook peas only briefly to minimize loss of color and flavor.

:: **Boiled:** 10-15 min, depending on size.
:: **Steamed or braised:** place between two layers of wet lettuce leaves.

SNOW PEAS
:: **Boiled or steamed:** 6-15 min.

WHOLE DRIED PEAS
:: **Boiled:** cook on a low simmer for 1-2 hr, after soaking.

SPLIT PEAS
:: **Boiled:** 1-1½ hr, until tender. If cooked for too long, they tend to disintegrate.
Don't cook in the pressure cooker, as they produce too much scum, which can block the safety and pressure valves (see *Introduction*, p. 118).

fresh green peas

STORING

Do not keep green pea pods longer than 12 hr.

:: **In the fridge:** place fresh podded green peas, 4-5 days, in a non-airtight container or a loosely closed or perforated bag.
:: **In the freezer:** blanch green peas and snow peas before freezing (1-2 min, depending on size).

Chickpea

Cicer arietinum, Leguminosae

The fruit of a plant probably originally from the Middle East. Chickpeas grow on a plant of bushy appearance. The short and swollen pods contain 1-4 seeds. These can be cream-colored, greenish, yellowish, reddish, brownish or almost black. Depending on the variety, their consistency can be more or less pasty; some have a nutty flavor.

chickpeas

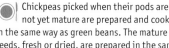

NUTRITIONAL INFORMATION

	dry, boiled
water	60%
protein	8.9 g
fat	2.6 g
carbohydrates	27.4 g
fiber	3.5 g
calories	164
	per 3.5 oz/100 g

EXCELLENT SOURCE: folic acid and potassium.
GOOD SOURCE: iron, magnesium, copper, zinc and phosphorus.
CONTAINS: thiamine, niacin, vitamin B_6 and calcium.
PROPERTIES: diuretic, stomachic and anthelmintic.
Chickpeas are a source of fiber.
As they are deficient in certain amino acids, their proteins are incomplete (see *Food Complementarity Theory*, p. 277).

PREPARING

 Soak chickpeas for 12-16 hr before cooking. They can also be left to soak overnight and frozen in their soaking water, defrosted the next day and cooked. This reduces the cooking time by about 1 hr.

COOKING

Chickpeas generally require 2-2½ hr of cooking time after soaking.
:: **Pressure-cooked:** 20-25 min with soaking; 35-40 min without soaking.

SERVING IDEAS

Chickpeas picked when their pods are not yet mature are prepared and cooked in the same way as green beans. The mature seeds, fresh or dried, are prepared in the same way as the seeds of other legumes; unlike most of these, however, they do not disintegrate when cooked.

Chickpeas are, along with common beans, the legumes with the most variety of uses; they are used in appetizers, soups and main dishes. They are delicious cold in mixed salads or puréed. Two Middle Eastern specialties, hummus (a chickpea purée eaten cold) and falafel (spiced bean croquettes), are based on chickpeas. They are also an ingredient in several specialties from the south of France, in particular its stews, hot pots and braises, *puchero* (a Mexican hot pot dish) and *cocido* (a Spanish stew). Chickpeas are one of the traditional ingredients in couscous.

Chickpeas are made into flour, and can be roasted or sprouted. The flour is especially used for batters, unleavened breads and flatbreads; it is used very widely in India. Roast chickpeas, salted or unsalted, are often eaten as snacks in the same manner as nuts.

Peanut

Arachis hypogaea, Leguminosae

The fruit of a plant thought to be originally from South America (Brazil or Bolivia) or China. The peanut is usually considered to be a nut. It is in fact a legume belonging to the same family as peas, broad beans and common beans, and can be used in the same way.

Peanuts grow on a climbing or bushy plant. The fertilized floral stems bend over toward the ground and penetrate it; the end of these stems swells, ripens and produces the pod underground. The pods become brittle when they are dried and hold 2 or 3 edible seeds.

There are about 10 species of peanut and a very large number of varieties.

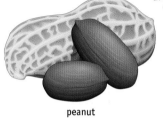

peanut

BUYING

:: Avoid: old, spotted, blackened, rancid or moldy peanuts, as they can be contaminated by a type of mold.

COOKING

Cook peanuts for about 30 min. Peanuts will lose their firm texture if the dish is reheated or if they are cooked for too long. To keep peanuts crunchy, only add them if possible to the portion of food that will be eaten immediately.

STORING

Raw peanuts deteriorate more quickly than roasted peanuts.

:: At room temperature: place roasted peanuts in a cool and dry spot.

:: In the fridge: raw, in an airtight container (9 months in the shell or 3 months shelled).

:: In the freezer: in the shell, 6 months; shelled, 3 months.

Peanut

NUTRITIONAL INFORMATION

	raw	dry roasted
water	5.6%	1.4%
protein	13 g	11.8 g
fat	23.8 g	24.8 g
carbohydrates	9.3 g	10.7 g
fiber	1.2 g	3.9 g
calories	282	293
		per 1.8 oz/50 g

RAW PEANUTS

EXCELLENT SOURCE: thiamine, niacin, magnesium and potassium.
GOOD SOURCE: pantothenic acid, copper, zinc and phosphorus.
CONTAIN: iron.

DRY OR OIL-ROASTED PEANUTS

EXCELLENT SOURCE: magnesium, niacin and potassium.
GOOD SOURCE: zinc, copper, thiamine and phosphorus.
CONTAIN: pantothenic acid, iron and vitamin B_6.
Dry-roasted peanuts are high in fiber.
PROPERTIES: peanuts are high in protein, calories and fat (85.5% unsaturated fatty acids, of which 57% are monounsaturated and 28.5% are polyunsaturated, see *Fats and oils,* p. 579). The proteins are said to be incomplete, as lower levels of certain amino acids are present in relation to others (see *Food Complementarity Theory*, p. 277).

SERVING IDEAS

Peanuts are left whole, crushed, ground or made into a paste. They are available salted or unsalted, peeled or unpeeled, dry or honey roasted, coated in chocolate or oil. They are often eaten as appetizers or snacks. They can replace almonds or pistachios in pastries. Peanut butter (an excellent source of protein) is not really an American invention, although it is a popular and important food in North America. Africans, South American Indians and Indonesians have been preparing a similar paste for a long time.

Peanuts occupy a privileged position in cooking, accompanying meat, fish and poultry or flavoring soups, sauces, salads, simmered dishes and desserts. They are the basis of satay sauce, a spicy sauce, and *gado gado*, a vegetable dish flavored with a sauce containing peanuts, coconut milk, pepper and garlic. Peanuts yield an excellent oil with a neutral flavor that is suitable for all purposes and can tolerate high temperatures and several fryings without deteriorating (see *Oil,* p. 590).

Alfalfa

Medicago sativa, Leguminosae

The fruit of a plant thought to be originally from Southwest Asia. Its sprouted seeds especially are used for human consumption. Sprouting increases the nutritional value of alfalfa by making it more digestible and raising the level of its various nutrients. The young leaves are used as a vegetable or to make infusions.

alfalfa

BUYING

::Choose: firm alfalfa sprouts with green leaves.

:: Avoid: waterlogged, discolored or moldy-smelling sprouts.

Buy the dry seeds sold especially for sprouting in small quantities, as they have a high yield.

PREPARING

:: Sprouting in a glass jar:
   1. Measure about 1 tablespoon (10-15 ml) of dry alfalfa seeds and leave them to soak in water overnight.
2. Drain, rinse and place the seeds in a large sterilized jar with a wide mouth. Cover the top of the jar with a straining cloth (for example, cheesecloth) and keep in place with an elastic band. Turn the jar upside down and place in a dark and warm environment.
3. Twice a day for 3-4 days, rinse the seeds in tepid water, then drain and put the jar back in the same place, so that the liquid drains completely (it is important that the seeds do not dry out).
4. When the sprouts are 1½-2 in. (4-5 cm) long, expose them to sunlight so that the leaves turn green. Serve or refrigerate.

NUTRITIONAL INFORMATION

	raw sprouts
water	91%
protein	1.4 g
fat	0.2 g
carbohydrates	1.3 g
fiber	1 g
calories	10
	per 1 cup/250 ml

RAW ALFALFA SPROUTS
CONTAIN: folic acid and zinc.
PROPERTIES: antiscorbutic, diuretic, stimulant and useful against peptic ulcers and urinary or intestinal problems.

STORING

:: At room temperature: dried seeds, 1 year, in a cool and dry place in an airtight container (1 year).
:: In the fridge: sprouts, 1 week.

SERVING IDEAS

Alfalfa sprouts are eaten raw (in salads, sandwiches and hors d'oeuvres), as they are very delicate with a subtle taste. They are added at serving time to soups, stews, omelettes, vegetables and tacos.
Alfalfa flour can be added in small quantities to cereals.

Soybean

Glycine max, Leguminosae

dried soybeans

The fruit of a plant originally from eastern Asia. Soybean pods enclose very hard seeds of variable color. Soybeans are the only legume from which a liquid can be extracted, "soy milk" (or "soy drink"), which is used to make tofu, among other purposes. They can be pressed for oil (see *Oil,* p. 587) and fermented (see *Tempeh,* p. 146; *Miso,* p. 459; *Soy sauce,* p. 460). They are made into textured protein products (see *Textured vegetable proteins,* p. 147). Processed soybean products (miso, tamari, soy milk and tofu) are especially consumed in Asian cultures.

Soy granules are soybeans whose outer husk has been removed before being milled into granules. Soybean sprouts are ready to eat after germinating for a few days. They are used in the same way as mung bean sprouts. Soy flour is a gluten-free (non-rising) flour. It contains 2-3 times more protein than wheat flour and 10 times more fat in the case of full-fat soy flour (which must be kept in the fridge).

soybean sprouts

PREPARING

Soybeans require a period of soaking beforehand, which slightly reduces the cooking time, preserves the vitamins and minerals and reduces flatulence.

soy flour

COOKING

Dried soybeans require at least 3 hr of cooking time, sometimes up to 7-9 hr, depending on the variety. They are cooked when they can be easily crushed with a fork. Use a little more water than for other legumes and check during cooking that they have enough.

:: Pressure cooked: bring the soybeans to a boil (uncovered), remove any scum, then lower the heat and let simmer. Cover with the lid. When the required pressure is reached, time 30 min for soybeans that have already been soaked. Do not fill the pressure cooker by more than one-third.

Soybean

NUTRITIONAL INFORMATION

	boiled soybeans	full-fat soy flour	defatted soy flour
water	62.5%	5.2%	7.2%
protein	16.6 g	34.5 g	47 g
fat	9 g	20.6 g	1.2 g
carbohydrates	9.9 g	35.2 g	38.4 g
fiber	2 g	-	-
calories	173	436	329
			per 3.5 oz/100 g

Soybean contains more protein and calories than other legumes. Its proteins are of excellent quality. Soybean is an ideal complement to grain foods (see *Food Complementarity Theory*, p. 277). The fats are 78% unsaturated, with no cholesterol, and contain lecithin. Soybean is beneficial for the liver, mineralizing and energizing. It contains several potentially anticancerous compounds.

SOYBEANS

EXCELLENT SOURCE: potassium, magnesium, iron and folic acid.

GOOD SOURCE: phosphorus, copper, niacin and riboflavin.

CONTAIN: vitamin B_6, zinc, thiamine and calcium.

SOY FLOUR (FULL-FAT OR DEFATTED)

EXCELLENT SOURCE: potassium, magnesium, folacin, copper, niacine, iron, phosphorus, thiamine, zinc and vitamin B_6.

GOOD SOURCE: calcium.

FULL-FAT SOY FLOUR

EXCELLENT SOURCE: riboflavin.

GOOD SOURCE: pantothenic acid.

DEFATTED SOY FLOUR

EXCELLENT SOURCE: pantothenic acid.

GOOD SOURCE: riboflavin.

SERVING IDEAS

FRESH SOYBEANS

Fresh soybeans contain antinutritional elements that are neutralized by cooking and fermentation. It is important to cook them well. Fresh soybeans are eaten by themselves or in their pods. They are often used as a vegetable or can be cooked in the same way as dried soybeans. To pod them more easily, blanch for about 5 min or cook in their pods. They are excellent in simmered dishes.

DRIED SOYBEANS

Dried soybeans are prepared in the same way as other legumes. It is important to cook them well.

SOY GRANULES

Soy granules cook much more quickly than the whole bean; use 4 parts water to 1 part granules. They are added to soups, stews, spaghetti sauces, cookies and bread. Cover with boiling water beforehand or boil for a few minutes (not necessary if being cooked for a long time).

SOYBEAN SPROUTS

These are eaten raw or lightly cooked.

SOY FLOUR

Soy flour is used in small quantities to bind sauces or to make cakes, muffins and cookies, and as an enriching ingredient.

Soy milk

A liquid that resembles milk, extracted from ground soybeans or made using full-fat soy flour. Soy milk is almost always pasteurized or sterilized. It is sold as a liquid (often artificially flavored and very sweet) or in powder form. Manufacturing soy milk results in an edible by-product called "okara" (see *Okara*, p. 145).

soy milk

SERVING IDEAS

 Soy milk is used to make soups, sauces, yogurt, sorbets, ice creams, puddings, beverages and pastries.

PREPARING

:: **Making soy milk:**
1. Wash 1 cup (250 ml) of soybeans, cover with water to allow for expansion; leave to soak 10 hr.
2. Heat ½ cup (125 ml) of water in a saucepan.
3. Meanwhile, purée the soybeans, adding 2-2½ cups (500-750 ml) of water.
4. Pour the mixture into the saucepan, bring to a boil, lower the heat and simmer 12-25 min (30 min for milk with a milder flavor).
5. Pour this mixture into a colander lined with a straining cloth (for example, cheesecloth) set over a container.
6. Press or wring the cloth to extract the liquid.
7. Open up the cloth and pour over ½ cup (125 ml) of water, close and wring well once again.

STORING

 :: **At room temperature:** keep powder in an airtight container.
:: **In the fridge:** liquid, several days.

NUTRITIONAL INFORMATION

water	93.3%
protein	7 g
carbohydrates	4.6 g
fat	4.8 g
calories	84
	per 8 oz/250 ml

EXCELLENT SOURCE: thiamine and potassium.
GOOD SOURCE: magnesium and copper.
CONTAINS: phosphorus, riboflavin, iron, niacin and vitamin B_6.
Soy milk proteins are of excellent quality, but they are low in the amino acid methionine (see *Food Complementarity Theory*, p. 277). They contain mostly unsaturated fatty acids, which, being plant-derived, have no cholesterol and contain lecithin. Soy milk contains no lactose, a substance to which some people have an intolerance (see *Milk*, p. 527).
PROPERTIES: alkalinizing and beneficial for the digestive system. It is said to be effective against anemia, for stimulating the production of hemoglobin, lowering triglyceride and blood cholesterol levels. Exclusive or excessive use of soy milk in combination with a strict vegetarian diet can lead to calcium and vitamin B_{12} deficiencies.

Tofu

The Japanese name of the curd obtained from the milky liquid extracted from soybeans. Tofu is originally from China. It occupies an important place in Asian cuisine.

Tofu is sometimes referred to as bean curd (the literal meaning of its name). It has a somewhat gelatinous but firm consistency; its texture can be compared to a firm custard. It has a bland flavor, but it absorbs the flavors of the foods with which it is cooked.

tofu

BUYING

Tofu is sold loose, immersed in water, individually wrapped (often vacuum-packed), dried or frozen. If it is sold loose, make sure it is quite fresh and kept in adequately hygienic conditions. Sealed packaging eliminates risks of contamination and extends its keeping time (90 days).

The use-by date on the packaging is valid as long as the packaging has not been opened.

COOKING

:: **Boiled:** whole or cut into cubes (4-20 min, depending on the size of the pieces and the desired texture).

Eat fresh tofu as soon as possible after it is made or bought. Aged tofu is firmer with a stronger taste, and benefits from being well seasoned. Firm tofu keeps its shape better and can be sliced and cubed more easily than soft tofu, which crumbles and mashes more easily.

NUTRITIONAL INFORMATION

	firm tofu
water	69.8%
protein	15.7 g
fat	8.6 g
carbohydrates	4.3 g
fiber	0.1 g
calories	146
	per 3.5 oz/100 g

EXCELLENT SOURCE: iron and magnesium.
GOOD SOURCE: potassium, niacin, copper, calcium, zinc and phosphorus.
CONTAINS: folic acid, thiamine, riboflavin and vitamin B_6.

Tofu proteins are rich in lysine, which makes tofu an ideal complement to grains (see *Soybean,* p. 139). Its fats are 78% unsaturated and do not contain cholesterol. 3.5 oz (100 g) of tofu contains 50% less protein than 2 oz (60 g) of cooked meat. Other sources of protein eaten during the day are enough to fulfill protein requirements.

Tofu contains 2-3 times more iron than a portion of cooked meat. It will be absorbed more easily and effectively if a good source of vitamin C is eaten at the same meal.

fresh tofu

Tofu

STORING

:: **In the fridge:** place fresh tofu whose packaging has been opened 1 week in an airtight container filled with water. Refresh the water every 2 days. This process can be used with vacuum-packed tofu whose use-by date has passed; make sure it still has a pleasant smell when it is opened and that it isn't viscous.

:: **In the freezer:** without water, in an airtight container with the air pushed out or in its vacuum packaging. Defrost in the fridge. Freezing makes tofu more rubbery and its white color may become yellowish.

firm tofu

PREPARING

1 Rinse ½ lb (250 g) of soybeans under cold water. Cover with water in a bowl and leave to soak 8 hr.

2 Rinse again, drain, then purée in the food processor with 3 cups (750 ml) of water.

3 Bring 8 cups (2 l) of water to a boil and add the purée. Cook on medium heat 10 min, stirring constantly.

4 Pour the whole mixture into a colander lined with a straining cloth (for example, cheesecloth) over a bowl, then wring the cloth to extract the soy milk.

5 Heat the milk until just under boiling point; add ⅓ of the coagulating agent dissolved in cold water (nigari or others). Stir, add the remaining ⅔, stir and let rest 5 min.

6 When the curd has formed, remove the remaining liquid (the whey) with a ladle.

7 Place the curd in a colander lined with a cloth and wrap.

8 Place a heavy object on the curd and rest 15-30 min, depending on the desired firmness.

SERVING IDEAS

Tofu is served hot or cold. It is used in soups, pasta dishes, pizzas, cakes, pies, cookies and muffins. Raw, ground and seasoned tofu is added to sandwiches, salads and hors d'oeuvres. Soft tofu can be liquidized in the blender and can replace sour cream, yogurt and soft curd cheeses. It can be used in place of scrambled eggs. Firm tofu can be sautéed, braised, stewed, fried and broiled.

Tofu is the base ingredient of frozen desserts similar to ice cream. It is made into croquettes, burgers and sausages. These products are high in protein and low in fat, salt and additives. The flavor of tofu can be enhanced by adding Worcestershire sauce, hot pepper sauces and soy sauce as well as with garlic, fresh ginger, curry powder, chili powder and strong mustard.

Okara

okara

The drained pulp of soybeans, okara is the residue of the manufacture of soy milk. Beige in color, it has a shredded texture reminiscent of freshly grated coconut.

SERVING IDEAS

Okara lightens the texture of breads and pastries and extends their storage life. It absorbs other flavors and can be added to grains, batters, crepes, muffins, cookies, croquettes and stews. It is used as a meat substitute, to coat foods for frying and to thicken soups (except clear soups, which will become muddy) and sauces. Okara is used wet or dried. Its moisture levels depend on the level of milk extraction and this influences the way it can be used. It can be dried in the sun, in a dehydrator or in the oven at 250°F-455°F (120°C-235°C). Stir occasionally; to obtain a finer mixture, process afterward in a food processor.

NUTRITIONAL INFORMATION

water	82%
protein	3.3 g
fat	1.8 g
carbohydrates	12.6 g
fiber	4.1 g
calories	77
	per 3.5 oz/100 g

GOOD SOURCE: potassium.
CONTAINS: magnesium, iron, calcium and phosphorus. It is very high in fiber.

STORING

:: **At room temperature:** indefinitely, dried, in a cool and dry place.
:: **In the fridge:** wet, 1 week.

Tempeh

A fermented product originally from Indonesia with a slightly rubbery texture and a strong flavor. Tempeh is traditionally made with soybeans. It can be prepared using other legumes (peanuts, red kidney beans, small white beans), grains (wheat, oats, barley) and coconut.

The beans need to be split in two and their skin removed; they are then partially cooked before being cultured with the fermenting agent *Rhizopus oligosporus*. White molds form around the product. The texture of tempeh is similar to nougat.

tempeh

BUYING

:: **Choose:** fresh tempeh covered with a thin whitish layer, with a mushroom smell. Black or gray marks indicate higher levels of fermentation; do not let tempeh ferment to this extent.

:: **Avoid:** tempeh with pink, yellow or blue spots or with an ammonia-like or rotten smell. Tempeh is bought in Asian groceries or natural food stores.

SERVING IDEAS

 Tempeh is only eaten cooked. It can replace or be combined with tofu in several recipes. It is more tasty when it has been marinated (at least 20 min) or if garlic and fresh ginger or strong mustard is added to it. Tempeh can be added to soups, sauces, stuffings, dips, sandwiches, mixed salads, stews, lasagna and pizzas.

STORING

:: **In the fridge.**
:: **In the freezer:** blanch before freezing.

NUTRITIONAL INFORMATION

	soy tempeh
water	55%
protein	18.9 g
fat	7.7 g
carbohydrates	17 g
fiber	3.0 g
calories	199
	per 3.5 oz/100 g

EXCELLENT SOURCE: vitamin B_{12}, niacin, copper, potassium and magnesium.
GOOD SOURCE: folic acid, zinc, phosphorus, vitamin B_6 and iron.
CONTAINS: thiamine, calcium, vitamin A, riboflavin and pantothenic acid.
Tempeh is a source of fiber. It is high in nutrients and easily digested and assimilated.

COOKING

 :: **Sautéed** or **fried:** 5-10 min.

Textured vegetable proteins

Proteins extracted from certain vegetables using a chemical process. Textured vegetable proteins (often referred to as "TVP") are ingredients in various food products and are mainly used as a meat substitute and a food additive (compulsory labeling).

They are made mostly from soybeans, sometimes wheat, sunflower or alfalfa. Depending on the manufacturing method, the extracted proteins are more or less gelatinous, slimy and soluble.

textured vegetable
proteins

BUYING

 Check the list of ingredients on the label to avoid food additives.

SERVING IDEAS

 Textured vegetable proteins come in various forms (granules, powder, cubes, slices); they are sold plain or flavored (meat, vegetable, nut, fish, seafood, etc.). They absorb other flavors and are used in making sauces, stews, lasagna, hamburgers, frozen desserts, cereal products, etc.

In powder form, vegetable proteins are used in making charcuterie (sausage and deli meats), cereals, pastries and factory-made breads.

STORING

:: **At room temperature:** dehydrated.
:: **In the fridge:** rehydrated, 1 week.

NUTRITIONAL INFORMATION

The range of commercial cooking uses is so wide that it is difficult to know the nutritional value unless this is indicated on the label. Textured vegetable proteins are very low in fat.

PREPARING

:: **For homemade proteins without additives:** use frozen tofu; defrost in a colander and extract the water. Mash the drained tofu with a fork or using a mortar and pestle and season with stock, tomato juice, tamari sauce, fresh herbs, etc. Mix well and serve as is or dehydrate (250°F-275°F/120°C-135°C) for future use.

:: **To rehydrate proteins:** add ⅚ cup (200 ml) of boiling water to 1 cup (250 ml) of granules; let stand 10-15 min. Wet hands before shaping to stop the rehydrated proteins from sticking.

Introduction
Fruits

Botanically speaking, the fruit of a plant is what develops when the flower's ovary has been fertilized, and is what protects the ovules that have become seeds. The word "fruit" is usually applied to sweet foods eaten for dessert, breakfast or as snacks. Some vegetables, however, such as eggplant, tomato, squash, olive, avocado and nuts, are also fruits. Until the 18th century, vegetables were also called "fruits," as they formed part of what were called the "fruits of the earth."

TIPS FOR STORING FRUITS

Fruits are fragile; they continue living after they are picked and are said to "breathe."

:: At room temperature

Environmental temperature has a great impact on fruits' breathing rhythm. The higher the temperature, the more the fruits breathe, which leads to water loss and speeds up the ripening process. Not all fruits are fragile, however; oranges, for example, keep more easily than strawberries. Fruits need a certain level of humidity and coolness to stay fresh for longer periods; the more humid the surrounding air, the slower the dehydration rate. To speed up the ripening process, keep fruits at room temperature away from sunlight, while making sure they do not become too ripe, as many fruits spoil very quickly. Fruits are ripe when they yield to gentle finger pressure and become fragrant. They should then be kept in the fridge and used quickly.

Fruits produce a large amount of ethylene, a gas that speeds up the ripening process. Place fruit in a bag to trap the gas and accelerate ripening. Remove fruits from the bag when they are ready to eat, otherwise they will become overripe. Do not keep fruits in a plastic airtight container, as plastic keeps in air and humidity, which will lead fruits to rot. Fruit juices are best kept in sealed, nontransparent containers to limit the loss of nutrients.

:: In the fridge
The ethylene gas emitted by fruits affects vegetables, so it is better to store fruits and vegetables separately. (Ethylene gas can, however, be used to stimulate flowering in plants that are not blooming. Placing a plant in a bag with a fruit, especially an apple or banana, will encourage blooming.) Handle fruits carefully, as any bruising leads them to deteriorate more quickly and accelerates the ripening process. Keep fruits away from strong-smelling foods, as most fruits have a tendency to absorb odors.

:: In the freezer
Almost all fruits can be frozen, with the exception of pears and sweet cherries, which become too soft when defrosted. During the freezing process, certain enzymes cause fruits to brown, so they should be sprinkled with sugar or acidic substances (lemon juice, ascorbic acid) to slow down this process. This is especially the case with small fruits, such as strawberries, raspberries and blackberries.

:: Canned
To can good-quality fruits, it is essential to use a sterilizer with boiling water, even if fruits are very acidic, to destroy all bacteria, molds and yeasts. Make sure to only use ripe, firm and well-formed fruits. Well-made home-canned fruits keep for up to a year, preferably kept in a dark and cool place.

:: Dried
Drying ensures the keeping quality of fruit because dried fruits no longer contain enough water to enable microorganisms to grow. The most commonly dried fruits are apricots, dates, figs and grapes (raisins). Drying fruits involves a certain amount of preparation, as enzymes in fruits can affect their color and flavor during the drying process. They are thus either blanched or treated with sulfur for a certain period of time. Fruits are then dried until there is no more water at their center. They then have a flexible texture, like leather. Drying times range from 5 to 15 hr, depending on the variety of the fruit and the size of the pieces.

Dried fruits

Fruits from which part of the water content has been removed. In previous times, fruits were dried in the sun. These days, commercial dehydration is highly mechanized and carried out under controlled heating conditions.

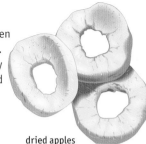

dried apples

dried apricots

BUYING

:: Choose: dried fruits from stores with a high turnover of merchandise to ensure quality and freshness.

:: Avoid: fruits with sulfite additives and that are hardened.

Dried fruits are bought loose or packaged.

SERVING IDEAS

Dried fruits are eaten as is or rehydrated, cooked or uncooked. They are eaten as a dessert or a snack. They can also be made into a purée. They are added to cereals, fruit salads, mixed salads, sauces, stuffings, rice, cakes, cookies, puddings and pastries (reduce the amount of sugar in dishes to which the fruits are added).

NUTRITIONAL INFORMATION

Dried fruits usually contains 4-5 times more nutrients than the same weight of fresh fruits, which makes them a high-energy food. They often (but not always) contain preservatives, such as sorbic acid, potassium sorbate, potassium bisulfite or sodium bisulfite.

STORING

:: At room temperature: 6-12 months, in a cool and dry place, protected from drafts.

:: In the freezer.

PREPARING

:: To rehydrate dried fruits: soak in water, juice or alcohol (6-8 hr in a cold liquid and about 30 min in a hot liquid).

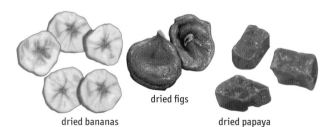

dried figs

dried bananas

dried papaya

Candied fruits

Fruits preserved in sugar: the water content of the fruits is replaced with sugar. The fruits are picked when still slightly underripe. The traditional process consists of first blanching the fruits to soften them (with the exception of strawberries and apricots). They are then macerated in a series of increasingly concentrated sugar syrups, which impregnate the flesh of the fruit with sugar without damaging it. Once drained, the fruits are dried. They are sold as is or glazed with sugar, which makes them less sticky and easier to store. Most fruits can be candied whole or in pieces. Citrus fruit rind, angelica stems and violet petals are also candied.

candied cherries

candied apricots

SERVING IDEAS

 Candied fruits are used to decorate pastries or eaten as sweets. They are an essential ingredient in English puddings and fruit cakes. In Italy, they are added to ice cream.

STORING

:: **At room temperature:** 6 months, in a cool and dry spot, protected from heat.

NUTRITIONAL INFORMATION

	candied apricot
water	12%
protein	0.6 g
fat	0.2 g
carbohydrates	86.5 g
	per 3.5 oz/100 g

Candied fruits are high in sugar, and thus high in calories.

candied orange

Rhubarb

Rheum rhaponticum, Polygonaceae

A plant originally from northern Asia. Usually eaten as a fruit, rhubarb is a vegetable belonging to the same family as sorrel and buckwheat. There are about 20 varieties, and only the thick, crunchy stems are edible. Rhubarb reaches its optimal flavor in springtime.

rhubarb

BUYING

:: **Choose:** rhubarb with firm, stiff stems, with no marks.

SERVING IDEAS

Raw rhubarb is dipped in sugar or salt. Cooked rhubarb can be found in compotes, marmalade and marinades. It is used in cakes, muffins, punch, sorbets, ice cream and pies. Rhubarb can be combined with other fruits (especially strawberries or apples). It works well with cinnamon, lemon and ginger. Rhubarb can also be used in savory dishes and accompany meat and fish. It can replace cranberries in most recipes.

STORING

:: **In the fridge:** a few days.
:: **In the freezer:** in pieces or as a compote. Rhubarb can be preserved in heat- or cold-sterilized containers (alternate layers of rhubarb and sugar in the bottles, close, then sterilize in boiling water).

NUTRITIONAL INFORMATION

water	94%
protein	0.9 g
fat	0.2 g
carbohydrates	4.5 g
calories	21
	per 3.5 oz/100 g

EXCELLENT SOURCE (RAW): potassium.
CONTAINS (RAW): vitamin C and calcium.
PROPERTIES: purgative and tonic, aperitive, cholagogic, antiputrefactive and anthelmintic. As it is often eaten with a large quantity of sugar, rhubarb can be high in calories.

PREPARING

Cut off the leaves and the base of the rhubarb, wash the stems, then cut into pieces about ¾ in. (2 cm) long. Peel the stem if it is too woody.

COOKING

:: **Boiled:** over moderate heat in a small amount of water until the fibers soften (20 min).

Currant

Ribes spp, Saxifragaceae

The fruit of the currant bush, a dense shrub with thorny branches. Currants are covered in a thin, translucent skin. Their juicy, aromatic and slightly tart flesh contains tiny seeds. Currant varieties are divided into three categories. The **red** or **white currant** is originally from northern Europe and Asia. It is a round berry, white or red, no bigger than ¼ in. (5 mm) in diameter. The **gooseberry** is larger than red or white currants and grows as a single berry on a thorny shrub. It is said to be originally from Europe, where it is especially enjoyed. The **blackcurrant** is a black-colored currant from the blackcurrant bush. It is originally from northern Europe.

gooseberries

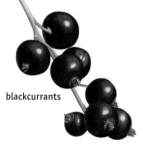
blackcurrants

BUYING

:: **Choose:** intact and well-colored currants and gooseberries. For jams or jellies, choose currants that are slightly underripe (their pectin content is higher).

PREPARING

Clean currants only when using. To remove red and white currants from a bunch, use fingers, a fork or a wide-toothed comb.

STORING

:: **In the fridge:** fresh, 2-3 days.
:: **In the freezer:** whole, with or without sugar. Use before they have completely defrosted, as they will have more flavor.

COOKING

Cook currants and gooseberries slowly in a small quantity of water or juice, just enough to prevent them from sticking (3-5 min). Add sugar after cooking.

Currant

NUTRITIONAL INFORMATION

	red or white currants	blackcurrants	gooseberries
water	84%	82%	88%
protein	1.4 g	1.4 g	0.9 g
fat	0.2 g	0.4 g	0.6 g
carbohydrates	14 g	15 g	10 g
fiber	4.3 g	5.4 g	4.3 g
calories	55	64	45
			per 3.5 oz/100 g

RED OR WHITE CURRANT

GOOD SOURCE: vitamin C and potassium.

CONTAINS: iron and magnesium.

TRACES: phosphorus, calcium and sodium.

BLACKCURRANT

EXCELLENT SOURCE: vitamin C and potassium.

CONTAINS: iron, magnesium, pantothenic acid, phosphorus and calcium.

TRACES: vitamin A.

GOOSEBERRY

GOOD SOURCE: vitamin C and potassium.

TRACES: pantothenic acid, vitamin A and phosphorus.

PROPERTIES: aperitive, digestive, diuretic and depurative. Currants are laxative, especially blackcurrants.

SERVING IDEAS

Red and white currants are eaten plain, by themselves or in salads. They are used in puddings, cakes and pies. They work well with pears, plums, raspberries and pineapple. Red and white currants are mainly made into compote, jelly, jam, syrup and wine. Currant juice is excellent in a vinaigrette as a substitute for vinegar.

Gooseberries are eaten raw with sugar. They are made into pies, sorbets, jellies and syrups. They can be used in puddings, chutneys and fruit salads. They are used as a garnish for meats and fish.

Blackcurrants are used to make liqueurs, wines, coulis (sauce made from strained purée) and jellies.

red currants

Blueberry/Bilberry

Vaccinium spp., Ericaceae

The blueberry and bilberry both belong to the same berry family. The **blueberry** is originally from North America. Its sweet flesh contains small seeds. The dwarf blueberry tends to be sweeter and tastier than the giant blueberry. It is often covered with a thin, naturally waxy film, its "bloom," which gives it a dull appearance.

The **bilberry** is originally from Europe and Asia. It resembles the blueberry, but is from a different species.

blueberries

BUYING

 :: Choose: well-colored blueberries and bilberries that are not wrinkled and have no mold.

SERVING IDEAS

 Blueberries and bilberries are excellent plain. They are eaten as is or used in fruit salads, cereals, pancakes and waffles. They are eaten dressed with whipped cream, orange juice, orange liqueur or vodka. They are used to make muffins, pies, cakes, ice cream, yogurt and sorbets. Blueberries are delicious in jelly and jam. They are made into juice or alcoholic drinks. They can be dried.

STORING

:: In the fridge: a few days, unwashed, remove any damaged berries.

:: In the freezer: as is, washed and dried. Freezing affects the flavor and texture (not important if the berries are being cooked). Cook without completely defrosting. Blueberries can be preserved.

NUTRITIONAL INFORMATION

water	85%
protein	0.7 g
fat	0.4 g
carbohydrates	14 g
fiber	2.3 g
calories	56
	per 3.5 oz/100 g

GOOD SOURCE: vitamin C, potassium and sodium.
Blueberry and bilberry are good sources of fiber.

PROPERTIES: astringent, antibacterial and antidiarrheal. Blueberries contain several acids that are said to be effective for treating urinary infections.

PREPARING

Blueberries and bilberries are fragile. Wash briefly before eating.

bilberries

Blackberry

Rubus spp., Rosaceae

The fruit of a bramble bush belonging to the same family as the raspberry bush and the strawberry plant, the blackberry is originally from temperate regions. The blackberry is a berry composed of many small juicy fruits connected together. It can be black, purple-red or yellowish-white. Crosses between the blackberry and raspberry have produced new fruits that are often named after their creator (loganberry, boysenberry).

blackberries

BUYING

:: **Choose:** firm and shiny blackberries.
:: **Avoid:** soft, dull blackberries or ones that are packed too tightly.

STORING

Blackberries are fragile and highly perishable. Avoid exposing them to sunlight or keeping them at room temperature.
:: **In the fridge:** a few days, unwashed and loosely packed; remove any damaged berries.
:: **In the freezer:** as is or as a coulis, with or without sugar. Blackberries can be frozen individually; spread on a cookie sheet in a single layer, then place in a sealed bag when frozen. Blackberries are better if they are defrosted before using.

PREPARING

Washed blackberries become waterlogged and soft. If it is absolutely necessary to wash them, do so quickly, delicately and only when they are about to be used.

NUTRITIONAL INFORMATION

water	86%
protein	0.7 g
fat	0.4 g
carbohydrates	13 g
fiber	4.6 g
calories	51
	per 3.5 oz/100 g

GOOD SOURCE: vitamin C and potassium.
CONTAIN: magnesium and copper.
PROPERTIES: astringent, depurative and laxative.

SERVING IDEAS

Blackberries are used in the same way as raspberries. They are delicious plain or with ice cream, yogurt or crème fraîche. They are used in fruit salads, crepes, pies and breakfast cereals. They are made into jams, jelly, juice, syrup, wine or eau-de-vie (ratafia). Made into a coulis, they are used in cakes, puddings, ice cream, sorbets, flans and bavarois (custard cream dessert) or as a garnish. To make a coulis, purée blackberries in a blender, then strain to eliminate the small seeds. Blackberries can be dried.

Raisin

A dried grape. Table grapes in particular are dried. Grapes suitable for drying have a soft skin, rich flavor and high sugar content. Muscat, Malaga, sultana and Thompson seedless grapes are among the most popular commercial varieties. Dried grapes may or may not contain seeds, depending on the variety. Most are sun-dried in the vineyard. Dried currants are miniature black seedless grapes (Black Corinth or Zante), much sought after for pastries. Golden-colored raisins are made from the Thompson grape variety.

raisins

BUYING

 If the packaging is transparent, check that the raisins are intact and not too dry.

SERVING IDEAS

Raisins are eaten as is, often as a snack. They are used in cereals, salads, sauces (port sauce), fricassees, poultry stuffing, meat loaves, pâtés, pies, breads, muffins, cookies, brioches and puddings. They are used in stuffed vine leaves, couscous, *tajines* and pilafs. They are mixed with other dried fruits in the cooking of northern and eastern Europe, as is or rehydrated with water, juice or alcohol.

STORING

 :: **At room temperature:** 1 year, in a cool and dry place.

NUTRITIONAL INFORMATION

water	15%-19%
protein	3-4 g
fat	0.3-0.5 g
carbohydrates	74-80 g
fiber	3.7-6.8 g
calories	283-302
	per 3.5 oz/100 g

Raisins are nutritious, as their nutrients are concentrated (fast source of energy).

EXCELLENT SOURCE: potassium.

GOOD SOURCE: iron, magnesium and copper.

CONTAIN: calcium, phosphorus, zinc and vitamin C.

Golden yellow raisins are treated with sulfites to prevent oxidation.

Grape

Vitis spp., Vitaceae

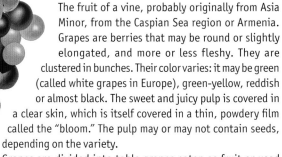

The fruit of a vine, probably originally from Asia Minor, from the Caspian Sea region or Armenia. Grapes are berries that may be round or slightly elongated, and more or less fleshy. They are clustered in bunches. Their color varies: it may be green (called white grapes in Europe), green-yellow, reddish or almost black. The sweet and juicy pulp is covered in a clear skin, which is itself covered in a thin, powdery film called the "bloom." The pulp may or may not contain seeds, depending on the variety.

Grapes are divided into table grapes eaten as fruit or used in pastries or cooking, wine grapes and grapes for drying to produce raisins.

Muscat grapes

The most well-known European varieties are the **Cardinal**, **Black Muscat**, **Lival** and **Ribier** grapes, whose skin is purple-blue or dark blue, which are classed as blue or black grapes; and the **Chasselas**, **Muscat Blanc**, **Gros-vert** and **Servant** grapes, classed as green or white grapes.

In North America, there are the **Concord** grape, a blue-black, seeded grape; the **Flame**, **Delaware** and **Ruby** grapes, red seedless grapes; and the **Thompson** and **Niagara** grapes, green seedless grapes.

Unlike European varieties, the skin of American grape varieties does not adhere to the pulp. **Black Corinth** grapes are distinguished from other grapes by their tiny size. They are also called "**Zante** grapes" or "champagne grapes." They are decorative, seedless and very sweet and tasty.

Grapes are the main ingredient in wine and various alcoholic drinks (armagnac, cognac, port, champagne, etc.). The European species, *Vitis vinifera*, produces the preeminent wine grape. It has thousands of varieties, called *cépages* in French.

Black Corinth grapes

green grapes

Grape

There are two main North American species: *Vitis labrusca* and *Vitis rotundifolia*. The **Concord grape** (black), **Niagara grape** (green) and **Catawba grape** (red) are *labrusca* varieties. The **Delaware grape** (red) is a cross between the *vinifera* species and the *labrusca* species. The skin of *labrusca* species grapes separates easily from the pulp. A third species covers the hybrids, also called "French hybrids," that have been developed from the European species *Vitis vinifera*.

Thompson grapes

BUYING

:: Choose: firm, intact, well-colored grapes that still have their bloom and are firmly attached to the bunch. Green grapes with hints of yellow are sweeter.

:: Avoid: soft, wrinkled, spotted grapes, or ones that are white at the end attached to the stem.

PREPARING

Wash grapes carefully, as they have almost always been treated with chemicals (copper sulfate and calcium hydrate). Don't confuse treatment residues (which stops well before harvesting) with the grape's bloom. Detach small clusters of grapes from the bunch using scissors. Don't pick grapes off at random from all over the bunch, as the stems dry out and the grapes that are still attached become soft and shrivel.

NUTRITIONAL INFORMATION

	American	European
water	81%	81%
protein	0.7 g	0.7 g
fat	0.3 g	0.6 g
carbohydrates	17 g	18 g
fiber	0.9 g	1.2 g
calories	63	71
		per 3.5 oz/100 g

GOOD SOURCE: potassium.
CONTAINS: vitamin C, thiamine and vitamin B_6.
PROPERTIES: diuretic, energizing, cholagogic, laxative, tonic and mineralizing. Black grapes are an excellent tonic in virtue of their coloring agent, oenocyanin. Grape cures purify the body because of their reinvigorating and depurative properties.

SERVING IDEAS

 Grapes are eaten as is or used in fruit salads, pies, flans and jams. In pastries, they can be used in place of cherries or apples. Grapes are made into jam and jelly. They are used in sauces, stuffings, curries, stews and mixed salads. They work well with poultry, game, rabbit, fish and seafood. Grapes are a particularly good accompaniment to calf's liver and duck, as well as quail.

Grape juice is widely enjoyed, plain or fermented. A cooking oil is extracted from grape seeds (see *Oil*, p. 587).

Grapevine leaves are used in North Africa, Greece, Israel and Iran, often stuffed with rice or meat.

STORING

:: **In the fridge:** a few days, bunches wrapped in paper towel in a loosely closed or perforated plastic bag after removing any damaged grapes. For better flavor, let stand at room temperature for about 15 min before eating.

Grapes are suited to being macerated in alcohol.

BERRIES

Chasselas grapes

Cardinal grapes

Strawberry

Fragaria spp., Rosaceae

The fruit of the strawberry plant, the most widespread temperate-climate plant in the world. Some strawberry varieties are originally from the temperate regions of Europe, while others are from North and South America. Strawberry varieties vary in size, texture, color and flavor. The smaller, juicier and tastier wild strawberry is the ancestor of the cultivated strawberries.

cultivated
strawberries

BUYING

:: **Choose:** firm, glossy and well-colored strawberries. Check the condition of strawberries at the bottom of the container.
:: **Avoid:** soft, dull and moldy strawberries.

SERVING IDEAS

 Strawberries are very often eaten plain, whole, cut or crushed. They can be eaten raw with yogurt or ice cream, dressed with whipped cream or alcohol, or dipped in a chocolate fondue. Strawberries can also be added to fruit salads, crepes, ice cream or sorbets. Less attractive strawberries can be cooked in pies, cookies, mousses, soufflés, flans, puddings and cakes. Strawberries are used decoratively, to garnish hors d'oeuvres or cheese platters.

NUTRITIONAL INFORMATION

water	92%
protein	0.6 g
fat	0.4 g
carbohydrates	7 g
fiber	2.6 g
calories	30
	per 3.5 oz/100 g

EXCELLENT SOURCE: vitamin C.
GOOD SOURCE: potassium.
SOURCE: folic acid, pantothenic acid and magnesium.
PROPERTIES: tonic, depurative, diuretic, mineralizing and astringent. Eaten in quantity, strawberries are a laxative. Strawberry essence is used in beauty treatments.
Infused strawberry leaves counteract diarrhea, while an infusion made from the roots is said to have a diuretic effect.

PREPARING

Wash strawberries before hulling, when about to use. Use cold water without letting them soak.

STORING

Strawberries are perishable. Avoid exposing them to sunlight or leaving them at room temperature.
:: In the fridge: 2-3 days, packed loosely, unwashed and unhulled, after removing any damaged strawberries. Cover to avoid their smell being absorbed by other foods.

:: In the freezer: whole, sliced, quartered or crushed, with or without sugar, after removing any underripe or overripe strawberries. Strawberries will keep their shape if not completely defrosted.

wild strawberries

Raspberry

Rubus spp., Rosaceae

The fruit of the raspberry bush, a bramble bush probably originally from eastern Asia. Usually red, raspberries can also be black (without being blackberries), yellow, orange, amber-colored or white. Sweet and finely perfumed, they are moderately tart and more fragile than strawberries. Wild raspberries are smaller than cultivated raspberries.

raspberries

BUYING

:: Choose: firm, glossy raspberries.
:: Avoid: soft, dull raspberries, or ones that are packed too tightly.

PREPARING

To prevent raspberries from becoming soft and waterlogged, only wash if necessary and do so delicately and quickly, when about to use. When they are freshly picked, shake gently to remove any insects that might be in their cavity.

Raspberry

NUTRITIONAL INFORMATION

water	87%
protein	0.9 g
fat	0.6 g
carbohydrates	11.5 g
fiber	4.7 g
calories	50
	per 3.5 oz/100 g

GOOD SOURCE: vitamin C.
CONTAINS: potassium and magnesium.
TRACES: calcium and vitamin A.
Raspberries are high in fiber.
PROPERTIES: diuretic, tonic, depurative, aperitive, sudorific, stomachic and laxative. Raspberries are said to relieve heartburn and constipation.
Infused raspberry leaves are said to have astringent, diuretic, emmenagogic and laxative properties.

STORING

Raspberries are fragile and highly perishable. Avoid exposing them to sunlight or leaving them at room temperature.
:: In the fridge: 1-2 days, unwashed and only loosely packed raspberries, after removing any damaged berries.
:: In the freezer: as is or made into a coulis, with or without sugar. Raspberries will keep their shape if they are not completely defrosted.

SERVING IDEAS

 Raspberries are used in the same way as strawberries, and the two fruits are in fact interchangeable in most recipes. Raspberry coulis is used in cakes, puddings, ice cream, sorbets, flans and bavarois (custard cream desserts). It is also used as a sauce with various foods. Adding a little lemon or orange juice intensifies the color of cooked raspberries or raspberry coulis. Raspberries are delicious plain or eaten with ice cream, yogurt or crème fraîche. They work well as a garnish on fruit salads, cereals, cakes and crepes. They are made into fermented drinks, liqueurs, pies, syrups, jams, jelly, compote, wine or beer.
Raspberry juice is used to flavor ice creams and sorbets. Raspberries can be preserved in syrup, eau-de-vie or as is. They give a pleasant flavor to vinegar.

Cranberry

Vaccinium spp., Ericaceae

A berry from North America and Europe, cranberry belongs to the family that includes the blueberry, bilberry, arbutus berry and heather. In Canada, cranberries are often called by their American Indian name, "*atoca*." Cranberries resemble small cherries. They are juicy, very tart and contain small edible seeds.

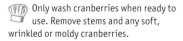

cranberries

BUYING

:: **Choose:** fleshy, firm and shiny cranberries.

:: **Avoid:** soft, wrinkled or crushed cranberries, with white marks or dull, discolored skin.

SERVING IDEAS

Cranberries are rarely eaten plain (because of their tartness). They are added to muffins, breads or cakes or they are cooked just until they burst to make pies, sorbets, mousses or crepes. Cranberries are made into compote, jelly, jam or chutney, which are served with poultry. They work well with citrus fruits, apples and pears. They are used to flavor pâtés, sausages and terrines. Baked apples can be garnished with cranberries and squash can be stuffed with cranberry jam or compote. Cranberry juice is excellent.

PREPARING

Only wash cranberries when ready to use. Remove stems and any soft, wrinkled or moldy cranberries.

COOKING

:: **Boiled:** in a covered saucepan with a small quantity of water.

NUTRITIONAL INFORMATION

water	87%
protein	0.4 g
fat	0.7 g
carbohydrates	13 g
fiber	1.4 g
calories	46
	per 3.5 oz/100 g

CONTAINS: vitamin C and potassium.

PROPERTIES: astringent. Cranberry is beneficial for blood circulation, skin and the digestive system. It is used to treat urinary infections. Cranberry contains various acids, in particular oxalic and citric acid, which are responsible for its tart taste.

STORING

Cranberries quickly deteriorate at room temperature.

:: **In the fridge:** up to 2 months, in a sealed plastic bag.

:: **In the freezer:** as is. Simply wash them without defrosting when ready to use. Cranberries can be dehydrated in a slow oven, slightly ajar, until dry. To rehydrate, soak for a few hours in water, juice or alcohol.

Winter cherry

Physalis alkekengi, Solanaceae

The fruit of a plant of uncertain origin that belongs to the same family as the tomato, eggplant, bell pepper and potato. The winter cherry is a red, orange or yellow-green colored berry, the size of a cherry, with a fine, inedible membrane (calyx). The fruit is not very juicy, and sweet with a slightly tart and astringent aftertaste. It contains edible seeds. The winter cherry is also called "alkekengi," "Cape gooseberry" and "Chinese lantern."

winter cherries

BUYING

:: **Choose:** firm, evenly colored winter cherries without mold. If the calyx is still attached, it should be brittle (a sign of maturity).

SERVING IDEAS

Winter cherries are usually cooked, but can be eaten raw (as is or in fruit salads and mixed salads). They are used to make pies, sorbets and ice cream. Very high in pectin, they are made into jam, jelly and marinades. They are also turned into juice.

PREPARING

Remove the membrane, then wash the fruit and the part surrounding the stem, which holds a waxy substance.

NUTRITIONAL INFORMATION

water	85%
protein	2 g
fat	0.7 g
carbohydrates	11 g
calories	53
	per 3.5 oz/100 g

SOURCE: iron, niacin and vitamin A.
PROPERTIES: antipyretic, diuretic and antirheumatic.

STORING

:: **At room temperature:** for ripening.
:: **In the fridge:** 2 days, covered with a cloth.
:: **In the freezer:** without the calyx.

Plum

Prunus spp., Rosaceae

The fruit of the plum tree, a tree probably originally from China. The different varieties are usually grouped into six main species. The **European plum**, also called the "common plum," is oval-shaped, dark blue (such as the quetsche plum) or red in color and medium sized. The thick skin holds firm flesh that is yellow or yellow-green in color. It is eaten fresh, canned or dried. The **Japanese plum** is yellow, crimson, purple or greenish in color. Its size varies, and its flesh is pale, juicy and sweet. It is round or heart-shaped. It is eaten fresh or canned. The Santa Rosa plum is the most well-known Japanese plum in North America. The **American plum** forms a group that includes several cold-resistant species with amber-colored skin and flesh. The **Damson plum**, with blue skin and a rather sharp, tart taste, is ideal for making jams and jellies. This group includes the mirabelle plum, among others. The **ornamental plum**

Japanese plums

is a red fruit, also used for making jams and jellies. The **wild plum** is small, spherical, blue-black in color and tart in flavor.

Dried plums are called prunes.

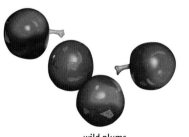

wild plums

BUYING

:: **Choose:** perfumed plums with well-colored skin that yields to light finger pressure. A plum that still has its "bloom" (a powdery layer that covers some fruits) is a sign that it has not been overhandled.

:: **Avoid:** hard plums with little color, ones that are not yet ripe, and very soft, bruised or spotted plums.

Plum

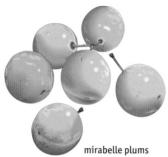

mirabelle plums

NUTRITIONAL INFORMATION

water	85%
protein	0.8 g
fat	0.6 g
carbohydrates	13 g
fiber	1.6 g
calories	55
	per 3.5 oz/100 g

GOOD SOURCE: potassium.
CONTAINS: vitamin C and riboflavin.
PROPERTIES: laxative. Plums are said to be energetic, diuretic and disintoxicating.

SERVING IDEAS

 Plums are eaten as is or added to fruit salads. They may be cooked into jam, jelly or compote, among other preparations. They work very well with pork, game and poultry. They are made into sweet-and-sour sauce. Plums are delicious in pies, cakes, puddings, muffins and ice cream. They can replace fresh cherries in most desserts. Plums are preserved, candied, dried, pickled in vinegar, made into juice, eau-de-vie (*prunelle, mirabelle*) or wine.

PREPARING

To peel plums, plunge into boiling water for 30 sec, then cool immediately in cold water but do not let them soak.
Avoid overcooking plums, as they quickly turn to mush.

STORING

Plums are moderately perishable.
:: At room temperature: for ripening.
:: In the fridge: ripe, a few days.
:: In the freezer: pitted (the pit gives a bitter taste).

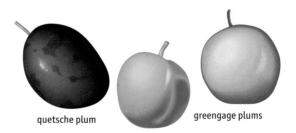

quetsche plum

greengage plums

Prune

Prunus domestica, Rosaceae

A dried plum. Only certain varieties of plums are suited to being dried, such as the "French prune" (also called *prune d'Agen* and *prune d'ente*) and greengage plums. These firm-fleshed plums with a high sugar content are dried with their pit intact. Prunes are also used to produce juice.

prune

BUYING

 :: Choose: black, shiny, soft and fleshy prunes that are not sticky or moldy. If they are dryish, they are either old or have not been treated with additives.
Prunes of various size and quality can be sold pitted or unpitted.

SERVING IDEAS

 Prunes are eaten as is or cooked as a compote (add sugar at the end of cooking). They are used whole or chopped in sauces, cakes, cookies, muffins and puddings. Prunes are a classic accompaniment to rabbit, pork, poultry and game, as well as lamb (in the Near East and Iran). Prunes can be soaked in water, juice or alcohol instead of being cooked or to reduce cooking time. When they are too dry, soak in boiling water, drain and wipe dry before using.
The kernel inside the prune pit contains a toxic substance. It can be eaten, but only in small quantities.

NUTRITIONAL INFORMATION

water	32%
protein	2.6 g
fat	0.5 g
carbohydrates	63 g
fiber	7 g
calories	239
	per 3.5 oz/100 g

EXCELLENT SOURCE: potassium.
GOOD SOURCE: copper, vitamin A, iron, magnesium and vitamin B_6.
CONTAINS: vitamin B_{12}, niacin, pantothenic acid, phosphorus, zinc, vitamin C and calcium.
PROPERTIES: laxative, particularly if the fruit is soaked and eaten before sleeping. Prune juice has similar properties.

STORING

:: At room temperature: in an environment that is not too humid or dry.
:: In the fridge: keeps for an extended period.

Nectarine

Prunus persica var. *nectarina,* Rosaceae

A fruit originally from China, the nectarine resembles the peach and belongs to the same family. Both freestone and clingstone varieties of nectarine are sold under the same name. The nectarine is distinguished from the peach by its smooth and more colorful skin and its slightly tastier flesh. Its white or yellow flesh is firm, juicy, sweet and slightly tart.

nectarine

BUYING

:: **Choose:** perfumed nectarines that are not too hard, and have no spots, cracks or bruises.

:: **Avoid:** fruit with a green tinge.

SERVING IDEAS

Nectarines are excellent plain. They can be cooked, dried, preserved, candied or frozen. They are prepared in the same way as peaches, which they can replace in most recipes. They are used in pies, fruit salads, cakes, yogurt, ice cream, sorbets and crepes. They are made into jelly, jam, marinades, juice and liqueur.

PREPARING

To prevent nectarine flesh from oxidizing, eat immediately or sprinkle with lemon or lime juice, wine, vinegar or vinaigrette, depending on how it is going to be used. It isn't necessary to peel nectarines, but if this is preferred, plunge them for about 1 min in boiling water, then cool in cold water to stop the effect of the heat, without letting them soak.

NUTRITIONAL INFORMATION

water	86%
protein	0.9 g
fat	0.4 g
carbohydrates	12 g
fiber	1.6 g
calories	49
	per 3.5 oz/100 g

GOOD SOURCE: potassium.
CONTAINS: vitamin C and vitamin A.

STORING

Handle nectarines carefully, as they become damaged easily. Do not store them piled up on each other and wash only before using.

:: **At room temperature:** a few days. Place nectarines in a paper bag to accelerate ripening.

:: **In the fridge:** extended keeping time. For more flavor, let stand at room temperature for a while before eating.

:: **In the freezer:** pitted, blanched and peeled. When the fruit is very ripe, freeze as a compote or purée. Add lemon juice to prevent discoloration. Nectarines can be preserved.

Peach

Prunus persica, Rosaceae

The fruit of the peach tree, a tree originally from China. The peach is a close relative of the apricot, almond, cherry and plum. The peach's edible skin may be more or less thin, and is velvety and yellowish in color. Some varieties of peach have crimson tints, even when the fruit is not ripe.

The peach has a juicy, sweet and perfumed flesh that can be more or less firm and yellow or green-white in color. The white-fleshed varieties are more fragile, but sweeter and juicier. The flesh contains an oval, woody pit.

peach

BUYING

 :: Choose: perfumed peaches that are not too hard.

:: Avoid: peaches with a green tinge, spots, cracks or bruises.

Peaches rot easily, even when they are not ripe. It is best to only buy peaches in quantities that will be eaten quickly.

PREPARING

To peel peaches, plunge for a minute in boiling water, then cool immediately in cold water, without letting them soak. Using a colander will make this easier. To prevent the flesh from oxidizing, eat or cook the peach immediately, or sprinkle with lemon, orange or lime juice, or alcohol.

NUTRITIONAL INFORMATION

	fresh	*dried*
water	88%	31%
protein	0.7 g	3.6 g
fat	0.1 g	0.8 g
carbohydrates	11 g	61 g
fiber	1.6 g	8.2 g
calories	43	240
		per 3.5 oz/100 g

FRESH PEACH

GOOD SOURCE: potassium.

CONTAINS: vitamin C, vitamin A and niacin.

PROPERTIES: diuretic, stomachic and slightly laxative.

DRIED PEACH

EXCELLENT SOURCE: potassium and iron.

GOOD SOURCE: vitamin A, niacin, copper, magnesium and riboflavin.

CONTAINS: phosphorus, vitamin C and zinc.

Peach

SERVING IDEAS

Excellent plain, peaches can also be cooked, dried, preserved, candied or frozen. They are used to make pies, crepes, cakes, fruit salads, yogurt, ice creams, sorbets or soufflés. They are made into jelly, jam, marinades, juice, compote and liqueur. They are served with savory dishes, in particular seafood, poultry and pork. They are delicious dressed with vinaigrette.

STORING

Handle peaches carefully, as they deteriorate quickly once damaged. Wash peaches only just before using.

:: At room temperature: 3-4 days. Place peaches in a paper bag to speed up the ripening process.

:: In the fridge: do not store piled on top of each other. For more flavor, take out of the fridge before eating.

:: In the freezer: pitted (the pit gives a bitter taste). When the fruit is very ripe, freeze as a compote or purée. Adding lemon juice will prevent peaches from blackening.

Peaches are well suited to being preserved.

Date

Phoenix dactylifera, Palmaceae

The fruit of the date palm, a tree originally from the Middle East. The date palm is a member of the palm family. The flesh of the unripe date is green; it becomes amber or brown-colored when it ripens. Dates vary in flavor, level of sugar and consistency. They are usually classified as soft, semisoft or firm. There are more than 100 varieties, only some of which are commercially significant. The varieties eaten in the United States, usually dried, include the **Deglet Noor**, one of the most popular varieties worldwide, and the **Medjool**, **Khadrawi**, **Zahidi**, **Halawi** and **Bardhi** date varieties.

dates

Bardhi dates

Medjool dates

NUTRITIONAL INFORMATION

water	24%
protein	1.9 g
fat	0.5 g
carbohydrates	72 g
fiber	2.3 g
calories	271
	per 3.5 oz/100 g

DRIED DATES

EXCELLENT SOURCE: potassium.
SOURCE: copper, pantothenic acid, vitamin B_6, niacin, magnesium and iron.
PROPERTIES: mineralizing and tonic.
Dates are nourishing due to their high level of carbohydrate. They are often sulfur-treated or coated in syrup (corn or other syrup) to keep them moist, which increases their already very high sugar content.

STONE FRUITS

BUYING

 :: Choose: plump, soft and well-colored dates.

:: Avoid: dull, dry, moldy or fermented dates. Dates are sold pitted or unpitted.

PREPARING

 To rehydrate dates, soak for a few hours in water.

STORING

:: At room temperature: 6-12 months, depending on the variety, in a cool and dry place.

:: In the fridge: 2 weeks. Wrap fresh dates so that they don't absorb odors.

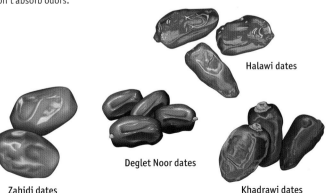

Halawi dates

Zahidi dates

Deglet Noor dates

Khadrawi dates

Cherry

Prunus spp., Rosaceae

The fruit of the cherry tree. The cherry tree belongs to a large family that includes the apricot, apple, plum and peach trees. Cherries are round, fleshy, juicy *drupes* (stone fruit), with smooth skin. They are divided into three groups. The **sweet cherry** is fleshy and sweet. It is sometimes yellow-colored, but is usually light or dark red. The **sour cherry** or "pie cherry," such as Montmorency and morello cherries, is usually dark red. These cherries are more often cooked than eaten fresh. The **wild cherry** is small and not very fleshy, and leaves a fuzzy taste in the mouth.

wild cherries

BUYING

:: Choose: fleshy, firm, glossy and well-colored cherries whose stalks are not dried-up.

:: Avoid: hard, small and pale cherries (as they are not mature), soft, bruised, wrinkled cherries or those with brown spots.

NUTRITIONAL INFORMATION

	sweet	*sour*
water	81%	86%
protein	1.2 g	1 g
fat	1 g	0.3 g
carbohydrates	17 g	12 g
fiber	1.6 g	1.2 g
calories	72	50
		per 3.5 oz/100 g

SWEET CHERRY

GOOD SOURCE: potassium.

SOUR CHERRY

EXCELLENT SOURCE: potassium.

WILD CHERRY

PROPERTIES: diuretic, mineralizing, antirheumatic, antiarthritic, disintoxicating and mildly laxative.

The stems can be made into an infusion that is said to have diuretic properties.

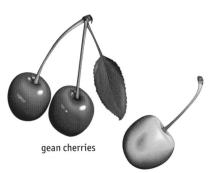

gean cherries

Montmorency cherry

morello cherries

PREPARING

Wash cherries without letting them soak. To remove the pit, make a slice with the point of a knife and remove the pit, cut the cherries in two or use a cherry pitter.

Using a cherry pitter, make a hole in the flesh to extract the pit.

STONE FRUITS

STORING

Cherries are fragile and perishable.
:: In the fridge: a few days, in a loosely closed or perforated plastic bag. Keep them away from foods with a strong smell.
:: In the freezer: pitted or unpitted, covered in sugar or syrup; use frozen cherries for cooking. Dried cherries keep 1 year in a closed container in a cool and dry place.

SERVING IDEAS

Cherries are eaten plain, cooked, dried, candied, preserved, macerated in alcohol or distilled. They are used in fruit salads, flans, sorbets, pies, *clafoutis* (a baked batter dessert), ice cream and yogurt. They are an essential ingredient of black forest cake and cakes using candied fruit. Cherries can be turned into compote or jam. They are also made into wine or eau-de-vie. Cherries are an accompaniment to game and poultry.

Bing cherries

bigarreau cherries

Apricot

Prunus armeniaca, Rosaceae

The fruit of the apricot tree, a tree originally from China. The apricot's edible skin is slightly velvety and becomes smooth when mature. Its orange flesh is tender, sweet and very aromatic.

apricot

BUYING

:: **Choose:** intact apricots that are neither too firm nor too soft, without white spots, cracks or bruises.

SERVING IDEAS

 Apricots are eaten as is or used in fruit salads. They are cooked in the same way as peaches and nectarines and can replace them in most recipes. They are used in pies, cakes, sorbets, ice creams, yogurt and crepes. They are cooked into jam or chutney, and made into compote or juice. They can be macerated in alcohol, candied, preserved or dried (and used as is or after soaking in water, juice or alcohol). In Arab countries, a paste called *kamraddin* is made from apricots.

The kernel enclosed within the pit of the apricot contains a toxic substance. It can be eaten, but only in small quantities.

STORING

Handle apricots with care, as they deteriorate quickly. Wash before using.

:: **At room temperature:** for ripening.

:: **In the fridge:** ripe, 1 week.

:: **In the freezer:** blanch (30 sec), peel and pit. If they are very ripe, freeze them as a compote or purée.

NUTRITIONAL INFORMATION

	fresh	*dried*
water	86%	31%
protein	1.4 g	3.7 g
fat	0.4 g	0.5 g
carbohydrates	11 g	62 g
fiber	0.6 g	2.9 g
calories	48	237
		per 3.5 oz/100 g

FRESH APRICOT

EXCELLENT SOURCE: vitamin A.

GOOD SOURCE: potassium.

CONTAINS: vitamin C.

PROPERTIES: antianemic, astringent and aperitive.

DRIED APRICOT

EXCELLENT SOURCE: vitamin A, potassium, iron and riboflavin.

GOOD SOURCE: copper and magnesium.

CONTAINS: sulfites that preserve the freshness and color of the fruit.

PROPERTY: slightly laxative when consumed in large quantities.

PREPARING

To prevent apricot flesh from oxidizing, eat or cook immediately, or sprinkle with citrus juice or alcohol.

Apple

Malus spp., Rosaceae

The fruit of the apple tree, thought to be originally from southwestern Asia. The very large number of apple varieties concerns their shape, color, flavor, texture, nutritional value, time of harvesting, uses and keeping qualities. Apple flesh may be more or less firm, crunchy, tart, juicy, sweet and aromatic.

Some varieties are called summer or early apples; other varieties, winter or late apples. Summer apples do not keep well and should be eaten quickly. Winter apples keep longer. Depending on how they are to be used, consider in particular the firmness of the apple, its cellulose, pectin and sugar levels, degree of acidity and how quickly the flesh discolors in contact with the air. Some varieties do not tolerate cooking well, others become bitter when cooked in the oven.

McIntosh apple

BUYING

:: **Choose:** firm, well-colored apples, without bruises (the damaged parts will make the fruit rot as well as those around it). If the flesh gives way to finger pressure, the apple will be mealy. It is best to buy apples from a refrigerated display, unless you know when they were picked, as they ripen very quickly at room temperature.

Fresh apples are available throughout the year. Check for ripeness by flicking the apple near the stem: a dull sound indicates that the apple is ripe, whereas a hollow sound means that it is becoming overripe.

SERVING IDEAS

Apples are eaten plain, cooked, dried or candied. They are made into compote, jelly, jam, marmalade, bottled sweet preserves, apple butter, chutney or vinegar. They are used in cakes, muffins, crepes, flans, strudels, *clafoutis* (a baked batter dessert), charlottes, pies and puddings. Cooked apples work very well with cinnamon and vanilla. They accompany savory foods, in particular cheese, meat, poultry and game. They are used in salads, as in the Waldorf salad. Apples are used in distilling to make calvados and for making cider and apple juice.

PREPARING

Before eating or cooking, wash the apple by brushing under cold water. To prevent the flesh from oxidizing in contact with the air, eat or cook the apple immediately, or sprinkle with citrus juice (lemon, lime, orange), vinegar or vinaigrette, depending on how the apple is to be used.

Spartan apple

1 Using an apple-corer, pierce the center of the fruit down to the work surface; turn and pull the corer out.

2 Cut the apple in two and remove the core with a peeler.

NUTRITIONAL INFORMATION

water	84%
protein	0.2 g
fat	0.4 g
carbohydrates	15 g
fiber	2.2 g
calories	59
	per 3.5 oz/100 g

GOOD SOURCE: potassium and vitamin C.
CONTAINS: pectin (plays a role in controlling cholesterol and blood sugar levels), cellulose (aids proper intestinal function).
PROPERTIES: diuretic, laxative, antidiarrheal, muscular tonic, antirheumatic, stomachic, digestive and liver decongestant.
Raw apple cleans the teeth and massages the gums. Most of its nutrients are located under the skin, which is why it should be consumed unpeeled as much as possible.

3 Depending on the dish, the cored apples can now be chopped.

Empire apple

Apple

COOKING

To keep the shape of cooked apples, choose a variety with a lower water content, such as Rome Beauty or Cortland. Cook apples gently and use only a little liquid, just enough to stop the apples from sticking.

:: **Baked:** core apples without cutting completely through, leaving a base that can hold a stuffing in the middle (raisins, coconut, nuts, honey, tahini, etc.).

:: **Microwaved:** to make a quick compote, dice a few apples and cook for 2 min.

Depending on the variety of apple used, a compote does not necessarily need any sugar; to adjust to this, the amount of added sugar can gradually be decreased. For variety, cook new types of apples, combine different varieties or add to strawberry, cranberry or rhubarb compote.

STORING

:: **At room temperature:** for ripening. Keep ripe apples several weeks in a dark, very cool (35°F-40°F/1°C-4°C) and very humid (85%-90%) environment. To slow down the dehydration of apples and maintain the humidity level, cover with a loosely closed or perforated plastic bag. Discard overripe or damaged apples or separate from the rest.

:: **In the fridge:** a few weeks, in the fruit compartment or in a loosely closed or perforated bag.

:: **In the freezer:** made into a purée, with or without sugar. Raw apples should be peeled, trimmed, sliced and sprinkled with lemon juice or ascorbic acid to prevent browning.

Granny Smith apple

Cortland apple

Red Delicious apple

Melba apple

Russet apple

Yellow Delicious apple

Pear

Pyrus communis, Rosaceae

The fruit of the pear tree, a tree originally from the northern region of central Asia. The pear tree is related to the apple, almond and apricot trees. The pear's edible skin is colored yellow, brown, red or green; it is usually soft and thin. The pear has a fine white or cream-colored flesh, sometimes slightly grainy around and inside the core. The flesh can be more or less juicy, melting and aromatic depending on the variety.

The **D'Anjou pear** is originally from France. It has very juicy, smooth flesh.

The **Bartlett pear** is an English pear known in Europe as a "Williams pear." Its skin goes from light green to golden yellow when mature. Its white flesh is not grainy and very aromatic.

Bartlett pear

The **Red Bartlett**, or "red Williams," has the same taste as the Bartlett. Both tolerate cooking very well.

The **Bosc pear** is originally from Belgium; its skin is thicker and rougher than other pears. Its white, juicy, grainy and very aromatic flesh is well suited to cooking and poaching.

The **Comice pear** is originally from France. Its tender yellow-green skin often shows hints of pink or brown when the fruit is ripe. Its yellow-white flesh is one of the most juicy and sweet, and is very aromatic. It is considered the best and most refined variety of pear. It works very well with delicate cheeses.

The **Conference pear** has white, creamy and juicy flesh that is sweet and refreshing.

The **Packham pear** is originally from Australia. It resembles the Bartlett pear in color and flavor, but has a less regular shape. Its green skin becomes slightly yellow when ripe. Its white flesh is juicy and sweet.

The **Passe-Crassane pear** is originally from France. It keeps well. Its skin is thick and its flesh is white, slightly grainy, very juicy and tasty, melting in the mouth.

The **Rocha pear** is originally from Portugal. Its flesh becomes creamy and smooth when mature.

BUYING

:: Choose: smooth pears that are firm but not too hard, with no bruises or mold.

STORING

:: At room temperature: for ripening. Several varieties remain green when mature; they are ready to eat if the flesh yields to light finger pressure around the stem. Eat quickly, as their flesh tends to rot easily.

:: In the fridge: ripe, a few days. As pears are fragile, do not store on top of one another and avoid placing them in a bag or airtight container. Keep them away from apples, onions, potatoes, cabbages and other strong-smelling foods, as they easily absorb odors.

:: In the freezer: cooked.

NUTRITIONAL INFORMATION

	fresh	dried
water	84%	27%
protein	0.4 g	1.9 g
fat	0.4 g	0.6 g
carbohydrates	15 g	70 g
fiber	1.4 g	6.4 g
calories	59	262
		per 3.5 oz/100 g

FRESH PEAR

CONTAINS: potassium and copper.

DRIED PEAR

EXCELLENT SOURCE: potassium.

GOOD SOURCE: copper and iron.

CONTAINS: magnesium, vitamin C, phosphorus and sodium.

PROPERTIES: diuretic, mineralizing, stomachic and sedative.

Pear represents a rich source of fiber. The nutrients in dried pear are more concentrated. Unripe pear can be indigestible and have a laxative effect.

POME FRUITS

Conference pear

Rocha pear

Passe-Crassane pear

Pear

Packham pear

Bosc pear

D'Anjou pear

Comice pear

SERVING IDEAS

Pears are eaten plain, cooked, dried or candied. They are made into compote, coulis, jelly, jam, juice, vinegar, eau-de-vie and liqueur (*Poiré*, *Poire William*, an eau-de-vie made using the Williams variety). Pears work well with apples, quince, chocolate and ginger. They are cooked as a compote or poached in wine or syrup (choose fruits that are slightly underripe). They are used in fruit salads, sorbets, yogurts, soufflés, pies and charlottes as well as served with various sauces and flavorings. Pears are used in chutneys and marinades. They add an unusual touch to mixed salads. They are delicious with sweet onions and slightly bitter vegetables (cress, radicchio, dandelion and Belgian endive). Pears work well with brie, camembert, cheddar, goat cheese and roquefort. They are delicious with prosciutto or Parma ham.

PREPARING

To prevent pear flesh from oxidizing, eat or cook pears immediately, or sprinkle with lemon, lime or orange juice.

Quince

Cydonia oblonga, Rosaceae

The fruit of the quince tree, a small tree thought to be originally from Iran. Quince has a firm, dry, very aromatic flesh that is high in pectin. It cannot be eaten raw. Its harsh taste, due to its high tannin content, disappears when cooked.

quince

BUYING

:: **Choose:** fleshy, firm, intact quince, with partly yellow skin. Very ripe fruit is often marked, which is not important if it is to be cooked immediately.
:: **Avoid:** hard and very green quince.

SERVING IDEAS

To prevent its flesh from oxidizing, sprinkle quince with lemon juice or cook immediately once it is cut. The flesh becomes pink or red when cooked. Quince keeps its shape and texture when cooked. It is cooked in the same way as apples, after being trimmed and, if desired, peeled. It is made into jam, jelly, compote, syrup and wine. It is combined with apples, pears, strawberries or raspberries. Europeans enjoy quince paste, called *cotignac;* this paste is also popular in Hispanic cultures, where it is called *dulce de membrillo*. In eastern Europe, the Near East and northern Africa, quince is used with meat and poultry. It is used in simmered dishes.

NUTRITIONAL INFORMATION

water	84%
protein	0.4 g
fat	0.1 g
carbohydrates	15 g
fiber	1.7 g
calories	57
	per 3.5 oz/100 g

GOOD SOURCE: potassium.
CONTAINS: vitamin C and copper.
PROPERTIES: astringent and aperitive. Quince is said to be beneficial for the gastrointestinal system.

STORING

:: **At room temperature:** for ripening.
:: **In the fridge:** a few weeks, individually wrapped.
:: **In the freezer:** peeled, trimmed, sliced and sprinkled with lemon juice or ascorbic acid, or puréed, with or without sugar.

loquats

Loquat

Eriobotrya japonica, Rosaceae

The fruit of the loquat tree, a tree originally from China and Japan which grows in temperate areas and belongs to the same family as the pear, peach and apple trees. The skin of the loquat is edible. It contains a small quantity of cream- or orange-colored flesh, which is firm or melting, depending on the variety. It is tart, juicy, somewhat sweet and refreshing. Its flavor is reminiscent of cherry or plum. It contains inedible seeds. The loquat is only edible when very ripe.

BUYING

:: **Choose:** tender, smooth loquats. They are tastier when covered with brown spots.

SERVING IDEAS

Loquat is delicious plain or cooked, with or without its skin. It is added to fruit salads and pies. It is cooked into jam or jelly. It is particularly suited to being poached. Loquats are made into alcohol. They can also be candied or preserved.
The whole or ground seeds are used as an aromatic flavoring.

NUTRITIONAL INFORMATION

water	87%
protein	0.4 g
fat	0.2 g
carbohydrates	12 g
calories	47
	per 3.5 oz/100 g

GOOD SOURCE: potassium and vitamin A.
CONTAINS: magnesium.
PROPERTIES: diuretic and tonic.

STORING

Eat as soon as possible.

Pomelo

Citrus maxima, Rutaceae

The fruit of the pomelo tree, a tree thought to be originally from Asia. The pomelo is also called a *"pummelo"* or *"shaddock"* and *"chadèque"* in French Creole countries (Guadeloupe and Martinique). It can be spherical or pear-shaped. Its thick rind peels easily and is very perfumed. Depending on the variety, its pulp is bland or tasty, very sour or very sweet, and may or may not contain seeds.

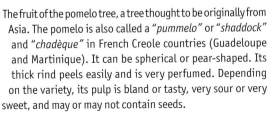

pomelo

Pomelo

BUYING

:: **Choose:** a pomelo that is heavy for its size and relatively firm. Marks on the skin do not affect the quality of the fruit.

:: **Avoid:** a pomelo that is too soft, that has a dull rind or that yields too easily to finger pressure, and that appears dry at the stem end.

SERVING IDEAS

Pomelo is eaten with a spoon less often than grapefruit. It is cooked or candied. It can be peeled, its membranes removed and the segments used in a fruit salad or in a vegetable salad with a vinaigrette.

NUTRITIONAL INFORMATION

water	89%
protein	0.7 g
carbohydrates	9.6 g
calories	37
	per 3.5 oz/100 g

EXCELLENT SOURCE: vitamin C.
GOOD SOURCE: potassium.
PROPERTIES: aperitive, digestive and stomachic.

STORING

:: **At room temperature:** a few days.
:: **In the fridge:** 1 week.
:: **In the freezer:** the juice and the zest.

Grapefruit

Citrus paradisi, Rutaceae

A fruit often confused with the "pomelo" (which is also sometimes called a grapefruit), eaten in the West. The pomelo is a larger, pear-shaped fruit and closely related to the grapefruit, which can lead to confusion. The grapefruit is thought to be originally from Jamaica and the result of a natural cross-fertilization between the pomelo and the sweet or bitter orange. Its yellow, pink or red pulp can be more or less mild, sour, sweet and perfumed (the yellow pulp less so than the others). It is juicier than the pulp of the pomelo and usually contains seeds.

white grapefruit

pink grapefruit

BUYING

:: Choose: a grapefruit that is heavy for its size, relatively firm, with taut, shiny skin. Scars or hard patches on the skin do not affect the quality of the fruit.

:: Avoid: a grapefruit that is too soft, with a dull rind.

SERVING IDEAS

Grapefruit is cut in two and eaten with a spoon plain or sprinkled with sugar. Wash the grapefruit before cutting. For ease of eating, separate the segments using a serrated knife with a curved point or a serrated spoon. Broiled grapefruit can accompany duck, chicken, pork and shrimp. It is added to mixed salads. Grapefruit is used in cheesecakes, flans, fruit salads and sorbets. It can be used in place of orange or pineapple in many recipes. Grapefruit juice is refreshing. The peel can be candied.

NUTRITIONAL INFORMATION

water	91%
protein	0.7 g
fat	0.1 g
carbohydrates	8 g
fiber	0.6 g
calories	30-33
	per 3.5 oz/100 g

The nutritional value of grapefruit varies, depending on the color of its flesh. It is slightly less nutritious than the orange.

EXCELLENT SOURCE: vitamin C.

CONTAINS: potassium and folic acid.

PROPERTIES: aperitive, digestive, stomachic, antiseptic, tonic and diuretic.

STORING

:: At room temperature: 8-15 days.
:: In the fridge: extended storage.
:: In the freezer: the juice and the zest.

Lemon

Citrus limon, Rutaceae

The fruit of the lemon tree, a tree thought to be originally from China or India. The size and acidity of the lemon varies, depending on the variety. Its yellow rind can be more or less thick and rough. The juicy flesh may or may not contain seeds.

lemon

Lemon

PREPARING

1 Remove the zest using a zester.

2 Strips of zest can also be obtained using a peeler.

3 Chop the strips with a knife.

BUYING

:: **Choose:** a firm, heavy lemon, with a finely grained and slightly glossy yellow rind. Lemon that shows hints of green is more acidic. A lemon with rough skin won't contain much pulp.

:: **Avoid:** a wrinkled lemon with hardened or softened parts or whose color is dull or too dark a yellow.

NUTRITIONAL INFORMATION

water	89%
protein	1 g
fat	0.3 g
carbohydrates	9.3 g
fiber	2.1 g
calories	29
	per 3.5 oz/100 g

EXCELLENT SOURCE: vitamin C.
CONTAINS: potassium and folic acid.
PROPERTIES: expectorant, antiseptic, antiscorbutic, antirheumatic, diuretic, fortifying, anthelmintic. It also soothes insect bites.

SERVING IDEAS

The lemon can be used as an ingredient as well as for decorative purposes. It sharpens the flavor of foods and can be used in place of salt; it prevents certain fruits and vegetables from discoloring. Lemon flavors soups, sauces, meat, vegetables, cakes, pastry creams, ice creams and sorbets. It is made into marmalade and jelly. Lemon can also replace the vinegar in vinaigrette. It is used to marinate and tenderize meat, poultry, fish and game. It is made into lemonade and added to tea. The zest of lemons can be grated or sliced. It is candied or dried.

STORING

:: **At room temperature:** about 1 week. Candied and dried zest can be kept in a cool and dry place, protected from drafts.
:: **In the fridge:** extended storage.
:: **In the freezer:** the juice and the zest.

Orange

Citrus spp., Rutaceae

The fruit of the orange tree, a tree originally from China. Oranges are classed into two groups covering the bitter oranges and the sweet oranges.

The **bitter orange** is the ancestor of the sweet oranges. It is also called a "bigarade" or "Seville" orange. It has a thick, rough rind with tints of green or yellow. It is also smaller than the sweet orange. Its flesh, low in juice, is very bitter.

The **sweet orange** is the juicy orange that is so widely enjoyed, sweet and tart. There are several varieties of sweet oranges.

Valencia orange

The **Valencia orange** is the preeminent juicing orange. Its very juicy and tart flesh contains few or no seeds. The **navel orange** has a thick, rough rind and is easy to peel. Its firm-textured flesh is sweet, tasty and almost always seedless. The **blood orange** is a hybrid with red flesh and usually without seeds. Its flesh is sweet, juicy and very perfumed.

Commercial practices have resulted in some oranges being identified by brand name, such as Sunkist, Jaffa or Outspan.

BUYING

:: Choose: a firm orange that is heavy for its size, with smooth skin.

:: Avoid: an orange with soft parts, black spots and mold.

navel orange

NUTRITIONAL INFORMATION

water	87%
protein	0.9 g
fat	0.1 g
carbohydrates	12 g
fiber	1.8 g
calories	47
	per 3.5 oz/100 g

EXCELLENT SOURCE: vitamin C.
GOOD SOURCE: potassium.
PROPERTIES: diuretic, antiscorbutic, tonic, digestive and slightly laxative. Its flowers are antispasmodic and the water they contain is said to aid sleep. The leaves, used as an infusion, are said to have digestive and antispasmodic effects.

CITRUS FRUITS

bitter orange

STORING

:: **At room temperature:** about 1 week.
Keep candied or dried zest in a cool and dry place.

:: **In the fridge:** extended storage.

:: **In the freezer:** the juice and the zest.

The skin of the orange must be rinsed if the zest will be used.

SERVING IDEAS

Oranges are eaten plain, cooked or made into various drinks. They are used in fruit salads, soufflés, flans, crepes, ice creams, sorbets and punches. Orange adds an unusual touch to sauces, vinaigrettes, vegetables and salads of rice, chicken or seafood. It works well with fish, duck, beef and pork. Oranges are cooked into marmalade. The zest and flesh of the orange is candied. An essential oil and an essence used in pastries and sweets are extracted from oranges.

The flowers are distilled to make essential oils (for example, Neroli Bigarade) and the orange flower water that flavors crepes, flans, syrups, pastries and herbal teas. The bigarade (bitter orange) especially is used to make preserves or cooked (marmalade, jam, jelly, syrup, sauce). Cointreau®, Curaçao and Grand Marnier® owe their orange flavor to bigarade orange zest.

blood orange

Mandarin

Citrus reticulata, Rutaceae

The fruit of the mandarin tree, a tree originally from China or Indochina. The mandarin resembles a small, slightly flattened orange. Its skin peels very easily. Its sweet, perfumed and delicate flesh is less acidic than most citrus fruits. It may contain several seeds or be seedless.

mandarin

A number of hybrids have been produced. The **tangerine** is a cross between the mandarin and the bitter orange. Its skin is usually darker, often verging on red. The **clementine** is a cross between the mandarin and the bitter orange. Its fine skin is reddish-orange, nonclinging and sometimes puffy and bumpy. Its juicy and tart flesh is slightly less aromatic than that of the mandarin. The **tangor** is a cross between the tangerine and the sweet orange. It peels easily. Its flesh is both semisour and semisweet. The **tangelo** is a cross between the mandarin and the grapefruit. This fruit is often identified by the name of the variety (Minneola, Seminole, Orlando). The **ugli fruit** has thick, wrinkled skin, is nonclinging and peels easily. Depending on the variety, it is a yellowish-red, orange-yellow or green color. It contains a pink or orange-yellow pulp, sweeter than grapefruit pulp, slightly acidic and almost seedless.

BUYING

 :: **Choose:** an intact mandarin that is heavy for its size.

:: **Avoid:** a mandarin with black marks or showing mold or soft spots.

Do not be concerned by the existence of marks on ugli fruit.

STORING

:: **In the fridge:** 1-2 weeks.

NUTRITIONAL INFORMATION

water	88%
protein	0.6 g
fat	0.2 g
carbohydrates	11 g
fiber	1 g
calories	44
	per 3.5 oz/100 g

EXCELLENT SOURCE: vitamin C.
CONTAINS: potassium, vitamin A and folic acid.

SERVING IDEAS

 The mandarin and its hybrids are very often eaten as is, as a snack or dessert. They are used in fruit salads, sauces and sweet-and-sour dishes. They decorate cakes, puddings, desserts and pies, and add an unusual touch to salads of rice, chicken or seafood. They are delicious with ice cream, sprinkled with orange liqueur or plain, or in a chocolate fondue. Mandarin peel is thinner than orange peel and less pressure needs to be applied when grating it or extracting the mandarin's refreshing and delicious juice.

tangerine

tangelo

ugli fruit

tangor

Kumquat

Fortunella spp., Rutaceae

The fruit of a tree originally from China. The kumquat has edible, tender, thin, sweet and perfumed skin. Its tart flesh contains a few seeds.

kumquat

BUYING

:: **Choose:** firm, unbruised kumquats with a shiny skin and without marks.
:: **Avoid:** soft kumquats.

PREPARING

 Wash the skin carefully. Kumquats can be blanched in boiling water (20 sec), then rinsed in cold water to tenderize the peel.

STORING

Kumquats are fragile.
:: **At room temperature:** 5-6 days.
:: **In the fridge:** 3 weeks.

NUTRITIONAL INFORMATION

water	82%
protein	1.1 g
fat	0 g
carbohydrates	16 g
fiber	3.7 g
calories	63
	per 3.5 oz/100 g

EXCELLENT SOURCE: vitamin C.
GOOD SOURCE: potassium.
CONTAINS: copper.

Kumquat

SERVING IDEAS

Kumquat is eaten as is, with its peel. It is used in fruit salads and mixed salads, stuffings, cakes and muffins. It is used for decoration. Kumquats enhance the flavor of sweet-and-sour sauces. It is a fruit that is candied, marinated, cooked into jam or marmalade, poached in syrup or preserved in alcohol. It works well with fish, poultry, lamb and duck.

Lime

Citrus aurantifolia, Rutaceae

The fruit of the lime tree, a thorny shrub probably originally from an area close to India and Malaysia. The lime has green, juicy flesh that is very acidic and very perfumed, and may or may not contain seeds, depending on the variety. Some are known as "Key limes," "finger limes" or "kaffir limes." Other varieties are called "sweet limes." Key limes have yellow flesh and peel and are smaller than the Persian lime.

lime

NUTRITIONAL INFORMATION

water	88%
protein	0.8 g
fat	0.2 g
carbohydrates	10.6 g
fiber	2.1 g
calories	30
	per 3.5 oz/100 g

EXCELLENT SOURCE: vitamin C.
CONTAINS: potassium.
TRACES: iron, folic acid and calcium.
PROPERTY: antiscorbutic.

BUYING

:: **Choose:** a firm lime that is heavy for its size, with a smooth and shiny skin of a fairly dark green color.
:: **Avoid:** a dull, dry or soft lime.
Brown marks on the skin do not affect the flavor.

STORING

Handle lime with care.
:: **At room temperature:** 1 week. Light will turn limes yellow and affect their flavor. The candied or dried peel can be kept in a cool and dry place, protected from drafts.
:: **In the fridge:** extended storage.
:: **In the freezer:** the juice and the zest.

SERVING IDEAS

Lime is used in the same way as lemon, which it can replace in most recipes. It is used in main meals, soups, vinaigrettes, salsas, sauces, cakes, desserts, ice creams or sorbets. It adds flavor to punches and tropical cocktails and enhances the flavor of chicken, fish and bean dishes, and vegetable soups.

Citron

Citrus medica, Rutaceae

The fruit of the citron tree, a tree from a family of citruses thought to be originally from China. The green or yellowish flesh of the citron is acidic and not very juicy. It is divided into several segments, contains a lot of seeds and is covered with a thick white membrane.

citron

BUYING

 Citron is rarely sold fresh. It is mostly available in candied form.

STORING

 Candied citron keeps in a cool place protected from drafts.

NUTRITIONAL INFORMATION

GOOD SOURCE: vitamin C.
PROPERTIES: antiscorbutic. Citron juice is said to be sudorific, antipyretic and digestive. The crushed seeds are used as an anthelmintic remedy.

SERVING IDEAS

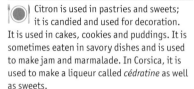 Citron is used in pastries and sweets; it is candied and used for decoration. It is used in cakes, cookies and puddings. It is sometimes eaten in savory dishes and is used to make jam and marmalade. In Corsica, it is used to make a liqueur called *cédratine* as well as sweets.

Bergamot

Citrus bergamia, Rutaceae

The fruit of the bergamot tree. Bergamot resembles a small orange; it is thought to be the result of a cross between the lime and the bitter orange. Bergamot is very juicy, but too sour and too bitter to be edible. Its rind, which is very rich in essential oil, emits a delicate aroma.

bergamot

SERVING IDEAS

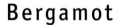 Bergamot cannot be eaten as is. Its zest is used in pastries and sweets, and its essential oil in confectionery, perfumery and distilling.

Bergamot gives its perfume to Earl Grey tea. In France, bergamot-flavored barley sugar is a specialty of the town of Nancy.

Banana

Musa spp., Musaceae

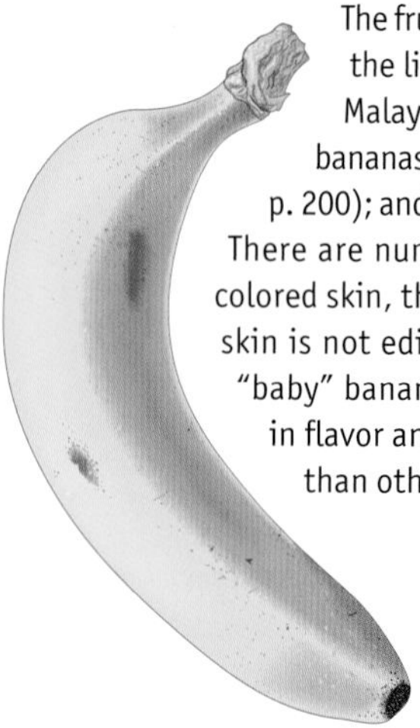

The fruit of the banana plant, a giant plant in the same family as the lily and the orchid. The banana is probably originally from Malaysia. There are three groups: **sweet bananas** (or dessert bananas); **cooking bananas**, also called "plantains" (see *Plantain*, p. 200); and **inedible bananas**.

There are numerous varieties of sweet banana; most have yellow-colored skin, though some varieties have red, pink or purple skin. The skin is not edible. Some banana varieties are very small. These are "baby" bananas (also called "lady finger bananas"). Bananas vary in flavor and texture, some varieties being more mealy or sweeter than others.

banana

BUYING

:: **Choose:** an intact banana that is not too hard.

:: **Avoid:** a very green banana, a split or very soft banana, unless using it for cooking.

Banana is also commercially available as a flour or as dried chips, which are very high in calories.

PREPARING

Peel banana at the last minute to avoid oxidation, or sprinkle with citrus juice to prevent browning.

NUTRITIONAL INFORMATION

water	74%
protein	1 g
fat	0.5 g
carbohydrates	23 g
calories	92
	per 3.5 oz/100 g

EXCELLENT SOURCE: vitamin B$_6$ and potassium.

SOURCE: vitamin C, riboflavin, folic acid and magnesium.

PROPERTY: slightly laxative when overripe.

lady finger bananas

red banana

STORING

Bananas are fragile.

:: At room temperature: to speed up their ripening, place in a paper bag or in newspaper.

:: In the fridge: very ripe, a few days. Their skin will blacken but not their flesh.

:: In the freezer: 2 months, puréed. Mix in a little lemon juice to prevent the bananas from discoloring and developing an unpleasant taste. Defrosted bananas are cooked in cakes, muffins or other desserts. Partially defrosted bananas will become mousse-like when whipped, resulting in a dessert resembling ice cream.

SERVING IDEAS

Bananas are eaten as is. They can be cooked in the oven, quick-braised, boiled, sautéed or fried. They are used as a fruit or a vegetable (green banana breaks up less and is not as sweet as ripe banana). Bananas are delicious sprinkled with ginger or cinnamon, dressed with brown sugar that has been mixed with a little lemon or lime juice, and flambéed with rum or orange liqueur. Bananas work well with dairy products. They are used in sundaes, yogurts, ice creams, sorbets, milkshakes, tapioca and flans. Bananas are made into a purée that is eaten as is or used for pies, cakes, muffins, puddings and fritters.

An essence is extracted from bananas that flavors numerous dishes. Bananas can be dehydrated or distilled.

Plantain

Musa paradisiaca, Musaceae

The fruit of the banana plant, a plant probably originally from Malaysia. The plantain (also called "cooking banana" and "flour banana") is related to the sweet banana, but its flesh is firmer and not as sweet. Its skin yellows then blackens when ripe. Plantain is not edible raw.

plantain

BUYING

:: **Choose:** a firm and intact plantain.

SERVING IDEAS

Plantain is mainly used as a vegetable. Its flavor and consistency are slightly reminiscent of sweet potato, or, when very ripe, banana. It is used in soups and stews. It is combined with apples, sweet potatoes and squash.

COOKING

Plantain is cooked whole or sliced, and it keeps its shape.
:: **Boiled:** 25 min.
:: **Broiled:** 45 min at 4 in. (10 cm) from the heat source.
:: **Fried**.
:: **Baked:** unpeeled, 1 hr at 350°F (175°C). The two ends can be cut off and the skin removed, or a lengthwise slice can be made in the skin.

NUTRITIONAL INFORMATION

water	65%
protein	1.3 g
fat	0.4 g
carbohydrates	32 g
fiber	2.3 g
calories	122
	per 3.5 oz/100 g

EXCELLENT SOURCE: potassium.
GOOD SOURCE: vitamin C, vitamin B_6 and magnesium.
CONTAINS: vitamin A and folic acid.

STORING

:: **At room temperature:** for ripening.
:: **In the fridge:** when very ripe, 2 weeks.
:: **In the freezer:** when very ripe, can peel and individually wrap.

Durian

Durio zibethinus, Bombaceae

The fruit of a tree originally from the Malay Archipelago related to the baobab, the cacao, and the cotton and mallow plants. The sweet, creamy and dense flesh of the durian possesses a particular flavor and contains edible seeds.

durian

BUYING

:: **Choose:** a durian with intact skin. The yellowing of the skin indicates that the fruit is ripe.

SERVING IDEAS

Durian is eaten plain, with a spoon. It is combined with yogurt and ice cream, and cooked into jam. In Asia, durian is enjoyed with sticky rice, and in China, it is used in pastries.
Durian seeds are roasted, toasted or ground to make sweets.

STORING

:: **At room temperature:** for ripening.
:: **In the fridge:** wrapped and isolated from other food items. Eat quickly.
In Malaysia, it is preserved in salt so it can be eaten year-round.

NUTRITIONAL INFORMATION

water	81.1%
fat	0.8 g
carbohydrates	15 g
fiber	1.6 g
calories	81
	per 3.5 oz/100 g

EXCELLENT SOURCE: potassium.
GOOD SOURCE: vitamin C.
PROPERTY: aphrodisiac. Do not prepare or eat durian with alcohol (this results in an unpleasant fermentation).

PREPARING

Open the durian by inserting a well-sharpened knife into its grooves. Take out the flesh using a spoon and remove the seeds.

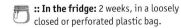

Jaboticaba

Myrciaria cauliflora, Myrtaceae

jaboticabas

The fruit of a tree originally from Brazil. The black or purple skin of the jaboticaba is thick. Its flesh is juicy, sweet and flavorful.

BUYING

:: **Choose:** firm, intact, shiny and well-colored jaboticabas.

SERVING IDEAS

The jaboticaba is eaten as is, in fruit salads, as a jelly, jam, juice and wine. It decorates cheese platters and hors d'oeuvres.

NUTRITIONAL INFORMATION

water	87%
carbohydrates	13 g
calories	46
	per 3.5 oz/100 g

CONTAINS: vitamin C.

STORING

:: **In the fridge:** 2 weeks, in a loosely closed or perforated plastic bag.

Carambola

Averrhoa carambola, Oxalidaceae

A fruit originally from Sri Lanka and the Malaku Islands. The **carambola** is formed of 5 protruding ridges (sometimes 4 or 6) arranged in star-formation. It is also called "star fruit." Its fine skin is edible and its color ranges from light yellow to golden yellow when mature. Some varieties are sweet and slightly acidic, while other are sour-tasting. Its sugar content does not increase after picking.

carambola

The **bilimbi**, a close relative, is originally from Malaysia. It is smaller than the carambola and the 5 ridges are barely visible. Its juicy flesh is firmer and much more acidic than the carambola.

BUYING

:: **Choose:** a firm, well-colored carambola, with no bruises and a fruity aroma.

SERVING IDEAS

Raw or cooked carambola can be combined with fruits or vegetables. It is sprinkled with vinaigrette, served as a side dish or cooked with seafood and vegetables, Asian-style. Cook very briefly to preserve its flavor. Cut into thin decorative slices, carambola can accompany seafood and fish. It garnishes drinks and decorates hors d'oeuvres, cheeses, cakes and pies. Carambola is cooked into marinades or jelly. It is used in sorbets or puddings and made into juice. The bilimbi is usually cooked. It is made into marinades, jam or jelly. It is used in soups, sauces or sweet-and-sour dishes, and made into juice. It is used in place of mango in Indian chutneys.

NUTRITIONAL INFORMATION

water	91%
protein	0.6 g
fat	0.3 g
carbohydrates	7.8 g
calories	33
	per 3.5 oz/100 g

GOOD SOURCE: vitamin C.
SOURCE: vitamin A and potassium.
CONTAINS: several acids, including oxalic acid, tartaric acid and malic acid.

PREPARING

Wash the carambola. If the edges of the ridges are blackened, remove them with a knife or peeler. Remove the seeds. The carambola is often sliced to highlight its star shape.

STORING

:: **At room temperature:** for ripening or if eating within the next few days.
:: **In the fridge:** about 15 days.

Cherimoya

Annona cherimola, Anonaceae

A fruit originally from the Andes, of which there are several varieties. The cherimoya belongs to the *Annona* genus, along with the soursop, sugar or custard apple and bullock's heart. Depending on the variety, these fruits are oval, conical, spherical or heart-shaped. The white flesh is juicy, sweet, a little grainy, slightly acidic and very perfumed. The cherimoya is often considered to be one of the finest and most flavorful of fruits.

cherimoya

BUYING

:: **Choose:** an aromatic, intact cherimoya that is not too firm.

:: **Avoid:** a cherimoya with blackened or bruised skin.

SERVING IDEAS

Cherimoya is mainly eaten raw, as cooking affects its flavor. It is eaten chilled, with a spoon. It is served with orange juice to prevent oxidation (a classic way of serving cherimoya in Chile). Cherimoya is used in fruit salads, sorbets, ice creams, yogurts, pastries and cookies. It is cooked into compote, jam and jelly. It is also made into juice.

PREPARING

Wash the cherimoya briefly. Peel, then cut into two or more sections. Remove the central fiber if it seems hard. Remove the seeds immediately or when eating the fruit. They should also be removed before puréeing the cherimoya or cutting it into pieces.

NUTRITIONAL INFORMATION

water	74%
protein	1.3 g
fat	0.4 g
carbohydrates	24 g
fiber	3.4 g
calories	94
	per 3.5 oz/100 g

Cherimoya is a nourishing fruit, as it has a high level of carbohydrate.

CONTAINS: vitamin C and niacin.

STORING

:: **At room temperature:** for ripening. It must not ripen too much, as it ferments.

:: **In the fridge:** ripe, 1-2 days.

:: **In the freezer:** 4 months maximum, puréed once the flesh reaches a certain level of maturity, which is not easily identified.

Jackfruit

Artocarpus heterophyllus, Moraceae

The fruit of the jackfruit tree, a tree probably originally from the region between India and Malaysia. The jackfruit is a close relative of the breadfruit tree. Jackfruit are divided into two groups: those with soft, juicy and sweet flesh and the varieties with firm flesh that are less juicy and not as sweet. The white or yellowish flesh becomes a golden yellow when mature. It holds numerous large white seeds.

jackfruit

The fertilized flowers are edible. Jackfruit continues to ripen after picking.

BUYING

:: **Choose:** a jackfruit with intact skin. When mature, it will emit a strong smell. Jackfruit is often sold in cut pieces because of its large size.

SERVING IDEAS

Jackfruit is eaten as a vegetable when not ripe and as a fruit when mature. It is eaten raw (as is, grated, cut into pieces, in fruit salads and ice creams) or cooked (as purée and jam). It is made into juice, frozen, dried or made into flour. Boiled or fried jackfruit is cooked by itself, with vegetables, in chutneys or added to curries. It can be preserved with sugar or salt. The skin is cooked into jelly or candied, and pectin is extracted from it.

The seeds, often boiled, are used as vegetables or eaten roasted. They are canned, by themselves or with other vegetables, in brine or tomato sauce. They are dried and milled into flour. In India, this flour is used to make chapatis and papadums.

NUTRITIONAL INFORMATION

	jackfruit	seeds
water	72%	
protein	1.5 g	19 g
fat	0.3 g	1 g
carbohydrates	24 g	74 g
fiber	1 g	4 g
calories	98	383
		per 3.5 oz/100 g

JACKFRUIT
EXCELLENT SOURCE: potassium.
DRIED SEEDS
CONTAIN: B-complex vitamins, calcium, potassium, magnesium, phosphorus, iron and sulfur.

PREPARING

Oil fingers and the knife that will be used to cut the jackfruit so that its sticky sap does not adhere to them. Cut the fruit and take out the seeds and the flesh covering them.

STORING

:: **At room temperature:** 3-10 days.
:: **In the fridge:** ripe or cut.
:: **In the freezer:** cover in syrup (half water and half sugar with citrus juice).

Tamarillo

Cyphomandra betacea, Solanaceae

A fruit originally from South America. The skin of the tamarillo (also named "tree tomato") is not edible. Its firm and tart flesh contains several edible seeds. Its sweet-and-sour taste is reminiscent of gooseberry, tomato and winter cherry.

tamarillo

BUYING

:: **Choose:** intact and firm tamarillos with smooth, bright red skin, with no marks and yielding to slight finger pressure.

SERVING IDEAS

When very ripe, tamarillo is eaten raw, cut in two, with salt or sugar or sprinkled with lemon or lime juice. Puréed tamarillo is used to flavor yogurts, ice creams, sorbets and drinks. Unripe tamarillo is cooked like a vegetable. Use in moderation when cooking with other fruits, as its flavor will dominate. It is cooked in the same way as tomato, which it can replace. It accompanies meat, poultry and fish. It is also delicious in sauces and cooked into jam, jelly or marinades.

PREPARING

Peel tamarillos or blanch them to remove their skin easily. Its red juice leaves indelible marks.

NUTRITIONAL INFORMATION

water	86%
protein	2 g
fat	0.9 g
carbohydrates	10 g
fiber	1.6 g
calories	50
	per 3.5 oz/100 g

EXCELLENT SOURCE: vitamin A, vitamin C, calcium, potassium, phosphorus, sodium and magnesium.

STORING

:: **At room temperature:** for ripening.
:: **In the fridge:** 2 weeks, in a loosely closed or perforated plastic bag.
:: **In the freezer:** whole or cut, peel and sprinkle with sugar. It can also be cooked and puréed.

Rambutan

Nephelium lappaceum, Sapindaceae

A fruit originally from Malaysia, the rambutan is related to the lychee and the longan. Its pulp is juicy, whitish and translucent with a sweet, mild and perfumed flavor, sometimes tart or acidic, depending on the variety. The seed inside is not edible.

rambutan

Rambutan

BUYING

:: **Choose:** rambutan with light red skin, greenish hairs, without moist spots on their peel.

:: **Avoid:** rambutan with dark and dry skin leaking a sour-smelling juice.

SERVING IDEAS

Rambutan is used in the same way as the lychee, which it can replace. It is delicious as is, in fruit salad or with ice cream. Cooked rambutan accompanies vegetables and meat or is used to stuff meat.

STORING

Eat rambutan as soon as possible.
:: **In the fridge:** a few days.
They can be preserved 3-4 months in a light syrup or made into jam.

NUTRITIONAL INFORMATION

water	82%
protein	1.0 g
fat	0.1 g
carbohydrates	16.5 g
fiber	1.1 g
calories	64
	per 3.5 oz/100 g

EXCELLENT SOURCE: vitamin C.
CONTAINS: iron and potassium.

PREPARING

Rambutan peels easily. Remove its shell by splitting it carefully with the fingers or a knife, avoiding breaking the flesh. For an original presentation, leave the rambutan in its skin, remove only the upper half of the shell and serve like an egg in its shell.

Longan

Dimocarpus longan, Sapindaceae

The fruit of a tree thought to be originally from India, the longan is a close relative of the lychee and the rambutan. It is covered with a shell that becomes brown and fairly rigid when mature. It encloses a white translucent flesh that is a little less aromatic than the lychee. A large inedible seed is found at the center of the fruit.

longan

PREPARING

Remove the longan's shell by splitting it at the stem end, then peeling. Depending on how it is to be used, pit the longan or leave this to the eater.

SERVING IDEAS

The longan is delicious as is. It is added to fruit salads, and used with rice, vegetables, salads or sauces. It is poached or stir-fried. It is available canned in syrup or dried.

BUYING

 :: Choose: well-colored longans with no cracks.

COOKING

Add longans at the end of cooking, and cook only briefly.

STORING

Eat longans as soon as possible.
:: In the fridge: 2-3 weeks, in a loosely closed or perforated plastic bag with a sheet of paper towel.
:: In the freezer: as is in their shell.

NUTRITIONAL INFORMATION

	fresh
water	83%
protein	1.3 g
fat	0.1 g
carbohydrates	15 g
fiber	0.4 g
calories	286
	per 3.5 oz/100 g

EXCELLENT SOURCE: vitamin C and potassium.
CONTAINS: magnesium and copper.

TROPICAL FRUITS

Pepino

Solanum muricatum, Solanaceae

The fruit of a plant originally from Peru. The pepino has an orange or yellowish flesh holding edible seeds. The flesh is a little mealy and slightly sweeter than the melon.

pepino

NUTRITIONAL INFORMATION

water	93%
protein	0.6 g
fat	0.1 g
carbohydrates	5 g
fiber	1 g
calories	22
	per 3.5 oz/100 g

EXCELLENT SOURCE: vitamin C.
PROPERTY: antirheumatic. The pepino is said to be useful for treating bronchitis and various skin problems.

BUYING

 :: Choose: a firm and intact pepino with a delicate perfume.

STORING

 :: At room temperature: for ripening.
:: In the fridge: ripe, 1-2 days.

SERVING IDEAS

 Unripe pepino is prepared like squash. It is delicious flavored with ginger, sprinkled with lemon or lime juice, Grand Marnier® or Cointreau®. It is used in hors d'oeuvres, fruit salads and mixed salads.

Persimmon

Diospyros spp., Ebenaceae

The fruit of the persimmon tree, a tree probably originally from China. The different varieties of persimmon are classed into two groups: the **Asian persimmon** and the **American persimmon**.

There are two more well-known varieties of Asian persimmon: the *hachiya* and the *fuyu*. They are the size of a tomato. The *hachiya* persimmon (also called "Japanese persimmon" or "Kaki") is heart-shaped and has very sweet, soft flesh colored red or bright orange. Hachiya is the most widely available persimmon in the United States. It is eaten very ripe (completely soft). Its skin is edible. When ready to eat, the flesh becomes sweet, almost liquid, slightly sticky, nonacidic, fairly fragile and very aromatic.

The *fuyu* persimmon is eaten firm or ripe. Israel is a major producer of a type of *fuyu* persimmon called *Sharon*. The flesh holds brown, inedible seeds.

Asian persimmon

BUYING

:: **Choose:** an intact persimmon.
:: **Avoid:** a yellow or greenish persimmon. Find out what variety it is; do not judge by the color, which is not a sign of maturity.

SERVING IDEAS

Persimmon is eaten with a spoon. The *fuyu* variety can be bit into like an apple. Persimmon can be puréed (add lemon juice to keep its color). It forms a sauce for ice cream, cakes and crepes. Persimmon decorates salads of fruit, rice, seafood or poultry. It accompanies cheese and flavors yogurt, flans and other desserts. It is cooked into jam, dried or preserved.

NUTRITIONAL INFORMATION

water	80%
protein	0.6 g
fat	0.2 g
carbohydrates	19 g
fiber	1.6 g
calories	70
	per 3.5 oz/100 g

GOOD SOURCE: vitamin A.
CONTAINS: potassium, vitamin C and copper.
PROPERTY: slightly laxative.

STORING

:: **At room temperature:** for ripening. Place the persimmon in a paper bag to speed up the ripening process; to stimulate this even further, add fruits that emit ethylene (banana or apple).
:: **In the fridge:** ripe.
:: **In the freezer:** whole or puréed (add 2 tablespoons/30 ml of lemon juice).

kaki >

Lychee

Litchi chinensis, Sapindaceae

The fruit of a tree originally from southern China. The lychee is covered with a rough shell that hardens after picking. When mature, this shell is red or pink-colored; it becomes duller and browner as the fruit becomes older. The translucent, pearly-white and firm-textured flesh is juicy, refreshing, very sweet and very perfumed. It surrounds a large nonclinging inedible seed. The flavor of the lychee evokes strawberry, rose and muscat all at the same time. The flavor varies, depending on the degree of maturity.

lychee

BUYING

:: **Choose:** intact, colorful lychees with no cracks.
Lychees are bought fresh, canned in syrup and sometimes dried, candied or in bunches.

SERVING IDEAS

The lychee forms a delicious dessert by itself. It adds an exotic note to a fruit salad. It can accompany or flavor rice, vegetables, stuffings or sauces. In Chinese cooking, it is partnered with meat and fish.

PREPARING

The lychee peels easily. Split the shell carefully with the fingers or a knife, avoiding breaking the flesh, then peel. Depending on how it is going to be used, you may need to remove pit.

NUTRITIONAL INFORMATION

water	82%
protein	0.8 g
fat	0.4 g
carbohydrates	16.5 g
fiber	0.5 g
calories	66
	per 3.5 oz/100 g

EXCELLENT SOURCE: vitamin C.
GOOD SOURCE: potassium.
CONTAINS: copper and magnesium.

COOKING

Cook lychee only briefly so that it keeps its delicate flavor. Add at the end of cooking.

STORING

:: **In the fridge:** a few weeks, in a loosely closed or perforated plastic bag with a sheet of paper towel.
:: **In the freezer:** as is in their shell.

Papaya

Carica papaya, Caricaceae

The fruit of the papaya tree, a tree probably originally from Central America. The papaya is spherical or cylindrical in shape. The Hawaiian "Solo" variety is one of the most common. The papaya has a thin nonedible skin colored orange-yellow, red-yellow or yellow-green. Its juicy flesh, orange-yellow in color, can also be yellow or reddish. Its texture, similar to cantaloupe, is softer. Its central cavity holds a number of edible seeds. The papaya has a mild flavor, more or less sweet and perfumed, depending on the species, which is reminiscent of melon. Most species in the *Carica* genus are not edible. The mountain papaya and the babaco are more rare.

papaya

BUYING

:: **Choose:** a papaya with orange-yellow skin over most of its surface that yields to slight finger pressure. The presence of black spots or mold does not affect the flavor.
:: **Avoid:** a papaya that is hard and very green, or one that is very soft or very bruised.

STORING

:: **At room temperature:** for ripening. Place the papaya in a paper bag to speed up the ripening process. Eat as soon as it is ripe.
:: **In the fridge:** ripe, a few days.
An unripe papaya kept at under 45°F (7°C) or in the fridge will not ripen any further.

NUTRITIONAL INFORMATION

water	89%
protein	0.6 g
fat	0.1 g
carbohydrates	10 g
fiber	0.9 g
calories	39
	per 3.5 oz/100 g

EXCELLENT SOURCE: vitamin C.
GOOD SOURCE: potassium and vitamin A.
PROPERTIES: stomachic and diuretic. The seeds are used as an anthelmintic remedy. In Brazil, a syrup is made with papaya juice that has a sedative effect.

Papaya

SERVING IDEAS

Papaya is eaten with a spoon, with or without sugar, sprinkled with lemon or lime juice, port or rum. It is used in yogurt, puddings, sorbets and ice cream. Papaya is added at the last moment to fruit salads, as it softens the other fruits. It is made into juice or purée. It is cooked into jam, chutney or ketchup. Papaya works well with ham, prosciutto and smoked salmon. It can be stuffed with fruit, chicken or seafood salad. Green papaya is used in the same way as winter squash, which it can replace in most recipes, though it needs to be "bled" (that is, drain the white sap and acid it contains) before using.

It can be dressed with vinaigrette, stuffed, cooked in a fricassee or ratatouille, and marinated.
Papaya seeds can be ground and used like black pepper. A few can be eaten when eating the papaya.
The babaco is cooked into jam or canned. In South America, it is used in cakes. This fruit is rarely made into juice, as it is too acidic.

babaco

Pomegranate

Punica granatum, Punicaceae

The fruit of the pomegranate tree, a shrub that is probably originally from Persia. The pomegranate's tough skin is not edible. Usually colored bright red, some varieties have yellow skin. Inside, there are white, thick, bitter and inedible membranes that separate 6 sections filled with a multitude of small edible seeds with a very juicy fleshy pulp, both sweet and tart.

pomegranate

BUYING

:: **Choose:** a large-sized, colorful pomegranate that is partially tinted brown, heavy and without spots.
:: **Avoid:** a wrinkled pomegranate with dull or low-colored skin.

STORING

:: **At room temperature:** a few days.
:: **In the fridge:** 3 weeks.
:: **In the freezer:** only the seeds.

Pomegranate

PREPARING

Cut off the upper part of the pomegranate, taking care not to cut into the seeds, because the juice will leak out. Peel the pomegranate, open it carefully (in a large bowl of cold water to prevent splattering), then eat the berries or pile them into a bowl to eat with a spoon. Discard the membranes that hold the berries. To get the benefit of the juice, roll the pomegranate, squashing it slightly. Collect the juice with a straw after making a hole in the skin, or by squeezing the fruit.

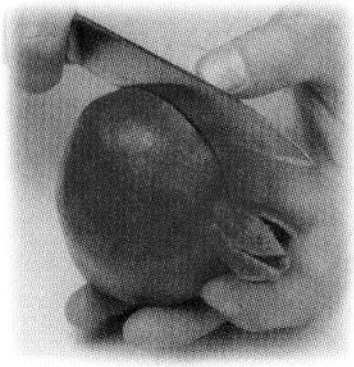

1 Make four slices into the skin of the pomegranate.

2 Divide the pomegranate in half, then into quarters.

3 Take out the seeds and pile them in a bowl in order to eat them.

NUTRITIONAL INFORMATION

water	81%
protein	1 g
fat	0.3 g
carbohydrates	17 g
fiber	0.2 g
calories	68
	per 3.5 oz/100 g

GOOD SOURCE: potassium.
CONTAINS: vitamin C and pantothenic acid.
TRACES: sodium and niacin.

SERVING IDEAS

Pomegranate berries are often eaten plain. They decorate and flavor fruit salads, mixed salads, soups, sauces, cheeses, vegetables, poultry, fish or seafood. They are consumed as juice. Pomegranate syrup (grenadine) is used to make aperitifs, drinks, molasses, ice creams, sorbets and other desserts.

TROPICAL FRUITS

Kiwifruit

Actinidia chinensis, Actinidiaceae

A fruit originally from China. The kiwifruit is a berry with emerald green flesh that is juicy, sweet and slightly tart. It contains small black edible seeds. The skin is edible but most people prefer to remove it. In North America, the Hayward variety of kiwifruit is the most common.

kiwifruit

BUYING

 :: Choose: an intact kiwifruit with no marks. Soft flesh yielding to slight finger pressure indicates it is ready to eat.
:: Avoid: very soft or damaged kiwifruit.

SERVING IDEAS

 Kiwifruit is delicious peeled and eaten as is or cut in two and eaten with a spoon. It is used in cereals, yogurts, ice creams, sorbets and fruit salads (add at the last moment). It decorates hors d'oeuvres, cheese platters, cakes, pies and desserts. It works well with meat, poultry and fish. It is added to certain soups and sauces. It is delicious in mixed salads. Kiwifruit can be made into juice, but avoid grinding the small seeds.

STORING

:: At room temperature: for ripening. Place the kiwifruit in a paper bag to speed up the ripening process; to stimulate it further, add fruits that emit ethylene (banana or apple).
:: In the fridge: ripe, several days; unripe, 2-3 weeks.

NUTRITIONAL INFORMATION

water	83%
protein	1 g
fat	0.4 g
carbohydrates	15 g
fiber	3.4 g
calories	61
	per 3.5 oz/100 g

EXCELLENT SOURCE: vitamin C and potassium.
CONTAINS: magnesium.
TRACES: phosphorus, iron and vitamin A. Kiwifruit contains almost double the amount of vitamin C of the same weight of orange and lemon.
PROPERTIES: diuretic, antiscorbutic and laxative. Kiwifruit contains enzymes that tenderize meat or the fruit itself when it is not quite ripe (peel and leave in the open air). On the other hand, it softens other fruits in a fruit salad, prevents gelatin from solidifying and curdles milk (but not yogurt or ice cream).

COOKING

Cook kiwifruit only briefly to keep its color and flavor.

Feijoa

Feijoa sellowiana, Myrtaceae

feijoa

The fruit of a shrub originally from South America, the feijoa belongs to the same family as the guava, clove and eucalyptus. Its cream-white-colored flesh is sweet, aromatic and has a slightly grainy texture. It is sometimes slightly tart, depending on its maturity. The center of the fruit is slightly gelatinous and holds tiny soft and edible seeds. Its skin is too bitter to be eaten.

BUYING

:: **Choose:** a perfumed feijoa that is tender to the touch, without spots.
:: **Avoid:** a very firm feijoa.

SERVING IDEAS

Peeled feijoa is eaten plain (as is or incorporated into fruit salads, yogurts and other desserts) or cooked (into jam or jelly). Use in moderation, as it is very perfumed. Puréed feijoa flavors ice creams, sorbets, flans and puddings. It works well with apples and bananas, which it can replace in most recipes.

PREPARING

To prevent the flesh of the feijoa from oxidizing, sprinkle with citrus juice.

NUTRITIONAL INFORMATION

water	87%
protein	1.2 g
fat	0.8 g
carbohydrates	10.6 g
fiber	4.3 g
calories	50
	per 3.5 oz/100 g

GOOD SOURCE: folic acid.
CONTAINS: vitamin C and potassium.

STORING

:: **At room temperature:** for ripening. Eat as soon as it is ripe.
:: **In the fridge:** a few days.
:: **In the freezer:** plain or cooked.

Jujube

Ziziphus jujuba, Rhamnaceae

The fruit of the jujube tree, a tree originally from China. Depending on the variety, the jujube can be the size of an olive or a date. It contains a long, hard pit. Its white or greenish flesh is not very juicy. Slightly mealy with a crunchy texture, it is sweet, slightly tart and mucilaginous. Dried jujube becomes sweeter and somewhat spongy.

jujubes

Jujube

BUYING

 :: Choose: firm and intact jujubes. Dried jujubes should be wrinkled and heavy. Canned jujubes can be found in gourmet food stores.

SERVING IDEAS

Jujube is eaten fresh or dried, plain or cooked (as a compote, jam or paste). It is used in the same way as the date, which it can replace, as is or in desserts, soups, stuffings and simmered dishes. It is marinated or made into juice. An alcoholic drink is extracted from fermented jujubes.

STORING

 :: At room temperature: almost indefinitely, dried, in an airtight container.
:: In the fridge: fresh.

NUTRITIONAL INFORMATION

	fresh	dried
water	78%	19.7%
protein	1.2 g	3.7 g
fat	0.2 g	1.1 g
carbohydrates	20 g	74 g
fiber	1.4 g	
calories	70	287
		per 3.5 oz/100 g

FRESH JUJUBES
EXCELLENT SOURCE: vitamin C.
GOOD SOURCE: potassium.
CONTAIN: magnesium, niacin, copper and iron.
DRIED JUJUBES
EXCELLENT SOURCE: potassium.
GOOD SOURCE: magnesium.
SOURCE: vitamin C, copper, iron, phosphorus and calcium.
PROPERTIES: expectorant, emollient, calmative and diuretic.

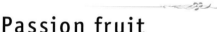

Passion fruit

Passiflora spp., Passifloraceae

 A fruit originally from Brazil. Passion fruit has a nonedible skin, colored yellow, purple or orange. It contains a jellylike substance, whose color varies from pinkish green to yellow or orange and can even be white or colorless. This flesh surrounds small black edible seeds. It is juicy, sweet, tart, very aromatic and refreshing.

passion fruit

BUYING

 :: Choose: a wrinkled passion fruit without bruises, as heavy as possible.

STORING

:: In the fridge: ripe, 1 week.
:: In the freezer: several months. Freeze as is or with the skin removed with the pulp in an ice cube tray.

SERVING IDEAS

 Passion fruit is good to eat when fully ripe as is, with a spoon. It is used to flavor fruit salads, flans, crepes, yogurts, ice creams, sorbets, cakes, puddings and drinks. Put the pulp through a strainer if you wish to remove the seeds. It is cooked into jelly or jam, and it is made into an alcoholic drink.

NUTRITIONAL INFORMATION

water	73%
protein	2.2 g
fat	0.7 g
carbohydrates	23 g
calories	100
	per 3.5 oz/100 g

EXCELLENT SOURCE: vitamin C, potassium and sodium.
GOOD SOURCE: iron, magnesium, niacin, vitamin A and phosphorus.
PROPERTIES: antispasmodic and narcotic (leaves and flowers), anthelmintic (seeds).

TROPICAL FRUITS

Guava

Psidium spp., Myrtaceae

The fruit of the guava tree, a tree originally from the American tropics. The edible skin of the guava encloses a very aromatic and slightly tart flesh that contains edible seeds.

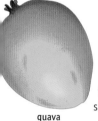
guava

BUYING

 :: Choose: a smooth, unbruised guava, neither too soft nor too hard.

SERVING IDEAS

Guava is eaten plain or cooked, in sweet or savory dishes. It is cooked into jam, jelly or chutney. It is added to sauces, fruit salads, pies, puddings, ice creams and drinks.

PREPARING

Remove the skin or leave it on; cut the fruit into two then, according to taste, remove the seeds.

NUTRITIONAL INFORMATION

water	86%
protein	0.8 g
fat	0.6 g
carbohydrates	12 g
fiber	5.6 g
calories	50
	per 3.5 oz/100 g

EXCELLENT SOURCE: vitamin C and potassium.
CONTAINS: vitamin A and niacin.
TRACES: phosphorus and calcium.
PROPERTIES: astringent and laxative.

STORING

 :: At room temperature: for ripening.
:: In the fridge: ripe, a few days.

Asian pear

Pyrus spp., Rosaceae

The fruit of a tree originally from Asia. The Asian pear is probably the ancestor of the pear, and is part of the same family. Most Asian pears are round; only a few are pear-shaped. Their fine, smooth and edible skin can be yellow, green or golden brown. Their flesh is very juicy, slightly sweet and mild like that of the pear with a very crunchy texture like that of the apple. It is sometimes grainy, depending on the variety.

Asian pear

BUYING

:: **Choose:** a perfumed Asian pear with no marks and relatively heavy for its size. It stays firm when ripe, but its thin skin makes it fragile. Surface bruising will not affect the flesh.

SERVING IDEAS

The Asian pear is mainly eaten plain, as its flavor is easily masked by other foods. It is added to fruit salads and mixed salads. Asian pear adds an unusual texture to sautéed or stir-fried dishes. It works well with cream cheese and yogurt. Its juice is excellent and refreshing.

PREPARING

The Asian pear is often sliced into rounds to highlight its star-shaped core. It is often eaten peeled so that the flesh can be better appreciated.

NUTRITIONAL INFORMATION

water	88%
protein	0.5 g
fat	0.3 g
carbohydrates	11 g
calories	42
	per 3.5 oz/100 g

CONTAINS: potassium.

COOKING

The Asian pear requires a slightly longer cooking time than the pear; it keeps its shape when **poached** or **baked.**

STORING

:: **At room temperature:** a few days.
:: **In the fridge:** 2 months, individually wrapped in paper towel, then in a loosely closed or perforated plastic bag.
Brown-skinned Asian pears keep longer than green-skinned ones. Yellow-skinned pears are the most fragile.

Mango

Mangifera indica, Anacardiaceae

The fruit of the mango tree, a tree thought to be originally from India. It is related to the pistachio and cashew trees. The mango is round, oval or kidney-shaped, depending on the variety. Its thin, smooth skin is green, yellow or scarlet. It can be tinted with red, purple, pink or orange-yellow. Its orange-yellow flesh is often mild-flavored like the

mango

peach, which has earned it the nickname "the peach of the tropics." It is sometimes fibrous but more often smooth, melting, juicy, sweet and aromatic, depending on the variety. The flesh clings to a large, flat seed. Its slightly acidic and spicy taste can be surprising.

BUYING

:: Choose: a mango that is neither too hard nor too wrinkled, with a pleasant smell. A ripe mango emits a sweet perfume and yields to gentle finger pressure. There may be black spots on the skin, a sign of advanced maturity.

SERVING IDEAS

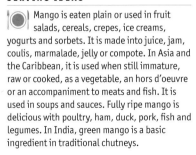

Mango is eaten plain or used in fruit salads, cereals, crepes, ice creams, yogurts and sorbets. It is made into juice, jam, coulis, marmalade, jelly or compote. In Asia and the Caribbean, it is used when still immature, raw or cooked, as a vegetable, an hors d'oeuvre or an accompaniment to meats and fish. It is used in soups and sauces. Fully ripe mango is delicious with poultry, ham, duck, pork, fish and legumes. In India, green mango is a basic ingredient in traditional chutneys.

NUTRITIONAL INFORMATION

water	82%
protein	0.5 g
fat	0.3 g
carbohydrates	17 g
calories	65
	per 3.5 oz/100 g

EXCELLENT SOURCE: vitamin A and vitamin C.
GOOD SOURCE: potassium.
CONTAINS: copper.
PROPERTIES: mango that is not quite ripe is said to be laxative. Mango skin can cause allergic cutaneous reactions and irritate the skin and the mouth.

STORING

:: At room temperature: for ripening. Place mango in a paper bag to accelerate the ripening process.
:: In the fridge: ripe, 1-2 weeks.
:: In the freezer: cook in a syrup or purée, with or without added sugar, lemon or lime juice.

Mango

PREPARING

Remove the skin before eating the mango. Mango juice leaves indelible marks on clothes.

1 Cut in two, passing the blade of the knife close to the pit. Do the same on the other side.

2 With the point of the knife, trace lines in the flesh down to the skin.

3 Turn out the skin to separate the cubes of mango flesh.

4 Cut the mango cubes away from the skin with the blade of a knife.

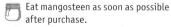

Mangosteen

Garcinia mangostana, Guttiferae

The fruit of the mangosteen tree, a tree originally from Malaysia, the Philippines and Indonesia. The skin of the mangosteen is not edible. It covers a reddish inedible membrane that encloses the flesh. This pearly white flesh is juicy and sweet, with an exquisite flavor. It divides into segments that sometimes contain an edible pit.

mangosteen

BUYING

:: **Choose:** purple-skinned mangosteens that yield to gentle finger pressure.
:: **Avoid:** mangosteens with very hard skin.

STORING

Eat mangosteen as soon as possible after purchase.
:: **At room temperature:** 2-3 days.
:: **In the fridge:** 1 week.

PREPARING

Peel the mangosteen by cutting into the skin around the circumference of the fruit, toward the center, taking care not to cut the flesh (cut about ½ in./1 cm deep). Rotate gently and remove the shell.

NUTRITIONAL INFORMATION

water	84%
protein	0.5 g
fat	0.3 g
carbohydrates	14.7 g
fiber	5.0 g
calories	57
	per 3.5 oz/100 g

CONTAINS: potassium and vitamin C.
TRACES: iron and niacin.

SERVING IDEAS

Mangosteen is eaten as is, peeled and divided into segments. It is delicious with a strawberry or raspberry sauce. It can be used for jams and fruit salads. Puréed mangosteen is used to flavor yogurts, ice creams, sorbets, cakes or puddings. In Asia, a vinegar is made from mangosteen and oil is extracted from its seeds. Cooking softens the flavor of the mangosteen.

TROPICAL FRUITS

Horned melon

Cucumis metuliferus, Cucurbitaceae

The horned melon was originally from southwestern Africa. The emerald green flesh of the fruit contains soft, edible seeds. Its flavor is reminiscent of melon and cucumber, with a hint of lime and banana.

horned melon

BUYING

:: **Choose:** a firm, intact horned melon colored yellow or orange. When ripe, it has a brilliant orange color.
:: **Avoid:** a dull or spotted horned melon.

SERVING IDEAS

Horned melon juice can be used instead of vinegar in a vinaigrette. For a thirst-quenching drink, add lemon or lime juice, sugar and orange liqueur to horned melon juice. Its flesh can be used in sauces, soups, salads, sorbets and yogurts.

STORING

:: **At room temperature** or **in the fridge:** 10 days.

NUTRITIONAL INFORMATION

water	90.4%
protein	0.9 g
carbohydrates	3.1 g
fiber	4 g
calories	24
	per 3.5 oz/100 g

EXCELLENT SOURCE: vitamin C.
CONTAINS: iron and potassium.

PREPARING

Rinse, peel, then cut horned melon into thin slices or cubes, or make into juice.

Sapodilla

Manilkara zapota, Sapotaceae

The fruit of the sapodilla tree, a tree originally from Mexico and Central America. The rough, gray or brown-colored skin of the sapodilla peels easily. Its translucent flesh, reddish or brownish yellow in color, is sometimes slightly grainy. It is juicy, melting, sweet and very aromatic. Its flavor is often compared to honey or apricot. Flat, oblong seeds are found at the center of the fruit. They contain a white bitter kernel that is used in an herbal tea. Sapodilla is eaten when very ripe.

sapodilla

BUYING

:: **Choose:** firm and intact sapodillas.

SERVING IDEAS

Sapodilla is eaten raw or cooked. It is used in fruit salads, sauces, ice creams and sorbets. Sapodilla is made into purée, juice or wine. It is cooked into jam or poached.

PREPARING

Wash the sapodilla, peel, then eat as is or cut the flesh and remove the seeds. Sapodilla can be cut in two and eaten with a spoon or the flesh can be taken out.

NUTRITIONAL INFORMATION

water	78%
protein	0.4 g
fat	1.1 g
carbohydrates	20 g
fiber	5.3 g
calories	82
	per 3.5 oz/100 g

GOOD SOURCE: potassium.
CONTAINS: vitamin C, sodium and iron.
Sapodilla is a rich source of fiber.

STORING

:: **At room temperature:** for ripening.
:: **In the fridge:** ripe.

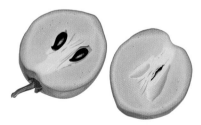

Prickly pear

Opuntia ficus-indica, Cactaceae

The fruit of the prickly pear cactus, a cactus originally from the tropical regions of America. Prickly pear is a berry. The color of its skin ranges from green to yellow, orange, pink or red, depending on the variety. Its swollen parts are covered with fine spikes. The orange-yellow, green or quite dark red flesh is juicy, tart, fairly sweet and perfumed. It contains numerous edible seeds.

prickly pear

BUYING

:: **Choose:** intact prickly pears that are not wrinkled and have no marks.
Pears that still have their spikes must be handled carefully.

SERVING IDEAS

 Prickly pear is eaten plain, in salads or sprinkled with lemon or lime juice.
When it is cut, strain to remove its numerous seeds, which will harden when heated. It is used to flavor sorbets, yogurts, fruit salads and other desserts. It is made into juice or purée, and cooked into jam.
The flattered stems of the prickly pear plant are also edible. They are eaten raw or cooked as a vegetable. Remove the spikes, peel and cut. Steam for a few minutes, sautée, quick-braise. Mexicans add them to salads, omelettes and puréed beans. Add them to a soup about 10 minutes before the end of cooking time.

STORING

 :: **At room temperature:** for ripening. Eat as soon as it is ripe.
:: **In the fridge:** ripe, a few days.

NUTRITIONAL INFORMATION

water	81%
protein	0.8 g
fat	0.5 g
carbohydrates	17 g
fiber	1.1 g
calories	67
	per 3.5 oz/100 g

EXCELLENT SOURCE: magnesium.
GOOD SOURCE: potassium.
CONTAINS: calcium, vitamin C and sodium.
PROPERTY: astringent.

PREPARING

Prickly pear is ripe when it yields to gentle finger pressure. To peel, slice a round section off one end, then make shallow slices lengthwise into the skin and remove the skin. If the pear has spikes, remove before cutting by rubbing with a cloth or thick paper, or by brushing under running water. Gloves can be worn to protect the hands.

Fig

Ficus carica, Moraceae

The fruit of the fig tree, a tree thought to be originally from the Mediterranean region. Botanically speaking, the fig is not a true fruit, but a fleshy container holding a large number of small crunchy seeds, called *achenes*, which are the true fruits. The most prominent commercial varieties of fig are the **black fig**, which is sweet and rather dry, and is the least fragile of the three; the **green fig**, which is juicy, with a fine skin; and the **purple fig**, the sweetest, juiciest, most fragile and rarest fig.

black fig

green fig

purple fig

BUYING

 :: Choose: soft, plump figs whose stems are still firm.

:: Avoid: waterlogged, bruised, moldy figs, or ones that have a sour smell.
Dried figs should emit a pleasant smell without being too hard.

PREPARING

 Wash fresh figs briefly and gently before eating. Cut stem; eat peeled or unpeeled. Dried figs can be used as is or rehydrated in water, juice or alcohol.

STORING

 Fresh figs are very fragile.
:: At room temperature: dried figs, in a cool and dry place.
:: In the fridge: fresh, wrapped, 1-2 days.

SERVING IDEAS

 Fresh or dried figs are used in fruit salads or hors d'oeuvres. They accompany cheese and ham. They are cooked into jam or made into compote. Dried figs can be stuffed with almonds, walnuts and pieces of orange. They are used in desserts.
Figs work well with rabbit, poultry and game. They can be used in place of prunes in most recipes; they can also be used as a coffee substitute. Figs are delicious poached or marinated in whisky, port or moderately dry sherry.

NUTRITIONAL INFORMATION

	fresh	dried
water	79%	28%
protein	0.8 g	3 g
fat	0.4 g	1.2 g
carbohydrates	19 g	65 g
fiber	3.3 g	9.3 g
calories	74	255
		per 3.5 oz/100 g

FRESH FIG
GOOD SOURCE: potassium.
Fresh fig is a source of fiber.
DRIED FIG
EXCELLENT SOURCE: potassium.
GOOD SOURCE: magnesium, iron and copper.
CONTAINS: calcium, vitamin B_6, sodium, phosphorus, pantothenic acid, riboflavin, zinc and thiamine.
PROPERTIES: diuretic and laxative. The milky sap of fig branches and leaves is said to remove corns and calluses.

Pineapple

Ananas comosus, Bromeliaceae

The fruit of a plant originally from the tropical and subtropical regions of America, probably Brazil. The pineapple is an amalgam of individual fruits that are joined together. It has no seeds. Its yellowish flesh is fibrous, juicy and sweet. The flesh is more tender, sweet and colored at the bottom of the fruit. The following four varieties of pineapple are of commercial importance. The **Cayenne pineapple**, whose firm and fibrous flesh is juicy, acidic and very sweet, is the most common variety. The **Queen pineapple**'s flesh is firmer and yellower than the Cayenne variety; it is a little less juicy, acidic and sweet. The **Red Spanish pineapple** has a pale, tart, slightly fibrous and very aromatic flesh. The **Pernambuco pineapple** is a medium-sized pineapple with yellowish or whitish flesh. Its tender, sweet flesh is moderately acidic.

Cayenne pineapple

Pineapple

Pineapple canning is a major industry (the Cayenne variety lends itself well to canning). The skin, core and ends of the pineapple are made into compote, alcohol, vinegar and cattle fodder.

Red Spanish pineapple

BUYING

 :: Choose: a pineapple that is heavy for its size and has a pleasant smell, with no spots, mold or moist parts, whose flesh yields slightly to finger pressure. The leaves should have a good green color. Tap the pineapple lightly with the palm of the hand; a muffled sound indicates a ripe fruit, a hollow sound indicates that it is low in juice.

:: Avoid: a pineapple with an overly strong smell, blackened "eyes," soft parts and yellowed leaves.

STORING

Pineapple is very fragile; eat as soon as possible after purchase.

:: At room temperature: 1-2 days.

:: In the fridge: 3-5 days, in a loosely closed or perforated plastic bag. Take out of the fridge a few minutes before eating for more flavor. Cover cut pineapple with liquid and place in an airtight container to keep it several days.

:: In the freezer: cut, in its own juice or in a sweet syrup (reduced flavor).

SERVING IDEAS

Pineapple is excellent plain or sprinkled with rum or kirsch. It is used in sauces, pies, cakes and fruit salads, yogurts, ice creams, sorbets, confectionery and punches. Pineapple upside-down cake is a classic North American recipe. Pineapple can accompany savory foods. It is often part of sweet-and-sour dishes, accompanying seafood, duck, chicken or pork. Ham with pineapple is a classic combination in Canada and the United States. Pineapple works well with cottage cheese, rice and salads of cabbage, chicken or shrimp. Dried pineapple is used as is or after soaking in water, juice or alcohol.

PREPARING

 The skin must be removed before the pineapple is edible. Several methods can be used:

- Cut off the two ends, then slice the skin off thinly, from top to bottom. Remove the remaining eyes by cutting around them with the point of a knife. Cut the pineapple into slices, then, if desired, into cubes. It is not necessary to remove the core if the pineapple is very ripe.

- Cut off the two ends, then cut the pineapple in two lengthwise. Separate the flesh from the skin with a knife, remove the core if desired, then cut the flesh. One can also keep the pineapple whole and only remove the top, then take out the flesh with a knife. The cut-up flesh can be put back into the shell.

- A cylindrical utensil can be used to remove the skin. It can't be adjusted to the size of the pineapple, so this sometimes results in the loss of a large amount of flesh.

Pineapple loses juice when it is peeled and cut. It can be saved by cutting the fruit in a deep plate.

NUTRITIONAL INFORMATION

water	87%
protein	0.4 g
fat	0.5 g
carbohydrates	12 g
fiber	0.5 g
calories	50
	per 3.5 oz/100 g

CONTAINS: vitamin C, potassium, magnesium and folic acid.

PROPERTIES: diuretic, stomachic and disintoxicating.

Pineapple contains an enzyme that can tenderize meat, prevent gelatin from setting, curdle milk (but not yogurt or ice cream) and soften other fruits in a fruit salad (unless added at the last moment). Cooking removes these properties, so canned pineapple can be used with gelatin or in fruit salads.

Queen pineapple

Melon

Cucumis melo, Cucurbitaceae

A fruit originally from India or Africa that belongs to the same family as cucumbers, pumpkins, squash, watermelons and bottle gourds. Winter melons are distinguished from summer melons by their oblong shape and better keeping qualities.

Charentais melon

SUMMER MELONS

The true **cantaloupe** with orange flesh is recognized by its rough, marked ridges; it is rarely found in North America. The most widely cultivated variety is the **Charentais melon**. What North Americans call "cantaloupe" is in fact a variety of muskmelon.

The **muskmelon** is usually not ribbed, although several hybrids combine the characteristics of the cantaloupe and the muskmelon. These very flavorful melons have salmon-pink or orange-yellow flesh.

WINTER MELONS

The **Honeydew melon** has a cream-yellow rind when mature. Its green flesh is very sweet.

The **Prince melon** resembles the Honeydew melon but has orange-colored flesh.

The **Casaba melon** has creamy white flesh, which is less perfumed than other melons.

The **Persian melon**, when mature, is covered with a brownish netting pattern. It has firm orange flesh.

The **Juan Canary melon**, or "Brazilian melon," has a whitish flesh that is very tasty and sweet, and colored pink close to the central cavity. It is very aromatic when ripe.

The **Ogen melon** is a hybrid. Its very juicy flesh is dark pink or pale green.

The **Galia melon** is another hybrid. Its pale green flesh is very aromatic.

The **Santa Claus melon** or "Christmas melon" has pale green flesh.

Santa Claus melon

Casaba melon

Galia melon

Juan Canary melon

BUYING

:: **Choose:** a heavy melon with no bruises, marks or parts that are soft or moist.

:: **Avoid:** a soft melon with an abnormal color and a strong smell.

If the spot where the melon was attached to the plant is very hard and unevenly colored, or a part of the green stem is still present, this is a sign of immaturity. When mature, this part of the melon becomes flexible and the part opposite the stem emits a delicate scent. Melons sound hollow when lightly tapped with the palm of the hand.

PREPARING

Cut the melon in half or in quarters. Remove the seeds from the central cavity, but leave those in the part of the melon that is not being eaten (which keeps it fresh). Serve the melon as is, chop the flesh into cubes or take out balls of flesh using a melon baller.

NUTRITIONAL INFORMATION

water	90%
protein	0.5-1 g
carbohydrates	8-9 g
calories	35
	per 3.5 oz/100 g

PALE OR WHITE-FLESHED MELON

EXCELLENT SOURCE: potassium.

GOOD SOURCE: vitamin C and folic acid.

PROPERTIES: refreshing, aperitive, diuretic and laxative.

Some people find melon difficult to digest.

SERVING IDEAS

Melon is often eaten plain, but is delicious flavored with ginger, lemon juice, lime juice or sherry. It is eaten with cereal and in fruit salads. Juiced or puréed melon is used to flavor sorbets and ice creams. Melon is cooked into jam, marmalade or chutney. It works well with ham, charcuterie (sausages and deli meats), prosciutto or any other dried meat, smoked fish and cheese. It accompanies meat, poultry or seafood. It adds an unusual note to salads of vegetables, rice or chicken. It can be dried, marinated and distilled.

STORING

Melon is very fragile and spoils quickly.
:: At room temperature: for ripening. Keep away from other fruits and vegetables.
:: In the fridge: ripe and covered. Take out of the fridge a little while before eating.
:: In the freezer: only the flesh; in slices, balls or cubes, sprinkled with sugar (1 cup/240 ml per 4 cups/1 l of fruit) and lemon juice, then sealed in an airtight container. The flesh softens when defrosted.

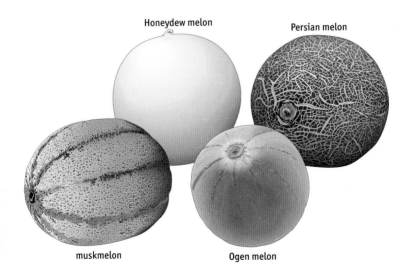

Honeydew melon

Persian melon

muskmelon

Ogen melon

watermelons

Watermelon

Citrullus lanatus, Cucurbitaceae

A variety of melon thought to be originally from Africa. Watermelon can be round, oblong or spherical. Its usually red flesh is sometimes white, yellow or pink. It contains smooth seeds that may be black, brown, white, green, yellow or red. Some varieties are seedless. Watermelon flesh breaks up more easily (because of a higher water content) than that of other melons, and is crunchier and more thirst-quenching.

watermelon

BUYING

:: **Choose:** a firm, heavy watermelon with a slightly waxy appearance, without being dull. A paler section on the rind or a muffled sound when lightly tapped are signs of maturity. Fresh, cut watermelon has firm, juicy flesh with a good red color, without white streaks.

:: **Avoid:** a cracked watermelon or that has soft sections.

SERVING IDEAS

Watermelon is eaten plain, in slices or quarters, cut into chunks or balls. It is used in fruit salads or cooked into jam after removing the seeds. Puréed watermelon is made into sorbet or a delicious juice that is the basis of a widely enjoyed Russian wine. Unripe watermelon is used in the same way as summer squash.

Watermelon seeds are edible. In some areas of Asia and China, they are eaten plain, roasted or salted, and sometimes milled for use in making bread.

Watermelon rind can be marinated or candied.

NUTRITIONAL INFORMATION

water	92%
protein	0.6 g
fat	0.4 g
carbohydrates	7 g
calories	31
	per 3.5 oz/100 g

CONTAINS: vitamin C and potassium.
PROPERTIES: depurative, diuretic and disintoxicating.

STORING

Watermelon is sensitive to cold and temperatures below 50°F (10°C).

:: **In the fridge:** cover cut watermelon with plastic wrap. Eat as soon as possible after purchase.

Nuts and seeds

Seeds are contained in the fruit of the plant and are used for its reproduction. "Nut" is the name given to various fruits with a hard casing (shell) that encloses a kernel. Nuts and seeds are quite popular, as they are nourishing and require a minimal amount of preparation. They are eaten whole, chopped or ground, plain or roasted, salted or unsalted, coated with chocolate, sugar or a variety of spices. They are also cooked in various ways or used for decoration. Nuts and seeds are often served salted and are high in fat and calories: eat in moderation.

TIPS FOR BUYING NUTS AND SEEDS

Nuts and seeds are sold in several forms: shelled or unshelled, whole, halved, finely sliced, slivered, chopped, ground, plain, roasted with or without their brown skin, salted, smoked, sugared, coated with sugar or chocolate, with butter, oil, or as a sweetened or unsweetened paste. Unshelled nuts are protected by their shell and keep for a longer period without turning sour. Choose shelled nuts sold in vacuum-packed or sealed containers for maximum freshness. Buy nuts and seeds from stores with a constant turnover of stock.

TIPS FOR USING NUTS AND SEEDS

Nuts and seeds are eaten as snacks or appetizers or to enhance meat dishes. Nuts that still have their skin have a stronger flavor than blanched nuts. Nuts and seeds are cooked as often with savory foods as sweet foods. Flavorful oils are extracted from nuts, which are also made into butter and flour.

TIPS FOR STORING NUTS AND SEEDS

Unshelled nuts keep frozen for about 1 year. Leave nuts that are shelled, cut, chopped or ground at room temperature if they are in airtight packaging.

Walnut

Juglans spp., Juglandaceae

The fruit of the walnut tree, a tree originally from the shores of the Caspian Sea and northern India. There are several species of walnut tree. The walnut is made up of a seed (kernel), called the "meat" when it is still green. This very bumpy seed is formed of two parts, about one-third of which is connected, the rest being separated by a membrane. White in color, the kernel has a strong flavor and is covered with a fine yellow skin that can be more or less dark in color. It is enclosed in a hard, bulging shell that can be woody, rounded or oblong in shape. This shell is encased in a smooth, green, clinging husk called the "shuck."

whole walnut

BUYING

UNSHELLED WALNUTS
:: Choose: nuts that seem relatively heavy and full, with intact shells.
:: Avoid: walnuts with split or pierced shells.

SHELLED WALNUTS
:: Choose: crisp nuts sold in vacuum-sealed glass jars or cans.
:: Avoid: soft, shrivelled or sour nuts.

NUTRITIONAL INFORMATION

water	3.6%
protein	7.2 g
fat	31 g
carbohydrates	9.2 g
fiber	2.4 g
calories	326
	per 1.8 oz/50 g

EXCELLENT SOURCE: copper, magnesium.
GOOD SOURCE: potassium, vitamin B_6, folic acid and thiamine.
CONTAINS: phosphorus, niacin, iron, riboflavin and pantothenic acid.
The walnut is a source of fiber.
PROPERTIES: dried walnut is said to be slightly laxative and an anthelmintic remedy.
Walnut leaves contain an antibiotic substance that acts as a bactericide.

shelled walnut

SERVING IDEAS

Walnuts are used whole, chopped or ground, plain or roasted. They are often eaten as an appetizer. They are used in desserts (cakes, brioches, muffins, pies, cookies, ice creams) and in sauces, sandwiches, and main dishes (omelettes, legumes, Asian and Middle Eastern dishes). Walnuts can be used as a condiment in stuffings, pâtés or pasta sauces. They are a good accompaniment to cheese.

Green walnuts can be preserved in vinegar or added to jams and marinades. An expensive and strongly flavored oil is extracted from walnuts, which is commonly used in salads. The shuck is used in the making of certain liqueurs.

STORING

:: **At room temperature:** 2-3 months, unshelled, in an airtight container, protected from heat and humidity.
:: **In the fridge:** shelled, 6 months.
:: **In the freezer:** shelled, 1 year.

whole walnut
covered in its shuck

Pecan

Carya spp., Juglandaceae

The fruit of the pecan tree, a large tree originally from the Mississippi Valley in the United States. The pecan is made up of a seed (kernel) formed of two lobes that resemble the walnut. These whitish seeds are covered in a thin dark-brown skin. They are enclosed in a brown, smooth, oval shell that is easy to crack, surrounded by a fleshy green-colored casing that breaks into four pieces when the fruit is ripe. The pecan varies in size and this is not an indication of quality. It has a slightly milder flavor than the walnut.

whole pecans

Pecan

shelled pecans

NUTRITIONAL INFORMATION

	dried	*roasted with oil*
water	4.8%	4%
protein	3.9 g	3.5 g
fat	33.8 g	35.6 g
carbohydrates	9.1 g	8.1 g
fiber	3.3 g	3.6 g
calories	345	357
		per 1.8 oz/50 g

BUYING

:: **Choose:** unshelled, relatively heavy pecans that seem full when shaken and whose shell has no cracks, spots or holes. Buy shelled pecans in vacuum-sealed glass jars or cans.

SERVING IDEAS

Pecans are eaten whole, ground or chopped, plain, salted, sugared or spiced. They are part of many dishes (pecan pie, cookies, ice creams, cakes and confectionery), and can be coated in chocolate. They are used in stuffings for game or poultry. A clear, mild-tasting oil is extracted from pecans that is equal in quality to olive oil; this expensive oil is mainly used in salads.

STORING

:: **At room temperature:** unshelled, 3 months.

:: **In the fridge:** 6 months, shelled, in an airtight container.

:: **In the freezer:** 1 year.

PLAIN PECAN

EXCELLENT SOURCE: thiamine, zinc, copper and magnesium.

GOOD SOURCE: potassium.

CONTAINS: phosphorus, pantothenic acid, niacin, folic acid, iron and vitamin B_6. Plain pecans are a source of fiber.

PECAN ROASTED WITH OIL

EXCELLENT SOURCE: zinc, copper and magnesium.

GOOD SOURCE: potassium.

CONTAINS: phosphorus, pantothenic acid, thiamine, folic acid, niacin, iron and vitamin B_6.

Pecans roasted with oil are a rich source of fiber. Pecans roasted with oil and dried pecans have substantially the same nutritional value. Their fats are made up of 87% unsaturated fatty acids (62% monounsaturated fatty acids and 25% polyunsaturated fatty acids) (see *Fats and oils*, p. 579).

Cashew

Anacardium occidentale, Anacardiaceae

The fruit of the cashew tree, a tree originally from Brazil. The cashew "apple" is soft and very juicy. Its fine, yellow and refreshing flesh is very high in vitamin C, much more so than the orange. Each apple produces a single nut.

The cashew nut is encased in two shells—a smooth, fine outer shell, which changes color as the fruit develops from olive green to red-brown, and an inner shell that is difficult to crack. Between the two shells is a resinous and highly caustic oil, called "cashew balm" or "urushiol."

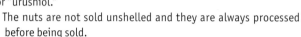

cashew nuts

The nuts are not sold unshelled and they are always processed before being sold.

cashew apple

BUYING

:: **Choose:** cashews in vacuum-sealed jars or cans for maximum freshness.

:: **Avoid:** very shrivelled nuts, with a sour smell.

STORING

Cashew nuts become rancid quickly.

:: **In the fridge:** in an airtight container, 6 months.

:: **In the freezer:** 1 year.

Cashews are difficult to keep, as they spoil quickly.

NUTRITIONAL INFORMATION

	dry-roasted
water	1.7%
protein	7.7 g
fat	23.2 g
carbohydrates	16.4 g
fiber	0.9 g
calories	287
	per 1.8 oz/50 g

EXCELLENT SOURCE: copper, magnesium and zinc.

GOOD SOURCE: potassium, phosphorus, iron and folic acid.

CONTAINS: niacin, pantothenic acid, thiamine, vitamin B$_6$ and riboflavin.

Dry-roasted cashew nuts are the least fatty nut. The fats are made up of 60% monounsaturated fatty acids and 16% polyunsaturated fatty acids (see *Fats and oils*, p. 581).

Cashew

SERVING IDEAS

Cashews are used whole, in pieces, chopped, roasted, dry-roasted, salted or unsalted. Ground cashews turn into a creamy butter that is used in the same way as peanut butter, but with a much milder flavor. They are eaten as appetizers, alone or with dried fruit, seeds and other nuts. They are used in salads, rice, pasta dishes, cakes, cookies, puddings and stir-fried dishes. In Indian cuisine, they are used in lamb curries, certain stews and rice.

They are used for cooking less often than other nuts, as they soften more easily; add them at time of serving.

The cashew apple is eaten raw or cooked and it has a sweet-and-sour flavor. It is mainly made into juice, which is mostly used to make alcoholic drinks (wines and liqueurs). It is made into jams or canned. In Brazil and the Caribbean, where cashew trees are cultivated, the apple is often preferred to the nut.

Kola nut

Cola spp., Sterculiaceae

The fruit of the kola tree, a tree probably originally from western tropical Africa. The kola nut is a capsule-shaped fruit composed of fleshy, irregularly shaped seeds. The seeds are pink, red or white when fresh, and become brown and hard once they are dried. Their bitter and astringent taste is why these seeds are called nuts.

kola nuts

NUTRITIONAL INFORMATION

CONTAINS: the stimulants caffeine (up to 2%), theobromine and kolanin.
PROPERTIES: diuretic and aphrodisiac. The effect of kola is less abrupt and longer-lasting than that of coffee.

SERVING IDEAS

Kola nuts are used for chewing by many indigenous populations in Africa. They ease hunger and thirst, eliminate fatigue and provide energy by stimulating the muscles and nerves. Elsewhere the nuts are used to make refreshing drinks called "colas." Coca-Cola™ is one of the most well-known of these drinks.

Coconut

Cocos nucifera, Palmaceae

The fruit of the coconut palm, a tree that belongs to the palm family and is probably originally from Southeast Asia and Melanesia. The edible parts of the coconut are the flesh, called "copra" (or coconut "meat") and the sweet and very refreshing liquid (coconut water) that is found in its cavity. Coconut water is not to be confused with coconut milk, which is obtained after crushing the pulp.

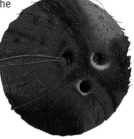

coconut

BUYING

:: **Choose:** an uncracked coconut that still contains some water (easily checked by shaking the nut), with "eyes" that are intact and firm, with no mold.
Coconut is sold whole, as a sweetened or unsweetened cream, roasted, as canned milk, dried, shredded or flaked. It is often sweetened, which makes it higher in calories.

coconut milk

STORING

:: **At room temperature:** unopened, 2-4 months. Dried, in a cool place, sheltered from drafts.
:: **In the fridge:** opened, 1 week. Cover the fresh pulp with water to prevent it from drying out.
:: **In the freezer:** 9 months, opened and the fresh pulp.

PREPARING

To open a coconut, first pierce the soft spots on top (the "eyes") using a pointed instrument. Collect the water that flows out in a container. Strike the nut one-third of the way along the nut from the eyes with a hammer or a heavy knife, slowly turning, to split the outer shell; keep tapping until the coconut breaks in two. Remove the white flesh.
The coconut can also be placed in a hot oven at 350°F (175°C) for 30 min after piercing the eyes and draining the liquid, which will make it burst and enable the flesh to be removed more easily.

Coconut

NUTRITIONAL INFORMATION

	raw	grated, sweetened dried pulp	grated, unsweetened dried pulp	coconut milk	coconut water
protein	1.7 g	1.7 g	3.5 g	4.6 g	1.8 g
fat	16.8 g	16.1 g	32.3 g	48.2 g	0.5 g
carbohydrates	7.6 g	23.8 g	12.2 g	6.3 g	9.4 g
fiber	4.5 g	2.7 g	2.6 g		
calories	176	250	330	535	46
			per 1.8 oz/50 g		per 1 cup/250 ml

FRESH COCONUT
GOOD SOURCE: potassium.
CONTAINS: copper, iron, magnesium, folic acid, zinc and phosphorus.
DRIED, UNSWEETENED COCONUT
GOOD SOURCE: potassium, copper and magnesium.
CONTAINS: iron, zinc, phosphorus, vitamin B_6 and pantothenic acid.
Dried unsweetened coconut is a source of fiber.
PROPERTIES: laxative and diuretic. Coconut water is said to be an anthelmintic remedy.

SERVING IDEAS

Coconut is a basic ingredient in Asian, African, Indian, Indonesian and South American cooking. The fresh or dried pulp is used, as well as the milk and cream.
The dried pulp is used to prepare many dishes, both sweet and savory (appetizers, soups, main dishes, desserts).
Coconut milk is used in an equally varied number of ways, comparable to cow's milk. It is used a great deal in Indian cuisine to make curries and sauces and for cooking rice. Coconut milk is used to make soups and marinades, to cook meat, poultry, seafood, stews, flans and puddings, as well as to make drinks.
Coconut cream is used for simmering meats and poultry.
Copra oil (see *Oil*, p. 587) is used as is or made into butter.

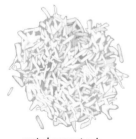

grated coconut pulp

Macadamia nut

Macadamia integrifolia, Proteaceae

The fruit of the macadamia tree, a tree originally from Australia. The macadamia nut is formed of a kernel enclosed in a thick and very hard shell. This shell is covered in a thin, green and fleshy envelope that needs to be removed to crack the shell. When mature, the nuts are crunchy and flavorful, and tolerate cooking better. Depending on the variety, the nuts can be more or less high in fat, tender, sweet and flavorful. Its coconut-like flavor relies to a great extent on its oil content. When the oil content is lower, the nuts become heavier, darker and less flavorful. The oilier nuts are generally plump, smooth and light-colored.

macadamia nuts

BUYING

:: **Choose:** plump, crunchy and light-colored nuts. Macadamia nuts sold in vacuum-sealed glass jars or cans keep fresh for a longer period.

Macadamia nuts are often sold shelled, raw or roasted, plain or salted, coated in chocolate, honey or carob. They are also available whole, halved, chopped, ground or powdered.

SERVING IDEAS

Macadamia nuts add an unusual crunchy note to dishes. They are used in curries, salads and stews, and with vegetables, rice, cookies, cakes, confectionery, chocolates, ice creams and other desserts. They can be used in place of Brazil nuts. Macadamia nuts are ground into a creamy butter that is used in the same way as peanut butter.

NUTRITIONAL INFORMATION

water	2.9%
protein	4.3 g
fat	37.3 g
carbohydrates	6.9 g
fiber	2.5 g
calories	355
	per 1.8 oz/50 g

GOOD SOURCE: magnesium and potassium.
CONTAINS: thiamine, zinc, iron, copper, phosphorus and niacin.
The fat in macadamia nuts is made up of 81% unsaturated fatty acids (see *Fats and oils*, p. 579).

PREPARING

Crack macadamia nuts using a nutcracker or a hammer.

STORING

:: **In the fridge:** 2 months, shelled, in an airtight container.
:: **At room temperature:** unshelled, 1 year.

Brazil nut

Bertholletia excelsa, Lecythidaceae

The fruit of a tree originally from Brazil and Paraguay. The Brazil nut is composed of a crunchy seed (kernel) whose flavor is reminiscent of coconut. This kernel is covered in a thin skin that clings to a rough, hard and fibrous shell. It has three irregular sides that give it a shape similar to an orange segment. Between 12-20 nuts are crowded together in a sort of capsule that looks somewhat like a coconut. Brazil nuts are shelled by manually operated machines.

Brazil nuts

BUYING

When buying shelled nuts, preferably choose nuts that are vacuum-sealed in glass jars or cans.

PREPARING

To shell Brazil nuts more easily, put them in a steam bath for a few minutes, or freeze them and crack them when slightly defrosted. Ideally they should be subjected to a minimum of treatments.

SERVING IDEAS

Brazil nuts are eaten whole, sliced, chopped or ground. They are served as appetizers and used in fruit cakes, cookies, salads, stuffings and ice creams. They are used in confectionery coated in chocolate. They can be used in place of coconut and macadamia nuts, and have a similar flavor and texture. A pale yellow oil is extracted from Brazil nuts, which is used in the manufacture of soap and for other industrial purposes.

NUTRITIONAL INFORMATION

	dried, unblanched
water	3.3%
protein	7.2 g
fat	33.1 g
carbohydrates	6.4 g
fiber	5.7 g
calories	328
	per 1.8 oz/50 g

EXCELLENT SOURCE: magnesium, copper, thiamine, phosphorus, potassium and zinc.
CONTAINS: niacin, iron, calcium and vitamin B_6.
The Brazil nut is a very rich source of fiber. After the macadamia nut, it is one of the nuts with the highest level of fat, which is made up of 71% unsaturated fatty acids (see *Fats and oils*, p. 579).

STORING

:: **At room temperature:** 2 months, unshelled, in a fresh and dry place.
:: **In the fridge:** shelled, in an airtight container.

Pine nut

Pinus spp., Coniferae

A seed produced by several species of pine tree, including the umbrella or "parasol pine." The pine nut is lodged between the scales of the pine cone. It has a soft texture and its delicate and sweet flavor can be more or less resinous depending on the variety. It is protected by a hard shell. The araucaria is a species that produces large seeds covered in a fine, slightly woody and red-tinted casing.

pine nuts

BUYING

:: **Choose:** pine nuts without any sour smell.

Pine nuts are almost always sold shelled. Buy them in stores with a constant turnover of stock as they become rancid quickly.

SERVING IDEAS

Pine nuts are eaten whole, ground or chopped, raw or roasted. They can be roasted in the oven (10 min at 350°F/175°C) or in a frying pan. They are used in salads, stuffings, sauces, puddings and cookies. They are a basic ingredient of the Italian pesto sauce. They decorate and flavor flans, cakes, pastries, meat and fish. They are made into a flour used in sweets. They occupy a privileged place in the cooking of the Middle East, India, south of France and the southern United States.

Araucaria nuts are mostly eaten cooked, most often boiled (30 min).

NUTRITIONAL INFORMATION

	dried
water	6.7%
protein	18 g
fat	38 g
carbohydrates	10.7 g
fiber	10.7 g
calories	505
	per 2.6 oz/75 g

EXCELLENT SOURCE: magnesium, iron, copper, potassium, phosphorus, zinc and niacin.
GOOD SOURCE: folic acid.
CONTAINS: riboflavin and vitamin B_6.
Pine nuts are a very rich source of fiber.
Their fats are made up of 80% unsaturated fatty acids (38% monounsaturated fatty acids and 42% polyunsaturated fatty acids) (see *Fats and oils*, p. 579).

STORING

:: **In the fridge:** 1 month, shelled, in an airtight container.
:: **In the freezer:** shelled or unshelled, 2-3 months.

Ginkgo nut

Ginkgo biloba, Ginkgoaceae

The fruit of the ginkgo tree, a tree originally from Asia. Rarely sold commercially, the ginkgo nut is practically unknown in the West. It is covered in a pulpy yellow-orange colored casing that is removed before being sold, as it quickly produces a sour smell after being picked and the juice it contains can cause itching. This casing encloses a smooth and very hard cream-colored oval shell that contains a green-yellow seed (kernel), the size of a small plum or olive. This kernel is covered in a brown skin; it has a mild, waxy flavor.

ginkgo nuts

BUYING

 :: Choose: nuts that are heavy for their size. Ginkgo nuts are mostly available canned, in water.

PREPARING

To peel ginkgo nuts easily, plunge them in just-simmering water for a few seconds.

SERVING IDEAS

Ginkgo nuts are usually roasted and eaten as is, or cooked. They are stir-fried, cooked with vegetables, fish, seafood, pork or poultry. They are used in soups. In Japanese cuisine, in which they are used a great deal, they are also eaten as a dessert fruit.

NUTRITIONAL INFORMATION

	dried
water	12.5%
protein	5.2 g
fat	1.1 g
carbohydrates	37 g
fiber	0.3 g
calories	174
	per 1.8 oz/50 g

EXCELLENT SOURCE: potassium and niacin.
GOOD SOURCE: thiamine.
CONTAINS: vitamin C, copper, phosphorus, magnesium, pantothenic acid, iron, riboflavin and vitamin A.

STORING

:: At room temperature: in an airtight container, protected from heat and humidity.

Chestnut

Castanea spp., Fagaceae

The fruit of the chestnut tree, a tree thought to be originally from the Mediterranean basin and Asia Minor. In cooking, chestnuts are sometimes called by their French name, *marron*, especially when candied (*marrons glacés*).

whole chestnuts

BUYING

:: **Choose:** heavy and firm chestnuts, with skin that is shiny and quite taut.
:: **Avoid:** soft chestnuts that are light in weight, whose skin is dull and wrinkled, which are no longer fresh.

SERVING IDEAS

Chestnuts are eaten boiled, quick-braised, braised or roasted. They are used in soups, stuffings and salads. They are canned whole, peeled, plain or in syrup, candied in sugar or glazed (*marrons glacés*), steeped in alcohol, cooked into jam or a sweetened or unsweetened purée. Chestnuts are ground into a flour that is used in cakes, flatbreads, crepes, waffles, porridge or bread. The purée flavors, among other things, ices, puddings, pastry creams, bavarois (custard cream dessert) and pies. In Europe, chestnuts are traditionally associated with game and poultry; in France and Italy, they are served as a vegetable side dish.

NUTRITIONAL INFORMATION

	fresh	boiled
water	52%	68.2%
protein	3 g	2 g
fat	1.2 g	1.4 g
carbohydrates	44.2 g	28 g
fiber	20 g	0.7 g
calories	211	243
		per 3.5 oz/100 g

FRESH CHESTNUT
GOOD SOURCE: vitamin C and potassium.
CONTAINS: folic acid, copper, vitamin B$_6$, magnesium and thiamine.
COOKED CHESTNUT
EXCELLENT SOURCE: potassium.
CONTAINS: vitamin C, copper, magnesium, folic acid, vitamin B$_6$, iron, thiamine and phosphorus.
PROPERTIES: antianemic, antiseptic and stomachic.

STORING

:: **At room temperature:** fresh with their skin, 1 week; dried, 2 months. Keep chestnuts in a cool and dry place.
:: **In the fridge:** peeled and cooked, a few days. Fresh chestnuts with their skin, 1 week in a loosely closed or perforated plastic bag.
:: **In the freezer:** 6 months, raw, cooked or dried, with or without their skin.

PREPARING

Remove the skin and the thin brown membrane covering the chestnut, as it is bitter. Chestnuts are easier to peel when they are cooked and still hot. Make a cross-shaped cut in the skin on the rounded side of the nut with the point of a knife before cooking to prevent them bursting.

The chestnuts can be cooked completely or partially. Make sure they are completely cooked later so that they are more digestible. There are three methods for peeling chestnuts:

• Use a small, well-sharpened knife to remove the skin and the membrane, so the chestnut can be used raw.

• Pierce a hole in each chestnut, then roast them until they burst. Cool, then peel.

• Boil the chestnuts in water after making a slice in the skin. Peel while still hot.

1 Make a cut in the skin of the chestnut with the point of a knife or a peeler.

2 Remove the skin and make sure the thin membrane covering the chestnut is also removed.

3 The raw chestnuts can be used according to the chosen recipe.

peeled chestnut

dried chestnuts

‹ chestnuts

Beechnut

Fagus spp., Fagaceae

The fruit of the common beech tree, a tree that grows in the forests of the temperate regions of the Northern Hemisphere. The beechnut has a flavor reminiscent of hazelnut. Two or three seeds are enclosed in a capsule that opens at maturity and reveals the beechnut.

beechnut

SERVING IDEAS

 Beechnuts can be eaten raw but they are better roasted. Very high in fat, an edible oil is extracted from beechnuts, which keeps for a long time and whose flavor and cooking qualities are similar to olive oil.

STORING

Place beechnuts in an airtight container, protected from heat and humidity.

NUTRITIONAL INFORMATION

water	7%
protein	6 g
fat	50 g
carbohydrates	34 g
fiber	4 g
calories	575
	per 3.5 oz/100 g

The fats in beechnuts are made up of 75% unsaturated fatty acids (see *Fats and oils*, p. 579).

Hazelnut

Corylus spp., Betulaceae

The fruit of the common hazel tree, a small tree probably originally from Asia Minor. Some varieties of hazel tree are called "filbert trees." The filbert is slightly larger than the hazelnut. Hazelnuts are round or oblong achenes covered in a leafy green casing that is removed before cracking the nut. The seed, covered in a brown skin, is found encased in a yellowish shell.

BUYING

:: **Choose:** hazelnuts in shells that are not split and have no holes. Buy shelled hazelnuts in vacuum-sealed glass jars or cans. Hazelnuts are sold shelled or unshelled, with or without their brown skin, whole or ground, plain, roasted or salted.

hazelnuts

NUTRITIONAL INFORMATION

water	5%
protein	6.6 g
fat	32 g
carbohydrates	8 g
fiber	3 g
calories	315
	per 1.8 oz/50 g

EXCELLENT SOURCE: magnesium and copper.
GOOD SOURCE: thiamine, potassium, vitamin B_6 and folic acid.
CONTAINS: phosphorus, zinc, iron, calcium and pantothenic acid.
Hazelnuts are a source of fiber. Its fats are made up of 88% unsaturated fatty acids (see *Fats and oils*, p. 579).

STORING

Hazelnuts do not spoil as quickly as pecans, Brazil nuts and macadamia nuts. Shelled hazelnuts are highly perishable and easily become bitter and shrivelled.
:: At room temperature: 1 month, unshelled, in a cool and dry place, protected from the sun.
:: In the fridge: shelled, 3-4 months.
:: In the freezer: 1 year.

SERVING IDEAS

Hazelnuts are used whole, ground or chopped. They are delicious fresh or dried, as an appetizer or snack. They are added to cereal, salads, sauces, muffins, puddings and ice creams. Finely ground hazelnuts are used in cakes and cookies. Finely crushed hazelnuts can be made into a butter to dress fish and crustaceans. They can accompany poultry and game. Hazelnuts are made into a paste or butter similar to almond paste and butter. They are used in nougat and paired with chocolate. The oil extracted from hazelnuts must not be heated. It is excellent in salads.

PREPARING

To roast hazelnuts, spread them on a cookie sheet and put them in the oven (300°F-350°F/150°C-175°C) until they are golden, moving them around occasionally. They are rubbed in a cloth while still hot to remove their brown skin covering.
Roasting, milling or chopping hazelnuts enhances their flavor.

sesame seeds

Sesame

Sesamum indicum, Pedaliaceae

An oil-producing plant originally from Indonesia and eastern Africa. The sesame plant is a bushy plant with attractive white or pink flowers that produce pods. These pods enclose several tiny flat seeds that are cream-white, yellow, red or black in color, depending on the variety. These seeds have a nutty taste and are covered in a thin edible husk.

Sesame

BUYING

 Sesame seeds are sold hulled or unhulled, raw or roasted.

SERVING IDEAS

 Sesame seeds are used as is, raw or toasted. They are often used to decorate breads and cakes. They are the basic ingredient of halvah, a Middle Eastern confection that also includes honey and almonds. Sesame seeds are milled into a flour, which contains no gluten, so it doesn't rise. It is combined with other flours or used by itself. Raw or roasted sesame seeds are ground and made into a thick paste (sesame butter) or liquid (tahini). Tahini is greatly appreciated in the Middle East and Asia, where it is used in particular to flavor sauces, main dishes and desserts. Lemon juice, salt and pepper and spices are often added to tahini to make a dressing that enhances the flavor of vegetables, salads and hors d'oeuvres. The oil extracted from sesame seeds is excellent for frying, and is used as a cooking fat, flavoring or condiment. In Lebanon, sesame oil is used to make the chickpea-based spread hummus.

STORING

 :: At room temperature: keep unhulled sesame seeds in an airtight container, protected from heat and humidity.
:: In the fridge: hulled.
:: In the freezer: 1 year.

NUTRITIONAL INFORMATION

	whole dried seed
water	4.7 %
protein	13.3 g
fat	37.3 g
carbohydrates	17.6 g
fiber	7.6 g
calories	290
	per 2.6 oz/75 g

DRIED SESAME SEEDS

EXCELLENT SOURCE: copper, magnesium, iron, calcium, zinc, phosphorus, thiamine, niacin, vitamin B_6, folic acid and potassium.

CONTAINS: riboflavin.

Dried sesame seeds are a very rich source of fiber. Their fats are made up of 82% unsaturated fatty acids (38% monounsaturated fatty acids and 44% polyunsaturated fatty acids) (see *Fats and oils*, p. 579).

PROPERTIES: laxative, emollient, antiarthritic and beneficial for the nervous system.

Sesame is used to assist blood circulation and digestion. The oil is an excellent massage oil. It is best to grind sesame seeds, as they are difficult to chew properly because of their tiny size and they will pass straight through the digestive system without being assimilated. Their nutrients are better absorbed when they are made into an oil, paste or butter.

Almond

Prunus amygdalus or *Prunus dulcis*, Rosaceae

The fruit of the almond tree, a tree probably originally from Asia and northern Africa and belonging to the same family as the peach tree. The almond is made up of an oval seed (kernel) nestled in a shell. This shell is enclosed in a fibrous and leathery green-colored casing (the shuck), which bursts open at maturity.

Almonds are divided into two groups. The **bitter almond** often contains various less toxic substances. An essential oil is extracted from the bitter almond, which is treated to eliminate the toxic elements and used as a flavoring agent (almond essence) as well as in the making of liqueurs. The **sweet almond** is usually eaten dried. It is edible fresh, when it is green and its shell is firm but still tender.

almonds

BUYING

:: **Choose:** unshelled almonds with intact shells and shelled almonds sold in vacuum-sealed glass jars, cans or sealed bags. Almonds are sold in various forms: shelled or unshelled, whole, in pieces, sliced or slivered, chopped, ground, plain, roasted, with their brown skin or blanched, salted, smoked, sugared, sugar-coated or chocolate coated, as a butter or oil, or as a sweetened or unsweetened paste.

COOKING

Almonds can be roasted whole, in pieces or sliced, blanched or unblanched.

:: **Dry-roasted in the oven:** heat the oven to 350°F (175°C). Arrange the almonds on a cookie sheet in a single layer. Cook them, moving them about from time to time until they are evenly roasted or golden. Remove the almonds from the oven and transfer them to another container to cool.

:: **Oil-roasted in the oven:** proceed as for dry-roasting, heating the oven to 300°F-350°F (150°C-175°C) and coating the almonds with a small amount of oil.

:: **Roasted in a pan on the stove-top:** dry-roast the almonds in a nonstick frying pan or with a small quantity of oil. Cook over a medium heat and stir the almonds continuously.

Almond

NUTRITIONAL INFORMATION

	dried and unblanched
water	4.4%
protein	9.9 g
fat	26 g
carbohydrates	10.2 g
fiber	3.4 g
calories	298
	per 1.8 oz/50 g

SWEET ALMOND
EXCELLENT SOURCE: magnesium
and potassium.
GOOD SOURCE: phosphorus, riboflavin, copper,
niacin and zinc.
CONTAINS: folic acid, iron, calcium
and thiamine.
Its fats are made up of 86% unsaturated fatty
acids (65% monounsaturated fatty acids and
21% polyunsaturated fatty acids) (see *Fats and
oils*, p. 579).
PROPERTIES: mineralizing. Almond milk is said
to be effective against intestinal and stomach
inflammations.
Almond oil is said to encourage the elimination
of gallstones and, used externally, the healing of
burns and split skin as well as soothing dry skin.

SERVING IDEAS

Almonds are used in cereal, salads,
cakes, cookies, pastries, ice cream
and sweets.
Whole, split or finely ground, almonds work
well with fish and chicken.
They can also be made into a paste (marzipan),
which is used for decorating cakes and making
candies, and in chocolate fillings. Almonds are
eaten as a snack or appetizer, by themselves or
with dried fruit, seeds and other nuts.
Ground almonds are made into a creamy butter
that is used as a spread or to flavor sauces,
soups and stews. This butter has a much milder
flavor than peanut butter.
Almond milk perfumes various dishes, and is
the main ingredient in *orgeat* syrup, a syrup
flavored with orange flowers that is diluted
with water to make a refreshing drink.
Dry-ground almonds are used in stuffings and
as an ingredient in desserts.
Various sweets are made from almonds, such as
dragées (sugared almonds), pralines, nougat
and filled chocolates.
An edible oil is extracted from sweet almonds;
this oil, which must not be heated, is mainly
used in salads, but also for pharmaceutical,
cosmetic and massage-therapeutic purposes.
Almond essence flavors numerous foods, such
as cakes, cookies, flans, pies, puddings and
drinks. It also flavors Amaretto, a delicious
Italian liqueur.

whole almond

PREPARING

To blanch almonds, plunge them in boiling water and let them soak 2-3 min, until their skin puffs up. Drain the almonds, run them under cold water to cool them, remove the skins by pinching the almond between thumb and forefinger, then dry or roast the almonds.

STORING

:: **At room temperature:** 1 year, shelled, in an airtight container protected from sunlight and humidity.
:: **In the fridge:** shelled, 6 months.
:: **In the freezer:** shelled or unshelled, 1 year.

shelled almond

Sunflower seed

Helianthus annuus, Compositae

The fruit of the sunflower, a plant originally from Mexico and Peru. This magnificent plant is crowned by a large yellow flower that tops a long, thick, hairy stem. The yellow flowers (*capitula*) contain thousands of flowers forming a flat disc surrounded by yellow petals. These flowers produce the sunflower seeds. These seeds have a mild flavor slightly reminiscent of Jerusalem artichoke.

sunflower seeds

BUYING

:: **Avoid:** yellowed seeds and raw hulled seeds.
Sunflower seeds are sold hulled or unhulled, raw, roasted, salted or unsalted. Buy sunflower seeds in stores with quick turnover of stock.

STORING

:: **At room temperature:** keep sunflower seeds in a cool and dry place.
:: **In the fridge:** hulled, ground, chopped or as a butter.
:: **In the freezer:** 1 year.

Sunflower seed

PREPARING

Sunflower seeds can be hulled in a seed mill or an electric blender.

:: **In a seed mill:** pass the seeds through the largest opening, most of the hulls should open. To get rid of the hulls, immerse the whole mixture in cold water; the hulls will float and can be removed easily. Drain the seeds quickly, then dry them.

:: **In a blender:** process a small amount of seeds at a time and activate the blender for a few seconds; then separate the seeds from the hulls using the flotation method outlined above.

SERVING IDEAS

Sunflower seeds are used plain or roasted, whole, chopped, ground or sprouted. They increase the nutritional value and fat content of dishes, making them higher in energy. Whole sunflower seeds are added to salads, stuffings, sauces, vegetables, cakes and yogurts. Ground sunflower seeds are combined with flour to make crepes, cookies and cakes.

The floral buds of the sunflower can be eaten like artichokes.

COOKING

The seeds can be roasted at home.

:: **Sautéed:** over medium heat, stirring constantly (not necessary to add oil).

:: **In the oven:** at 300°F-350°F (150°C-175°C), stirring them from time to time.

The seeds can be coated with a small amount of oil after cooking to make salt stick to the seeds.

NUTRITIONAL INFORMATION

	dried	roasted with oil
water	5.4%	2.6%
protein	17.1 g	16.1 g
fat	37.2 g	43.1 g
carbohydrates	14.1 g	11 g
fiber	9.9 g	5.1 g
calories	426	460
		per 2.6 oz/75 g

DRIED SUNFLOWER SEEDS

EXCELLENT SOURCE: thiamine, magnesium, folic acid, pantothenic acid, copper, phosphorus, potassium, zinc, iron, niacin and vitamin B_6.

CONTAINS: riboflavin and calcium.

Dried sunflower seeds are a very rich source of fiber.

OIL-ROASTED SUNFLOWER SEEDS

EXCELLENT SOURCE: folic acid, phosphorus, pantothenic acid, copper, zinc, magnesium, iron, vitamin B_6, niacin and potassium.

GOOD SOURCE: thiamine.

CONTAINS: riboflavin.

Oil-roasted sunflower seeds are a rich source of fiber.

Their fats are made up of 85% unsaturated fatty acids (19% monounsaturated fatty acids and 66% polyunsaturated fatty acids) (see *Fats and oils*, p. 579).

PROPERTIES: sunflower seeds are said to have a beneficial effect on blood pressure in hypertensive individuals. They are used as an expectorant and to relieve colds, coughs and asthma. They are also used to treat anemia and gastroduodenal ulcers, and to improve eyesight.

Pistachio

Pistacia vera, Anacardiaceae

pistachios

The fruit of the pistachio tree, a tree originally from Asia Minor. The pistachio is formed of a small, mildly flavored seed (kernel) covered in a brown skin. It is found within a shell whose side seam opens down its whole length when the fruit is ripe. This cream-colored shell becomes pink when dried, an effect reproduced by the food industry, which often dyes the shell pink.

BUYING

Pistachios are sold roasted, salted or in their shell. Buy shelled pistachios in vacuum-sealed glass jars or cans.

PREPARING

To remove the skin from the pistachios, blanch the pistachios 2-3 min, drain, then rub them while they are still lukewarm to remove the brown skin.

SERVING IDEAS

Pistachios are eaten whole, ground or chopped, salted or unsalted. Do not use red pistachios for cooking. They are used in salads, sauces, stuffings, terrines, pâtés, cereals, cakes, puddings, ice creams and pastries. They are also used in the making of confectionery and charcuterie (sausages and deli meats). Mediterranean and Asian cooking uses pistachios with meat, poultry and in several pastries. Puréed pistachios are used as a condiment for rice and vegetables in Indian cuisine.

STORING

 :: In the fridge: 3 months, in an airtight container.
:: In the freezer: in their shell, 1 year.

NUTRITIONAL INFORMATION

	dried	dry-roasted
water	4%	2.1%
protein	10.3 g	7.5 g
fat	24.2 g	26.4 g
carbohydrates	12.4 g	13.8 g
fiber	5.4 g	2.9 g
calories	278	285
		per 1.8 oz/50 g

DRIED PISTACHIO
EXCELLENT SOURCE: potassium, magnesium, thiamine and copper.
GOOD SOURCE: iron and phosphorus.
CONTAINS: folic acid, niacin, pantothenic acid, zinc, vitamin B$_6$, calcium, vitamin C and riboflavin.
Dried pistachio is a rich source of fiber.
DRY-ROASTED PISTACHIO
EXCELLENT SOURCE: potassium, copper and magnesium.
GOOD SOURCE: phosphorus and thiamine.
CONTAINS: folic acid, iron, niacin, pantothenic acid, riboflavin, zinc, vitamin B$_6$ and vitamin C.
Dry-roasted pistachio is a source of fiber.
Its fats are made up of 68% monounsaturated fatty acids and 15% polyunsaturated fatty acids (see *Fats and oils*, p. 579).

Introduction
Seaweeds

Seaweeds are plants (*algae*) that are generally aquatic, and grow in bodies of salt water or freshwater. They are sometimes called "sea vegetables." Japan is where the most seaweed is eaten per capita; it is also the biggest producer and exporter of seaweed, which explains why seaweeds are often known by their Japanese names (kombu, wakame, hijiki, arame, etc.).

Seaweeds have no leaves, stems or roots. Their size and shape vary depending on whether they grow in warm, temperate or cold waters. Warm-water seaweeds are grasses or bushy plants that rarely measure more than 1 ft (30 cm), whereas cold-water seaweeds often measure 3-33 ft (1-10 m), sometimes more, and are a lush form of vegetation.

The texture and flavor of seaweeds vary greatly; in particular, they can be rubbery, tender or crunchy. Of the 25,000 existing species of seaweeds, only a tiny fraction are pleasant to eat (40-50 species). These seaweeds are divided into four groups: brown seaweeds (Pheophyceae), green seaweeds (Chlorophyceae), red seaweeds (Rhodophyceae) and blue-green seaweeds.

• The **brown seaweeds** are the most abundant and most frequently used types of seaweeds. In Japan, arame, hijiki, kombu and wakame, in particular, are harvested. In North America, kelp is an especially harvested seaweed. Brown seaweeds grow at medium depths.

• The **green seaweeds** include the ulvas or sea lettuces and the caulerpas.

• The **red seaweeds** represent an important group of seaweeds from which galactose (a carbohydrate) is extracted to make agar-agar and carrageenan, substances that are particularly used in the food industry as gelling agents, emulsifiers and stabilizers.

• The **blue-green seaweeds** are primitive microscopic plants that are sometimes classified as bacteria. Spirulina, often taken as a dietary supplement, belongs to this group.

TIPS FOR PREPARING SEAWEEDS

Wash seaweeds before using them, as they often contain sand and small shells. Dried seaweeds are almost always soaked before eating or cooking (5-60 min or more). The soaking water can be saved for making stocks or sauces or for cooking pasta or grains.

TIPS FOR STORING SEAWEEDS

Most fresh seaweeds keep for a few days in the fridge. Dried seaweeds are placed in an airtight container (such as a glass jar) and kept in a cool, dry place away from light. Cooked seaweeds are kept in the fridge.

Most seaweeds can be frozen, except for kelp, which does not freeze well.

Seaweeds are low in fat and calories. They represent an important source of minerals (about 5%-20% of their dried weight), in particular calcium and iodine. They also contain a good quantity of several vitamins, including vitamin A (in the form of beta-carotene), certain B-complex vitamins (in particular, thiamine, riboflavin and niacin) and vitamin C.

Arame

Eisenia bicyclis, Pheophyceae

A thick seaweed that is cooked for several hours before being dried. A yellow-brown color when fresh, arame turns almost black when cooked. Its texture is slightly less crunchy than hijiki and it has a milder and sweeter taste. Young arame is more tender.

arame

SERVING IDEAS

Arame is used in soups (miso soup, in particular) and in salads, with vinegar, soy sauce and sugar. It is served with tofu and vegetables, or as a side vegetable.

NUTRITIONAL INFORMATION

	raw
protein	8.8 g
fat	0.1 g
carbohydrates	56 g
	per 3.5 oz/100 g

PREPARING

Wash arame twice in cold water, stirring it at the same time. Soak for 5 min to eat it raw. It can also be boiled (5-10 min) or sautéed for a few minutes.

Wakame

Undaria pinnatifida, Pheophyceae

A seaweed that grows at a depth of 20-40 ft (6-12 m). A thick, gelatinous ridge is located in the middle of the upper part of the seaweed. It has a delicate texture and flavor.

SERVING IDEAS

Wakame is edible raw after being soaked for 3-5 min. It is often cooked (a few minutes). It works well with rice, pasta dishes, vegetables, tofu, meat, poultry, fish and seafood. It is used in soups, salads and marinades. It can accompany legumes (and shorten their cooking times).

wakame

NUTRITIONAL INFORMATION

	dried
protein	13 g
fat	2.7 g
carbohydrates	46 g
	per 3.5 oz/100 g

EXCELLENT SOURCE: calcium.

Kombu

Laminaria spp., Pheophyceae

A large, popular seaweed measuring 3-10 ft (1-3 m). Kombu is rich in glutamic acid, an amino acid that, in contact with water, enhances flavors, improves the digestibility of foods and tenderizes their fibers.

PREPARING

Wash the kombu well. Use 1.5-1.75 oz (20-50 g) of dried kombu to make 4 cups (1 l) of stock. Let it soak for 30 min in a container containing 10%-20% more water than the amount needed to make the stock. Heat the water gently and remove the kombu before it comes to a boil.

SERVING IDEAS

Kombu is mainly used to make stocks. Do not boil it too much (10-15 min), or else the stock will have an unpleasant taste and become sticky. Keep the kombu after boiling to make other dishes or tea. It is found in various dishes, pickled, boiled, roasted or fried. Kombu works well with legumes (and shortens the cooking time).

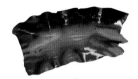

kombu

NUTRITIONAL INFORMATION

	dried
protein	6 g
fat	1 g
carbohydrates	56 g
	per 3.5 oz/100 g

EXCELLENT SOURCE: calcium, iron and potassium.
CONTAINS: iodine.
PROPERTIES: the Chinese use kombu to treat goiter.

Agar-agar

A transparent sticky substance obtained from certain species of red seaweed. Agar-agar can replace gelatin. Agar-agar makes foods firmer and more difficult to melt than gelatin.

agar-agar

BUYING

Agar-agar is bought as powder, flakes, bars or threads.

Agar-agar

PREPARING

Agar-agar is used in bar form or in small pieces. It absorbs water, softens and swells. Bring the liquid containing the agar-agar to a boil and melt it over a gentle heat. The quantity of agar-agar needed varies depending on the firmness desired and the product it is mixed with (the thicker or more acid the liquid, the larger the amount required). About 0.3 oz (10 g) of agar-agar is needed per 4 cups (1 l) of liquid. A jelly forms when cooled.

SERVING IDEAS

Agar-agar is used to make jellies using juice or purées. It is used in the food industry as a stabilizer.

NUTRITIONAL INFORMATION

	dried
protein	6 g
fat	0.3 g
carbohydrates	81 g
calories	306
	per 3.5 oz/100 g

EXCELLENT SOURCE: iron.
PROPERTIES: slightly laxative. The power of agar-agar as a gelling agent is 8-10 times greater than gelatin. It is much lower in calories than gelatin. It sometimes causes an allergic reaction.

Hijiki

Hizikia fusiforme, Pheophyceae

A seaweed that grows on rocks just below sea level. Hijiki is dried, then boiled or steamed, dried again, then soaked in arame juice and dried in the sun. It is slightly crunchy and has a stronger flavor than arame.

hijiki

SERVING IDEAS

Hijiki works well with root vegetables, grains, fish and crustaceans. It is eaten in soups, sandwiches, salads and crepes. It is used as a vegetable or an infusion.

PREPARING

Soak hijiki in lukewarm water (20-30 min) before eating raw or steaming, boiling or frying it.

NUTRITIONAL INFORMATION

	dried
protein	8 g
fat	0.1 g
carbohydrates	56 g
	per 3.5 oz/100 g

COOKING

:: **Steamed:** 20 min, then sauté or simmer.

Kelp

Macrocystis pyrifera, Pheophyceae

A seaweed that grows on the Pacific and Atlantic coasts of North America. Giant kelp, the largest of all seaweeds, can measure almost 200 ft (60 m) in height.

SERVING IDEAS

Dried, ground kelp compressed into capsules is used as a dietary supplement. Ground kelp is used as a condiment. Kelp fronds are high in alginic acid. The salt from this acid, alginate, is used by the food industry as a thickening, stabilizing and emulsifying agent.

NUTRITIONAL INFORMATION

	raw
protein	1.7 g
carbohydrates	10 g
fat	0.6 g
	per 3.5 oz/100 g

EXCELLENT SOURCE: iodine.

Sea lettuce

Ulva lactuca, Chlorophyceae

A tender seaweed with a flavor identical to lettuce.

sea lettuce

PREPARING

Rehydrate the sea lettuce in water for 3-4 min. Eat cooked (5 min), added to soups, or raw, in salads.

NUTRITIONAL INFORMATION

	raw
protein	17 g
fat	0.9 g
carbohydrates	37 g
calories	223
	per 3.5 oz/100 g

Dulse

Palmaria palmata, Rhodophyceae

A seaweed that grows in the cold waters along rocky coastlines. Dulse has a soft texture and strong flavor.

dulse

 Raw or cooked, dulse is used after soaking in the same way as other seaweeds, which it can replace in most recipes. It is delicious in soups and salads.

NUTRITIONAL INFORMATION

	dried
protein	20 g
fat	3 g
carbohydrates	44 g
	per 3.5 oz/100 g

EXCELLENT SOURCE: iron.

Irish moss

Chondrus crispus, Rhodophyceae

A seaweed that grows abundantly in the North Atlantic. Irish moss is a yellow-green, brown or purple seaweed. It is only edible after cooking. A viscous polysaccharide, called *carrageen*, is extracted from it (a gelling agent). It is used in the food industry as a stabilizer, thickener and gelling agent in the manufacture of ice creams, sorbets, cheeses, evaporated milk, instant soups, cakes, cookies and sweets.

Irish moss

SERVING IDEAS

Irish moss is added to soups and simmered dishes or used as a vegetable.

NUTRITIONAL INFORMATION

	raw
protein	1.5 g
fat	0.2 g
carbohydrates	12 g
	per 3.5 oz/100 g

Spirulina

Spirulina spp., Cyanophyceae

One of the most well-known blue-green seaweeds that grows in the fresh, alkaline waters of certain lakes, in particular in Mexico, Peru and Africa. Spirulina is considered to be a nutritional concentrate of great interest.

spirulina

BUYING

Spirulina is available in powder form, as flakes, tablets, capsules or gel capsules. It is best to buy it in a glass container or a laminated polyester sachet.

SERVING IDEAS

Spirulina is often dissolved in juice or water or mixed with yogurt or cereal. It is added to stocks, soups, sauces, rice and pasta, just before eating. Some dislike its flavor and color (it colors other foods green), and many prefer to take it in tablet form. The recommended starting dose of spirulina is 0.03 oz (1 g) (dry) over a week, then increase the daily dose by 0.03 oz (1 g) per week until one is taking 0.17-0.35 oz (5-10 g) per day.

NUTRITIONAL INFORMATION

	dried
protein	60 g
fat	6 g
carbohydrates	18 g
	per 3.5 oz/100 g

The nutritional value of spirulina varies according to the season, the growing environment, the harvest and drying process.

EXCELLENT SOURCE: chlorophyll, beta-carotene and other carotenoids (vitamin A precursors), iron (10 g provides 10 mg), thiamine, riboflavin, magnesium and protein (it contains a small amount of methionine, an essential amino acid).

The quality of these nutrients is inferior to those from animal-derived products but superior to those derived from grains and legumes, including soybean. Spirulina contains gamma-linolenic acid, a fatty acid found principally in breast milk. It is low in sodium (1-9 mg/g) and doesn't contain any iodine. Studies suggest that 95% of the vitamin B_{12} content of spirulina remains inactive in humans.

PROPERTIES: revitalizing. Spirulina is said to suppress or reduce the appetite.

Nori

Porphyra spp., Rodophyceae

A seaweed mostly known by its Japanese name, *nori*. Red or purple nori turns dark purple when dried, and green when cooked.

nori

NUTRITIONAL INFORMATION

	dried
protein	17 g
fat	0.8 g
carbohydrates	36 g
	per 3.5 oz/100 g

EXCELLENT SOURCE: vitamin A.

BUYING

:: **Choose:** dried nori that is shiny and crackly, green in color and translucent when exposed to the light.
Nori is sold in packets of dried sheets folded in two, in toasted sheets and in pieces.

SERVING IDEAS

Nori is eaten fresh, dried or rehydrated. Roasted nori has a sardine-like taste. Nori is used to make sushi. It is used in soups, salads, appetizers and breads. It is cooked with fish, tofu, vegetables, pasta dishes and rice. It is also used as a condiment and an infusion.

Glasswort

Salicornia sp., Chenopodiaceae

A wild plant that is technically not a seaweed. Glasswort is formed from green stems with no leaves.

glasswort

BUYING

:: **Choose:** firm and well-colored glasswort, without soft or damaged parts, whose center and base are neither hard nor fibrous.

PREPARING

Cut off the roots as well as the hard parts of the base if they are attached.

SERVING IDEAS

Glasswort is eaten raw, as a salad or cooked with butter. It accompanies fish, seafood and poultry. Glasswort preserved in vinegar is served as an hors d'oeuvre. If glasswort is added to a stew, salt can be omitted, as glasswort is salty.

COOKING

:: **Steamed** or **boiled:** a few minutes. Do not add salt.

Introduction
Mushrooms

A plant without roots, stems, leaves, flowers and chlorophyll. The absence of chlorophyll forces the mushroom to survive on already-made organic matter, which is why mushrooms are found attached to an extremely wide range of objects, such as wood, dirty glass, rusty metal, manure, humus or rotting fabric.

The mushroom family includes several genera (in particular the molds and the yeasts) and more than 50,000 species; some are hallucinogenic, 1%-2% are poisonous and several are used for their medicinal properties. Without being poisonous, several varieties can cause illness, stomach ache and vomiting. Therefore, it is important to know the exact type and edibility of any mushroom before consuming it.

TIPS FOR PREPARING MUSHROOMS

Only clean and prepare mushrooms when using. Some recipes suggest peeling the mushrooms, but this involves a loss of flavor and nutritional value. It is mainly recommended for aged mushrooms. The stem (or "foot") of the mushroom is usually edible. Some species have a tough and fibrous stem that needs to be removed. In other cases, simply cut off the base of the stem if it is dry or has traces of soil.

TIPS FOR STORING MUSHROOMS

Mushrooms are fragile. Handle them with care and refrigerate them as soon as possible. Place fresh mushrooms in a nonairtight container, as lack of ventilation encourages the mushrooms to rot as well as the emergence of the *C. botulinum* bacterium, which is naturally present in the soil and can cause a serious toxic condition (botulism). Mushrooms freeze easily; simply slice and wrap them carefully. Blanching, which toughens mushrooms, is unnecessary if the mushrooms are to be kept for less than 3 months. If they are being kept for a longer period, sprinkle them with lemon juice diluted in water, then blanch them for 2½ min before freezing. Use the mushrooms without defrosting. Mushrooms can be dried and kept up to 1 year.

TIPS FOR COOKING MUSHROOMS

Cook mushrooms in stainless steel, glass, cast iron or terra-cotta pots to avoid their browning. Only salt them at the end of cooking to prevent their losing their water. To extract the maximum amount of flavor from mushrooms, it is best to add them at the end of cooking to dishes that simmer for a long time. Omit mushrooms if possible from dishes that will be frozen and only add them when using the dish. Freezing affects their texture and reduces their aroma.

Cultivated mushroom

Agaricus bisporus, Agaricaceae

The **white mushroom** is the most widely cultivated and eaten mushroom. It is found in North and South America, Europe, Australia and New Zealand. A variety found less often is coffee-colored; it is sometimes called **coffee mushroom**. It has a little more flavor than white mushrooms. Among the common varieties of cultivated mushroom is the **portobello mushroom**; it has an impressive size, an exceptional flavor and a strong aroma that is reminiscent of wild mushrooms. It is delicious broiled or grilled and incorporated into sauced dishes.

cultivated mushrooms

BUYING

:: **Choose:** fresh mushrooms that are intact, firm and fleshy.

:: **Avoid:** mushrooms that are shrivelled, slimy or marked, or with split caps.

Cultivated mushrooms are sold fresh, canned or dried.

Sliced fresh mushrooms are often sold in the refrigerated section of food stores. They keep for 90 days. The flavor and nutritional value of these mushrooms is somewhere between fresh and canned mushrooms.

SERVING IDEAS

 Cultivated mushrooms are eaten raw (in hors d'oeuvres, salads and with dips) or cooked. They are traditionally paired with meat and work well with onions and rice. Mushrooms are used in soups, sauces, stuffings, stews, omelettes and quiches. They are excellent sautéed with butter, garlic and parsley.

NUTRITIONAL INFORMATION

	raw
water	91%
protein	3 g
fat	0.2 g
carbohydrates	0.3 g
calories	14
	per 3.5 oz/100 g

EXCELLENT SOURCE: potassium.
GOOD SOURCE: riboflavin.

COOKING

:: **Sautéed:** sauté over a high heat, stirring continuously (a few minutes). Remove from heat as soon as they start to produce liquid.

:: **Baked:** 12-15 min.

:: **Broiled** or **grilled.**

STORING

:: **In the fridge:** 1 week, in a paper bag or wrapped in a clean cloth.

:: **In the freezer.**

Cultivated mushrooms are also preserved or dried.

Cultivated mushroom

PREPARING

When using, wash mushrooms briefly under running water or in slightly vinegared water, using a soft brush if desired. Do not let them soak. Mushrooms can be brushed delicately or wiped with a cloth or damp paper towel.

The base of the stem must often be removed.

Mushrooms can be left whole, cut into pieces, sliced, diced, chopped or puréed. Sprinkle cut mushrooms with an acidic ingredient (lemon juice, vinegar, vinaigrette) to prevent them from discoloring if they are to be eaten fresh.

Enoki mushroom

Flammulina velutipes, Collybiaceae

An edible mushroom with a delicate flavor. The cultivated enoki mushroom is paler in color than the wild mushroom. Its white flesh is soft and resistant. It has a slightly fruity aroma.

enoki mushrooms

BUYING

:: **Choose:** white, firm and shiny enoki mushrooms.

:: **Avoid:** enoki mushrooms with a slimy or browned base.

Fresh enoki mushrooms are sold in bunches in plastic containers, especially in Asian grocery stores. They are also sold in jars or cans.

PREPARING

Cut off 1-2 in. (3-5 cm) of the base of the mushrooms, which is tough.

NUTRITIONAL INFORMATION

	raw
water	90%
protein	2.4 g
carbohydrates	7 g
calories	34
	per 3.5 oz/100 g

SERVING IDEAS

 Enoki mushrooms are delicious raw. They decorate and flavor salads and sandwiches. They are added to soups, pasta dishes, vegetables and stir-fried dishes at the end of cooking time.

STORING

:: **In the fridge:** 1 week, in their packaging.

Morel

Morchella spp., Discomycetes

An edible spring mushroom that is relatively rare. The morel is highly sought after for its savory flavor. Morel flesh, which is thin and fragile, is highly perfumed. The darker the cap color, the more they are valued.

morels

BUYING

The morel is usually sold dried or canned.

SERVING IDEAS

The morel should always be eaten cooked, as it irritates the stomach when raw. Delicious in a sauce, stuffed or partnered with cream, it accompanies meat, poultry, game and fish. Morel is added to soups and stews. It is cooked with rice, pasta dishes and eggs.

COOKING

:: Sautéed: sauté over a gentle heat in butter or oil (5-7 min).
:: Simmered: in a sauce, soup or stew (15-20 min).

STORING

:: In the fridge: fresh, 2-3 days.

NUTRITIONAL INFORMATION

water	90%
protein	2 g
carbohydrates	0.3 g
calories	9
	per 3.5 oz/100 g

EXCELLENT SOURCE: potassium.

PREPARING

Rinse the morel delicately and quickly under water several times. If necessary, clean the cavities with a small brush. Do not let them soak. Dry immediately.
Cover dried morels with lukewarm water, leave them to soak for 10 min, drain, renew the water and leave them to soak again for 10-15 min.

Pleurotus mushroom

Pleurotus spp., Agaricaceae

A mushroom of which most species are edible. The oyster mushroom is a species of pleurotus mushroom that is highly valued. Its white and tender flesh has a mild flavor and may have a strong aroma.

oyster mushrooms

Pleurotus mushroom

BUYING

 :: Choose: nonslimy and evenly colored pleurotus mushrooms, with a smooth cap and no black spots.

STORING

Pleurotus mushrooms are highly perishable and absorb the flavor of surrounding foods. Eat them immediately.
:: In the fridge: a few days, in a paper bag or in a dish covered with a cloth. Remove the cloth if the pleurotus mushrooms become humid or moisten them slightly if they become dry.

PREPARING

It is not usually necessary to wash pleurotus mushrooms.

SERVING IDEAS

 Pleurotus mushrooms are a pleasant substitute for cultivated mushrooms. They are added to soups and sauces, and work well with rice, pasta dishes, eggs, tofu, poultry and seafood. Do not mask their flavor by pairing them with strongly flavored foods or cooking them in a large amount of fat or oil. The firm, al dente flesh is tastier when the mushroom is young.

COOKING

 :: Sautéed or **broiled:** 3-5 min.
:: Quick-braised or **baked:** 10-15 min.
The mushroom stems require a longer cooking time and benefit from being chopped.

Wood ear mushroom

Auricularia auricula-judae, Auriculariales

An edible mushroom that grows on tree trunks (beech, elder, walnut). The wood ear mushroom has translucent flesh with a firm, gelatinous texture. It has little flavor.

wood ear mushroom

BUYING

The wood ear mushroom is sold fresh in Asian grocery stores or dried.

PREPARING

Wash in cold water. Remove any sticky parts. Cover dried wood ear mushrooms with lukewarm water and soak them for 10 min, drain, change the water, then soak them again for 10-15 min.

NUTRITIONAL INFORMATION

water	93%
protein	0.5 g
carbohydrates	7 g
calories	25
	per 3.5 oz/100 g

EXCELLENT SOURCE: iron, potassium and magnesium.
GOOD SOURCE: riboflavin.

SERVING IDEAS

Wood ear mushrooms are eaten raw, blanched (1 min) or cooked (fried or boiled). They give an unusual texture to soups, salads, vegetables, stews and pasta dishes. They absorb the cooking liquid and flavor of the foods they are combined with.

STORING

:: **In the fridge:** unwashed, 1 month. Use them preferably within 1 week.
:: **In the freezer:** as is.

COOKING

:: **Sautéed** or **broiled:** 3-5 min.
:: **Quick-braised** or **steamed:** 10-15 min.

Chanterelle

Cantharellus spp., Agaricaceae

Golden chanterelles

An edible mushroom that grows in coniferous or deciduous forests of temperate regions. Depending on the variety, the cap of the chanterelle mushroom can be yellow, orange, white, gray-brown or near-black and its underside is formed of irregular folds. Some species have soft flesh. The best species, such as the Golden chanterelle or "girolle mushroom," have a firm, fruity, yellow-white flesh. Cooking softens the peppery taste of its flesh.

BUYING

:: **Choose:** fresh chanterelles with spongy, firm and fleshy caps.
:: **Avoid:** translucent chanterelles; these are toxic.
Chanterelles are also sold dried or canned.

SERVING IDEAS

Chanterelles accompany meat and omelettes. They are delicious in soups and sauces, with pasta dishes, rice, buckwheat and millet.

NUTRITIONAL INFORMATION

water	92%
protein	2 g
fat	0.5 g
calories	10
	per 3.5 oz/100 g

EXCELLENT SOURCE: potassium and iron.

COOKING

:: **Sautéed** or **broiled:** 3-5 min.
:: **Quick-braised:** 15-20 min.
:: **Baked:** 10-15 min.

Chanterelle

PREPARING

Wash chanterelles quickly under running water. Drain them immediately, then dry. Cover dried chanterelles with lukewarm water and leave them to soak for about 1 hr.

STORING

:: **In the fridge:** fresh, 1 week.
:: **In the freezer:** 1 year.
Dried chanterelles keep in an airtight container in a cool and dry place.

Bolete

Boletus spp., Polyporeae

An edible mushroom also called "cep." Bolete mushrooms usually grow in coniferous or deciduous forests of temperate regions. The underside of their cap is covered with vertical tubes resembling pores. There are several species of bolete mushroom, including the porcini mushroom.

porcini mushrooms

BUYING

:: **Choose:** fresh and young bolete mushrooms.
Bolete mushrooms are often sold dried.

SERVING IDEAS

 Bolete mushrooms can be eaten raw, especially porcini mushrooms. They are better cooked. They can replace and are used in the same way as other mushrooms. Do not mask their flavor with strongly flavored foods. Bolete mushrooms are delicious braised or cooked in oil, complemented with shallots, garlic, parsley and white wine.

PREPARING

Bolete mushrooms are usually clean except for the base of the stem, which often must be removed (too ripe or containing worms) or brushed. Remove the pore surface underneath the cap if it is slimy.

NUTRITIONAL INFORMATION

water	89%
protein	3 g
fat	0.4 g
calories	14
	per 3.5 oz/100 g

EXCELLENT SOURCE: potassium.
GOOD SOURCE: riboflavin.

COOKING

:: **Sautéed** or **broiled:** 5-7 min.
:: **Quick-braised:** 20-30 min.
:: **Baked:** 15-20 min.

STORING

Eat bolete mushrooms as soon as possible after purchase.
:: **In the fridge:** a few days, in a paper bag or a dish covered with a clean cloth. Some species quickly turn blue if left cut or broken.

Shiitake

Lentinus edodes, Polyporaceae

An edible mushroom sometimes called a "Black Forest mushroom." Rounded or almost flat, the shiitake mushroom is topped with a cap measuring 2-8 in. (5-20 cm) in diameter. The stems are woodier than the stems of most other mushrooms. Its white flesh is slightly acidic but pleasant-tasting and it has a stronger smell when it is dried. In the West, it is often only sold in dried form.

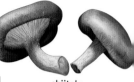

shiitake

SERVING IDEAS

The shiitake mushroom is used in the same way as other mushrooms, for which it can be a beneficial substitute. It absorbs the flavor of the dishes it is added to. It is delicious in soups, sauces, pasta dishes, rice, stews and stir-fried dishes.

PREPARING

Clean fresh shiitake mushrooms with a cloth or damp paper towel, or a soft brush. They can be washed briefly under running water. Do not let them soak. Dry them immediately.

Cover dried shiitake mushrooms with lukewarm water and leave them to soak (1 hr). This water can add flavor to stocks, soups and sauces. Dried shiitake mushrooms have a stronger flavor than fresh ones. Chop or finely slice the stems and cook them separately.

NUTRITIONAL INFORMATION

	dried
protein	9 g
fat	1 g
carbohydrates	75 g
calories	293
	per 3.5 oz/100 g

GOOD SOURCE: potassium.
PROPERTIES: treats hypertension, influenza, tumors, stomach ulcers, diabetes, anemia, obesity and gallstones.

COOKING

Cooking enhances the flavor of shiitake mushrooms.
:: **Sautéed** or **broiled:** brush with oil (5-7 min).
:: **Quick-braised** or **baked:** 15-20 min.

STORING

Shiitake mushrooms are a little less fragile than other mushrooms.
:: **In the fridge:** 1 week, unwashed, in a paper bag.

Truffle

Tuber spp., Tuberaceae

An edible underground mushroom. The truffle enjoys an esteemed reputation. There are several species of truffles, most of which are very expensive to purchase. The **black Perigord truffle** is the most sought after. Its near-black flesh marbled with white veins is very aromatic. The **white truffle** is known under various names ("white Piedmont truffle," "precious white truffle"). It is also highly valued, especially the white truffle that grows around Alba, in Italy. Its white or ochre-colored flesh veined with white has a garlicky and cheesy flavor. It is the largest of the edible truffles. The **black summer truffle** is less flavorful. Its light or beige-colored flesh is not very aromatic.

black Perigord truffles

BUYING

:: **Choose:** firm, fleshy truffles, without bruises.

Fresh truffles are usually sold in the areas from which they are harvested.

Truffles canned in water are also available in some stores.

SERVING IDEAS

Truffles are used raw, cooked, in the form of a concentrate, juice, *fumet* (reduced stock) or essence. They are a component of several dishes, such as pâtés, terrines and foie gras dishes. They can flavor salads, stuffings, sauces, pasta dishes, rice and eggs. Truffles are delicious raw or cooked alone. They are associated with game and poultry, especially the Christmas turkey. A few slivers are enough to flavor a whole dish.

COOKING

:: **Sautéed:** 2-3 min.
:: **Quick-braised:** 10-15 min.
:: **Braised:** 45-60 min.

NUTRITIONAL INFORMATION

	raw
water	76%
protein	6 g
fat	0.5 g
calories	25
	per 3.5 oz/100 g

EXCELLENT SOURCE: potassium.
GOOD SOURCE: iron.

PREPARING

Do not wash truffles—rub them gently with a soft brush. Cut them in slices, slivers, cubes or shavings.

STORING

Eat them as soon as possible.
:: **In the fridge:** fresh, 1 week. Place cut truffles in an airtight container and cover them with Madeira or white wine. Canned truffles that are cut and covered with Madeira or a little oil keep for 1 month.

Introduction
Cereals and grains

Cereals and grains belong to the Graminaceae family. Buckwheat, often considered to be a cereal grain, belongs to another family, the Polygonaceae family. The grain itself is formed of an outer casing, the bran, the endosperm and the germ.

The **outer casing** (husk) is the indigestible part that holds the grain. The grain must have its husk removed in order to be considered "hulled."

The **bran** (pericarp) covers the kernel. It is high in vitamins and minerals. It plays a role in regulating the gastrointestinal system by helping to prevent constipation.

The **endosperm** (kernel) is the largest part of the grain, mostly made up of starch. This complex carbohydrate is absorbed slowly by the digestive system and results in a feeling of fullness.

The **germ** (embryo) is located in the lower part of the grain. It is what would eventually be the source of a new plant. It is small, but it is the part of the grain that is highest in nutrients. It is very high in fats, which makes it perishable. Different cereals and grains are made up of various substances in varying proportions. This is especially true with gluten. This substance becomes sticky and elastic when in contact with liquid. It is gluten that makes dough rise, as it stretches under the pressure of the gases produced by fermenting the milled flour and activated by kneading.

TIPS FOR COOKING FOR CEREALS AND GRAINS

Cereals and grains are usually cooked in 2-3 times their volume of water, milk or stock. They are cooked directly over the heat, in a double-boiler or, less often, in the oven. A larger quantity of liquid results in a soft, pasty grain, while less liquid leaves the grain harder and drier. The final texture of a given grain will be different depending on whether it has been added to boiling liquid or cold liquid; boiling liquid results in a lighter and less pasty grain. Small grains cook quickly and form a sticky mass. To avoid this tendency to stick, first mix the grains with a small amount of cold liquid before adding them to the boiling liquid. Roasting grains for 4-5 min also prevents them from sticking together, improves their digestibility and gives them a slightly nutty taste. Avoid overroasting them, or they will taste bitter. Soaking whole grains for 12-24 hr will reduce the cooking time. Use the soaking water for cooking. Most whole cereals and grains remain slightly firm to the bite after cooking.

Cook cereals and grains in a heavy-based pot; slowly pour the grain into lightly salted liquid, stirring constantly. Let them boil 1-2 min, lower the heat, cover and simmer until the liquid is absorbed, stirring occasionally. It is also possible to finish cooking the grain in a double boiler once it starts to thicken, meaning less worry about stirring the mixture. If any liquid is left over, it can be used for cooking, as it will be high in nutrients. Cereals and grains increase 3-4 times in volume during cooking.

FOOD COMPLEMENTARITY THEORY

This theory states that vegetarians should include foods in their diet that complement or "complete" each other with respect to their amino acid content. Amino acids are the main components of the proteins that play a fundamental role in maintaining good health.

Proteins contain 20 amino acids, 8 of which are called essential amino acids because the human body cannot synthesize (produce) them. It therefore has to obtain them from food. Meat protein differs from plant protein, as it contains all of the 8 essential amino acids together in sufficient quantity and adequate proportions. Amino acids are not balanced as well in plants, which means that plant proteins are not effective by themselves and can only be partially used by the human body. Thus, when a plant protein is low in amino acid X, this amino acid is considered to be a limiting factor, as even though it is present, its low quantity reduces the overall effectiveness of the protein.

Animal proteins are described as complete and plant proteins as incomplete.

The knowledge we have today of the composition of foods enables us to compensate for the deficiencies in amino acids of one food using the high levels in another. For example, most legumes are deficient in methionine, cystine and tryptophan, but high in lysine. They thus complete and enrich cereals and grains, seeds and nuts, which are low in lysine. Cereals and grains, seeds and nuts themselves are high in methionine and tryptophan, and thus complete legumes. More concretely, to create a perfect pairing of plant proteins, one combines cereals and grains with legumes (bread and peanut butter) or legumes with nuts and seeds to obtain a complete protein. The same concept applies to the combination of cereals and grains with dairy products. These pairings are effective for all of the foods within the one family.

The complementary proteins can be paired with each other within the same meal and also within the same day. However, pregnant and breastfeeding women, children and growing adolescents should complement their proteins within the same meal, as should vegans (who eliminate all animal products from their diet, versus vegetarians, who usually eat dairy products and eggs). Vegans reduce their safety margin with respect to their nutritional balance, as they eliminate dairy products and eggs.

Wheat

Triticum spp., Gramineae

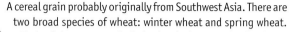

A cereal grain probably originally from Southwest Asia. There are two broad species of wheat: winter wheat and spring wheat. Each of these groups includes hard wheats and soft wheats (determined by the hardness of the grain). **Hard wheat**, used to make bread and pasta, has a higher protein content than "soft wheat," which is used to make cake and pastry flour.

The "**soft wheat**" species are the most widely cultivated throughout the world.

Spelt is a variety of wheat that can be used in the same way as rice once it is hulled (it cooks in 1 hr). Mixed with hard wheat, spelt is suitable for bread-making. Its nutritional value is similar to that of soft wheat.

grains of wheat

The wheat grain must be hulled, as its outer casing (the chaff) is indigestible for human beings. The hulled grain is made up of three main parts: the endosperm, the bran and the germ.

The **endosperm** (the kernel or albumen) is mainly made up of grains of starch. In the presence of water, most of the wheat proteins form a gummy, sticky mass: gluten. It is this gluten that is responsible for the size, appearance and texture of dough. Without gluten, dough cannot rise. The elasticity of gluten varies depending on the variety of flour. The more the dough is kneaded, the more the gluten develops, making the structure of the dough stronger.

spelt

Wheat gluten is used to make monosodium glutamate (MSG), a flavor enhancer.

The **bran** covers the endosperm; it is the outer casing made up of several fibrous layers. Wheat bran is mainly made up of insoluble fiber. It is high in fiber, protein, vitamins (especially niacin and the B-complex vitamins) and minerals. One of the properties of bran is that it can absorb up to three times its weight in water.

whole wheat flour

The **germ** is the embryo of the plant. It is the part that contains the most nutrients. It is very high in fats, and is therefore highly perishable. Its fats are made up to a large extent of linoleic acid (see *Fats and oils*, p. 579).

SERVING IDEAS

Wheat grains can be eaten whole, cracked, puffed, in flakes, as semolina (couscous) and as bulgur. The germ can be used to make an oil.

Wheat germ or bran are added to cereals. They are used in stuffings, pâtés, pastries, crepes, muffins and bread. Replacing ¼ cup (60 ml) of flour with ¼ cup (60 ml) of wheat germ for each cup (250 ml) of white flour improves its nutritional value. Wheat germ is sprinkled on vegetables, omelettes, legumes and yogurt; it can replace nuts in cakes and cookies.

Whole wheat grains can be cooked as is or added to soups, simmered dishes and legumes. Leave them to soak for 12 hr in lukewarm water before cooking them in just-simmering water for 60-90 min. Hard wheat needs 3-4 cups (750-1,000 ml) of liquid per cup (250 ml) of grains, and soft wheat, 3 cups (750 ml).

Whole wheat grains can be eaten raw, coarsely milled, after being soaked for 12 hr. They are added to mueslis, used in baked goods, salads and pilafs. They are used to make alcohol (whiskey) and starch. They can also be sprouted.

Cracked wheat is made from whole grains that are broken into several pieces; it is used in the same way as whole grains and should also be soaked. It cooks in 30-40 min and needs 2 cups (500 ml) of liquid per cup (250 ml) of grains. A little cracked wheat is sometimes added to bread dough. It can be used in the same way as rice, cooked into a cream dessert or eaten as a cereal.

Puffed wheat is made from the grain, which has had its outer casing removed, then heated and subjected to very high pressure. It is used in cereals and sweets.

Wheat flakes, cooked or raw, are also available. Soak them for several hours before cooking them for 1 hr in about 2 cups (450-500 ml) of liquid for 1 cup (250 ml) of flakes.

The term **semolina** refers to the product obtained from milling grains of wheat, rice, corn or other cereals and grains. It is made using the endosperm. Very fine semolina is used as a farina, in soups or as a dessert. Semolina is also made into **couscous**, a term that refers to the seed or national dish of Algeria, Morocco and Tunisia. Couscous can be cooked by itself and used in the same way as

semolina

rice or any other cereal grain. It can be served as a side dish, added to soups and salads, and prepared as a dessert. Since it has been precooked, it cooks quickly. Traditionally, couscous is steamed in a *couscoussière* (a special two-part cooking pot).

Bulgur is a whole grain of wheat from which the bran has been removed. It has a nutty taste. There are two ways of cooking bulgur: by rehydration or by cooking. If the bulgur is to be used in cold dishes or salads, soak it in a boiling liquid (2 cups/500 ml of liquid per cup/250 ml of grain) for 1 hr, then drain. If it is not soft enough, add a small amount of liquid and wait for it to be absorbed. If too much liquid is left over, drain. If it is to be served hot or used in stews and pilafs, simmer the bulgur for 30 min over low heat, using 2 cups (500 ml) of liquid for 1 cup (250 ml) of bulgur. Any surplus liquid that isn't absorbed can be used for cooking (soup, fricassee, sauce). Bulgur is eaten as a cereal or used in tabbouleh, a salad of Lebanese origin, which also includes parsley, tomatoes, mint, oil and lemon juice. In Turkey, it is used to make stuffed vine leaves.

Bulgur can be used in the same way as rice, which it can replace. It is used in soups, salads and stuffings. It can constitute a main dish, accompanied by legumes or meat.

Wheat germ oil is obtained from cold-pressing the germ or by using solvents. It is added to food as a vitamin supplement; it serves as an excellent source of vitamin E.

STORING

:: At room temperature: keep whole wheat in a cool and dry place.

:: In the fridge: bulgur, bran, semolina and wheat germ, if the wheat germ is not in a vacuum-sealed container.

:: In the freezer: the best mode of storing wheat germ. Use it without defrosting.

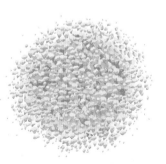

couscous

bulgur

grains of wheat >

Wheat

NUTRITIONAL INFORMATION

	raw wheat bran	raw wheat germ	hard durum wheat	cooked couscous	cooked bulgur
water	9.9%	11.1%	10.9%	72.6%	10%
protein	4.7 g	6.9 g	10.2 g	3.8 g	11.2 g
fat	1.3 g	2.9 g	1.9 g	0.2 g	1.5 g
carbohydrates	19.4 g	15.5 g	53.3 g	23.2 g	75.7 g
fiber	12.7 g	4.5 g	1.8 g	1.4 g	1.7 g
	per ½ cup/ 125 ml	per ¼ cup/ 60 ml	per ⅓ cup/ 100 ml	per 3.5 oz/ 100 g	per 3.5 oz/ 100 g

RAW WHEAT BRAN

EXCELLENT SOURCE: magnesium, potassium and phosphorus.
GOOD SOURCE: niacin, zinc, iron, vitamin B_6 and copper.
CONTAINS: thiamine, riboflavin, folic acid and pantothenic acid.
Raw wheat bran is a very rich source of fiber.

COOKED BULGUR

CONTAINS: magnesium, folic acid, niacin, iron, zinc, potassium, pantothenic acid, vitamin B_6 and thiamine.

RAW WHEAT GERM

EXCELLENT SOURCE: thiamine, zinc, folic acid, magnesium and niacin.
GOOD SOURCE: phosphorus, potassium and vitamin B_6.
CONTAINS: iron, copper, pantothenic acid and riboflavin.
Raw wheat germ is a rich source of fiber.
A limiting essential amino acid in the rest of the grain, lysine is present in high amounts in the germ.

COUSCOUS

CONTAINS: niacin, folic acid, pantothenic acid, potassium and thiamine.

DURUM WHEAT

EXCELLENT SOURCE: magnesium, phosphorus, zinc, niacin and potassium.
GOOD SOURCE: thiamine, copper, iron, vitamin B_6 and folic acid.
CONTAINS: pantothenic acid and riboflavin.
Its main essential amino acid deficiencies are in lysine, tryptophan and methionine. A varied diet can compensate for this deficiency (see *Food Complementarity Theory*, p. 277). The cross-fertilization of certain varieties has enabled a hybrid to be created that contains higher amounts of lysine and protein.
Wheat may cause food allergies in some people. The main symptoms can affect the following systems: gastrointestinal, skin, respiratory, circulatory and central nervous. These symptoms may indicate an allergy to gluten.

Seitan

A spongy food made from wheat protein (gluten). Gluten turns into seitan only after being cooked in soy sauce. It becomes very digestible, with a high nutritional value. The longer gluten is cooked, the firmer it becomes.

seitan

NUTRITIONAL INFORMATION

protein	18 g
calories	118
	per 3.5 oz/100 g

Since it is derived from a plant, fresh seitan does not contain any cholesterol, and is low in fat and carbohydrates. To provide a complete protein meal (as would a meat meal), seitan should be accompanied by legumes or dairy products.

BUYING

 Seitan is found in natural food stores and gourmet delicatessens.

SERVING IDEAS

 Seitan is used in the same way as meat. It is roasted, made into meat loaf, hamburger and kebabs. It is used in soups, stuffings, pies, stews, croque-monsieur (grilled sandwiches), lasagna and tacos. It is also stir-fried.

STORING

:: **In the fridge:** 1-2 weeks.
:: **In the freezer:** 2-6 months.

PREPARING

 TO MAKE SEITAN
Preferably use hard wheat flour.

:: **Kneading:**

1. Pour 4 cups (1 l) of water in a large bowl and add enough flour to obtain the consistency of a thick soup.
2. Stir vigorously using a wooden spatula and add the rest of the flour, for a total of 2 lb (1 kg) (8 cups/2 l) of hard whole wheat flour.
3. Form into a ball of dough; this quantity will give about 2½ cups (625 ml) of raw seitan, which will expand further when cooked.
4. Knead the dough (10-20 min), adding flour or water so that it can be worked well.
5. Rest the dough (30 min-8 hr), covering it with cold water; this step is not essential, but it will reduce the rinsing time.

Seitan

:: Rinsing:

1. Fill a large bowl with cold water; place a strainer in the bowl and place the dough inside of it.
2. Knead the dough gently until it thickens and becomes whitish.
3. Keep refreshing the water until it is clear.
4. The rinsing water can be used to thicken soups, sauces, quick-braised dishes and desserts. The water can be poured out slowly, keeping only the starch that accumulates at the bottom of the container, which can be used in the same way as cornstarch when it is dried.

:: Cooking:

1. Prepare a stock with 8 cups (2 l) of water, ½ cup (125 ml) of tamari sauce or more, according to taste, 1 piece of kombu seaweed 2¾ in. (7 cm) long and a pinch of salt.
2. Flavor the stock with vegetables, spices and fresh herbs according to taste (garlic, onion, ginger, thyme, bay leaf, etc.).
3. Cut the gluten into pieces the size of a potato.
4. Bring the water to a boil, add the seasonings and the gluten, cover the pot, lower the heat and let simmer.
5. Stir occasionally and add water if necessary. The cooking time varies according to the size of the pieces and the way they will be used: about 30 min for seitan that will be cooked again in a dish, and 1 hr for seitan that will be eaten in slices.

Buckwheat

Fagopyrum esculentum and *Fagopyrum tataricum*, Polygonaceae

Considered a cereal grain, buckwheat is in fact the fruit of a plant related to red currant and rhubarb. Buckwheat is originally from northern Europe and Asia. The buckwheat seed needs to be hulled before being edible.

STORING

:: **At room temperature:** keep roasted buckwheat groats (kasha) in an airtight container, in a cool and dry place. The whole grains keep for 1 year, the flour for several months.

:: **In the fridge:** place unrefined buckwheat flour in an airtight container.

roasted buckwheat (kasha)

buckwheat flour

NUTRITIONAL INFORMATION

	whole grain flour	cooked and roasted grains
water	11.2%	75.7%
protein	15.1 g	3.4 g
fat	3.7 g	0.6 g
carbohydrates	84.7 g	19.9 g
	per 1 cup/ 250 ml	per 3.5 oz/ 100 g

SERVING IDEAS

Whole or cracked roasted buckwheat, called "kasha," can be used in the same way as rice or potatoes. It is used in particular as a side dish or added to soups, stews and muffins. Unroasted buckwheat has a delicate flavor, making it suitable for using with fish or desserts. It can be eaten as a cereal. It is also cooked as a porridge or combined with other cereals and grains to vary their flavor. Buckwheat flour has no gluten and doesn't rise when cooked; wheat flour must be mixed with it if it is to be made into bread, cakes or other foods that rise. Buckwheat flour is used to make noodles, flatbreads, polentas, cakes and cookies. It is also used to make blinis (small Russian crepes that are served with caviar) and the Japanese noodles called "soba."

WHOLE GRAIN BUCKWHEAT FLOUR
EXCELLENT SOURCE: magnesium, potassium, zinc, vitamin B_6, thiamine, phosphorus, iron, niacin, copper and folic acid.
CONTAINS: riboflavin, pantothenic acid and calcium.
COOKED AND ROASTED BUCKWHEAT GRAINS
GOOD SOURCE: magnesium.
CONTAINS: potassium, copper, zinc, phosphorus, folic acid, iron and pantothenic acid.
PROPERTIES: buckwheat contains rutin (1%-6%), which is used in the treatment of certain kinds of hemorrhages and chilblains. It is considered to be digestible, nourishing and energy-giving.

COOKING

Add the buckwheat to a boiling liquid (2 parts liquid to 1 part buckwheat) and boil 30 min (whole) or 15-20 min (cracked grains). It needs less liquid if it has been sautéed beforehand in fat or oil. Buckwheat can easily become a bland mush if it isn't cooked well. To avoid this, mix it with a beaten egg and cook in a frying pan until golden before cooking in water. Buckwheat and white rice can also be cooked together.

CEREALS AND GRAINS

285

Oats

Avena sativa, Gramineae

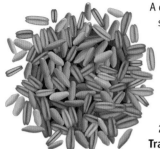

oats

A cereal grain probably originally from Asia. There are several varieties of oats, divided into winter oats and summer oats. Depending on the variety, the grains can be white, gray-yellow, red or black, and covered in numerous hairs.

Irish oats are made from hulled and roasted grains, passed between steel blades, then cut into thin slices. The finer they are cut, the more quickly they cook. Add 2-3 parts water to 1 part oats.

Traditional rolled oats are made from hulled grains that are steamed and rolled into flat flakes. For cooking, 2-3 parts water are used to 1 part oats and they are cooked for 10-25 min.

Quick-cooking rolled oats are simply traditional rolled oats cut into smaller pieces to reduce the cooking time. The nutritional value of quick-cooking oats is the same as traditional rolled oats, but they have less flavor. The quicker cooking process takes 3-5 min for 2½ parts liquid to 1 part oats.

Instant porridge oats are made from grains that are partly boiled, dried, then rolled very thinly. The porridge is ready to eat with the addition of boiling water. The nutritional value of this product is similar to quick-cooking oats. Several instant porridge products are flavored and sold as breakfast cereals. The porridge almost always contains added salt and sugar, and often contains food additives.

Oat bran is found in the outer layers of the grain beneath the inedible husk. It is sold as a separate product, but it can also be present in rolled oats and Irish oats. It can be cooked like porridge or added to other foods in the same way as wheat germ.

Oat flour contains no gluten and does not rise when cooked. It must be combined with wheat flour in order to make bread and other foods that rise.

NUTRITIONAL INFORMATION

	uncooked oat bran	dry porridge
water		8.9%
protein	5.4 g	4.3 g
fat	2.2 g	1.7 g
carbohydrates	20.5 g	18.1 g
fiber	4.9 g	2.8 g
calories	76	104
		per 1 oz/30 g

Oats retain almost all of their nutrients after being hulled, as the bran and the germ cling to the kernel. They are very nourishing. They contain proteins of good nutritional value.

PORRIDGE

GOOD SOURCE: magnesium and thiamine.
CONTAINS: phosphorus, potassium, iron, pantothenic acid and copper.
Porridge is a source of fiber.

UNCOOKED OAT BRAN

EXCELLENT SOURCE: magnesium, thiamine and phosphorus.
GOOD SOURCE: potassium.
CONTAINS: iron, zinc, folic acid, pantothenic acid and copper.
PROPERTIES: diuretic. The soluble fiber content of oats helps lower cholesterol levels. Its auxin (a growth hormone) content is said to make it beneficial for children.

SERVING IDEAS

Porridge is probably the most well-known use of oats. Oats are also used in granolas, mueslis, muffins, cookies, flatbreads, crepes and bread; in this case, it must be mixed with wheat flour in the proportions of about 4 cups (1 l) for 1 cup (250 ml) of oats. Oats are used to thicken soups, meat loaves, pâtés and puddings and to make date squares, fruit crumbles, cakes, jellies, beers and drinks.

CEREALS AND GRAINS

rolled oats

Barley

Hordeum vulgare, Gramineae

A plant probably originally from the mountainous regions of Ethiopia and Southeast Asia. Barley is not used very much for human consumption in western countries. In Asia, northern Africa and the Middle East, it is used as a flour or as grains to make porridge. In industrialized countries, barley is mainly used as cattle feed, in bread making, brewing (beer) and distilling (whiskey). The barley grain is oval-shaped and a milky-white color; it can also be black or purple. It must have its outer husk removed to be edible.

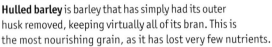

barley

Hulled barley is barley that has simply had its outer husk removed, keeping virtually all of its bran. This is the most nourishing grain, as it has lost very few nutrients.

Scotch or **pot barley** has undergone three processes of polishing by abrasion. The grain loses various nutrients, especially vitamins and minerals, as well as virtually all of its bran.

Pearl barley has been subjected to five or six abrasions and then standardized. The grain loses its germ as well as a certain amount of vitamins, minerals, fiber, fat and protein.

Barley flakes are produced and used in the same way as rolled oats.

Barley flour can be more or less refined. Whole grain barley flour has a nutty flavor. It is darker than whole-grain wheat flour.

Some varieties of barley are the primary material for making **malt**, which is mostly used to make beer and whiskey. To obtain malt, the barley grains are sprouted, dried, roasted, then ground. The longer the malt is roasted, the darker the resulting beer will be.

SERVING IDEAS

Barley is often added to soups and stews. It is used in the same way as other cereals and grains. It is cooked as is or at the same time as rice (in the case of pearl barley) or is added to pâtés, croquettes, puddings and desserts. The slightly rubbery texture of barley adds an unusual touch to mixed salads. Barley can be used in the manufacture of miso (p. 459).

Barley flour thickens soups and sauces; it adds a slightly sweet taste to foods. It is used in particular in cookies, bread, crepes and cakes. It contains no gluten, so it must be combined with wheat flour in order for it to rise.

When roasted and ground, barley provides the malt that is used as a coffee substitute and is also used to enrich certain foods. It is made into malt syrup, which flavors milkshakes and some industrially made cakes. Malted barley cereals are also available.

COOKING

Hulled barley cooks in about 1 hr over a low heat; use 3-4 cups (750 ml-1 l) of liquid for 1 cup (250 ml) of grains. It is best to soak barley for several hours before cooking (use the same liquid to cook the barley), in the case of hulled barley and Scotch barley only. If desired, drain the barley, then roast it before cooking. Pearl barley requires about 30 min cooking time and does not need to be soaked.

NUTRITIONAL INFORMATION

	cooked pearl barley
water	68.8%
protein	2.3 g
fat	0.4 g
carbohydrates	28.2 g
fiber	6.5 g
	per 3.5 oz/100 g

COOKED PEARL BARLEY

CONTAINS: niacin, iron, zinc, magnesium, potassium, folic acid, vitamin B_6, thiamine, copper and phosphorus.

Barley is an excellent source of soluble fiber, and more generally a rich source of fiber.

PROPERTIES: fortifying, emollient, regenerating, beneficial for the respiratory system and antidiarrheal. Barley tea has been used for a very long time to relieve coughs.

CEREALS AND GRAINS

Millet

Panicum miliaceum and *Setaria italica*, Gramineae

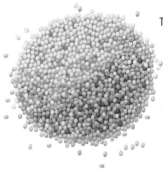

millet

The name given to several species of cereal grain. Millet is thought to be originally from eastern or central Asia. Most species have panicles rather than ears like most other cereals and grains. Millet grains are small and round. They can be gray, straw-yellow, red, white or reddish-brown. The grains are hulled, then left as is, made into flakes or ground. The main varieties of cultivated millet vary widely from a botanical point of view. The **common millet** (*Panicum miliaceum*) is mainly cultivated for human and animal consumption. The **foxtail millet** (*Setaria italica*) is the most well-known variety. It is mostly cultivated for animal pastures. In Russia, it is used to make beer, whereas in England, it is used as birdseed. The **pearl millet** is mainly cultivated in India.

Sorghum is the most eaten cereal grain in the world after wheat, rice, corn and barley.

Teff is used as much for its annual hay, used for animals, as for its grains, which are used for human consumption.

Sorghum and teff are sometimes called millets.

COOKING

Let millet simmer for 30-40 min in 2 parts liquid to 1 part grains. Soak before cooking or toast the millet in a dry pan or with a small amount of oil to slightly alter its flavor.

:: **Toasted:** to give millet a delicious nutty taste.

:: **Roasted:** on low to medium heat, moving the grains about continuously to prevent them from burning, until they become golden, then add the cooking liquid.

To cook teff grains into a porridge, add 3 parts water or milk to 1 part teff and cook for about 15 min.

‹ millet grains

Millet

SERVING IDEAS

Millet can be used in place of most cereals and grains, though its strong flavor is not always appreciated. It is added to, among other things, soups, omelettes, croquettes, pies, puddings and muesli.

Millet does not contain any gluten, so bread made with millet does not rise. Millet is cooked as a porridge or it is made into an alcoholic drink, like beer. It can also be sprouted in the same way as alfalfa. Ground, sprouted millet is used to enrich foods; it is added in particular to breads, pies, muffins and cookies.

Sorghum flour cannot be used for making bread, as it contains no gluten. It is nevertheless used to make bread by being mixed with wheat flour or by itself to make flatbreads. Sorghum is eaten whole or as a semolina and it is used in the same way as rice or millet. It is cooked into a porridge or made into a flatbread. It is also used in cakes.

Teff is used as a whole grain or ground. The slightly grainy flour does not rise, but it produces delicious flatbreads or dessert breads. In Africa, a flatbread called *injara* is made from teff. A fortified food product, *faffa*, is also made based on teff mixed with chickpeas, skim milk, sugar and salt.

STORING

:: **At room temperature:** keep millet and sorghum grains several months in an airtight container in a cool, dry and dark place.

NUTRITIONAL INFORMATION

	cooked
water	71.4%
protein	3.5 g
fat	1.0 g
carbohydrates	23.7 g
calories	119
	per 3.5 oz/100 g

MILLET
GOOD SOURCE: magnesium.

CONTAINS: zinc, phosphorus, niacin, folic acid, thiamine, copper, vitamin B_6, potassium, riboflavin and iron.

The quality of the proteins in millet is generally superior to the protein in wheat, rice and corn. It is one of the rare alkalinizing cereal grains; it is very easy to digest and not very allergenic.

PROPERTIES: slightly laxative. Its high silica content is said to have a positive effect on blood cholesterol levels and on bones.

Millet is said to prevent the formation of gallstones, stomach ulcers and colitis. It is said to be beneficial for the bladder, kidneys and gastrointestinal system.

SORGHUM
CONTAINS: iron, potassium, phosphorus, niacin and thiamine.

The nutritional value of sorghum is similar to corn, but it contains more protein, less fat and more starch.

Rice

Oryza sativa, Gramineae

A plant originally from Southeast Asia, with branching stems ending in a panicle formed of flowers or "spikelets," from which the grains are formed.
Most varieties grow in flooded fields. The different varieties are categorized based on the length of the grains ("wild rice" is from a different species; see p. 298).

basmati rice

Short-grain rice is almost as wide as it is long. Because of its high starch content, the grains cling together when cooked.

Medium-grain rice is shorter and plumper than long-grain rice; it stays firm and light. The grains will stick together when cooled.

Long-grain rice is light and nonsticky; it can become sticky if overcooked or stirred frequently.

In order to be edible, the hard casing, or husk, that covers the rice grain must be removed. The process used for this determines its flavor, nutritional value and keeping properties. Rice is sold in several forms.

Brown rice is a whole grain of rice with its outer husk removed. It often contains green (immature) grains. It is the most complete rice. Its nutlike flavor is stronger than white rice.

Quick-cooking brown rice is brown rice that has been treated in the same way as instant white rice. The cooking time is reduced to 5 min plus 5 min resting time, instead of 45 min for brown rice.

Parboiled brown rice (ready in 25 min) is treated to reduce its cooking time, using the same process as for parboiled white rice. The parboiling improves its keeping properties. In contrast to parboiled white rice, parboiled brown rice retains the bran and the germ.

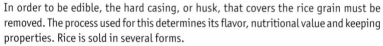

white rice

Rice

White rice is hulled and polished. It has lost a large portion of its nutrients.

Quick-cooking or "precooked white rice" is a white rice that has been cooked, then dried to reduce cooking time. It has a dry and light appearance when cooked. It does not have much taste, has less nutritional value and is more expensive than white rice.

Parboiled white rice has undergone a steam treatment before being hulled in order to keep its nutrients. Parboiled rice becomes white when cooked, keeps its appearance and doesn't stick together. It is lighter and has a more delicate flavor than brown rice. Even if it does not contain as much fiber, it is the most nourishing rice after brown rice. It has the same yield after cooking as the same quantity of brown rice.

arborio rice

Arborio rice, considered to be one of the finest rices, is a high-starch short grain rice. It is essential for making the Italian rice dish *risotto*.

Perfumed rices are much tastier than other varieties. **Basmati rice** is one of the most well known and highly valued; essential in Indian cuisine, it has a light, dry and perfumed texture and flavor. **Jasmine rice** is also highly regarded.

Flavored rices are almost always precooked or parboiled rices, highly seasoned and salted and containing additives.

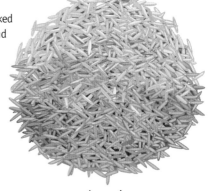

brown rice

NUTRITIONAL INFORMATION

	cooked long-grain brown rice	*cooked parboiled long-grain white rice*	*cooked long-grain white rice*	*precooked long-grain white rice*
water	73%	72.5%	68.7%	76.4%
protein	2.6 g	2.3 g	2.7 g	2.1 g
fat	0.9 g	0.3 g	0.3 g	0.2 g
carbohydrates	23.0 g	24.7 g	27 g	21.3 g
fiber	1.7 g	0.5 g	0.4 g	0.8 g
calories	112	114	129	98

per 3.5 oz/100 g

CEREALS AND GRAINS

RICE
GOOD SOURCE: magnesium.
CONTAINS: niacin, vitamin B$_6$, thiamine, phosphorus, zinc and copper.
TRACES: pantothenic acid, potassium and thiamine (except brown rice).

COOKED PARBOILED LONG-GRAIN WHITE RICE
CONTAINS: niacin, magnesium, copper and pantothenic acid.
TRACES: phosphorus, zinc and potassium.

COOKED LONG-GRAIN WHITE RICE
CONTAINS: pantothenic acid, vitamin B$_6$, magnesium and zinc.
TRACES: phosphorus, niacin and potassium.
Rice is one of the cereal grains lowest in protein. As for all cereals, the proteins are incomplete, lysine being the limiting factor (see *Food Complementarity Theory*, p. 277). Its starch has the property of swelling during cooking and being very digestible.
PROPERTIES: astringent. Rice is said to be effective against diarrhea (especially its cooking water) and hypertension.

rice flour

STORING

:: **At room temperature:** 1 year, in an unopened packet, away from heat and humidity.
:: **In the fridge:** a few days, cooked, in a closed container. Keep brown rice in an airtight container (to prevent it from spoiling).
:: **In the freezer:** cooked, 6-8 months.

Rice

flavored rice

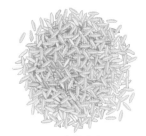

parboiled rice

COOKING

:: Boiled: rice is cooked in water, stock, juice or milk (especially to make desserts). Several methods can be used:

1. Measure out 1 part rice to 2 parts liquid. The rice can be cooked in two ways: place both rice and liquid in a pot and bring to a boil, lower the heat, cover and cook gently; or bring the water to a boil before adding the rice. Cook until the liquid is completely absorbed.

2. Put the rice in a pot, cover with a large quantity of water and bring to a boil; lower the heat, cook uncovered and drain when the rice is done. If desired, dry the rice in the oven (300°F/150°C) for 7-15 min.

3. Soak brown rice for 1 hr (for a nonsticking rice). Cook in its soaking water for 35 min, turn off the heat and leave the pot covered for 10 min, or cook for 45 min.

4. The absorption or "Indian" method produces a light and nonsticky rice. Put the rice in a pot and cover with cold water until the water level is ½ in. (1 cm) above the rice. Bring to a boil covered over high heat and then cook over medium heat without stirring, until small holes appear in the rice. Reduce the heat and let simmer, covered, for 15 min. Be careful not to overcook the rice, as it will stick to the base of the pot.

Do not stir the rice (or stir once) after the small holes appear, if a nonsticky steamed rice is desired.

5. Basmati rice cooks in 1⅓ cups (300 ml) of liquid (water or milk) for 1 cup (250 ml) of grains if it has been soaked, a little more if not soaked. Soak the rice for 30 min in 2 cups (500 ml) of water, drain and let rest for 10 min. Put the rice in the pot, add the liquid and cook, covered, for 20 min over very low heat. Turn off the heat and let rest for 10 min.

The cooking times below are only approximate: brown rice, 40-45 min; parboiled rice, 25 min; white rice, 15 min; instant rice, 5 min.

When cooking rice in a pot:

- Reduce the quantity of water and be careful not to overcook the rice if firmer rice is preferred, or slightly increase the quantity of liquid to obtain a softer rice.

- If the rice is not served immediately, reduce the cooking time slightly. The larger the quantity of rice, the longer the heat remains trapped and the more the cooking time should be reduced. Uncover the pot once the cooking is finished.

- If some liquid remains after the rice is cooked, remove the cover and increase the heat so that the liquid evaporates quickly

jasmine rice

(be careful that the rice does not stick).

- If there is a larger amount of cooking liquid left over, drain the rice (use the cooking liquid to make soup, sauce, stew). The rice can be heated for a few moments to dry it out.
- Avoid stirring rice while it is cooking unless sticky rice is desired.

:: Steamed: put the rice in a steaming basket, place above boiling water, cover and keep the water boiling over medium-high heat. The rice can be blanched for a few minutes beforehand, but this reduces its vitamin and mineral content.

:: In fat or oil: rice is cooked for a few minutes in fat or oil and constantly stirred. Twice its volume in liquid is then added, the rice is covered and the cooking continues until the liquid has been absorbed. This rice retains its firmness and shape better (it is the traditional method for preparing risotto, paella, Greek rice, pilaf and Creole rice).

SERVING IDEAS

Rice is used in soups, croquettes, stuffings, salads, puddings, pies and cakes. It is used to stuff vegetables. It is the basis for risotto, pilaf, paella and curries. It is made into noodles (rice noodles), dried cereal, syrup, wine, vinegar, miso and alcoholic drinks. Rice can replace potato and accompany meat, poultry, fish and seafood. It is traditionally served with broiled fish and kebabs. It is served plain, cooked or stir-fried. Milled into a flour, rice gives a slightly al dente texture to cakes and pastries and can be used to bind sauces. This flour is not suitable for making bread, as it does not contain any gluten.

PREPARING

It is not necessary to soak parboiled rice, white rice or quick-cooking rice before cooking. Medium- and short-grain rice should be washed before using so that the grains don't stick together during cooking. Put the rice under running water until the water that runs from the rice is clear.

Basmati rice (and Thai rice or perfumed rices, according to taste) should be soaked in cold water before being cooked. Stir the rice and when the water becomes milky, drain and refresh the water 4 or 5 times until it is clear. Rinsing the rice gives it a lighter rather than a creamier consistency.

Wild rice

Zizania aquatica, Gramineae

The seed of an aquatic plant originally from North America, specifically the Great Lakes region. Highly sought after, wild rice is expensive. Grains of wild rice acquire their blackish color after being hulled, cleaned and dried. They have a fairly strong, nutty flavor and a crunchy texture.

wild rice

SERVING IDEAS

Wild rice accompanies poultry, seafood and game. It is served by itself or mixed with other types of rice. Cooked wild rice is used in stuffings and crepes. It works well with mushrooms, vegetables, fruit and nuts. It can be popped like corn or milled into flour.

COOKING

:: **Boiled in water** or **stock:** soak wild rice for several hours or quick-soak for 1 hr. In a pot, put 4 parts of water for 1 part of rice and bring to a boil; add the rice then let it boil for 5 min; remove from the heat. Cover and leave to soak for 1 hr. Drain. Put the pot back on the heat, add 3 times its volume in water (or less if a drier rice is desired), add ½ teaspoon of salt and bring to a boil, reduce the heat and simmer until tender (about 20 min).

Avoid overcooking wild rice.

The cooking time for unsoaked grains is about 40 min (cook the rice in 3 times its volume of water).

NUTRITIONAL INFORMATION

	cooked
water	73.9%
protein	4 g
fat	0.3 g
carbohydrates	21.3 g
	per 3.5 oz/100 g

GOOD SOURCE: zinc.

CONTAINS: magnesium, folic acid, niacin, potassium, vitamin B_6, phosphorus, copper and riboflavin.

Wild rice is highly nutritious. It contains a greater quantity and better quality of proteins than regular rice, as it contains more lysine (see *Food Complementarity Theory*, p. 277).

PREPARING

Wash the wild rice to remove any foreign matter. If the grains have not been hulled already, they can be spread on a cookie sheet and dried for 2-3 hr in a 200°F (95°C) oven, stirring them occasionally, or leave them 2-3 days in a warm place. They can also be dried in a pan, stirring continuously. Hull them by beating or rubbing the grains; the light husk will separate from the grain. Dry these again for 1 hr in the oven at 250°F (120°C).

Quinoa

Chenopodium quinoa, Chenopodiaceae

A plant originally from South America that produces tiny grains about 1/16 in. (2 mm) in diameter. Depending on the variety, the outer layer of the quinoa grain can be transparent, pink, orange, red, purple or black. Quinoa found in food stores is generally yellowish. Quinoa grains contain a large germ that holds most of its nutrients. They are covered in saponin, a soapy and bitter resin that needs to be removed before they are edible.

quinoa

STORING

:: **At room temperature:** place the quinoa in an airtight container, in a cool and dry place.

:: **In the fridge:** ground, 3-6 months.

COOKING

Cook 1 part quinoa grain to 2 parts liquid (about 15 min). The grains stay slightly crunchy after cooking and do not stick together. The texture is reminiscent of caviar and the taste is nutty.

NUTRITIONAL INFORMATION

	raw
water	9%
protein	5.2 g
fat	2.3 g
carbohydrates	27.6 g
	per 3.5 oz/100 g

EXCELLENT SOURCE: magnesium, iron and potassium.

GOOD SOURCE: copper, zinc and phosphorus.

CONTAINS: riboflavin, thiamine and niacin. Quinoa contains more protein than most cereals, and these proteins are higher quality, as their amino acids are more balanced. It is higher in lysine, methionine and cystine; it is a food that complements other cereals, legumes, nuts and seeds well (see *Food Complementarity Theory*, p. 277).

Quinoa

SERVING IDEAS

Quinoa can be substituted for most other cereals and grains and replaces rice. It is cooked as a porridge or added to soups, pies and croquettes. Ground quinoa is added to breads, cookies, puddings, crepes, muffins and pasta dishes. Quinoa grains are very low in gluten. They can be grown and used in the same way as alfalfa sprouts.

Quinoa leaves are cooked in the same way as spinach.

In South America, quinoa is used to make the alcoholic drink *chicha*.

PREPARING

Rinse the quinoa under running water and let it drain; if it leaves a bitter taste in the mouth when it is raw, it is because it still contains saponin. To remove this substance, wash carefully, rubbing it under running water until the water no longer froths up.

Rye

Secale cereale, Gramineae

A cereal grain originally from Asia that is mostly used to feed cattle. The rye grain resembles a grain of wheat, while being longer and not as plump. Its sides are also slightly compressed and it is topped by a tuft of hairs. It takes on hues ranging from yellow-brown to gray-green. Once its husk is removed, it is left whole, cracked or turned into flakes or flour. Among the species of rye, several varieties are divided into winter rye and summer rye.

Rye flour is suitable for making bread, but its gluten is less elastic than the gluten in wheat and holds less moisture; rye bread does not rise very much and is more dense and compact than wheat bread. It keeps for a longer time, as it dries out more slowly.

rye grains

rye flour

NUTRITIONAL INFORMATION

	dark rye flour	light rye flour
water	11%	8.8%
protein	14 g	8.4 g
fat	2.6 g	1.4 g
carbohydrates	68.8 g	80.2 g
fiber	2.4 g	0.4 g
		per 3.5 oz/100 g

DARK RYE FLOUR
EXCELLENT SOURCE: magnesium, potassium, zinc, phosphorus, iron, copper, folic acid and vitamin B$_6$.
GOOD SOURCE: thiamine, pantothenic acid, niacin and riboflavin.
CONTAINS: calcium.
LIGHT RYE FLOUR
EXCELLENT SOURCE: magnesium and thiamine.
GOOD SOURCE: potassium, zinc and phosphorus.
CONTAINS: iron, vitamin B$_6$, copper, folic acid, pantothenic acid, riboflavin and niacin.
PROPERTIES: rye is said to help prevent hypertension, arteriosclerosis and vascular afflictions. Ergot, a rye parasite, is used to relieve migraines and headaches, control bleeding and facilitate childbirth.

STORING

 **:: At room temperature:** keep rye grains and flour in an airtight container, and store it in a cool and dry place.

BUYING

 When buying rye bread, be sure to check the list of ingredients.

SERVING IDEAS

Whole rye grains can be cooked and eaten as is. They should be soaked overnight in 2-3 parts water to 1 part rye, then boiled until tender. They are very nourishing. The flakes are cooked as a porridge or added to mueslis and granolas.

Coarsely ground and retaining all of its nutrients, rye flour is used in particular to make the famous pumpernickel bread of German origin, with its sour taste and heavy texture. It is also used in the preparation of crispbreads, spice breads, crepes, pâtés and muffins. Rye grains are used in the manufacture of alcoholic drinks. They are grown and used in the same way as wheat sprouts.

Amaranth

Amaranthus spp., Amarantaceae

A plant originally from Mexico whose large red leaves and tiny seeds are edible. Only the white-seeded varieties of amaranth are cultivated as food.

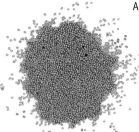

amaranth

CEREALS AND GRAINS

SERVING IDEAS

Amaranth leaves are used in the same way as spinach, which they can replace. The grains are cooked as is (about 30 min in 2-3 parts water for 1 part amaranth) and are eaten as a cereal. They have a slightly spicy flavor. They can be puffed, sprouted or milled into flour.

Amaranth flour makes pastries moister and sweeter; it does not contain any gluten, so it does not rise when cooked. It is used by itself to make cookies, crepes or waffles, but must be combined with wheat flour to make rising breads and cakes.

STORING

:: At room temperature: place amaranth flour and seeds in a nontransparent container, and store in a cool and dry place (amaranth flour keeps for a longer time than wheat flour).
:: In the fridge: the leaves, a few days.
:: In the freezer: the leaves (in the same way as spinach).

NUTRITIONAL INFORMATION

	seeds
water	9.8%
protein	10.8 g
fat	4.9 g
carbohydrates	49.6 g
fiber	11.4 g
calories	280
	per 2.6 oz/75 g

EXCELLENT SOURCE: magnesium, iron, phosphorus, copper and zinc.
GOOD SOURCE: potassium and folic acid.
CONTAINS: pantothenic acid, calcium, riboflavin, vitamin B_6, vitamin C, thiamine and niacin. Amaranth contains twice as much iron and four times more calcium than hard wheat. It contains more protein than most cereals, and the protein is of a better quality. It is a food that complements cereals, legumes, nuts and seeds well (see *Food Complementarity Theory,* p. 277).

Triticale

Triticale (Triticum x secale), Gramineae

A cereal grain resulting from a cross between wheat and rye. Triticale contains high levels of wheat protein and high levels of rye lysine. It thus has a high nutritional value.

triticale

SERVING IDEAS

Triticale is used in the same way as wheat or rye. The grain is eaten whole, cracked, sprouted, in flakes or ground. The flour has a nutty flavor; it improves the fiber and nutrient content of the dishes it is used in. Its gluten is difficult to make into bread because it can only tolerate a single kneading. The bread is thus smaller in volume. Wheat flour (which is finer) absorbs more water than triticale flour (which is coarser). They can therefore be substituted for each other in most recipes, as long as one adjusts the quantity of liquid.

Triticale is used to make pasta dishes, tortillas, crepes, muffins, cakes, pies, eau-de-vie and beer.

COOKING

:: **Boiled:** cook the triticale grains in 2-3 times their volume of water (45-60 min).

NUTRITIONAL INFORMATION

	whole grain triticale flour
water	13%
protein	17 g
fat	2.4 g
carbohydrates	95.1 g
fiber	19 g
	per 1 cup/250 ml

WHOLE-GRAIN TRITICALE FLOUR

EXCELLENT SOURCE: magnesium, potassium, folic acid, pantothenic acid, zinc, phosphorus, thiamine, copper, iron and vitamin B_6.

GOOD SOURCE: niacin.

CONTAINS: riboflavin and calcium.

This flour is higher than whole wheat flour in folic acid, copper, pantothenic acid and vitamin B_6, and slightly lower in niacin. Triticale contains a little more protein than wheat; its essential amino acids are more balanced, in particular in lysine (see *Food Complementarity Theory*, p. 277). Its concentration of gluten is somewhere between the levels found in rye (low) and wheat (high).

Corn

Zea mays, Gramineae

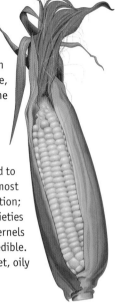

Probably originating from Mexico or Central America, corn is sometimes also called "Indian wheat." The corn kernels grow on ears that are 6-12 in. (15-30 cm) long. They are yellow, white, orange, red, purple, blue, black or brown, depending on the variety.

The kernel comprises three main parts: the pericarp (envelope), the endosperm (contains 90% starch) and the embryo (the germ, rich in nutrients). Corn species are grouped into six categories. The most important species commercially is used to feed animals, and is referred to as **dent corn**. The second most important species is the **sweetcorn** used for human consumption; the kernels are tender, milky and sweet. Among the other varieties are **popping corn** or "popcorn"; this is a variety with small kernels (see p. 308). There is also **ornamental corn**, which is not edible. Depending on the species, the kernels are more or less sweet, oily and tasty.

corn

BUYING

:: **Choose:** very fresh corn that releases white juice under simple finger pressure.
:: **Avoid:** colorless or shrivelled corn, whose silky threads are dark and dry, or whose husk leaves are faded or yellowed. Don't buy corn from displays that are exposed to sunlight or high temperatures, as heat accelerates the process that makes corn floury.

fresh corn kernels

COOKING

Ears of corn are cooked with or without their leaves.
:: **Baked** or **grilled:** wrap husked corn in aluminum foil (35 min at 425°F/220°C).
:: **Steamed:** 20 min. Avoid salting or overcooking as it toughens and loses flavor.
:: **Boiled:** immerse the ears in boiling water to which a very small amount of sugar has been added, leaving on a few leaves from the husk and adding a little milk or beer (3-4 min for small ears and 5-7 min for larger ones).
:: **Pressure-cooked:** in 1 cup (250 ml) of liquid (3-5 min).
:: **Microwaved:** 3 min on the highest setting for 1 ear. Let stand for 5 min.

NUTRITIONAL INFORMATION

	fresh, cooked	creamed	cornmeal (whole grain)	cornmeal (de-germed)	corn flour (whole grain)	bran
water	69.6%	78.7%	10.3%	11.6%	10.9%	4.8%
protein	3.3 g	1.7 g	8.1 g	8.5 g	6.9 g	2.5 g
fat	1.3 g	0.4 g	3.6 g	1.6 g	3.9 g	0.2 g
carbohydrates	25.1 g	18.1 g	76.9 g	77.7 g	76.8 g	25.7 g
fiber	3.7 g	1.3 g	11.0 g	5.2 g	13.4 g	25.4 g
calories	108	72	362	366	361	67.2
					per 3.5 oz/100 g	*per 1 oz/30 g*

Corn is mainly made up of polyunsaturated fatty acids (46%), monounsaturated fatty acids (28%) and saturated fatty acids (15%) (see *Fats and oils,* p. 579). The floury varieties are higher in starch, which results in kernels that are not very sweet. In the sweeter varieties, the sugar begins to turn into starch as soon as it is picked, quickly resulting in a loss in flavor.

FRESH COOKED CORN
GOOD SOURCE: folic acid, potassium and thiamine.
CONTAINS: magnesium, pantothenic acid, vitamin C, phosphorus, niacin, zinc and riboflavin.
Rich source of fiber.

CREAMED CORN
GOOD SOURCE: folic acid.
CONTAINS: potassium, vitamin C, magnesium, zinc, niacin and phosphorus.

YELLOW CORNMEAL (WHOLE GRAIN)
EXCELLENT SOURCE: magnesium, thiamine, iron and potassium.
GOOD SOURCE: phosphorus, zinc, niacin and vitamin B$_6$.
CONTAINS: riboflavin, folic acid, copper, pantothenic acid and vitamin A.
Very rich source of fiber.

CORNMEAL (DEGERMED)
GOOD SOURCE: folacin and magnesium.
CONTAINS: vitamin B$_6$, potassium, niacin, thiamine, zinc, iron and phosphorus.

CORN FLOUR (WHOLE GRAIN)
EXCELLENT SOURCE: magnesium, potassium and phosphorus.
GOOD SOURCE: vitamin B$_6$, thiamine, zinc and iron.
CONTAINS: niacin, copper, folic acid, pantothenic acid, riboflavin and vitamin A.
Very rich source of fiber.

CORN BRAN
CONTAINS: magnesium and iron.
Very rich source of fiber.

CORN GERM
EXCELLENT SOURCE: magnesium, phosphorus, thiamine, potassium and zinc.
GOOD SOURCE: vitamin B$_6$ and iron.
CONTAINS: riboflavin, folic acid and copper.

Fresh corn, boiled or dried, is deficient in lysine and tryptophan, the amino acids that make up proteins (see *Food Complementarity Theory,* p. 277). It is the only cereal that contains vitamin A (yellow varieties). People who get almost all their nutrients from corn often suffer from a niacin deficiency.

Corn

corn flour

STORING

Eat fresh corn as soon as possible, preferably on the same day as it is bought.

:: **At room temperature:** keep cornmeal and corn flour in a cool and dry place, in airtight containers.

:: **In the fridge:** if eating at a later time. Do not remove the husks. If it is husked, keep in a plastic bag. Keep whole grain cornmeal and corn flour in airtight containers.

:: **In the freezer:** 1 year, blanch 7-11 min, depending on size; 3 months, blanch 4 min then remove the kernels. Whole grain cornmeal and corn flour keep 1-2 years. Fresh corn can be canned.

SERVING IDEAS

Fresh corn is eaten cooked as is on the cob, or the kernels are removed, then cooked and eaten.

Corn on the cob is often seasoned with butter and salt.

Corn kernels can be removed from the cob before or after cooking. Raw corn kernels are used in soups, stews and relishes. Cooked kernels are served as a side dish or added to salads.

Hominy is made by soaking corn kernels in lye to remove the hulls; hominy is soft and creamy, and slightly puffy, and is used as a side dish or in casseroles and stews. *Pozole* is the Mexican name for hominy, and is available fresh or dried.

Hominy grits are ground dried hominy, eaten as a porridge but more commonly as a side to eggs and bacon.

The fine corn flour called **masa harina** is milled from dried hulled corn kernels that have been soaked and kneaded into dough, then dried and ground to make tortillas.

Cornstarch is obtained by extracting the starch from the endosperm. It has gelling properties and is used in the same way as wheat flour or to thicken foods. Before adding cornstarch to a hot mixture, blend it with some cold liquid to prevent it from forming lumps.

corn flakes

dried kernels

cornmeal

Cook it for at least 1 min. The food industry uses this starch to thicken sauces, desserts, pastries, vinaigrettes, sour cream, peanut butter, confectionery, baby foods, charcuterie (sausages and deli meats), etc. The starch can be processed to control its effect. It is called "modified starch."

Cornmeal is obtained by milling degermed and dried corn kernels into more or less fine granules. It gives a slightly crunchy texture to cookies, muffins, cakes, breads. It is boiled into a thickened porridge to make polenta; it is added to and thickens soups and sauces, and is made into tamales—a meat-filled corn "roll" baked in a corn husk— tortillas and corn chips. It is difficult to knead and results in a crumbly product.

Corn flour results from the finest milling of the dried corn kernel, from which the germ is often removed. It is used in crepes, cakes, muffins and breads. As it is gluten-deficient, it must be combined with wheat flour to obtain foods that will rise (cakes, muffins, breads).

The **corn germ** is the embryo; it contains several nutrients and 46% of its calories comes from its fats. The germ is almost always removed from the kernels so that the products made from corn keep for a longer time. The corn germ has a crunchy texture and a nutty flavor. It is used by itself with milk as a cold cereal, added to foods to enrich them (salads, legumes, simmered dishes). Highly perishable, it is often sold in airtight packaging that is stored in the fridge or freezer once opened.

Corn oil is dark gold when unrefined and pale amber when it is refined. It contains polyunsaturated fatty acids (58.7%), monounsaturated fatty acids (24.2%) and saturated fatty acids (12.7%) (see *Fats and oils*, p. 579).

Cornflakes are ready-to-eat cold cereal. Corn is used in the manufacture of beer, bourbon (whiskey), gin and *chicha* (an indigenous South American drink made from fermented corn sprouts).

corn oil

Popping corn

Zea mays var. *everta*, Gramineae

Popping corn is produced from a variety of corn with small **and hard** ears and kernels. Heated to a high temperature, the moisture contained in the kernel's endosperm turns to steam, which creates a great amount of pressure. This pressure makes the outer casing burst open, revealing the inside of the kernel, which is now puffed up and crunchy (popcorn or **"popped corn"**). The varieties of popping corn are classified according to their shape. The kernels, usually white or yellow, can be red or brown, but they all turn white or yellow when popped.

popping corn

popped corn

BUYING

Buy popping corn from stores with a quick turnover of stock.

PREPARING

Popcorn is made in an airtight container. A small amount of oil and salt can be added once the cooking is finished.

SERVING IDEAS

Popcorn is eaten plain or coated with butter, unseasoned or seasoned with salt and spices. It can also be coated with caramelized sugar.

STORING

:: **At room temperature:** keep popping corn in an airtight container (the kernels must retain their moisture, or else they won't pop).

COOKING

Cook the corn over medium heat, shaking the pot often. Once all of the kernels have popped, take the popcorn off the heat quickly so that it doesn't burn. Packets of ready-made popping corn for microwaving can be more expensive. The kernels can be popped in a specially made appliance.

NUTRITIONAL INFORMATION

	with oil and salt	sweetened	plain
water	3.1%	4.0%	4.0%
protein	1.8 g	4.6 g	2.8 g
fat	4.2 g	2.6 g	1.0 g
carbohydrates	11.2 g	63.2 g	16.8 g
fiber	1.6 g	4.4 g	1.8 g
	per 2 cups/500 ml	per 2 cups/500 ml	per 2 cups/500 ml

CONTAINS: magnesium, zinc, copper, thiamine, phosphorus and potassium. Corn is a source of fiber.

Popcorn coated with sugar or butter is much higher in energy than plain popcorn.

Bread

A food essentially made from flour, water and salt that has been kneaded, allowed to rise, shaped or molded, and cooked in the oven. Bread can contain a fermenting agent that makes it rise (a sourdough starter or yeast), or have none, in which case it is an **unleavened bread** (such as the Middle Eastern "pita" or the Indian "chapati," etc.).

A "**starter**" is a portion of uncooked, fermented dough removed from a previous mixture. It is made up of yeasts and bacteria. To make a starter, 0.25 oz (7 g) of dried yeast is dissolved in 2½ cups (600 ml) of lukewarm water with 1 tablespoon (15 ml) of sugar. Two cups (500 ml) of hot water and about ½ lb (250 g) of white flour are added. The resulting dough is covered with a cloth and left to ferment for 3-5 days away from drafts. The starter is acidic, which prevents the development of pathogenic bacteria (those that lead to infections or illness). It must be used within a week, and flour and lukewarm water need to be added to it if one wishes to extend its storage life. In a recipe, ½ cup (125 ml) of starter replaces 0.25 oz (7 g) of dried yeast. Starters are now commonly replaced by **baker's yeast** (also called "brewer's yeast"), which is easier to use and acts more quickly and consistently.

Yeast is composed of microscopic fungi; like a starter, it is a living culture. Yeast feeds on sugar (the sugar added to the dough or the starch in the flour). It converts this sugar into carbon dioxide and alcohol, which stay trapped in the gluten. Gluten has the property of holding the gas produced by the fermentation of the dough, which makes it rise. During cooking, the alcohol evaporates, and the bubbles of gas trapped in the dough form cells; this gas will be dislodged by the environmental air when the bread cools. A sourdough starter also transforms starch, but because it contains a

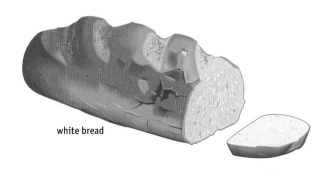

white bread

Bread

greater number of lactic acid bacteria, it does not produce as much alcohol. Bread that uses a starter (sourdough bread) does not rise as much as yeast-leavened bread, its crumb consists of irregular and smaller cells, its taste is slightly sour and more flavorful, it is more digestible and it keeps better.

rye bread

multigrain bread

BUYING

 :: Choose: bread with a firm, golden and fairly thick crust, and a tender crumb.

STORING

 :: At room temperature: 5-7 days maximum, sliced, in a plastic bag.

:: In the fridge: unsliced (a few days). If it is cut, put the cut edge flat against a wood or marble surface.

:: In the freezer: about 2 months.

NUTRITIONAL INFORMATION

	enriched white bread 1 oz/30 g (slice)	cracked wheat bread 1 oz/30 g (slice)	whole grain bread 1 oz/30 g (slice)	dark rye bread 1 oz/30 g (slice)	light rye bread 1 oz/30 g (slice)
water	35.8%	34.9%	36.4%	34%	35.5%
protein	2.4 g	2.2 g	2.5 g	2.9 g	2.3 g
carbohydrates	14.1 g	13.0 g	13.8 g	17.0 g	13.0 g
fat	0.9 g	0.6 g	0.7 g	0.4 g	0.3 g
fiber	0.5 g	1.0 g	1.6 g	1.7 g	0.7 g
calories	75	66	67	79	61

The protein, carbohydrate, fat and calorie content of different kinds of bread is relatively similar, as indicated by the table. The vitamin, mineral and fiber content varies greatly from one bread to another.

WHITE BREAD (ENRICHED)

GOOD SOURCE: thiamine, niacin, iron and folic acid.

CONTAINS: riboflavin, phosphorus, potassium, calcium and pantothenic acid.

WHOLE WHEAT BREAD

CONTAINS: folic acid, phosphorus, thiamine, iron, potassium and niacin.

DARK RYE BREAD

CONTAINS: potassium, phosphorus, magnesium, iron, thiamine, copper and zinc.

Whole grain, cracked grain and dark rye breads are very nutritious breads. It is also possible to find rice, corn or oat breads. They can be eaten with cumin or poppy seed flavorings, or salted like the pretzels enjoyed by Germans. In France, one eats brown bread, prepared with grayish-brown whole flour, white bread made with refined flour and black bread, a rye and wheat mix.

Eating bread daily provides the complex carbohydrates, fiber, B-complex vitamins and minerals like iron and zinc that are difficult to find in other foods.

CEREALS AND GRAINS

whole grain bread

PREPARING

It is best not to slice bread until using it so that it doesn't dry out as quickly and it keeps all of its flavor.

When bread is stale, place it in the oven (200°F/95°C) for about 10 min so that it regains some freshness.

1 Mix 1½ teaspoon (8 ml) of yeast with 2 cups (500 ml) of lukewarm water and 1 teaspoon (5ml) of sugar.

2 Pour the yeast and the water in a mix of 3½ cups (875 ml) of flour, 2 teaspoons (10 ml) of sugar and 1 teaspoon (5 ml) of salt. Add ⅛ cup (30 ml) of oil.

3 Mix until the dough forms a crude mass. If the dough is too dry, add a little water.

4 Knead the dough on the work surface using a regular movement, until it no longer sticks.

5 Leave the dough to rise in a warm place, covered with food wrap, until it has doubled in size (1½-2½ hr).

6 Punch down the dough to push out its gas, and return it to the work surface.

7 Divide the dough, taking care to cover the remainder with a damp cloth so that it doesn't become dry.

8 Form rounded balls and place them on a cookie sheet. Cover with a cloth, leave to rise again for 30-50 min, then bake.

Bread

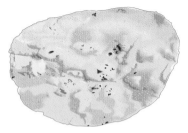

chapati

pita

tortillas

SERVING IDEAS

Bread is used in a wide variety of ways. It can be found on the table from the first course to dessert and it is served as an accompaniment to all meals. Essential for sandwiches, canapés, toast and croutons, bread is used as an ingredient in certain soups (French onion soup, gazpacho, garlic soup), and is indispensable for cheese fondue. It is very popular in the morning, toasted or untoasted. Bread is cooked in charlottes and bread pudding, as well as French toast. When it is stale, it is dried to make crispbreads, breadcrumbs and breadcrumb dressings. It is used for stuffings and *panzanella* (an Italian bread salad). It is best not to eat bread straight out of the oven, as it is more difficult to digest. Wait until the next day, in the case of a large sourdough country loaf, or until it is slightly stale, in the case of rye bread. Toasting bread lowers its nutritional value. The more it is toasted, the higher the loss.

Flour

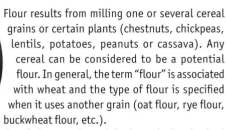

all-purpose flour

Flour results from milling one or several cereal grains or certain plants (chestnuts, chickpeas, lentils, potatoes, peanuts or cassava). Any cereal can be considered to be a potential flour. In general, the term "flour" is associated with wheat and the type of flour is specified when it uses another grain (oat flour, rye flour, buckwheat flour, etc.).

Grains of wheat are cleaned, finely crushed, pulverized and sifted to remove their bran (outer layers) to obtain a finer flour. The germ is removed for better keeping qualities. The endosperm, or albumen, is used to make the flour.

Soft wheat is low in gluten; soft wheat flour is especially recommended for making cakes. Hard wheat contains a higher proportion of gluten; this is why hard wheat flour is used to make breads.

To compensate for the loss of nutrients during the milling process (if the grain has lost its bran and germ), the flour is enriched by adding various vitamins (thiamine, riboflavin, niacin) and minerals (iron) (mandatory in Canada and the United States for white flour).

Whole wheat flour is produced from milling the whole grain (the endosperm, germ and bran of the grain), which gives it a slightly nutty flavor. It is important to read the label carefully and look for the words "whole wheat" if you want a whole wheat product. This flour can replace white flour in most recipes, but it is sometimes necessary to slightly increase the quantity. The resulting mixture will be more nourishing, have a darker color, a stronger flavor and be smaller in size. For light results, sift the flour several times before using it, taking care to put the bran collected in the sieve back into the flour.

Graham flour usually contains finely milled bran flakes, and the germ is usually removed. This flour is used by itself or combined with others.

All-purpose or **"plain" flour** comes from the milling and combination of various varieties of hard and soft wheat. It has a variety of uses both in bread- and pastry-making.

Flour

Cake flour is a white flour made exclusively from soft wheat milled very finely. It has a very soft feel. It almost always comes from the last millings, so it is very refined. With a higher percentage of starch and lower levels of gluten, it results in very light cakes and can't be used to make leavened breads. It can be used in place of all-purpose flour; 1 cup (250 ml) of all-purpose flour can be replaced by about 1¼ cups (300 ml) of cake flour.

Pastry flour is mostly derived from soft wheats, sometimes hard wheats. Low in gluten, it is finely milled but not to the same extent as cake flour. It is used to make pastries, cookies, cakes, etc.

unbleached flour

Self-rising flour is all-purpose flour to which salt and raising agents have been added. These food additives increase its sodium content. Self-raising flour is designed to save time, as, depending on the recipe, it eliminates the need to add baking powder or baking soda and salt; 1 cup (250 ml/125 g) of self-rising flour contains 1½ teaspoons (7 ml) of baking powder and ½ teaspoon (2 ml) of salt. Self-rising flour is not recommended for yeast breads.

Unbleached flour is flour that is not artificially whitened. The oxidation of the flour makes the gluten stronger or more elastic and leads to better cooking results. Moreover, some bleaching agents contain calcium or phosphorus and can thus somewhat improve the nutritional value of the flour; unbleached flour has a more natural taste, as it contains no food additives. The presence of bleaching agents results in a lighter product that is larger in volume, with a finer grain and a lighter color, as more sugar and fat or oil can be used.

gluten flour

Gluten flour is a flour made from whole grains of wheat from which the starch has been removed and contains a high level of gluten. To make this flour, hard, high-protein wheat flour is washed to remove its starch, dried, then remilled. Gluten flour is usually composed of 45% gluten and 55% white flour. It can be used with whole wheat flour or with low-gluten flours (rye, barley, oat).

Bread flour is derived from a mixture of hard flours. It is slightly grainy and its higher level of protein (gluten) is useful for homemade breads.

CEREALS AND GRAINS

BUYING

:: **Choose:** flour from stores with a rapid turnover of stock to ensure maximum freshness.
Genuine whole wheat flour is usually found in natural food stores. Read labels carefully, as not all flours have the same nutritional value.

STORING

:: **At room temperature:** keep refined flour in a cool and dry place, protected from light.
:: **In the fridge:** whole wheat flour, stone-ground or not stone-ground.
:: **In the freezer:** whole wheat flour. Place in a paper bag when defrosted.

whole wheat flour

bran flour

Flour

cake flour

NUTRITIONAL INFORMATION

	whole wheat flour	enriched white flour
water	10.3%	11.9%
protein	13.7 g	10.3 g
fat	1.9 g	1 g
carbohydrates	72.6 g	76.3 g
fiber	12.6 g	3.1 g
calories	339	364
		per 3.5 oz/100 g

The nutritional value of flour varies in relation to the cereal grain used, the maturity of the flour and its extraction rate. The extraction rate indicates the amount of germ and bran present after the milling of the grain; a 100% extraction rate refers to a whole grain flour. The lower the figure, the less nutritious the flour.

WHOLE WHEAT FLOUR

EXCELLENT SOURCE: magnesium, niacin, thiamine, potassium, zinc, phosphorus and iron.

GOOD SOURCE: folic acid, vitamin B$_6$ and copper.

CONTAINS: pantothenic acid and riboflavin.

ALL-PURPOSE WHITE FLOUR

EXCELLENT SOURCE: thiamine, niacin and iron.

GOOD SOURCE: riboflavin.

CONTAINS: folic acid, phosphorus, potassium, magnesium, zinc, copper and pantothenic acid.

GLUTEN FLOUR

EXCELLENT SOURCE: niacin.

CONTAINS: phosphorus, folic acid and potassium.

SERVING IDEAS

Flour is used in the baking and pastry industry as well as in cooking to make crepes and pancakes, waffles, brioches, donuts, pies, puddings, muffins, cookies and tempura. As a thickening agent, flour gives consistency to cheese fondues, sauces, soups, syrups and pastry creams.
It is also used to make modeling paste and craft glues.

Pasta

Products made essentially from milled cereals and water. In the West, good quality pasta is made from a hard wheat variety, durum wheat, which has a high protein (and thus gluten) content and is low in starch. It can also be made from soft wheat flour, a mixture of hard and soft wheat, buckwheat flour, rice flour or, less often, corn flour. Small quantities of soy or mung bean flour, vegetables (spinach, tomatoes, beets, carrots), gluten, whey, eggs, flavors, fresh herbs, spices and colors can be added. Some pasta can be colored using a coloring agent rather than a vegetable purée. "Egg" pasta is made with soft wheat flour. In some countries, pasta is enriched with B-complex vitamins (thiamine, riboflavin and niacin) and sometimes iron. Protein and fiber-enriched pastas are also available.

tortellini

To make pasta, semolina is mixed with water, then kneaded to make a dough. This dough is rolled into thin sheets or forced through holes to create different shapes. Sheets of pasta are cut into the desired shape. Shaped pastas are ready to be sold (fresh pasta) or dried. The choice of pasta shape is a matter of taste and how it will be used. Small pastas are used particularly for clear or hearty soups. Curved, twisted or tube-shaped pastas are perfect for sauces. Ridged pastas are ideal for meat-based sauces, while smooth pastas are ideal for cream- or cheese-based sauces.

penne

ravioli

farfalle

rigatoni

Pasta

BUYING

:: **Choose:** unbroken pasta with a smooth and regular appearance, evenly colored, or ivory verging on yellow. Fresh pasta should have a pleasant smell.

SERVING IDEAS

Pasta accompanies meat, poultry and seafood. In Asia, pasta is enjoyed roasted. Dishes served with pasta are usually based on tomato, to which ground meat, seafood, cheese, poultry, vegetables or ham is added. Pastas can be stuffed with ground meat, spinach, cheeses, fresh herbs or mushrooms. To reduce calories:

- Replace cream-based sauces with ones based on vegetables or fresh herbs.
- Replace cream with skim milk.
- Use low-fat cheeses (cottage cheese, ricotta) and reduce the amount of high-fat cheeses (for gratins).
- Reduce the amount of meat used in the sauces and choose poultry instead.
- Replace butter with olive oil (see *Oil*, p. 587).

STORING

:: **At room temperature**: keep dried bought pasta indefinitely in a dry place, protected from drafts.

:: **In the fridge**: fresh pasta, covered, 1-2 days; cooked pasta, 3-5 days; fresh egg pasta and stuffed pasta, 1 day.

:: **In the freezer**: 2 months, fresh pasta and cooked pasta; fresh egg pasta and stuffed pasta.

fusilli

fettucine

whole wheat spaghetti

rotini

NUTRITIONAL INFORMATION

	cooked durum wheat pasta	cooked whole wheat spaghetti	cooked egg noodles
water	63.6%	67.2%	68.7%
protein	4.8 g	5.3 g	4.8 g
fat	0.7 g	0.5 g	1.5 g
carbohydrates	28.3 g	26.5 g	24.8 g
fiber	0.1 g	0.1 g	2.2 g
calories	141	124	133

per 3.5 oz/100 g

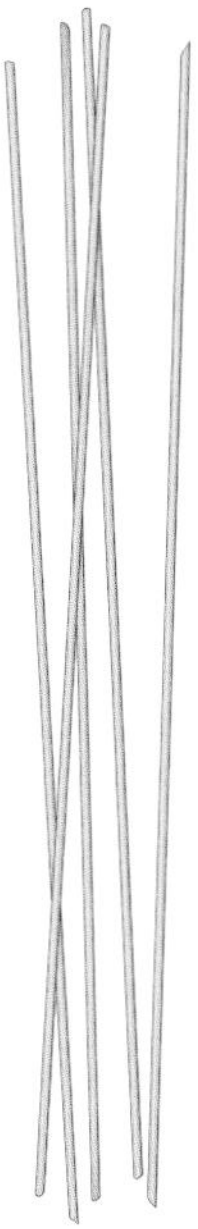

CEREALS AND GRAINS

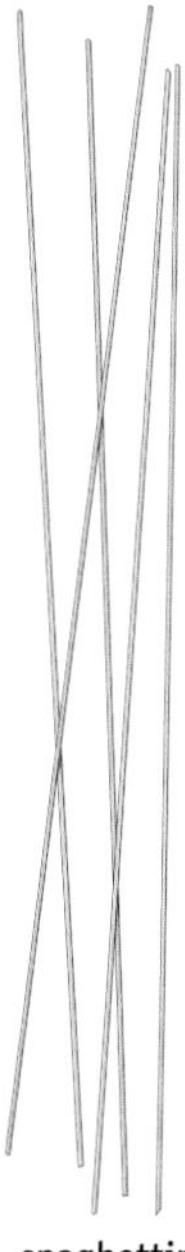

Despite its reputation for being high in calories, it is not pasta itself that is high in calories, but rather what is added to it (butter, cream and cheese). Its nutritional value varies depending on what its ingredients are (whole grains, eggs, milk powder, vegetables) and the amount of cooking. Pasta that is cooked for a long time contains slightly fewer B-complex vitamins than firm pasta. Pasta is a good source of energy and protein, and it is low in fat. Its high level of carbohydrate is mostly in the form of complex carbohydrates (which are easy to digest and are absorbed more slowly by the body). This is why pasta is recommended for people who need sustained energy.

COOKED WHOLE WHEAT SPAGHETTI
CONTAINS: magnesium, zinc, thiamine, niacin, phosphorus, copper, iron and pantothenic acid.

COOKED EGG NOODLES
CONTAIN: magnesium, zinc, phosphorus, niacin and vitamin B_{12}.

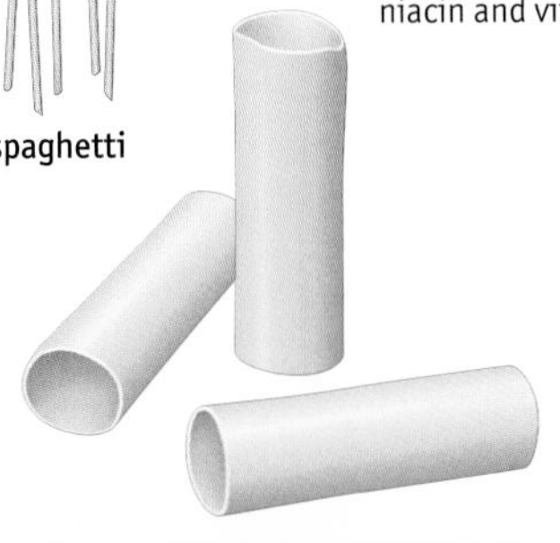

spaghetti

spaghettini

cannelloni

Pasta

PREPARING

1 Make a crater in ¾ cup (180 ml) of flour and place 2 eggs, 1 tablespoon (15 ml) of oil and 1 teaspoon (5 ml) of salt in it.

2 Incorporate the flour and work it in; if necessary, add a little water to mix well.

3 Form an elastic ball of dough. Let it rest 30-60 min.

4 Flour the work surface, then flatten the dough slightly with a rolling pin and divide it into 2 pieces.

5 Roll out the dough into a round shape.

6 Reduce the thickness further for a thin sheet of pasta dough.

7 Sprinkle the dough with flour and roll the sheet up.

8 Cut into strips about ⅕ in. (5 mm) wide.

9 Unroll the fresh pasta and let it dry on a cloth before cooking.

conchiglie (shells)

ziti

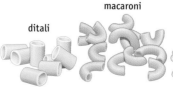

macaroni

ditali

gnocchi

spinach tagliatelle

spinach lasagna

COOKING

 :: Boiled: pour small pasta in a stream, or push long pasta gradually into the water as it softens. Add pastas to water that is already at a full boil to obtain Italian-style pasta cooked al dente (pasta that is still firm to the bite without tasting uncooked). The cooking water should be salted (1 tablespoon/15 ml of salt for 1 lb (500 g) of fresh or dried pasta). A small amount of oil can be added to prevent the pasta sticking together and some professional cooks believe that this also prevents the water from boiling over. Stir pasta gently as it softens. A large pot should be used so that the pasta can be cooked at a full boil (as pasta swell) and cooked evenly. Use about 2 quarts (3 l) of water for 1 lb (500 g) of pasta, and 1 more quart for every extra ½ lb (250 g) of fresh or dried pasta.

The cooking time is a matter of taste, but also depends on the quantity of pasta, its size and the hardness of the water. For al dente pasta, it is best to taste pasta during cooking so that it can be stopped at the right time.

The cooking time also varies depending on the moisture content of the pasta.
- Hard wheat pasta takes longer to cook than soft wheat pasta.
- Fresh pasta cooks more quickly than dried pasta.
- Pasta that will be cooked a second time or frozen should be cooked for a shorter time.
- Drain the pasta as soon as the cooking is finished.
- Once cooked, pasta should not be rinsed in cold water unless it is high in starch (soft wheat pasta, for example), to stop it from sticking, or if one wants to cool it down immediately (to make into a salad) or stop the cooking process (for dishes that require a second cooking process).

Some pastas can be used without being precooked, in dishes cooked in the oven (lasagna, manicotti, cannelloni, etc.), where it is a matter of increasing the amount of liquid or sauce.

Asian noodles

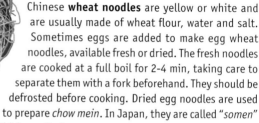

Noodles form an essential component in Asian cuisines. They are usually divided into groups according to their ingredients.

Chinese **wheat noodles** are yellow or white and are usually made of wheat flour, water and salt. Sometimes eggs are added to make egg wheat noodles, available fresh or dried. The fresh noodles are cooked at a full boil for 2-4 min, taking care to separate them with a fork beforehand. They should be defrosted before cooking. Dried egg noodles are used to prepare *chow mein*. In Japan, they are called "*somen*" (thin noodles) or "*udon*" (thick noodles).

fresh egg noodles

Rice noodles are made from rice flour and water and are found most notably as very thin, brittle noodles (rice vermicelli) or wide ribbons. They are often fried or added to soup. They need to be soaked for about 20 min in cold or lukewarm water before being cooked in boiling water or in a wok.

Mung bean noodles are transparent and are usually available in 3.5 oz (100 g) packets. They need to be soaked in lukewarm or hot water for about 10 min before being added to a dish, except if being added to a soup.

rice noodles
(ribbons)

Buckwheat and wheat noodles, called "*soba*" in Japan, are available fresh or dried. They are cooked at a full boil. They are often served cold with a soy sauce or added to soups.

Wonton noodles are very thin sheets of pasta based on wheat, water, eggs and salt, which are stuffed with meat, fish, seafood or vegetables. They are available fresh or frozen.

mung bean noodles

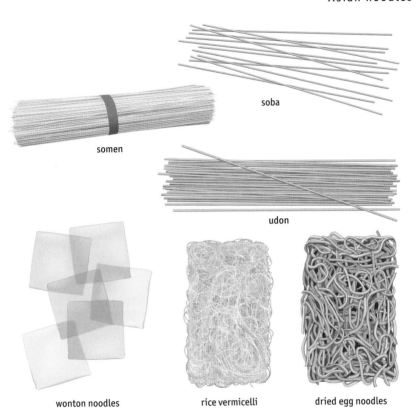

soba

somen

udon

wonton noodles

rice vermicelli

dried egg noodles

BUYING

:: **Choose:** fresh noodles that are supple and not sticky, neither too moist nor brittle; dried noodles without added artificial ingredients or preservatives.

STORING

:: **At room temperature:** dried noodles, indefinitely, in a dark, cool and dry place.
:: **In the fridge:** fresh egg noodles, 3-4 days.
:: **In the freezer:** fresh egg noodles, 1 month.

Introduction
Fish

The overwhelming majority of fish are saltwater species; the rest are freshwater species. Fish can also be divided into three other groups:
• lean fish, which contain less than 5% fat
• semifatty fish, which contain 5%-10% fat
• fatty fish, which contain more than 10% fat
Fish is a good source of protein, and fatty fish like salmon, tuna, sardines, herring, mackerel and lake trout are a good source of omega-3 fatty acids, which helps heart health.

As much as possible, avoid eating fish that live in polluted waters, as the flesh of some fish easily absorbs various very toxic substances, such as DDT (dichlorodiphenyl trichloroethane), PCB (polychlorinated biphenyl) and mercury.

TIPS FOR BUYING FISH

WHOLE FRESH FISH
• The gills should be moist and bright red.
• The eyes should be full, shiny and flush with the head.
• The skin should be glistening, pearly, tight and adhere to the flesh.
• The flesh should be firm and elastic; it should not be marked, retain finger impressions or separate easily from the bones.
• The scales should cling to the skin, and be shiny and intact.
• The belly should be neither swollen, nor dull, and should have a sweet and pleasant odor (a strong fish smell indicates lack of freshness).
• A muddy smell can impregnate various fish, depending on where they live, but it does not mean that the fish is not fresh.

FRESH FISH PORTION
• Fillets (pieces of flesh cut from along the spine).
• Steaks (thick cross-cuts) or pieces.
• The flesh should be firm, elastic and shiny, it should cling well to the bones and have a pleasant smell. It should not be brown, yellow or dried out.
• A defrosted fish will have a slightly different flavor and texture from a fresh fish. It should be eaten as soon as possible and should not be refrozen without being cooked beforehand.

FROZEN FISH
The flesh should have a fresh, firm and glistening appearance without evidence of drying or freezer burn. It should also be solidly frozen and enclosed in intact, watertight packaging, without frost or ice crystals on the inside.

SALT-CURED FISH
The flesh should have a good color and pleasant smell, and not be dried out.

SMOKED FISH
The flesh should have a pleasant smell and must retain its juice.

TIPS FOR STORING FISH

Wipe the fish well with a damp cloth, wrap in waxed paper and place in an airtight container in the fridge (2-3 days).

Fish can also be cold- or hot-smoked. Cold-smoked fish is not cooked; it is not as fine or flavorful as hot-smoked fish. Hot-smoked fish and fish that is salt-dried then cold-smoked are eaten as is, whereas fish that is brined, then cold-smoked needs to be cooked before storing. Smoked and salt-cured fish keep for a few days in the fridge or 3-4 weeks in the freezer.

FREEZING
Fish should always be cleaned before freezing and should be as fresh as possible. There are four possible methods:

:: Freezing in an ice block
Wash the fish in salted water (1 tablespoon/15 ml of salt per 4 cups/1 l of water), then place it in a container and cover with fresh water, up to 1 in. (2 cm) from the edge. Cover and freeze.

For steaks or fillets, remove the skin, rinse the fish under cold water, then put the slices or fillets in a container, separating them using a sheet of aluminum foil or plastic wrap. Cover them with water and freeze them as described above.

:: Freezing in layers of ice
Wash the fish, then freeze unwrapped. When it is frozen, plunge into ice water and return to the freezer. Repeat this process several times until the fish is covered in a layer of ice $1/8$ -$1/5$ in. (4-5 mm) thick, then wrap the fish airtight.

:: Lemon-flavored fish
Place the fish in a bowl containing lemon juice, moisten and turn the fish, repeat the process, then wrap and freeze.

:: Airtight-wrapped fish
Wash the fish, wrap carefully in food wrap and then in a freezer bag, taking care to expel all of the air. Freeze the fish quickly at a low temperature (0°F/-18°C or less).

TIPS FOR PREPARING FISH

FROZEN FISH

It is generally not necessary to defrost the fish before cooking; if it is thick, defrost it partly or completely so that it cooks as evenly on the inside as on the outside. Defrost the fish completely if it is to be grilled or fried.

To defrost a fish, place it in the fridge, in its original wrapping, for 18-24 hr (for 1 lb/500 g). Never defrost at room temperature; if time is short, place the fish in cold water (1-2 hr for 1 lb/500 g), but do not use hot water, as the fish will cook.

FRESH FISH

You can ask the grocer to prepare fresh fish for you. It is not necessary to remove the head, as the eyes and cheeks are edible and keeping the head attached limits loss of juices during cooking.

:: Scaling

Scale the fish without gutting it, using a fish scaler, the back of a knife, a fork or a blunt knife (to avoid cutting yourself). Hold the fish firmly by the tail, then remove the scales by holding the scaling implement at 45 degrees and moving it along the fish toward the head. Scale the fish under a stream of water to prevent the scales from scattering. If the fish is going to be cooked with the skin on, avoid damaging it. Do not scale the fish if it will be skinned.

:: Trimming

To trim the fish, cut the fins against their direction of growth. It is not necessary to remove the fins, particularly the back fins, which hold the flesh in place during cooking.

:: Gutting

The simplest way to gut a fish is through the belly. It can also be cleaned by making a small slice of ½-¾ in. (1-2 cm) near the gills and removing the insides with the index finger or a small spoon. The head can be cut at the base of the gills, then pushed gently toward the back. Large live fish (halibut, turbot, brill) must be bled before being cleaned. To do this, cut off the end of the fish near the tail.

CLEANING A FISH THROUGH THE BELLY

1 Make a slice from the anus to the gills using scissors.

2 Detach the guts and remove them.

3 Remove the gills.

4 Rinse the cavity and scrape the inside with a spoon.

:: Filleting

To avoid dirtying the flesh, wash the fish well under running water, working quickly after the fish has been gutted. If the stomach cavity is not open, force the water into it.

FILLETING A ROUND FISH

1 Rest the fish on its side and cut along the middle of the back (down to the spinal column) from the tail to the base of the head.

2 Separate the flesh from the backbone from the tail to the head.

3 Remove the fillet from the head by cutting behind the gills.

4 Hold the end of the tail firmly; make a slice about ¾ in. (2 cm) from the tail and carefully detach the fillet from the skin using the knife. Turn the fish over and repeat the process for the second fillet.

FILLETING A FLAT FISH

1 Start by cutting into the skin close to the tail.

2 Using a cloth, pull back the skin to the head.

3 Make a slice along the middle of the fish to divide the 2 fillets.

4 Insert the blade along the backbone and remove the fillet with a series of small cuts.

5 Detach the fillet from the lateral bones by making a slice along its length.

6 Turn the fish over and repeat the process to remove the other fillet. 4 fillets are obtained using this method.

TIPS FOR COOKING FISH

Fish can be prepared in a multitude of ways: marinated, smoked, stuffed, cooked in a sauce, as a mousse, as *quenelles* (dumplings), pâtés, terrines and rolled around a filling. Allow about 1 lb (500 g) of fish per person for whole fish, 9 oz (250 g) per person for trimmed fish (cleaned and scaled with its fins, head and gills removed), and close to 7 oz (200 g) if using fillets or steaks.

Fish can be cooked whole (gutted), in pieces, steaks or fillets. Cooking time should be short to prevent the fish from becoming dry and bland. To estimate cooking time, measure the thickest part of the fish and allow for 5-7 min per ½ in. (1 cm) of thickness for fresh fish cooked in the oven at 425°F (220°C) or partly defrosted fish cooked in the oven at 450°F (230°C), and 10-12 min per ½ in. (1 cm) of thickness for fish that is frozen solid.

The flesh is cooked when it becomes opaque but is still moist, has an even color and flakes easily. Serve immediately, as the fish can easily become overcooked in a hot dish.

:: Baked

1. Make a few cuts into whole fish so that the heat penetrates it well and, if desired, season the inside of the cavity.
2. Place the fish in a dish, lightly coat in fat or oil, cover (to taste) with finely sliced vegetables and thin rounds of lemon (or place on a bed of vegetables), dress with sauce, white wine or cream.
3. Set the oven to 450°F (230°C). If the fish is covered in a sauce containing milk, eggs or cheese, cook at 350°F (175°C).

:: Grilled or barbecued

Consists of cooking on a grill or spit-roast.

1. Use flour to coat fish that is lean or that has a tendency to dry out.
2. Slash the flesh of larger fish for faster cooking.
3. Brush the fish with fat or oil, or with sauce. Season the fish before and during cooking.
4. Place skinned fish, fish steaks or fillets on a very hot, lightly oiled grill. Cook fillets on the skinless side first. Place fish 6-8 in. (15-20 cm) from the heat source (3-4 in./7-10 cm for large fish). Turn thicker fish over in the middle of cooking, but not thin fish. When broiling fish in the oven, leave the door slightly ajar.

:: Poached

Consists of cooking slowly in a just-simmering liquid (court bouillon, milk, salted water, etc.). This method suits firm fillets and small whole fish particularly well.

- The liquid should contain an acidic ingredient (vinegar, dry wine, beer or lemon juice) to reduce the strong fish smell released during cooking, enhance the flavor and give a firm flesh.
- If the fish is salt-cured, do not add salt to the cooking liquid. Reduce the amount of salt if the fish is poached for a long time (to prevent the fish from becoming too salty).
- Poach the fish in only just enough liquid to cover it.
- Place the fish in cold liquid and heat until the liquid is just simmering so that the flesh cooks evenly. Don't cook fish in water at a full boil, as the bubbling breaks up the flesh and flavor is lost more quickly.
- Fish with exposed flesh (fillets, steaks) can be cooked in a court bouillon (vegetable broth or fish stock), which preserves the flavor and prevents the flesh from breaking up.
- Reduce cooking time by a few minutes for fish that will be served cold and let it cool in the cooking liquid.

:: Steamed

Consists of cooking fish using the steam released from a boiling liquid in the bottom of a saucepan. To avoid bland-tasting fish, place seasonings on top of or inside the fish (fresh herbs, spices, ginger, etc.). The cooking liquid should ideally contain an acidic ingredient.

1. Bring water (2 in./5 cm) to a boil, then place the fish on a rack, in a steaming basket or suspended in a fine cloth (such as cheesecloth) so that it is not in contact with the liquid.
2. Cover and cook according to the required cooking time.

:: "Au bleu"

Consists of poaching small fish, still alive or dead for less than 2 hr, in a vinegared, salted and flavored liquid. It is absolutely essential that the fish still have its slimy coating—that is, that it not be scaled (but it can be gutted). They turn blue during cooking as the result of a chemical reaction between the vinegar and the slimy liquid that coats them.

1. Sprinkle the fish on both sides with about ⅓ cup (100 ml) vinegar, then cook in a very vinegary court bouillon. If desired, the fish can be sprinkled with vinegar in the pot that will be used to cook it. The vinegar will then mix with the vinegared court bouillon, which will give a more acidic flavor.
2. Cook for 8-10 min.

:: "En papillote"

Consists of wrapping a fish airtight so that it cooks in the steam from its own natural moisture and that of any vegetables and liquids added.

1. Place the fish on a sheet of aluminum foil or parchment paper on a layer of thinly sliced vegetables and seasonings, or scatter the vegetables and seasonings over the fish.
2. Add a small amount of liquid (wine, soy sauce, broth or stock, sauce, cream or water).
3. Add lemon slices to taste and a small amount of fat or oil.
4. Fold the wrapper so that the package is airtight, and place in an oven dish.
5. Cook at 450°F (230°C) for the required time.

:: Braised

Consists of cooking food for a long time over a low heat in a covered container with very little liquid. This method suits firm-fleshed fish well.

1. Place the fish in a saucepan or fish casserole with a layer of various vegetables and fresh herbs in the bottom (if the fish is large, make a few slashes in its flesh so that the heat penetrates it well). Add a liquid (fish stock, white wine or court bouillon) to moisten the fish to halfway only. Cover and cook over a low heat on the stove top or in the oven.
2. Serve the fish as is or thicken the sauce. To thicken the sauce, remove the fish, strain the juices and reduce slightly over heat, or add a mixture of butter and flour (1 tablespoon/15 ml of each), 1 or 2 egg yolks, or a little cream.

FRYING

This is the most popular method of cooking fish, but also the least favorable from a nutritional point of view, as it increases the fat content of the fish.

Frying can be done in two ways: deep frying or shallow frying. In both cases, the fish is first floured, breaded or coated in batter.

:: Deep-fried

Consists of cooking fish by immersing it in boiling fat or oil.

1. If only cooking a small quantity of fish, or if the fish is small in size, use only a very small quantity of oil.
2. Heat the fat or oil to 375°F (190°C).
3. Soak the fish for 5 min in salted milk or dip it in a mixture of beaten egg and 1 tablespoon (15 ml) of water, or soak it in citrus juice (leave to soak 30 min for an impressive flavor). Drain the fish lightly, then coat well in flour, breadcrumbs or batter, with or without added seasonings or cheese.

Use oil with a high smoke-point (see *Oil*, p. 587). The temperature must be 350°F-370°F (175°C-190°C). Fry only a small quantity of fish at a time. When cooked, drain the fish, then place on a paper towel before serving.

:: Shallow-fried (**pan-fried** or **à la meunière**—fried with a pan sauce of lemon, parsley and flour)

1. Use only a very small amount of fat or oil. Butter or margarine can be used, especially if they are clarified (see *Butter*, p. 536).
2. Bread or flour the fish.
3. Ensure that the fat or oil is very hot but not smoking. If the fish sticks, it is because the pan is not hot enough.
4. Cook for the required time. Turn the fish once only, in the middle of the cooking time.
5. At the end of cooking, place the fish on paper towels.

The fish can also be cooked in the oven instead of a pan. This means that even less fat or oil can be used, the fish does not need to be turned and it cooks more quickly and evenly. Set the oven to 500°F (260°C).

MICROWAVING

This cooking method enhances the delicate flavor of fish, gives it a light and moist texture, and preserves its nutrients well.

1. Cook only one layer of fish at a time, placing larger or thicker pieces toward the outside of the dish. If the whole fish is too large for the container, bend it or remove the head and tail. Unless otherwise indicated in the recipe, cover the container loosely with one corner open to allow excess steam to escape.
2. Coat the fish lightly with fat or oil and season.
3. Make a few cuts into the skin of large fish so that it doesn't split during cooking. Make slashes in the flesh of large fillets if they are thick, so that they keep their shape.
4. Cook on the highest setting, allowing 8-10 min for a whole fish (1.5 lb/750 g) or 4-5 min for 1 lb (500 g) of fillets or steaks (for a 700 watt microwave), turning the dish in the middle of the cooking time.
5. Let the fish rest for 2-3 min in the microwave before serving.

Kamaboko

A Japanese word that refers to seafood substitutes made from *surimi*, a paste made from fish flesh.

kamaboko

BUYING

Here are some tips to help distinguish imitation seafood products from genuine seafood:
• Their shape is too perfect.
• Their flesh is formed of long, regular threads.
• The very white flesh has a pink or red surface.

PREPARING

To make the imitation seafood, the surimi paste is ground, then water, starch, egg white, monosodium glutamate and natural or artificial flavor are added and the whole mixture is combined. This paste is partly cooked and put through various equipment to give it its final shape (sticks, crab flesh pieces, shrimp, etc.). It undergoes a final cooking, then it is pasteurized and sterilized. Sometimes a small quantity of real seafood is added to the surimi. The flavor of the final product is sometimes quite close to the flavor of the imitated food. Kamaboko is less expensive than the natural product and it is often used as a replacement.

NUTRITIONAL INFORMATION

	steamed
protein	12 g
fat	1 g
calories	52
	per 3.5 oz/100 g

Kamaboko is high in protein and low in fat and calories. It is low in cholesterol if no crustaceans have been used in the surimi paste. It contains several additives and up to 3-4 times more sodium than the seafood it imitates. The frequent presence of monosodium glutamate can cause allergic reactions in some people.

STORING

:: **In the fridge:** a few days.
:: **In the freezer:** if it has not already been frozen.

SERVING IDEAS

Kamaboko is eaten hot or cold. Because it is precooked, it can be used as is in salads, sandwiches and canapés. It can replace genuine seafood in most recipes.

Eel

Anguilla spp., Anguillidae

A fish measuring up to 5 ft (1.5 m) long and weighing more than 9 lb (4 kg) (the male is smaller than the female). Eel flesh is fine, firm and fatty; its bones are easily removed. Only the **American eel** is found in North America, whereas the **European eel** is found near the coasts of Europe, Australia and New Zealand. It is especially enjoyed in Europe and Japan.

When the eel is close to 3 years old, it measures 2-3½ in. (6-9 cm) in length and is transparent. It is called an "elver" or "glass eel," and its tasty flesh is highly regarded.

European eel

BUYING

 Eel is sold as fillets, steaks or pieces, fresh, smoked, marinated or canned. In some countries, it is kept alive in water tanks.

SERVING IDEAS

Avoid preparing eel with products that increase its fat content.

PREPARING

Skin the eel before cooking to remove its excess fat. To do this, cut the eel into thick slices and poach for 1-2 min in boiling water to soften the skin. They can also be grilled without being cooked (the skin blisters and is easily removed).

STORING

 :: **In the fridge:** 1-2 days.

NUTRITIONAL INFORMATION

	raw
protein	18 g
fat	12 g
calories	184
	per 3.5 oz/100 g

GOOD SOURCE: vitamin A and vitamin D.

COOKING

:: **Grilled, baked, smoked, poached** or **sautéed**.

:: **Fried:** first poach the eel for 8-12 min in salted water to which 1-2 teaspoons (5-10 ml) of lemon juice has been added.

Eel can also be cooked in stews or soups (for example, the fish soup *bouillabaisse*). The heat takes a certain time to penetrate the eel flesh.

Bass

Micropterus spp., Centrarchidae

A fish that lives in the rivers and lakes of North America and is considered part of the "sunfish" family, which is different than the sea bass family (page 346). Bass reaches a maximum length of 2 ft (65 cm). Its white flesh is lean, flaky and very tasty. The **smallmouth bass** is found in the rocky parts of lakes and rivers. It usually measures 8-15 in. (20-38 cm) in length and weighs no more than 3 lb (1.5 kg).

The **largemouth bass**, with a slightly more solid body than the smallmouth bass, prefers warm waters, slow-moving bodies of water and muddy lakes. The largemouth bass is also called "black bass" or "green trout."

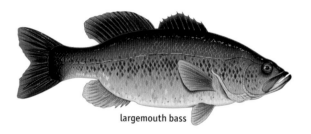

largemouth bass

BUYING

 Bass is a game fish; it is rarely sold commercially.

SERVING IDEAS

 A medium-sized bass is prepared in the same way as trout, while a large bass is prepared in the same way as carp or shad. The older the fish (the larger in size), the higher its potential level of contamination. Limit consumption unless the cleanliness of its habitat is known.

NUTRITIONAL INFORMATION

	raw
protein	19 g
fat	4 g
calories	114
	per 3.5 oz/100 g

COOKING

Bass is suited to all cooking methods.

PREPARING

Before scaling, plunge the bass for a few moments in boiling water to which some lemon juice has been added (this will make scaling easier). The skin can also be removed.

Pike

Esox spp., Esocidae

A fish that lives in the rivers, lakes and ponds of North America, Europe and Asia. The white flesh of the pike is lean, firm and flaky. There are several species of pike. The **northern pike** is the most common. It weighs on average 2-4 lb (1-2 kg); it measures 1-2 ft (35-70 cm) in length. The **chain pickerel** is rather small (16-20 in./40-50 cm), with very tender flesh. The **grass pickerel** is often too small (5-8 in./15-20 cm) for good eating. The **muskellunge**, or "muskie," is the largest of the whole family. It measures 2-4 ft (70-120 cm) in length and weighs 4-35 lb (2-16 kg).

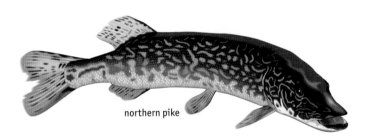

northern pike

BUYING

Pike is sold fresh or frozen, whole or in fillets. Small pike is more tender and thus better than large pike.

PREPARING

Pike flesh sometimes has a muddy taste. To remove this, soak the fish for 1-2 hr in fresh or vinegared water (1-2 tablespoons/20-30 ml of vinegar for 1 cup/250 ml of water). Pike can be cooked without being scaled, whole, in fillets or steaks (remove the skin before serving). Do not overwash the fish before cooking, as its slimy coating retains moisture, which keeps it more tender.

NUTRITIONAL INFORMATION

protein	19 g
fat	0.7 g
calories	88
	per 3.5 oz/100 g

SERVING IDEAS

Because it contains many soft, small bones, pike is often made into pâté, *quenelles* (dumplings) or fish loaf.

COOKING

 Pike is suited to all cooking methods.

Carp

Cyprinus carpio, Cyprinidae

A fish inhabiting the warm, shallow waters of the rivers, lakes, ponds and canals of North America, Europe, Africa and Asia. Carp can measure 13-18 in. (35-45 cm) in length and often weighs more than 15 lb (7 kg). Its white flesh is firm and semifatty.

carp

BUYING

Carp is sometimes sold smoked.

SERVING IDEAS

Carp is cooked whole, in fillets or in sections. The eggs, cheeks, tongue and lips are highly sought after.

COOKING

Carp is suited to all cooking methods. It is often quick-braised, roasted, poached, grilled or fried.

NUTRITIONAL INFORMATION

protein	18 g
fat	4.6 g
calories	127
	per 3.5 oz/100 g

EXCELLENT SOURCE: niacin, phosphorus and vitamin B_{12}.

PREPARING

Carp varies in flavor. Wild species of carp often have a muddy taste. To remove this, soak the scaled and gutted carp (remove the bladder from underneath the head) for 1-2 hr in slightly vinegared water, refreshing the water occasionally. To make scaling easier, plunge the carp in boiling water for a few moments.

Pike-perch

Stizostedion spp., Percidae

A fish that lives in freshwater lakes and large rivers, whose white, lean flesh is firm, delicate and tasty. In Europe, pike-perch is called "zander."

Zander is found in Scandinavia, Europe (where it is also called "pike-perch") and England; it measures 2-3¼ ft (60-100 cm) in length and can weigh 22 lb (10 kg).
Walleye, or "yellow walleye," has smooth cheeks. It measures 13-20 in. (33-50 cm) in length and weighs 2-4 lb (1-2 kg). **Sauger**, or "Canadian pike-perch," has cheeks covered with rough scales. It measures 10-16 in. (25-40 cm) in length and weighs 1 lb (0.5 kg) on average. Some consider its flesh superior to the yellow walleye.

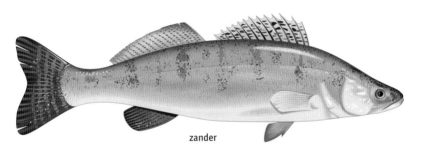

zander

BUYING

Pike-perch is sold whole, trimmed or as fillets, fresh or frozen.

SERVING IDEAS

Pike-perch is prepared in the same way as any firm-fleshed fish (for example, perch or pike), whole or in fillets.

NUTRITIONAL INFORMATION

	sauger
protein	17 g
fat	1 g
calories	83
	per 3.5 oz/100 g

COOKING

Pike-perch is suited to all cooking methods.

Perch

Perca spp., Percidae

A fish that lives in fresh or briny waters. Perch is found almost everywhere in the world. It measures ¾-1½ ft (25-50 cm) in length and weighs up to 7.5 lb (3.5 kg); its average weight is about 1 lb (500 g). Perch contains a lot of bones. Its white, lean and firm flesh has a delicate taste.

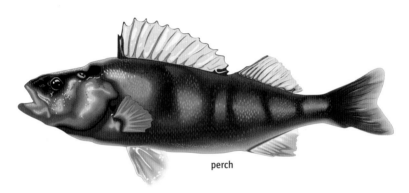

perch

BUYING

Perch is a game fish; it is rarely sold commercially.

COOKING

Perch is cooked whole or in fillets.
:: Poached, quick-braised or **à la meunière** (shallow fried with a pan sauce of flour, lemon and parsley), **broiled, fried** and **baked.**

SERVING IDEAS

Perch works well in recipes for carp or trout. Avoid masking the delicate nature of its flesh.

NUTRITIONAL INFORMATION

	raw
protein	19 g
fat	0.9 g
calories	91
	per 3.5 oz/100 g

EXCELLENT SOURCE: niacin, vitamin, B$_{12}$, phosphorus and potassium.

PREPARING

Scale perch as soon as it comes out of the water; otherwise, this becomes a more complicated process and it is often necessary to remove the skin. Perch can be poached or plunged for a few moments in boiling water before being scaled. Be careful of the spikes in its fins.

Trout

Salmo spp., Salmonidae

A fish that lives in the cold waters of lakes and rivers and in the sea; in the latter case, it returns to freshwater to spawn. The trout is a close relative of the char and grayling, highly sought-after fish with very fine flesh. The various species of trout have flesh that is semifatty, very fine and very aromatic. Its especially delicate flavor varies slightly depending on the species. Its coloring also varies, being white, ivory, pink or reddish.

The **brown trout**, or "European trout," has pink flesh which is delicious. The **rainbow trout** owes its name to the horizontal band of color, varying from dark pink to bright red or even purple, that features on its metal-blue back and sides. The **lake char**, or "American char," is distinguished from the others by its more elongated body, usually spotted with pale, sometimes yellowish, markings and by its forked tail. It varies in color. The **brook trout**, or "speckled trout," is smaller. The **Arctic char** is distinguished by the beauty of its colorings, often dark blue or blue-green on the back, silver-blue on the sides and white on its belly. Its sides are flecked with large red, pink or cream spots. Its size varies depending on its habitat. The **grayling** has a scent of thyme when freshly caught. Its whole body is flecked with a variable number of lozenge- or V-shaped markings. It is a very beautiful fish than can measure 16-20 in. (40-50 cm) in length.

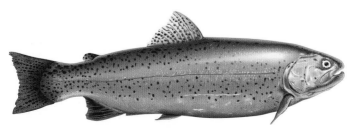

rainbow trout

brook trout

BUYING

Trout is sold fresh or frozen, whole, trimmed, as fillets and sometimes as steaks. It is also found smoked or in cans.

SERVING IDEAS

Prepare trout as simply as possible so as not to mask its delicate flavor. Trout is delicious smoked. All recipes for salmon are suitable for trout.

NUTRITIONAL INFORMATION

protein	21 g
fat	7 g
calories	148
	per 3.5 oz/100 g

PREPARING

The scales on the skin can be left on. The fillets are very easy to remove.

SALTWATER FISH

Mullet

Mugil spp., Mugilidae

A fish found in the waters of the Atlantic, Mediterranean and Pacific, as in coastal rivers. It usually measures 12-16 in. (30-40 cm) in length. The most common species of mullet is the gray mullet.

mullet

NUTRITIONAL INFORMATION

	raw
protein	19 g
fat	4 g
calories	116
	per 3.5 oz/100 g

SERVING IDEAS

 Mullet is eaten smoked, hot or cold. Its eggs are used to make *bottarga* (a Provencale specialty of salted, pressed and dried fish eggs) and *taramasalata* (a pink dip from Greece).

COOKING

Mullet is suited to all cooking methods (cook without gutting if small).

< rainbow trout

Bluefish

Pomatomus saltatrix, Pomatomidae

A fish that lives in the Atlantic and Pacific oceans. Bluefish generally measures 16-24 in. (40-60 cm) in length and weighs 10-15 lb (4.5-6.8 kg). It has lean and tasty flesh.

bluefish

SERVING IDEAS

 Bluefish is prepared in the same way as mackerel, which it can replace. Fry bluefish only if small.

PREPARING

Bleed bluefish as soon as it is caught so that its flesh retains its flavor and stays firm. Fish measuring 4-6 in. (10 - 15 cm) in length do not need to be scaled.

NUTRITIONAL INFORMATION

	raw
protein	20 g
fat	4 g
calories	124
	per 3.5 oz/100 g

STORING

:: **In the fridge:** eat as soon as possible.
:: **In the freezer:** 3 months.

Shad

Alosa spp., Clupeidae

A fish that is sought after for both its flesh and eggs. One of the most important fish in North America, shad is also fished in western Europe and on the Mediterranean. Its white flesh is fatty, tender and flaky. The female shad carries delicious eggs. Its bones are larger, and thus more easily avoided, than those of the male shad.

The **American shad** lives in the Atlantic and the Pacific. It measures 16-30 in. (40-75 cm) in length and weighs 2-6.5 lb (1-3 kg). The **twaite shad** measures 8-16 in. (20-40 cm) and reaches a maximum length of 20 in. (50 cm). It lives in the Atlantic, the Baltic Sea, the North Sea and the Mediterranean. The **allis shad** reaches a maximum length of 28 in. (70 cm). It is found on the European Atlantic coasts and in the Mediterranean. The **alewife** measures 10-12 in. (25-30 cm) and can reach a maximum length of 16 in. (40 cm).

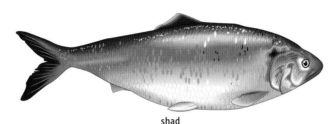

shad

BUYING

Shad is sold fresh or frozen, whole or as fillets.

SERVING IDEAS

Shad is prepared with acidic ingredients (sorrel, rhubarb and gooseberries). It can replace herring and mackerel in most recipes.

STORING

Cook shad as soon as possible, as it deteriorates quickly.

NUTRITIONAL INFORMATION

	raw
protein	17 g
fat	14 g
calories	197
	per 3.5 oz/100 g

COOKING

Cook shad whole if one has little practice removing fillets. Cooking shad briefly allows the bones to be removed more easily.

Monkfish

Lophius spp., Lophiidae

A fish that dwells at the muddy bottoms of the Atlantic and the Mediterranean. Monkfish, often called "lotte," can measure 20 in.-7 ft (50 cm-2 m) in length and reach a weight of 90 lb (40 kg). The only edible parts are the tail, whose boneless flesh is often compared to lobster, and for some, the liver.

monkfish

BUYING

Monkfish is sold fresh, frozen or smoked. It is usually skinned, with its head removed. Have any membrane on the tail removed.

COOKING

:: **Braised:** 30 min.
:: **Poached** or **grilled:** 20 min.
Monkfish flesh has a tendency to become dry. Baste often when grilling or roasting and serve with a sauce.

NUTRITIONAL INFORMATION

protein	14 g
fat	1.5 g
calories	75
	per 3.5 oz/100 g

SERVING IDEAS

Monkfish can replace lobster. It is excellent cold, dressed with vinaigrette. Its head can be used to flavor soup.

Sea bass

Disentrarchus labrax, Serranidae

A fish of the North Atlantic and Mediterranean whose prized white flesh is lean, delicate, tasty and has few bones. Includes striped bass. "Chilean sea bass" is really Patagonian tooth fish. Sea bass can reach 3 ft (1 m) in length.

Sea bass

PREPARING

Do not scale sea bass if it is to be poached or grilled whole. Once cooked, remove the skin; the scales will be removed at the same time and the flesh will be less dry.

NUTRITIONAL INFORMATION

	raw
protein	18 g
fat	2 g
calories	96
	per 3.5 oz/100 g

COOKING

:: **Poached, roasted, grilled, braised, fried** or **stuffed.**
Prepare simply; it is excellent cold.

Sturgeon

Acipenser spp., Acipenseridae

A fish found in both the fresh and sea waters of the Northern Hemisphere. Sturgeon can weigh over a ton and reach 13 ft (4 m) in length. The different species of sturgeon include the **white sturgeon**, the **shortnose sturgeon**, the **starry sturgeon** (or "serruga"), the **Beluga sturgeon** and the **sterlet**. Sturgeon is sought after for its flesh and especially for its eggs, which are used to make genuine caviar (see page 348).

Its white, blue-veined flesh, which contains very few bones, is lean, and more or less moist, firm and tasty, depending on the species.

white sturgeon

BUYING

Rarely sold fresh commercially, sturgeon is frozen or canned. It can be smoked, salt-cured or marinated. Its flesh becomes pink, veined with brown or yellow as it loses freshness.

PREPARING

As the flesh is rather firm, it is best to let it rest 48 hr when the sturgeon is freshly caught. The flesh is also marinated before cooking to tenderize it. To skin the sturgeon or make it more digestible, poach for a few minutes.

NUTRITIONAL INFORMATION

	raw
protein	16 g
fat	4 g
calories	106
	per 3.5 oz/100 g

EXCELLENT SOURCE: niacin, phosphorus, vitamin B_{12} and potassium.

SERVING IDEAS

Sturgeon flesh is prepared in the same way as that of land animals. It works well in recipes for swordfish or tuna. It is delicious cold and smoked.
The dried spinal marrow of the sturgeon (*vesiga*) is used in Russia to make pie fillings (the fish pie *coulibiac*).

Caviar

Salted sturgeon eggs from the Black or Caspian seas. Caviar enjoys enormous prestige. The size, flavor and color of the sturgeon eggs varies depending on whether they are "Beluga," "Ossetra" or "Sevruga" varieties. The eggs can be golden, black, brown, dark green or gray. They are classified according to their size, color, firmness and flavor. The salting process determines the quality of the caviar, so the quantity of added salt is carefully monitored. Salmon, carp, cod, whitefish, herring, pike and tuna eggs are also edible, but they must be sold under another name. Caviar is low in fat.

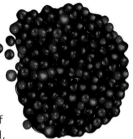

Beluga caviar

SALTWATER FISH

BUYING

Caviar is available as separate granules or pressed (riper eggs pressed together), in glass or metal containers. The best-quality caviar is called *malassol* and contains less than 5% salt. Pressed caviar is called *payusnaya* and contains 10% salt.

SERVING IDEAS

Caviar is only eaten raw at a cool (not cold) temperature. Remove from the fridge 15 min before serving (place the container on ice). Caviar is eaten as is, alone or accompanied by toast, butter and lemon juice. Russians like to spread caviar on blinis (small buckwheat pancakes), accompanied by sour cream and vodka.

NUTRITIONAL INFORMATION

protein	2.5 g
fat	1.8 g
calories	25
	per .35 oz/10 g

EXCELLENT SOURCE: vitamin A, vitamin B$_{12}$, magnesium, iron and sodium.

STORING

:: **In the fridge:** keep unopened caviar at a temperature of 30°F-45°F (0°C-7°C) (a few weeks). Opened caviar must be eaten quickly.

Sardine

Sardina pilchardus, Clupeidae

A fish that lives in schools in the temperate waters of the Atlantic, Mediterranean and Pacific. In North America, what is sold, canned, under the name "sardine" is in fact a small herring. In several countries, adult sardines are called "pilchards." In France, this term refers to canned herrings or sardines prepared in an oil- or tomato-based sauce. Sardines measure 6-8 in. (15-20 cm) in length. They have delicious, semifatty flesh.

sardine

BUYING

Sardines are rarely sold fresh, but if found, choose firm fish with bright eyes and skin. They can be sold smoked or salt-cured. Sardines, with their head and insides removed and cooked in their own juices, are canned. Sardines in oil improve with age.

SERVING IDEAS

Canned sardines are often eaten as is, with or without a sprinkling of lemon juice and accompanied by buttered bread. They are also marinated or made into a pâté with lemon juice and butter or with cream cheese and spices.

PREPARING

Scale, gut, clean and remove the heads of fresh sardines before cooking. Very fresh small sardines can simply be wiped.

NUTRITIONAL INFORMATION

protein	19 g
fat	5 g
calories	85
	per 3.5 oz/100 g

EXCELLENT SOURCE: phosphorus, vitamin B_6, niacin and calcium when the bones are eaten.

COOKING

:: **Grilled, roasted**.
Avoid cooking methods that increase its fat content.

STORING

Turn unopened cans of sardines over occasionally so that the sardines are always immersed in the liquid.
:: **In the fridge:** opened can.

Anchovy

Engraulis encrasicolus, Engraulidae

A fish that prefers warm waters; it is common in the Mediterranean but it also lives in other seas, including the Atlantic and the Black Sea. Anchovies measure 5-8 in. (12-20 cm) in length; 20 anchovies are usually needed to make 2 lb (1 kg). Anchovies are fatty and high in calories.

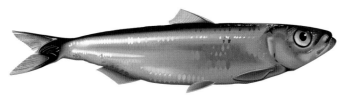

anchovy

BUYING

Highly perishable, anchovies are rarely sold fresh. They are sold in jars or cans, in brine, oil or salt. They are also sold as a paste, cream, butter or in the form of an essence.

SERVING IDEAS

In the Mediterranean, anchovies are used in several dishes (*pissaladière*—an onion tart; *tapenade*—an olive paste; *anchoïade*—an anchovy dip; and the classic Caesar salad). Its essence flavors soups and sauces. Anchovy paste and butter are used to baste meat and fish before cooking and for spreading on brown bread.

NUTRITIONAL INFORMATION

	canned, in oil
protein	29 g
fat	10 g
calories	210
	per 3.5 oz/100 g

PREPARING

To desalt anchovies, run them carefully under cold water. They will have more flavor if they have been steeped in milk, dry wine or wine vinegar for 30-90 min.

Herring

Clupea harengus, Clupeidae

A fish from the Atlantic and Pacific oceans. The herring is one of the most plentiful and harvested saltwater fish in the world. Herring measures 6-12 in. (15-30 cm) in length and can attain a maximum length of 17 in. (43 cm). It weighs 0.5-1.5 lb (250-750 g). The shape of the herring varies slightly, depending on species and habitat. Its white, fatty and tasty flesh contains many bones that are easily removed.

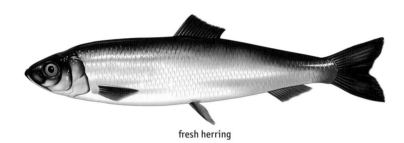

fresh herring

BUYING

Herring is sold fresh and frozen, whole or as fillets, but also canned, marinated, salt-cured and smoked.

- **Marinated herring:** whole herring with its bones removed, fried and immersed in a marinade. In North America, canned sardines are in fact herring.
- **Smoked herring:** cold- or hot-smoked herring.
- **Cured herring:** herring that is cold-smoked over a long period of time and salt-cured. It can be cleaned or uncleaned. Whole cured herring is sold by the piece. As fillets, it is sold in cans, sachets or marinated. It keeps 12-15 days. Its smoked eggs are sold in cans.
- **Bloater:** usually a whole herring, ungutted, barely salted, semismoked (hot or cold). It keeps for about 5 days.

- **Buckling:** lightly brined herring, hot-smoked and thus partly cooked, which can be eaten without further cooking. This treatment is especially popular in Germany and Holland. Buckling keeps for about 4 days.
- **Kipper:** a large herring with its head removed, split in two along the back, boned, flattened, barely smoked (cold). Kippers can be eaten as is or they can be cooked for a few moments. They are sold fresh in cans, frozen or in ready-to-cook sachets. They keep for 4 days.

SERVING IDEAS

Herring can replace mackerel in most recipes. It is very often marinated, smoked and canned.

PREPARING

To scale herring, it is usually enough to simply wipe it. Herring can be gutted via the gills or by cutting through the spinal column behind the head.

NUTRITIONAL INFORMATION

	raw
protein	18 g
fat	9 g
calories	158
	per 3.5 oz/100 g

EXCELLENT SOURCE: B-complex vitamins, phosphorus, potassium and fat.

COOKING

:: **Grilled**, **baked** or **pan-fried**.
Herring is not well suited to steaming or poaching, as it is too fragile. Avoid overcooking.

SALTWATER FISH

smoked herring

Mackerel

Scomber spp., Scombridae

A fish that lives in most seas and oceans, including the Pacific, Atlantic and Mediterranean.

The **common** or **Atlantic mackerel** measures 12-22 in. (30-55 cm) in length and weighs 1-2 lb (0.5-1 kg) (maximum 4.5 lb/2 kg). Atlantic mackerel is the most common species in North America. A similar species lives in the warm waters of the Pacific, from Japan to Australia.

The **Spanish mackerel**, whose maximum length is 20 in. (50 cm), lives in the east Atlantic, the Mediterranean, the Black Sea and the Pacific.

Mackerels have tasty white flesh that is fairly fatty. It has a fatty strip that is darker on the outside, which makes it bitter and more difficult to digest.

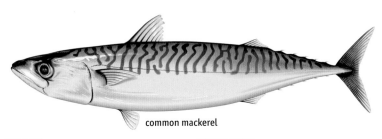

common mackerel

BUYING

:: **Choose:** a firm, stiff mackerel with metallic glints, bright eyes and a rounded belly that is quite white.

:: **Avoid:** mackerel whose stomach has burst (it will no longer be edible).

Mackerel is sold whole or as fillets, fresh or frozen, canned in its own juice, in sauce, white wine or oil. It is also available salt-cured or smoked under the name of "buckling."

COOKING

:: **Baked, poached in stock, grilled** or **en papillote.**

PREPARING

Remove the dark fatty strip, marinate the flesh or baste it with a marinade while cooking to make it more digestible. To remove the fillets, insert the knife between the flesh and the bones that jut out in the middle of the ribs to separate them properly.

STORING

:: **In the fridge:** eat mackerel as soon as possible, as its flesh spoils quickly.

:: **In the freezer:** mackerel loses a great deal of flavor when frozen.

SERVING IDEAS

Mackerel can be prepared any way, but avoid increasing its fat content. It can be eaten hot or cold, smoked or marinated. It is served with gooseberry sauce. It is greatly enjoyed as a *ceviche* (a lime juice and onion marinade); check, however, that it doesn't contain any parasites. It can be used in place of canned tuna, herring or shad in most recipes.

NUTRITIONAL INFORMATION

	raw
protein	19 g
fat	14 g
calories	205
	per 3.5 oz/100 g

EXCELLENT SOURCE: vitamin B_{12}.
CONTAINS: omega-3 fatty acids that offer protection agains cardiovascular diseases by thinning the blood and preventing the formation of clots.

Gurnard

Trigla spp., Triglidae

A fish that lives in the Atlantic, Mediterranean and Pacific. Its slightly flaky pink flesh is delicious.

The **gray gurnard** can measure about 20 in. (50 cm) in length. It is found near the coasts of Iceland and Norway down to the Mediterranean. Its flesh is firm and tasty.

The **red gurnard**, which usually measures 12 in. (30 cm) in length, lives in the Mediterranean, Atlantic and Pacific. As it is not very fleshy, it is often cooked in soup.

The **American gurnard**, or "northern sea robin," can reach 15 in. (37 cm) in length and weighs about 1.8 lb (800 g). It lives close to the American Atlantic coasts. Its flesh is lean, firm and tasty.

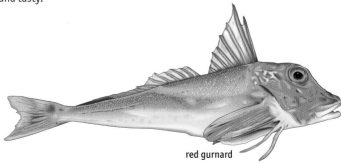

red gurnard

Gurnard

NUTRITIONAL INFORMATION

	raw
protein	17 g
fat	3 g
calories	100
	per 3.5 oz/100 g

EXCELLENT SOURCE: potassium and calcium.

SERVING IDEAS

 Gurnard is often used in the fish soups *bouillabaisse* and *matelote*.

PREPARING

Remove the spiky fins to avoid injuries. Leave gurnard whole or cut into fillets or sections. The skin is easily removed.

COOKING

:: **Grilled** or **baked:** brush the skin with oil or marinade.
:: **Poached, fried** or **smoked.**
Gurnard dries out when exposed to excessively high heat.

Sea bream

Chrysophrys aurata, Sparidae

A coastal fish found in the tropical waters of the Atlantic and Mediterranean. Sea bream measures 8-14 in. (20-35 cm) in length and weighs 0.5-6.5 lb (0.3-3 kg). It has lean, very fine and tasty white flesh.

sea bream

NUTRITIONAL INFORMATION

protein	16 g
fat	0.5 g
calories	73
	per 3.5 oz/100 g

BUYING

Sea bream is sold fresh, gutted, or frozen, as fillets.

SERVING IDEAS

Sea bream is prepared in all ways, in particular as sashimi, ceviche or smoked. Its eggs are excellent.

PREPARING

The sea bream has large, numerous, adhesive scales. It is important to scale sea bream as soon as possible. To avoid scaling the fish, remove the fillets, then pull on the skin, which should come away easily, as it is thick. Sea bream has lots of bones. They can be removed when the fish is skinned and filleted. It is then possible to simply locate the bones with the fingers and pull them out, taking care not to damage the flesh.

Conger

Conger spp., Congridae

A fish that can measure 10 ft (3 m) in length and weigh up to 110 lb (50 kg). The conger lives in the Atlantic, Mediterranean and Pacific. Its white, lean and firm flesh has no bones, except near the tail. The smaller specimens are bland. The black conger is considered to be the best.

conger

BUYING

Conger is sold whole (gutted, with its head removed), in sections or in slices.

SERVING IDEAS

Often an ingredient in fish soups such as *bouillabaisse* and *matelote*, conger can be cooked any way, especially the flesh from the middle of the body up to the head.

NUTRITIONAL INFORMATION

protein	20 g
fat	3 g
calories	100
	per 3.5 oz/100 g

EXCELLENT SOURCE: potassium and magnesium.

Swordfish

Xiphias gladius, Xiphiidae

A fish that lives on both sides of the Atlantic, in the North Sea, Baltic Sea and Mediterranean. Swordfish measures 7-10 ft (2-3 m) in length and weighs 200-350 lb (90-160 kg). Its very firm white flesh is tasty and highly regarded.

swordfish

COOKING

Swordfish steaks or fillets can be cooked marinated or unmarinated.
:: **Roasted, grilled:** 5-7 min on each side.

:: **Braised:** 20-30 min.
:: **Sautéed:** 4-6 min on each side.
Avoid overcooking, as it dries swordfish out.

Swordfish

BUYING

 Swordfish is sold fresh as steaks, frozen, smoked or canned.

SERVING IDEAS

 Fresh swordfish is more digestible if it is poached for 10-15 min before being prepared. It is cooked in the same way as other firm-fleshed fish (halibut, sturgeon and tuna). The tail and fins are edible.

NUTRITIONAL INFORMATION

	raw
protein	20 g
fat	4 g
calories	121
	per 3.5 oz/100 g

EXCELLENT SOURCE: vitamin B$_{12}$, niacin, potassium and phosphorus.

Goatfish

Mullus spp., Mullidae

A fish often called simply "mullet," found in the warm, shallow waters of the Mediterranean Sea and the Pacific, Atlantic and Indian oceans as well as the Gulf Coast. Goatfish is often tinted red or pink. Its flesh is lean, firm and contains several small bones. It quickly loses its brightness, which indicates lack of freshness. The most common Mediterranean species include the **striped red mullet**, which usually measures 8-10 in. (20-25 cm) in length; the **red goatfish**, which resembles the striped red mullet; and the **red mullet**, which measures 4-8 in. (10-20 cm) in length.

striped red mullet

SERVING IDEAS

Goatfish is highly prized, especially in the south of France. Prepare simply so as not to mask its flavor. It can be cooked whole (when small) or gutted; but in this case, leave the liver inside, as it is very tasty.

NUTRITIONAL INFORMATION

	raw
protein	20 g
fat	2 g
calories	88
	per 3.5 oz/100 g

PREPARING

 Scale goatfish carefully, as its skin is fragile.

Redfish

Sebastes spp., Scorpaenidae

A fish also called "red drum" that lives in the deep waters of the North Sea and the shallow southern waters. Redfish measures 8-22 in. (20-55 cm) in length and weighs 1-4 lb (0.5-2 kg). Its flesh, sometimes pink, is lean, firm, flaky and very tasty.

large redfish

The **large redfish** measures 14-22 in. (35-55 cm) in length and can reach 3¼ ft (1 m). It lives on both sides of the North Atlantic.

The **large-scaled scorpionfish** reaches a maximum length of 20 in. (50 cm). It lives in the deep waters of the Mediterranean and east Atlantic. Scorpionfish are also referred to by their French name, "*rascasse*."

The **blade scorpionfish** measures 6 in. (15 cm) on average and reaches a maximum length of 10 in. (25 cm). It lives in the shallower waters of the Mediterranean.

BUYING

 Redfish is sold fresh or frozen, whole or as fillets.

COOKING

 Whole or as fillets, redfish and scorpionfish are suited to all cooking methods.

:: Poached in fish stock or **grilled:** leave the skin on.

PREPARING

 Remove the spiky fins as soon as possible.

NUTRITIONAL INFORMATION

	raw
protein	19 g
fat	2 g
calories	94
	per 3.5 oz/100 g

SERVING IDEAS

 Redfish is eaten raw, cooked, smoked or cold. It is used in a classic Cajun dish: "blackened" redfish is highly seasoned and pan-charred in butter. In the south of France, a genuine *bouillabaisse* must contain scorpionfish. Large-scaled scorpionfish is also used in the fish soup *matelote*. If it is fleshy, it can be cooked in a more elaborate manner.

Salmon

Oncorhynchus spp. and *Salmo salar*, Salmonidae

Five species of salmon live in the Pacific (*Oncorhynchus spp.*); one lives in the Atlantic (*Salmo salar*); and one is a permanent freshwater fish (the ouananiche, or landlocked, salmon, *Salmo salar ouananiche*).

The **chinook salmon**, or "king salmon," measures 33-36 in. (84-91 cm) in length and weighs 30-40 lb (13.5-18 kg). The color of its flesh varies from light pink to dark orange. The most prized of the Pacific salmon, it is especially sold fresh, frozen or smoked. Chinook salmon is the fattiest of the salmon.

The **red salmon**, or "sockeye salmon," is the most sought-after species after the chinook salmon. It measures on average 24-28 in. (60-70 cm) in length and weighs 4-7 lb (2-3 kg). Its matte red flesh is firm, semifatty and very tasty. It keeps its color when canned. It is most commonly found in this form, but also smoked or salt-cured.

The **coho salmon**, or "silver salmon," measures 18-24 in. (45-60 cm) in length and weighs 4-10 lb (2-4.5 kg). It is the third most commercially important species. Its orange-red flesh is almost equal to the flesh of red or chinook salmon. It is paler than the flesh of the red salmon. The flesh of the coho salmon is semifatty. Used a great deal in canning, coho salmon is also sold fresh, frozen, smoked or lightly brined.

The **pink salmon**, is the smallest of the group. It measures 17-19 in. (43-48 cm) and weighs 3-5 lb (1.3-2.3 kg). For a long time, it has been considered as a species of inferior quality (like the chum salmon), as its pink flesh is rather soft and breaks up into small pieces. Pink salmon is lean. Mostly used for canning, it is also sold fresh, smoked or frozen.

The **chum salmon**, or "dog salmon," measures 25 in. (64 cm) in length on average and weighs 11-13 lb (5-6 kg). Its flesh is the least attractive and lowest in quality. Barely pink, it is spongy and soft, and breaks up into small pieces, but it is lean. Better fresh, it is also canned, frozen, dry-cured or smoked. It is the least expensive salmon.

Pacific salmon

< salmon filets (marinated)

Salmon

The **Atlantic salmon** is the only salmon that lives in the Atlantic. It is recognized by its pink and deliciously aromatic flesh, which is semifatty. It measures 32-34 in. (80-85 cm) in length and weighs 10 lb (4.5 kg) on average. Atlantic salmon is sold fresh, frozen or smoked. It is best prepared as simply as possible so as not to mask its flavor.

The **ouananiche**, or "landlocked salmon," is a small, delicious freshwater salmon. It is found on the East Coast of North America as well as in Scandinavia. This fish represents a whole separate species, both because of its habitat and because of certain bodily features that distinguish it from salmon. It is smaller (8-24 in./20-60 cm) and rarely weighs more than 13 lb (6 kg). It is prepared in the same way as salmon or trout.

BUYING

Salmon is sold fresh, frozen, smoked, salt-cured, dried and canned. Its eggs are often sold in glass jars. Fresh or frozen salmon can be whole, in steaks, pieces, cutlets or fillets. Smoked salmon is often sold sealed under plastic or frozen. Buy smoked salmon from a grocer with a quick turnover of stock.
:: Avoid: smoked salmon with dried or browned edges, that appears shiny or that leaks slightly. Dark salmon may be very salty.

PREPARING

Scale and gut salmon before preparing it. It does not need to be washed and can simply be wiped.

COOKING

All cooking methods suit salmon. It is often cooked as steaks or fillets. It is as good hot as cold.

STORING

Salmon spoils quickly, as its flesh is fatty.
:: In the fridge: 2-3 days.

Atlantic salmon

NUTRITIONAL INFORMATION

	chinook salmon	red salmon	coho salmon	pink salmon	chum salmon	Atlantic salmon
protein	20 g	21 g	22 g	20 g	20 g	20 g
fat	10 g	9 g	6 g	3 g	4 g	6 g
calories	180	168	146	116	120	142
						per 3.5 oz/100 g

salmon steak

SERVING IDEAS

The flesh close to the head of the salmon is more delicate than the flesh nearer to the tail. Smoked salmon is often served with capers and thin slices of mild onion. It is used to give a special touch to sandwiches, salads, omelettes, pasta dishes, mousses and quiches. Avoid masking its flavor. Canned salmon is cooked and canned in its own juice. The bones and vertebrae can be eaten if present (source of calcium). Canned salmon is used in sandwiches, salads, sauces, omelettes and quiches. It is cooked in mousses, soufflés, pâtés and crepes. As a spread, it is used on sandwiches and canapés. Salmon eggs are often wrongly called "red caviar." Genuine caviar comes only from sturgeon eggs.

SALTWATER FISH

smoked salmon

Cod

Gadus spp., Gadidae

A fish found in the cold, deep waters of the North Atlantic and North Pacific. Cod weighs 4-9 lb (2-4 kg) and measures 16-32 in. (40-80 cm) in length. Its flaky, milky-white flesh is lean and delicate. Its firmness depends on the freshness and size of the cod (the smaller it is, the tenderer its flesh will be). The large Gadidae family includes several species with similar flesh.

Haddock resembles cod but is smaller. It measures 15-25 in. (38-63 cm) and weighs 2-4 lb (1-2 kg). It lives on both sides of the North Atlantic. Its lean, white and tasty flesh is milder than cod. In France, the English word "haddock" refers to smoked haddock.

Hake lives at various depths. There are several species called hake. The common hake lives on the European coasts of the Atlantic, from Norway to Portugal. It measures 12-28 in. (30-70 cm) in length and reaches a maximum length of 4 ft (1.2 m). Its flesh is tasty. Silver hake lives on the North American Atlantic Coast. It measures 9-14 in. (23-35 cm) and weighs 1.5 lb (0.7 kg) on average. Its tender, flaky flesh is very tasty.

Whiting measures 12-16 in. (30-40 cm). It lives in the Atlantic, the Mediterranean, the Black Sea and Baltic Sea. Its very tasty flesh flakes easily.

Black pollock measures 20-35 in. (50-90 cm) and weighs 2-15 lb (1-7 kg). It lives on both sides of the Atlantic. It is a very common fish in Europe, particularly in England. It has firm, white, inferior quality flesh.

Atlantic tomcod is very small, measuring 8-12 in. (20-30 cm) in length (14 in./35 cm maximum). It is found in the salt or brackish waters on the west coast of the Atlantic. Its white, lean flesh is highly prized.

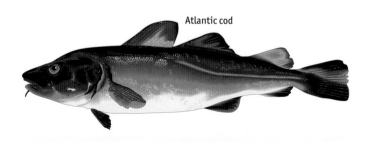

Atlantic cod

COOKING

All cooking methods suit cod.
:: Poached: cook in a just simmering fish stock for 8 min (it must not boil) or add after the liquid has come to a boil. Remove the pot from the heat immediately, cover with a lid and let stand for 15 min. Cod tongues are often poached before being prepared following the chosen recipe (sauced, floured, etc.). Place them in a cold liquid and remove as soon as it comes to a boil. Atlantic tomcod is often fried.

SERVING IDEAS

Cod is canned, air-dried (stockfish) or salt-cured (kipper). Its eggs are eaten fresh, smoked or salted. Its tongue, cheeks and liver are edible. More fragile than cod, haddock is more often smoked than salt-cured. Cod is delicious cooked in a sauce.

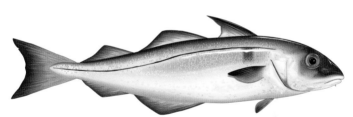

haddock

black pollock

Cod

NUTRITIONAL INFORMATION

	cod	haddock	hake	whiting	pollock	tomcod
protein	18 g	19 g	17 g	18 g	19 g	17 g
fat	0.7 g	0.7 g	0.9 g	1.3 g	1 g	0.4 g
calories	82	87	76	91	92	77

per 3.5 oz/100 g

The oil extracted from cod's liver is an important source of vitamin D.

PREPARING

Dried salt cod needs to be soaked for 8-12 hr before being prepared. To desalt salt cod, place in a strainer, skin-side up (if it has skin) so that the salt doesn't gather between the flesh and the skin. Place the strainer in a large container filled with water; the salt will gather at the bottom of the container. The container can also be placed in the sink with a thin stream of water running into it, which allows the salt to be eliminated as the water overflows.

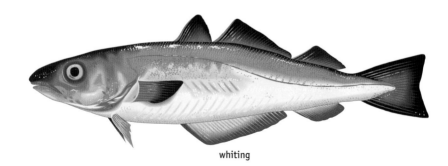

whiting

Smelt

Osmerus spp., Osmeridae

A fish from the cold or temperate waters of seas and lakes. Smelts measure 6-14 in. (15-35 cm) in length. Their white flesh is fine, tasty and rather fatty; it has a cucumber scent. The smelt is part of a family that includes several species. The **American smelt** lives on the American and Canadian sides of the Atlantic and also in several lakes. It measures 7-8 in. (18-20 cm) on average and can reach a maximum length of 13 in. (32 cm). The **European smelt** is found in the Atlantic, the North Sea and the Baltic Sea. It is particularly enjoyed in the north of France. It usually measures 8 in. (20 cm) in length. The **capelin** reaches a maximum length of 9 in. (23 cm). It is different from the Mediterranean capelin, or poor cod, which belongs to the Gadidae family.

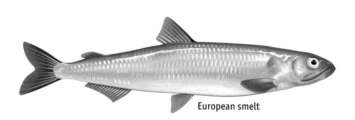

European smelt

BUYING

 Smelt is sold fresh, frozen, lightly smoked, salt-cured or dried. Capelin, a rarer fish, is mostly used as food for cod and other commercial fish.

SERVING IDEAS

 All parts of the smelt are edible.

COOKING

:: **Fried** or **grilled**.
Larger smelts are easier to cook in a more elaborate way.

NUTRITIONAL INFORMATION

	raw
protein	18 g
fat	2 g
calories	98
	per 3.5 oz/100 g

PREPARING

Smelt is most often gutted and pan-fried. It is often marinated for about 10 min in lemon juice with salt and pepper, or dipped in milk and flour before cooking.

Lamprey

Petromyzon spp., Petromyzontidae

A fish that measures 6-40 in. (15 cm-1 m) in length, living in seawaters. More delicate than eel flesh, the flesh of the lamprey is fatty and boneless. There are various species of lamprey. The **sea lamprey** is common on both sides of the Atlantic. It measures 20-35 in. (50-90 cm) in length. The **river lamprey** is found on the European coasts and spreads as far as the cold waters of Siberia. It measures 12-18 in. (30-45 cm) in length. The **Pacific lamprey** is common close to the American coastline.

The sea lamprey is finer than the river lamprey, and the males taste better.

lamprey

SERVING IDEAS

 Lamprey is prepared in the same way as eel. Lamprey à la bordelaise is a famous French recipe, in which the lamprey is stewed in red wine with vegetables, herbs and spices.

COOKING

:: **Grilled** or **cooked in a fish soup** or served as **pâté**.

NUTRITIONAL INFORMATION

	raw
protein	21 g
fat	18 g
calories	252
	per 3.5 oz/100 g

John Dory

Zeus faber, Zeidae

A fish also called "St. Peter" or "St. Pierre" that lives in the temperate waters of both hemispheres. John Dory is found in the Mediterranean Sea, and in the Atlantic, Indian and Pacific oceans, in particular near the coasts of Japan, Australia and New Zealand. It usually measures 8-20 in. (20-50 cm) in length and weighs 1.75-2 lb (800-900 g). Its flesh is white, firm and tasty.

John Dory

SERVING IDEAS

 Prepare gutted and definned John Dory simply so as not to mask the delicate nature of its flesh. Recipes for whole or filleted sole or turbot suit John Dory very well. Its gelatinous bones make excellent stock.

STORING

:: **In the freezer:** 3 months.

NUTRITIONAL INFORMATION

	raw
protein	18 g
fat	1 g
calories	80
	per 3.5 oz/100 g

Shark

Selachians

SALTWATER FISH

A boneless fish that lives in most seas. Shark flesh has no bones and cooks without any wastage and without breaking up. Depending on the species, it is firm, more or less moist, sometimes slightly gelatinous and more or less tasty. The larger the shark, the more intense its flavor.

The **hammerhead shark** lives in the warm waters of temperate seas, in particular on both sides of the Atlantic, in the Pacific and in the Mediterranean. It reaches a length of 13 ft (4 m). Its white flesh is excellent. The **spiny dogfish**, or "picked dogfish," is found in most cold seas. It measures 2-3.25 ft (60-100 cm) and can reach a maximum length of 4 ft (125 cm). The flavor of its flesh is not very strong and is often considered to be the best. The **smoothhound shark** lives in particular in the Mediterranean Sea, and in the Atlantic and Pacific oceans. It measures 1½-3 ft (50-100 cm) (5 ft/150 cm maximum) and weighs 6-9 lb (3-4 kg). Its white flesh has an ammonia smell. The **mako shark** is found in the Atlantic, Mediterranean and Caribbean. It measures 6-9 ft (2-3 m) and can weigh hundreds of pounds (kg).

smoothhound shark

Shark

The **larger spotted dogfish** is common in the Mediterranean Sea and Atlantic Ocean. It reaches a length of 5 ft (160 cm), but usually measures 4 ft (130 cm). Its flesh benefits from being cooked when very fresh. The **school shark** lives in temperate and subtropical seas, in particular on both sides of the Atlantic Ocean, in the Pacific Ocean and in the Mediterranean Sea. It measures 4½-6 ft (140-180 cm) in length and weighs 11-33 lb (5-15 kg). It has firm, white flesh.

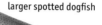

larger spotted dogfish

BUYING

Shark is usually sold skinned. It is cut into fillets, steaks or pieces, and sold fresh or frozen.

PREPARING

Shark is best eaten within 2 days of being killed. To remove the shark's skin, freeze quickly, then plunge into boiling water. The urea that shark contains turns into ammonia after their death. Any trace of ammonia will disappear during cooking. To improve its flavor, run shark under cold water, soak the flesh for 4 hr in milk, or in water to which some lemon juice or vinegar has been added, before cooking.

NUTRITIONAL INFORMATION

	raw
protein	21 g
fat	4 g
calories	131
	per 3.5 oz/100 g

COOKING

:: **Grilled, broiled, braised, fried, poached in fish stock** or **baked**.
Dogfish is often used for "fish and chips."

SERVING IDEAS

 Shark is delicious dressed with a well-flavored sauce.

Tuna

Thunnus spp., Scombridae

A large fish common in warm waters, tuna is frequently found in the Mediterranean Sea and the Pacific, Atlantic and Indian oceans. Tuna flesh is firm and dense. Tuna is classified into several species with distinct names according to their particular features.

The **bluefin tuna** is the giant of the tuna family. It generally measures 3-7 ft (1-2 m) in length and weighs 220-400 lb (100-180 kg). It can sometimes measure more than 13 ft in length and weigh more than a ton (900 kg). Its brownish-red flesh has a strong flavor.

The **albacore tuna** measures 22-40 in. (55-100 cm) in length and weighs 66-88 lb (30-40 kg). Its white flesh, barely tinged with pink, and its eggs are highly regarded. The French give the name "albacore" to yellowfin tuna.

The **bonito tuna**, which reaches a length of 20 in. (50 cm) and a weight of 4 lb (2 kg), is the most fished species of tuna in the world. It is highly consumed in Japan in the form of dried flakes, which keep indefinitely. Like the albacore and yellowfin tuna, bonito tuna is mostly used for canning. Its flesh is dark red.

The **yellowfin tuna**, which measures 24-60 in. (60-150 cm) in length, has very good pale flesh that is used especially for canning.

The color of these fish varies depending on the species, as does their flavor, which can be very strong. The flesh between its flanks is highly sought after, as it is the finest flesh of the fish. It is also the most expensive.

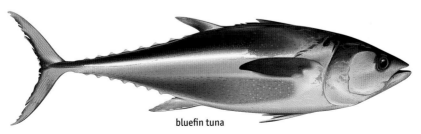

bluefin tuna

Tuna

BUYING

Fresh tuna is sold as steaks, fillets or pieces. Several varieties of tuna are canned and rarely sold fresh.

Canned tuna can be whole, in chunks, flaked or shredded. It can be canned in vegetable oil, stock or water. Whole tuna is always more expensive.

Shredded tuna is often less expensive, but it is also the form of tuna most likely to contain skin and bone residue.

Tuna in oil is less dry but is higher in fat. The label very rarely indicates the precise species, but in the United States, only albacore tuna can be labeled as "white meat tuna." Cans of bluefin and yellowfin tuna must be labeled "pale meat." Bonito tuna must be mentioned on the label by name.

COOKING

Strong-flavored species of tuna benefit from being soaked for several hours in lightly salted water and being marinated in lemon juice seasoned with fresh herbs before cooking. Tuna is more easily digested if it is poached (10 min) before being cooked.

:: **Quick-braised, poached in fish stock** and **steamed:** these are recommended cooking methods.

:: **Poached, braised, grilled, baked** or **cooked en papillote**.

albacore tuna

NUTRITIONAL INFORMATION

	fresh	*pale-fleshed, in oil*	*pale-fleshed, in water*
protein	23 g	29 g	30 g
fat	1-5 g	8 g	0.5 g
calories	105-145	198	131
			per 3.5 oz/100 g

Depending on the species, fresh tuna is lean or semifatty. Pale-fleshed tuna in cans (in oil, drained) is semifatty. Pale-fleshed tuna in cans (in water, drained) is lean.

PREPARING

Bleed freshly caught tuna as quickly as possible. To do this, make a slice about 1 in. (2-3 cm) above the tail. Tuna has a row of bones that jut out in the middle of its ribs, which can be separated from the flesh by passing the blade of a knife between them. A band of darker, fattier and very strong-tasting meat is located near the flanks. Removing this softens the flavor of the fish.

SERVING IDEAS

The Japanese prepare raw tuna as sashimi and sushi. Tuna is also one of the basic ingredients of *vitello tonnato*, an Italian dish that also includes cold veal, anchovies, capers and mayonnaise. Canned tuna is used in salads, sandwiches, sauces, omelettes and casseroles. Avoid increasing the fat content of tuna when preparing it.

SALTWATER FISH

tuna steak

Skate

Raja spp., Rajidae

A fish that lives in the shallow waters of most seas. Skate measures from 12 in. (30 cm) to more than 20 ft (6 m) in length, depending on the species (the manta ray is the largest and can weigh over 1 ton/900 kg). Its wings, cheeks and liver are edible. It has white or pink flesh with no bones.

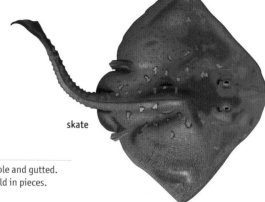

skate

BUYING

 Small skate are sold whole and gutted. Larger specimens are sold in pieces.

PREPARING

Skate contains urea, which turns into ammonia after the death of the fish. This substance disappears during cooking, but skate is better 1 or 2 days after being killed, as the smell is less strong. To improve the flavor, rinse skate before cooking by soaking it for 2 hr in water to which some lemon, vinegar or milk has been added.

To skin skate, cover with boiling water and poach for 1-2 min. Lay the skate out flat and scrape off the skin with a knife; turn it over and repeat the process. Proceed with care, as the wings can contain spikes.

NUTRITIONAL INFORMATION

protein	22 g
fat	1 g
calories	98
	per 3.5 oz/100 g

COOKING

 Remove the skin of the skate.
:: Poached: 15 min.
:: Baked: 15-25 min.
:: Sautéed: in a *beurre noir* (browned butter with a little lemon juice or vinegar) (4-6 min each side).

SERVING IDEAS

 Skate is cooked in the same way as scallops. Cook well or it will be slimy. It should also be served very hot to avoid its becoming gelatinous.

Halibut

Hippoglossus spp., Pleuronectidae

A cold-water fish from the northern seas of the
Atlantic and Pacific. Halibut measures
20-55 in. (50-140 cm) in length
and weighs 11-155 lb (5-70 kg).
Halibut is lean. Its fine, firm and
flaky flesh contains very few bones; it is
often sold and served as steaks.

halibut

NUTRITIONAL INFORMATION

	raw
protein	21 g
fat	2.4 g
calories	109
	per 3.5 oz/100 g

SERVING IDEAS

Halibut can be prepared with red or
white wine. Grilled or poached, one
should avoid masking its fine flavor. Halibut
poached in olive oil or served with anchovy
butter is delicious.
Avoid preparations that might dry out the flesh.

Sole

Solea spp., Soleidae

A fish from the sandy beds of the English Channel, the eastern Atlantic, the
Mediterranean, the North Sea and the Pacific. Sole usually measures 8-18 in. (20-
45 cm) in length. The most sought after species is **common sole**, also called "Dover
sole." It lives close to the English coasts and in the
Mediterranean up to the coasts of Norway. Sole
is lean and very tasty.

common sole

NUTRITIONAL INFORMATION

	raw
protein	18 g
fat	1.4 g
calories	77
	per 3.5 oz/100 g

SERVING IDEAS

Sole is prepared in a multitude of ways,
similar to flounder, fluke, dab, plaice
and other flatfish. It is suited to all cooking
methods.

Turbot

Psetta maxima, Scophthalmidae

A fish measuring 16-20 in. (40-50 cm) in length and able to weigh up to 55 lb (25 kg). Turbot lives in the Mediterranean and North seas, and the Atlantic and Pacific oceans. Its white, firm flesh is lean and very tasty. In North America, the Greenland halibut is often incorrectly referred to as Greenland turbot.

turbot

BUYING

 Turbot is sold whole, cleaned or uncleaned, as skinned fillets or cut into cutlets, depending on its size. A more costly fish, it is one of the finest saltwater fish.

COOKING

:: **Poached** or **grilled**.

NUTRITIONAL INFORMATION

	raw
protein	16 g
fat	3 g
calories	95
	per 3.5 oz/100 g

Plaice

Pleuronectidae

A flat fish that is abundant in the Atlantic and Pacific. Plaice is often confused with sole, which only lives near the European coasts. A wide variety of fish are sold under the name "plaice." These fish rarely measure more than 24 in. (60 cm) in length and usually weigh 1-4 lb (0.5-2 kg). Plaice is lean.

American plaice is abundant in New England, Canada and both sides of the Atlantic. It reaches a maximum length of 24 in. (60 cm).

Common plaice rarely measures more than 16 in. (40 cm) in length. It is the most abundant flatfish on the European coasts.

Winter flounder usually measures 18 in. (45 cm) in length. It is especially abundant in New England and in the Gulf of Saint Lawrence. It is the fleshiest species of plaice. Commonly called "fluke."

Summer flounder, which is a member of the Bothidae family, can reach a length of 37 in. (94 cm). It is the largest species of plaice. It is abundant in the United States, from the coasts of Maine to those of South Carolina.

common plaice

Yellow-tailed flounder measures 10-16 in. (25-40 cm) in length. It is common from Labrador in Canada down to southern New England in the United States.

Common flounder rarely measures more than 12 in. (30 cm) in length. This flounder, especially abundant in the Baltic Sea, is fished in the Mediterranean. Its flesh is not quite as tasty as plaice.

Witch flounder has an average length of 12-18 in. (30-45 cm). It is found on both sides of the Atlantic.

Common dab measures 8-10 in. (20-25 cm) in length. It lives along the European coasts (in particular the French coasts). Its flesh is less tasty than plaice.

Lemon sole reaches a maximum length of 26 in. (65 cm). It lives on the European coasts, from France up to Iceland. It is particularly abundant near the French coasts. Its flesh is bland and stringy.

FLATFISH

BUYING

Plaice, flounder and dab are generally sold as fillets, fresh or frozen and are often interchangeable. Buy what's freshest. Their flesh contains many bones.

COOKING

Plaice is cooked with or without its skin, but scaled beforehand. Be careful not to mask the delicacy of its flesh.
:: **Grilled** or **fried**.

NUTRITIONAL INFORMATION

	raw
protein	19 g
fat	1.2 g
calories	92
	per 3.5 oz/100 g

Introduction
Crustaceans

Crustaceans are invertebrate animals with a hard shell (its "carapace"), most of which live in the sea (crab, shrimp, lobster, spiny lobster, scampi). Some, however, live in freshwater, such as crayfish and some species of shrimp and crab. Crustaceans move by walking, on the seabed in most cases. Their red-colored eggs ("coral") are edible. Crustaceans can cause allergic reactions in some people.

TIPS FOR BUYING CRUSTACEANS

Live crustaceans should be heavy and vigorous (lobsters and crabs move their legs), with a pleasant smell and an intact shell. After cooking, the shell should be pink or bright red, without any greenish or blackish marks; the meat should be firm with a pleasant smell; and the tail should be curled, a sign that the crustacean was still alive when it was cooked. The freshness of frozen crustaceans (raw, cooked or prepared as a dish) is shown by the absence of frost on the inside of the packaging or any drying-out of the meat (freezer burn). Raw or cooked, crustaceans may have been defrosted. It is best to check, as, if this is the case, they should not be refrozen and do not keep as long.

TIPS FOR COOKING CRUSTACEANS

Crustaceans should be alive until the moment they are cooked. Almost all crustaceans change color and become pink when plunged into boiling water. Before cooking, fill in any holes in the shell of lobsters and crabs using pressed pieces of crustless bread.

There are several ways to boil live crustaceans. Generally, they are plunged headfirst into boiling water to kill them instantly (be careful of splashes caused by the tail curling). Some claim that crustaceans killed this way are tastier; others consider this method to be cruel, and find that it toughens the meat. In this case, crustaceans are placed in the freezer for an hour (to put them to sleep so that they die gently) or into freshwater, seawater, fresh salted water (add 1-2 tablespoons/15-30 ml of salt per 4 cups/1 l of water) or a fish stock that is then brought slowly to a boil. Cooking time varies depending on the species and its size, but overcooked crustacean meat becomes tough and loses its flavor.

Shrimp

Pandalus spp., Crustacea

A small crustacean, also called "prawns," that lives in most seas and fresh or brackish waters in the world. Cold-water shrimp, from the northern Atlantic and Pacific oceans, are smaller and tastier. Their firm, translucent meat can be pink, yellow, gray, brownish, reddish or dark red. They become opaque and tinged with pink when cooked. Warm-water species are found in the South Atlantic, Gulf of Mexico and along Latin American and Asian coastal waters. **Pink shrimp**, colored pink-red, measure 3-4 in. (7.5-10 cm) in length. **Giant tiger shrimp** measure 6-12 in. (15-30 cm) in length. They are the most common and most widely eaten shrimp in Asia.

pink shrimp

BUYING

:: **Choose:** fresh, firm-bodied shrimp with a mild sea smell; frozen shrimp with no frost or drying. Shrimp are better if they have not been completely defrosted or if they have been defrosted slowly in the fridge.

:: **Avoid:** soft, slimy shrimp, those whose body is separated from the shell and those with an ammonia smell or with black spots. Highly fragile, shrimp are frozen, covered with ice on the fishing boat, or cooked immediately. They are sold whole or with their head removed, fresh or frozen, cooked or smoked, shelled or unshelled. They can be dried or canned. The largest shrimp are the most expensive.

Shrimp are often labeled small, medium, large, extra-large or jumbo but there is little consistency in what the terms mean. Choose by number of shrimp per pound—for example, "16/20" refers to 16 to 20 shrimp per pound.

NUTRITIONAL INFORMATION

water	76%
protein	20 g
fat	2 g
carbohydrates	0.9 g
cholesterol	153 mg
calories	106
	per 3.5 oz/100 g

EXCELLENT SOURCE: vitamin B_{12} and niacin. To extend their keeping qualities, shrimp are sometimes treated with sodium bisulfite.

Shrimp

PREPARING

When using whole shrimp, remove its shell. Hold the head in one hand and the body in the other, and pull so that the head tears off, taking the shell with it. Any parts of the shell still attached to the body can then be removed. For headless shrimp, the shell can be cut with scissors before being removed, or just removed as is. It is easier to shell a slightly frozen shrimp than an unfrozen one. Two pounds (1 kg) of unshelled shrimp only gives 1 lb (500 g) of cooked meat, as there is 50% wastage for whole, raw, unshelled shrimp.

The shell makes an excellent stock, which can be used for cooking the shrimp. To prepare the stock, cover the shells with boiling water and simmer (10 min), then strain the liquid before adding the shrimp. Uncooked shells can be ground and added to butter as a flavoring. Shrimp can be eaten with their intestine—a dark vein along the back—still intact. Some people prefer deveined shrimp (some are sold deveined). Make a small slice into the flesh with the point of a knife parallel to the vein, then pull out the intestine.

CRUSTACEANS

1 Remove the shell of the shrimp.

2 Make a small slice into the flesh with the point of a knife.

3 Carefully pull out the intestine.

SERVING IDEAS

Shrimp is delicious hot or cold, as an hors d'oeuvre, appetizer or main dish (by itself or with meat, poultry, vegetables or pasta dishes). It is used in soups, sauces, stuffings and salads. Shrimp can replace other crustaceans in most recipes. In Southeast Asian cuisine, fermented shrimp, in paste or powder form, is used as a seasoning.

STORING

:: **In the fridge:** 1-2 days.
:: **In the freezer:** 1 month.

COOKING

The body of a shrimp curls when cooked. Overcooking makes shrimp tough and dry.

:: **Boiled in water** or **fish stock:** cook shelled or unshelled shrimp in seawater or fresh salted water (2 tablespoons/30 ml of salt per 4 cups/ 1 l). The fish stock can consist of salted water flavored with a slice of lemon and a little thyme, or other variations, depending on taste and the inspiration of the moment.

1. Bring the chosen liquid to a boil, add the shrimp, return to a boil, lower the heat and let simmer for 3-5 min if they are small, fresh shrimp (the cooking time for larger or nondefrosted shrimp is longer). To check for doneness, run a shrimp under cold water, then taste. (It should be slighty tender, but not soft.)
2. Drain shrimp as soon as they are cooked, then run them under cold water to stop the cooking process and keep their flavor.

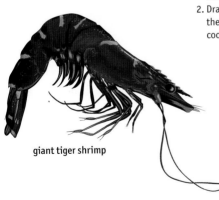

giant tiger shrimp

CRUSTACEANS

Crab

Cancer spp., Cancridae

A crustacean that lives in the sea, freshwater or brackish water. Crab does not contain very much meat. The meat found in its body, legs and claws, and the liver and creamy substance under its shell, are edible. Its white meat is lean, stringy and tasty.

The **green crab** is the most common species. Its fairly small green shell usually reaches 3½ in. (8.5 cm) across. It weighs about 0.4 lb (200 g) and does not contain very much meat. It is usually sold as a bait for game fishing.

The **Atlantic common crab** prefers rocky or sandy seabeds along the coasts. It measures 4-8 in. (10-20 cm) in diameter. It has excellent meat.

The **velvet swimming crab** measures 3-6 in. (8-15 cm) across and has a brown-red shell marked with blue, velvety legs. It has powerful claws. Its meat is highly prized.

The **spider crab** lives in sandy seabeds. It measures 4-8 in. (10-20 cm) in diameter. Its fine meat is tastier in the female than the male.

The **snow crab** belongs to the spider crab family and lives in cold, deep waters. Its almost circular body is slightly wider at the back. Its shell is often orange-brown in color. Its long legs are slightly flattened. The male is much larger than the female. Its shell reaches an average size of 5 in. (13 cm) across, and its weight almost 3 lb (1.25 kg). Its unique-tasting meat is highly sought after.

The **Pacific common crab** including Dungeness crab lives in cold waters and belongs to the rock crab family, like the Atlantic common crab. It reaches a maximum width of 9 in. (23 cm) and weighs 2-4 lb (0.5-2 kg). It is sold whole, live, cooked, canned or frozen. Its delicious meat is available frozen or fresh.

Pacific common crab

The **blue crab** is highly regarded in the United States. It measures 6-8 in. (15-20 cm) and lives on the Atlantic Coast. It has excellent, sweet meat.

The **soft-shelled crab** is a blue crab that has molted. It is usually sold live, but sometimes frozen. Almost transparent, it is cleaned (the gills and tail are removed and it is rinsed under cold water) and sautéed in butter or fried and served with a tartare sauce. Other species of crab are also eaten as soft-shelled crabs.

Atlantic common crab

BUYING

 :: Avoid: a frozen crab that is dried out or covered in frost.

Sometimes sold live, crab meat is mostly sold cooked, frozen or canned. Imitation crab products are also available on the market (see *Kamaboko*, p. 334).

Do not buy (and do not cook) a live crab unless it moves its legs. Grasp the crab from behind to avoid its claws.

SERVING IDEAS

 Crab is delicious hot or cold. It is prepared in the same way as other crustaceans, which it can replace in most recipes. It is used in hors d'oeuvres, salads, sandwiches and soups. Crab is tasty in a sauce or in pasta dishes. It is often fried in its shell.

COOKING

 Live crab is cooked in the same way as lobster (p. 388).

:: Boiled: plunge the crab into boiling salted water for 10-20 min for a 6 in. (15 cm) crab, or up to 30 min, if it is very large.

:: Broiled, fried.

NUTRITIONAL INFORMATION

	snow crab
protein	18 g
fat	1 g
cholesterol	60 mg
calories	89
	per 3.5 oz/100 g

EXCELLENT SOURCE: vitamin B$_{12}$, niacin, copper and zinc.

STORING

 Crab dies quickly away from its natural habitat.

:: In the fridge: place live crab in a damp cloth for up to 12 hr; cooked, 1-2 days.

:: In the freezer: cooked lump or claw crab meat, 1 month.

Crab

PREPARING

To prepare cooked crab, make a slice between its underside and shell, and tear the shell off the top of the crab. Take care not to damage the shell if it will be used as a container for serving the crab. Detach the legs and claws, then break them with a nut-cracker or a heavy instrument. All that remains is to remove the meat. There are other methods, including the following.

spider crab

1 Detach the crab's legs and claws.

2 Break the claws and legs with a lobster cracker or nutcracker, then extract the meat.

3 Remove the tail found underneath the crab by unbending and twisting it, then discard.

4 Remove the plastron (the hard crab "belly") and set aside.

5 Take out the meat found inside the shell. Discard the intestines and other appendages located behind the crab's mouth.

6 Cut the plastron in two with a kitchen knife.

7 Remove the meat found in the cells of the plastron.

CRUSTACEANS

Scampi

Nephrops norvegicus, Nephropsidae

A crustacean that lives in the deep waters of the Atlantic coasts. Species related to scampi live in the Pacific. "Scampi" is the commercial name given to the Norway lobster. It is also called a "langostine." In the United States "scampi" more commonly refers to shrimp cooked in garlic butter. Scampi measures 3-10 in. (8-25 cm) in length. Unlike other crustaceans, scampi changes very little in color during cooking. Its meat, more delicate than that of lobster, is excellent.

scampi

BUYING

 :: Choose: firm scampi with no ammonia smell.

Scampi is sold raw (with its head removed and frozen or kept in crushed ice) or cooked.

SERVING IDEAS

 Scampi is often served with garlic butter. It is suitable for most recipes for crustaceans. It is often used in place of giant shrimp (shell raw scampi in the same way as shrimp), and is one of the ingredients in paella. Avoid masking its delicate flavor.

COOKING

Scampi is cooked in the same way as shrimp, lobster or spiny lobster. Avoid overcooking.
:: Boiled: 3-5 min.
:: Steamed: 6-7 min.
:: Grilled: 3 min each side.

NUTRITIONAL INFORMATION

protein	17 g
fat	2 g
carbohydrates	0.5 g
calories	91
	per 3.5 oz/100 g

EXCELLENT SOURCE: calcium, phosphorus and iron.

STORING

:: In the fridge: raw or cooked, 1-2 days.
:: In the freezer: raw or cooked, 1 month.

Spiny lobster

Palinurus spp., Palinuridae

A crustacean that lives on the rocky beds in the warm or temperate waters of the Adriatic and Mediterranean seas, and the Atlantic and Pacific oceans. The species of spiny lobster found in the Atlantic are usually reddish-brown, whereas those in the Pacific are more greenish. It measures 12-20 in. (30-50 cm) in length and weighs 1-4 lb (0.5-2 kg). Its white meat is not quite as tasty as lobster.

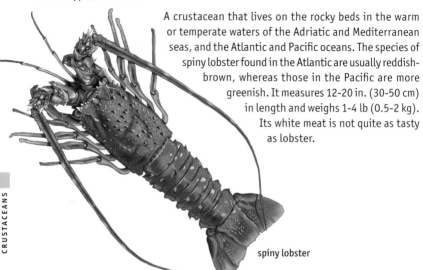

spiny lobster

BUYING

 Usually only the tail of the spiny lobster is sold, raw or cooked, generally frozen.

SERVING IDEAS

Spiny lobster can be used in place of lobster in most recipes. It is often dressed with garlic butter. It is delicious in salads. Avoid masking its fine flavor.

STORING

:: **In the fridge:** raw or cooked, 1-2 days.
:: **In the freezer:** 1 month.

NUTRITIONAL INFORMATION

protein	21 g
fat	2 g
carbohydrates	2.4 g
cholesterol	70 mg
calories	112
	per 3.5 oz/100 g

EXCELLENT SOURCE: niacin, vitamin B$_{12}$ and zinc.

COOKING

 Overcooking spiny lobster makes its meat rubbery and tough.
:: **Boiled:** 15 min.
:: **Grilled:** 5 min.

Crayfish

Astacus and *Cambarus spp.*, Crustacea

A small freshwater crustacean, also called "crawfish," that lives in rivers, lakes, streams and ponds. Some species of crayfish are identified by the coloring of their claws ("white-clawed crayfish," "red-clawed crayfish"). Crayfish usually measure 2-6 in. (6-14 cm) in length. Its white meat tinged with pink is lean, delicate and more or less compact, depending on the species.

crayfish

BUYING

 :: Choose: cooked crayfish with a pleasant smell, firm shell and claws intact.
Crayfish is sold live or cooked, frozen or canned.

PREPARING

Remove the intestine at the time of cooking (it is usually already removed from frozen crayfish). Pull gently on the small fin underneath the tail and the intestine should come out; if not, remove by making a lengthwise slice with the point of a knife.

SERVING IDEAS

Crayfish is prepared in the same way as lobster, crab and shrimp, which it can replace in most recipes. It is cooked as a bisque, gratin, soufflé or mousse, used in salads or gratinéed.
Only the tail of the crayfish is eaten.
Crushed crayfish shell can flavor fish stock, bisque or butter.

NUTRITIONAL INFORMATION

	raw
protein	19 g
fat	1 g
cholesterol	139 mg
calories	89
	per 3.5 oz/100 g

EXCELLENT SOURCE: niacin, vitamin B$_{12}$, potassium, phosphorus and copper.

COOKING

 :: Poached in fish stock: 5-8 min for whole crayfish.
:: Steamed: 10-12 min.
:: Grilled: 3-5 min to cook the tails.

STORING

 :: In the fridge: live, 12 hr. Cover it with a damp cloth. Cooked, 1-2 days.
:: In the freezer: cooked, 1-2 months.

Lobster

Homarus americanus (America) and *Homarus vulgaris* (Europe), Crustacea

A crustacean with an elongated body that lives in the deep waters of the Atlantic. Some claim that the meat of the female lobster is better, especially at egg-laying time, thus it is more sought after. The edible parts of the lobster are the meat of the abdomen (or tail), the legs (even the very small ones that are chewed to extract the meat), the claws, the coral and the greenish liver located inside the thorax. The white and pink-tinged meat of lobster is lean, firm, delicate and very tasty.

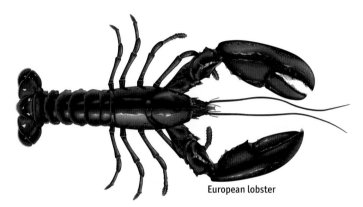

European lobster

BUYING

:: **Choose:** a lively lobster (when grasped by the sides, it should curl its tail abruptly beneath its body). A cooked lobster should have black, shiny eyes, firm meat and a pleasant smell.

Lobster is bought live, frozen or canned (in pieces or as a pâté).

NUTRITIONAL INFORMATION

water	77%
protein	19 g
fat	1 g
cholesterol	95 mg
calories	91
	per 3.5 oz/100 g

EXCELLENT SOURCE: potassium, zinc and niacin.

The nutritional composition of lobster meat varies according to the season and the part of the body it comes from; the tail contains more nutrients than the claws.

COOKING

For maximum freshness, it is suggested that lobster be cooked live.

:: Boiled (in seawater, fresh salted water, fish stock): plunge the lobster headfirst into a boiling liquid. Some find this method cruel and believe that it toughens the meat. They prefer to place the lobster in the freezer for 1 hr, which puts it to sleep and lets it die gently. Lobster can also be placed in fresh water and brought slowly to a boil. For either cooking method, allow 12 min of cooking time per pound (500 g), adding 1 min for each additional 4.5 oz (125 g).

When lobster is cooked in boiling water, time the cooking from the moment the lobster is plunged into the water. When it is cooked in cold water, time the cooking from the moment the liquid comes to a boil. Always cover lobsters completely in liquid to cook them. Before serving the lobster, make a hole in its head so that the liquid contained underneath the shell can drain.

:: Steamed.

:: Grilled: cut the lobster in two lengthwise. Brush the flesh with oil, lemon juice and, if desired, ground pepper (10 min).

Do not defrost a frozen cooked lobster. It will be tastier if it is simply reheated for 2 min in boiling water.

STORING

Lobster can live 3-5 days away from its natural habitat if it is placed in a saltwater fish tank. After buying, avoid keeping lobster at room temperature. Cook immediately, or cover with a damp cloth and place in the fridge, briefly.

:: In the fridge: cooked, 1-2 days.

:: In the freezer: 1 month, cooked, drained, then left as is or, preferably, remove the meat from the shell. Cool the meat in the fridge, then place in freezer containers, covered in a brine (2 teaspoons/10 ml of salt per cup/250 ml of water) and closed with a lid. The whole lobster, cooked and cooled, can also be placed in a sealed, airtight freezer bag.

CRUSTACEANS

American lobster

PREPARING

For tastier lobster, before boiling, block the holes in the shell with fresh crustless bread, preferably pressed between the fingers. To cut lobster in two, position the tip of a knife in the center of the head and pierce down to the board. Turn the lobster around and, beginning at the head, split the lobster in half, lengthwise. Remove the intestines located underneath the tail and the pockets near the start of the head.

1 Place the lobster on a chopping board. Insert the point of a knife in the center of the head, down to the board.

2 Turn the lobster around and cut it lengthwise down to the tail.

3 Divide the lobster in two by cutting the head lengthwise.

4 Set aside the coral (black when uncooked) and the liver (green) for use in a sauce, if desired.

5 Remove the gravel pouch located near the head.

6 Remove the intestine carefully.

SERVING IDEAS

Lobster is eaten cooked, hot or cold (in salads and sandwiches. It is greatly enjoyed with garlic or lemon butter, with mayonnaise or plain. To get the meat out of the claws, use a lobster cracker or nutcracker, the handle of a heavy knife or even a hammer. Lobster is prepared as a bisque, soufflé or in sauce and can be gratinéed.

Lobster thermidor, *lobster à l'américaine* and lobster Newburg are classic lobster dishes. The shell can be used to make fish stock and to flavor bisques, stews and sauces.

Introduction
Mollusks

A soft-bodied animal without a skeleton (invertebrate), often covered with a shell. Mollusks are divided into three main branches: gastropods, bivalves (or lamellibranchia) and cephalopods. Gastropods and bivalves are often referred to as shellfish.

Gastropods (periwinkles, whelks, abalone) are covered in a single shell (univalve), in the form of a coiled spiral in the case of the periwinkle and the whelk. They move using a flat, ventral "foot."

Bivalves, or "lamellibranchia" (oysters, clams, great scallops, scallops, mussels, quahogs, queen scallops, carpet shells, soft-shell clams), have a shell formed of two valves joined by a hinge ligament. Their gills resemble thin blades (Latin lamella), hence their name. Most are sedentary, sitting on the seabed or on rocks, or bury themselves in the sand.

Cephalopods (squid, octopus, cuttlefish, little cuttle) don't have an outer shell. In its place they may have internal cartilage or even a bone, in the case of cuttlefish. Cephalopods have tentacles (8-10) that end in suckers, which they use to grasp their prey or for moving around.

Mollusks can become inedible when the water they live in is polluted or when they ingest a microscopic algae that produces toxins, such as *Gonyaulax tamarensis* (or *Alexandrium spp.*). This algae has already caused several cases of fatal poisoning. Never eat these creatures if they have been harvested from prohibited areas.

TIPS FOR USING MOLLUSKS

Mollusks must stay quite fresh until the time they are eaten or cooked. Several mollusks are as good eaten raw as cooked (oysters, scallops, clams, carpet shells), whereas others are only eaten after cooking (periwinkles, whelks). Do not overcook mollusks, as they become shriveled and tough or, if they are cooked in a liquid, soft and pasty.

Abalone

Haliotis spp., Haliotidae

A gastropod mollusk, also called "sea-ear." The edible part of the abalone is a gray-brown muscle, called its "foot," which attaches itself to rocks. When mature, abalone measures 4-10 in. (10-25 cm) across. It is mainly found in the Pacific and Indian oceans. Its firm and compact meat is usually white and very tasty. It is similar in shape to the scallop, though larger.

BUYING

Rare and expensive, abalone is mostly sold tenderized and canned, dried or frozen. If it is sold living in the shell, touch the foot: it should still move.

PREPARING

To shell fresh abalone, insert the blade of a knife into the thinnest end of its shell, under the meat. Move the blade around to detach the muscle. Take out the foot. Wash raw abalone well to remove the intestine and dislodge any sand; use a small brush if necessary. Leave whole or cut into slices. Abalone becomes stiff when it is harvested and its muscle stays contracted, even after it is separated from the shell. For meat that is less firm, it is important to tenderize the abalone before cooking. To do this, place the abalone between two clean cloths or sheets of food wrap, and flatten it using a rolling pin, a mallet, a rock or any other heavy object. It can also be placed in a tough bag and beaten against a hard surface for a few minutes. Abalone can be tenderized by cooking in a pressure cooker. Cook for 20 min in 2 cups (500 ml) of water, then let it cool in the liquid or simmer for up to 4 hr. Prepare according to the chosen recipe.

abalone

NUTRITIONAL INFORMATION

	raw
carbohydrates	6 g
protein	17 g
fat	1 g
calories	105
	per 3.5 oz/100 g

EXCELLENT SOURCE: vitamin B_{12}, niacin and pantothenic acid.

COOKING

:: **Boiled, grilled, braised** or **fried**.
:: **Sautéed:** in thin slices (30 sec on each side).
Only add abalone at the last minute to cooked dishes and don't salt until the end of cooking.

SERVING IDEAS

Raw or cooked, abalone is excellent in appetizers, salads, soups and quick-braised dishes.

Abalone

STORING

:: **In the fridge:** fresh abalone in its shell, 3 days, in a container covered with a damp cloth; shelled and cooked, 1-2 days.

Freshly harvested abalone, 2 days, in salted water, refreshing the water often.
:: **In the freezer:** shelled, 3 months.

Cockle

Cardium spp., Cardiidae

A mollusk that lives on sandy and muddy seabeds near the coast. Cockles can reach ½-3 in. (1-8 cm) in length. Their pale meat is lean, firmer and stronger-tasting than oysters or mussels.

cockles

BUYING

:: **Choose:** live cockles that are tightly closed or if, partly open, that close again when tapped. If they don't close, discard them.

SERVING IDEAS

Cockles are eaten raw or cooked, hot or cold. They can be used in place of mussels and clams in most recipes. They are delicious in chowder.
:: **Avoid:** discard cockles that don't open after cooking.

STORING

:: **In the fridge:** fresh cockles, 3 days (cover with a damp cloth); shelled cockles, 1-2 days, in an airtight container (cover with their own liquid).
:: **In the freezer:** shelled cockles, 3 months, in a container (cover with their juices).

NUTRITIONAL INFORMATION

	raw
protein	17 g
fat	1 g
calories	81
	per 3.5 oz/100 g

PREPARING

Wash and brush cockles well and discard any dead ones. If the cockles are full of sand, salt them for 1 hr or more in fresh salted water (4 teaspoons/15-20 ml of salt per 4 cups/1 l of water) or in seawater for 12 hr. Open cockles using an oyster knife or by heating them for a few minutes in a pot with no water, by steaming them, or for a few seconds in the microwave oven (30 sec for 6 cockles) at the highest setting.

Scallop

Pecten spp., Pectinidae

A mollusk with round shells of almost equal dimensions joined by a small hinge. Scallop rests on seabeds. All species of scallop are edible. The most well-known species in Europe are the great scallop (the *coquille Saint-Jacques*, known in North America as a scallop dish) and the queen scallop. In North America, scallop is the name given to several different local species. The meat of these species is quite similar; they differ mainly in their size and external appearance.

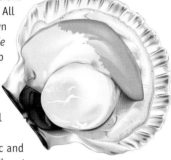

scallop

The **great scallop** lives in Europe, in the Atlantic and Mediterranean. It measures 3½-6 in. (9-15 cm) in diameter and weighs about 4 oz (115 g).

The **scallop** has two valves decorated with radiating ridges. Some species are characterized by shell-halves of different size. The meat resembles that of the great scallop. Three species are common along the North American Atlantic coastline. The **sea scallop** is the largest member of the family. It can reach 6-12 in. (15-30 cm) in diameter. Its shell-halves are equal in size. In Canada, it is the most commercially important mollusk. The **bay scallop** is quite small (2-3 in./5-8 cm). It has identical shell-halves. One of the **Iceland scallop**'s shell-halves is longer than the other.

The **queen scallop** is very similar to the North American scallop species. Quite small (1½-2¾ in./4-7 cm), it has whitish valves flecked with brown with several quite wide radiating ridges and shell-halves of unequal size.

The edible parts of these mollusks are their delicate and tasty meat, which is in fact the large white muscle that opens and closes the shell, and the coral or roe, the more fragile, orange-colored sexual glands. The coral is almost never available in North America.

Scallop

BUYING

:: **Choose:** fresh, live scallops whose shell closes as soon as it is touched; fresh, shelled scallops with white, firm meat without any smell. Ask whether the scallops are defrosted, as they should not be frozen again without being cooked. Frozen scallops should be firm, glistening and moist. The inside of the packaging must not contain any frost. Scallops are highly perishable. They are often shelled as soon as they are harvested, washed, then covered in ice or frozen immediately.

SERVING IDEAS

Raw or cooked, scallops are delicious dressed with a little lemon juice in sashimi or a ceviche. They are prepared in a multitude of ways: grilled, poached, breaded, sautéed, gratinéed, quick-braised, fried or marinated.
The shells of these mollusks are often used as a serving dish (they can withstand the heat of an oven).

PREPARING

To open scallops, proceed as for oysters, after rinsing the closed shells under cold water. Detach the meat by sliding the blade of a knife beneath the "beard" (the gray outer edge). Remove the small black pouch and the beard (these can be used in fish stock). Cut the small, tough muscle from the side of the meat, and separate the white part of the scallop from the coral. Wash these carefully.

NUTRITIONAL INFORMATION

	raw
protein	17 g
fat	1 g
carbohydrates	2.4 g
calories	88
	per 3.5 oz/100 g

EXCELLENT SOURCE: vitamin B_{12} and potassium.

COOKING

Small scallops are cooked whole. Cut large scallops into pieces or slices. Cook scallops only briefly (3-4 min); otherwise they become tough, dry and quickly lose flavor.

STORING

:: **In the fridge:** 1-2 days, fresh or cooked, placed in a closed container.
:: **In the freezer:** 3 months. To defrost them, plunge them in boiling milk, off the heat, or place them in the fridge. It is preferable, however, to cook scallops without defrosting, for better flavor.

great scallop

Clam

Venus spp., Veneridae

A mollusk that lives in seas all over the world, particularly in the shallow waters of the Atlantic Ocean. The name "clam" is a generic term covering several species, some of which are cultivated. Most, like the **quahog** and the **surf clam**, have very hard shells. Some have smooth shells, which is the case with the surf clam and the **razor clam**. Others, such as the **venus clam**, have striated shells. The shells vary in color, shape and size. They are often tinted brown, brown-black, pale gray or chalk white. Razor clams are long and thin. Most of the other species have an elliptical shape.

One of the largest clams, the surf clam, can measure up to 7 in. (18 cm). The ocean quahog reaches up to 5 in. (13 cm); the **hard-shell clam**, 6 in. (15 cm); and the **soft-shell clam**, 5 in. (13 cm).

The lean meat of the clam varies in color, depending on the species, ranging from cream-white to gray and dark orange.

hard-shell clams

BUYING

:: Choose: live clams in their shell. Their shell will then be closed tightly, or, if slightly open, will close slowly when tapped. Choose clams with a fresh and mild smell.

:: Avoid: clams whose shells don't close when tapped or clams that give off an ammonia smell.

Clams are sold fresh (in or out of their shells), cooked, frozen or canned.

STORING

:: In the fridge: 3 days, fresh in their shell (cover with a damp cloth); 1-2 days, out of their shell, fresh or cooked.

:: In the freezer: 3 months, shelled, in a freezer container (cover with their own liquid). Cook them without defrosting; they will have more flavor.

NUTRITIONAL INFORMATION

protein	13 g
fat	1 g
carbohydrates	3 g
cholesterol	34 mg
calories	74
	per 3.5 oz/100 g

EXCELLENT SOURCE: vitamin B_{12}, potassium and iron.

COOKING

Avoid overcooking clams.

:: Poached, steamed or **microwaved:** until the shells open.

Clam

SERVING IDEAS

Small clams can be eaten raw or cooked; they are excellent plain, dressed with lemon juice. The larger clams are tougher and more often eaten cooked. They are chopped and used in sauces and chowders. Clam chowder is popular in the United States. In Italy, they are used to make spaghetti *alle vongole*.

Clams work well with shallot, tomato, white wine and thyme. They are used in dips, sauces, salads, croquettes, vinaigrettes, paella, soufflés, quiches and stews. They are stuffed and marinated. Clams can be used in place of other mollusks in most recipes.

PREPARING

Eat clams as soon as possible. Clams in the shell almost always contain sand, so it is preferable to soak them in seawater or salted water (4-5 tablespoons/60-75 ml of salt per 4 cups/1 l of water) before cooking. Leave to soak 1-6 hr, refreshing the water occasionally, as clams will die from lack of oxygen in the water if they soak for a long time. Before opening or cooking clams, rub and brush the shells to eliminate all traces of sand or alga. They are difficult to open. It is useful to let them rest for a certain time in the fridge. Their adductor muscle then relaxes and it is easier to insert the blade of a knife between the two shells. Be careful not to damage the shells and to save the liquid they contain for cooking and keeping them. They can also be opened by exposing them to dry heat for a few minutes (in the oven or barbecue), placing them for a few seconds in the microwave oven on the highest setting or heating them over steam.

quahog

Mussel

Muscullus spp. and *Mytilus spp.*, Mytilidae

A mollusk that lives close to sea coasts all over the world (it prefers cold waters). Most mussels found on the market are cultivated. Mussels are formed of two thin oblong shells of equal size. The shells of the **blue mussel**, or "common mussel," a very widespread mussel, are usually smooth but sometimes have concentric striations. They are blue-black and often have purple eroded sections. The meat of the mussel is more or less fleshy and firm, depending on the species, of which there are many.

blue mussels

NUTRITIONAL INFORMATION

	raw
protein	12 g
fat	2 g
calories	86
	per 3.5 oz/100 g

GOOD SOURCE: riboflavin, niacin, folic acid, vitamin B_{12}, phosphorus, iron and zinc.

SERVING IDEAS

Mussels are rarely eaten raw, except sometimes when they are harvested out at sea and are very fresh and unpolluted. Mussels are prepared as *moules marinière* (steamed in their own juices with white wine and seasonings), grilled, gratinéed, sautéed, fried, cooked on a kebab, marinated or stuffed. They are used in both delicate and hearty soups, sauces, hors d'oeuvres, salads, paella, stews and omelettes.
Canned mussels are eaten as is, cold or hot.

COOKING

:: Poached or **steamed:** until they open (2-5 min), then cook as directed in the recipe. Discard mussels that stay closed after cooking.

STORING

:: In the fridge: fresh unshelled mussels, 3 days in a container (cover with a damp cloth); shelled mussels, 24-48 hr in a sealed container (cover with their own liquid). It is best to eat them as soon as possible.
:: In the freezer: 3 months, shelled in a freezer container (cover with their own juices).

BUYING

Mussels are sold fresh (either shelled or unshelled) or canned. Only buy mussels in the shell if they are live. In this case, the shells are shut; if they are partly open, they close slowly when they are tapped.
Canned mussels are available in their own juices, in oil, tomato, white wine or smoked.

PREPARING

Wash and brush the mussels. It is not necessary to remove all of the beards, as they add flavor to the cooking stock. Remove any open mussels that don't close again when tapped, or that have damaged shells, as they are no longer edible. Particularly heavy mussels may be filled with mud or sand. Discard them or soak them for 1 hr or longer in fresh salted water (4-5 tablespoons/60-75 ml of salt per 4 cups/ 1 l of water). Sometimes after soaking or being brushed, the mussel's adductor muscle escapes from the shell and it seems to be dead. Slide the two shell-halves over each other; if they don't move, the mussel is live; if not, discard.

MOLLUSKS

Oyster

Ostrea spp. and *Crassostrea spp.*, Ostreidae

A mollusk found in tropical or temperate seas, highly regarded for its flavor. Oysters are fleshy. Their glistening meat takes on tints of gray-white, passing through pearly gray and beige; it can have a hint of green when the oyster feeds on algae. Oysters are tastier from September to April. In North America, oysters are often named after the area they live in. In the United States, the Blue Point (the most well-known species) and Cape Cod oysters are greatly enjoyed. In eastern Canada, the Caraquet oyster (from a bay of the same name in New Brunswick) and the Malpèque oyster (cultivated on Prince Edward Island) are highly regarded.

Pacific cupped oysters

Oysters produce magnificent iridescent pearls that are used in jewelry. The most beautiful pearls are produced by the *Pinctadine* species, which lives in warm waters.

MOLLUSKS

BUYING

:: Choose: fresh, unshelled oysters that are still alive and full of water. A live oyster is closed or, if it is partly opened, closes if tapped. (Discard those that don't close when tapped.) Fresh oysters should be firm, plump and glistening, and bathed in a clear liquid that is not milky. Shucked oysters cost more, but there is no waste.

Oysters are sold by the dozen or by the case. Shucked oysters can also be sold fresh or frozen, by weight.

Oysters are classed according to their size and shape.

NUTRITIONAL INFORMATION

	raw
water	80%
protein	7 g
fat	3 g
carbohydrates	4 g
cholesterol	55 mg
calories	65
	per 3.5 oz/100 g

EXCELLENT SOURCE: vitamin B$_{12}$, iron, zinc and copper.

PROPERTIES: regenerative, revitalizing and nourishing. Oysters are said to be an aphrodisiac.

SERVING IDEAS

Oysters are most often eaten raw, seasoned with lemon juice, a vinaigrette or left plain. Cooked oysters are delicious hot or cold. They can be cooked as a soup, stew, gratin or in a sauce or stuffing. Oysters that are bought shucked can be eaten raw. Less tasty than oysters in the shell, they are perfect for cooking.

Smoked, canned oysters are ready to eat, but they may be rinsed and marinated.

COOKING

:: Boiled: add oysters to boiling water, remove the pot from the heat and let rest for a few minutes. For oysters that are more cooked, simmer them without letting them boil (5 min maximum). Stop cooking as soon as the edges of the oysters start to look crimped.

:: Grilled, baked, stuffed.

Cooking oysters for too long makes them rubbery and pasty.

STORING

:: In the fridge: 10 days, shucked (covered with their juices); 6 weeks, in shell (cover with a damp cloth). Never put oysters in a sealed bag or container.

:: In the freezer: 3 months, shucked (covered with their juices).

MOLLUSKS

flat oysters

Oyster

PREPARING

It is suggested to use an oyster knife, which is a tool especially designed for opening oysters; it has a solid handle and a thick blade. Use a stainless steel instrument so as not to give the oyster a metallic taste. Before shucking the oyster, brush it under a stream of cold water. Never let oysters soak in water, as they could open, lose their juices and die. Hold the oyster firmly in one hand, rounded side downward, so that less liquid is lost. Insert the blade of the knife between the shell halves, near the hinge. Twist the blade, separate the shell halves, then cut the muscle that joins them. Pass the blade over the base of the oyster to detach it from the shell. Remove any shell fragments (if necessary). A glove, cloth or thick paper can be used to protect the hand in case the knife slips. Oysters also open when placed in a medium oven for 30-60 sec, after being steamed for a few seconds or in the microwave oven for 1 min on the highest setting, which helps to soften the adductor muscle.

The freshness of oysters can only be judged once they are open. Only eat firm, plump oysters that are bathed in a clear liquid and have a pleasant smell.

1 Hold the shell with a cloth. Insert the oyster knife between the two valves.

2 Twist the blade and separate the valves.

3 Cut the muscle. It is now only necessary to remove any shell fragments.

4 Pass the blade along the base of the shell to remove the meat.

shucked oyster >

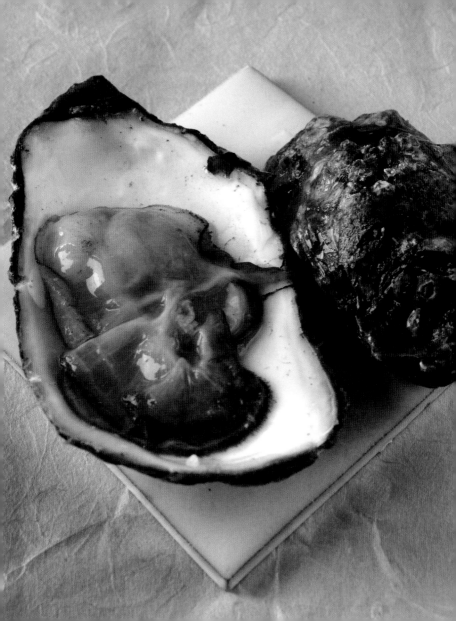

Squid

Loligo spp., Loliginidae

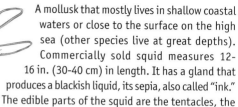

squid

A mollusk that mostly lives in shallow coastal waters or close to the surface on the high sea (other species live at great depths). Commercially sold squid measures 12-16 in. (30-40 cm) in length. It has a gland that produces a blackish liquid, its sepia, also called "ink." The edible parts of the squid are the tentacles, the pouch forming its body and the ink. Its white meat is lean, firm and slightly rubbery. Also called "calamari."

BUYING

:: **Choose:** firm, moist squid with a mild sea smell.

Squid is sold fresh, frozen, canned or dried.

SERVING IDEAS

Squid is eaten hot or cold. Very small squid is eaten raw. It is marinated, smoked, stuffed, used in soups, sauces, salads and pasta dishes. The ink is used in some recipes.

PREPARING

To prepare whole squid, take out the transparent cartilage (the pen) from the inside of the body and discard. Separate the head from the body by pulling on it firmly but carefully. Spread the tentacles out flat, cut them off beneath the eyes and remove the hard part (the beak) located in the middle. Wash the tentacles and the body and remove the membrane covering them by scraping with the fingernails or a butter knife under running water. Keep the body whole (for stuffing) or cut it into cross-sections.

NUTRITIONAL INFORMATION

	raw
protein	16 g
fat	1 g
carbohydrates	3 g
calories	92
	per 3.5 oz/100 g

EXCELLENT SOURCE: riboflavin and vitamin B_{12}.

COOKING

:: **Grilled, braised, poached** or **quick-braised.** Cook in a sauce (10 min) or in the oven at 350°F (175°C) (15-20 min).

:: **Sautéed** or **fried:** 1-2 min over moderate heat. Cooking squid briefly prevents it from becoming tough and doesn't change its flavor.

STORING

:: **In the fridge:** 1-2 days, fresh or cooked. If it is freshly caught, leave squid 1-2 days in the fridge to tenderize its meat.

:: **In the freezer:** 3 months.

Octopus

Octopus spp., Octopoda

A mollusk related to the squid and cuttlefish. The octopus lives in most seas. It can reach almost 30 ft (9 m). Its meat is firm and tasty (especially small octopi). Some species are poisonous. This mollusk occupies an important place in Mediterranean and Asian cuisines. In several countries, including the United States and Australia, octopus is not as highly regarded except in ethnic neighborhoods.

octopus

BUYING

:: **Choose:** firm-fleshed octopus with a mild sea smell.

SERVING IDEAS

Octopus is delicious marinated, stir-fried or quick-braised. It works well with garlic, tomato, onion, lemon, ginger, olive oil, cream, wine or soy sauce.

PREPARING

Octopus is usually sold clean and tenderized; if not, cut the body to separate it from the tentacles, turn over the ventral pouch and pull out the intestines. Remove the eyes, locate the beak at the center of the octopus and remove it, then skin the octopus. Tenderized octopus is easier to skin than octopus that has not been tenderized. Blanching octopus for 2 min also makes skinning easier.

STORING

:: **In the fridge:** 1-2 days, washed, fresh or cooked.

:: **In the freezer:** washed, 3 months.

NUTRITIONAL INFORMATION

	raw
protein	15 g
fat	1 g
calories	73
	per 3.5 oz/100 g

COOKING

:: **Grilled, poached, sautéed, fried** or **quick-braised:** Cook already-blanched octopus over a low heat for 45 min (if it weighs 2 lb/1 kg or more). Simmer unblanched octopus for 60-90 min.

Small octopus can be grilled or fried with its skin on. To evaporate the liquid produced during cooking, sauté octopus over a low heat in a small saucepan with no added liquid until it evaporates, then prepare according to the chosen recipe.

Cuttlefish

Sepia officinalis, Sepiidae

A mollusk that lives in the deep or shallow waters of most seas. Cuttlefish measures 6-10 in. (15-25 cm) in length. Its white meat is very firm.

cuttlefish

BUYING

:: Choose: fresh cuttlefish with firm, moist meat and a mild sea smell.
Cuttlefish is found fresh, frozen or canned.

SERVING IDEAS

Cuttlefish is used in the same way as octopus and squid, which it can replace. It is delicious stuffed. Its sepia (ink) is sometimes saved and used in certain recipes.

PREPARING

Cuttlefish is prepared in the same way as octopus. Like octopus meat, it is necessary to tenderize cuttlefish before cooking.

NUTRITIONAL INFORMATION

protein	16 g
fat	1 g
calories	81
	per 3.5 oz/100 g

COOKING

:: Poached or **fried:** 2-3 min each side.
:: Pan-fried: 1-2 min each side.
:: Quick-braised: 30-60 min.
Cook cuttlefish quickly, as it can become tough.

STORING

:: In the fridge: 1-2 days, cleaned, fresh or cooked.
:: In the freezer: cleaned, 3 months.

Whelk

Buccinum spp., Buccinidae

A large mollusk found all along the coasts of the Atlantic, Pacific and Arctic. The whelk is better known in Europe than in North America.

whelk

PREPARING

 Shake whelks before washing them so that they retreat into their shell.

COOKING

Only cook live whelks whose shells are intact. When overcooked, the meat becomes tough.

:: Poached: 8-10 min in fresh salted water (1 tablespoon/15 ml of salt per 4 cups/1 l of water), in seawater or in a court bouillon. Place whelks in a pot, cover them with liquid, cover the pot with a lid and bring to a boil. Drain, then take the whelks out of their shell using a pin, first removing the operculum (the cap covering the shell opening).

The larger species (6 in./15 cm) require longer cooking; poach until the whelks come out of their shell, extract them, then remove the soft intestine that connects the body to the shell, keeping only the firm meat that will still need further cooking.

NUTRITIONAL INFORMATION

	raw
protein	24 g
fat	0.4 g
calories	138
	per 3.5 oz/100 g

SERVING IDEAS

Whelks are prepared in the same way as periwinkles. They are eaten dressed with lemon juice or marinated. They are delicious in a salad or cooked in white wine sauce.

STORING

:: In the fridge: fresh, 3 days maximum.
:: In the freezer: 3 months, shelled, in a container (cover with a damp cloth).

MOLLUSKS

Periwinkle

Littorina spp., Littorinidae

A small mollusk that is abundant in the Atlantic and Pacific oceans. The color of the periwinkle varies according to the species. It can be eaten when it measures about 1 in. (2-3 cm) in length and width.

periwinkles

COOKING

Only cook periwinkles that are still alive with their shell intact.

:: Poached: 5 min in fresh salted water (1 tablespoon/15 ml of salt per 4 cups/1 l of water), in seawater or in a fish stock. Place periwinkles in a pot, cover them with liquid, put the lid on and bring to a boil. Drain, then take them out of their shell using a pin.

NUTRITIONAL INFORMATION

protein	20 g
fat	2 g
calories	100
	per 3.5 oz/100 g

PREPARING

Shake periwinkles so that they retreat into their shell before washing them.

Periwinkle

SERVING IDEAS

 Periwinkles are eaten hot or cold, as is, dressed with lemon juice or vinegar. They can be used in place of snails in most recipes. They are prepared in white wine sauce, in salads or as appetizers. They can be marinated or grilled over a wood fire (avoid overcooking them).

STORING

:: **In the fridge:** 3 days maximum, in a container (cover with a damp cloth).

:: **In the freezer:** shelled, 3 months.

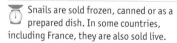

Snail

Helix spp., Helicidae

A herbivorous land animal housed in a spiralled shell. The species most used for eating are the **Roman snail**, or "Burgundy snail," 1½-1¾ in. (40-45 mm) in length, and the **brown garden snail**, measuring 1-1¼ in. (25-30 mm). Snail meat is more or less firm and delicate depending on the species.

Roman snail

BUYING

 Snails are sold frozen, canned or as a prepared dish. In some countries, including France, they are also sold live.

PREPARING

:: **Preparing live snails:**

1. Wash them in cold water; if necessary, remove the hard stopper that covers the opening of the shell.

2. Reduce some of the liquid in the snails by soaking for 3 hr in a mixture of coarse salt (a handful), vinegar (½ cup/120 ml) and flour (1 tablespoon/15 ml), these amounts being enough for 3 or 4 dozen snails (some claim that this negatively affects the quality of the meat). Cover the container, place a weight on top so that the snails do not escape and mix from time to time.

3. Take the snails out of the container and wash them well in cold water so that any mucous secretions are removed.

4. Place the snails in a pot and cover them with cold water; bring the water to a boil and boil gently for 5 min; drain and run under cold water.

5. Shell the snails and remove the black part (the cloaca) at end of their tails; leave the glands and the liver, which are tasty and nutritious parts of the snail.

6. Cook according to the chosen recipe.

SERVING IDEAS

 Snails can be grilled, sautéed, cooked in a sauce, in a court bouillon, as a kebab and in flaky pastry. Snails bathed in garlic butter is a classic appetizer.

NUTRITIONAL INFORMATION

	raw
protein	16 g
fat	1.5 g
carbohydrates	2 g
calories	90
	per 3.5 oz/100 g

STORING

 :: In the fridge: fresh or cooked, 3 days maximum.
:: In the freezer: shelled, 3 months.

shelled snail

Frog

Rana spp., Amphibia

An amphibian that lives in fresh waters and humid areas. Only the frog's legs are eaten; the white, tender and delicate-tasting flesh is compared to chicken. These usually come from farmed frogs. In Europe, the **green frog** (the tastiest) and the **common frog** occupy the majority of the market. In North America, it is mostly the larger species that are eaten.

frog legs

BUYING

 :: Choose: fresh frog's legs that are plump and moist, slightly tinged with pink. Frog's legs are sold skinned, fresh, frozen or canned.

COOKING

:: Grilled, broiled or **fried:** 2-3 min.
:: Sautéed: 1-2 min.
:: Poached: 3-5 min.
:: Baked: 5-8 min.

STORING

:: In the fridge: 2-3 days, fresh or cooked and wrapped well.
:: In the freezer: 2-3 months, as per above.

NUTRITIONAL INFORMATION

	raw
protein	16 g
fat	0.3 g
cholesterol	50 mg
calories	73
	per 3.5 oz/100 g

SERVING IDEAS

 Frog's legs are often fried or sautéed and prepared Provencale-style (with tomato, wine, olives, etc.), lyonnaise-style (with onions), with garlic or parsley. They are also cooked in soup and pies.

Sea urchin

Echinodermata

A small invertebrate marine animal that lives close to the coasts of most seas. The sea urchin's shell usually reaches between 2¾-3 in. (7-8 cm) across. It is sometimes referred to by its older name, "sea hedgehog." The edible part of the urchin is located under its mouth (beneath the shell), namely the sexual glands, called the "coral" and the liquid it bathes in. The orange-colored coral has a strongly iodized flavor and consistency.

sea urchin

BUYING

:: **Choose:** whole sea urchins with firm spikes, whose mouth opening is closed. One can buy whole sea urchins (packaged in small wooden boxes) or sea urchins ready to serve (just the coral). They are highly perishable.

SERVING IDEAS

Sea urchin is often eaten raw, with or without the liquid in which it bathes, seasoned with lemon or lime juice, shallots and salt, and accompanied by buttered bread or placed on canapés. As a purée, it flavors sauces, mayonnaises and dips. It is used in omelettes, scrambled eggs and crepes. It is used to prepare *oursinade*, a fish soup with sea urchins. It can be cooked for a few minutes in boiling salted water, like a boiled egg.

NUTRITIONAL INFORMATION

protein	12 g
fat	4 g
calories	126
	per 3.5 oz/100 g

PREPARING

To open the sea urchin, use a thick cloth or a sturdy glove. Hold the sea urchin so that one is able to make an opening near the mouth and all around the soft part with no spikes that surround it, using small scissors. Discard the blackish intestines. Remove the coral using a spoon and pour the liquid into a bowl, then remove any shell fragments if required.

STORING

:: **In the fridge:** 1-2 days, in an airtight container without the crunchy parts of the mouth.

Herbs, spices and seasonings

The word "seasoning" is often used to refer to both spices and herbs; they both enhance the taste of food. Spices are aromatic substances derived from plants that grow in tropical regions, whose flavors are more or less perfumed, warm and pungent. Herbs are herbaceous plants with green leaves from temperate regions, often grown in vegetable gardens.

TIPS FOR BUYING HERBS AND SPICES

HERBS

Fresh herbs should be moist and fragrant. Avoid any trace of mold, dry stems or discolored leaves. It is preferable to buy dried herbs whole or crushed, as in powdered form they become stale more quickly and can contain foreign matter.

Avoid mixes of salt with dried herbs, as they are expensive and, as a rule, contain more salt than seasoning.

SPICES

It is better to buy spices whole or in their original state (seeds, stems, roots) so that they keep the strength of their aroma for much longer. Don't grind until you are ready to use them.

TIPS FOR PREPARING HERBS AND SPICES

Chop fresh herbs finely, this way they release more flavor and aroma compounds into the food. Use dried herbs and spices as is or soak them for about half an hour in water, milk, oil or stock. Crushing herbs and spices gives them a stronger flavor, as the crushing process releases their essential oils. Gentle heating before using for cooking also releases more flavor.

TIPS FOR USING HERBS AND SPICES

It is useful to remember that 1 tablespoon (15 ml) of fresh herbs can be replaced by 1 teaspoon (5 ml) of dried herbs.

Most herbs lose their aroma and flavor over long periods of cooking, especially in an uncovered dish at a full boil. Simmering, however, suits rosemary, thyme, sage, bay leaf and savory very well. Add more fragile herbs at the end of cooking.

Most spices can be added at the beginning of cooking so that they give their flavor to the dish.

For cold dishes, add herbs and spices well in advance so that they have time to release their flavor; add a larger quantity than for hot dishes.

Spices and herbs help to reduce the use of salt, or can replace salt altogether.

TIPS FOR STORING HERBS AND SPICES

Herbs can be dried by spreading them on a mosquito net or piece of nylon netting away from the sun or direct light. Leaves should be very dry when stored, or else they will become moldy. If necessary, finish the drying process in the oven 200°F/90°C) for about 15 min.

Herbs that don't dry easily (basil, parsley, fennel, cilantro, bay leaf and juniper) can be dried in a microwave oven. Spread the herbs evenly between two sheets of paper towels, about ½ cup (125 ml) at a time. Heat for about 1½-2½ min on a high setting and move the herbs around until they break up. Return leaves that aren't dry enough to the microwave and check every 30 sec until they are quite dry. Dried herbs and spices keep in airtight, opaque containers in a dry place protected from light and heat.

Keep fresh herbs with or without their roots for a few days in the fridge wrapped in damp paper towels and placed in a plastic bag. (One can also stand them in a glass with water and cover the leaves with a plastic bag.) Don't wash them until ready to use, unless they are soiled with dirt or sand. Fresh herbs will keep better if their roots are still attached.

Herbs freeze easily, whole or chopped, washed or unwashed (if they have been washed, dry them well). Freezing especially suits herbs that do not take well to being dried. They can be frozen in an ice cube tray by covering them with water or stock; these cubes can then be added to soups, sauces and stews. It is better to use the herbs without defrosting them, as they will have more flavor. An old method of storing herbs is to cover fresh herbs (whole or chopped) with salt in glass or stone jars with airtight seals. Place the containers in a cool spot. Avoid salting dishes that have been seasoned in this way.

A simple practice combines a storage method and flavoring process: storing fresh herbs in vinegar, oil or alcohol. The liquid absorbs the flavor of the herb, which it then lends to foods and this allows one to have a seasoning on hand when the herb is no longer available or too expensive.

Spices should be stored away from sunlight and protected from heat and moisture (so keep them away from the stove). Keep spices in airtight containers. Whole spices last longer than pre-ground spices (6 months to 1 year).

Add dates to the spice packaging or containers to keep track of how long you have stored them.

Dill

Anethum graveolens, Apiaceae

An aromatic plant originally from the Mediterranean basin and western Asia. Dill is related to fennel. It is especially enjoyed in Scandinavia, Russia, central Europe and North Africa.

The sweet and pungent smell of the seeds is evocative of fennel, caraway and mint.

fresh dill

BUYING

 When buying fresh dill, don't be concerned if the leaves are wilted.

SERVING IDEAS

Dill seeds flavor vinegars, soups, gherkins, marinades, cold sauces and various salads. Dill is excellent for fish marinades, especially salmon and herring. It flavors tomato, celeriac, beet, cucumber, cabbage, fresh and sour cream, cream cheese, white sauces, melted butter, vinaigrettes, eggs, stews and seafood. Add the leaves (milder tasting) only at the end of cooking.

NUTRITIONAL INFORMATION

	dried seeds
potassium	25 mg
calcium	32 mg
magnesium	5 mg
fiber	0.4 g
zinc	0.1 mg
	per 1 tsp/5 ml

PROPERTIES: diuretic, carminative, antispasmodic and mildly stimulating.

STORING

:: At room temperature: keep the dried seeds in an airtight container, in a dark, cool and dry place.

:: In the fridge: 2 days. Place the stems in a bowl of water or wrap the leaves in slightly damp paper.

For more flavor, it is better to freeze fresh dill than to dry it.

Dill responds very well to drying in the microwave oven.

dill seeds

Anise

Pimpinella anisum, Apiaceae

An aromatic plant originally from the countries of the eastern Mediterranean and Egypt. Several plants have an aniselike flavor, to various degrees, such as fennel, dill, caraway and cumin. True anise comes from a species called **anise** or "aniseed."

Star anise has a stronger and more peppery flavor than ordinary anise. A whole dish can be flavored using just a few seeds. It keeps its flavor for a longer period than ordinary anise.

star anise

star anise seeds

anise

NUTRITIONAL INFORMATION

	seeds
potassium	30 mg
calcium	14 mg
phosphorus	9 mg
iron	0.7 mg
	per 1 tsp/5 ml

BUYING

Unless you plan to use a large quantity of anise, buy only a small quantity at a time so that the seeds are more flavorful.

PROPERTIES: diuretic, carminative, digestive, antispasmodic, expectorant, stomachic and stimulating. Anise is used as a heart tonic, for stimulating digestion, treating flatulence and relieving coughs and asthma.

The essential oil of anise contains anethole. It used as an herbal tea for a tonic effect on the nervous system and digestive apparatus.

SERVING IDEAS

 Anise leaves, more delicate than the seeds, are excellent cooked or raw. They are used to season salads, soups, cream cheese, fish, vegetables and tea. The fruits (seeds, star anise) flavor or decorate compotes, cakes, cookies, breads (focaccia, pretzels, gingerbread), salads, soups, vegetables, fish and poultry.

The roots are used to make wine.

Anise can be used instead of or combined with spices such as cinnamon and nutmeg in compotes, cakes, pies and breads, in particular. Anise is used a great deal in making sweets and liqueurs.

anise seeds

In India, anise can be an ingredient in curry powders and garam masala. It is chewed to freshen the breath. In Asia, star anise flavors pork, chicken, duck, rice, coffee and tea. It is also one of the ingredients in Chinese "five-spice powder."

Bay laurel

Laurus nobilis, Lauraceae

A tree originally from the Mediterranean basin whose persistent, lanceolate (spear-shaped) leaves, dark green in color, are used for their flavor. In cooking, these are usually referred to as bay leaves. The bay laurel tree produces small flowers that form berries.

bay laurel

BUYING

 :: Choose: dried bay leaves that are well colored and a light green.

STORING

Dry freshly picked leaves to keep their flavor. Keep them away from drafts and light and they will keep up to 1 year.

NUTRITIONAL INFORMATION

vitamin A	4 RE
calcium	5 mg
potassium	3 mg
iron	0.3 mg
	per 1 tsp/5 ml

PROPERTIES: bay leaves and berries are said to be antiseptic, digestive, expectorant and antirheumatic.

Its essential oil is said to be effective as a pomade to relieve sprains and bruises.

Bay laurel

SERVING IDEAS

Bay leaves are used whole or in pieces, fresh (bitter) or dried. In cooking, they are usually used dried. As they are highly perfumed, quite often only a single leaf is needed for a whole dish. The longer they cook in a liquid, the more flavor they give to the dish. They flavor sauces, soups, stews, meats, poultry, fish, vegetables, legumes, terrines, pâtés, marinades, in short, almost everything, but especially simmered dishes. Ground bay leaf flavors stuffings and marinades. Along with parsley and thyme, bay leaves are an essential component of *bouquet garni*.

Tarragon

Artemisia dracunculus, Compositae

An aromatic plant originally from central Asia or Siberia. It is highly valued in French cuisine. There is also a variety of tarragon called "Russian tarragon" that is more pungent and doesn't have the same delicacy as common or "French" tarragon.

tarragon

BUYING

Fresh tarragon has a finer flavor and better aroma than dried tarragon.

SERVING IDEAS

Tarragon flavors eggs, fish, seafood, turkey, salads, sauces, stuffings, mustard, vinegar and gherkins. Its slightly aniseed flavor, somewhat bitter and peppery, is a seasoning for bland foods. Tarragon tolerates cooking well. It is often paired with chicken and it is an essential ingredient in béarnaise sauce and other sauces. Use dried tarragon in moderation to avoid masking the taste of other foods or herbs.

NUTRITIONAL INFORMATION

potassium	48 mg
calcium	18 mg
magnesium	6 mg
phosphorus	5 mg
iron	0.5 mg
	per 1 tsp/5 ml

PROPERTIES: stimulating, diuretic, antiseptic, carminative, emmenagogic, anthelmintic, aperitive, digestive and antispasmodic.
Its essential oil has a turpentine taste and aniseed perfume.

Chervil

Anthriscus cerefolium, Apiaceae

An aromatic plant probably originally from Russia. Chervil looks somewhat similar to curly parsley, a close relative. It is more fragile and not as intensely green. Chervil has a subtle, slightly aniseed flavor; it is a particularly refined aromatic ingredient.

chervil

BUYING

:: **Choose:** firm chervil without dark spots.
:: **Avoid:** chervil with yellowed, browned or wilted leaves.

SERVING IDEAS

Chervil is used in the same way as parsley, which it can replace. Along with parsley, tarragon and chives, chervil makes up the traditional *fines herbes* mix in French cuisine. It flavors soups, vinaigrettes, sauces, salads, vegetables, raw vegetables, omelettes, stews, cold dishes and fish.
Dried or boiled, it quickly loses its taste. Use chervil that is as fresh as possible and add at the end of cooking.

NUTRITIONAL INFORMATION

	dried
potassium	28 mg
calcium	8 mg
iron	0.1 mg
	per 1 tsp/5 ml

PROPERTIES: aperitive, stomachic, depurative and diuretic.

STORING

Chervil is fragile.
:: **In the fridge:** place stems in a bowl of water or wrap the chervil in a slightly damp paper towel.
:: **In the freezer:** it keeps more flavor frozen than dried.

HERBS, SPICES AND SEASONINGS

Rosemary

Rosmarinus officinalis, Labiaceae

A shrub originally from the Mediterranean region whose highly perfumed leaves are used as a condiment. Rosemary is an excellent natural preservative. It has a slightly camphorous smell and quite a strong aromatic and pungent flavor.

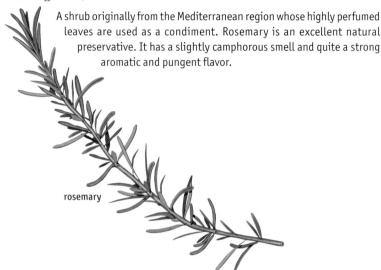

rosemary

SERVING IDEAS

Use rosemary in moderation so that it doesn't mask the flavor of other foods. Highly regarded in the south of France and in Italy, it is used in soups, stuffings, sauces and marinades. It flavors pasta dishes, stews and fish as well as lamb, poultry and roasted or skewered game meats.

Rosemary flowers flavor wines and salads. Milk can be lightly perfumed by infusing a few leaves in it; this milk can be used to make various desserts. Rosemary is used in *herbes de Provence* herb mixes.

It is used in perfumery, and is a basic ingredient in ointments, soaps and shampoos.

NUTRITIONAL INFORMATION

	dried
calcium	15 mg
potassium	11 mg
magnesium	3 mg
vitamin C	1 mg
iron	0.3 mg
vitamin A	4 RE
	per 1 tsp/5 ml

PROPERTIES: antispasmodic, antirheumatic, antiseptic, diuretic, stimulant, sudorific, stomachic, carminative, cholagogic and emmenagogic. Rosemary is said to soften wrinkles. It is used a great deal in herbal medicine.

In high doses, rosemary can irritate the stomach and intestines.

Marjoram/Oregano

Origanum spp., Labiaceae

Aromatic shrubs. One of these varieties, originally from northern Europe, is wild and commonly called oregano. Marjoram is a close relative of the *vulgare* variety. It is thought to be originally from North Africa and southwestern Asia. Marjoram is also called "wild marjoram," "sweet marjoram" and "knotted marjoram." The aroma and flavor of marjoram is reminiscent of mint and basil.

BUYING

:: **Choose:** fresh marjoram and oregano with firm stems.

SERVING IDEAS

Marjoram and oregano are used fresh, dried or ground. Marjoram has a slightly milder flavor than oregano. These herbs are essential in Mediterranean cuisines. They flavor vinaigrettes, sauces, stuffings, vegetables (tomato, onions, spinach, zucchini and eggplant), fish, seafood, legumes, eggs, meat, poultry and charcuterie (sausages and deli meats)—in short, almost everything. They are used (separately or together) in the herb mix called *herbes de Provence*. A sprig of marjoram or oregano in a bottle of oil or vinegar will perfume it.

marjoram

NUTRITIONAL INFORMATION

	dried marjoram	ground oregano
calcium	12 mg	24 mg
potassium	9 mg	25 mg
magnesium	2 mg	4 mg
phosphorus	1.8 mg	3 mg
iron	0.5 mg	0.6 mg
vitamin A	5 RE	10 RE
		per 1 tsp/5 ml

PROPERTIES: antispasmodic, antiseptic, bactericidal, carminative, stomachic, expectorant, calmative and aperitive. These herbs assist digestion, are said to be beneficial for the respiratory system and relieve migraines, travel sickness, insomnia and bronchitis.

oregano

Basil

Ocimum basilicum, Labiaceae

An aromatic plant originally from India. There are several varieties of basil, each with a different flavor from the other. The flavor of basil can be reminiscent of lemon, camphor, jasmine, clove, aniseed and thyme.

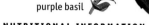

purple basil

green basil

NUTRITIONAL INFORMATION

	dried	fresh
potassium	48 mg	24 mg
calcium	30 mg	8 mg
vitamin C	1 mg	traces
iron	0.5 mg	0.1 mg
phosphorus	7 mg	4 mg
magnesium	6 mg	4 mg
vitamin A	13 RE	10 RE
		per 1 tsp/5 ml

PROPERTIES: antispasmodic, antiseptic, tonic and stomachic. Basil is said to help treat migraines, digestive difficulties and insomnia.

STORING

:: At room temperature: keep dried basil in an airtight container, in a dry place away from light and heat. Fresh leaves can be kept in olive oil or mixed with oil to form a smooth paste.

:: In the fridge: wrapped in slightly damp paper towel. Only wash when ready to use.

:: In the freezer: whole or chopped. It can also be put in an ice cube tray and covered with water or stock; these cubes are then added to liquid dishes. For more flavor, don't defrost before using.

SERVING IDEAS

Basil works very well with tomato, pasta dishes, garlic, onion and olive. It also flavors salads, eggs, cheese, vegetables, fish, seafood, poultry and pork. Some varieties perfume desserts and drinks. Basil is made into pesto sauce, which is used in pasta and soups. Basil leaves and stems give a delicate flavor to oil. Basil combines well with olive oil and lemon. It must never be simmered, and should only be added at the end of cooking. It can be made into herbal tea.

Sage

Salvia officinalis, Labiaceae

An aromatic plant originally from the Mediterranean region, of which there are several varieties. The most widespread is common sage. It has a pungent, intense and slightly camphorous flavor.

common sage

BUYING

Dried sage leaves are sold whole, crushed or ground.

SERVING IDEAS

Sage flavors meat, poultry, charcuterie (sausages and deli meats), marinades, hams, stuffings, vegetables, omelettes, soups, stews and cheese. It works as well with dairy products as with fatty fish. It perfumes wine, beers, teas and vinegars. It flavors white meats and vegetable soups (France), roast pork (Provence), ham, sausages and beer (Germany), roast mutton and tea (China). In England, it flavors and colors a cheese and is paired with onion in stuffings and sauces. In Italy, it is an essential ingredient in *saltimbocca* and *osso buco*. Use sage in moderation, as it has a robust flavor. Only add at the end of cooking.
It can be made into herbal tea.

NUTRITIONAL INFORMATION

	ground
calcium	12 mg
potassium	7 mg
magnesium	3 mg
iron	0.2 mg
vitamin A	4 RE
	per 1 tsp/5 ml

PROPERTIES: tonic, antispasmodic, antiseptic, diuretic, emmenagogic, aperitive, carminative and depurative. Sage is said to be effective against sore throats and to soothe mouth ulcers.

STORING

Dried sage keeps easily 1 year without any great loss of flavor.

ground sage

Thyme

Thymus spp., Labiaceae

A woody aromatic plant originally from the Mediterranean region. **Common thyme** has leaves that emit a penetrating scent and produce an essential oil with a warm, pungent taste. **Wild thyme** is a wild variety with a climbing stem. It emits a strongly perfumed scent. Its spicy taste is slightly bitter. **Lemon thyme** adds a hint of lemon to the dishes it seasons. It does not respond well to cooking.

common thyme

lemon thyme

BUYING

Whole thyme leaves have more flavor than ground leaves.

SERVING IDEAS

Fresh thyme works well with dried beans, sauces, eggs, tomato sauce, vegetables, stuffings, meats and grilled fish. It stands up well to lengthy cooking and is thus an ideal addition to stews, slow-cooked meats, soups, tomato sauces and stocks. When it is used whole, remove the stems before serving.

Thyme is one of the ingredients in *bouquet garni* (with parsley and bay leaf) and it flavors vinegar very well. It is used in making charcuterie (sausages and deli meats) and marinades. Its essential oil is used in the cosmetic industry. Thyme can be made into herbal tea.

NUTRITIONAL INFORMATION

	ground
calcium	26 mg
potassium	11 mg
magnesium	3 mg
phosphorus	3 mg
iron	1.7 mg
vitamin A	5 RE
	per 1 tsp/5 ml

PROPERTIES: diuretic, stimulating, antispasmodic, carminative, emmenagogic, aphrodisiac, sudorific, anthelmintic and expectorant. Its essential oil contains thymol and carvacrol, excellent antiseptics and anthelmintic remedies.

HERBS, SPICES AND SEASONINGS

Mint

Mentha spp., Labiaceae

An aromatic plant originally from the Mediterranean region.
Peppermint has oval, lanceolate leaves. It has a strong, penetrating smell. A small quantity is quite enough to flavor dishes.
Spearmint has highly scented leaves colored bright gray-green.

spearmint

peppermint

BUYING

:: **Choose:** dried mint leaves that are a blackish-green (unless they have been dried in a microwave oven). Buy them in a store with a quick turnover of stock.

SERVING IDEAS

Mint is used fresh or dried. It flavors cold or hot soups, sauces, certain vegetables (eggplant, cabbage, cucumber, peas, tomato), potato salads, meat, game, fish, ice cream, vinaigrettes and mayonnaises. It can be delicious mixed with lemon. It accompanies lamb in the form of a jellied sauce. Fresh spearmint is wrapped around Vietnamese summer rolls and is used in Lebanese salad tabbouleh. It is a part of North African, Middle Eastern, Indian, Chinese, Thai and Indo-Chinese cuisines. Mint perfumes curries, chutneys, shish kebabs, yogurt, salads, sauces and tea.
Its essential oil flavors chewing gum, chocolate, liqueurs, toothpastes and medicines.
Mint is also made into herbal tea.

NUTRITIONAL INFORMATION

Peppermint contains menthol.
PROPERTIES: carminative, antispasmodic, antiseptic, cholagogic, tonic, expectorant, stomachic and digestive. Applied as a balm, menthol is said to be beneficial in treating headaches and muscular pains. In high doses, mint can cause insomnia, whereas in low doses, it promotes sleep.

STORING

:: **At room temperature:** 2 years, dried, in an airtight container away from light and moisture.
:: **In the fridge:** fresh, a few days.

Parsley

Petroselinum spp., Apiaceae

An aromatic plant originally from southern Europe. There are three main species of parsley. **Curly parsley** has very green leaves and long stems. **Flat parsley**, or Italian parsley, has smooth leaves and a flavor reminiscent of celery. **Hamburg parsley** is mostly cultivated for its white roots, which resemble salsify.

curly parsley

BUYING

:: **Choose:** firm parsley with a good green color.
:: **Avoid:** parsley with yellowed, browned or limp leaves.

SERVING IDEAS

Parsley is used fresh, dried, frozen or marinated. Fresh parsley has more flavor and nutritional value. Add at the last minute to cooked dishes to preserve its properties. The stems are edible as well as the leaves. Parsley is part of *bouquet garni*, along with thyme and bay leaf. It is used in sandwiches, omelettes and salads. It is the main ingredient in the Lebanese salad tabbouleh.

Parsley roots are prepared in the same way as turnip or carrot and are especially used in soups and stews.

Hamburg parsley is used as an ingredient in soups and sauces and can also be cooked and eaten in the same way as asparagus or celeriac.

PREPARING

Wash parsley by plunging it in fresh water and shaking it gently. Avoid leaving it to soak. Refresh the water if necessary.

NUTRITIONAL INFORMATION

	fresh	dried
potassium	55 mg	49 mg
calcium	14 mg	19 mg
vitamin C	13 mg	2 mg
phosphorus	6 mg	5 mg
iron	0.6 mg	1.2 mg
vitamin A	52 RE	30 RE
		per 2 tsp/10 ml

PROPERTIES: antiscorbutic, stimulating, diuretic, depurative, stomachic, aperitive and anthelmintic. Parsley freshens the breath.

STORING

:: **At room temperature:** keep dried parsley in an airtight container in a dark, cool and dry place.
:: **In the fridge:** place the roots or stems of fresh parsley 1 week in water; cover leaves with a plastic bag or place parsley in a loosely closed or perforated plastic bag 2-3 days.
:: **In the freezer:** it loses its firmness. Preferably use without defrosting.

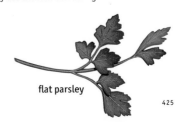

flat parsley

Clove

Syzygium aromaticum, Myrtaceae

A dried floral bud of the clove tree, a tree with persistent leaves, originally from the Maluku Islands in the Indonesian archipelago. Cloves have a sharp, tenacious and pungent flavor.

cloves

NUTRITIONAL INFORMATION

potassium	23 mg
calcium	14 mg
magnesium	6 mg
vitamin C	2 mg
iron	0.18 mg
	per 1 tsp/5 ml

PROPERTIES: tonic, antineuralgic, antispasmodic, stomachic, antiseptic and carminative. The essential oil of the clove contains 70%-85% eugenol. It is said to be of benefit against toothaches and earaches. It contains stimulants that, in high doses, can irritate the digestive system.

BUYING

:: **Choose:** whole cloves (ground cloves quickly lose their flavor and do not keep as long). A good-quality clove should float vertically in water.

SERVING IDEAS

Whole clove is traditionally associated with cooking ham. Oranges and onions studded with cloves are used in broths and braises. Cloves season fruit compotes, marinades and gherkins in vinegar, and perfume coffee.

Ground cloves flavor stuffings, blood pudding, charcuterie (sausages and deli meats), beef, lamb, pot roast, meat loaves, head cheese, marinades, soups, vegetables, cakes, cookies, pies, puddings, pastries with honey and dried fruit, fruits preserved in eau-de-vie, compotes, juices and mulled wines. It is one of the ingredients of gingerbread.

Cloves are often paired with cinnamon and nutmeg. They are used in spice mixes (garam masala and Indian curry powder, the North African *ras-el-hanout* and Chinese five-spice powder). They work well with *bouquet garni*, garlic, onion and pepper, but one should avoid using them with herbs.

The essential oil of cloves is extracted from the floral buds, leaves and stems. It is used in the production of vanillin, a synthetic form of vanilla. It is used in perfumes, soaps, medicines (dental analgesics), mouthwashes and chewing gum.

ground cloves

Allspice

Pimenta dioica, Myrtaceae

A very aromatic fruit used as a spice, produced by the Jamaica pepper tree, a tree originally from the Caribbean and Mexico. Allspice is also called "Jamaica pepper" or "myrtle pepper." Its flavor is reminiscent of cinnamon, clove, pepper and nutmeg at the same time, hence its name.

allspice grains

BUYING

:: **Choose:** whole allspice grains and grind them when needed for more flavor.
Allspice is sold as grains or ground.

SERVING IDEAS

Use allspice sparingly. This spice is used in the same way as cloves, which it can replace. It seasons roast meats, game, marinades, sauces, apple compote, pies, fruit cakes, flans, rice, onions, cabbage and poultry.
It is used to make charcuterie (sausages and deli meats) and certain liqueurs.
The leaves can be used in the same way as bay leaves.

NUTRITIONAL INFORMATION

	ground
potassium	20 mg
calcium	13 mg
magnesium	3 mg
iron	0.1 mg
	per 1 tsp/5 ml

PROPERTIES: aperitive, digestive, carminative and antirheumatic. Its essential oil contains eugenol. Its leaves are a source of vanillin.

ground allspice

Cardamom

Elettaria cardamomum and *Amomun kravanh*, Zingiberaceae

A very aromatic seed growing on a plant originally from India. Cardamom is part of the same family as ginger; it has a fine, warm, slightly peppery flavor. Cardamom is one of the most expensive spices.
Malabar cardamom (*Elettaria cardamomum*, var. *minuscula*) is the most sought after of all the varieties and the most expensive. **Ceylon cardamom** (*Elettaria cardamomum* var. *major*) resembles the previous variety a great deal, but produces seeds of lesser quality.

brown cardamom

Cardamom

Cambodian cardamom (*Amomun kravanh*) produces seeds similar in shape and flavor to Malabar cardamom.

The color of the pods varies. Green cardamom has been dried in the sun (India), brown cardamom has been dried in an oven (Asia and Europe) and white cardamom has been bleached (United States).

BUYING

Cardamom is sold in pods, as podded seeds or ground. It is preferable to buy cardamom pods and grind as needed, to preserve its flavor and extend its usability.

SERVING IDEAS

In the West, cardamom is mostly used to add aroma to cakes, cookies, fruit compotes, marinades, charcuterie (sausages and deli meats), wines and liqueurs. In the East, it flavors meats, fish, rice, omelettes and desserts. Cardamom is one of the main ingredients of Indian curry powder and garam masala. It is also used to flavor coffee in Arab countries. In Scandinavia, it is used to flavor mulled wine, compotes and pies, as well as some charcuterie products (sausages and ground meat). Cardamom can replace ginger or cinnamon in most recipes.
It is made into herbal tea.

NUTRITIONAL INFORMATION

potassium	22 mg
calcium	8 mg
iron	0.3 mg
zinc	0.2 mg
	per 1 tsp/5 ml

PROPERTIES: digestive, aperitive, carminative and stimulating. Chewing the seeds gives fresher breath.

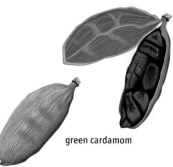

green cardamom

Nutmeg

Myristica fragrans, Myristicaceae

nutmeg

The fruit of the nutmeg tree, thought to originally be from the Maluku Islands in Indonesia. Its kernel, enveloped in a scarlet covering, the mace, encloses a brown seed, the nutmeg. The flavor of mace is not as pungent and strong as nutmeg, which is warm and spicy. Mace has an aroma of cinnamon and pepper.

BUYING

:: **Choose:** a hard, heavy nutmeg without any insect holes. To check for freshness, make a tiny shallow cut or press a needle into the nutmeg a few millimeters deep: a thin oily film or drop should appear.

Mace is sold in "blades" (blade mace) or as a powder. Buy mace and nutmeg in a store with a quick turnover of stock.

SERVING IDEAS

Nutmeg is used to flavor potato, egg and cheese-based dishes as well as cakes, puddings, pies, compotes, cabbage, spinach, sauces, onion soup, snails, meat and marinades. Its perfume is used in several drinks. It works well with dairy products, but doesn't stand up well against other perfumed spices.

Mace is used in pastries, charcuterie (sausages and deli meats) and in spice mixes. It can replace nutmeg in omelettes, béchamel sauce or mashed potatoes.

NUTRITIONAL INFORMATION

	ground nutmeg	ground mace
calories	12	8
fat	0.8 g	0.6 g
potassium	8 mg	8 mg
phosphorus	5 mg	2 mg
calcium	4 mg	4 mg
magnesium	4 mg	3 mg
iron	0.1 mg	0.2 mg
		per 1 tsp/5 ml

PROPERTIES: digestive, stimulating and carminative. Nutmeg contains myristin, a narcotic substance with a euphoric effect that causes headaches and stomachaches if not consumed in moderation.

mace

nutmeg

Savory

Satureja spp., Labiaceae

An aromatic plant originally from the Mediterranean region. There are two species of savory: **perennial savory**, or "winter savory," and **annual savory**, called "summer savory," which is more common. It has very strong-smelling green leaves. Pale-mauve or white flowers appear at the base of the leaves where they join the stem. These have a scent reminiscent of mint or thyme prior to flowering.

summer savory

SERVING IDEAS

Savory leaves are used fresh or dried. Dried savory is found either in packets or ground. Add at the end of cooking. A pinch of dried savory is enough to flavor a whole dish. It is used to flavor vinegar and goat cheeses. It enhances the taste of legumes, sauces, salads, soups, stews, marinades, meats, game, stuffings, pâtés, vegetables and vinaigrettes. It is the ideal companion to chervil and tarragon.

NUTRITIONAL INFORMATION

	ground
calcium	30 mg
potassium	15 mg
vitamin A	7 RE
magnesium	5 mg
phosphorus	2 mg
iron	0.5 mg
	per 1 tsp/5 ml

PROPERTIES: carminative, antispasmodic, antiseptic, anthelmintic, expectorant and stimulating. Savory is often associated with legumes, as it combats flatulence.

Lemon balm

Melissa officinalis, Labiaceae

An aromatic plant originally from southern Europe, lemon balm is related to mint. Called "lemon balm" because of the lemon smell emitted by its leaves, it is also known as "balm mint," "sweet balm" or just "balm." The upper part of its leaves is covered in tiny hairs. Small flowers tinged with white or pink produce long oval seeds.

lemon balm

BUYING

:: **Choose:** fresh lemon balm with firm stems and leaves, without any dark spots.

SERVING IDEAS

Lemon balm is used fresh or dried. It is a good accompaniment to pungent, bitter foods. Highly prized in Asian countries, it is used to flavor Indian curries, soups and sauces. Add lemon balm just before serving. Lemon balm seasons mixed salads, omelettes, rice, fish, stuffings, orange- or lemon-flavored pastries, fruit salads, compotes and fruit juices. It is used in the manufacture of liqueurs, including Benedictine and Chartreuse. In the Netherlands, it flavors and softens the taste of marinated herring and eel. The Spanish use lemon balm to perfume milk, sauces and soups.

NUTRITIONAL INFORMATION

PROPERTIES (ESSENTIAL OIL): carminative, tonic, stomachic, sudorific, anthelmintic, bactericidal, antispasmodic and digestive. A folk tradition ascribes the power of extending longevity to lemon balm.

Infused as a tea, fresh lemon balm is said to be effective against headaches, minor gastric ailments, nervousness and dizziness. Taken after a meal, lemon balm tea is said to help reduce flatulence and colic pains.

One of the elements of its essential oil, citral, is used to perfume deodorant creams, hair-styling products and insecticides.

Lemon grass

Cymbopogon citratus, Gramineae

A plant probably originally from Malaysia. Lemon grass (or "citronella grass") has a mild lemony flavor. The base of the stem is the most tender part.

lemon grass

BUYING

:: **Choose:** fresh lemon grass with a firm bulb.

Lemon grass is sold fresh, dried or canned.

PREPARING

Peel the lemon grass stems, then cut them about 2-3 in. (6-7 cm) from the base (the edible part). The outside of the stem and its upper part are too fibrous to be edible, but they can be used to flavor stocks, sauces, soups, stews, fish, poultry and herbal teas. Discard them after cooking.

Lemon grass

SERVING IDEAS

 Fresh lemon grass is more flavorful than dried. Use in moderation, especially if not familiar with its flavor. It works well with ginger, chile pepper, coconut, garlic, shallot and pepper. It is prized in Southeast Asian cuisines, being used to season soups, vegetables, curries, poultry, seafood, fish and marinades. It is often used as an infusion.

NUTRITIONAL INFORMATION

The essential oil of lemon grass contains geraniol and citral, which give it its lemony smell.

STORING

:: **In the fridge:** fresh, individually wrapped.

:: **In the freezer:** as is, the base and the top of the stems kept separately.

Caper

Capparis spinosa, Capparidaceae

capers

The floral bud of the caper bush, a shrub originally from the Mediterranean region.

BUYING

 Capers are sold preserved in vinegar, brine or canned in wine. The smaller they are, the more expensive, and the more delicate their flavor and stronger their smell.

STORING

Pickled capers keep indefinitely.
:: **In the fridge:** the opened container.

NUTRITIONAL INFORMATION

PROPERTIES: aperitive and digestive. Capers contain glucocapparin, a bitter and irritating glucoside that has tonic and diuretic effects.

SERVING IDEAS

Capers enhance the flavor of mayonnaises, salads and cold sauces like remoulade sauce. They are one of the essential ingredients in steak tartare. They are especially used to flavor sauces, hors d'oeuvres, mustard, sandwiches, pizza, rice, pasta dishes, meat, poultry, fish and seafood. For maximum flavor, add capers at the end of cooking.
The combination of capers, olives and onions is typical of Mediterranean cuisine.

Coriander/Cilantro

Coriandrum sativum, Apiaceae

An aromatic plant originally from the Mediterranean region. In the United States, the leaves of the coriander plant are usually called "cilantro" (from the Spanish name for coriander), while the term "coriander" is used to refer to its seeds. It is a highly regarded herb in Latin America and Asia, especially India, China and Thailand. Its dried fruits have a mild musky and lemony scent.

cilantro

BUYING

:: **Choose:** fresh cilantro that is firm and crisp with a good green color. Dried coriander seeds should be whole.

:: **Avoid:** cilantro with yellowed, browned or wilted leaves.

SERVING IDEAS

Fresh cilantro is used in the same way as parsley and chervil, which it can replace. It is a key ingredient in Mexican salsas and other dishes. In Asia, it is used in salads, soups, sauces and sandwiches. Ground coriander seeds are used similarly to salt in the Middle East.

Whole or ground coriander seeds are used to season seafood, fish, rice, charcuterie products (sausages and deli meats), omelettes, potatoes, cheeses, curries, marinades, chutneys, cookies, cakes and gingerbreads. It works well with parsley, lemon and ginger. Coriander seeds are an ingredient in Indian curry mixes and garam masala. Coriander is used to make liqueurs, as well as in the production of lower-quality cocoa.

Crushed coriander root can be used as a flavoring combined with or as a replacement for garlic.

NUTRITIONAL INFORMATION

	fresh	seeds
vitamin A	11 RE	
potassium	22 mg	23 mg
calcium	4 mg	7 mg
phosphorus	1.4 mg	7 mg
magnesium	1 mg	6 mg
	per 1 tbsp/ 15 ml	per 1 tsp/ 5 ml

PROPERTIES: carminative and stomachic. Coriander is used to relieve rheumatism, joint pains, flu and diarrhea. Chewing coriander grains is effective for neutralizing the smell of garlic. It is used as an herbal tea after meals.

STORING

:: **At room temperature:** keep dried cilantro leaves away from sunlight and dried seeds, 1 year, in an airtight container, in a dark, cool and dry place.

:: **In the fridge:** place the roots or stems of fresh cilantro 1 week in water like a bunch of flowers and cover the leaves with a plastic bag. Or, place the cilantro in a loosely closed or perforated plastic bag for 2-3 days.

:: **In the freezer:** use without defrosting, as it quickly loses its firmness.

HERBS, SPICES AND SEASONINGS

Coriander/Cilantro

PREPARING

Wash fresh cilantro at the last minute in cold water by shaking it gently. Macerate the dried seeds for about 10 min in cold water, then drain them.

coriander seeds

Cumin

Cuminum cyminum, Apiaceae

An aromatic plant originally from the Mediterranean region. Cumin leaves sliced into thin strips resemble strips of fennel, a species in the same family. Each of the flowers contains two small seeds, which are often confused with caraway, another species in the same family. They have a strong smell and a warm, slightly bitter and penetrating flavor. Use them sparingly at first, as it may take some time to get used to their taste.

cumin seeds

BUYING

:: **Choose:** whole cumin seeds, as they will have more flavor than the ground seed and keep for a longer time.

PREPARING

Crush and roast cumin seeds to release their flavor. For a more delicate flavor, sauté them briefly in fat or oil before crushing them.

NUTRITIONAL INFORMATION

potassium	38 mg
calcium	20 mg
phosphorus	10 mg
magnesium	8 mg
iron	1.3 mg
	per 1 tsp/5 ml

PROPERTIES: carminative, diuretic, digestive, anthelmintic and sedative.

SERVING IDEAS

Arab, Indian and Mexican cuisines use cumin in abundance. It is used to flavor soups, vegetables, cheese, eggs, rice, legumes, sausages, stews, pâtés, beef, marinades, pastries and bread. It is one of the basic ingredients in chili powders, curry mixes and *ras-el-hanout*, a North African spice mix. It is one of the major spices in North African cuisines, where it is called *kamoun* and used in *tajines* and couscous.

In eastern Europe, it is used as a classic seasoning for bread, certain charcuterie products (sausages and deli meats) and some cheeses.

Arabs ascribe aphrodisiac properties to a liquid paste made from crushed cumin seeds with pepper and honey.

Saffron

Crocus sativus, Iridaceae

A variety of crocus thought to be originally from Asia Minor whose flower's stigmata are used as a food seasoning and coloring. Saffron has a pungent smell and a warm and bitter flavor. It is the most expensive spice.

saffron

BUYING

:: **Choose:** orange-colored saffron threads with a mildly spicy smell.

:: **Avoid:** cheap ground saffron, which may be mixed with lesser spices.

PREPARING

Soak the saffron for about 15 min in a hot liquid before adding to food to distribute the color more effectively. Use a small amount of the liquid in the recipe. Add at the beginning of cooking. To keep its flavor, avoid cooking in butter or oil on a high heat.

NUTRITIONAL INFORMATION

water	11.9%
calories	3.1
carbohydrates	0.7 g
potassium	17.2 mg
phosphorus	2.5 mg
	per 1 tsp/5 ml

PROPERTIES: carminative, antispasmodic, digestive, emmenagogic, stomachic and stimulating. Saffron contains a bitter substance called picrocrocin and a perfumed essential oil. Its very powerful yellow coloring (crocin) can't be used for dying, as it is water-soluble.

Saffron

SERVING IDEAS

Use saffron sparingly. It is used to season Arab and Indian dishes, and adds color to soups, stews, poultry, seafood, fish, rice, curries, couscous, pastries, liqueurs and cheeses. It is an essential ingredient in the fish soup *bouillabaisse*, paella and risotto *alla milanese*.

STORING

:: At room temperature: keep saffron in an airtight container away from light, heat and humidity.

Caraway

Carum carvi, Apiaceae

An aromatic plant originally from Europe and western Asia. Caraway seeds have an acrid and pungent taste that is not as strong as cumin, but stronger than dill.

caraway

BUYING

:: Choose: whole caraway seeds, for better flavor and keeping qualities.

SERVING IDEAS

In India, caraway is used in curries, lentils and rice. In eastern Europe and Germany, it flavors charcuterie (sausages and deli meats), sauerkraut, stews, fish, potato salad, pastries and apple compote. Caraway is candied, used to decorate bread and flavors cheeses and drinks. Arab cultures use caraway in their salads and kebabs. The roots can be boiled. The leaves and young sprouts flavor soups and salads.

NUTRITIONAL INFORMATION

potassium	28 mg
calcium	14 mg
phosphorus	12 mg
iron	0.3 mg
zinc	0.1 mg
	per 1 tsp/5 ml

PROPERTIES: carminative, stimulating, anthelmintic, antispasmodic and stomachic. The seeds are said to assist digestion. They are made into herbal tea.

PREPARING

Crush and roast caraway seeds to release all of their flavor. For a more delicate taste, sauté the seeds briefly in fat or oil before crushing them.

caraway seeds

HERBS, SPICES AND SEASONINGS

caraway seeds >

Juniper berry

Juniperus communis, Cupressaceae

The fruit of the juniper tree, a tree originally from the boreal regions of the Northern Hemisphere. The flowers produce small fleshy berries that are first green, then turn blue-black or violet with a dusty bloom during the second year. The berries have a resinous perfume, a sharp taste and slightly bitter flavor.

juniper berries

BUYING

:: Choose: whole berries (more flavor) that are almost black and with no mold. They can be slightly shrivelled.

:: Avoid: brown or greenish berries.

SERVING IDEAS

Juniper berries are used whole or cracked. They are popular in northern Europe. They are used to flavor game, poultry, pork, rabbit, sauerkraut, pâtés, marinades, stuffings, charcuterie (sausages and deli meats), cabbage dishes and stocks.

Juniper berries are used in the making of gin, certain beers, Scandinavian aquavits and certain German schnapps.

NUTRITIONAL INFORMATION

PROPERTIES: antiseptic, diuretic, tonic, depurative, stomachic and antirheumatic. Juniper berries are said to help combat arthritis, biliary disorders and bladder stones. Do not use the essential oil of juniper without seeking professional advice if pregnant or if one has kidney problems.

The berries, bark and needlelike leaves of the juniper can be used as an infusion.

Borage

Borago officinalis, Borraginaceae

An aromatic and medicinal plant probably originally from Syria. Borage leaves have a flavor reminiscent of cucumber.

borage

SERVING IDEAS

Borage is eaten raw or cooked. Raw young borage leaves, or less tender leaves that have been marinated in a vinaigrette (about 30 min), are used in salads. Borage can flavor yogurt, cream cheese or vinaigrette. Preferably use the fresh leaves and flowers (more aromatic).

The candied flowers can be used to decorate pastries. Fresh borage flowers can be infused in the same way as mint (which they can replace) or be macerated in wine or iced tea.

COOKING

Borage is cooked and prepared in the same way as spinach, which it can replace in most recipes. Avoid boiling borage, which makes it lose a great deal of flavor.

NUTRITIONAL INFORMATION

	cooked
water	92%
protein	2.1 g
fat	0.8 g
carbohydrates	3.6 g
calories	25
	per 3.5 oz/100 g

EXCELLENT SOURCE: vitamin C, vitamin A, potassium and iron.
GOOD SOURCE: magnesium.
CONTAINS: riboflavin, calcium and phosphorus.
PROPERTIES: diuretic, laxative, depurative and sudorific.
The infused flowers are effective against colds and bronchitis.

STORING

:: In the fridge: place unwashed borage leaves in a loosely closed or perforated plastic bag.

Angelica

Angelica spp., Apiaceae

A giant aromatic plant that is abundant in northern Europe, where it originally comes from. Angelica looks a little like celery. The more developed it is, the more flavor it has. Angelica has a characteristic, highly perfumed scent that is warm and musky and resembles that of juniper berries.

angelica

Angelica

SERVING IDEAS

Angelica is widely used in pastry-making, where its candied stems are used to flavor or decorate cakes, gingerbreads, puddings and soufflés. It can be used to season fish or flavor vinegar. Its chopped, raw leaves can be added to a salad. When cooked with acidic fruits, it makes them sweeter.
Liqueur-makers use its essential oil or its stems and roots macerated in alcohol to make various alcoholic drinks (Chartreuse, Benedictine, angelica liqueur, gin and *eau de mélisse*). Angelica is also made into herbal tea.

NUTRITIONAL INFORMATION

PROPERTIES: tonic, digestive, aperitive, antispasmodic, expectorant and carminative. Angelica is used against asthma, chronic bronchitis, cough, colic pains and nervous migraines. It can be used as a mouthwash.

angelica stems

Ginger

Zingiber officinale, Zingiberaceae

A tuberous rhizome from a plant originally from Southeast Asia. The fleshy ginger rhizomes vary in size and color (golden sand, yellow, white or red) depending on the variety, of which there are many. Their highly aromatic pulp is pungent, peppery and sometimes very hot. It is covered in a thin skin that is edible when the rhizome is young and fresh.

fresh ginger

BUYING

:: **Choose:** fresh, firm ginger that isn't shrivelled or moldy. If ginger skin scratches off easily, it should be fresh. Ginger is sold fresh, dried or canned; it is ground, candied, crystallized or sliced finely and pickled in vinegar.

COOKING

For maximum flavor, add ginger at the end of cooking. The flavor will be more subtle if it is added at the beginning of cooking.

NUTRITIONAL INFORMATION

	ground
potassium	24 mg
magnesium	3 mg
phosphorus	3 mg
	per 1 tsp/5 ml

PROPERTIES: tonic, antiseptic, diuretic, antipyretic, aperitive, stomachic and aphrodisiac. Ginger is said to stimulate digestion, combat flatulence and be effective against colds, coughs, travel sickness and rheumatism pains. It can irritate the digestive system, so it is preferable to use ginger in moderation.

STORING

 :: At room temperature: keep ground ginger in an airtight container in a dark, cool and dry place.
Candied ginger keeps indefinitely.
:: In the fridge: fresh, 2-3 weeks (only peel at time of using); canned, when the container is open.
:: In the freezer: as is. It can be peeled and cut without being defrosted.

PREPARING

Fresh ginger can be peeled, sliced, grated, chopped or cut into fine sticks.

SERVING IDEAS

 Fresh ginger is used to flavor sauces, meat, poultry, fish, seafood, vegetables, rice, tofu, marinades, stocks, soups, fruits, cakes and drinks. It is made into jam and candied sweets.
Pickled ginger is served with sushi and sashimi. Ginger is used to flavor Asian dishes. In the West, it is more often used ground to flavor cakes, cookies, gingerbreads, compotes and curries. It works particularly well with apples and bananas.
Its essential oil is used in the production of beers and soft drinks (ginger ale). It is not easy to replace fresh ginger with dried or ground ginger, as the flavor will be much less strong. Ginger is also made into herbal tea.

ground ginger

1 Peel the fresh ginger.

2 Cut into fine slices.

3 Chop finely.

HERBS, SPICES AND SEASONINGS

Curry

The word "curry" refers to a mix of spices as well as the dishes of fish, meat, lentils or vegetables that are flavored with this seasoning. It is originally from India. Curry usually contains a mixture of the following spices: cinnamon, coriander, cumin, turmeric, pepper, cardamom, ginger, nutmeg and cloves. Sometimes mace, aniseed, caraway, fennel, fenugreek, bay leaf, poppy seed, saffron, Cayenne pepper and mustard seeds are added. In Sri Lanka, coconut milk is added; in Thailand, shrimp paste. The color of Indian curry varies from white to golden brown and red, to green; these curry mixes can be liquid, dry or in powder form. Depending on the amount of pepper or chile pepper used, one can buy mild, medium, hot and very hot curry mixes.

curry powder

BUYING

 Curry is sold as a powder or a paste.

SERVING IDEAS

 Curry is used to season main dishes of meat (chicken, pork, lamb) or vegetarian dishes (chickpeas, lentils, fish), appetizers, soups, vegetables, pasta dishes, rice, sauces, mayonnaise and butter.
To bring out its flavor well, heat curry powder in fat or oil before adding to a sauce or dish.

NUTRITIONAL INFORMATION

This varies according to the variety and quantity of ingredients used.

STORING

 :: At room temperature: keep curry powder in an airtight container in a cool and dry place.
:: In the fridge: opened containers of curry paste.

Turmeric

Curcuma longa, Zingiberaceae

The rhizome of a plant probably originally from Indonesia and Malaysia. Turmeric is related to ginger. The rhizomes are colored yellow or lemon-yellow, depending on the variety. They are mostly sold in powder form. Turmeric is a highly aromatic spice with a pungent taste reminiscent of ginger. It has a more bitter taste than saffron; this difference is accentuated during the cooking process, which blackens turmeric.

fresh turmeric

BUYING

The color of turmeric varies according to the variety and is not an indication of quality.

SERVING IDEAS

Use turmeric in moderation so that it doesn't mask the taste of other foods. Turmeric is prized in Southeast Asia, where it adds color and flavor to soups, sauces, salads, legumes, rice, eggs, fish and crustaceans. In India, it is one of the main ingredients in curry mixes and in the spice mix garam masala, as well as chutneys. It is one of the ingredients in Worcestershire sauce. Turmeric adds color to sauces, syrups, certain liqueurs, American mustard, marinades, sweets, butter, margarines, cheeses and shortenings.

NUTRITIONAL INFORMATION

potassium	56 mg
phosphorus	6 mg
calcium	4 mg
magnesium	4 mg
iron	0.9 mg
	per 1 tsp/5 ml

PROPERTIES: turmeric is said to be useful in treating coughs, indigestion and conjunctivitis.

STORING

:: **At room temperature:** away from light.

ground turmeric

Cinnamon

Cinnamomum spp., Lauraceae

The dried bark of the cinnamon tree, a tree in the same family as the bay laurel and avocado trees. Commercially, there are two important species. **Ceylon cinnamon**, whose thin, smooth and fine bark is a light, matte brown, is the most aromatic cinnamon. The paler it is, the better its quality. **Chinese cinnamon**, whose bark is called "cassia" or "false cinnamon," has a less fine flavor, a more pungent taste and is thicker than Ceylon cinnamon. Less expensive, it captures almost all of the North American market.

cinnamon sticks

BUYING

Cinnamon is sold in sticks, as a powder or as an essential oil. Ground cinnamon has a stronger flavor than cinnamon sticks, but it deteriorates more quickly.

SERVING IDEAS

Cinnamon is used to flavor cakes, cookies, apple pies, donuts, brioches, puddings, crepes, compotes, yogurts and confectionery. In central Europe, Italy, Spain and Canada, it is used to season soups, meats, tomato sauces, vegetables, pot roast, couscous, pasta dishes and marinades. In English-speaking countries, it is traditionally used to season baked squash. In France and Nordic countries, it is added to mulled wine. In Asia, dried cinnamon buds, leaves and berries are also used. Cinnamon is used in pharmacy to flavor various preparations, including toothpaste.

NUTRITIONAL INFORMATION

calcium	28 mg
potassium	11 mg
iron	0.8 mg
	per 1 tsp/5 ml

PROPERTIES: antispasmodic, antiseptic, stimulating and anthelmintic. Ground cinnamon added to tea or any other liquid is said to relieve gastric ailments and combat diarrhea.

STORING

:: **At room temperature:** keep cinnamon in an airtight container, away from light and moisture.

powdered cinnamon

Mustard

Brassica and *Sinapis spp.*, Cruciferae

A plant originally from the Mediterranean basin. There are several species of mustard. **Black mustard** (*Brassica nigra*) produces small seeds that become black at maturity. They have an extremely rich and pungent flavor, stronger than yellow mustard. **White mustard** (*Sinapis alba*) produces large yellow-colored seeds with a bitter taste that is not as pungent as other varieties. **Indian mustard** or mustard greens (*Brassica juncea*) is a green vegetable whose very tasty leaves are used in the same way as spinach.

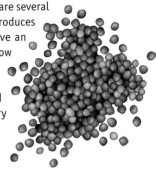

white mustard seeds

BUYING

:: **Choose:** mustard greens with fresh, supple and well-colored leaves.
:: **Avoid:** dry, yellowed or withered leaves as well as leaves with thick and hard stems, as they are woody.

STORING

:: **At room temperature:** keep powdered mustard and whole seeds dry and away from heat.
:: **In the fridge:** place prepared mustard and mustard oil in an airtight container. Keep unwashed mustard leaves a few days in a loosely closed or perforated plastic bag.
:: **In the freezer:** in the same way as spinach.

PREPARING

Dijon mustard is prepared with verjuice (unripe grape juice) and white wine; Bordeaux mustard with unfermented grape must (juice); and Meaux mustard with vinegar. American mustard is sweet and is prepared using black and white seeds, to which turmeric is added.

Indian mustard

Mustard

NUTRITIONAL INFORMATION

water	91%
protein	2.7 g
fat	0.2 g
carbohydrates	5 g
fiber	1.1 g
calories	26
	per 3.5 oz/100 g

MUSTARD LEAVES
EXCELLENT SOURCE: vitamin C, vitamin A, iron and potassium.
PROPERTIES: aperitive, stimulating, digestive, disinfectant, antiseptic, laxative and emetic. The leaves contain substances that can provoke an increase in the size of the thyroid gland; eat in moderation and be sure to eat foods that provide good amounts of iodine, such as seafood, fish and seaweeds.

MUSTARD OIL
PROPERTIES: antibacterial and antifungal. Mustard is used in foot baths or as a poultice to decongest the sinuses and lungs. It is used to treat pneumonia and bronchitis, among other ailments.

SERVING IDEAS

 Mustard leaves are prepared in the same way as spinach, which they can replace in most recipes. They are delicious in soups or puréed, combined with potato or legume purées to soften their pungent flavor. Avoid cooking them in an aluminum or iron container, as they will blacken.

The whole seeds can be used as is, roasted or sautéed in very hot oil; they pop in the same way as popcorn. The whole grains flavor marinades, legumes, sauces and curries. Powdered mustard can be added to vinaigrettes or mayonnaise; it is also used to season ham for cooking. It can be blended with liquid to make a paste. Prepared mustard is used with rabbit, pork, chicken and some fatty fish before cooking. Several hot or cold sauces are based on mustard.

black mustard seeds

Pepper

Piper nigrum, Piperaceae

The fruit of the pepper plant, a climbing bush originally from India. There are several hundred species of pepper. Whole pepper is often referred to as peppercorn. **Green pepper** is not very pungent and is slightly fruity. It is preserved in brine or vinegar, or dried. **Black pepper** is the most pungent and aromatic of peppers. **White pepper** is milder than black pepper. **Gray pepper** is quite rare on the market, and is always ground. It can also consist in a mixture of black and white pepper. Gray pepper is fairly mild. **Pink pepper** (or "red pepper") is a dried berry with a delicate, perfumed and slightly pungent flavor, which deteriorates quickly.

black peppercorns

BUYING

:: **Choose:** heavy, compact peppercorns that don't crumble easily and have a uniform color. Preferably buy ground pepper in a place where the turnover of stock is rapid. Pepper is sold whole, cracked or ground, plain or seasoned. Green pepper is sold in brine, vinegar or dried. For best flavor and aroma, buy whole peppercorns and grind them as needed.

NUTRITIONAL INFORMATION

	ground black pepper	ground white pepper
potassium	26 mg	2 mg
calcium	9 mg	6 mg
phosphorus	4 mg	4 mg
magnesium	4 mg	2 mg
iron	0.6 mg	0.3 mg
		per 1 tsp/5 ml

PROPERTIES: tonic, stimulating, carminative and antibacterial. Pepper can irritate the mucous lining of the stomach. It activates the production of saliva and gastric secretions and helps digestion. In high doses, pepper becomes an irritant and can overheat the body.

ground black pepper

Pepper

SERVING IDEAS

Pepper is added to almost all savory dishes, hot or cold: sauces, meats, vegetables, charcuterie products (sausages and deli meats), vinaigrettes and even certain desserts.

White pepper is used to season white sauces, poultry and fish.

Whole peppercorns flavor marinades, pâtés, charcuterie, cheeses and soups, stocks and stews. The flavor of pepper is enhanced when food is frozen.

COOKING

Ground pepper loses its flavor and aroma if cooked for over 2 hr. Add ground pepper right at the end of cooking, so that it doesn't become bitter.

STORING

:: **At room temperature:** whole, indefinitely; ground, 3 months; green, 1 week once the container is opened, otherwise, 1 year.

green peppercorns

pink peppercorns

white peppercorns

Fenugreek

Trigonella foenum-graecum, Papilionaceae

The fruit of a plant originally from southeastern Europe and India. Fenugreek is part of the pea and clover family. The fruits are long and thin pods that harbor tiny seeds. Both the plant and the seeds emit a strong, spicy smell. The seeds have a sweet-and-sour flavor with an aftertaste of caramel and maple syrup that becomes stronger when the seeds are roasted. The food industry uses fenugreek to make an artificial flavor that imitates maple syrup.

fenugreek seeds

BUYING

 Fenugreek is sold in specialty food stores.

SERVING IDEAS

Fenugreek seeds are used dried, whole, ground, cracked or sprouted, roasted or unroasted. They are more flavorful when they have been roasted and ground. They are cooked in the same way as porridge or used as a seasoning. They are used to flavor soups, vegetables, cheeses, chutneys, gherkins and simmered dishes.

The sprouted seeds are eaten as a salad. The seeds, leaves and young sprouts are made into herbal tea; the leaves and young sprouts are eaten as vegetables in some countries in Africa and India.

NUTRITIONAL INFORMATION

water	7.5%
protein	0.9 g
fat	0.2 g
carbohydrates	2.2 g
calories	12
	per 1 tsp/5 ml

Fenugreek seeds are high in mucilage.
PROPERTIES: galactogenic, aphrodisiac, emollient, stomachic, aperitive and tonic. The seeds are used to treat stomachaches and abscesses, and as an emollient poultice. The leaves are used as an expectorant, emollient, astringent and diuretic.

STORING

:: **At room temperature:** keep fenugreek in an airtight container in a cool and dry place away from light.

ground fenugreek

Chile pepper

Capsicum spp., Solanaceae

The fruit of plants originally from South and Central America. Chile peppers belong to the same family as eggplant, winter cherry, potato, tamarillo and tomato. The chile pepper is a pod that encloses multiple seeds inside its cavity. The different species of chile pepper have different sizes, shapes, colors and flavors.

paprika pepper

Some chile peppers are green (jalapeño, serrano, poblano); others are coppery, purple or red (ancho, cascabel or cherry pepper, cayenne pepper, japone, hontaka, pasilla); others are yellow (caribe, guero). Some chile peppers are so strong that they cause tears when they are cut (guero, habanero, japone).

Cayenne pepper, originally from around the Cayenne River in French Guyana, is a powder of dried red chile peppers with a very hot taste. Its rather small fruits are elongated and thin. Greatly used in Latin America and India, it is used to make Tabasco® sauce, chili powder and curry mixes.

Paprika is a powder made from dried red peppers that grow on a shrub originally from America. The sweeter version of this spice occupies a very important place in Hungarian cuisine. Smoky Spanish *pimentón* is a key ingredient in chorizo sausage and on everything from eggs to sauces. Its color and flavor can vary (check the label).

Harissa is a condiment based on chile peppers that is especially enjoyed in the Middle East and North Africa; it is the national condiment of Tunisia. It contains a purée of small red chile peppers, cayenne pepper, oil, garlic, coriander, mint leaves, caraway and sometimes several other spices.

paprika

Chili powder is a mixture of spices based on dried ground hot peppers originally from Mexico. It can contain black pepper, cumin, oregano, paprika, clove and garlic. The heat of the peppers determines the strength of the seasoning.

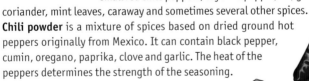

dried chile peppers

Tabasco pepper is a variety of chile pepper that has given its name to a very hot sauce originally from America.

chili powder

crushed chile peppers

BUYING

:: **Choose:** fresh or dried chile peppers that are well colored with shiny skin that has no marks or soft spots. Ground chile peppers should have an even color and good aroma. Dried whole chile peppers are often wrinkled, which is normal.

PREPARING

Avoid touching the face, lips and eyes when cutting up chile peppers, as it can cause irritations. Simply handling chile peppers can cause tears due to the capsaicin, which is highly volatile; wash hands with soap and clean the knife and chopping board in hot water. If your hands are very sensitive, wear gloves. If you wish to reduce the heat of chile peppers, do not use the seeds or white membranes from inside the pepper. Chile peppers can be soaked in cold water with a little vinegar for 1 hr.

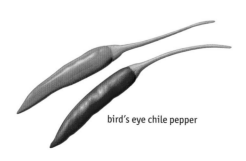

bird's eye chile pepper

Chile pepper

jalapeño pepper

fresh red chile pepper

fresh green chile pepper

NUTRITIONAL INFORMATION

	fresh, whole
water	88%
protein	2 g
fat	0.2 g
carbohydrates	9.6 g
fiber	1.8 g
calories	40
	per 3.5 oz/100 g

Chile peppers contain more vitamin C than oranges. The amount used, however, is often very small, and most of the time chile peppers are cooked, which reduces its vitamin C content. If the seeds are removed, they contain 50% less fiber.

The proportion of various nutrients is strongly influenced by the variety. Red chile peppers generally contain more vitamin A and vitamin C than green chile peppers.

Their heat comes from capsaicin. This substance stimulates the production of saliva and activates digestion. To soften its hot taste in the mouth, have some yogurt, milk, bread, cooked rice, sugar or candy, rather than water.

STORING

:: At room temperature: keep chili powder in an airtight container, in a dark, dry and cool place; Tabasco® sauce, indefinitely.

:: In the fridge: unwashed chile peppers, 1 week, in a paper bag; paprika powder in an airtight container; opened containers of harissa.

:: In the freezer: grill or blanch (3 min) chile peppers, then peel.

Chile peppers can be marinated or dried. Dried chile peppers will keep for 1 year.

harissa

Chile pepper

SERVING IDEAS

Chile peppers are used dried, marinated or cooked, then made into a paste so that they mix through foods more evenly. In China, a red chile paste with salt and oil called *öt* is served with numerous dishes. Ground chile pepper is used as an ingredient in curry powders and ketchups.

A pinch of cayenne pepper is usually enough to season a whole dish. It is used to flavor appetizers, soups, butter or cream sauces and main dishes with crustaceans or eggs.

Paprika and chili powder are used to flavor and color rice, pasta dishes, sauces and potato salads. Paprika is used with eggs, poultry, seafood, mayonnaise and cheese dips or fresh cheeses. It is an essential ingredient in goulash, a Hungarian beef stew.

Harissa is an essential ingredient in couscous. It enhances the taste of soups, salads, meats, fish, stews, rice, sauces, mayonnaises and eggs. It is used as is or blended with some stock or olive oil and lemon juice. Use in moderation, if not accustomed to its strong flavor.

Tabasco® sauce flavors soups, vinaigrettes, sauces, dips, mixed salads, beans, lentils, stews, meat, poultry and seafood. One to three drops is enough to season a whole dish.

COOKING

Use chile peppers in small doses, as their flavor develops during cooking. A "safe" way of giving a chile flavor to a dish consists of sautéeing a chile pepper in oil and then using the oil for cooking.

Do not heat paprika for too long, to prevent it losing its flavor and color.

Tabasco® sauce

tabasco pepper

serrano pepper

Horseradish

Armoracia rusticana, Crucifereae

A plant originally from eastern Europe, horseradish is a root from which wavy and jagged leaves grow. Its very firm flesh is cream-white in color. Horseradish contains an essential oil similar to mustard, which gives it its hot and acrid taste. Horseradish, which belongs to the same family as the cabbage, mustard, turnip and radish, contains more vitamin C than an orange.

horseradish root

BUYING

:: **Choose:** a firm horseradish, without mold or soft parts.

SERVING IDEAS

Horseradish is eaten raw, marinated or cooked. Its leaves are used in salads. It can be used in place of mustard. Usually grated, it can also be cut into cubes, julienne strips or slices. Chopped finely, it can be added to sauces, vinaigrettes, soups and sandwich preparations. Added to sauces, it enhances the taste of stews, boiled meats, smoked fish and seafood. It works well with potatoes, beets, celery, parsnip, tuna, legumes, apple sauce served with roast meat, charcuterie products (sausages and deli meats) and eggs. Added to cream, yogurt or mayonnaise, its flavor is softened and it makes a delicious sauce. Its leaves can be eaten raw or cooked, in the same way as the leaves of other cruciferous vegetables.

COOKING

Avoid cooking horseradish.

NUTRITIONAL INFORMATION

	prepared
protein	0.2 g
carbohydrates	1.4 g
calcium	9 mg
phosphorus	5 mg
iron	0.1 mg
calories	6
	per 1 tbsp/15 ml

PROPERTIES: antiseptic, antigout, antiscorbutic, antispasmodic, antirheumatic, stomachic, expectorant, cholagogic, diuretic, stimulating and purgative.

STORING

:: **In the fridge:** a few weeks, wrapped in slightly damp paper towel and a plastic bag. If the root becomes soft or soft spots appear (remove them), prepare the horseradish immediately. Prepared horseradish sauce keeps for a long time but gradually loses its flavor.

:: **In the freezer:** grated (gradually loses its flavor).

Horseradish can be dried. It keeps 6 months in vinegar.

HERBS, SPICES AND SEASONINGS

PREPARING

Wash horseradish, then peel. If green flesh appears when peeling, remove it, as it is bitter. Discard the core of a large horseradish when it appears very hard and woody. To prevent horseradish flesh from oxidizing, sprinkle with lemon juice, vinegar or vinaigrette as soon as it is cut or grated. Use a stainless steel grater. When grating horseradish using a food processor or blender, grate very finely and only when ready to eat or cook for maximum flavor.

Poppy

Papaver somniferum, Papaveraceae

A plant thought to be originally from Asia Minor. The opium poppy used for poppy seeds is part of the same family that includes the field poppy. Its flowers produce seeds that have narcotic properties, as do its flower capsules, from which opium is extracted (used to produce morphine and codeine).

poppy

BUYING

Poppy seeds are sold in most grocery stores. Buy them in a store with a quick turnover of stock.

SERVING IDEAS

The gray-blue colored poppy seeds have a mild nutty flavor that is brought out by cooking. They are used to flavor breads, cakes, pastries (especially in Turkey, Egypt and central Europe), as well as for vegetables, pasta dishes, potato salads, cheeses and marinades.
Poppy seed oil can be used in salads. The leaves are prepared in the same way as spinach. The ground grains have a thickening effect.

NUTRITIONAL INFORMATION

calcium	41 mg
phosphorus	24 mg
potassium	20 mg
magnesium	9 mg
zinc	0.3 mg
iron	0.3 mg
	per 1 tsp/5 ml

PROPERTIES: the seeds and latex extracted from the green capsules are said to have a sedative, calming, antispasmodic and hypnotic effect.

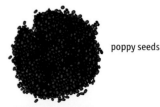

poppy seeds

Tamarind

Tamarindus indica, Leguminosae

The fruit of the tamarind tree, a tree originally from India. Tamarind is used a great deal in the cuisines of several Asian and Middle Eastern countries. The tamarind is enclosed in pods that hold hard seeds. The pulp of the seeds is compact and contains fibrous threads. With a bitter flavor, it is sweet and very acidic.

tamarind pods

BUYING

Tamarind is usually sold in specialty food stores as an instant paste (that needs to be blended with a little water) or pressed into a compact block.

SERVING IDEAS

Tamarind is used fresh, dried, preserved, pickled in brine, as a juice, paste or syrup. It is used as a food or condiment. It is added to soups, sauces, marinades, stews, cakes and confectionery. It accompanies meat, game and fish. Its flavor enhances the flavor of fruits. It is used to make jams, sorbets, chutneys, drinks and condiments. It is made into thirst-quenching drinks.

Its flowers and leaves are eaten as a vegetable in salads.

Tamarind can be replaced by lemon juice in most recipes, but the result will be different. The juice of a lemon is equivalent to 1 tablespoon (15 ml) of tamarind pulp dissolved in ⅕ cup (50 ml) of water.

PREPARING

Soak pressed tamarind in hot water (about 15 min) until it softens and can be separated with the fingers. Strain to remove the fibers.

Tamarind seeds need to soak overnight and be completely cooked.

NUTRITIONAL INFORMATION

	raw
water	31.4%
protein	2.8 g
fat	0.6 g
carbohydrates	62.5 g
fiber	3 g
calories	239
	per 3.5 oz/100 g

EXCELLENT SOURCE: potassium, magnesium and thiamine.

GOOD SOURCE: iron.

CONTAINS: phosphorus, riboflavin, niacin, calcium and vitamin C.

Tamarind is a source of fiber.

PROPERTIES: choleretic and laxative.

STORING

:: **At room temperature.**

tamarind seeds

Vanilla

Vanilla planifolia, Orchidaceae

The fruit of a climbing orchid originally from Mexico or Central America. The most highly regarded vanilla comes from Mexico. True vanilla is derived from the species of vanilla tree *Vanilla planifolia*. The fruits, elongated capsules, contain an aromatic pulp and numerous small seeds. The pods are dried until they become dark brown, soft and covered in a film of vanillin crystals, a substance responsible for the flavor of vanilla. Vanillin is also produced synthetically using eugenol, clove essence. It is often used in place of the vanillin derived from vanilla, although it does not have the same fineness.

vanilla pods

NUTRITIONAL INFORMATION

PROPERTIES: tonic, stimulating, digestive and antiseptic.

BUYING

Vanilla is sold as pods, powder, liquid or as vanilla sugar. The pods are sold in glass tubes, jars or sachets. Dried or liquid vanilla is not always pure (read the label carefully). Pure vanilla is much more expensive and has a better taste than artificial vanilla.

STORING

:: **At room temperature:** keep vanilla pods in an airtight container, in a dry place. To make vanilla sugar, bury a pod or a piece of pod in sugar.

SERVING IDEAS

Vanilla is used to flavor tapioca, compotes, ice creams, yogurts and puddings. Almost indispensable for making pastries, it is also used in confectionery and chocolate-making. Used in very small quantities, it can enhance the flavor of certain savory dishes, in particular fish soups, mussels and poultry. It is added to punches, wines, sangria and hot chocolate and is used in distilling. Liquid vanilla extract loses a great deal of flavor during cooking. Add once cooking is finished.

Vanilla pods are used as is, reduced to a powder (in the blender) or finely chopped. Use as is to flavor milk, syrup or fruits. Split in two lengthwise and infuse in the cold liquid, heating to the desired temperature. Whole pods can be reused up to four times. Remove them at the end of cooking, rinse and sponge them, then store until they are used again.

Miso

A fermented paste originally from Asia. Miso is usually very salty (sometimes sweet, although this is more rare), made from soybeans, mainly used as a flavoring. In Japan alone, there are more than 50 varieties of miso. Rice miso is the most popular there. Each miso has its characteristic color, texture, flavor, aroma and nutritional value. As a general rule, a dark miso will be more fermented and therefore saltier. Conversely, a pale miso is less fermented and sweeter. Barley usually produces a miso that is darker than rice miso and paler than soybean. The texture of miso can be more or less moist and more or less smooth.

There is also a wide variety of misos to which diverse ingredients are added (honey, sugar, water, sake, nuts, seeds, vegetables, seafood, spices, seaweeds).

rice miso

HERBS, SPICES AND SEASONINGS

BUYING

Miso is usually sold in a sealed bag or loose, in plastic or glass containers. When buying, read the label carefully to check its ingredients, whether the miso has been pasteurized and if it contains additives.

COOKING

Avoid cooking miso, as cooking destroys the microorganisms it contains. Add miso at the end of cooking once any boiling has finished. Preferably blend miso first separately with a small quantity of stock or hot water.

SERVING IDEAS

Miso enhances the flavor and nutritional value of foods. It can be used in place of salt and tamari sauce in most recipes. Miso is added to almost everything (soups, sauces, stocks, vinaigrettes, pasta dishes, mixed salads, vegetables, tofu, seafood, meat, poultry, eggs, crepes, marinades).

Sweet misos lend themselves more easily to being used with vegetables, sauces, spreads, crepes and desserts.

STORING

:: **At room temperature:** unless it is very hot, keep salted miso away from drafts, to prevent drying.

:: **In the fridge:** sweet miso.

Miso

NUTRITIONAL INFORMATION

	rice miso
water	41%
protein	11.8 g
fat	6.1 g
carbohydrates	28 g
fiber	2.5 g
calories	206
	per 3.5 oz/100 g

The nutritional value of misos varies greatly; it depends on the ingredients and manufacturing process.

SOYBEAN MISO

EXCELLENT SOURCE: zinc.

GOOD SOURCE: iron, riboflavin and folic acid.

CONTAINS: vitamin B_6, thiamine and calcium. Soybean miso is a source of fiber.

MISO

Unpasteurized miso is of great nutritional value. It contains lactic acid bacteria (0.5%-1%), enzymes, yeasts and various other microorganisms. Its fats are mostly unsaturated.

PROPERTIES: miso is said to be beneficial for the digestive system; it helps the organism rid itself of toxic substances, including heavy metals, and it protects against pollution and illnesses.

Soy sauce

soy sauce

A condiment originally from China. Soy sauce occupies a preeminent position in the cuisines of Asian countries. Its Japanese name is *shoyu*. Traditionally, soy sauce, shoyu and tamari refer to the liquid formed during the manufacture of miso.

Traditional Chinese **soy sauce** (or *chiang-yu*) is made using whole soybeans and ground wheat. It can be more or less dark depending on its age and whether caramel or molasses has been added.

Tamari is made exclusively using soybeans or soybean meal (the residue from pressing the beans when oil is extracted); therefore, it contains no cereal grain. It sometimes contains additives such as monosodium glutamate and caramel. Tamari is dark and has a thicker consistency.

Shoyu is lighter in color than Chinese soy sauce and slightly sweet.
Soy sauce (Chinese or Japanese) contains some of the alcohol produced during the fermentation of the cereal grains, whereas tamari has none. The soy sauce found in supermarkets is usually a synthetic product that is a pale imitation of the original.

NUTRITIONAL INFORMATION

	soy sauce	tamari
water	71%	66%
protein	0.8 g	1.5 g
carbohydrates	1.2 g	0.9 g
calories	7.5	8.8
		per 1 tbsp/15 ml

tamari

Most of these condiments are very salty and to be used in moderation. However, over the last few years, reduced-salt versions of these sauces have been produced. The properties of tamari and shoyu sauces made according to traditional methods are identical to those of miso.

STORING

 :: At room temperature: synthetic soy sauce, indefinitely.
:: In the fridge: an opened bottle of shoyu or tamari.

SERVING IDEAS

Shoyu, tamari and soy sauce can be used in place of salt, giving a new flavor to dishes. Only add shoyu at the end of cooking. These sauces can be used as marinades or dips and they season and color foods. They give taste to tofu and form its traditional minimal accompaniment. Garlic, onion, fresh ginger, vinegar and oil can be added to them. Shoyu, tamari or soy sauce are a basic ingredient of numerous sauces, including teriyaki sauce and Worcestershire sauce.

Vinegar

A liquid obtained from the action of bacteria that transforms an alcoholic liquid into a solution containing 4%-12% acetic acid. All foods that can produce an alcoholic fermentation can be used to make vinegar (wine, ethyl alcohol, cider, sugar cane, malt, dates, oranges, bananas, rice, coconut milk, for example). Wine and cider are the best base ingredients for making vinegar.

Traditional method or "Orleans method"

Vinegar is produced in oak barrels. The wine can ferment for several weeks, after which vinegar is obtained. It is unpasteurized and keeps all of its flavor and color.

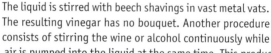

Industrial method

The liquid is stirred with beech shavings in vast metal vats. The resulting vinegar has no bouquet. Another procedure consists of stirring the wine or alcohol continuously while air is pumped into the liquid at the same time. This produces a clarified vinegar that has lost much of its bouquet.

balsamic vinegar

Balsamic vinegar is a highly renowned vinegar; the variety from Modena has the best reputation. A sweet white grape (*Trebbiano*) is used in its fabrication. Usually sold when it has been aged for 4-5 years, it is possible to find some that have been aged 10-40 years, resulting in indescribable fineness and flavor. Balsamic vinegar is a dark brown color, with a fluid, slightly syrupy consistency, low acidity and a characteristic flavor.

white wine vinegar

NUTRITIONAL INFORMATION

Vinegar is composed of 95% water. It contains no protein, fat or vitamins, very little carbohydrate and very few calories (2 per tablespoon/15 ml).

Unpasteurized vinegar contains very small quantities of minerals. Pasteurized vinegar has almost no minerals.

The higher its level of acetic acid, the more acidic the vinegar will be.

PROPERTIES (particularly if unpasteurized): vinegar soothes wounds, insect bites, burns, headaches and chronic fatigue. It stimulates the appetite and digestion and helps prevent gastroenteritis conditions or treat them. Consumed in a too great quantity, it can irritate the mucous membranes. Replace vinegar with lemon juice if one has digestive problems.

STORING

:: **At room temperature:** indefinitely.
:: **In the fridge:** homemade vinegar. It is still edible even if it becomes cloudy and a slime ("mother of vinegar") forms; it can be filtered out or left in.

PREPARING

:: **Homemade vinegar:** to make one's own vinegar, pour the chosen liquid into a wooden, glass or stoneware container and leave at room temperature. One can begin with a mixture of unpasteurized vinegar and alcohol (white or red wine, cider, etc.) (3 cups/750 ml of wine and ¾ cup/200 ml of vinegar), but this method takes a long time (3-4 months). It can be shortened to 1-2 months if one uses a mother of vinegar mixture. In this case, cover the container with a double thickness of a straining cloth (like muslin) to allow air to pass through and let it rest in a warm place; it is important to avoid moving the container. When the wine has become vinegar, filter and bottle.

If you wish to keep the mother of vinegar for later use, keep it in a small amount of vinegar. When the mother of vinegar becomes too large, remove a portion that can be used to make another vinegar.

Herbs can be added to taste to a sterilized container in which previously heated vinegar can be poured. Let rest for 2 weeks, shaking occasionally; filter by pouring into a new sterilized bottle and keep in a cool place, away from light.

flavored
vinegar

1 Place herb sprigs in a pot containing white wine vinegar, heat gently then let infuse off the heat for 30 min.

2 Pour the flavored vinegar into a jug, taking care to keep back the herbs.

3 Fill a sterilized bottle with flavored vinegar, then add a fresh herb sprig.

4 In this way, one can make vinegars flavored with thyme, tarragon, etc.

SERVING IDEAS

Vinegar is used as a condiment, seasoning vinaigrettes, mayonnaises and mustards. Its acidifying action prevents the oxidation of fruits and vegetables, slows down the action of enzymes that destroy vitamin C, extends the storage of foods by maceration, pickling and preserving, and gives foods a sweet-and-sour flavor. It is used for meat, chicken and game marinades and for dried beans (add vinegar at the end of cooking for legumes). It is useful for deglazing. Added to the poaching water of eggs, it helps coagulate the white. Most vinegars can be used in place of each other. **White vinegar,** which is less perfumed, is ideal in pickles and other preserves. **Cider and malt vinegars** are used in dark and spicy pickles and chutneys. Cider vinegar gives a slight apple taste to foods.

wine
vinegar

Cider and white wine vinegars are excellent with fish, crustaceans and shellfish, fruits and fine sauces (hollandaise and béarnaise).
Red wine vinegar adds piquancy and enhances the taste of slightly bland foods (calf liver and red meat dishes).
Chinese or Japanese rice vinegar is generally mild and is used to flavor crudités, soups and sweet-and-sour dishes.
High-quality **balsamic vinegar** shouldn't be boiled, although less expensive balsamic can be boiled and reduced to a thicker consistency such as a syrup; the flavor mellows. For cooked dishes, high-quality balsamic is added a little before the end of cooking. It can be added to grilled meats and sauces before serving. It is used on salads (in place of or combined with red wine vinegar), or to flavor beef fillet, foie gras, fish, lobster and mussels. Cut strawberries can be sprinkled with balsamic vinegar and left to macerate for a few minutes.

Salt

A crystallized, odorless and flaky substance with a pungent taste and soluble in water. Salt is made up of sodium (40%) and chlorine (60%), hence its scientific name, *sodium chloride*.

Salt, like water, is essential to the functioning of the human body; it is precious as a condiment and as a food preservative.

There are two types of salt.

Rock salt comes from mines exploited for their natural salt

coarse salt

deposits, which are the result of the sea retreating over the course of geological

epochs. Refined salt or "table salt" comes from rock salt.

Sea salt or "marine salt" is derived from salt marshes, basins in which seawater is trapped and whose salt content becomes concentrated through the combined evaporating action of the sun and wind. It can also be derived from inland seas or salt lakes (Red Sea, Dead Sea, Great Salt Lake), which contain higher concentrations of salt. Sea salt is white, pink or grayish in color, as it contains various minerals in very small quantities. Some people consider it to have a purer and stronger taste than rock salt.

sea salt

STORING

:: **At room temperature:** keep salt away from drafts and moisture. A few grains of raw rice in a salt shaker prevent the formation of lumps.

BUYING

Salt is generally sold as coarse salt, fine salt, crystallized salt and table salt. Table salt can contain both rock salt and sea salt. It is very often iodized, which is to say potassium iodide has been added to it, which has no effect on its flavor. Salt is almost always treated with additives to prevent it from absorbing moisture and clumping instead of staying in grain form.

Kosher salt, which gets its name from its use in making meats Kosher, has a larger grain than table salt and usually has no additives, like iodine.

Coarse salt, which can be more or less refined, is used in the food industry and certain culinary preparations (beef or poultry with coarse salt, degorging vegetables, marinades).

Several salts are available on the market for more specialized uses. Tenderizing salt is a salt to which enzymes have been added for tenderizing meat. Nitrite salt contains a mixture of sodium nitrate or potassium nitrate and sodium nitrite; it is especially used in charcuterie (sausages and deli meats) and in canning, and acts as a preservative. Flavored salts are also available (garlic salt, spiced salt, onion salt, etc.).

Salt substitutes are also available. These are partly or totally devoid of sodium chloride. This is often replaced with potassium chloride, a substance that leaves a bitter aftertaste in the mouth and can cause imbalances in the body, especially when consumed in large quantities.

HERBS, SPICES AND SEASONINGS

Salt

SERVING IDEAS

Salt inhibits the action of bacteria and molds, which makes it an excellent preservative (charcuterie products, pickles, cheeses, fish, etc.). It stabilizes the color, flavor and texture of foods (vegetables, in particular). It controls the development of yeasts (breads, cakes, cookies, etc.). It hides the bitterness of foods and enhances their flavor. It stimulates the appetite.

To reduce salt consumption, monitor intake of processed foods, restaurant food and certain medications that are high in salt (laxatives, analgesics, antacids). Also:

- Avoid commercially made soups and stocks; smoked, salted and canned meats; smoked, salted and canned fish (anchovies, sardines); pickles, sauerkrauts and seaweeds; commercially made sauces (soy sauce, chili sauce, ketchup, prepared mustard); potato chips, crackers, pretzels, etc.; celery salts, garlic salts, onions salts, monosodium glutamate.
- Avoid adding excess salt when cooking food.
- Avoid adding salt at the table.
- Rinse canned vegetables before using.
- Read the labels of commercially produced foods, which can contain several salt substitutes, such as sodium bicarbonate, monosodium glutamate, sodium alginate or sodium benzoate.

It is generally easier to gradually reduce salt consumption to allow the taste buds to get used to the reduced amount.

NUTRITIONAL INFORMATION

PROPERTIES: sodium plays a role in the metabolism of proteins and carbohydrates, the transmission of nerve impulses, the contraction of muscles, the regulation of hormones, the consumption of oxygen by the cells, the control of the production of urine and the sensation of thirst and the production of liquids (blood, saliva, tears, sweat, gastric juices, bile). Salt is essential for the production of hydrochloric acid in the stomach.

Eating very salty foods produces thirst.

Excessive consumption of salt contributes to hypertension and cardiovascular illnesses in individuals at risk.

It is recommended to consume salt in moderation. There is no need to fear developing a salt deficiency, as this element is present in drinking water and most natural foods. However, those on a nonsalt vegan diet, or someone subject to a major and extended case of diarrhea, vomiting or sweating, could become salt deficient.

Most salt in the diet comes from foods produced by the food industry (77%).

table salt

There are three types of meat:
- red meat (beef, lamb, mutton, bison)
- white meat (veal, pork, rabbit, poultry)
- dark meat (game)

A distinction is also made between butcher's meat (beef, veal, mutton, pork and variety meats [offal]), poultry and game.

TIPS FOR BUYING MEATS

The tenderness of meat varies depending on which part of the animal the cut comes from. The area around the ribs and loin (back) of the animal provides the most tender cuts. The rear end of the animal (thigh or leg) produces cuts of medium tenderness, while the toughest cuts come mostly from the front end (flank, shank, breast, shoulder, neck and the ends of the ribs). The older the animal, the less tender the meat will be. Use tender cuts for short cooking methods, tough cuts for long cooking. Allow for about 2-3.5 oz (55-100 g) of cooked meat per person.

Choose meat that is fine-grained, firm and smooth to the touch. Beef should be a bright, shiny red, mutton a dark pink, lamb a paler pink, pork pink and veal more or less pink (grain-fed veal is pink, milk-fed veal is white). Avoid meat that is dull or has an unusual color; it is probably not fresh.

TIPS FOR PREPARING MEATS

Some cuts of meat require more elaborate preparation in order to tenderize them and enhance their flavor, or to ensure they do not dry out during cooking.

:: Marinating
Consists of letting the meat rest for a few hours in a liquid mixture that is usually acidic and flavored in order to improve its taste. The container in which the meat and marinade are placed should be well-covered and refrigerated.

:: Larding
Consists of inserting thin strips of fat in the piece of meat using a larding needle. This provides a lean piece of meat with sufficient fat so that it doesn't dry out during cooking.

:: Barding

Consists of wrapping a wide strip of fat (a "bard") around a piece of roasting meat to prevent it from drying out during cooking.

1 Wrap the bard of fat around the piece of meat and tie a piece of string around it.

2 Starting from one end, make a loop around one hand and slide it around the roast; pull on the string with the other hand to tighten the loop. Continue the process to the other end.

3 Turn the roast over and thread the string through the loops all along its length.

4 Tie firmly at the other end.

TIPS FOR STORING MEATS

Meat is highly perishable. Raw or cooked, it should never remain at room temperature for more than 2 hr. Various methods are used to extend its keeping quality. Meat treated in these ways must be of good quality and in good condition.

Smoking consists of impregnating the meat with smoke. It dries the meat and gives it a darker color and smoky taste. Smoked meats keep for 6-7 days in the fridge and 1-2 months in the freezer.

Curing or **salting** consists in salting raw meat to reduce moisture content and enhance flavor. It can be combined with smoking or drying. The meat should be desalted before cooking.

Drying was originally carried out using the sun in countries where the air is dry and hot. It is also done industrially using freeze-drying. Drying can be combined with smoking and curing.

Freeze-drying is a recent, fairly expensive method that turns the meat's water content from an ice state into a gas state. Freeze-dried meat contains less than 2% water.

Irradiation uses radiation to kill the pathogenic bacteria present on the meat. It is a relatively little-used method, as its health repercussions are not yet known.

Freezing must be carried out quickly to prevent large ice crystals from forming, which affect the quality of the meat. Wrap the meat well to prevent its drying out and its fat becoming rancid in contact with air. Defrost the meat slowly, preferably in the fridge, to avoid the loss of juices that results in reduced flavor and nutritional value. Never refreeze completely defrosted meat unless it is cooked beforehand.

Remove excess fat before cooking. Monitor meat for dryness; add minimal fat or other liquid as needed. Degrease the sauce: place it in the fridge (a layer of fat forms on the surface that can easily be removed), or use paper towels placed gently on the surface to soak up the fat.

Tenderize meat: using a utensil to break its fibers, enzymes (certain fruits contain these, including papaya, kiwifruit, fig and pineapple) or an acidic ingredient (vinegar, yogurt, cider, wine, beer, citrus or tomato juice).

:: Roasting

Consists of cooking meat in an oven or a closed barbecue; it suits tender roasts, thick meat cuts and poultry. Place meat on rotisserie grill or in oven, placing a container underneath to collect the juices. To make sauce base, place meat directly on meat bones or trimmings. Season. Roast in 350°F (175°C) oven; semitender or tougher roasts, however, are best cooked slowly at 325°F (160°C). Once cooked, let meat rest for 5-15 min or wrapped in aluminum foil (shiny side facing the meat).

:: Broiling (oven) or Grilling (barbecue)

Consists of cooking meat under the broiler of an oven or on the barbecue; it suits tender cuts and poultry. If needed, tenderize meat. Make cuts in fat surrounding meat and season it if desired (only add salt at the end of cooking). Preheat oven broiler or barbecue to a high temperature. Place meat about 4-5 in. (10-12 cm) from heat source and cook a few minutes on each side, turning (using tongs to limit loss of juices) when droplets appear on surface (no more than twice). Leave oven door slightly open and do not cover barbecue. Do not prick meat, and wait a few moments before serving so juices settle evenly.

:: Pan-frying

This method suits tender or tenderized steaks, ground meat and poultry. Season meat and brown it in pot with a thick base and sides using a small quantity of fat (omit if using a nonstick pan). Cook uncovered over medium-high heat a few minutes on each side; avoid stewing meat (heat too low) or letting it stick (heat too high). Turn when droplets appear on surface of meat (no more than twice). Add salt at the end of cooking, if desired.

:: Braising

Consists of cooking meat on a low temperature and using wet heat; it suits semitender and tougher steaks and roasts. Trim meat of fat and season or flour. Sauté meat in a little hot fat or oil on all sides to brown it. Season (salt after cooking unless meat is breaded or floured), insert thermometer if using a roast, then add a little liquid. Cover and cook over low heat or in the oven at 325°F (160°C). Degrease cooking liquid before serving. If it is not concentrated enough, bring to a boil (without the meat) and reduce.

:: Poaching

Similar to braising but using more liquid; it suits roasts or other pieces of meat that are tougher. Before poaching, if desired, flour and sauté meat on all sides over medium-high heat; only salt at the end of cooking. Immerse meat in a cold or just-simmering liquid. For richer stock, add salt at the beginning of cooking, don't sauté the meat in fat or oil, and immerse it in a cold liquid. Add desired seasonings and simmer gently until meat reaches the desired tenderness. Degrease before serving.

:: Microwaving
Suits most meats. Use pieces similar in size and arrange in a circle inside microwave, the thickest part toward the outside. Cook covered. Most meats can be cooked on the highest setting, but less tender cuts benefit from being cooked slowly. Baste meat with marinade or various sauces to improve flavor and appearance. Check internal temperature at several points.

MEAT DONENESS
Doneness, when referring to meat, signifies two things:

• First, the cooking temperature (gauged with a food thermometer) at which potential harmful pathogens on the meat are killed, making the meat safe to eat.

• Second, the desired look, taste, and texture of the meat for the person consuming it.

Below are temperatures for different degrees of doneness. The amount of time it takes to reach a certain degree of doneness depends on the thickness of the meat, amount of fat and bone, starting temperature of the meat and pan, and other factors. Check the meat periodically. A thermometer works better for thick roasts than for thinner steaks and chops. Note: Roasts will continue to cook after being removed from the oven, so the temperature will rise slightly.

Meat		Internal Temperature	
Beef, Veal, Lamb	chops, steaks, roasts	125°F–135°F/52°C–57°C	rare
		135°F–145°F/57°C–63°C	medium-rare
		145°F–155°F/63°C–68°C	medium
		155°F–165°F/68°C–71°C	medium-well
		170°F/77°C	well done
*The USDA recommends cooking these roasts to 145 °F/63° C for safety.			
Pork	chops or roasts	155°F–165°F/68°C–71°C	medium
		170°F/77°C	well done
*The USDA recommends cooking pork roasts to 160 °F/71°C for safety.			
Ground meat		160°F/71°C	

Beef

Bos, Bovidae

The flesh of a bovine animal. In butchery, "beef" is used generally to refer to the meat of a heifer, cow, bull, young bull, bullock or steer, even if the tenderness and flavor vary greatly. Bison (buffalo) meat can be used as well. The older the animal and the more it has worked, the tougher the meat.

beef

BUYING

About 30% of the animal represents the tender parts that are in demand and more expensive than the less tender parts. These latter parts, prepared properly (using a marinade, a mallet or tenderizer, or cooked slowly in a liquid) can yield equally good results. The composition and fat content of the ground beef available on the market is variable. Beef containing more fat is less expensive to buy, but has a lower yield. Standard ground beef (highest fat content) can prove to be a good buy if the cooking fat can be drained (in a meat tomato sauce, for example). When it is not possible to drain the fat (in the case of a meat loaf, for example), choose leaner ground beef.

It is available in portions for braising or stewing, as chops or steaks for sautéeing, broiling or grilling, in fillets or roasting cuts.

SERVING IDEAS

Beef is eaten hot or cold, raw (steak tartare) or cooked. Ground beef used in burgers, meat loaves, meat balls and sausages should be eaten well cooked, as it can carry a bacterium, *E. coli*, whose toxin can lead to serious and potentially fatal food poisoning. Beef is delicious cured and smoked. It can also be stir-fried, combined with vegetables and grains or noodles.

NUTRITIONAL INFORMATION

The nutritional value of beef varies according to the breed of the animal and how it has been reared, as well as the cut, the cooking method and whether it has been degreased.

EXCELLENT SOURCE: protein, potassium, zinc, niacin and vitamin B_{12}.

GOOD SOURCE: iron and phosphorus.

Beef can be a major source of saturated fatty acids and cholesterol.

Marbling (the layers of fat spread throughout the muscle of the meat) helps to make beef more tender, tasty and juicy, without significantly increasing the fat content of the cooked meat. In the United States, beef grading is based on the age of the animal, the proportion of meat to bone, and the amount of marbling.

To reduce fat intake:

• choose lean cuts (inside round, eye of round, sirloin, etc.) and cooking methods that require less fat (grilling, roasting, braising, etc.)

• reduce the portion-size of meat and remove visible fat before cooking

• degrease the sauce by skimming the fat from the surface

MEATS

Beef

COOKING

Beef is eaten blue (raw on the inside with a slightly cooked outside), rare, medium-rare, medium (pink) or well done. A low temperature is recommended for semitender or tougher cuts. A higher temperature allows tender cuts to cook quickly.

STORING

:: **In the fridge:** ground, 1-2 days; steaks, 2-3 days; roasts and cooked beef, 3-4 days.
:: **In the freezer:** ground and cooked, 2-3 months; steaks and roasts, 10-12 months.

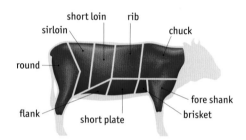

sirloin · short loin · rib · chuck · round · flank · short plate · fore shank · brisket

FLANK & SHORT PLATE

skirt steak   flank steak

FORE SHANK AND BRISKET

brisket (whole)   shank (cross cut)

ROUND

tip roast   rump roast   eye round roast   top round roast

SHORT LOIN

T-bone steak

boneless top loin steak

tenderloin roast

porterhouse steak

RIB

back ribs

rib eye roast

rib roast (large end)

SIRLOIN

sirloin steak (flat bone)

top sirloin steak

CHUCK

short ribs

flanken-style ribs

boneless top blade steak

under blade pot roast

chuck eye roast

boneless shoulder pot roast

arm pot roast

blade roast

Veal

Bos, Bovidae

The young of the cow up to 1 year in age. Older than this, the neutered male is called a "steer" and a female that has not yet calved a "heifer." In butchery, it is mostly the males that are slaughtered, the females being used for producing milk.

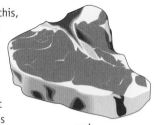

veal

Milk-fed veal is almost exclusively fed on milk. Its pale pink flesh, almost white, is very tender and delicate. It is slaughtered at the age of 4-5 months and its carcass weighs about 300 lb (135 kg).

Grain-fed veal is fed on milk until the age of 6-8 weeks. It is then fed a grain-based diet until the age of 5-5½ months, when it is slaughtered. Its carcass weighs about 340 lb (155 kg). Its flesh is more pink in color, with a stronger flavor and is slightly less tender than milk-fed veal.

SERVING IDEAS

Veal can be prepared as a pan-fried steak or cutlet, sautéed, roasted, rolled, stewed or cooked in a white sauce. It is used to make veal Milanese and veal Marengo (with white wine, tomato and garlic). Veal shanks are slow cooked to make the Italian dish Osso Buco. Calves' liver and sweetbread (pancreas and thymus glands) are sautéed or stewed in many cuisines. Veal works well with the following ingredients: cream, cheese, herbs (thyme, tarragon, rosemary, sage, basil and others), mushrooms, eggplant, spinach, onion, garlic, tomato, apples, citrus fruits and alcohol (wine, calvados, madeira, cognac and others).

NUTRITIONAL INFORMATION

	raw loin	*roast loin*
protein	20 g	26 g
fat	3 g	7 g
cholesterol	80 mg	100 mg
calories	116	175
	per 3.5 oz/100 g	

The nutritional value of veal is linked to the age, diet and living conditions of the animal. Veal meat contains less fat and calories, but a little more cholesterol than beef, pork or lamb. The flesh of grain-fed veal contains more iron than milk-fed veal.

COOKING

:: **Roasted, broiled** or **grilled, pan-fried:** tender pieces from the ribs, loin and sirloin. Also semitender pieces from the leg, especially if marinated or tenderized with a mallet.

:: **Braised, simmered:** the less tender pieces from the neck, shoulder, flank, shank and breast.

Being lean, veal flesh dries out and becomes tough easily. It is therefore a good idea to bard it or coat it in fat or oil and cook it at a fairly low temperature (300°F-350°F/150°C-180°C), basting it from time to time and avoiding overcooking it. Veal is better when it is still slightly pink.

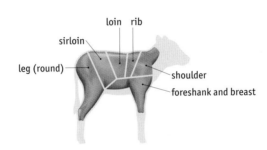

loin rib

sirloin

leg (round)

shoulder

foreshank and breast

FORESHANK AND BREAST

riblet

cross-cut shank

shank

breast

LEG

leg cutlet

round steak

boneless rump roast

Veal

RIB

rib chop

short ribs

rib roast

crown roast

SIRLOIN

top sirloin steak

sirloin roast

LOIN

loin chop

butterfly chop

kidney chop

loin roast

top loin chop

SHOULDER

shoulder steak

shoulder roast

blade steak

boneless shoulder arm roast

boneless shoulder eye roast

blade roast

Pork

Sus, Suidae

The meat from the pig, an omnivorous mammal. The male is called a "boar," the female a "sow" and the young a "piglet" or "feeder." There are various breeds of pig, including Yorkshire, Duroc and Landrace. The demand for a less fatty meat has led to the development of breeds with 30%-50% less fat.

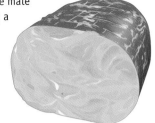

pork

BUYING

The most tender pork meat comes from the loin (back), from which tenderloin, roasts and chops are taken. The meat from the leg and shoulder is less tender. Roasts are also taken from this area as well as different pieces: trotters, hocks, tail, etc.

Smoked picnic shoulder is sometimes incorrectly called "picnic ham"; the name "ham," however, only applies to leg cuts. Bacon comes from the loin (back bacon or "Canadian bacon") or the belly (slab or sliced bacon). Cured pork and fat pork (lardoons and bacon pieces), taken from the back fat found between the flesh and the rind, come from the shoulder. The lean fat, where the fat is mingled with lean meat, is taken from the side. Pork lard is melted pork fat.

STORING

:: **In the fridge:** ground, 1-2 days; fresh chops and sausages, 2-3 days; roasts, deli cuts (opened containers) and cooked meat, 3-4 days.

:: **In the freezer:** chops and roasts, 8-10 months; sausages, 2-3 months; bacon and ham, 1-2 months; deli cuts, 1 month.

NUTRITIONAL INFORMATION

Pork is distinguished nutritionally by its levels of thiamine (especially), riboflavin and niacin (B vitamins), which are higher than in other meats.

EXCELLENT SOURCE: zinc and potassium.
GOOD SOURCE: phosphorus.

The nutritional value of pork varies, depending on the cut and whether the visible fat is removed or not. Cooked lean pork is no fattier or higher in calories than other meats.

SERVING IDEAS

Pork is eaten fresh, salted or smoked. It is eaten hot or cold and always cooked (slightly pink). Ground pork used in burgers, meat loaves, meatballs and sausages should be eaten well-cooked to prevent food-borne illness. It is delicious prepared with fresh or dried fruits (chestnuts, pineapple, apple, orange, prune, grapes, apricots).

Pork

COOKING

Always cook pork, as cooking is the only way (apart from irradiation) to kill the parasites that are potentially present in the flesh; cook until the internal temperature reaches 155°F-165°F (68°C-71°C) (the flesh will then be slightly pink).

To enhance the flavor of pork, season it before cooking or marinate it with green peppercorns, mustard, onion, garlic, citrus juice, soy sauce and herbs.

Avoid overcooking and, if the visible fat is removed, protect the flesh with a little fat, as it can dry out and become tough during cooking. Pork should be cooked at a gentle heat (250°F/120°C in the oven or medium heat in a pan or on the barbecue, for example).

:: Roasted, broiled or **grilled, pan-fried:** tender cuts (taken mainly from the loin).

:: Braised, simmered: less tender cuts (from the shoulder, leg or side).

:: Microwaved: this method can result in uneven cooking: take the internal temperature of the meat at different places using a thermometer to ensure it is completely cooked.

MEATS

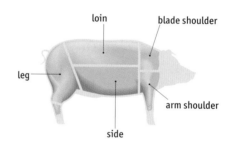

loin

blade shoulder

leg

arm shoulder

side

SHOULDER

blade roast

boneless shoulder picnic roast

smoked hock

smoked picnic

SIDE

spareribs

sliced bacon

LOIN

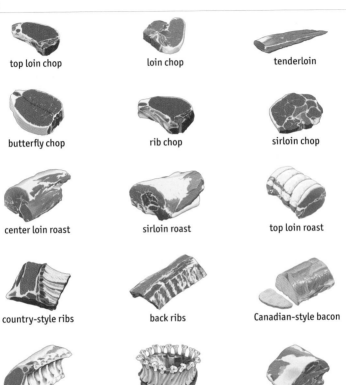

top loin chop

loin chop

tenderloin

butterfly chop

rib chop

sirloin chop

center loin roast

sirloin roast

top loin roast

country-style ribs

back ribs

Canadian-style bacon

center rib roast

crown roast

blade roast (loin)

LEG

smoked ham
(center slice)

smoked ham
(shank portion)

smoked ham

smoked ham
(rump portion)

Lamb

Ovis, Caprinae

lamb

The young of a sheep. In butchery, the term "mutton" is used for the meat of the adult male sheep (ram), neutered or not, and the adult female (ewe). Lamb meat comes from an animal less than 12 months old (the standards vary in different countries).

Milk-fed lamb (or "sucker lamb") is killed at about 2 months of age and has been fed almost exclusively on its mother's milk. Its carcass, sold with the skin, head and offal, weighs about 30 lb (14 kg). Its skin is delicate and tender.

Heavy lamb is reared on a diet made up of grains and fodder. It is killed at 3-8 months and its carcass weighs more than 40 lb (18 kg). Its flesh is tender and its flavor is stronger than milk-fed lamb.

Light lamb has qualities that lie in between the types of lamb described above.

Mutton (and "hogget") comes from adult breeds; the older the animal, the more the meat is red, tough, marbled with fat and stronger in taste.

Both lamb and mutton have a fat called "hard fat." It is called this because the fat congeals as it cools (serve them on a very hot plate).

MEATS

BUYING

The color, texture and flavor of the meat depend on the breed, age, diet and living conditions of the animal. The joints of the back limbs are cartilaginous in lamb and bony in mutton. Mutton flesh is red-hued, whereas lamb flesh is pink-hued. The bone in a lamb leg roast represents about 25% of its weight. A lamb leg weighing 5-6 lb (2-3 kg) serves 6-8 people.

STORING

:: **In the fridge:** portions, 3 days; ground, 1-2 days.

:: **In the freezer:** portions, 8-10 months; ground, 2-3 months.

NUTRITIONAL INFORMATION

	roast leg
protein	28 g
fat	7 g
cholesterol	100 mg
calories	181
	per 3.5 oz/100 g

The older the animal, the fattier and higher in calories its meat will be; however, a large proportion of the fat is visible and can be removed easily. Leg roasts, rib roasts and the loin (back) are leaner than shoulder cuts.

EXCELLENT SOURCE: protein, zinc and B-complex vitamins (niacin, riboflavin and vitamin B_{12}).

GOOD SOURCE: iron, potassium and phosphorus.

< lamb chops

Lamb

SERVING IDEAS

 The following seasonings work well with lamb and mutton: garlic, mustard, basil, mint, rosemary, sage, and lemon, lime or orange zest. The meat benefits from being marinated, especially less tender parts (shoulder, breast, shank) to be cooked using dry heat. Roast leg of lamb is a traditional Easter dish in several countries. *Méchoui*, a whole gutted lamb or sheep spit-roasted over a wood fire, is a customary dish in North Africa and Middle Eastern countries. Middle Eastern cuisine incorporates lamb (or mutton) into kebabs and meatballs and couscous.

COOKING

LAMB

:: Broiled, grilled or roasted: lamb can be eaten rare (145°F/63°C), medium (155°F/68°C) or well done (about 165°F/73°C). It has maximum flavor when it is still slightly pink. Since the meat dries out and becomes tough easily, cook at a moderate heat (325°F-350°F/160°C-175°C) and avoid overcooking.

MUTTON

:: Braised or **poached.**

:: Roasted: leg roast and bin of lamb.

:: Broiled or **grilled:** chops, especially if they have been marinated.

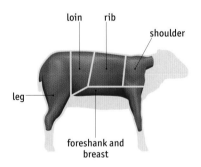

loin   rib

shoulder

leg

foreshank and breast

LOIN

loin chop

double loin chop

loin roast

MEATS

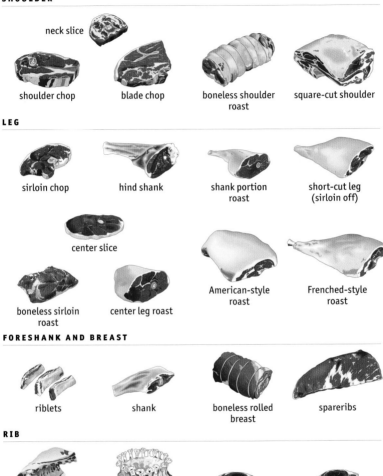

SHOULDER

neck slice

shoulder chop

blade chop

boneless shoulder roast

square-cut shoulder

LEG

sirloin chop

hind shank

shank portion roast

short-cut leg (sirloin off)

center slice

boneless sirloin roast

center leg roast

American-style roast

Frenched-style roast

FORESHANK AND BREAST

riblets

shank

boneless rolled breast

spareribs

RIB

rib roast

crown roast

Frenched rib chop

rib chop

MEATS

Venison

A term referring to the meat of large game animals, usually deer, white-tailed deer, moose, fallow deer and sometimes wild boar. Today, game called "wild" is often wild only in name, unless you have hunted it yourself. Many animals are now farmed, which provides a more tender, but often less tasty, meat, as their diet is not the same as that of wild game. In the United States, game animals available for sale have been farm-raised; wild game cannot be sold. The flavor of venison varies according to the animal's diet: wild fruits, young shoots, grains and cereals, barks, etc. Deer and white-tailed deer are the varieties of game that are most sought after by connoisseurs.

loin

BUYING

:: **Choose:** white-tailed deer less than 2 years old, and deer less than 3 years old. As a general rule, the fat of a young animal is whiter than that of an older animal; the flesh is dark and the grain very fine. Venison meat is usually available fresh, vacuum-packed or frozen. It is available in portions for braising or stewing, as chops or steaks for sautéeing, broiling or grilling, in fillets or roasting cuts.

NUTRITIONAL INFORMATION

	roasted
protein	25 g
fat	3.3 g
calories	159
	per 3.5 oz/100 g

Venison is an especially lean meat; it has about 5 times less fat than beef.

STORING

:: **In the fridge:** 1-2 days.
:: **In the freezer:** individually wrapped portions, 3-6 months. Defrost in the fridge; allow 4-6 hr per 2 lb (1 kg).

PREPARING

Venison bought from the butcher has usually been aged and doesn't need to be hung. The only stage of preparation that cannot be skipped is the barding of a piece intended to be roasted. The visible fat on the venison, which tastes foul, is removed and replaced by a strip of lard or bacon fat.

SERVING IDEAS

Capers, mushrooms, pepper, madeira, wine, lemon juice and small fruits such as cranberries and cherries work well with venison. It is often accompanied by a purée of potatoes or chestnuts. Venison is also used in terrines and pâtés.

COOKING

As venison is lean, it is important not to overcook it, since it quickly becomes tough and dry. It must be juicy and still pink.

:: Roasted: the haunch or saddle. Enclose the piece of venison in a covered oven dish and roast in a hot oven (350°F-400°F/175°C-200°C), basting every 15 min. Allow 25-35 min per 2 lb (1 kg) for a piece weighing over 3 lb (1.5 kg) and 35-40 min for a piece less than 3 lb (1.5 kg).

:: Sautéed: medallions, the loin and chops.

:: Braised: the shoulder and less tender pieces.

MEATS

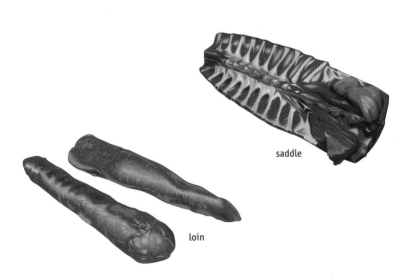

saddle

loin

Rabbit

Oryctolagus, Leporidae

A furry mammal thought to be originally from southern Europe and northern Africa. Rabbit is a relative of the hare, a wild species considered a game meat, whose flesh is darker with a stronger flavor.

Wild rabbit has lean and dark meat with a gamey taste. In the United States, only farmed rabbit is sold for food. They are generally imported Scottish hares, Chinese rabbits or a cross between Belgian and New Zealand varieties. The flesh of farmed rabbit is similar in texture and taste to chicken. Young rabbit, or "fryers," refer to rabbit that weigh 1-3 lbs and are less than 12 weeks old. Young rabbit has tender, finely grained flesh, which can be prepared in the same way as most poultry. Mature rabbit, or "roasters," weigh 4-8 lbs and are over 8 months in age. They have firm, coarsely grained flesh, best suited for braising or stewing.

rabbit

BUYING

:: **Choose:** a rabbit with glistening and slightly pink-tinged flesh, with a good red, unmarked liver and visible kidneys surrounded by fat that is quite white.
Rabbit is sold fresh or frozen, whole or cut into 4 or 6 pieces, depending on its size. It is almost always skinned and gutted. If it is fresh and whole, the flexibility of its paws is a sign of freshness.

STORING

:: **In the fridge:** fresh or cut, 1 week.
:: **In the freezer.**

NUTRITIONAL INFORMATION

	roasted
protein	29 g
fat	8 g
cholesterol	821 mg
calories	197
	per 3.5 oz/100 g

EXCELLENT SOURCE: protein, B-complex vitamins, calcium and potassium.
GOOD SOURCE: iron and phosphorus.

COOKING

Rabbit flesh dries out easily. This is why it is often cooked in a liquid; it is recommended to bard it or baste it before cooking. It needs 1-1½ hr cooking at 325°F (162°C). If roasting or broiling the rabbit, baste during cooking.

SERVING IDEAS

Rabbit compares favorably to chicken; like chicken, it suits a wide variety of cooking methods and there is a wide choice of ingredients and seasonings that can accompany it. Older rabbit is less tender and is best cooked using wet heat (braised, simmered); it is often made into a pâté or terrine.

Hare is prepared in the same way as rabbit; it is often accompanied by acidic fruits or a sweet-and-sour or spicy sauce, which softens its flavor.

PREPARING

To joint the rabbit, detach the 4 legs, then cut the saddle (the fleshy part that extends from the base of the ribs to the tail, often considered to be the best part) across into 2 or 3 parts. If desired, when the rabbit is quite large, cut the back legs in 2 (they are the most fleshy part).

Before cooking the rabbit, wash, then if desired, soak it for a few hours in slightly salted cold water to whiten the flesh and soften its flavor. Rabbit and hare can be marinated, which moistens and whitens the flesh while simultaneously enhancing its flavor. The marinade should contain an acidic ingredient (red or white wine, lemon juice, vinegar) and oil; vegetables and aromatics can be added. Farmed rabbit, which is naturally tender, does not need to be tenderized before cooking.

MEATS

Ground meat

Ground meat comes from various parts of the animal (shoulder, loin, leg, breast and flank). Ask the butcher to grind the meat at the time of purchase (more freshness) or grind it at home using a grinder or food processor. It can also be bought wrapped from the meat section of supermarkets.

ground beef

BUYING

The more the meat is flecked with white, the more fat it contains. In the United States, a maximum of 30% fat is allowed in ground beef, though a fat content of no more than 22% is recommended. The beef used for steak tartare must not contain more than 5% fat. Less fresh meat has a brownish color. The inside of packaged ground meat is darker than on the surface, as the color pigment in the meat reacts when it is not in contact with the oxygen in the air.

SERVING IDEAS

Raw or cooked, ground meat can be cooked well in both simple and elegant ways. A staple item in the cuisines of many countries, it is used in several ways: the American hamburger, Greek moussaka, meat loaf, meatballs, sausage and steak tartare are among the most well-known dishes.

STORING

Ground meat is highly perishable.
:: **In the fridge:** wrapped, 1-2 days.
:: **In the freezer:** 2-3 months.

NUTRITIONAL INFORMATION

The more fat ground meat contains, the higher in calories it is.

COOKING

Make sure ground meat is cooked until it loses its pinkness and its juices run clear. The USDA suggests cooking until 160°F (71°C), although you may want to cook it less for more flavor and moistness.

PREPARING

Meat can be ground raw or cooked, which means one can use leftovers and the less tender or appetizing parts of meat. A good ground meat should be quite fresh, without cartilage, tendons and nerves.

Lean meat tends to have less flavor than fattier meat. Ground meat that is higher in fat is cheaper to buy than lean ground meat, but it has a lower yield, as part of the fat melts from the heat.

The best way to control the quality, freshness and fat content of ground meat is to grind it at home.

Introduction
Variety meats

Variety meats (offal) are the edible parts of butchered animals apart from the flesh. A distinction is usually made between red variety meats (heart, liver, tongue, lungs, spleen and kidneys) and white variety meats (brains, udder, spinal marrow, testicles, trotters, sweetbreads, head and tripe).

TIPS FOR BUYING VARIETY MEATS

Make sure the variety meats are very fresh, as they are much more perishable than meat. They should have the characteristic color, smell and appearance of the particular variety meat and not be sitting in a large quantity of liquid. For one serving, allow about 4 oz (125 g) raw or 3 oz (90 g) cooked.

TIPS FOR USING VARIETY MEATS

Some variety meats need to be cooked for long periods using moist heat (braising, poaching) until they are tender, such as heart and tongue. Others cook quickly using dry heat, in particular liver, kidneys and brains. Marrow, mostly beef marrow, can be poached by itself or in the bone. It can also be melted like butter and used to cook meat and vegetables.

Variety meats such as brains, heart, liver, sweetbreads and kidneys are rich in purines, the precursors to uric acid. For this reason, people afflicted with gout, a disorder affecting the metabolism of uric acid, should limit their consumption of these variety meats.

TIPS FOR STORING VARIETY MEATS

Variety meats are highly perishable. Prepare them within 24 hr of purchase. Variety meats can be frozen for 3-4 months. However, freezing affects their flavor, texture and appearance in most cases.

Heart

Heart is a red variety meat. Calf, lamb and chicken hearts are small and tender, and therefore the most sought after. Pig heart is moderately tender. Beef heart is larger, firmer and has the strongest flavor.

beef heart

BUYING

:: **Choose:** a fleshy heart with a fresh appearance and red-brown (lamb and beef), bright red (pig and chicken) or pale red (calf) in color.

:: **Avoid:** a gray heart.

PREPARING

Remove the fat around the heart, the membranes and veins, wash and, if desired, soak the heart for at least 1 hr in the fridge in cold water to which 1 tablespoon (15 ml) of vinegar per 4 cups (1 l) of water has been added (to tenderize, especially for beef heart). Rinse well, then wipe.

COOKING

:: **Braised** or **simmered:** pig and beef hearts (3-4 hr, add liquid as needed). The hearts of young animals (2-3 hr).

:: **Broiled, grilled** or **roasted**.

:: **Sautéed:** sliced heart (5-7 min). Serve slightly pink.

SERVING IDEAS

Heart is often cooked as a stew or a casserole. Peruvians are fond of *anticuchos*, marinated and grilled beef hearts.

VARIETY MEATS

NUTRITIONAL INFORMATION

	simmered beef heart	braised lamb heart	braised pig heart	braised calf heart	simmered chicken heart
protein	29 g	25 g	24 g	29 g	26 g
fat	6 g	8 g	5 g	7 g	8 g
cholesterol	193 mg	249 mg	221 mg	176 mg	242 mg
calories	175	185	148	186	185

per 3.5 oz/100 g

EXCELLENT SOURCE: protein, iron, zinc, copper and B-complex vitamin.
GOOD SOURCE: phosphorus and potassium. Its cholesterol content is higher than fresh meat, but less than other variety meats.

STORING

:: **In the fridge:** 1-2 days.
:: **In the freezer:** 3-4 months.

Liver

An edible red variety meat from butchered animals, poultry, game and certain fish (cod, monkfish, skate). The liver of young animals is tastier and more tender; the most sought after is calf's liver. Lamb, heifer, poultry and rabbit livers are highly regarded for their tenderness and delicate flavor. Beef, sheep, pig and poultry livers have a stronger flavor and a pastier texture after cooking.

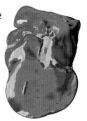

calf liver

BUYING

:: **Choose:** a liver that glistens, does not have a strong smell and is not sitting in a large quantity of liquid.

The color of liver varies from pinkish brown to reddish brown, depending on the particular animal and its age.

PREPARING

Remove the fine membrane that covers the liver so that it keeps its shape during cooking, and remove the tubes. Soak beef and pig livers in milk for 1-2 hr in the fridge to soften their flavor. Dry well. Cut the liver into slices of equal size so that they cook evenly.

COOKING

Liver should not be eaten rare; it is tastier if it is slightly pink in the middle.

:: **Grilled**, **broiled** or **sautéed:** tender liver (5-8 min).

Use as little fat as possible to avoid increasing its fat content. Cook less tender liver slowly and in a small amount of liquid.

NUTRITIONAL INFORMATION

	braised calf's liver
protein	22 g
fat	7 g
cholesterol	561 mg
calories	165
	per 3.5 oz/100 g

EXCELLENT SOURCE: protein, iron, vitamin A, vitamin B$_{12}$, folic acid, vitamin C, phosphorus, zinc and copper.

Its high iron content helps to prevent anemia. An oil is extracted from cod liver that is high in vitamin D, which helps prevent rickets.

SERVING IDEAS

Liver is sautéed, grilled or broiled, pan-fried or marinated; it is accompanied by mushrooms, wine, cream or onions. Pig liver especially is used for charcuterie products (pâtés and terrines).
Cod liver is often smoked.

STORING

Liver is highly perishable.
:: **In the fridge:** 1-2 days.
:: **In the freezer:** 3-4 months.

VARIETY MEATS

Tongue

A fleshy and muscular organ that is pink or grayish. Tongue is covered with a thick and rough mucous membrane that is not eaten. Beef tongue is the thickest and largest. Calf tongue is the most tender and tasty. Pig tongue is soft to the touch. Bird tongues and those of certain fish (cod) are also edible.

beef tongue

BUYING

:: **Choose:** a tongue without any marks. Buy 6-7 oz (165-200 g) of raw tongue for a cooked 3 oz (90 g) serving.

SERVING IDEAS

Cooked tongue is breaded and fried, smoked or marinated. It can be eaten cold (seasoned with mustard, dressed with vinaigrette or brined, in salads and sandwiches).

PREPARING

Brush the tongue under cold water and soak for 4-12 hr (preferably) in cold water (refresh the water 2 or 3 times).

COOKING

 :: **Poached** then **braised:** beef tongue is poached for 2 hr, then braised 4 hr; calf, lamb or pig tongues are poached for 45 min, then braised for 2 hr. Once cooled, remove the tongue's skin.

STORING

:: **In the fridge:** 1-2 days.
:: **In the freezer:** 3-4 months.

NUTRITIONAL INFORMATION

	simmered beef tongue	braised pig tongue	braised calf tongue
protein	22 g	24 g	26 g
fat	21 g	19 g	10 g
cholesterol	107 mg	146 mg	238 mg
calories	283	271	202
			per 3.5 oz/100 g

EXCELLENT SOURCE: vitamin B$_{12}$ and zinc, iron (pig and beef tongues).

Sweetbreads

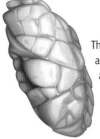

The name given to the thymus and pancreas glands of a calf and lamb, a gland located at the start of the chest, in front of the trachea and only present in young animals. Sweetbreads contain a central lobe called the "heart lobe" and two side lobes called "throat lobes." They have a very delicate taste and are very tender. Calf sweetbreads are the most valued.

sweetbread

BUYING

 :: Choose: plump, shiny sweetbreads with a good smell and a creamy white color verging on pink.

PREPARING

Wash the sweetbreads and soak them for 2-3 hr in cold, slightly salted water (refresh several times). Blanch before cooking to make them firmer and easier to handle (lamb sweetbreads, 2-3 min; calf sweetbreads, 7-10 min). Cool and remove the membrane, the veins and the fat covering them. Dry well.

STORING

:: In the fridge: 1-2 days.
:: In the freezer: blanched.

NUTRITIONAL INFORMATION

protein	32 g
fat	4 g
cholesterol	469 mg
calories	174
	per 3.5 oz/100 g

BRAISED SWEETBREADS

EXCELLENT SOURCE: protein, niacin, vitamin C (rare in the animal world), phosphorus and zinc. As they are lean, sweetbreads are easy to digest.

COOKING

 :: Grilled or **broiled:** 6-8 min.
:: Sautéed: 3-5 min.
:: Braised: 30-40 min.
:: Poached: 20-30 min.
:: Fried: 3-4 min.
Sweetbreads are cooked as kebabs, in flaky pastry and as a gratin. They are used in stuffings. Avoid lengthy cooking.

VARIETY MEATS

Brains

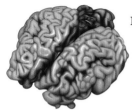

In cooking, the most valued brains are those of lambs and sheep. Calf brains are comparable in flavor. Beef brain is firmer. Pig's brains are rarely eaten.

calf brains

VARIETY MEATS

BUYING

:: **Choose:** plump, gray-pink brains with a pleasant smell, without marks or blood clots. Allow 4 oz (125 g) of raw brains per serving.

PREPARING

Soak brains for 30 min in cold salted water (½ teaspoon/2½ ml of salt per 2 cups/500 ml of water), which is refreshed several times. Remove the membrane that covers the brains, then blanch for 15-18 min in salted water (½ teaspoon/2½ ml of salt per 4 cups/1 l of water) with 1 tablespoon (15 ml) of vinegar or lemon juice added. Cool in cold water and dry.

STORING

:: **In the fridge:** 1-2 days.
For eating later, soak and then blanch brains in salted water to which vinegar or lemon juice has been added.

NUTRITIONAL INFORMATION

	braised calf brains	braised lamb brains
protein	12 g	13 g
fat	10 g	10 g
cholesterol	3,100 mg	2,040 mg
calories	136	145
		per 3.5 oz/100 g

EXCELLENT SOURCE: vitamin B_{12} and phosphorus.
Brains are very high in cholesterol.

COOKING

:: **Poached in meat stock:** whole (sheep and lamb's brains, 10 min; calf brains, 15 min).
:: **Sautéed:** sliced (3-4 min).
:: **Fried:** 2-3 min.
The most tender brains are served as is or in salads; others are prepared as gratins, croquettes, sauces, stuffings and soups.

Kidneys

calf kidneys

The kidneys of butchered animals. Calf, lamb and heifer kidneys are tender and tasty. Pig, sheep and beef kidneys have a sharp and strong taste and a firmer texture. Beef and lamb kidneys are dark brown, pig's kidneys are pale red-brown, and calf kidneys are brown and paler than beef kidneys.

NUTRITIONAL INFORMATION

	braised lamb kidneys	simmered beef kidneys	braised pig kidneys	braised calf kidneys
protein	24 g	26 g	25 g	26 g
fat	4 g	3 g	5 g	6 g
cholesterol	565 mg	387 mg	480 mg	791 mg
calories	137	144	151	163

per 3.5 oz/100 g

EXCELLENT SOURCE: protein, vitamin A (beef), vitamin B$_{12}$, riboflavin, niacin and folic acid (lamb and beef), iron, phosphorus and zinc. Kidneys are lean, but they contain a great deal of cholesterol.

BUYING

:: **Choose:** plump, firm and shiny kidneys that have the characteristic color for the particular animal, without any ammonia smell.

PREPARING

Remove the skin covering the kidneys, cut them in two and remove the fat and internal tubes. To remove any unpleasant odor, boil them briefly, then drain before cooking, or soak for 1-2 hr in the fridge in salted water (1 tablespoon/15 ml of salt per 4 cups/1 l of water), rinse in cold water then, dry them.

COOKING

:: **Broiled, sautéed** or **roasted:** for the most tender kidneys.
:: **Braised:** for less tender kidneys. Cook just until they are no longer red in the middle.

SERVING IDEAS

Kidneys are served in stews and pies. They work well with tomatoes, mushrooms, mustard, lemon juice, cream, red wine, Madeira and sherry.

STORING

:: **In the fridge:** 1 day.
:: **In the freezer:** use kidneys as soon as they are defrosted.

Tripe

paunch

Dishes using the stomach lining of beef, sheep and calf. There are 3 kinds of tripe, all with tough flesh that require long cooking times.

Honeycomb tripe is favored for its tender meat and subtle flavor. **Pocket tripe** is shaped like a pocket. **Plain or smooth tripe** has a smooth texture on both sides. It is the least desirable of the 3 varieties.

VARIETY MEATS

BUYING

:: **Choose:** tripe that is white or cream-yellow in color with a good smell. Tripe is often sold blanched.

SERVING IDEAS

 Tripe can be accompanied by potatoes; it is cooked with beef, pig or calf trotters, pig's head, pork fat, vegetables, wine, cream and seasonings. The most common tripe dish is tripe *à la mode de Caen* (stewed in cider with vegetables, garlic and herbs). *Trippa alla romana,* or tripe roman style, involves stewing the tripe with wine, tomato sauce, pecorino romano cheese and fresh mint.
Gras-double (scalded pieces of beef paunch cooked in water) is marinated before being grilled or fried; they are also served as a stew, a gratin or braised (20 hr). In Spanish cuisine, *menudo,* or tripe soup, is popular.

PREPARING

Before cooking tripe, soak it in cold water (10 min), rinse, brush to remove the fat and slice.

NUTRITIONAL INFORMATION

	raw beef tripe
protein	15 g
fat	4 g
cholesterol	95 mg
calories	98
	per 3.5 oz/100 g

EXCELLENT SOURCE: vitamin B$_{12}$ and zinc.

COOKING

:: **Poached** (1-2 hr), then **sautéed** or **fried** (10 min).
:: **Blanched** (15 min), then **braised** (3-4 hr).

STORING

:: **In the fridge:** 1-2 days.
:: **In the freezer:** 3-4 months.

Delicatessen meats

"Delicatessen meats" refers to pork products using the flesh or variety meats of the pig, but also products made using other meats. They are often high in fat, cholesterol, calories and sodium, and often contain additives. It is recommended that they be eaten in moderation.

There are numerous methods for making deli meats. In Europe, it is common for regions to be distinguished by their special recipe. The term "charcuterie" is often used to describe preserved meats. It is not easy to definitively classify deli meats, as there is such a variety of ingredients and preparation methods. The meat is usually treated so that it preserves well; it is raw or cooked and can be cured, smoked and dried. Some products are eaten as is (foie gras, dry and cooked sausage meats, cooked ham, rillettes, terrines), others after cooking (fresh and smoked sausages, bacon and others). Deli meats enjoy great popularity, as they are generally ready to eat; they are very often eaten on bread or in a sandwich.

TIPS FOR STORING DELI MEATS

Keep deli meats in the fridge; wrap them well so that they do not dry out or absorb the smell of surrounding foods. Place them in the meat compartment; their storage life is about 3-4 days.

For maximum flavor, take deli meats out of the fridge about 15 min before eating.

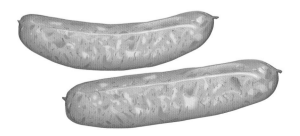

Bacon

Cured, generally smoked pork, taken from the belly (slab or sliced bacon) or loin (back bacon). It is usually sold in thin slices. In North America, bacon and eggs is a common morning meal. **Pancetta,** or "Italian bacon," is a flavorful, salty bacon sold in a sausage-like roll. **Canadian bacon,** or "back bacon," comes from the lean part of the loin, or back.

sliced bacon

SERVING IDEAS

Bacon works well with eggs (in quiches, omelettes, crepes and pancakes), as well as in salads. It is often added to vegetable dishes, stuffings and wrapped around roasts and fish to add flavor and moisture.
Bacon substitutes based on hydrolyzed soy protein (in granule form) are used to flavor soups, salads, vinaigrettes, dips and various prepared foods.

COOKING

:: **Broiled, grilled** or **sautéed:** cook on a low heat or for less than 10 min, draining away the fat. Drain the cooked bacon on paper towels before serving.

NUTRITIONAL INFORMATION

protein	4 g
fat	6 g
cholesterol	10 mg
calories	72
per 0.4 oz/12 g (Two cooked slices)	

Bacon is high in fat and sodium (about 1,600 mg of salt per 3.5 oz/100 g of cooked bacon) and contains sodium nitrite.

STORING

:: **In the fridge:** vacuum-packed (until the use-by date indicated on the packaging). Open, 1 week.
:: **In the freezer:** 1-2 months.

pancetta

Canadian bacon

Ham

French ham (*jambon de Paris*)

Cured pork (or boar or bear meat), often smoked and dried. True ham comes from the upper part of a pork leg. Similar products use shoulder meat (cottage roll, smoked picnic shoulder, etc.). Shank-end ham is taken from the fore or hind shank. Hams are sold in various forms. **Ready-to-eat hams** ("white" ham in Europe) are cured, then cooked. They can be smoked. They can be further cooked and seasoned, if desired. Fully-cooked hams are heated to an internal temperature of 160°F (70°C). Some are sold in cans. **Hams for cooking** have been precooked. They need to be cooked further, however, before eating them. **Raw hams** (or "dry hams") are dry-cured hams. They can also be smoked. In this category are Bayonne, Savoie, Westphalian, Ardennes, Corsica and Parma (Italian raw ham or "*prosciutto di Parma*") hams. The names "Corsica," "Parma" and "Westphalian" are restricted, which guarantees consistent quality. Hams can be sold boneless, partially boned or bone-in. Most gourmet hams are sold bone-in, as the bone adds flavor to the meat during cooking.

SERVING IDEAS

Ham can be eaten hot or cold. It can be served as the main dish of a meal or used in various dishes: quiches, omelettes, croquettes, gratins, pâtés, grilled ham and cheese sandwiches, mixed salads, sandwiches, canapés, terrines, stuffings and other dishes. Braised ham with pineapple and ham cooked in pastry are classic dishes. The bone is used to make soups.

PREPARING

Ham can be soaked to reduce its salt content. The length of the soaking time varies, depending on the size of the piece and how salty it is; it can be soaked overnight.

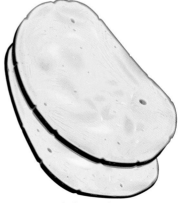

Black Forest ham

Ham

smoked ham

NUTRITIONAL INFORMATION

	lean baked ham meat
protein	25 g
fat	6 g
cholesterol	55 mg
calories	157
	per 3.5 oz/100 g

Ham generally has a high salt content (1,000-1,500 mg of salt per 3.5 oz/100 g of ham). Raw (or dry) ham is higher in fat and calories than cooked ham.

STORING

:: **In the fridge:** 1 week.
:: **In the freezer:** 1-2 months. Freezing results in loss of flavor and makes it more difficult to slice.

COOKING

:: **Roasted, broiled, grilled, braised** or **boiled:** if the ham is covered in its rind, make several incisions into it. To roast the ham, cook uncovered on a rotisserie grill or in a pan in a preheated oven at 325°F (160°C), until its internal temperature reaches 155°F (68°C) for fresh ham (for cooking), 165°F (71°C) for picnic shoulder or 135°F (57°C) for already-cooked ham. The bone is then easily detached from the flesh. Let stand for about 10 min before serving.

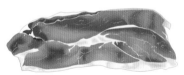

prosciutto

ROASTING TIME FOR HAMS NEEDING COOKING

cut	weight (lb/kg)	length of cooking time at 325°F (160°C)
Bone in		
Whole	7-10/3.5-4.5	3½ hr
Whole butt or shank end	5-7/2.5-3.5	3¼-3½ hr
Boned		
Whole	10-12/4.5-5.5	3½-4 hr
Half	5-7/2.5-3.5	2½-3½ hr
Picnic shoulder	4-6/2-3	2½-3 hr
	6-7/3-3.5	3-4 hr
	7-10/3.5-4.5	4-4½ hr

Sausage

Deli products formed from a casing filled with seasoned ground meat. There are innumerable varieties of sausage. Traditionally and still usually made from pork, sausages may also be made from beef, veal, lamb, mutton, poultry, variety meats or tofu. When the meat is boned mechanically, they can also contain pieces of nerve, tendon, blood vessel or bone. Sausages may also contain water, fillers, sugars, spices, smoke, preservatives and other ingredients.

Synthetic casings based on collagen (edible) or cellulose (nonedible) have virtually replaced natural casings.

There are four main types of sausages:

Fresh sausages are generally made from meat that has not been previously cured. They are comminuted, meaning they are made of meat that has been finely or coarsely pulverized into small pieces. They are usually seasoned, though they can also be cured, and many contain binders or extenders. Many are raw (long sausages, Toulouse sausages, *merguez*, chipolatas, breakfast sausages etc.).

Fresh sausages can be broiled, grilled, pan-fried, boiled or fried. Prick them with a fork before cooking, to allow the melted fat to drain away. Begin cooking over gentle heat. Add a small quantity of water to prevent the sausages from sticking. Fresh sausages must be kept refrigerated and be cooked fully before eating.

Cooked sausages (Frankfurt sausages, Polish sausages, *saveloy*, cocktail sausages, Chinese sausages, Vienna sausages, Bologna, liverwurst etc.), sometimes called "pre-cooked sausages," are made from fresh meat, seasoned and then fully cooked. They are sometimes smoked and dried. They must be kept refrigerated. The Frankfurt sausage, or "frankfurter" (hot dog) as it is more commonly known, is a cold-smoked pork sausage of German origin. Though it has been pre-cooked, cooking

Frankfurt sausages

Genoa salami

kielbasa

it again before eating is highly recommended. Many cooked sausages have also been **smoked** after cooking (kielbasa, Bologna). In the United States, fresh-cooked sausages are most popular, particularly those found in cased links (Italian sausage, bratwurst).

Dry sausages (Genoa salami, German salami, *sopressatta*, pepperoni, chorizo, rosette sausage) have been cured, then fermented and dried. Some are smoked. They are generally eaten cold and will keep for a long time. Dry sausages require more time to make, and are very concentrated.

Semi-dry sausages (Mortadella, Thuringer, summer sausage) are typically heated in a smokehouse to fully cook, but only partially dry them. They are generally semi-soft sausages, and like fully-dried sausages they have undergone a process of fermentation. Most are seasoned before cooking.

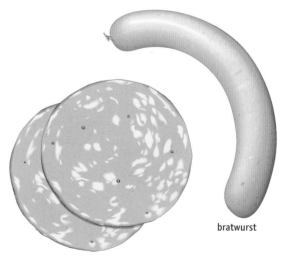

chorizo

mortadella

bratwurst

Sausage

weisswurst

BUYING

:: **Choose:** smooth sausages that are not sticky and have an even color. Dry sausage should be very firm, have a good aroma and be covered with a "bloom" (small white spots the size of a pinhead). Check the use-by date of vacuum-packed products.

SERVING IDEAS

Several dry and cooked sausages are generally served in thin slices. They are served as an hors d'oeuvre or main dish. They are used on canapés and sandwiches. Sauces such as Worcestershire, ketchups, mustard, chutneys and marinades work very well with sausages.

STORING

:: **At room temperature:** keep whole dry sausages in a cool and dry place, 3 months.
:: **In the fridge:** fresh or already-cooked sausages, 3 days. Keep ripe, open or sliced dry or cooked sausages covered and away from strong-smelling foods, 3-5 days. Sliced cooked sausages, 3-5 days.
:: **In the freezer:** fresh or cooked sausage in original sealed packaging, or wrapped, 3 months.

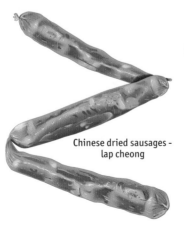

Chinese dried sausages - lap cheong

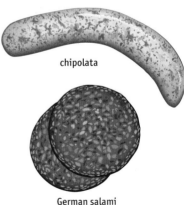

chipolata

German salami

NUTRITIONAL INFORMATION

	dry pork salami	Bologna sausage	smoked beef and pork sausage	fresh cooked pork sausage
protein	23 g	15 g	11 g	20 g
fat	34 g	20 g	29 g	31 g
cholesterol	79 mg	59 mg	50 mg	83 mg
calcium	407 mg	247 mg	320 mg	369 mg
sodium	2,260 mg	1,184 mg	1,120 mg	1,294 mg
				per 3.5 oz/100 g

The nutritional value of sausages varies according to the ingredients used and their proportions. They are generally fatty, salty and high in calories. They contain additives and less protein than meat. Water and fat account for almost three-quarters of the weight of smoked sausages.

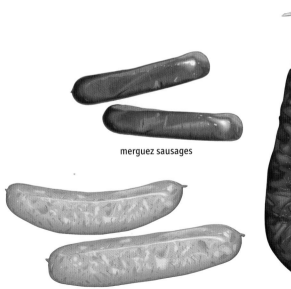

merguez sausages

Toulouse sausages

pepperoni

Andouille

A coarsely grained, smoked deli meat using the digestive tube of a pig, to which the head, heart, breast or throat may be added. Popular in Cajun cuisine, it is generally flavored with onions, pepper or wine. Andouilles measure 10-12 in. (25-30 cm) in length and andouillettes, 4-6 in. (10-15 cm). Andouillette is sometimes covered in breading, jelly or pork fat.

andouillette

SERVING IDEAS

 Andouille is eaten cold, cut into thin rounds (as an hors d'oeuvre). Andouillette is eaten grilled, broiled or pan-fried, served with mustard and accompanied by red beans or lentils, sauerkraut, red cabbage or fried potatoes.

STORING

 :: **In the fridge:** 3-4 days.

NUTRITIONAL INFORMATION

protein	10 g
fat	29 g
cholesterol	143 mg
calories	303
	per 3.5 oz/100 g

Simmered andouille is fatty and high in calories.

Rillettes

A dish made from meat cooked in fat until it acquires an unctuous texture. Rillettes are poured into pots, cooled and covered with a layer of fat (pork fat, goose fat or other fat). Traditionally made from pork or goose, rillettes can also be made from rabbit, poultry, duck, veal or fish.

rillettes

NUTRITIONAL INFORMATION

	beef, chicken, turkey
protein	16 g
fat	19 g
calories	280
	per 3.5 oz/100 g

SERVING IDEAS

 Rillettes are eaten cold, on canapés, in sandwiches or with toasted bread.

STORING

:: **In the fridge:** unopened, several weeks; opened, a few days.

Foie gras

The liver of a goose or duck that has been hypertrophied through a fattening process called *gavage*. Foie gras is considered to be a gastronomic dish. The name "foie gras" is regulated in several countries—in France, in particular. It refers to a product that contains at least 20% duck or goose foie gras. If the product contains the liver or meat from other animals, the name "foie gras" is accompanied by the words "pâté," "terrine" or "galantine."

Goose liver reaches an average weight of 1-2 lb (700-900 g) and duck liver 10.5-14 oz (300-400 g). It is only available in half-cooked or cooked form in the United States.

goose foie gras

SERVING IDEAS

 Foie gras is sold raw or ready to eat. It is placed in the fridge the day before eating; the container is opened 1 hr before serving, while still kept cool. The foie gras is then sliced using a knife whose blade has been run under hot water; it is eaten with a fork or on toasted bread.

COOKING

:: **Sautéed:** raw sliced foie gras (30 sec) in a very small amount of butter, the pan can then be deglazed with Madeira or cognac.

STORING

:: **In the fridge:** the opened container, 3-4 days, well wrapped.

NUTRITIONAL INFORMATION

	foie gras pâté
protein	11 g
fat	44 g
calories	462
	per 3.5 oz/100 g

The nutritional value of foie gras and related products varies according to the ingredients used: the livers of unfattened animals (including pork, calf and turkey liver), meat, pork fat, seasonings, truffles, alcohol, sugar, egg whites and various additives. These are almost always foods that are fatty and high in calories.

Blood sausage

Blood sausage, or *boudin noir* (the French version), are cooked deli meats based on pig's blood and fat that is seasoned and stuffed inside a casing. Cow, calf or sheep's blood can also be used. Onions, spinach, grapes, apples, prunes, chestnuts, milk, cream, eau-de-vie, semolina, bread crumbs, rolled oats, eggs, spices, herbs, etc. can also be used.

White-meat sausage, or *boudin blanc*, is a boiled mixture based on milk, eggs, white meats, fatty bacon and seasonings, inserted into natural casings. It is sold especially at Christmas time.

blood sausages

SERVING IDEAS

 Blood sausage is sliced, then pan-fried, poached, broiled or grilled (10 min). It is served with apples or a purée of potatoes. White-meat sausage is gently pan-fried, grilled or broiled, poached or baked, or cooked "en papillote" (in parchment or foil packages).

STORING

:: **In the fridge:** 3-4 days.

NUTRITIONAL INFORMATION

protein	15 g
fat	35 g
cholesterol	120 mg
calories	378
	per 3.5 oz/100 g

EXCELLENT SOURCE: iron and vitamin B$_{12}$. Blood sausage and white-meat sausage contain relatively high amounts of sodium (about 0.25 oz/700 mg per 3.5 oz/100 g). Check the list of ingredients to see if they contain additives.

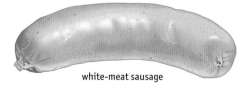

white-meat sausage

Poultry

In cooking, "poultry" refers to chicken meat; for other birds, recipes usually specify the particular variety of fowl. Chicken is the most popular form of poultry because it is tasty, economical to produce and can be prepared in a multitude of ways.

TIPS FOR BUYING POULTRY

Poultry is sold fresh or frozen, raw or cooked. Choose fresh poultry that is fleshy, with moist, flexible and intact skin, without any dark or dry patches. Avoid frozen poultry that is dry, has frosted or damaged packaging, or is covered in pink-colored ice.

TIPS FOR PREPARING POULTRY

Poultry is eaten hot or cold, but always cooked. Remove any feathers that are still attached by plucking them out with tweezers or pliers. Rinse the inside and outside of the poultry, then dry. If desired, rub the skin with lemon so that the flesh stays white during cooking. Remove the oil gland located at the back end of the bird's body (it is usually absent from the prepared available on the market). The wishbone can also be removed (the V-shaped or fork-shaped bone) to make carving the breast meat easier.

Poultry often carries salmonella bacteria, which causes an illness that can be serious, especially for children and older people. The handling and cooking of poultry therefore demands certain special precautions:

- Use a small area to prepare the poultry, to limit the risk of contamination.
- Before refrigerating poultry, take it out of its packaging, remove any organs from inside the cavity and store them separately; rinse the poultry and pat it dry with a paper towel; wrap loosely in waxed or aluminum paper and keep in the fridge no more than 2-3 days.
- Completely defrost the poultry; then cook it within 24-48 hr.
- Do not cook poultry at a low temperature (less than 300°F/150°C), since it must reach an internal temperature of 165°F (75°C) quickly to destroy any bacteria or viruses. Set the oven at 325°F (160°C) and insert a meat thermometer into the fleshiest part of the bird. Cook until the thermometer indicates 180°F (82°C), or 170°F (77°C) for an unstuffed turkey.
- Wash hands well and clean all the utensils and surfaces that were in contact with the poultry or its packaging with hot soapy water.
- Avoid leaving raw or cooked poultry at room temperature for more than 2 hr.
- Do not refreeze defrosted poultry before cooking it.

Only stuff poultry when ready to cook it. Immediately after the meal, remove the leftover stuffing from the poultry and refrigerate it separately in a closed container for up to 3 days. It can also be frozen for 3-4 weeks.

A whole bird bought frozen can be kept frozen for 12 months; pieces (bought frozen), for 6 months; and cooked poultry, for 1-2 months without any sauce or stock.

Defrosting in the fridge (the safest way) is the longest method (allow 1 hr per 2 lb/1 kg). Leave the poultry in its packaging and make a few holes beneath the back to allow the liquid to drain away.

To **defrost in the microwave oven**, leave the poultry in its packaging (remove any metal fastenings). Pierce the packaging so that the liquid can drain away. Place the poultry on a stand and heat at one-third of the highest setting, for 20-24 min per 2 lb (1 kg), or according to the time indicated by the manufacturer. When the poultry is half-defrosted, remove the packaging and cover the poultry so that it doesn't cook.

Defrosting by soaking in cold water is done by leaving the poultry in its packaging and in cold water. Refresh the water several times.

Defrosting at room temperature is not recommended.

TIPS FOR COOKING POULTRY

:: Roasting
Roasting consists of cooking whole birds or pieces in a conventional oven; it gives poultry a crispy skin. Coat the skin with a thin layer of oil or butter. Tie the bird with string to keep its shape; preheat the oven to 325°F (160°C). Place the bird on the grill of a rotisserie, breast side up (or skin side up for pieces). Cover with aluminum foil, with the shiny side facing the skin; roast. Remove the aluminum foil 30 min before the end of cooking, so the skin turns golden brown. Baste occasionally.

:: Grilling or broiling
Grilling consists of cooking pieces of poultry on the barbecue grill at a medium heat; broiling is done under the broiler of a conventional oven at 350°F (175°C). Do not place the poultry too close to the heat source (at least 4-5 in./10-12 cm away). Avoid pricking the poultry; baste and turn during cooking. Let the poultry rest for 10-15 minutes before serving; it will be tender and juicier.

:: Deep-fried
Frying poultry results in a tender, moist meat and crisp skin. Use a special deep-fryer with a basket. This frying is extremely dangerous and best performed outdoors in a well-ventilated area, not near anything flammable. Fill the pot with enough oil to about 1 inch below the top of the bird. Oil should be heated to 325°F-350°F (160°C-175°C). Allow 3-3½ min cooking time per lb.

:: Microwaving
Microwaving doesn't roast the skin; to improve its appearance, coat it with various seasonings. Cover the ends of the wings, the breast and thigh bones, and truss the bird by tying the joints close to the body. Pierce the bird's skin all over and place on a roasting stand so that the fat drains away. During cooking, remove the juice that accumulates. Turn the pieces or the whole chicken at least once during cooking. Check the internal temperature of the chicken in several places, after the waiting period.

Turkey

Meleagris gallopavo, Gallinaceae

A farmyard bird originally from North America. The head and neck of the turkey, colored purple-red, have no feathers and possess several growths. Wild turkeys have little flesh, in contrast to farmed turkeys, which have become fleshy through a great deal of crossbreeding. Domestic turkeys can weigh up to 40 lb (18 kg). Turkey meat is not as fine as chicken, and is more dry. The larger the animal, the less tasty it is.

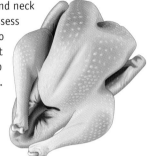

turkey

BUYING

Products that can be bought on the market include boned turkey, turkey pieces (breast, thighs, drumsticks, etc.), ground turkey, turkey scallops and cubes, and turkey rolled roast, as well as a whole range of processed products (sausage, salami, pastrami). Boned turkey can be sold skinless, with only the white meat or with both white and dark meat; it can also be cooked and smoked or given a ham flavor. Ready to cook or serve, these products are usually sold frozen; refer to the list of ingredients for information on what they contain. Turkey is also sold stuffed or injected with fat or oil, which is more expensive and contains a high proportion of saturated fats. Check that the skin, if any, is unbroken and free of cuts, bruises or blemishes.

NUTRITIONAL INFORMATION

	raw flesh (white and dark)	with skin	roast white and dark meat	with skin
protein	22 g	20 g	29 g	28 g
fat	3 g	8 g	5 g	10 g
cholesterol	65 mg	68 mg	76 mg	82 mg
calories	119	160	170	208
				per 3.5 oz/100 g

EXCELLENT SOURCE: protein, niacin, vitamin B$_6$, zinc and potassium.
GOOD SOURCE: vitamin B$_{12}$ and phosphorus. Turkey has almost twice as much white meat as dark. The white meat is less fatty and less moist. About 40% of the weight of the whole bird is edible. About 14 oz (400 g) of cooked meat is obtained for each 2 lb (1 kg) of raw turkey, 9 oz (250 g) of which can be served sliced.

Turkey

ROASTING TIME FOR TURKEY

Weight/(lb/kg)	Roasting time (hr)	
	Unstuffed	Stuffed
4-8/1.8-3.6	1½-3¼	2½-3
		(6-8 lb only)
8-12/3.6-5.4	2¾-3	3-3½
12-14/5.4-6.4	3-3¾	3½-4
14-18/6.4-8	3¾-4¼	4-4¼
18-20/8-9	4¼-4½	4¼-4¾
20-24/9-11	4½-5	4¾-5¼

Source: USDA

SERVING IDEAS

Turkey is traditionally roasted, often stuffed. It is prepared in the same way as chicken, which it can replace in most recipes. Like chicken, it is delicious cold, especially in salads and sandwiches.
Ground turkey is prepared in the same way as ground beef, and can be made into meat balls or burgers.

COOKING

Defrost the turkey completely before cooking, ideally in the fridge, in the original packaging; allow about 1 hr per 2 lb (1 kg). It can also be defrosted in cold water (allow 3 hr per 2 lb/1 kg) or in the microwave oven (see *Introduction*, p. 508) by following the manufacturer's directions.
The ideal cooking temperature is 325°F (160°C). The internal temperature of the breast should be 165°F (74°C), or 170°F (77°C) for thighs. Pierce the thickest part of the thigh; the juices should run clear, not pink. Let the turkey stand for 10 to 15 minutes before carving.

Goose

Anser anser, Anatidae

A web-footed bird with a long neck and a large beak. Some breeds of goose are raised for their tender and tasty flesh; they are killed when they weigh 6-11 lb (3-5 kg). Others are raised for their foie gras or liver; they can then weigh 22-26 lb (10-12 kg).

goose

NUTRITIONAL INFORMATION

	raw flesh	raw flesh with skin	roasted flesh	roasted flesh with skin
protein	23 g	16 g	29 g	25 g
fat	7 g	34 g	13 g	22 g
cholesterol	84 mg	80 mg	96 mg	91 mg
calories	160	370	238	305
				per 3.5 oz/100 g

Even if it is higher in fat, the nutritional value of goose is similar to duck.

BUYING

:: **Choose:** a goose with pink or pale flesh, a rounded breast and pale, smooth feet. An older goose has redder feet with more downy, a more rigid beak and firmer and drier flesh. Allow 1 lb (500 g) of meat per person.

COOKING

To reduce the fat, prick the skin in several places, place on a rotisserie grill and turn mid-cooking. Skim the fat from the surface of the sauce.
:: **Roasted:** about 30 min cooking per 2 lb (1 kg) at 325°F (160°C).

SERVING IDEAS

Goose is cooked in the same way as other poultry. Wild goose, which has firmer flesh, has maximum flavor when it is braised or prepared as a pâté. Dishes that use turkey or duck suit goose particularly well. Roast goose, stuffed or not, remains a traditional dish in Germany, England, central Europe and Scandinavia.

Goose stuffed with chestnuts and served with apples or sauerkraut is also a classic dish. The flesh of older or very large geese is made into *confit* (preserved in their own fat) and pâtés, or cooked as a stew or braised. Stuffings and accompaniments that contain fruit pair well with goose.

The fat drawn from goose is used in the same way as butter.

POULTRY

Chicken

Gallus gallus, Gallinaceae

chicken

The male or female offspring of a hen, 3-10 months of age. "Broilers" are chickens that are about 7 weeks old and weigh 2-4 lb (1-2 kg) cleaned; "roasters" are about 10 weeks old and weigh over 4.5 lb (2 kg). A "Rock Cornish game hen" is a cross between a White Rock chicken and Cornish hen; it weighs 1-2 lb (700 g-1 kg) cleaned. "Free-range" chickens are allowed to roam freely in the farmyard (rather than kept in coops) where they're raised. It is believed that this exercise keeps the meat tender and more flavorful.

Some chickens are called "grain-fed." In some countries, there are no regulations governing this name, and any chicken can be called "grain-fed," as all chickens are mostly fed on grain (wheat, barley, corn, etc.) and are produced using similar farming techniques. Chickens labeled "grain-fed" cost on average 30% more. Some "grain-fed" chickens are air-cooled rather than water-cooled when they are slaughtered. Those that are air-cooled lose less water when cooked, so their price is not as high as it appears. Air-cooling dries out the skin and gives it a darker color. A diet high in carotene also affects the color of poultry.

POULTRY

BUYING

It is better to compare the price of chicken based on the portion rather than the price per 1 lb (700 g) (taking into account waste during preparation and cooking). The price per 1 lb (700 g) of a whole chicken is usually lower than the price for pieces. A large chicken is a better value than a smaller chicken, since it has a higher proportion of flesh to bone. Look for the "sell-by" date on the store's label. This is usually 7-10 days after the chicken has been slaughtered, and is the last day recommended for sale.

SERVING IDEAS

Chicken is eaten cooked, hot or cold. All methods of cooking suit it and it can be accompanied by a multitude of ingredients and seasonings. Chicken is delicious roasted, grilled, broiled or sautéed. Marinating chicken for a few hours or stuffing it gives it more flavor. Given their young age, all chickens are tender and therefore cook very well using dry heat.

NUTRITIONAL INFORMATION

	raw without skin	raw with skin	roasted without skin	roasted with skin
protein	21 g	19 g	29 g	27 g
fat	3 g	15 g	7 g	14 g
cholesterol	70 mg	75 mg	89 mg	88 mg
calories	119	215	190	239

per 3.5 oz/100 g

Raw chicken flesh contains less fat and the same amount of cholesterol as the lean meat of butchered animals.

EXCELLENT SOURCE: protein, niacin and vitamin B_6.
GOOD SOURCE: vitamin B_{12}, zinc, phosphorus and potassium.

PREPARING

1 Insert a sharp chef's knife into the cavity of the bird and cut along the spinal column.

2 Turn over and open the chicken flat. Cut along the wishbone.

3 Cut the spinal column from the half it is attached to and discard.

4 Place the half-chicken flat on the work surface and insert the blade of the knife between the thigh and the breast.

5 Insert the point of a knife into the joint and cut to detach the wing.

6 This results in six pieces: two wings, two thighs and two half-breasts.

POULTRY

Hen

Gallus gallus, Gallinaceae

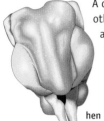
hen

A cock's female. The word "hen" also refers to the female of various other members of the Gallinaceae family. In this case, it is specified as being a "pheasant hen," "grouse hen" or "moorhen." About 12-24 months old, a hen weighs 3-6 lb (1-3 kg).

SERVING IDEAS

Hen flesh is firm and slightly fatty. It needs long and slow cooking using moist heat. It works well in soups and stews. It can be roasted after being braised in a very small amount of liquid (1 hr).

NUTRITIONAL INFORMATION

	boiled without skin	boiled with skin
protein	39 g	27 g
fat	12 g	19 g
cholesterol	83 mg	79 mg
calories	237	285
	per 3.5 oz/100 g	

EXCELLENT SOURCE: protein and niacin.
GOOD SOURCE: vitamin B$_6$, phosphorus, zinc and potassium.

Capon

Gallus gallus, Gallinaceae

A neutered, fattened rooster. Capon flesh is tender and succulent. It contains a higher proportion of white flesh than chicken. It tastes best when it weighs about 9 lb (4 kg).

capon

NUTRITIONAL INFORMATION

	raw with skin
protein	19 g
fat	17 g
cholesterol	75 mg
calories	234
	per 3.5 oz/100 g

COOKING

:: **Roasted:** stuffed or not.
Cook capon simply so as not to mask the delicate quality of its flesh.

Guinea fowl

Numida meleagris, Phasianidae

Guinea fowl is sometimes called "African pheasant." The most common
breed of Guinea fowl is the *Numida meleagris*. Domestic guinea fowl is
the size of a small chicken and has a slightly musky-tasting flesh.
It is particularly tasty when it weighs less than 2 lb (1 kg).

guinea fowl

SERVING IDEAS

Guinea fowl is cooked in the same way
as pheasant, partridge and chicken,
which it can replace.

COOKING

Brush with fat or oil or bard the meat
of the guinea fowl before cooking it,
and baste often during cooking.
:: **Roasted:** 1-1½ hr at 375°F (190°C).
:: **Braised**.

NUTRITIONAL INFORMATION

	raw without skin	raw with skin
protein	21 g	23 g
fat	3 g	7 g
cholesterol	63 mg	74 mg
calories	110	158
		per 3.5 oz/100 g

Guinea fowl is lean and low in calories.

Pigeon

Columba spp., Gallinaceae

Wild pigeon flesh is leaner and darker, and has a stronger flavor, than
domestic pigeon. Farmed pigeon is usually killed at about 4 weeks;
it weighs about 12 oz (350 g) and its flesh is very tender. It is
also called "squab."

pigeon

BUYING

 Allow one pigeon per person.

SERVING IDEAS

Pigeon is traditionally served with peas.
Cooked whole, it can be served as is,
without being cut up.

Pigeon

NUTRITIONAL INFORMATION

	raw without skin	raw with skin
protein	18 g	19 g
fat	8 g	24 g
cholesterol	90 mg	95 mg
calories	142	294
		per 3.5 oz/100 g

COOKING

Pigeon is cooked in the same way as other poultry.

:: Roasted, sautéed, grilled or **broiled:** young and tender pigeons.

:: Braised or **poached:** adult pigeons. Brown for 10-20 min at 425°F-475°F (220°C-245°C), then finish the cooking at 350°F (175°C). The liver can be left inside the bird during cooking.

Quail

Coturnix spp. and *Colinus spp.*, Gallinaceae

A small migratory bird thought to be originally from Asia or Africa.

American quail (*Colinus virginianus*) is a larger species closely related to the European quail, but are not migratory. It is also known as bobwhite, partridge or blue quail.

Farmed quail weighs 5-10 oz (150-300 g). Its flesh is delicate and tasty. Its tiny eggs are also edible.

quail

BUYING

Allow 2-3 quails per person.

SERVING IDEAS

Quail can be prepared as a pâté or terrine. The bones can be eaten, especially when the quail is well cooked. Grapes, cherries, olives, prunes and lemon are very good accompaniments to quail. Generally eaten hard-boiled, quail eggs are served as an appetizer or used as a garnish. They have a fine flavor and their texture is soft and creamy; they occupy a privileged position in Chinese and Japanese cuisine.

NUTRITIONAL INFORMATION

	raw without skin	raw with skin
protein	22 g	20 g
fat	5 g	12 g
cholesterol	70 mg	76 mg
calories	134	192
		per 3.5 oz/100 g

COOKING

Do not let quail flesh dry out during cooking.

:: Roasted, braised (with grapes), **cooked in a casserole, grilled** or **broiled:** 20-25 min.

STORING

:: In the fridge: 2-3 days, raw, in the coldest part.

chickens >

Pheasant

Phasianus colchicus, Gallinaceae

A bird originally from Asia. Farmed pheasant is fleshier and heavier than wild pheasant; its flesh is higher in fat and it has a less musky flavor. Usually 18-25 weeks old, farmed pheasant weighs 2-3 lb (800 g-1 kg).

pheasant

BUYING

 Allow 1 pheasant for 2 people or, if stuffed, for 3 or 4 people.

PREPARING

Traditionally, pheasant is aged (that is to say, it is hung so that the proteins start to break down, which tenderizes the flesh and gives it a certain bouquet) for 4-12 days, depending on the season. This practice is less often observed these days, especially if the pheasant is young and coming from a farm; it is usually just cooked 48 hr after being killed.

STORING

 :: In the fridge: 2-3 days, raw, in the coldest part.

NUTRITIONAL INFORMATION

	raw flesh	with skin
protein	24 g	23 g
fat	4 g	9 g
cholesterol	66 mg	71 mg
calories	133	181
		per 3.5 oz/100 g

COOKING

:: Roasted: young pheasant, often complemented with a moist stuffing that is placed in the bird just before cooking. It can also be barded or brushed with fat or oil.

:: Roasted (covered with bards)**, cooked in a casserole, prepared as a terrine** or **pâté:** older pheasant, whose flesh is drier and less tender. Wine and alcohol are particularly suitable for cooking pheasant. To roast, allow 1-1½ hr at 375°F (190°C). Baste often during cooking.

Duck

Anas platyrhynchos, Anatidae

A web-footed bird that is highly regarded in Europe, especially France (the largest European producer of duck) in particular because of the production of foie gras. Duck occupies an important place in Asian cuisine, especially Chinese cuisine. Among the breeds of farmed ducks, the **Barbary duck** has firm flesh and a strong taste, and the **Nantes duck** has fine but fattier meat. Among the wild species is the **mallard duck**, which is most common and whose meat is highly regarded. Usually only the thighs and breast fillets are eaten. Pekin, Long Island duck, is the most popular breed in America. They are white-feathered and full-breasted. The quantity of flesh, the flavor (more or less musky) and the nutritional value (particularly its fat content) vary from one species of duck to another. Market ducks are generally 7-12 weeks old, weigh 4-6 lb (2-3 kg) and have tender flesh. Most of the ducks on the market are available frozen year-round. In restaurants, the term "duckling" is used for animals less than 2 months old.

duck

BUYING

Duck does not yield a lot of meat. Allow 1-1.5 lb (500-750 g) raw meat per person.

COOKING

 :: Roasted: roasting allows the fat content in duck to be reduced: prick the skin in various places using a fork before cooking, and place the duck on a rotisserie grill. Allow 20-25 min cooking time per 1 lb (500 g) at 325°F (160°C). The fat makes the skin crispy and golden brown as it melts. Very large ducks, which are less tender, are often braised or made into pâtés and cassoulets.

SERVING IDEAS

Duck is often cooked with fruit such as oranges, cherries and apples, because their acidity works well with the fattiness of its flesh. Duck can be prepared as duck *à l'orange* or with chestnuts.

Duck eggs, not generally eaten in the West, are enjoyed in Asian countries.

Duck is also enjoyed for its foie gras, which some consider to be superior to goose foie gras. Duck fillets provide lean breast slices (*magrets*) that are grilled, pan-fried or smoked.

Duck

NUTRITIONAL INFORMATION

	flesh	roasted flesh and skin
protein	24 g	19 g
fat	11 g	28 g
cholesterol	89 mg	84 mg
calories	201	337
		per 3.5 oz/100 g

The nutritional value of duck varies according to how it is reared and its breed. The raw flesh of wild duck contains about 30% less fat than domestic duck. This difference is reduced during cooking, however, as some fat is lost.

EXCELLENT SOURCE: iron and B-complex vitamins.

Egg

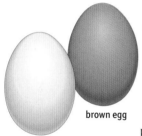

brown egg

white egg

An organic body of various sizes whose purpose is to ensure the reproduction of the species. Eggs are laid by the females of several animal species, in particular birds and reptiles. The usual use of the word "egg" refers to a hen's egg; in the case of other species, their name is mentioned. Eggs are composed of four main parts.

The **shell** is the rigid, porous and fragile casing that protects the egg. Its color depends on the breed of hen and has no influence on the nutritional value or the flavor of the eggs.

The shell **membrane** is made up of protein fibers that lightly adhere to the shell and act as a protective barrier against molds and bacteria. An air cell is found at one end of the egg. The larger the air cell is, the less fresh the egg.

The **albumen**, usually called the "white" of the egg, is made up of 87% water and 12.5% albumin. The *chalazae*, found on either side of the yolk, are threads of albumin that serve to keep the yolk in the middle of the egg. The fresher the egg, the denser and firmer the white around the yolk is.

The **yolk** is formed of several layers of a substance called "vitellus." The yolk is protected by a transparent membrane (the vitelline membrane). The overall color can be lighter or darker, and varies according to the hen's diet. The yolk contains about 50% solids, around 16% proteins and about 30% lipids.

POULTRY

BUYING

:: **Choose:** refrigerated eggs (they stay fresh longer), with intact shells. Check the use-by or sell-by date marked on the packaging.

Eggs are classified according to criteria that vary from country to country. In the United States, the USDA assigns one of three grades to eggs—AA, A or B—that indicate freshness and quality. Qualities such as cleanliness, shape and texture are used to determine which category the eggs are ranked in. The majority of eggs found in the supermarket are Grade AA or Grade A; most Grade B eggs are used to make egg-based products, such as mayonnaise, rather than be sold fresh. There are also established standards for classifying eggs according to weight, which is determined by the weight per dozen. "Small" eggs must weigh at least 1.5 oz (42 g); "medium" eggs 1.75 oz (49 g); "large" at least 2 oz (56 g); and "extra large" eggs at least 2.25 oz (64 g). The "peewee" egg, the smallest egg, must weigh less than 1.5 oz (42 g) and the largest egg, the "jumbo," at least 2.5 oz (70 g).

PREPARING

When breaking eggs, it is possible to come across a rotten egg. To avoid spoiling any already-broken eggs or the dish it was meant for, break each egg separately in a bowl and add it to the others or to the dish as you go along.

Eggs should be brought to room temperature before using for most recipes.

STORING

:: **In the fridge:** over 1 month, in their packaging or in a closed container. The fridge door is not a recommended storage place, as the door opening leads to changes in temperature. Place the eggs pointed-end down so that the yolk stays well-centered. Avoid washing eggs, as this removes their protective film; wipe soiled eggs with a dry cloth.

Place leftover raw egg whites and yolks 4 days, in an airtight container. Cover the yolks with cold water and place them up to 4 days in an airtight container. Whole hard-boiled eggs, 1 week.

:: **In the freezer:** egg whites and whole, lightly beaten eggs, 4 months. The yolks by themselves or beaten with the white.

POULTRY

goose egg

quail egg

Egg

SERVING IDEAS

Eggs are eaten as is or as an ingredient in crepes, quiches, cakes, pastries, drinks and ice cream. They are used both to thicken and bind foods, and to give them a smooth texture (sauces, soups, stuffings, flans, pastry cream, custard, puddings, purées, croquettes, pasta dishes). They are used to brown meat loaves, bread crumbs, breads, brioches and pies. They are emulsified (mayonnaise, sauces) and beaten into peaks (mousses, meringues, soufflés). Never add eggs directly to a hot liquid (soup, custard, pastry cream, etc.), especially the yolks, as they will coagulate and form lumps. Instead, the eggs should be heated slowly and a small part of the hot mixture beaten in. This mixture can then be poured back into the rest of the hot liquid, still beating, then finish the cooking. Mixtures such as custard or pastry cream, if cooked too quickly or too long, will curdle, so it is preferable to cook them in a double boiler. If the mixture is cooked in a saucepan, it must be taken off the heat as soon as it sets and the pan cooled immediately by being plunged in cold water.

Cracked or marked eggs should never be eaten raw, as they may contain toxic microorganisms that can only be destroyed by cooking. To check the freshness of eggs, place them in cold water: those that are not fresh will float.

NUTRITIONAL INFORMATION

	large egg
protein	6.3 g
fat	5 g
carbohydrates	0.6 g
calories	75
	per 1.8 oz/50 g

Eggs are highly nutritious. The total amount of nutrients varies according to the size of the yolk and the egg. The proteins in eggs are said to be "complete" as they contain the eight essential amino acids. Eggs are considered an excellent source of high-quality protein. The fats are made up of 32% saturated fatty acids, 38% monounsaturated fatty acids and 14% polyunsaturated fatty acids, and about 5% cholesterol.

1¾ OZ (50 G) EGG

EXCELLENT SOURCE: vitamin B_{12}.

GOOD SOURCE: riboflavin.

CONTAINS: vitamin D, folic acid, pantothenic acid, phosphorus, zinc, iron and potassium. The white provides just over half of the protein and the majority of the potassium and riboflavin. The yolk contains vitamins A and D, most of the other vitamins and minerals, three-quarters of the calories and all of the fat. Egg white can cause food allergies, which is why it is recommended that it only be introduced into an infant's diet after one year.

COOKING

:: Soft-, medium- or hard-boiled egg: An egg whose white has started to set and whose yolk is still liquid is a "soft-boiled" egg. An egg with a solid white and a still-runny yolk is a "medium-boiled" egg. An egg whose white and yolk are both firm is a "hard-boiled" egg.

It is better for the eggs to be at room temperature when they are immersed in water. A hole can also be made in the round end of the egg with a pin or special utensil to prevent the shell from cracking. Adding a pinch of salt or 1 tablespoon (15 ml) of vinegar allows the white to set immediately at the edge of the shell if the egg cracks.

- **To boil an egg starting with cold water:** Place the egg in a saucepan and cover with cold water. Heat until the water is just simmering. Count 3 min from this moment for a soft-boiled egg, 3-4 min for a medium-boiled egg and 7-10 min for a hard-boiled egg. Remove the eggs from the hot water immediately. When the hard-boiled egg is ready, run it under cold water immediately. To remove the shell, tap the egg gently to crack it and remove the shell under cold water.

- **To boil an egg starting with hot water:** Fill the saucepan with enough water to cover the eggs. Bring the water to a boil, then gently lower the eggs into the just-simmering water. Count 3-4 min for a soft-boiled egg, 7-9 min for a medium-boiled egg and 10-15 min for a hard-boiled egg. Run the hard-boiled egg under cold water.

Very fresh eggs require a slightly longer cooking time; eggs that are too old will be less tasty and tend to float. Avoid cooking on a high boil.

:: Poached egg: A shelled egg cooked in a boiling liquid to which a little vinegar has been added (2-3 tablespoons/30-50 ml per 4 cups/1 l). The goal is to allow the white of the egg to set quickly so that it doesn't spread. Do not add salt to the cooking water, as salt has a tendency to make the white and yolk separate. Break the egg into a small bowl and add it to the water all at once when the liquid is boiling. Reduce the heat and poach (3-5 min) in just-simmering water; the white will be firm and the yolk soft. Remove the egg using a slotted spoon, drain for a few moments or place it on a cloth, then serve immediately.

Depending on the size of the saucepan, it is possible to cook 2-4 eggs at the same time. Poached eggs can also be eaten cold.

:: Scrambled egg: An egg that is lightly beaten to break the yolk, to which seasonings are added; the addition of a little milk results in a creamier egg. Scrambled eggs are cooked in a thick-based frying pan containing fat or oil over a gentle and constant heat, stirring continuously with a wooden spoon for 6-10 min, depending on the quantity. The general serving suggestion is 2 eggs per person. When the eggs begin to set, vegetables, mushrooms, cheese, ham, poultry or seafood can be added. Add salt and pepper only at the end of cooking.

duck egg

Egg

:: **Egg sunny-side up:** An egg cooked over a gentle heat in a small frying pan (to prevent the white spreading too far), with a very small amount of fat. It is ready when the white is firm and the yolk liquid and shiny. When cooked, the yolk develops a thin transparent film; to avoid this, cover the eggs with a sheet of aluminum foil during cooking. If the egg is turned over, it is called "egg over easy."

:: **Shirred egg:** An egg baked in a custard cup, often with flavoring or sauce.

:: **Fried eggs:** Eggs cooked in hot oil (peanut or corn oil) for about 1 minute; the white is folded over the yolk so that the yolk doesn't over cook. It is ready when the white starts to brown; it is drained and placed on a paper towel before being served on toast.

:: **Egg threads:** Egg or egg white beaten to an omelette consistency, which is poured into boiling liquid through a fine strainer. The thin threads formed by the strainer set instantly in contact with the hot liquid. This preparation is widely used to garnish soups.

:: **Omelette:** Beaten eggs seasoned with salt and pepper and cooked in a frying pan, to which herbs can be added when the eggs are beaten. One can also make a filling (vegetables, meat, cheese) that is cooked beforehand and placed on the omelette before it is folded over. This is the classic omelette that is cooked over a high heat and remains runny inside.

A flat omelette consists of beaten eggs that are used to bind more substantial ingredients: potato, ham, onion, pepper. It is cooked gently and turned to brown on both sides.

pheasant egg

Omelettes can be hearty (like the Italian frittata and the Spanish tortilla), runny with a filling (French-style) or light (like the Chinese egg *foo yung*), where the egg is mostly used to bind the filling. Omelettes are cooked in a frying pan or skillet, or in a special omelette pan.

:: **Beaten egg whites:** Egg whites at room temperature that are beaten until they are thick and frothy. For successful beaten egg whites, one should:

- Use very clean utensils (avoid plastic utensils)
- Preferably use a copper or stainless steel bowl, not an aluminum container.
- Make sure no trace of egg yolk is mixed in with the white; separate the eggs in a separate bowl and only transfer the egg white if it is intact.
- Add a pinch of salt or cream of tartar at the beginning to make the froth firmer; add sugar when the consistency of the whites has started to change (the egg whites are ready when the mixture is firm enough to form peaks).
- Mix other ingredients into the egg whites gently so that the accumulated air stays in the whites.

Dairy products

Milk and products derived from milk, such as yogurt and cheese. Dairy products are considered to be the main dietary source of calcium. Calcium is an essential element for good health and bone and teeth density. In the United States, the daily recommended calcium intake is 500-1,300 mg for children, 1,000 mg for adults, and 1,200 mg for older people. These amounts could be obtained with approximately one dairy product per meal.

Milk

A liquid produced by the mammary glands of female mammals. Cow's milk is the most widely used, but sheep, goat, donkey, mare, camel and buffalo milk may also be consumed. The word "milk" without any mention of the animal species refers to cow's milk.

The consumption of cow's milk and dairy products is common in the United States, Canada, western and northern Europe, Australia and New Zealand.

homogenized milk

The ability to digest lactose (the sugar contained in mammals' milk) after early infancy is a genetic adaptation in populations that consume milk. The inability to digest lactose, known as lactose intolerance, is caused by a deficiency in lactase, an enzyme that turns lactose into a substance that can be absorbed in the intestine. Individuals who are lactose intolerant can suffer from abdominal pain, diarrhea, gas, bloating, nausea and cramps. Some show no symptoms when they consume small quantities of milk. These problems rarely result from eating yogurt and mature cheese. Cottage cheeses, cream cheeses and processed cheeses, however, contain a certain quantity of lactose that can cause symptoms. Whole milk is tolerated better than skim milk. Milk whose lactose content has been reduced by 50% should not cause symptoms in most adults who are unable to digest milk. Milk with a lactose content reduced by 90% is available on the market.

Pasteurized milk is heated to below boiling point to destroy the majority of disease-causing bacteria (99.4%), which extends its storage life. It is then cooled quickly. Pasteurization results in a small loss (less than 10%) of certain water-soluble vitamins.

Homogenized milk contains fat that is forced under pressure through very small openings. This breaks up the fat globules into very small particles that remain suspended in the liquid and don't clump together on the surface of the milk.

Microfiltered milk, or "ultrapasteurized milk," has undergone a filtration process before a minimal amount of pasteurization, which enables 99.9% of the bacteria to be eliminated. Microfiltration increases the storage life of the milk without diminishing its nutritional value.

Raw milk is untreated milk. Its sale is illegal in several American states, Canada and numerous European countries. Its consumption can lead to tuberculosis or salmonellosis.

Whole milk generally contains at least 3.25% milkfat and 8.25% milk solids. Approximately 50% of its calories are fat. Whole milk is generally recommended for infants and young children.

Low- and reduced-fat milk contains 1% or 2% fat. It has almost the same nutritional value as whole milk, with the exception of its reduced fat content, which lowers the calories. Its taste is not as rich as whole milk.

Skim milk contains a maximum of 0.3% milkfat and has half the calories of whole milk.

UHT milk undergoes pasteurization at a very high temperature or ultra-high temperature (UHT). Only the vitamin C content is reduced. It is packaged in sterile sealed containers and can be stored in its container at room temperature (3 months). Once opened, it should be consumed within 24-36 hr.

Evaporated milk is whole, skim or reduced-fat milk, from which about 60% of the water has been vacuum evaporated. It contains at least 7.5% milkfat and no less than 25.5% milk solids. It has a slightly darker color than ordinary milk and a caramelized flavor. It is nutritious and high in energy. Do not buy a can that bulges. Evaporated milk doesn't curdle much when cooked, making it suitable for preparing thick sauces and puddings. Whole, very cold evaporated milk can be whipped, but only just before serving, or it will quickly collapse. Because it has a sweeter taste, slightly reduce the suggested amount of sugar in recipes.

Condensed milk is essentially whole evaporated milk with added sugar and 60% of the water content removed. It contains 40%-45% sugar and has no less than 8% fat and 28% milk solids. With the exception of iron and vitamin C, which almost disappear, all the nutrients are concentrated. This milk is particularly high in calories and rich in fat. It is used to make desserts, sweets and cake fillings. Reduce the amount of sugar suggested in a recipe in order to reduce the energy content of the dish. To thicken and caramelize condensed milk, boil it in its sealed can (2-3 hr), in deep pot and covered with 1 in. water, and open when it has cooled.

Flavored milk is milk to which an ingredient (for example, chocolate) has been added to give it flavor. There are also malted milk, fruit-flavored milk and milk drinks containing fruit juice. Their nutritional value depends mainly on the milk used for its fat content, and the amount of sugar added. Malted milk, which contains milled barley and wheat, can be sold plain, flavored or dehydrated. Most flavored milk is manufactured using the UHT process.

Powdered milk is dehydrated milk that contains a maximum of 2.5% moisture, for whole milk, and 4%, for skim milk. Powdered skim milk keeps more easily than powdered whole milk. An unopened package can be stored at room temperature (1 year). An opened container will keep for longer if it is placed in a glass jar in the fridge (1 month).

Whole powdered milk contains a minimum of 26% fat; reduced-fat, 9.5%; and skim milk powder, 0.8%. Prepare the milk by following the instructions on the label. 10 quarts (10 l) of reconstituted milk is obtained from 2 lb (1 kg) of powdered milk. Powdered milk can be contaminated with bacteria that often cause intestinal problems.

DAIRY PRODUCTS

Milk

Non-instant powdered milk can be used in recipes to enhance their nutritional value or for thickening a liquid (sauces, puddings). In this case, 3 tablespoons (45 ml) of skim milk powder is equivalent to 1 cup (250 ml) of milk. Instant milk powder is easily mixed with water, cereals and drinks, but doesn't dissolve when it is added to dry ingredients.

Milk powder can be used in place of whipped cream: ¾ cup (175 ml) of powder beaten with ½ cup (125 ml) of ice water and 1 tablespoon (15 ml) of lemon juice yields about 1 quart (1 l) of whipped milk. Only beat it when serving, or it will quickly collapse.

Reconstituted powdered milk can be used in the same way as any other milk and the same precautions should be taken with storing it. Skim milk powder is often used in the manufacturing of baked goods, soups, processed meats, sweets and dairy products.

BUYING

Cow's milk is usually sold pasteurized, homogenized and, in some cases sterilized, whole, fat-reduced, skimmed, evaporated, flavored or powdered. The sale of raw milk is allowed in rural areas of Europe.

SERVING IDEAS

Milk occupies an important place in the cuisines of several countries, especially Western countries. It is consumed as a drink or cooked. It is used in the preparation of delicate and hearty soups, sauces such as béchamel sauce, crepes, cakes, pastries, desserts such as flans, custard, cooked creams or sweet dishes, purées and some cooked dishes. It is made into yogurt and cheese. Dairy products that are high in fat can be replaced by skimmed products in most recipes.

evaporated milk

NUTRITIONAL INFORMATION

	3.25% fat	2% fat	1% fat	skim
protein	8.5 g	8.6 g	8.5 g	8.8 g
fat	8.6 g	5.0 g	2.7 g	0.5 g
carbohydrates	12.0 g	12.4 g	12.3 g	12.6 g
cholesterol	35 mg	19 mg	10 mg	5 mg

per 1 cup/250 ml

EXCELLENT SOURCE: calcium, phosphorus and potassium.

GOOD SOURCE: riboflavin, B-complex vitamins, vitamin B_{12}, magnesium and zinc.

It contains a moderate amount of sodium. In North America and several European countries, vitamin D and vitamin A are added to liquid milk. In Canada, all types of milk must be vitamin D-enriched; reduced-fat and skim milk must also be vitamin A-enriched, while evaporated milk must be vitamin C-enriched. This enrichment is not required when the milk is used to make cheese or yogurt.

Beta-carotene is the pigment responsible for the yellow coloring of milk, more noticeable in butter.

The rich taste of milk comes from its fats, which are among the most easily digested dietary fats. They account for 49% of the calories of whole milk. They are made up of 62% saturated fatty acids, 29% monounsaturated fatty acids and 3.7% polyunsaturated fatty acids. In the case of skim milk, the proportions are 60% saturated fatty acids, 24% monounsaturated fatty acids and 4% polyunsaturated acids. Milk also contains an essential fatty acid, linoleic acid. Milk proteins are excellent. They represent 38% of the nonfatty solids in milk. Among these, casein represents 82% of the protein in milk. The lactoserum or "whey" (the liquid left over after the fat and casein have been extracted from milk) represents 18%. All the essential amino acids are present in milk. It is particularly high in lysine, which makes milk a good complement to cereals and grains, nuts and seeds (see *Food Complementarity Theory*, p. 277).

Lactose accounts for 97% of the carbohydrate in milk and 30%-56% of the calories, depending on the type of milk. It is the least sweet-tasting sugar.

Cow's milk has its supporters and its opponents. The supporters claim that it is an indispensable food, as it is plentiful, inexpensive and very nutritious, being an excellent source of protein, vitamins and minerals. The calcium it provides ensures good teeth development, acts on the functioning of the heart cells, nerves and muscles, encourages bone growth and plays a role in the prevention of osteoporosis, hypertension and, possibly, colorectal cancer and hypercholesterolemia. It is furthermore considered that, for the overall population, there is a greater risk of calcium, riboflavin, vitamin D and vitamin B_{12} deficiencies if dairy products are not part of the daily diet. The opponents maintain that milk is designed to nourish calves, animals that grow quickly and reach a large size, features that do not apply to human beings. They highlight the fact that milk is meant to nourish newborns and that adult animals in nature do not feed on milk. Another source of concern is the use of a hormone for stimulating an increase in the production of milk in cows of 10%-20%. Known under the scientific name of sometribove (rBST), this hormone is commonly called bovine somatotropin (BST). Over 25 countries allow this hormone to be used, including the United States. According to several researchers, this hormone doesn't present any danger to the consumer.

STORING

Heat, oxygen and light affect the nutritional value of milk. Milk must therefore be refrigerated as quickly as possible, preferably bought in a nontransparent container, which is closed tightly after use. Never return unused milk to the original container, as it may contaminate the rest.

:: **At room temperature:** milk powder, 6 months in a sealed package. The open container, kept cool and away from air and light.

:: **In the fridge:** 10 days, but it will not keep as long if it has been previously left at room temperature for long periods.

COOKING

It is better to heat milk over a low heat, in a double boiler, if possible, as it turns quickly once it reaches boiling point and sticks easily to the base of the saucepan. A skin forms on the surface of milk when it is heated without a lid or without being stirred (or after cooking, when it cools). To avoid curdling when an acidic ingredient is added, combine either the acidic ingredient or the milk with some cornstarch, then cook slowly. Homogenized milk curdles more quickly; its cooking time is longer and the resulting product has a sweeter and creamier texture.

powdered milk

Goat's milk

A milk that is whiter with a stronger flavor than cow's milk. Goat's milk does not need to be homogenized, as its fat globules tend to remain suspended.

goat's milk

BUYING

Goat's milk is usually available in natural food stores.

SERVING IDEAS

Goat's milk is used in the same way as cow's milk, for which it can often be substituted. It is drunk as is and used for cooking; it is made into cheese, yogurt and butter. Goat's milk is less stable than cow's milk when heated.

NUTRITIONAL INFORMATION

	whole
water	87%
protein	9.2 g
fat	10.7 g
carbohydrates	11.5 g
cholesterol	29 mg
sodium	128 mg
calories	177
	per 1 cup/250 ml

Goat's milk contains a little less cholesterol than whole cow's milk and the proportions of fatty acids are substantially the same.

EXCELLENT SOURCE: potassium, calcium and phosphorus.

GOOD SOURCE: riboflavin.

CONTAINS: vitamin A, magnesium, niacin, pantothenic acid, thiamine, zinc, vitamin B_{12}, vitamin B_6 and copper.

PROPERTY: more easily digested than cow's milk. The enrichment of goat's milk is not mandatory; however, if it is fortified, it must contain 35-45 IU of vitamin D and 140-300 IU (International unit) of vitamin A per 7 tablespoons (100 ml), according to the regulations.

DAIRY PRODUCTS

Buttermilk

buttermilk

A whitish liquid with a tart taste that separates from the cream during the making of butter. It is also produced by culturing skim or lowfat milk with a lactic-acid culture. Buttermilk has a consistency that is vaguely reminiscent of cream. When left standing, it separates into two layers: the lighter layer is made from whey and the heavier from casein that has curdled into fine lumps.

BUYING

 Check the use-by date marked on the packaging.

SERVING IDEAS

 Buttermilk is a natural emulsifier that is widely used, often in powder form, in baked goods, pastry-making and the production of ice cream. It is also used in soups and certain cheeses. It can be mixed with blended fruits to make drinks. It is used to make sauces, with the addition of herbs and lemon juice.
Buttermilk (and sour milk) can be replaced in most recipes by 1 cup (250 ml) of milk and 2 teaspoons (10 ml) of vinegar.

STORING

 :: **In the fridge:** unopened, 15 days; opened, 1 week. Reseal the container well.

NUTRITIONAL INFORMATION

protein	8.6 g
fat	2.3 g
carbohydrates	12.4 g
cholesterol	9 mg
sodium	272 mg
per 1 cup/250 ml	

The nutritional value of buttermilk is similar to skim or reduced-fat milk.
EXCELLENT SOURCE: potassium, vitamin B_{12}, calcium, riboflavin.
GOOD SOURCE: phosphorus.
CONTAINS: zinc, magnesium, pantothenic acid, niacin, thiamine, folic acid and vitamin B_6.
High in lactic acid and nitrogen, buttermilk is low in fat. It is a food that is well suited to people with digestive problems.

Sour cream

A cream with a sour flavor. Sour cream is made from pasteurized cream that is fermented using a bacterial culture. One can refer to "cultured sour cream" or "soured cream." It has a thick, smooth and even texture.

sour cream

BUYING

 Check the use-by date on the package.

PREPARING

Sour cream can be made at home by adding 2 tablespoons (30 ml) of buttermilk to 2 cups (500 ml) of fresh cream that is left to sour for at least 24 hr at room temperature, without being touched. It can then be stored in the fridge for 3 days.

SERVING IDEAS

Sour cream is widely used in German, English, Russian and Polish cuisine; it is used to flavor soups, dips, sauces, stuffed cabbage, goulash, breads and cakes. Smitane sauce, a classic Russian accompaniment to game, and eastern Europe borscht are typical uses. In the United States, baked potato is often served with sour cream. It can be replaced by plain yogurt in most recipes.

NUTRITIONAL INFORMATION

	14% fat	18% fat
water	78.1%	74%
protein	0.8 g	1.0 g
fat	4 g	5.2 g
carbohydrates	1.2 g	1.2 g
cholesterol	12 mg	12 mg
		per 2 tbsp/30 ml

Sour cream is made up of 63.5% saturated fatty acids. The fat in cultured soured cream with 18% fat is made up of 62.7% saturated fatty acids.

COOKING

When adding sour cream to hot foods, incorporate it at the end of cooking and heat gently without boiling; otherwise, it may curdle.

STORING

 :: In the fridge: 2-3 weeks.

Butter

A fatty, semi-solid substance with a greasy texture made by churning cream. Butter is mostly made from cow's milk. It consists of 80% milkfat and is graded by similar standards as milk, with consideration to flavor, texture, color and salt content.
Unsalted butter is recommended for baking. **Whipped butter** is softer and more easily spread because it has air beaten into it. **Margarine** and other butter substitutes are generally made with oils (see *Margarine,* p. 579).
The word "butter" also refers to other fatty substances extracted from various plants; in these cases, the origin of the butter is specified (peanut butter, cocoa butter, almond butter, coconut butter).

salted butter

SERVING IDEAS

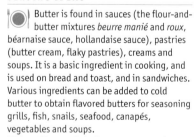 Butter is found in sauces (the flour-and-butter mixtures *beurre manié* and *roux*, béarnaise sauce, hollandaise sauce), pastries (butter cream, flaky pastries), creams and soups. It is a basic ingredient in cooking, and is used on bread and toast, and in sandwiches. Various ingredients can be added to cold butter to obtain flavored butters for seasoning grills, fish, snails, seafood, canapés, vegetables and soups.
Whipped butter, light butter or margarine should not be used in place of ordinary butters in recipes. These are generally used as a spread.

STORING

Butter quickly loses its quality if it is kept too long at room temperature or is poorly wrapped.
:: In the fridge: preferably in its original packaging or well covered. Keep it away from foods that might give it a bad taste. 8 weeks for unsalted butter and 12 weeks for salted butter, in their original packaging. Opened, 3 weeks.
:: In the freezer: 6 months. After this time, there is a slight loss of flavor. Freezing can also heighten its salty taste.

NUTRITIONAL INFORMATION

	light	*whipped*	*unsalted*	*salted*
protein	0.4 g	0.1 g	traces	traces
fat	3.9 g	7.8 g	8.2 g	8.2 g
carbohydrates	0.6 g	traces	traces	traces
cholesterol	12 mg	21 mg	22 mg	22 mg
sodium	69 mg	79 mg	82 mg	2 mg
				per 0.35 oz/10 g

Whipped butter, salted butter and unsalted butter all contain vitamin A.

Butter is a controversial food, defended by some, particularly its producers, and highly criticized by others, especially the manufacturers of oil and margarine. Butter should be consumed in moderation, since it serves as a major source of fat, saturated fatty acids and cholesterol.

COOKING

Avoid heating butter over high heat. It can be used in combination with oil, which means it won't break down as quickly (heat the oil first, then add the butter). Cold butter is more easily digested than melted butter. It doesn't lend itself well to high-temperature cooking, as its fats break down at temperatures of 250°F-270°F (120°C-130°C). Butter heated to this level turns brown and releases acrolein, an indigestible and toxic substance that may raise blood cholesterol levels.

PREPARING

 1 lb (500 g) of butter is equivalent to 2 cups (500 ml) of butter.

Butter can be "clarified," which is to say its whey solids can be removed. It then becomes limpid like oil and can stand up to frying. To clarify butter:

1. Melt the butter over a very gentle heat. It will then separate into three layers: a layer of froth on top; the pure fat in the middle (a thick, yellow liquid); and the whey beneath at the bottom of the saucepan.

2. Skim the froth with a spoon and slowly pour the butter into a straining cloth (like cheesecloth) or leave the liquid deposit at the bottom of the saucepan. The butter can then be refrigerated. Once it solidifies, the clarified butter forms a crust, whereas the whey deposit stays liquid; it can then be simply put aside.

Keep homemade clarified butter 2 months in the fridge or 3 months in the freezer. Industrially made clarified butter can be left at room temperature.

DAIRY PRODUCTS

Cream

cream

The milk fat that rises to the surface of nonhomogenized milk, created during the first stage of making butter. In Europe, the term "cream" is reserved for the product obtained from cow's milk containing at least 30% fat.

Cream is sold under various names, depending on its fat content.

Coffee cream contains 10% fat. **Half-and-half** is a mixture of equal parts cream and milk, which is then pasteurized and sometimes homogenized, and contains 10.5%-18% fat. **Double cream** contains about 40% fat. **Dehydrated cream** contains 40%-70% fat.

:: Cream substitutes

Artificially made creams are also available on the market. They are sold dehydrated or frozen, in liquid form or in pressurized aerosol cans. These products, which include coffee creams and whipped creams, are made from hydrogenated vegetable or animal fats, sweeteners and additives. Most have no vitamin content and are higher in saturated fatty acids than the products they replace.

BUYING

Cream is sold pasteurized after being homogenized and, in some cases, sterilized, by normal methods or using the ultra-high temperature (UHT) process. Only light creams and table creams are homogenized. Check the use-by date on the packaging.

SERVING IDEAS

Cream is particularly used in coffee, vinaigrettes, soups, sauces, omelettes, terrines, desserts, sweets and digestive liqueurs.

Whipped cream decorates and enriches pastries, soufflés, pies, ice creams, charlottes, sauces and fruits. When sugar and vanilla is added to whipped cream, it becomes Chantilly cream.

Cream is essential for making Boston cream pie and cream puffs.

Cream that has soured can still be used, especially for cooking.

PREPARING

:: Whipping cream: whip the cream at the last moment unless storing it in the fridge. Preferably use utensils that have been chilled beforehand for 30 min in the fridge, or in the freezer, if time is short. Only mix in other ingredients (sugar, vanilla) once the cream has started to froth. Whipping cream will double in volume once it has been whipped. Whipped cream that has started to turn yellow may turn into butter.

NUTRITIONAL INFORMATION

	table cream 15% fat	whipping cream 35% fat
water	77.5%	59.6%
protein	0.8 g	0.6 g
fat	4.6 g	10.6 g
carbohydrates	1.2 g	0.8 g
cholesterol	16 mg	38 mg
		per 2 tbsp/30 ml

Whipping cream (35% fat) contains vitamin A. Cream is a high-energy food, as it is rather high in fat. Its fats are made up of 62% saturated fatty acids.

COOKING

In soups and simmered dishes, add cream only at the end of cooking to avoid lumps appearing; the mixture also should not boil afterward.

STORING

:: At room temperature: unopened UHT cream, 45 days.

:: In the fridge: fresh cream, coffee cream and half-and-half, until the use-by date; whipped cream, a few hours.

DAIRY PRODUCTS

Yogurt

plain yogurt

Milk fermented by lactic fermentation process. Yogurt is thought to be originally from Bulgaria. It is made from cow, goat, sheep and soy milk to which bacteria are added that convert part of the lactose (the main sugar in milk) into lactic acid: *Lactobacillus bulgaricus* and *Streptococcus thermophilus*. The milk coagulates when enough lactic acid is produced. When the yogurt has fermented enough, it needs to be cooled. Whether it is plain, stirred or set, the basic yogurt mixture essentially remains the same. Commercial manufacturing processes result in a firmer yogurt that is less likely to release whey, the yellowish liquid sometimes found on the surface of natural yogurts. There is a wide range of yogurts, including set yogurt (the oldest kind), stirred yogurt (a Swiss-invented process) and various products such as frozen yogurt, drinking yogurt and dehydrated yogurt.

Plain yogurt is made with either whole, lowfat or nonfat milk. It contains no additional flavorings or ingredients.

Set yogurt has the appearance of a compact jelly. It is fermented in a container, then cooled; if it is flavored with natural or artificial products, they are generally found at the bottom of the container.

Stirred yogurt is mixed following the fermentation and cooling process, which makes the product smooth and even. It can be flavored with natural or artificial ingredients, such as fruit.

Drinking yogurt is made from fermented milk, to which a fruit-flavored syrup or sugar and fruit has been added, and is sometimes promoted as an alternative to carbonated soft drinks.

Frozen yogurt is similar to soft-serve ice cream in texture.

Several of these products have been pasteurized or treated using the ultra-high temperature (UHT) process, and may contain additives.

There are also other forms of fermented milk.

Curdled milk is milk that has been fermented at room temperature using just the action of the lactic flora present in the milk. Curdled milk separates into two distinct parts: the curds and the whey. It is consumed as is after being stirred or drained. It must be used as soon as possible and stored in the fridge.

Kefir, or "kephir," probably originally from the Caucasus, is whole or reduced-fat milk that is fermented using several species of bacteria and yeasts, making it slightly fizzy and alcoholic, with a sharp and somewhat bitter flavor. The alcohol level is generally 1%. Kefir can be liquid, creamy and alcoholic depending on the length of the fermentation period. It froths and bubbles in a way that is similar to beer. It can be made with dried fruits or lemon. Kefir keeps in the fridge and is more perishable than yogurt. It can still be used after it sours, especially for cooking. It is delicious served chilled and garnished with mint leaves, or poured over fruit. It can be a beverage, used or eaten in the same way as yogurt.

Kumis is similar to kefir, but it is more alcoholic, with up to 2.5% alcohol. It is made with mare, donkey or cow's milk and is traditionally popular in Central Asia. Its flavor is reminiscent of white wine.

fruit yogurt

Yogurt

BUYING

Check the use-by or sell-by date when buying. After the indicated date, the yogurt may still be edible as long as it has a good taste and no molds or bubbles have appeared. The formation of liquid is not a sign of spoiling.

SERVING IDEAS

Yogurt is eaten as is and can also be cooked. It is added to soups, salads, meat, poultry, fish, rice, pasta dishes, breads, cakes, pies, brioches, desserts and drinks. Yogurt is used as a basic ingredient in several hot or cold soups, as well as for making cold sauces for grilled skewers. It is used to marinate and tenderize meat, poultry and game.

It is an important ingredient in Middle Eastern and Indian cuisines (it is an accompaniment to curries and the basis of *raitas*—fruits or vegetables mixed with flavored yogurt).

Plain yogurt can be used in place of cream, whether liquid, whipped or sour, and it can be added to mayonnaise or vinaigrette, reducing the level of calories and fat. If using it in place of cream in dishes requiring cooking, yogurt needs to be stabilized by adding a little cornstarch. Bring it to room temperature for 1-2 hr before adding it to hot dishes and, if possible, add at the very end of cooking.

PREPARING

Making yogurt at home is easy and economical, and provides yogurt without any added sugar and containing vitamins A and D.

Utensils must be carefully washed and rinsed well in hot water or sterilized before using. Milk is heated to 185°F (85°C) for about 30 min, after adding 3%-5% powdered skim milk. The fresh milk used at the start can be whole, reduced-fat or even UHT milk.

The level of fat and milk solids in the milk will affect the texture, flavor and nutritional value of the yogurt. Whole milk results in a firmer, tastier yogurt that is higher in fat and energy than a yogurt made from skim milk. The addition of milk powder (3-8 tablespoons/45-120 ml per 4 cups/1 l of milk) thickens the yogurt, makes it creamier and increases its nutritional value.

Gelatin or pectin can be added to the milk when it reaches the boiling point, if desired; measure 1 teaspoon (5 ml) per 4 cups (1 l) of milk. Let it swell up completely in a small amount of milk before mixing it in (gelatin is not required if a dehydrated culture is used, as the resulting yogurt is firm).

The use of a thermometer helps to monitor the boiling and establishes the exact moment to add the ferment.

Cool the milk to 110°F-115°F (43°C-46°C), then culture the yogurt with a ferment or a dehydrated (freeze-dried) culture, plain commercial yogurt (2-5 tablespoons/30-75 ml per 4 cups/1 l of milk) that still contains live bacteria (but not starch or gelatin) and is as fresh as possible, or homemade yogurt prepared within the previous 5 days.

In order to minimize contamination risks, take care (before eating the yogurt) to set aside the amount needed for the next culture. Yogurt made with a dehydrated culture is

kefir

creamier, thicker and less acidic than a yogurt made with a commercial yogurt; moreover, it keeps these qualities for a longer time and it can be used more than once to make more yogurt. After about 1 month, or 3 batches, the yogurt degenerates and a new ferment must then be used.

Avoid stirring yogurt while it is setting, or it will separate and become watery. Leave it to incubate for 4-6 hr at a constant temperature of at least 105°F (40°C).

The incubation temperature of yogurt is crucial. The ideal temperature is 105°F-115°F (40°C-46°C); don't allow the temperature to go above 115°F (46°C), or the heat will destroy the bacteria and prevent it setting; it is slower under 105°F (40°C), when a lower temperature prolongs the setting time and makes the yogurt more sour.

The use of a yogurt-maker is practical but not essential. Any source of constant heat protected from drafts will fulfill the same function. Yogurt can be incubated in an oven preheated to 120°F (50°C) or an oven with a bulb that provides the necessary heat. One can also use an insulated bottle (thermos) that has been heated beforehand, a plate or frying pan filled with hot water and covered with a thick cloth to keep the heat in, or a container wrapped in a blanket and placed in a turned-off oven, on a heater or near a weak but constant heat source.

When the yogurt has set, or when the desired texture and taste have been reached, refrigerate immediately to stop the activity. Fruits or other ingredients are added just before eating.

If the yogurt does not thicken, there may be more than one factor responsible: the culture may be too old, the temperature may be too high or too low, the incubation time may not be long enough or the amount of dry extracts (milk powder) too low. Reintroduce a ferment, add some milk powder, if desired, and incubate again.

If the yogurt is sour or the whey separates, the incubation may have been too long or the cooling process too slow. Mix the whey back into the yogurt by beating it (the mixture will, however, be more watery).

Homemade yogurt can be kept for 3 weeks in the fridge.

DAIRY PRODUCTS

Yogurt

PREPARING

1 Heat the milk to 185°F (85°C) for about 30 min.

2 Cool the milk to 110°F-115°F (43°C-46°C), then culture with a ferment.

3 Pour the mixture into a container, cover with food wrap and keep warm for 4-8 hr. When it reaches the desired texture and taste, refrigerate for 12 hr before eating.

DAIRY PRODUCTS

NUTRITIONAL INFORMATION

EXCELLENT SOURCE: protein, calcium, phosphorus, potassium and vitamins A and B. The nutritional value of plain unsweetened yogurt is almost equivalent to milk with, along with the assumed benefits resulting from the fermentation process. The level of fat, carbohydrates and calories in commercial yogurts varies. Some yogurts contain up to 10% fat. The cholesterol level varies between 7.5 and 12.5 mg for 100 g (3.5 oz) for plain and flavored versions. Its carbohydrate level is generally 7% for plain yogurt and 11%-18% for fruit yogurts. Some yogurts can contain food additives.

PROPERTIES: yogurt is said to favor longevity, be beneficial for the digestive system, useful in treating vaginal inflammations and warding off cancer and, taken before bedtime, encouraging sleep.

Yogurt is more easily digested than milk and contains bacteria that facilitate the digestion of lactose.

STORING

 Avoid keeping at room temperature as much as possible.

:: **At room temperature:** dehydrated yogurt ferments, 6 months.

:: **In the fridge:** 2-3 weeks; dehydrated ferments, 12 months.

:: **In the freezer:** 1 month; dehydrated ferments, 18 months.

Preferably defrost yogurt in the fridge.

Ice cream

Ice cream is a sweet, flavored mixture based on dairy products that have turned solid through freezing. Traditional ice cream contains milk, cream, sugar, natural flavors and eggs (though not always). When it begins to freeze, the mixture is beaten to stop the formation of ice crystals, which results in a light and creamy product. For a product to be called "ice cream," it must contain at least 10% fat, or 8% if there is added cocoa, chocolate syrup, fruits or nuts. If a product contains less fat, it is called a "dairy dessert."

Industrially made ice cream is generally made from a mixture of cream, milk or evaporated milk (or both), to which nonfatty milk solids are added. It also contains sugar (14%-16%), emulsifiers, stabilizers, flavors and colorings, sometimes natural but most often artificial. The yield is the increase in volume of a frozen product by adding air, also known as the "overrun." Ice cream with an overrun of 20%-50% would yield creamier ice cream; above 50% would yield mushy, liquidy ice cream that melts quickly.

ice cream

Ice cream

BUYING

:: **Choose:** firmly frozen containers of ice cream, without any frost. Preferably buy frozen products from a store with a constant turnover of stock to ensure maximum flavor and freshness. Check the label for food additives.

SERVING IDEAS

Ice cream and other frozen products are eaten as desserts and snacks. Ice cream is often topped with caramel or chocolate sauce, or served blended as a milk shake. It accompanies cakes, pies, crepes, waffles, fruits and cookies. It can be served with fresh or canned fruits, like a banana split or a fruit coulis.

Ice cream can be put in the oven without melting, as in Baked Alaska, as long as it is completely covered with meringue.

NUTRITIONAL INFORMATION

	vanilla ice cream 11% fat	vanilla ice cream 16% fat	vanilla ice milk (soft-serve)	vanilla ice milk (firm)	orange sorbet
water	61%	57%	69.6%	68%	66%
protein	3.5 g	3.5 g	4.9 g	3.8 g	1.1 g
fat	11 g	16 g	2.6 g	4.3 g	2.0 g
carbohydrates	23.6 g	22.4 g	21.8 g	22.7 g	30.4 g
cholesterol	44 mg	61 mg	12 mg	14 mg	7.3 mg

per 3.5 oz/100 g

A medium-sized portion of ice cream provides about 1 tablespoon (15 ml) of sugar. Soft-serve ice cream contains 2%-3% less sugar.

VANILLA ICE CREAM WITH 11% FAT

GOOD SOURCE: vitamin B_{12}.

CONTAINS: potassium, riboflavin, calcium, zinc, vitamin A, phosphorus and pantothenic acid.

VANILLA ICE CREAM WITH 16% FAT

CONTAINS: vitamin B_{12}, vitamin A, potassium, riboflavin, calcium, zinc and phosphorus.

ORANGE SORBET

CONTAINS: potassium, zinc and calcium.

SOFT-SERVE VANILLA ICE MILK

EXCELLENT SOURCE: vitamin B_{12}.

GOOD SOURCE: potassium and riboflavin.

CONTAINS: calcium, phosphorus, pantothenic acid and magnesium.

FIRM VANILLA ICE MILK

GOOD SOURCE: vitamin B_{12}.

CONTAINS: potassium, riboflavin, calcium, phosphorus and pantothenic acid.

There are also many frozen preparations apart from ice cream.

Ice milk contains less fat than ice cream (2%-7%). It is made from a pasteurized mixture of cream, milk or other sweetened dairy products. Its sugar content is just as high, or higher. It is slightly less creamy and tasty, and is more dense than ice cream.

Gelato is Italian ice cream. It contains less milkfat than American ice cream, yet is typically more dense because it contains less air. Similar products exist in other countries, like "glace" in France.

Sorbet is traditionally made with fruit juice or purée. It can also have a base of wine, liqueur, alcohol or an infusion, to which a sugar syrup is then added. It is hardly beaten or not at all; it doesn't contain egg yolk or fat but can contain egg white that has been beaten into Italian meringue, which is mixed in once the sorbet starts to set. It can also contain milk or milk solids. Commercially made sorbet is often just a mixture of water and milk solids (about 5%), artificially flavored, which contains up to twice as much sugar as ice cream and has a calorie content between firm milk ice and ice cream.

Granita is a kind of Italian sorbet made from a light syrup flavored with fruit, liqueur or coffee. Semifrozen before its texture is too hard, granita has a grainy texture; it is often served between courses or as a refreshment.

"Frozen tofu" or **Tofutti**® is a soy milk-based product to which vegetable oil and sugar has been added. Therefore, this product has no lactose or cholesterol. Its calorie content is as high as ice cream since it contains more fat. Compared to ice cream, Tofutti contains very few saturated fatty acids and contains two times less protein. It contains natural or artificial flavors, isolated soy proteins, soy lecithin and, like ice cream, several stabilizers.

STORING

Frozen products left at room temperature lose flavor and are more likely to contain ice crystals if they are refrozen.

:: In the freezer: 1 month, in an airtight container in the coldest part of the freezer.

sorbet

Cheese

A product obtained from coagulating and draining milk, cream or a mixture of the two. The quality, nutritional value and characteristics of cheese vary according to the type of milk used (cow, goat, sheep, buffalo), the method of production and local preferences.

CHEESE MAKING

Coagulation ("curdling") is the curd-forming stage, when the casein (the protein contained in the milk) coagulates in response to bacteria or rennet.

Drainage consists of removing the water (the whey or lactoserum) from the curd and making it firmer. The amount of whey retained in the curd after draining will determine the firmness and texture of the cheese. It is during the draining stage that the curd is shaped in a mold.

Salting acts as an antiseptic, slows down the development of microorganisms, improves the storage life of the cheese and speeds up the drying process and the formation of a rind. Cheeses can be salted from the outside (dry salting) or in a brine bath. Some cheeses are fermented with molds to obtain a "bloomy" rind (the "croûte fleurie" of Brie and Camembert) or the veins of blue cheeses (Roquefort, Gorgonzola).

Ripening (or maturing) is the period during which the inside of the cheese is transformed through the biochemical action of the bacterial flora contained in the cheese. This is the crucial stage in which the consistency, aroma, flavor and, if desired, the rind of the cheese develop (fresh curd cheeses and process cheeses are not ripened). Ripening takes place under temperature and humidity conditions that vary according to the type of cheese. The longer the ripening process, the less moisture the cheese retains, and the firmer and stronger-tasting the cheese will be.

Cheeses are generally classified according to their firmness.

Fresh cheeses (unripened) are coagulated through the action of lactic acid bacteria.

They are simply drained (cottage, ricotta, mascarpone, cream cheese, Petit Suisse, quark). They are not aged and should be eaten quickly. They are generally low-fat (0.1%-13% fat) and low-energy foods. They become high in fat and energy when they are made with cream (up to 30% fat, in the case of cream cheese).

cottage

Several contain additives, thickeners and preservatives. Fresh cheeses are smooth, creamy or granular, with a mild or slightly acidic flavor. They are used mainly in pastries and desserts. They are available plain or flavored with vegetables, fruits or spices.

Unripened stretched curd cheeses are obtained by kneading and stretching the undrained curd until it acquires the desired consistency. This process gives them a supple texture. This category includes mozzarella, scarmoza, provolone, bocconcini and caciotta. Mozzarella is especially popular as a topping on pizza and pasta.

Soft cheeses are ripened for a relatively short period, drained and molded. Fats make up 20%-26% of the weight of the cheese. They acquire a velvet-like rind. The fermentation process begins on the surface of the cheese and moves toward the center. They are not used very much in cooking, because they lose a great deal of flavor when heated.

Soft cheeses are divided into two categories.

- **Bloomy-rind cheeses** are covered with a thin layer of white down or mold, with a velvety appearance (Camembert, Brie, Brillat-Savarin, Coulommiers); this rind is edible, but should be removed if its taste is too strong.
- **Washed-rind cheeses** are cheeses that undergo light brine washes (Munster, Pont-l'Évêque, Livarot, Bel Paese, Époisses). They have a delicate flavor and intense aroma. The ripening of some of these cheeses is finished by dipping them in alcohol, such as wine or beer.

Camembert

Semi-firm cheeses are pressed, uncooked cheeses that undergo quite a long ripening period. These cheeses (Cheddar, Cantal, Reblochon, Gouda, Edam, Fontina, Saint-Nectaire, Morbier, Tomme, Tilsiter, Monterey Jack) have a dense consistency and a pale yellow interior.

Firm cheeses (or hard cheeses) are cheeses that are pressed and cooked. These cheeses (Gruyère, Emmental, Jarlsberg, Comté, raclette, Beaufort, Parmesan, Romano) may or may not possess a hard rind. The texture of the interior is generally firm, but can sometimes be very grainy, as in the case of Parmesan and Romano.

DAIRY PRODUCTS

Cheese

Blue-veined cheeses (or "blue cheeses") are cheeses whose curd is first broken into pieces, molded, drained, salted, then fermented with molds. Fermentation begins on the inside and moves toward the outside. A whole network of blue-green veins forms through the action of the molds, and becomes more dense over time. These cheeses (Roquefort, Gorgonzola, Bleu de Bresse, Danish Blue, Stilton) have a peppery, strong, sharp taste and usually a crumbly texture.

Processed cheeses are cheeses made from one or several cooked or uncooked pressed cheeses that are re-melted, and to which milk, cream or butter is added; they keep for a long time. Depending on the product, stabilizers, emulsifiers, salt, colors, sweeteners and seasonings may be added. This results in a soft, elastic texture and mild flavor. In North America, these cheeses are mostly made using Cheddar cheese, whereas in Europe, Emmental and Gruyère are used most. Processed cheeses have different names depending on the quantity of cheese they contain (processed cheese, processed cheese food, cheese spread).

Cheese substitutes are imitation cheeses sometimes made from a single milk component, such as casein, to which artificial emulsifiers, flavors and colors are added. Some natural ingredients are also incorporated (soy, corn).

Goat cheeses (sometimes called *chèvre*, the French word for "goat") are cheeses with a soft interior and natural rind and can be made from 100% goat's milk ("pure chèvre") or goat's milk mixed with cow's milk ("mi-chèvre," if it contains at least 25% goat's milk). These cheeses may be fresh, soft with a bloomy rind or sometimes firm. They are more white than cow's milk cheese and have a stronger flavor. Goat cheese is generally moist, smooth and very salty in order to prolong its storage life. Some goat cheeses have evocative names (Chabichou, Crottin de Chavignol, Valencay, Chevrotin). Feta cheese is included in this category, made using sheep's milk, cow's milk or a mixture with goat's milk.

ricotta

fresh goat cheese

BUYING

SOFT CHEESES

:: Choose: cheeses that are soft inside as well as out, with a creamy, consistent interior that is even in color and completely fills the rind, which should be smooth and not dry or cracked.

:: Avoid: cheeses with a solid, firm, chalky-white center, a sticky rind, a dark color or an ammonia smell. A hard rind and dry interior are signs of a cheese that has not been properly stored.

SEMI-FIRM CHEESES

:: Choose: cheeses that are neither dried out nor too crumbly. The interior of the cheese close to the rind should not be darker in color. They should not taste spoiled or sharp.

FIRM CHEESES

:: Choose: cheeses with an even color and consistency and a firm rind.

:: Avoid: dried out or bulging cheeses that are pasty or too grainy, with a cracked rind. They should not taste too salty or too bitter.

BLUE CHEESES

:: Choose: cheeses with a smaller or greater number of veins, depending on the variety, spread evenly throughout the interior of the cheese. This interior, which is usually white, should not be crumbly, too dry or too salty. Check the use-by date on the packaging and avoid cheeses that are left at room temperature.

SERVING IDEAS

Cheese is used for stuffing, topping meats and vegetables or as the main ingredient of a dessert. It is prepared with savory dishes—salads, sauces, soups, croquettes, pizzas, pasta dishes, crepes, soufflés, fondues, raclette, grilled ham and cheese sandwiches, omelettes—and sweet dishes (cakes, pies, donuts). When seasoning a dish, take into account the fact that cheese is generally salty, particularly blue cheeses, whose salty taste is enhanced during cooking. One cheese may be replaced with another of the same kind. Cheese is often served at the end of a meal or as an appetizer accompanied with wine.

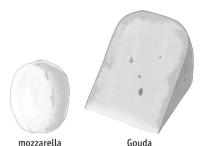

mozzarella   Gouda

Gruyère

DAIRY PRODUCTS

Cheese

NUTRITIONAL INFORMATION

The nutritional value of cheese varies according to the fat content of the liquid used (milk, cream) and the mode of production. The firmer the cheese, the more likely it contains a significant amount of calcium and protein, whereas fresh cheeses contain little calcium but are a source of protein; cream cheeses are low in both protein and calcium.

The quality of the protein in cheese, and its ability to be absorbed by the body, are excellent. Its carbohydrate content is generally minimal, whereas its fat (mostly made up of saturated fatty acids) and calorie content varies greatly. Soft cheeses are not necessarily the highest in fat—on the contrary. Fresh cheeses contain 5-51 mg cholesterol per 3.5 oz (100 g); cream cheeses can contain up to 110 mg; and blue cheeses, 75-90 mg. The higher the moisture content of a cheese, the lower it is in energy. Fresh cheeses contain up to 80% moisture; soft cheeses, 50%-60%; semi-firm cheeses, 40%-60%; and firm cheeses, a maximum of 35%. Fresh cheeses contain less calcium and phosphorus than firm cheeses.

Cheese contains fewer minerals than milk, but it still remains a good source. Sodium is usually present in considerable amounts; processed and blue cheeses are particularly high in sodium. Cheese remains a concentrated source of B vitamins. It still contains considerable amounts of vitamin A, except in the case of fresh and skim-milk cheeses, which have lower amounts. The rinds

process cheeses

feta

Roquefort

Munster

of certain soft-rind and bloomy-rind cheeses can contain more vitamins than the interior of the cheese.

Eating large amounts of cheese results in a high intake of fat, calories and salt, unless one chooses skim-milk and low-salt cheeses. It can also mean ingesting food additives, especially in the case of process cheese foods or cheese spreads. Some of these products, including colorings, play only an esthetic role; thus the only difference between a white Cheddar and a yellow Cheddar lies in the added coloring. Cheese cannot cause constipation. This condition is due rather to lack of fiber and water in the diet. Eating cheese after a meal can be beneficial as a form of protection against tooth decay.

Crottin de Chavignol

Monterey Jack

DAIRY PRODUCTS

cream cheese

Gorgonzola

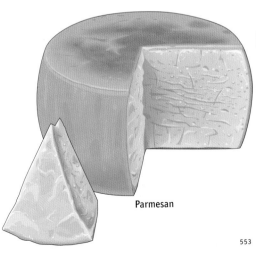

Parmesan

Cheese

STORING

 The storage life of cheeses mainly depends on their moisture content.

:: In the fridge: wrap the cheese well in a sheet of cheese paper or plastic wrap and place in the warmest area of the fridge.

- Fresh and blue-veined cheeses are placed 7-10 days in an airtight container or tightly wrapped.
- Soft cheeses keep a short time, especially when they have become ripe.
- Semi-firm cheeses keep for several weeks.
- Firm cheeses keep for 2 weeks.
- Grated cheeses keep for 1 week.

Cheeses can also be stored at a temperature of 50°F-55°F (10°C-12°C). Surface-ripened cheeses (bloomy-rind, washed-rind) should not be vacuum-packed or sealed airtight. For better flavor, remove cheeses from the fridge at least 30 min before eating them. If mold has developed on the surface of a firm cheese, cut off ½-¾ in. (1-2 cm) around the mold and cover with another piece of wrapping. Discard fresh and soft cheeses with such mold.

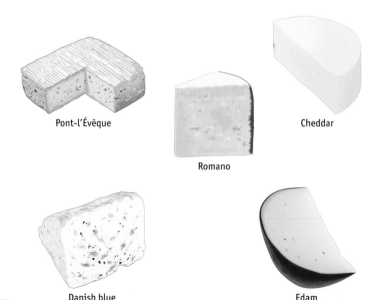

Pont-l'Évêque

Romano

Cheddar

Danish blue

Edam

sugar and molasses are almost entirely composed of carbohydrates. The main forms of carbohydrate include the simple carbohydrates, complex carbohydrates, fiber and sugar alcohols or polyols (sorbitol, mannitol and xylitol).

Simple carbohydrates are divided into monosaccharides and disaccharides.

Monosaccharides are made up of a single sugar molecule. They include glucose, fructose, galactose and mannose.

Disaccharides are formed from two monosaccharides and have one less water molecule. The most common are sucrose, lactose and maltose.

Glucose (or "dextrose") is the most abundant monosaccharide in nature. It is present in fruits, cereals and grains, honey, nuts, flowers and leaves. The glucose found in the blood serves to maintain body temperature and provide the necessary energy for vital processes.

Fructose (or "levulose") is found in natural form in fruits (2%-7%), honey (40%) and various other foods. It is the sweetest-tasting of all of the sugars, its sweetening power being one-and-a-half times greater than table sugar; it is also about three times sweeter than glucose. Fructose is refined into crystalline and syrup forms.

Generally speaking, any sugar solution that is heated with an acidic ingredient or added enzymes will cause the sugar molecule to break down into glucose and fructose; this mixture is called "invert sugar."

Invert sugar, like corn syrup, resists crystallization and holds moisture, which makes both of these products popular in the confectionery and baking industries. They are also used in making sweetmeats, preserves and glazes. Invert sugar is only sold in liquid form. It is also sweeter than sucrose.

Sucrose (or "saccharose") is made up of glucose and fructose. It occurs in plants that perform photosynthesis. It is particularly abundant in sugarcane, sugar beet and maple syrup. It is the common white sugar or table sugar.

Lactose is made up of glucose and galactose. It is only present in milk (5%-8% in breast milk and 4%-6% in cow's milk). It is used as a food additive in several food products, as a flavor enhancer among other things.

Maltose is made up of two glucose molecules. Maltose is created when the starch found in malt is hydrolyzed through the action of the diastase enzyme. Commonly used in the food industry, it is incorporated into beer, bread, infant foods and coffee substitutes.

SUGARS, COCOA AND CAROB

Sugar

White sugar (or "table sugar," "refined sugar," "granulated sugar") is the most well-known common sugar. It is made of pure dry sugar crystals obtained once the refining process is complete. It contains 99.9% sucrose and no vitamins or mineral salts.

Powdered sugar or **confectioner's sugar,** also called "icing sugar," is pulverized white sugar to which about 3% cornstarch is added to prevent lumps forming. It absorbs more quickly into liquids.

Molasses is a by-product of cane sugar refining. The molasses obtained from the first extraction (called "first molasses") is pale and very sweet. The molasses from the second extraction, called "second" or table molasses, is darker and moderately sweet. The molasses from the third and last extraction is black ("black-strap molasses") and less sweet with a strong flavor; it is the kind that contains the most nutrients. Molasses contains 35% sucrose and 20% glucose and fructose. It can be used to make alcohol and yeast, for human consumption and for making rum.

Liquid sugar is a sugar syrup in the form of a clear solution containing a highly refined sugar. It is used in canned foods, sweets, pastry-making, ice cream, etc.

white sugar

SERVING IDEAS

 Refined sugar is used to modify the texture of foods, to enhance their flavor, to sweeten acidic or tart-tasting foods, to feed yeast (when making bread, for example) and as a preservative.

Sugar is essential for making meringues, ice creams, sorbets, syrups and confectionery. It is used as a condiment (glazed vegetables, glazed ham, sweet-and-sour dishes) and is one of the main ingredients in pastries and sweets.

To reduce sugar intake:

• Gradually reduce the amount of sugar added to foods that do not really need it until it is completely eliminated (coffee, tea, vinaigrette, juice, yogurt and on grapefruit).

• Enhance the reduced amount of sugar using spices (cinnamon, ginger, nutmeg) or replace the sugar with fruit that give a natural sweetness to cereal, muffins and cookies.

• Reduce sugar by half in most recipes for cakes, muffins, quick breads, pastries and other desserts that call for more than ⅔ cup (175 ml).

• Read labels: generally the suffix "-ose" indicates the presence of sugar; if several names for sugar are found on the list of ingredients, the food will often contain too much sugar.

Significantly reducing sugar intake may lead to certain symptoms such as irritability and fatigue; these symptoms usually only last a week.

corn syrup

molasses

SUGARS, COCOA AND CAROB

Sugar

NUTRITIONAL INFORMATION

The nutritional value of sugar is very limited.
Sugar contains no protein, fat or fiber and has
no vitamins or minerals. It is essentially made
up of carbohydrates and provides 16 calories
per teaspoon (5 ml) for granulated sugar, or
9 calories per teaspoon (5 ml) for powdered
sugar.

Sugar and very sugary foods are often called
"empty calorie" foods because of their lack of
nutrients. Overconsumption of sugar, especially
saccharose, is thought to be a determining
factor in the appearance of tooth decay. This is
why brushing teeth is recommended after eating
sweet or sticky foods.

With regard to establishing a link between
sugar consumption and the development
of glucose intolerance, the current level
of sugar consumption does not represent
a risk factor. There is, moreover, no
conclusive proof linking dietary sugar to the
development of coronary illness or obesity or
behavioral changes in children.

Sugar can cause the retention of fluids,
which is why some people may feel thirsty
after eating sweet foods.

powdered sugar

STORING

:: **At room temperature:** indefinitely,
away from moisture, in a cool and dry
place and in airtight containers. Molasses can
be stored at room temperature, as well as in
the fridge, which makes it thicker and more
difficult to pour.

Sugar substitutes

Sugar substitutes are artificial sweeteners with high-level sweetening powers. They are used in place of sugar, as they contain very few or no calories. The use of high-intensity sweeteners goes back to 1879 with the discovery of saccharin. Its use dominated the market for almost 60 years, until cyclamates appeared in the 50s and 60s, finally superseded today by aspartame. At the beginning of the century, the aim of research into artificial sweeteners was to produce a substance with similar qualities to sugar, but at a lower cost. Today, the goal of this research is to create products that are lower in calories.

In several countries, certain sugar substitutes are subject to restrictions or are prohibited, as their safety for health is not yet proven. Artificial sweeteners are considered to be food additives as defined under United States and Canadian law concerning food and drugs, because they are synthetic substances that do not exist in food in its natural state. In Canada, only aspartame can be used as a food additive. Saccharin is still approved as a food additive and is used as such in the United States, whereas in Canada, saccharin and the cyclamates cannot be used as food additives. They can, however, be sold as table sweeteners.

cyclamate

Saccharin is a coal tar derivative; it contains no calories and its sweetening power is 300-500 times higher than sugar. It also does not increase the risk of tooth decay. The use of saccharin has been restricted in Canada since 1978, after research apparently showed that it caused bladder cancer in rats. The sale of foods containing saccharin is thus prohibited there, but the free sale of saccharin in the form of a table sweetener is still authorized. In various countries, including the United States, the use of saccharin as a food additive is allowed.

Cyclamates are a product derived from benzene. They have no calories, and have a sweetening power equivalent to 30 times that of sugar; they also do not cause tooth decay. Cyclamates are sold in about 40 countries, including Canada and France, where they are only used as table sugar. Cyclamates are available as table sweeteners in tablet, powder, cube or liquid form.

Aspartame is the result of combining two amino acids, aspartic acid and phenylalanine (sometimes glucose or lactose is added). It contains the same amount of calories as sugar, about 16 calories per teaspoon (5 ml), but its sweetening power is about 180 times higher. Aspartame does not cause tooth decay and leaves no aftertaste. On the other hand, it cannot be used for cooking because it will lose all of its sweetening power. It is the only sweetener approved for use as a food additive in both the United States and Canada. Despite everything, the safety of aspartame continues to be a preoccupation in both the scientific world and the media.

The daily allowable intake (DAI) (over a lifetime) has been set at 40 mg per 2 lb (40 mg/kg) of body weight, which is the equivalent of a 130 lb (58 kg) person consuming 16 10-ounce (300 ml) cans of diet soft drink every day. The only officially recognized contraindication regarding the consumption of aspartame concerns those suffering from phenylketonuria, a hereditary disorder of the metabolism in which phenylalanine, one of the main components of aspartame, accumulates in the blood. The difficulty is that about 2% of the population are carriers of one of the two genes that cause the disorder, without showing any symptoms. Those carrying the gene risk being affected by increased phenylalanine levels in their blood. These phenylalanine concentrations, however, are only slightly higher than the norm and are thus not considered to be neurotoxic. Pregnant women who are unaware of their condition could develop concentrations of phenylalanine in their placenta, thus exposing the fetus to higher concentrations than in the mother's blood. This is why pregnant women shouldn't consume more than 40 mg aspartame per 2 lb (1 kg) of body weight per day. It is recommended, moreover, that high-intensity sweeteners in general be avoided during pregnancy.

Aspartame is an ingredient in a number of products, including medications, vitamins and many foods, such as cereal, juice, cookies, puddings, cakes, pastries, pies, ice cream, yogurt, vinaigrette and gums. Some researchers recommend that pregnant women and children under six avoid aspartame; several studies also conclude that even for children, a moderate consumption of drinks containing this sweetener presents no risk. For the general population, limited intake is recommended, particularly for people who may be sensitive to it.

Sugar substitutes

Sucralose, the most recently developed artificial sweetener, is made from ordinary sugar and chlorine. This sweetener has the sweet taste of sugar, but its sweetening power is 600 times higher. It does not cause tooth decay. In the United States and Canada, sucralose is authorized for use in cereals, drinks, desserts, chewing gum and sweets, pastries and baked goods, among other things. Given its high sweetening power, only a very small quantity is needed; it must therefore be mixed with powdered starch to be measured. Calories from sucralose come from this starch. The daily allowable intake (DAI) is 9 mg per 2 lb (9 mg/kg) of body weight, or the equivalent of four packets per day. It is sold in granulated form and in packets.

Consuming artificially sweetened foods does not seem to contribute very much to the reduction of obesity levels. These products can help people who are monitoring their weight by allowing them to eat sweet foods, but it is only a quick-fix solution. In effect, sweetened foods without sugar only maintain the taste for sugar.

Honey

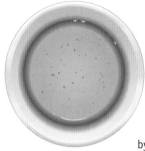

liquid honey

A sweet substance made from the nectar of flowers by bees, who use some of it as food.

The bees collect the nectar from flowers with their tongue and project it into their "crop" (a pouch located in the digestive tube). The nectar is transformed into honey through enzymes in the saliva and gastric juices. This transformed nectar is deposited by the bees in the cells of the hive and ventilated by vigorous wing-beating to reduce its moisture content by 14%-20%. The honey is then ready to eat.

About 10 pints (5 l) of nectar are necessary to obtain 4 cups (1 l) of honey. The quantity and quality of the honey are determined by geographical, seasonal and botanical factors. Names are not regulated in all countries: In the United States, the word "honey" must appear on its product label, though the name of the plant or blossom it came from only has to appear if it was the primary floral source for the honey.

There is a very wide variety of honeys. Some are made using the nectar of a single type of flower, while others are mixed; these honeys are called "polyflora" honeys (the bees have gathered nectar from several species of plant, or the producer has combined more than one honey variety). The floral origin of the nectar influences the color of the honey, its flavor and viscosity. The color varies from white to almost black, passing through brown, russet and blond hues. As a general rule, the darker the honey, the stronger the flavor. Among the most common honeys, clover, canola and alfalfa honeys are pale and moderate in flavor; heather honey is russet-colored and strong-tasting; and acacia honey is very mild, transparent and liquid.

SUGARS, COCOA AND CAROB

BUYING

 :: Choose: a 100% pure honey (read the label).

Honey is sold in liquid or creamed form and is often pasteurized. Creamed honey is obtained by adding finely crystallized honey, which sets off the crystallization process in the liquid honey. This honey should have a fine texture.

PREPARING

Honey has a tendency to crystallize at room temperature, but it becomes liquid again if the container is heated in hot water for about 15 min. Heating honey in the microwave oven is not recommended, as this increases its levels of hydroxy-methyl-furfural (HMF), which affects its taste.

Honey

NUTRITIONAL INFORMATION

water	14%-20%
protein	0.3%-0.5%
carbohydrates	76%-80%

The carbohydrates in honey contain on average 5% saccharose, 25%-35% glucose, 35%-45% fructose and 5%-7% maltose. Honey contains more calories than sugar for the same volume—1 teaspoon (5 ml) of honey has 64 calories while 1 tablespoon (15 ml) of sugar has 48 calories.

Honey only contains trace amounts of vitamins and minerals; from a nutritional point of view, the only advantage it has over sugar is its higher sweetening power.

PROPERTIES: purifying, antiseptic, tonifying, sedative, antipyretic, aperitive and digestive.

COOKING

In recipes, 1 cup (250 ml) of sugar can be replaced with ¾ or ⅔ cup (200 ml or 150 ml) of honey and the quantity of liquid reduced by 1.7 oz (50 ml). Monitor the cooking time and reduce the cooking temperature by 25°F (15°C). Honey can replace part or all of the sugar in jams and jellies, which will have a slightly different flavor.

STORING

:: **At room temperature:** almost indefinitely, in a cool and dry place. High temperatures can change its flavor and make its color darker.

:: **In the freezer**.

creamed honey

SERVING IDEAS

Honey is an ingredient in sweet dishes (pastries, cakes, flans, creams, yogurts, cookies, candies, nougat, syrups, gingerbread and Greek baklava) and savory ones (chicken, delicatessen meats, lamb, duck and couscous). It is used as a spread, and in tea, coffee and herbal teas. It is used to make sweet-and-sour sauces. Honey is more easily measured when it is lukewarm and if it is poured into an oiled container (the oil prevents it from sticking). It is the basic ingredient of mead, a drink obtained from the alcoholic fermentation of honey mixed with water. Mead can also be distilled or turned into vinegar. Honey is also used in the manufacture of medications and beauty products.

Giving honey to children less than one year old is not recommended, as it may contain a toxin, *Clostridium botulinum*. This type of botulism does not develop in children over the age of one or in adults.

Maple syrup

Maple syrup is obtained from reducing the sap of certain species of maple tree (sugar maple, red maple and black maple). These trees are found mainly in Quebec (the world's largest producer), New York and Vermont. The sap is collected at the end of winter, during the thawing period and before the appearance of buds, namely from January to April. The harvest is carried out by cutting into the tree; often a system of tubes collects the sap and channels it directly to the "sugar house," where it is boiled. The sap is a transparent and almost tasteless liquid containing 4%-10% sugar. About 30-40 quarts (30-40 l) of sap are needed for 4 cups (1 l) of syrup. This syrup then contains 66.5% sugar.

A recent procedure, reverse osmosis, enables 4 cups (1 l) of syrup to be obtained from only 10 quarts (10 l) of liquid.

BUYING

There are different grades, which relate to when the maple syrup is produced. "Light" or "#1 Extra Light" signifies early-season syrup (which is milder). "#2," "#3" or "Grade B" are produced late in the season and are dark and stronger in flavor. The name "maple syrup" can only be used for 100% pure products.

A syrup that is not very dense will be unstable and have a tendency to ferment and go sour, whereas a syrup that is too dense will crystallize more easily. The flavors vary as much as the colors.

STORING

:: **At room temperature:** keep unopened maple syrup in a cool and dry place.

:: **In the fridge:** an opened container. If molds appear on the surface, discard the whole container.

The crystallization of the syrup at the bottom and on the sides of the container may be caused by a product that is adulterated or has been stored for a long time.

:: **In the freezer:** maple syrup, maple butter, maple sugar and maple taffy.

maple syrup

NUTRITIONAL INFORMATION

water	34%
carbohydrates	32.5 g
	per 3 tbsp/40 ml

Maple syrup contains fewer calories than the same quantity of honey. It contains more minerals than honey and those it contains (calcium, iron, phosphorus and potassium) are slightly more concentrated.

SERVING IDEAS

Maple sap is made into syrup, taffy, sugar (hard or soft) and butter. The syrup is used to make maple syrup pies, soufflés, mousses and cakes. It is used to cook ham and eggs, for sweetening tea, coffee and herbal teas, and for topping pancakes and waffles. It is eaten by itself or on bread, as is maple sugar.

Maple taffy is eaten during the sugaring season and mainly in the sugar house, where it is poured on snow, while still hot, which hardens it immediately.
To replace sugar with maple syrup, reduce the quantity of liquid in the recipe by about ½ cup (115 ml) per 1 cup (250 ml) of syrup used.

Carob

Ceratonia siliqua, Leguminosae-Caesalpinioideae

The fruit of the carob tree, which likely originated in Syria. The food industry uses carob a great deal as a cocoa substitute and food additive, for its stabilizing, binding and gelling properties. Carob is also used as a coffee substitute and as animal feed.

The carob tree provides two quite distinct products, namely **carob powder**, similar to cocoa, which is obtained from the pods, and **carob gum**, which is obtained from the carob beans in the pod.

Unlike cocoa, carob doesn't contain theobromine, a stimulant similar to caffeine. Carob is very sweet so it is not necessary to add sugar when using it in place of cocoa. The flavor of carob is enhanced, however, by adding cinnamon or mint.

BUYING

Carob is generally bought in natural food stores. It is sold in solid (powder, chips) or liquid (syrup) form.

carob powder

NUTRITIONAL INFORMATION

	powder
water	3.6%
protein	1.4 g
fat	0.2 g
carbohydrates	26.7 g
fiber	3.7 g
	per 5 tbsp/75 ml

Carob powder contains much less protein and fat than cocoa. It is much lower in phosphorus, potassium and iron, but it is twice as high in calcium.

Carob powder is a rich source of fiber. It contains tannins. It is not allergenic and is easily digested.

The nutritional value of carob-based products depends on the ingredients they are made of, since sugar and vegetable oil, in particular, are often incorporated.

STORING

 :: At room temperature: keep carob in an airtight container away from moisture.

carob pods

SERVING IDEAS

Carob is used in the same way as cocoa and chocolate. It is used especially in cakes, cookies, drinks and sweets. It is used as is or combined with cocoa or chocolate. For each part cocoa, one can substitute 1½ to 2 parts carob by weight in most recipes. It is best, however, to add strong-tasting ingredients to enhance its flavor. When carob powder is used in place of cocoa, reduce the quantity of sugar in the recipe by about one-quarter. Carob is less soluble than cocoa. Blending the carob with hot water first allows it to dissolve better. Carob melts at a lower temperature than chocolate and becomes liquid more quickly, which can be a problem when making mousses, for example.

Cocoa

Theobroma cacao, Malvaceae

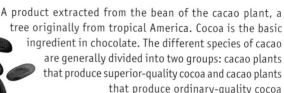

A product extracted from the bean of the cacao plant, a tree originally from tropical America. Cocoa is the basic ingredient in chocolate. The different species of cacao are generally divided into two groups: cacao plants that produce superior-quality cocoa and cacao plants that produce ordinary-quality cocoa (used mostly in industry).

The fruit of the cacao plant, its pod, is an oblong berry measuring up to 12 in. (30 cm) long and 3-5 in. (7-13 cm) wide. It contains a gelatinous pulp that harbors

cacao beans

30-40 pink or pale purple seeds (beans). These seeds are made up of a kernel, a seed coat and a germ. Only the kernels are eaten, and only after being processed, as they are very bitter.

The treatment process comprises the following stages:

- **Fermentation** alters the composition of the beans. It generally lasts 3-9 days at a temperature that may reach 125°F (50°C). The beans are then dried in the sun.
- **Sorting** removes the foreign matter (rocks and debris) and enables the beans to be graded.
- **Roasting**, which transforms some of the tannins, reduces bitterness and allows the flavor of the bean to develop, which will eventually determine the flavor and color of the final product.
- **Cooling**.
- **Cracking** allows the shells of the beans to be removed by crushing them between steel cylinders at a temperature of 125°F-165°F (50°C-72°C). The resulting paste is called cocoa mass, chocolate liquor or chocolate mass; it is made up of about 53% cocoa butter, a pale yellow fat.
- **Cocoa powder** is obtained from pressing the chocolate mass to extract the cocoa butter; the resulting paste (cake) is cooled, crushed, then sifted. Cocoa powder can contain 10%-25% fat.

MAKING CHOCOLATE

The chocolate mass (cocoa mass) is first mixed with sugar and cocoa butter; after being heated and stirred (conching), then cooled (or tempering), chocolate is obtained.

The regulation of the names given to chocolate products, depending on their composition, is a government matter and each country establishes its own standards.

Unsweetened chocolate, or cocoa mass, is the solidified chocolate mass without added sugar or milk solids. Chocolate makers and confectioners use this for cooking; its bitter flavor, which is chocolatey but not sweet, making it inedible as is.

Dark chocolate includes bittersweet chocolate and semisweet chocolate; these contain 35%-70% (or higher) cocoa mass as well as cocoa butter, sugar and sometimes emulsifiers. (Bittersweet has less sugar and more chocolate/cocoa mass than semisweet.) These chocolates are eaten plain or used in cooking.

Milk chocolate contains milk powder, sugar and flavorings (vanilla) that are mixed with the cocoa butter, resulting in a chocolate with a mild flavor and smooth texture; it should not, however, be used in cooking, as it burns when cooked.

White chocolate is made using cocoa butter (but no cocoa solids), which is combined with concentrated or powdered milk, sugar and vanilla essence. This chocolate has a milder flavor and creamier texture than darker chocolate. It is not used as much in sweets as dark chocolate.

cocoa powder

Numerous chocolate substitutes are also produced, which may or may not contain cocoa. Various additives are used in these to imitate the color, texture and flavor of genuine chocolate.

SUGARS, COCOA AND CAROB

Cocoa

BUYING

:: Choose: chocolate with a pleasant smell, brown or dark brown in color, shiny, that when snapped shows a clean, matte break, without small burst bubbles or white spots. It should melt evenly in the mouth or immediately in contact with the heat of the hand. Soft, tender chocolate contains more cocoa butter than hard, brittle chocolate.
:: Avoid: dull, grayish, whitish or crystallized chocolate.
Check the ingredients of chocolate to ensure that it is not a substitute.

PREPARING

Cocoa powder is high in starch, which makes it difficult to blend with other substances. Mix it with a cold liquid (if it is hot, lumps will form) or add sugar to it, which separates the starch particles; it can also be mixed after sifting.

STORING

:: At room temperature: wrap chocolate well and keep it away from moisture and heat (about 65°F/18°C).
:: In the fridge: well-wrapped.
:: In the freezer: freezing can lead to the appearance of a white "bloom" due to the cocoa butter rising to the surface; this doesn't affect the flavor of the chocolate at all and disappears when the chocolate is melted. Avoid moisture both when cooking and storing chocolate.

dark chocolate

NUTRITIONAL INFORMATION

	powder
protein	5.4 g
fat	7.8 g
carbohydrates	15.6 g
fiber	12.0 g
	per 6 tbsp/90 ml

The cocoa kernel or bean contains protein, fat (cocoa butter), carbohydrate, xanthines (caffeine and theobromine), tannins, cellulose, oxalic acid, small quantities of minerals, in particular phosphorus, potassium and iron, and negligible quantities of vitamins A and B. Cocoa and chocolate contain 10%-20% protein. Chocolate contains about 50% fat and cocoa 10%-22%. The industry frequently removes this fat (used especially in cosmetic products) and often replaces it with coconut butter or palm oil.

COCOA POWDER AND LOW-FAT COCOA POWDER

EXCELLENT SOURCE: copper, potassium, vitamin B_{12} and iron.

GOOD SOURCE: phosphorus.

CONTAIN: riboflavin, pantothenic acid, niacin and thiamine.

TRACES: calcium and vitamin B_6.

Cocoa powder and low-fat cocoa powder are very rich sources of fiber. The number of calories varies according to the ingredients in the chocolate.

Cocoa and chocolate contain theobromine, a stimulant similar to caffeine. The quantity of this stimulant is less than in coffee, which reduces their intensity, but their effects remain the same. Chocolate contains phenylethylamine, a chemical substance that releases serotonin in the brain; the effects on the neurotransmitters in the brain are said to be similar to those that are responsible for the euphoric state of being in love.

Cocoa contains the same antioxidants (phenols) as red wine, which are believed to be beneficial to heart function.

SUGARS, COCOA AND CAROB

white chocolate

Cocoa

milk chocolate

SERVING IDEAS

 Cocoa and chocolate are used to flavor cakes, pies, puddings, cookies, sauces, frostings, ice cream, mousses, flans, breads, candies, syrups, milk, drinks and liqueurs. Chocolate bars may contain peanuts, almonds, hazelnuts, caramel, cherries, cookies, nougat, fruit paste and alcohol. Chocolate truffles and molded Easter eggs are also found.

In some countries, Spain and Mexico, for example, chocolate is cooked with savory dishes. It flavors sauces used on seafood, chicken, duck, rabbit and turkey, including the famous *mole poblano*, a turkey stew with bittersweet chocolate, bell pepper and sesame.

Chocolate fondue, originally from Switzerland, is prepared using chocolate with almonds, nougat and honey that is melted, with cream and a dash of alcohol added. Fresh fruit, pieces of bread and dry cookies are dipped in it.

COOKING

Cooking improves the digestibility and flavor of cocoa.

To melt chocolate for a dish, the temperature of the chocolate must never exceed 115°F (45°C) for milk and white chocolate, or 120°F (50°C) for dark chocolate, and no water can come into contact with the chocolate. A double boiler is usually used, which is heated gently, uncovered, and into which the chocolate is placed, broken into pieces, and constantly stirred until it begins to melt. Remove from heat immediately after chocolate has melted. Do not overcook.

Fats and oils

Fats and oils may also simply be called "fats." They can be of plant origin (olive oil, sunflower oil, walnut oil, etc.) or of animal origin, such as duck fat or butter.
Fats and oils should form an essential part of the diet, as they represent an important source of energy and contribute to the body functioning well.

Margarine

A substance developed in France in 1869 to replace butter, which at the time was rare and costly. Most of the margarines sold in North America are based on vegetable oil or a combination of vegetable oils. Animal fat and certain oils, such as coconut oil, palm oil and palm kernel oil, are naturally highly saturated, which is why manufacturers use small quantities of them to achieve the desired texture; these margarines are thus not hydrogenated.

In Europe, the term "margarine" is used to refer to any food item with the appearance of butter and made to be used in the same way as butter. In the United States, margarine must contain at least 80% fat from any vegetable or animal source, natural or hydrogenated, although it is usually made from corn, cottonseed or soybean oil. It may also contain skim milk, water, salt and emulsifiers. To market margarine effectively, emphasis is put on the fact that it contains polyunsaturated fatty acids, which are considered beneficial for health. However, part of the oil contained in most margarines is hydrogenated. The harder the margarine, the more hydrogenated it is and the more "trans" fatty acids it contains.

margarine

FATS AND OILS

Margarine

Soft margarines containing less than 10% "trans" fatty acids are available on the market, as well as soft margarines based on nonhydrogenated fats. The potential effect these nonhydrogenated margarines (as well as those containing less than 10% trans fatty acids) have on elevating cholesterol levels is lower than butter and hard margarines.

BUYING

Margarine can be hard, soft, liquid or whipped, salted or unsalted. There are ordinary margarines, margarine spreads and diet margarines. To find out the fatty acid composition in a margarine, it is better to choose one with a nutritional information table. Also, choose a soft margarine over a hard one.

SERVING IDEAS

Since they have a high water content, diet margarines are not suitable for cooking or baking; they are only used as a spread.

Ordinary margarine can be used in place of butter in almost all recipes, as well as for cooking; the resulting flavor, however, is not always the same. Like butter, margarine is not appropriate for deep-frying. To prevent margarine from browning and burning during cooking, use a product that does not contain milk powder or whey.

NUTRITIONAL INFORMATION

Like butter, margarine is best consumed in moderation; it is high in fat and calories. It contains the same quantity of fat and calories as butter, about 11 g of fat and 100 calories per 1 tablespoon (15 ml), depending on the kind of margarine. Margarine made only from vegetable oil has no cholesterol.

Ordinary margarine contains 82% fat and 16% water. There are diet margarines whose fat content is lower (about 40%) and whose water content is higher (55%-59%).

A wide range of other ingredients is used in variable proportions during the manufacturing of margarine, including milk solids like buttermilk, vegetable colors, preservatives, emulsifiers, antioxidants, flavorings, sweeteners, modified starch and salt.

When used as a butter substitute, food regulations require that margarine be enriched with vitamins A and D.

STORING

:: **In the fridge:** margarine must be wrapped or stored in an airtight container.

:: **In the freezer:** the same as for refrigerated margarine.
Do not expose margarine to heat.

Fats

In food contexts, "fats" generally refers to liquid or solid substances used for cooking foods as well as seasoning, binding, emulsifying and preserving them. These fats can be of animal origin—butter, pork fat (lardo and lard), beef tallow, suet, goose fat, etc.—or plant origin—vegetable fat, most margarines, corn oil, sunflower oil and nut oils, etc., or as shortening, which is a fat based on several vegetable oils, sometimes with animal fats added and solidified through hydrogenation.

lard

FATS AND OILS

SERVING IDEAS

For a long time, it was believed that foods high in saturated fats (butter, red meat, cheese, etc.) could be replaced by foods containing mostly unsaturated fats (polyunsaturated oil and margarine, white meat, etc.) without concern for overall fat consumption. It has been discovered, however, that the amount of fat consumed, particularly, the amount of saturated fat, is the primary factor to be taken into consideration. It has also been discovered that polyunsaturated fatty acids are not as beneficial for health as previously believed. Monounsaturated fatty acids have been found to be equally, if not more, beneficial than polyunsaturated fatty acids. Therefore, it could be beneficial to incorporate olive oil, for example, which is high in monounsaturated fats, into the daily diet. For active people following a balanced diet, daily fat intake should not represent more than 35% of a total diet. People with a sedentary lifestyle should not eat more than 30%. It can prove difficult to reduce fat consumption, since the fat can often come from sources that may be "invisible." In effect, in many foods produced by the food industry or prepared in restaurants, a large part of the calories may come from fats.

Fats

Here are some tips to reduce fat consumption:

- Reduce portion sizes of meat, and choose lean meats or remove the fat before cooking: round, flank, rib-eye or sirloin in the case of beef; loin, shoulder or fillet for pork; escalope, chop or thigh for veal as well as for poultry, horse meat and game.
- Use a nonstick frying pan so that only a small amount or no fat is added.
- Opt for low-fat dairy products: choose cheeses containing less than 20% fat.
- Choose cooking methods that do not require much fat (baking, broiling and grilling, steaming or microwaving).
- Avoid hydrogenated fats: hard margarines, shortenings, deep-fried foods, crackers, cookies, cake mixes, snack foods, imitation cheese products, potato chips. Opt for nonhydrogenated margarine.
- Vary the types of fat in the diet. Choose a vegetable oil (cold-pressed or not), a small amount of butter and a nonhydrogenated margarine. Avoid foods that are high in tropical oils such as cookies, certain baked goods and certain cereals.

Read the list of ingredients, the nutritional information table and the fat content of the food on the product label carefully. Only foods of animal origin contain cholesterol and the term "light" on a food does not necessarily mean it is lower in fat. A "light" olive oil, for example, will simply have a light taste, and having the words "no cholesterol" on a vegetable oil is rather misleading. On the other hand, "light" butters and margarines genuinely contain half of the calories of the ordinary product, but cannot be used for cooking, as their water content is very high. They are thus reserved for spreading on bread or other uses.

ghee (clarified butter)

Reducing consumption of "added" fats represents the simplest and most effective way of managing dietary intake of fat in general. A reduction in dietary fat intake should, as a matter of necessity, be accompanied by a reduction in saturated fats, in order to reduce risk factors for coronary illnesses, since saturated fatty acids are the most associated with "high" cholesterol increasing the LDLs ("bad") and reducing HDLs ("good") cholesterol.

:: Fat substitutes

The use of a fat substitute was approved in the United States and Canada several years ago; it is a mixture of egg protein and milk. Its taste has the unctuous quality typical of fat. On labels, it is indicated by the words "protein microparticles." This substitute only contains 1 or 2 calories per gram, as opposed to 9 for fats. At the moment, this substitute is only used in the commercial food industry, particularly in the ice cream industry and as a thickener and textural modifier for frozen desserts. It does not tolerate very high temperatures, so it cannot be used for deep-frying.

A fat substitute has been created in the United States by manipulating the fat molecule. It is supposed to have the same properties with regard to taste, texture and appearance as fat, and tolerates frying; it does not contain any calories or cholesterol, but inhibits the absorption of vitamin E.

These substitutes could help to reduce the consumption of fats but, unlike fat, they do not contribute to the feeling of fullness that appeases the appetite. Foods that contain these fat substitutes, moreover, do not necessarily contain very many fewer calories, as some of the other additives and ingredients used can increase their calorie value.

NUTRITIONAL INFORMATION

In nutrition, the term "fats" is often used as a synonym for lipids. Fats are twice as high in energy (9 calories/g) as carbohydrates and proteins (4 calories/g). They provide energy and heat and contribute to the formation of body fat. All of the cells in the body (except the red blood cells and the cells of the central nervous system) use fatty acids directly as a source of energy.

Dietary fats add taste to foods and carry the fat-soluble vitamins (A, D, E and K). Without any fat in the diet, these vitamins would become ineffective in the body. Dietary fats provide two types of fat that the human body cannot produce by itself; they are called essential fatty acids, namely linoleic acid and alpha-linolenic acid. These fatty acids are especially found in polyunsaturated acids. The essential fatty acids enable the circulatory and immune systems to function harmoniously. They also contribute to the development of each cell.

Under the heading of the essential fatty acid alpha-linolenic acid are the omega-3 fatty acids found in fish. This type of fat is supposed to be beneficial for chronic inflammatory diseases, such as rheumatoid arthritis, as well as for the immune system and the incidence of atherosclerosis and cardiovascular diseases. Only small quantities of fats are necessary. High consumption of fat can raise blood cholesterol levels in susceptible individuals and contribute to the development of obesity. Fats are metabolized slowly, as they slow down the rate of gastric emptying, which spreads the digestive process over a longer period of time.

FATS AND OILS

Oil

Oil is an unctuous fat, nonsoluble in water and generally liquid at room temperature. The most used oils for food purposes are those from plants: legumes (soy, peanut), seeds (sunflower, canola seed, pumpkin), cereals and grains (corn), fruits (olive, palm, walnut, hazelnut, grapeseed, sweet almond) and cotton. There are also animal oils (for example, whale, halibut, cod, seal), mostly treated as dietary supplements, and mineral oils (hydrocarbons), among which only paraffin oil is edible but indigestible (never heat it).

OIL MAKING

The first stage of manufacturing oil is its **extraction**. This consists of cleaning and shelling certain oleaginous materials (for example, peanuts, sunflower seeds, almonds, hazelnuts). Next comes the **crushing**, which turns the substance into a paste that will then undergo mechanical extraction by cold- or hot-pressing.

Cold-pressing uses hydraulic presses at a maximum temperature of 140°F (60°C). Since they are not subject to any legal definition, oils said to be "cold-pressed" may not be. Oil from the "first pressing" refers to the oil obtained from the first extraction; "extra-virgin" oil indicates an oil from the first pressing that contains less than 1% acidity, whereas "virgin" oil is an oil from the first pressing that can contain up to 3% acidity. "Fino" oil is a mixture of the two. The name "100% pure" simply specifies that the oil is derived from a single source. It often comes from a second pressing.

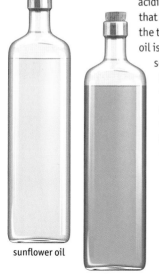

Hot-pressing is carried out mechanically by putting the paste through screw presses that are heated to a temperature of 175°F-250°F (80°C-120°C). The result is a crude oil that will need to undergo the following treatments:

- **Degumming** aims to remove free fatty acids, various substances that contribute to the instability of the oil and its production of froth and smoke during deep-frying.

sunflower oil

olive oil

< olive oil

Oil

- **Refining,** or "neutralization," consists of adding an alkaline substance in order to turn the free fatty acids in the oil into soap.
- **Bleaching** removes the pigments present in crude oil.
- **Hydrogenation** consists of adding hydrogen at the level of the unsaturated bonds; this process prevents oxidation and converts liquid oils into fluid or solid shortenings (see *Fats*, p. 581).
- **Fractionation** prevents the oil from crystallizing at cold temperatures.
- **Deodorization** produces a neutral-tasting oil and extends its storage life when it is stored after packaging.
- **Antioxidation treatment** usually consists of adding synthetic antioxidants that prevent oxidation for as long as the container remains sealed. Oil and vegetable fats contain a natural antioxidant, vitamin E. Cold-pressed oil contains more vitamin E than hot-pressed oils; oils are only protected against oxidation until their natural antioxidants are exhausted, after which the fatty acids start to deteriorate.

Unrefined oils are darker than refined oils and their flavor is stronger. Refining affects the nature and quantity of fatty acids in the oil, its vitamin and mineral content, and its color, flavor and cooking qualities. A hydrogenated oil can lose up to 50% of its polyunsaturated fatty acids, which reduces its level of linoleic fatty acid, an essential acid that the body cannot process.

peanut oil

corn oil

BUYING

There are a very wide variety of oils available on the market, refined or cold-pressed, with or without additives. Consult the list of ingredients on the label. For cold-pressed oils, check whether there is a date of pressing or a use-by date on the label.

STORING

:: **At room temperature:** keep oil away from drafts, light and heat, in a cool place and in an airtight, narrow and deep container.

:: **In the fridge:** keep cold-pressed oils in an opaque or dark small-sized container (1 year, but only a few months after opening). The oil will likely solidify and form white flakes. This phenomenon has no effect on its quality or taste; it will become liquid again at room temperature. Linseed oil keeps for a few months before being opened and a few weeks afterward.

COOKING

Certain oils do not tolerate heating, including walnut oil, linseed oil and cold-pressed safflower, corn and soybean oils. It is preferable not to heat cold-pressed oils too much using direct heat and reserve them for vinaigrettes. Avoid heating oil past its smoke-point, meaning the point at which a thin layer of smoke appears above the oil (a sign that the oil may catch fire at any moment). The higher the smoke-point of the oil, the more heat-resistant it is. An oil suitable for deep-frying should have a smoke-point above 425°F (218°C) (sunflower oil, peanut oil and canola oil). Polyunsaturated fatty acids do not tolerate high temperatures or repeated use for deep-frying well.

Certain conditions must be satisfied for oil to be reused safely:

- Do not go past the smoke-point—that is, maintain the temperature of the oil at 375°F (190°C).
- Filter the oil (using a coffee filter or a straining cloth such as cheesecloth) after use.
- Keep the oil in an opaque and airtight container in a cool place.
- Do not use the oil more than 5-7 times.
- Avoid using copper, bronze or brass utensils; preferably use stainless steel.
- Discard any oil that has smoked, that is too dark, that has a rancid smell, that does not bubble when food is added or that froths.

Adding fresh oil to oil that has already been used will not improve the quality of the used oil. Drain or wipe foods well before frying them to prevent the boiling oil from spitting.

A cooking thermometer helps determine the precise temperature at which foods should be immersed in the oil, to monitor the heat during cooking and to avoid reaching the smoke-point; deep-fryer thermostats also control the heat. It is best to cook foods in small batches so that they are cooked golden on the outside and well done on the inside.

sesame oil

Oil

SERVING IDEAS

Oil is the main ingredient in vinaigrettes. It is used in marinades for tenderizing meat, poultry, fish and game. Use it sparingly for brushing grilled or barbecued foods. Oil acts as a preservative, covering crushed garlic, dried tomatoes and herbs. When beaten, it emulsifies and produces a precursor to mayonnaise. Choose an oil that is not too strong-tasting.

To reduce fat intake, steam foods instead of pan-frying, deep-frying or sautéeing them. Oil can also be replaced with stock, tamari sauce or tomato juice.

Vegetable oil is often used in place of butter for browning certain foods or for making sauces, cakes, muffins and cookies. It sometimes alters the flavor and texture of foods.

oil	saturated fatty acids g/100 g	monounsaturated g/100 g	polyunsaturated fatty acids g/100 g	smoke-point
canola	7.2	55.5	33.3	refined: 470°F (240°C)
coconut	86.5	5.8	1.8	refined: 450°F (230°C)
corn	12.7	24	58.7	unrefined: 325°F (160°C) refined: 445°F (230°C)
grapeseed	9.6	16.1	69.9	420°F (215°C)
olive	13.5	73.7	8.4	extra virgin: 375°F (190°C) extra light: 475°F (245°C)
palm	49.3	37	9.3	450°F (230°C)
peanut	16.9	46.2	32	refined: 450°F (230°C)
sesame	14.2	39.7	41.7	unrefined: 350°F (175°C) refined: 450°F (230°C)
soybean	14.4	23.3	57.9	350°F (175°C) 450°F (230°C)
sunflower	10.1	45.2	40.1	unrefined: 225°F (105°C) refined: 450°F (230°C)
walnut	9.1	22.8	63.3	unrefined: 320°F (160°C) refined: 400°F (200°C)

NUTRITIONAL INFORMATION

Oil contains no proteins or carbohydrates. It contains fats (9 calories/gram) and vitamins (A, D and E), and is a source of energy (1 tablespoon/15 ml of oil provides 122 calories and contains 0.5 oz/14 g of lipids). Vegetable oils do not contain any cholesterol.

Fatty acids can be saturated, monounsaturated or polyunsaturated. Polyunsaturated and especially monounsaturated fatty acids are considered to be healthier than saturated fatty acids (see *Fats*, p. 584).

Oils that are high in monounsaturated fatty acids (olive, canola, peanut and hazelnut oils) or polyunsaturated fatty acids (peanut, safflower, canola, corn, linseed, walnut, sesame, soybean and sunflower oils) should be consumed in moderation. The use of oils that contain mostly saturated fatty acids (palm and coconut oils) should be kept to a minimum.

oxidation	uses	notes
slow	all	gives off an unpleasant smell at high heat, as it is high in linolenic acid
very slow	all	widely used in the food industry
moderately slow	all	unrefined: amber to dark golden color, often has a popcorn flavor; refined: pale amber
quick	only cold	striking taste
slow	all	widely used in the food industry
slow	cold, cooking	unrefined: yellow or green color with a strong flavor, tolerates high heat but has a persistent odor
slow	all	tolerates high heat
average	table	at high heat, gives off an unpleasant smell
average	table, cooking	unrefined: strong flavor and color, high in vitamin B; refined: whitish, milder flavor
very quick	especially cold	unrefined: amber color, strong flavor; refined: whitish, neutral flavor
quick	only cold	striking taste

FATS AND OILS

Introduction
Binders and leavenings

Certain ingredients, such as starches, are used in particular to bind foods or to assist in dough-rising (like yeast). They are often simple powders added to food preparation.

Arrowroot

Maranta arundinacea, Marantaceae

A starch originally extracted from maranta, a plant with tuberous roots probably originally from South America. The term "arrowroot" has also come to refer to the starch derived from various other species of rhizome, such as the *Zamia*, *Curcuma* and *Musa* varieties. Arrowroot is used in the same way as cornstarch or flour, which it can replace (use half as much). Unlike cornstarch, arrowroot retains the transparency of clear liquids and cooks in a short time; it does not change the taste of a sauce. It is also used in the production of low-protein foods for those with liver or kidney problems or with certain allergies.

arrowroot

SERVING IDEAS

 Arrowroot thickens soups, sauces, puddings, creams and flans. Blend it with a small amount of cold liquid before mixing it into a hot dish. It is used in cakes and cookies, especially cookies for infants.

NUTRITIONAL INFORMATION

protein	0.3 g
fat	0.1 g
carbohydrates	88.1 g
	per 3.5 oz/100 g

Arrowroot is easily digested.

STORING

:: At room temperature.

Baking powder

A fine white powder that reacts in contact with liquid and heat, forming carbon dioxide, which makes batters and other mixtures rise. It consists of a combination of alkaline and acid salts. Baking powder is more effective than baking soda, as it acts at a lower temperature and does not leave any aftertaste. The following baking powders are available on the market.

Quick-acting baking powder starts acting as soon as it comes in contact with a liquid, producing carbon dioxide. The mixture should be worked with quickly and cooked as soon as all of the ingredients are incorporated. It is used for angel food cake, crackers, donuts and pizza doughs.

Slow-acting baking powder produces maximum gas in the oven, through the effect of the heat. The mixture can be kept in the fridge until the next day.

baking powder

Double-acting baking powder contains two acids: one that starts acting very quickly, especially at room temperature; the other that acts slowly and only in the oven. It is useful for angel food cakes and donuts, as well as for mixtures that need to be refrigerated before cooking.

Low-sodium baking powder contains potassium salts instead of sodium salts; it is designed for those who need to limit their sodium intake.

PREPARING

Baking powder can be made at home by combining the following ingredients:

- 2 parts cream of tartar
- 1 part baking soda or potassium bicarbonate (containing no sodium, this product is of interest to those who need to monitor their salt intake; it is bought in pharmacies)
- 1 part cornstarch or arrowroot

STORING

:: At room temperature: keep baking powder away from moisture and heat. To find out if it is still effective, pour $2\frac{1}{3}$ tablespoons (50 ml) of hot water over $1\frac{1}{2}$ teaspoons (7.5 ml) of baking powder. If the powder is fresh, it will form lots of bubbles; if not, it will not react very much or at all.

Baking powder

SERVING IDEAS

Baking powder is used to make cakes, puddings, muffins, pancakes, waffles and cookies rise. One usually adds 1½ teaspoons (7.5 ml) of baking powder per 1 cup (250 ml—about 130 g) of flour.

Sift the baking powder with the flour and salt. At high altitudes, reduce the quantity of baking powder by 0.02 oz per teaspoon (0.5 ml per 5 ml) at 3,280 ft (1000 m); and 0.03-0.07 oz per teaspoon (1-2 ml per 5 ml) at 6,560 ft (2,000 m) altitude.

Cream of tartar

A fine white powder used as a raising agent, tartar is a by-product of wine-making. Cream of tartar reacts quickly in the presence of baking soda when it comes in contact with a liquid, making the mixture rise quickly. This mixture loses its volume in a short time if it is not baked immediately.

cream of tartar

SERVING IDEAS

Cream of tartar is often used to stabilize beaten egg whites in angel food cakes, sponge cakes, chiffon cakes, meringues and soufflés, and to prevent the sugar crystallizing in confectionery. It is also used in omelettes and cookies.

NUTRITIONAL INFORMATION

Cream of tartar contains potassium: 0.1 g of potassium per 0.1 oz/3 g of cream of tartar. A certain amount is lost during cooking.

STORING

:: **At room temperature:** keep cream of tartar away from heat and moisture.

BINDERS AND LEAVENINGS

Baking soda

A fine white powder formed from a mixture of alkaline salts that works as a raising agent. "Baking soda" (or "bicarbonate of soda" in British English) is the cooking name for sodium bicarbonate.

Baking soda only contains sodium: 1,370 mg per 1 teaspoon/5 ml. It breaks down into sodium carbonate, water and carbon dioxide when it is dissolved in water and heated, which makes the mixture rise, but these sodium carbonate residues are not very desirable, as they leave a bitter aftertaste. The use of an acid ingredient allows the sodium carbonate residue to be eliminated.

Molasses, honey, malt, fruits, cocoa, lemon juice, yogurt, sour cream, buttermilk and vinegar are the most commonly used acidic ingredients. It can happen, however, that despite everything, the sodium carbonate leaves an aftertaste in the food.

Depending on the type of recipe, 2 teaspoons (10 ml) of baking powder can be replaced by ½ teaspoon (2 ml) of baking soda and 1 cup (250 ml) of molasses, or by 1 rounded teaspoon (6 ml) of cream of tartar and ½ teaspoon (2 ml) of baking soda. The proportion of baking soda to the acid ingredient used is very important. Thus, if one uses ½ teaspoon (2 ml) of baking soda, it must be paired with 1 cup (250 ml) of buttermilk, sour milk or yogurt, or 1 tablespoon (15 ml) of an acidic substance (lemon juice or vinegar).

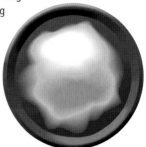

baking soda

SERVING IDEAS

 Baking soda is often used when fruits are incorporated into a mixture, as it neutralizes their acidity. It is usually sifted and mixed in with the other dry ingredients. When using an acid ingredient, the baking soda should be incorporated with the dry ingredients, then the acidic ingredient should be added just before baking the mixture.

COOKING

Added to the cooking water for vegetables and legumes, baking soda protects the color of vegetables and reduces the cooking time of legumes. This practice, however, leads to a loss in nutritional value and easily results in waterlogged and overcooked vegetables.

STORING

:: **At room temperature:** keep baking soda away from humidity.

Yeast

A microscopic mushroom used mainly in bread-making. The *Saccharomyces cerevisiae* yeast is the most frequently used; it is also called "brewer's yeast" or "baker's yeast."

yeast

When active yeast is added to a gluten-rich flour, the carbon dioxide stays trapped in the gluten, which makes the dough rise. Nonactive yeast is taken as a dietary supplement: brewer's yeast (very strong tasting) is a by-product of making beer. It is mainly used as a supplement, whereas torula yeast is specifically cultivated as a dietary supplement. It has a better taste than brewer's yeast.

BUYING

Live yeast is sold fresh and compressed, or dried. Compressed yeast is generally sold by weight. Dry yeast is an individual yeast or a mixture of several fast or regular-acting yeasts. It is found commercially in granulated or powder form.

Yeast used as a dietary supplement is nonactive and sold in powder form or as tablets.

SERVING IDEAS

Fresh, compressed yeast and dried yeast are used in identical ways. They are most effective at temperatures of 75°F-80°F (24°C-27°C). Yeast used as a dietary supplement is not used as a raising agent. This powder is blended with juice, water or stock, or added to soups, stews, breads and salads. Start with only a small quantity, especially in the case of brewer's yeast, to get used to its taste.

NUTRITIONAL INFORMATION

Yeast is of great nutritional value.

BREWER'S AND TORULA YEAST

EXCELLENT SOURCE: B-complex vitamins, iron and folic acid, potassium and phosphorus; vitamin B_{12} may also be added. They contain 5 g protein per 2 tablespoons (30 ml), which makes them a protein supplement between meals.

DRY TORULA YEAST

EXCELLENT SOURCE: high-quality protein, minerals and vitamin B including vitamin B_{12}. Avoid eating active yeast as a dietary supplement.

STORING

:: **At room temperature:** yeast used as a dietary supplement. Keep dried yeast 1 year, in a cool place.

:: **In the fridge:** fresh and compressed yeast, 1 week maximum.

ground coffee beans

PREPARING

Making coffee can be very simple, if using instant coffee, or less simple, if making a blend of different varieties, or grinding coffee for different types of coffeemakers, etc.

Maceration consists of putting coffee in contact with cold or hot water for a certain period of time, then separating out the coffee grounds after infusion. Turkish or Greek coffee and Mélior or Bodum French press coffeemakers use this method.

Percolation consists of passing the water through the coffee using either the force of gravity or pressure. This method is used by Moka pots and espresso coffeemakers. The amount of ground coffee needed for 1 cup (250 ml) of coffee depends on the grind, the type of coffee and the taste sought after; depending on the desired strength, 1-3 tablespoons (15-45 ml) of coffee are calculated for ¾ cup (180 ml) of water. The grind of the coffee varies according to the coffeemaker used, as each process requires a particular grind. The finer the grind, the stronger the coffee and the more flavor it has; the more economical it is as well, as a fine grind means that less coffee is needed for the same volume of water. There are various models of coffeemakers that operate according to different principles.

A **filter coffeemaker** exists in several different forms. The general process consists of pouring boiling water over coffee that is placed in a filter, and the water slowly drips through. A conical basket holding a paper or cloth filter and not too finely ground coffee is placed on top of a container. An overly fine grind will have the effect of blocking the pores of the paper and prevent the water from dripping through, whereas a coarse grind will result in an insipidly flavored coffee.

A **pressure coffeemaker** uses steam to operate—that is, the water is pushed through the coffee at high pressure for 20-30 sec. The coffeemaker is made up of two compartments resting on top of each other: a base with a valve into which water is poured and an upper compartment screwed onto the base, where the water is collected after rising in the form of steam and infusing the finely ground coffee it contains. The coffeemaker is placed on a heat source, brought to a boil and the heat is lowered. The coffeemaker is removed once the boiling stops. This type of coffeemaker produces a very dense coffee, which concentrates its taste and aromas.

A **Moka (or Cona) pot** is an Italian coffeemaker made up of three airtight sections resting on top of each other: the base that contains the water, the center that acts as a filter and contains the coffee, and the upper section that collects the finished coffee. The water is drawn from below toward the top by the pressure created inside the machine.

A **percolator** works by "washing" the coffee. It results in a more or less flavorful and often bitter coffee. The medium-grind coffee is placed in a container that is set on top of a small cylinder into which boiling water rises.

This water moistens the coffee then falls back down by slowly dripping; as the process is repeated over 7-10 min, the coffee runs the risk of boiling, which results in a great loss of aroma and a high extraction of tannins.

A **French press** (Bodum or Mélior) is a glass coffeemaker with a plunger that is pressed down to hold the coffee grounds; the coffee is infused, then filtered. Boiling water is first poured into the coffeemaker to warm it; this water is discarded and finely ground coffee is added. Boiling water is added and the mixture is stirred once, then left to infuse for 5 min. The plunger is pushed down just before serving. This coffeemaker results in a rich coffee with a great deal of body, whose strength varies, depending on the amount of water used.

An **ibrik**, or Turkish coffee pot, is a coffeemaker with a wide base and a conical shape that is used to make Turkish coffee, a very intensely flavored coffee that is best sipped to avoid swallowing the coffee grounds. Add coffee that has been ground to an extremely fine powder to just-simmering water with an almost equal quantity of sugar, and bring to a boil three times, adding a little cold water each time. A few drops of water are added at the end to make the grounds fall to the bottom, the coffee is immediately served scalding hot in small cups without being filtered.

For coffee lovers, making good coffee is an art governed by quite precise rules, the aim of which is to extract the maximum amount of caffeine and substances responsible for aroma and taste, while at the same time limiting the extraction of tannins. The Finnish consume on average over 4 cups (1 l) of coffee per day, whereas people in the United States and Canada consume around 2 cups (450 ml) per day.

To make a good coffee, follow these steps:

1. Grind the coffee at the last moment.
2. Use fresh water that hasn't been heated and let it just simmer (185°F-200°F/85°C-90°C) while avoiding boiling, as it then loses oxygen and becomes flat. Avoid water whose mineral or chlorine content is too high, or that tastes of sulfur or iron, as it will lend these flavors to the coffee.
3. Time the period of infusion, as the concentration of tannins increases if this period is prolonged; an infusion of 2 min is considered sufficient if the water temperature is 185°F-200°F (85°C-90°C) and if the water is in contact with all of the grounds at the same time.
4. Do not let coffee boil or reheat it; the brewing temperature should be 185°F-200°F (85°C-90°C) in order to extract the maximum amount of soluble substances without extracting too much of the substances that make coffee bitter.
5. Do not use metal coffeemakers or cups, which alter the taste of the coffee. Serve it in a stoneware or porcelain cup, as it retains heat better than glass.
6. Wash the coffeemaker well to remove the oil left by the coffee; this oil can become rancid and give an unpleasant taste to the coffee. Rinse it well to remove all traces of soap.

COFFEE, TEA AND HERBAL TEAS

< coffee cup and roasted coffee beans

Coffee

NUTRITIONAL INFORMATION

Coffee is low in protein, carbohydrate and fat. The most significant substances in coffee beans are caffeine, tannins (including chlorogenic acid), oils and nitrogenous substances. Caffeine is a stimulant that is one of the xanthines.

PROPERTIES: diuretic. Coffee stimulates the central nervous and respiratory systems, dilates the blood vessels, accelerates the heart rhythm, increases the work of the striated muscles and delays mental and muscular fatigue and increases wakefulness during periods of fatigue. People who are used to a high intake of caffeine can experience withdrawal symptoms after a period of abstinence (headaches, irritability, muscular and nervous tension; these symptoms disappear once some caffeine is ingested). The maximum amount of coffee to be consumed daily varies according to the variety of coffee, the method of making it, personal tolerance and whether other substances containing coffee are also consumed, such as tea (strong tea with 78-108 mg of caffeine per ¾ cup/180 ml), cocoa, soft drinks (colas) (28-64 mg caffeine per 1½ cup (355 ml) can) and certain medications (diuretics, analgesics and several anticold medications). A medium-sized cup of ordinary coffee (¾ cup/180 ml) contains 105-180 mg of caffeine in the case of filtered coffee, 70-145 mg in the case of percolated coffee, 60-90 mg in the case of instant coffee and 5-10 mg in the case of decaffeinated coffee.

The studies that have already been carried out do not conclude that the ingestion of caffeine is linked to hypertension, cancer or certain congenital malformations. However, moderation in caffeine consumption is recommended during pregnancy and breastfeeding, as caffeine passes through the placenta and is found in breast milk. The effect of coffee on sleep is undeniable. It affects the quality of sleep for the first 4 hr after consuming the coffee.

STORING

Storing coffee is a delicate matter, as the loss of flavor begins with the roasting process and becomes greater when the coffee is ground. Coffee should be kept in an airtight opaque glass container, away from drafts and light.

:: At room temperature: ground coffee, 7-10 days.

:: In the fridge: less desirable; ground coffee and unground coffee beans, several weeks.

:: In the freezer: ground coffee and unground coffee beans, 1 month.

unroasted green
coffee beans

Index

:: In the freezer: freeze pieces ¾ in. (2 cm) thick that weigh a maximum of 1 lb (500 g) (2½-3 months). Dry cheeses tolerate freezing better than moist cheeses (fresh cheeses don't freeze). Defrosting reduces the flavor of cheese, making it more crumbly. Defrost cheese in the fridge and use only for cooked dishes.

COOKING

Cheese melts more easily during cooking if it is shredded, grated or finely chopped. Added to a sauce, it is gently cooked until it just melts, not letting it boil. Firm cheeses withstand higher temperatures, in particular when used as a topping. Remove the cheese from the heat as soon as it is melted.

PREPARING

Only firm cheeses are grated. Cold cheese is easier to grate than cheese left at room temperature.

DAIRY PRODUCTS

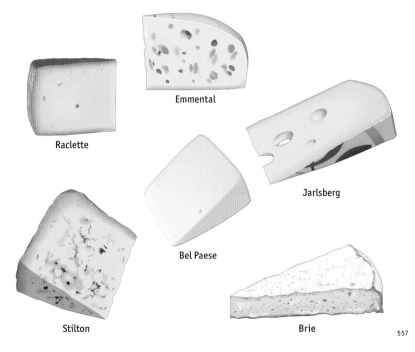

Emmental

Raclette

Jarlsberg

Bel Paese

Stilton

Brie

Introduction
Sugars, cocoa and carob

Sugar, cocoa and carob are products that essentially contain simple carbohydrates like glucose, saccharose or fructose. These carbohydrates are important sources of energy, all the more so because they are absorbed very quickly by the body. An indispensable part of the daily diet, simple carbohydrates are especially essential during exertion or when recovering from exertion. They have very little nutritional value, however. The energy derived from these carbohydrates should therefore be limited. If too many sugary foods are eaten, the body does not use the energy, storing it instead in the form of fat, which leads to weight gain.

Sugar

A water-soluble substance with a sweet flavor. Sugar is extracted from sugarcane and sugar beet. Its scientific name is "saccharose."

Sugarcane is originally from India or New Guinea. Its carbohydrates, containing 12%-15% saccharose, are found in the core of the stalks. One ton of sugarcane provides about 275 lb (125 kg) of sugar.

sugarcane

Sugar beet, originally from Europe, is related to the beet vegetable. It is a large root containing 15%-20% saccharose.

It is estimated that about 75%-80% of the sugar consumed comes from processed foods. Sugar is added to charcuterie products (sausages and deli meats), pizza, soy sauce, stock cubes, sauces, peanut butter and mayonnaise.

Approximately 100 sugars have been identified in food chemistry (glucose, fructose and maltose, in particular). They are grouped under the terms "carbohydrates" or "sugars." Most foods contain natural carbohydrates. Honey, maple syrup, corn syrup,

INDEX